"There will be no peace in Europe if States re-establish themselves on the basis of national sovereignty, with all that this implies by way of prestige policies and economic protectionism. . . . To enjoy the prosperity and social progress that are essential, the States of Europe must form a federation or a 'European entity' which will make them a single economic unit."

Jean Monnet, 1943

"For centuries, emperors, kings and dictators have sought to impose unity on Europe by force. For better or worse, they have failed. But under your inspiration, Europe has moved closer to unity in less than twenty years than it had done before in a thousand."

John F. Kennedy to Jean Monnet, 1963

"Europeans seemed to be the last to realize how great were these new proportions and prospects; but if their field of vision was too often limited by national horizons, at a distance the Community was revealed as an entity ever more present in the affairs of men and the calculations of States. . . . The new face of Europe was reassuring also to the less developed countries, some of whom were moving directly from having been colonies to becoming colleagues. For hundreds of millions of people in a number of continents, the Community was becoming a partner in freely negotiated agreements."

Jean Monnet, 1978

THE WORLD IN THE TWENTIETH CENTURY

VOLUME 2

Coming Apart, Coming Together

Edward R. Kantowicz

WILLIAM B. EERDMANS PUBLISHING COMPANY
GRAND RAPIDS, MICHIGAN / CAMBRIDGE, U.K.

© 2000 Wm. B. Eerdmans Publishing Co.
255 Jefferson Ave. S.E., Grand Rapids, Michigan 49503 /
P.O. Box 163, Cambridge CB3 9PU U.K.

Printed in the United States of America

05 04 03 02 01 00   7 6 5 4 3 2 1

Library of Congress Cataloging-in-Publication Data

Kantowicz, Edward R.
Coming apart, coming together / Edward R. Kantowicz.
p.   cm.   — (The world in the twentieth century; vol. 2)
Includes index.
ISBN 0-8028-4456-1
1. History, Modern — 1945-   I. Title.
II. Series: World in the twentieth century (Grand Rapids, Mich.); vol. 1.
D840.K27   2000
909.82′5 — dc21   99-34655
                                                        CIP

Maps are based on originals provided by
Mountain High Maps®
Copyright © 1993 Digital Wisdom, Inc.

Contents

PART THREE

THE MEDITERRANEAN ROAD TO NATIONHOOD

PART FOUR
THE SCRAMBLE OUT OF AFRICA

PART FIVE
NEW COMPLEXITIES, OLD RESPONSES

PART SIX
THE WALLS COME TUMBLING DOWN

Maps

Introduction

War, revolution, and genocide marked the first half of the twentieth century, as four terrible "isms" — nationalism, imperialism, socialism, and anarchism — ignited a bonfire of atrocities. Nationalism and socialism proved the most explosive of all, particularly in combination with each other. The phrases "terrible isms" and a "rage of nations," which I used in volume 1 of this history of the twentieth century, sound comfortingly impersonal and distant; but, in reality, individual human beings made the murderous choices. The dictators of the early twentieth century — Benito Mussolini, Adolf Hitler, and Joseph Stalin — all developed unstable amalgams of "national socialism" that ignited a war of extermination. Ordinary men and women issued commands or followed orders, hated, fought, and killed their perceived enemies, and consoled themselves with the belief that they were serving a higher cause, usually the good of the nation. A character in Walker Percy's novel *The Thanatos Syndrome* reminds us that neither impersonal ideologies nor supernatural demons committed the atrocities of the twentieth century. Satan did not need to send devils to torment us: "We did it."

The horrors of the century's first half had some salutary consequences. Though few individuals renounced war as an acceptable policy option and national leaders missed the chance to disarm or build a stronger world government, still the memory of world wars and genocide has chastened men and women throughout the world. The United States military dropped two atomic bombs on Japan at the end of World War II with very little forethought. Since then, however, no one has considered atomic explosives "just another weapon" and none have been used in anger. The full dimensions of the Holocaust in Nazi Germany were not appreciated during the war, but the horror of genocide has since become part of the world's consciousness. Regional wars and horrendous atrocities still abounded in the second half of the twentieth century, but no conflict on the scale of the two world wars occurred.

The second half of the twentieth century was dominated by two global events: the superpower Cold War between the United States and the Soviet Union; and the revolt against imperialism in Africa, Asia, and Latin America. The world came apart into three segments — the "First World" of free market trading nations, the "Second World," or Communist bloc, and the economically underdeveloped but politically emerging "Third World." The world wars discredited particular brands of nationalism, socialism, and imperialism, but other varieties remained potent. The European nations that had carved up Asia and Africa in the nineteenth century remained in control of their colonies and protectorates at mid-century, but not for long. Members of what I call the "intellectual proletariat," overeducated but underemployed individuals, felt frustrated by the lack of freedom, economic opportunity, and basic human respect that they faced as colonized subjects. Sukarno in Indonesia, Mohandas Gandhi in India, Kwame Nkrumah in Ghana, and their counterparts throughout Asia and Africa, led both violent and non-violent liberation movements against European imperialism. Sukarno coined the word "socio-nationalism" to describe the new, less murderous, blends of socialism and nationalism that the liberation leaders espoused.

Unfortunately, these nationalist struggles against imperialism often became entangled in the unrelated rivalries of the superpowers. The political leaders in Russia and the United States usually saw linkage between local, regional conflicts and the Cold War that distorted their understanding. Therefore, the typical war of the century's second half was a proxy battle between the superpowers, waged on the continents that Europeans had colonized a century earlier. The superpowers came close to a direct, nuclear confrontation in Korea, Cuba, and the Middle East, but they prudently backed off from the brink on each occasion. The murderous memory of the world wars may have been decisive. For that reason alone, it is worth recounting the history of the twentieth century.

Though the world came apart into three portions and over 180 nation-states, centripetal forces opposed this tendency as the century advanced. Ironically, Europeans, who had long considered themselves superior to the other peoples of the world, may have finally made a crucial contribution to world civilization after they lost their political and military preeminence. Out of the wreckage of World War II, a practical visionary, Jean Monnet, pushed European governments to create a common market, which grew over the decades. As the twentieth century ends, Europe is poised on the brink of full economic and political union, and many nations in the Americas and Asia see the

European Union as a model of peaceful change. As the world has been coming apart, it has simultaneously been coming together.

Looking back, it is clear that imperialism waned steadily throughout the whole century and is now a discredited, though far from irrelevant, force. Socialism experienced a spectacular rise and was considered the wave of the future by some; but the socialist bloc suddenly and unexpectedly collapsed toward the end of the century. Nationalism remains the most steady, consistent force for both good and evil. Nationalism blew apart the European empires and then the monolithic blocs of the Cold War.

A century ago ordinary people in Europe and North America seemed more afraid of anarchism than any of the other "isms," for anarchist terrorists were throwing bombs at heads of state and at random everyday locations. Besides the terrorists, anarchism inspired many thoughtful and courageous and even a few saintly individuals. At moments of catastrophic stress in widely separated places such as Ukraine, Mexico, and Spain, anarchists tried but failed to build small-scale, non-coercive societies. During most of the century the anarchists were spectacular losers, for it seemed that organized bigness was the leading world trend. However, in an indirect way, the anarchists have been proven partly right, for the failure of socialism was in large measure due to the inflexibility of organized bigness. As the world came apart, it seemed to many that "small is beautiful."

Perhaps the solution to these paradoxes — that the world has been coming apart yet straining to come together, that organized bigness has shown its ability to produce wealth and power yet appears soulless and stultifying — can be found in one further "ism," federalism. As the colonial empires and the socialist bloc fragmented into smaller and smaller nation-states, they did not literally come apart. States did not go anywhere in the physical sense, and the world was too tightly wrapped in a web of communications for them to disappear from view. The smaller states became, the more they needed each other for trade and political assistance. So the model of economic union and/or political federation should become increasingly attractive as the next century advances. With wise, just, and historically informed leadership, this process may abate the rage of nations and counter their tendency to come apart. A world government will not likely be forged during the next century, but groups of nations will probably continue coming together in new and unexpected ways.

PART ONE

ORIGINS OF THE
COLD WAR IN EUROPE

Once upon a time, in the middle decades of the twentieth century, a tiger broke loose from his cage and ravaged Europe. Alternately purring and snarling, the tiger roamed first to the East and then to the West, devouring anyone in his path, until he was stopped by a broad moat that he could not leap. On the far side of the moat, a bulldog growled and bared his teeth, but he could not cross over either. So the tiger turned east once again, raging into the domain of the bear. The huge brown bear was slow and stupid, seemingly an easy prey, but the tiger could not kill him. All his clawing and scratching just made the bear more angry and determined to protect his lair. Far across the sea, the fox looked on at this deranged animal farm and wondered what to do. The bear yowled for help. Finally, the fox and the bulldog built a bridge across the moat. When they reached the other side, they helped the bear kill the tiger.

Then the fox died. An old hound dog, who got along fine with the bulldog, took his place; but neither canine knew how to handle the bear. He still seemed stubborn and stupid but they feared he would turn out mean, like the tiger. Finally the bear and the dogs built a fence down the middle of Europe and divided the farm. The dogs yapped and yapped at the bear, who growled back ominously; but they lived together uneasily for fifty years.

This is not much of a tale, as fables go, but it is a true story. The greatest alliance in history, the bulldog (Churchill), the fox (Roosevelt), and the bear (Stalin), fell apart shortly after defeating the tiger (Hitler). When the hound dog (Truman) replaced the subtle fox, a snarling match called the Cold War ensued, lasting until nearly the end of the century.

CHAPTER ONE

The Grand Alliance Flies Apart

In February 1945, the Big Three, Franklin Roosevelt, Winston Churchill, and Joseph Stalin, met at Yalta, an old tsarist resort in the warm south of Russia near the Black Sea. This meeting, both the last wartime conference and the first of the postwar summits, marked the high point of cooperation between the leaders of the Grand Alliance against Hitler's Germany. A visibly frail Roosevelt played his usual role of mediator between the pugnacious Churchill and the scowling tyrant Stalin. All three leaders left Yalta believing they had obtained the assurances they needed for the postwar world.

Churchill rebutted any and all suggestions that the British ring down the curtain on their empire. Roosevelt secured the signature of the other two leaders on the Declaration on Liberated Europe, pledging that "the three governments will jointly assist people in any European liberated state or former Axis satellite state in Europe . . . to form interim governmental authorities broadly representative of all democratic elements in the population and pledged to the earliest possible establishment through free elections of governments responsive to the will of the people. . . ." Stalin construed this declaration simply as propaganda and believed he had tacit agreement to build a buffer zone of pro-Soviet states in the East European territory liberated from Hitler by the Red Army.

Within less than six months, however, Roosevelt was dead and Churchill was voted out of office. Their successors, Harry Truman and Clement Attlee, fell to arguing with Stalin over the Declaration on Liberated Europe and many other matters. Two years later, in mid-1947, the Grand Alliance fell apart and Europe was divided into two hostile camps led by the Soviet Union and the United States. By 1949 this bipolar division had hardened into a political and military rivalry known as the Cold War, which may be defined as a state of hostility falling short of actual military action but affecting, indeed poisoning, all relations between the two sides and numerous third parties.[1]

As the wartime alliance deteriorated, each side maneuvered to fix blame on the other. Strangely enough, though, many historians have tended to indict their own side for causing the Cold War. A generation of American scholars that came of age in the 1960s, under the impact of American intervention in the Vietnam War, taught that the United States had arrogantly tried to rearrange the world after Hitler's defeat and had pushed Stalin and the Russians into an unnecessarily hostile, defensive reaction. Since the end of the Soviet Union, newly liberated Russian scholars have placed all blame for the Cold War on their own discredited dictator Joseph Stalin.

In order to understand the origins of the Cold War, it seems best to adopt a more neutral stance. The Cold War was the product of an alliance gone bad, a messy divorce. As the former allies flew apart, both sides fell prey to exaggerated fears and suspicions, and both began to project their own behavioral traits onto the other. A similar situation occurs in personal relations. In nearly every lovers' quarrel or failing marriage, a man blames the woman for jealous behavior when he himself is burning with jealousy, or the woman accuses the man of selfishness and rigidity while she herself remains unwilling to give in. Each treats the other as a mirror image of himself or herself.

So too in the high politics of diplomacy. The wily Roosevelt saw in Stalin someone he could make deals with, and the next American president, Harry Truman, thought Stalin reminded him of his political patron back in Kansas City, the notorious city boss Tom Pendergast. Stalin, for his part, assumed that Roosevelt and Truman were as ruthless and cynical as he was. Any attempt at conciliation on their part was either a sign of weakness or a trick. Mutual misunderstandings made clear-eyed diplomacy extremely difficult.

Such a neutral stance in evaluating the origins of the Cold War does not imply a moral equivalence between the two sides. Stalin ranks alongside Hitler as one of the two most evil figures of the twentieth century. He committed genocide against Ukrainian peasants and prosperous landowners during the drive for collectivization in the 1930s. He not only slaughtered those he considered his enemies, but unlike Hitler he even murdered his friends, ruthlessly purging his own party supporters. As historian William Taubman has bluntly phrased it, "Stalin and his men were ultimately bastards."

Yet both in ordinary life and in international politics, people find ways to

---

1. The phrase "Cold War" is usually attributed to the Democratic elder statesman and financier Bernard Baruch. It was popularized in the second half of 1947 by journalist Walter Lippmann.

deal with "bastards" all the time; it is perfectly possible to work for or with one. The Big Three found that they worked well together during World War II. Two Russian historians, Vladislav Zubok and Constantine Pleshakov, have aptly summarized their relationship: "By the end of the war the Big Three behaved almost as a private club, with shared memories and jokes that only they could understand. At last Stalin felt that he had found the company of equals. . . . It was an important psychological motive that pushed him in the direction of postwar cooperation."

The wartime Grand Alliance, however, swiftly moved away from cooperation, partly because of mutual misunderstandings and psychological projection on the part of the leaders. More fundamentally, the Cold War took shape because the victorious allies invading Europe from East and West found a power vacuum in the middle and fell to arguing over how to fill it. The nations of Europe, whose power and culture had dominated the world for centuries, committed political suicide in the world wars. The two remaining great powers, the United States and the Soviet Union, had such different ways of life that conflict between them seemed inevitable. In the power vacuum of postwar Europe, both sides tried to create states and societies in their own image and likeness.

The Soviet Union desired centralized governments with command economies, a totalitarian top-down system; whereas the United States preferred decentralized, federalized governments, with open free-trading economies. A mix of idealism and self-interest motivated both sides. Americans assumed that democracy and free trade made for peace and prosperity, whereas the Russians believed that socialism would liberate the repressed energies of mankind. Russian Communists felt safer in a Europe dominated by party hierarchies and military structures, whereas American capitalists believed that an open, free-trading world would permit their own strong economy to prosper and flourish.

The two sides in the emerging Cold War held both maximum and minimum aims. Stalin, whose country had been invaded by Germany twice in the first half of the twentieth century, demanded as an absolute minimum the destruction of Germany's war-making potential and the payment of reparations by the defeated. In addition, he wished to build a security buffer zone of friendly states in Eastern Europe, to ensure that such countries as Poland, Hungary, and Romania would never again be used as invasion routes from the West. Having secured these minimums, Stalin also hoped to increase Communist influence in Western Europe, the Middle East, and Asia, laying the groundwork for the coming world revolution, which Marxist dogma predicted would follow the inevitable crisis of capitalism.

Soviet interests outside Germany and Eastern Europe, however, remained indirect and long-range. The Red Army was not poised to invade Western Europe. Russia was too devastated by World War II and Russians too war-weary, and American military leaders knew it. The Communists pursued their maximum goal of influence in Western Europe by economic and political, not military, means. If nations such as France and Italy became so economically desperate that communist parties gained power legally, the Russians would be happy to take advantage of this, but they never intended to invade Western Europe. For all his ruthlessness, Stalin had always acted cautiously and defensively in international affairs. The Soviet leader was probably more dangerous to his own people than Hitler had been to the Germans, but he proved less dangerous than Hitler to other nations. Ultimately, that is why the United States and Britain had allied with Russia against Germany, rather than the reverse.

The maximum goal for the United States was an open, free-trading world, without closed empires or economic spheres, that would allow American corporations to do business and American ideas of democracy and freedom to take root everywhere. Roosevelt's chief troubleshooter, Harry Hopkins, summed up this hope succinctly during World War II: "We not only need Russia as a powerful fighting ally in order to defeat Germany but . . . we need her as a real friend and customer in the postwar world." The Americans hoped for an open world filled with like-minded "friends and customers." If that were not possible, their minimum aim was a firm alliance of the English-speaking nations — the United States, Great Britain and her "white dominions" (Canada, Australia, and New Zealand) — plus other democratic, free-trading countries.

Both the Soviet Union and the United States, therefore, approached the postwar power vacuum in Europe with universalist, messianic ideologies. Each wanted to transform Europe, and eventually the whole world, into a mirror image of itself. Conflict was inherent in this situation, but so was a realistic sense of limits. Neither side wished a new shooting war. The devastation of World War II made such an overwhelming impression on all the peoples of the world that all sides wished to avoid a repetition. Since neither a continuance of the Grand Alliance nor the outbreak of a new world war seemed likely, therefore, postwar leaders faced two choices: competitive but peaceful coexistence between different forms of society, or a hostile, tension-filled Cold War. Conflict and disagreement were inevitable between Soviet Russia and liberal-capitalist America, but Cold War was not. Better leadership could not have made Russian Communists and American capitalists like each other, but it could have resulted in a different, and possibly more peaceful, political structure in Europe and the world.

Instead the Grand Alliance began to deteriorate even before the struggle against Germany and Japan had finished. The Russians concluded, quite rightly, that they were doing most of the fighting against Hitler's legions in Europe and constantly implored the Americans and the British to open a second front in the West. For a variety of valid technical reasons, the Western Allies were unable to land at Normandy until mid-1944, but the Russians suspected them of dragging their feet. Stalin and his lieutenants also feared that the An-glo-Americans might make a separate peace with the Germans, allowing them to concentrate the whole of their dwindling might against Russia and thus se-cure a favorable border in the East. This fear came to a head shortly after the Yalta Conference, in March 1945, when the chief of the American Office of Stra-tegic Services (the wartime intelligence service that was the precursor of the CIA), Allen Dulles, contacted a German SS general in Berne, Switzerland, to discuss surrender terms on the Italian front. The American ambassador in Moscow informed the Russians of these discussions, but Stalin still suspected a behind-the-back deal. The "Berne incident" illustrates how a suspicious ally projected its own behavior onto the other side. At several points during the war, when the Russian struggle against Germany was going badly, Stalin had secretly contacted German authorities to discuss the possibility of a separate peace. He assumed his allies were willing to do the same.

Disagreement over the Declaration on Liberated Europe proved a more important, and more enduring, cause of tension in the Soviet-American alli-ance. It is impossible to know how literally Franklin Roosevelt took the words "broadly representative" and "free elections" in the declaration. He knew very well at the time of the Yalta Conference that Eastern Europe was being liberated from the Nazis by Soviet armies and that neither Britain nor America could ex-ercise any decisive influence in that theater. Nevertheless, he needed a more ide-alistic statement for domestic political consumption. Several million Polish-Americans tended to vote Democratic in American elections, and smaller, but still significant, groups of Czechs, Slovaks, Romanians, and other East Euro-pean immigrants needed to be appeased. Stalin never believed Roosevelt when he invoked domestic political considerations, but he was willing to humor him. Therefore, the Declaration on Liberated Europe was conceived in a series of winks and nods.

Both Churchill and Roosevelt, however, protested when the Russian mili-tary began imposing pro-Soviet governments on Eastern Europe in the early months of 1945. The Soviet leader took this as betrayal of what the cozy club of three had agreed at Yalta. Stalin invoked a kind of parallelism in his defense: He did not interfere when Britain and the United States imposed their own form of government on defeated Italy or liberated Greece, so why should they protest when he arranged for friendly governments in Eastern Europe? In retaliation for the Anglo-American protests, he announced that his foreign minister, V. M. Molotov, would snub the organizing conference of the United Nations at San Francisco in May and send the Soviet ambassador in Washington, Andrei Gromyko, instead. In the final days of his life, Roosevelt lost much of his opti-mism about cooperation with Stalin, yet he still expressed to Churchill a hope that the alliance would endure.

FDR died on April 12, 1945, just before the final defeat and death of Adolf Hitler. Whether he could have sustained the alliance beyond VE-Day if he had lived is uncertain; but it is clear that Truman's succession did make a difference. As an accidental president, chosen vice president for political reasons just a few months before, Harry S. Truman from Missouri was an insecure leader with a combative personality and a short temper. Lacking foreign policy experience, Truman relied heavily on the advisors he inherited from Roosevelt, most of whom had become more pessimistic about Soviet-American relations than FDR.

In particular, Averell Harriman, the millionaire railroad heir serving as American ambassador in Moscow, had become disillusioned with the Russians at the time of the abortive Warsaw uprising in the summer of 1944. As the Red Army approached the capital of Nazi-occupied Poland, the Polish underground Home Army had mounted a revolt in Warsaw. The Russian troops, however, paused just short of the Vistula River while the Nazis reinforced their garrison in the capital and wiped out the Poles. Until the very end of the rising, Stalin refused American and British relief planes landing rights in Russia. Viewing Stalin's abandonment of the Poles, who were fighting against a common enemy, Harriman and his deputy, George F. Kennan, became increasingly suspicious of Soviet intentions.

Ambassador Harriman briefed Truman extensively about Russia and Eastern Europe on April 23, 1945, just before the president conferred with Foreign Minister Molotov. In a goodwill gesture after Roosevelt's death, Stalin had relented and sent Molotov to San Francisco for the UN conference after all. On April 23 the foreign minister was passing through Washington to pay a courtesy call on the new president. Instead of courtesy, he was treated to a tirade by the combative Truman, who protested the Russian refusal to allow exiled non-Communist Poles in the Warsaw coalition government. The president insisted, in short, staccato sentences and words of one syllable, that the Russians had violated the Yalta Declaration on Liberated Europe. According to Truman's own memoirs, Molotov then replied: "I have never been talked to like that in my life." Truman shot back: "Carry out your agreements and you won't get talked to like that." These may not have been the exact words of the exchange, for no contemporary account exists, but whatever Truman said to Molotov on April 23 he said it undiplomatically.

A few weeks later, the Americans delivered another rude shock to the Russians, when they abruptly terminated Lend-Lease aid on the very day of the German surrender in Europe, May 8, 1945. In fact, boats loaded with supplies for the Soviet Union turned around in the mid-Atlantic. This move, which affected England as well as Russia, was likely prompted by bureaucratic literal-mindedness rather than foreign policy; but the ever-suspicious Soviets interpreted it as an insult. It would be a mistake, however, to conclude that the new American president adopted a consistently rigid stance toward the Soviet Union after Roosevelt's death. In fact, the biggest problem with Truman's policy during the first year and a half of his presidency was inconsistency and uncertainty. In late May, after the Molotov interview and the Lend-Lease fiasco, Truman sent Roosevelt's most trusted advisor, Harry Hopkins, who was near death, on a goodwill mission to Moscow. The smooth-talking Hopkins confirmed for Stalin that only cosmetic changes in the Polish government were necessary to pacify American public opinion, and he also worked out with the Soviet leader several sticking points that had hampered progress at the UN founding conference in San Francisco. The Hopkins mission marked a retreat from confrontation on the part of the Truman administration, but it probably confused Stalin more than it reassured him. Stalin read such inconsistency as either weakness or a trick.

Stalin and Truman met in person at the Potsdam Conference of the Big Three in July 1945, held in a suburb of the conquered German capital. In the midst of this conference, a British general election voted Churchill's Conservative Party out of office, and his place was taken at Potsdam by the Labour Party prime minister, Clement Attlee. Stalin simply could not understand how the victorious Churchill could be so unceremoniously booted out at the end of the war. The British public had turned to the indomitable Churchill in their most desperate crisis, but they did not trust him or his party to build a welfare state after the war. Stalin did not hold either Truman, the failed storekeeper but successful small-town politician, or Attlee, a mild-mannered intellectual, in high regard. In the words of Russian historians Zubok and Pleshakov, "Stalin lost his two equals, the opponents with whom he knew he could play a grand game with a good chance of success."

The second event, after Roosevelt's death, which decisively shook the Grand Alliance, was the dropping of the atomic bomb on Japan. Truman informed Stalin of the first successful A-bomb test in New Mexico during the Potsdam Conference in July. Stalin already knew about the test from his intelligence network and he feigned unconcern when Truman mentioned it, but inwardly he was enraged and disturbed, especially a month later when the Americans dropped the bomb on Hiroshima. Zubok and Pleshakov remark: "Had Stalin entrusted his feelings to a diary, he would have filled the whole page of August 6 with profanities, directed at the Americans in general and Truman in particular." Just when the Soviet Union had finally been accepted as one of the great powers in the world and Stalin had negotiated as an equal with the leaders of the British Empire and the American Republic, the other two members of the exclusive Big Three club disappeared and were replaced by pygmies. Then, one of the three showed it had superior weaponry, rendering obsolete all previous notions of military security. Stalin's fears and suspicions came rushing back.

Despite the unfriendly atmosphere between Truman and Stalin, neither made an overt move to end the alliance. In fact, the foreign ministers of the Big Three (sometimes joined by France or other nations) met repeatedly to discuss postwar peace treaties and security arrangements. It is often remarked that no peace conference, like the World War I Versailles Conference, ever met after World War II. This is not completely accurate. No full-scale conference of all the warring nations convened, and no peace treaty between the Allies and Germany was ever written. But it was not for lack of trying. The Allied foreign ministers met on six different occasions — London, September 1945; Moscow, December 1945; Paris, April-July, 1946; New York, November-December, 1946; Moscow, March-April, 1947; and London, November-December, 1947 — in lengthy and exhaustive negotiations over the future of Germany and Europe before talks finally broke down. They managed to write peace treaties for the so-called Axis satellite states, Finland, Romania, Hungary, Bulgaria, and Italy, which had fought alongside Germany, and twenty-one nations met in Paris from July to October 1946 to discuss these treaties before they were signed the following year.

During 1946, while the foreign ministers talked endlessly, rhetoric outside the conference halls heated up. On January 5, 1946, after President Truman heard Secretary of State James Byrnes's report from the Moscow foreign ministers' conference, he exclaimed: "I'm tired of babying the Soviets." The president soon got some support for his instinctive reaction from the acting ambassador in Moscow, George F. Kennan. Ambassador Averell Harriman had just resigned from his post and his successor, General Walter Bedell Smith, had not yet arrived, so when the State and Treasury Departments cabled their embassy for background on recent Soviet policy in February 1946, Kennan, who was lying in bed with a fever and a toothache, had to answer it.

George Frost Kennan was born in Milwaukee in 1904. Educated at Princeton University and the Foreign Service School in Washington, D.C., he became a Russian expert, following in the footsteps of his grandfather's cousin, the first George Kennan, who had traveled across Siberia in the nineteenth century and written about tsarist prison camps. Since the United States had not yet recognized the Soviet regime when Kennan graduated in 1926, he began his diplomatic career at border "listening posts" in Estonia and Lithuania, then he helped establish the first American embassy in Moscow after U.S. recognition in December 1933. Following a number of other appointments, Kennan returned to Moscow in July 1944 as counselor to Averell Harriman. He confirmed Harriman's growing suspicions about Stalin's policy, but he often felt depressed and discouraged that his own views carried so little weight in Washington.

So in February 1946, despite his physical complaints, George Kennan recognized a golden opportunity to influence policy. Since he "felt his mind functioned better when his body was in a horizontal position," he stayed in bed and
dictated an eight-thousand-word "Long Telegram" on the "Sources of Soviet
Conduct." Kennan painted a vivid picture of traditional Russian xenophobia
and imperial expansionism, aggravated by Marxist dogma. He concluded that
"all Soviet efforts . . . will be negative and destructive in character. . . . We have
here a political force committed fanatically to the belief that with U.S. there can
be no permanent modus vivendi." This Long Telegram arrived in Washington
at a time when policymakers were either looking for enlightenment or for rationalizations of gut instincts. Hundreds of copies were mimeographed and
circulated. One State Department official later wrote: "There was a universal
feeling that 'This was It,' this was the appreciation of the situation that had been
needed." Kennan returned to Washington later that year, lectured at the Army
War College, then took up a newly created post as director of the State Department's policy planning staff in May 1947. A rewritten version of his seminal telegram appeared in the influential magazine, *Foreign Affairs,* in July 1947 under
the pseudonym of Mister X. Kennan became one of the crucial American
policymakers during the development of the Cold War.

While Truman fumed in private and pondered Kennan's advice, two
other members of the Big Three issued public blasts of rhetoric. Joseph Stalin,
going through the ritual of a Soviet "election" to the Politburo, delivered a
speech to his Kremlin supporters on February 9, 1946, announcing that there
would be neither a relaxation of discipline nor a turn toward consumer comfort now that the war was over. Instead, he urged his followers to greater sacrifice in reconstructing war damage and fulfilling yet another Five Year industrial
plan. Stalin was really aiming at an all-out drive to catch up with the United
States in the arms race by building an atomic bomb as soon as possible. There
would be no "return to normalcy" for good Communists. This election speech
was aimed primarily at an internal Russian audience, but panicky American
leaders read it as a virtual declaration of World War III.

Less than a month later, Winston Churchill, now out of office but on a tri-
umphal tour of the United States, traveled with President Truman to the small
town of Fulton, Missouri. On March 5, 1946, he delivered an address at tiny
Westminster College, declaring that "from Stettin in the Baltic to Trieste in the
Adriatic, an iron curtain has descended across the continent."[2] Truman had
read Churchill's speech in advance, so his Iron Curtain address may be regarded

2. Churchill had first used the "Iron Curtain" figure of speech in a cable to President
Truman on May 12, 1945. He apparently picked it up from a German official a few days after the Nazi surrender to the Russians and the Anglo-Americans.

The Division of Germany

as a trial balloon for a tougher policy toward Russia. The balloon proved un-ready to fly. The American press reacted negatively to Churchill's speech and the administration did not formulate any new, anti-Soviet policies, yet the mood in official Washington was changing. Truman's desire to quit babying the Soviets was now widely shared.

Similarly somber views were piling up in the other great power capitals. Kennan's British counterpart in Moscow, the acting ambassador Frank Roberts, sent three cables to his foreign minister, Ernest Bevin, in March 1946, warning of a "modern equivalent of the religious wars of the sixteenth century." Then on September 27, 1946, the Soviet ambassador in Washington, Nikolai Novikov, dispatched his own long telegram to Molotov concluding that "the foreign policy of the United States, which reflects the imperialist tendencies of monopolistic American capital, is characterized in the postwar period by a striving for world supremacy." The heated rhetoric of 1946 partially reflected reality. Both the United States and Soviet Russia harbored ambitions to remake the world, and their competing visions differed sharply. Yet neither side wanted war, and possibilities for compromise and peaceful coexistence still remained. Rhetoric had become inflamed but no irrevocable actions had been taken. The inability to agree upon a peace treaty for Germany, however, finally shattered the Grand Alliance.

The Cold War hostility between Russia and the United States has so dominated the last half of the twentieth century that it is easy to forget how much *Germany*, not Russia, was feared in the immediate postwar years. Initially all the Allies had considered partitioning Germany into either three or five parts after the war. The American secretary of the treasury, Henry Morgenthau, produced a plan that not only carved up Germany politically but removed all its heavy industry and reduced the country to a "pastoral" state. Roosevelt and Churchill actually approved this plan at their Quebec Conference in 1944 but soon backed off, postponing any firm decision until after the war.

The partition of Germany that finally resulted came about by force of circumstance rather than conscious policy. The Allies agreed at Yalta on the size and shape of temporary occupation zones within Germany. Stalin consented to include France as an occupying power, but only if her portion were carved out of the British and American zones. Little friction developed over the military occupation, with each side withdrawing from advanced salients to the agreed-upon positions shortly after V-E Day. Then the wrangling started. Two issues deadlocked the Allies: reparations and the nature of German government and society.

The Big Three signed a secret reparations protocol at Yalta declaring that "Germany must pay in kind for the losses caused by her. . . ." The United States insisted that reparations be in kind rather than cash to avoid the problem that arose after the last war. During the 1920s Germany could only meet its cash reparation payments by borrowing overseas, mainly in the United States, creating a nonsensical, vicious circle. To avoid that problem this time, the Yalta protocol stipulated three kinds of reparations: removals of heavy industrial equipment from Germany, annual deliveries of goods from current production after the war, and the use of German prisoners as laborers.

The three Allies at Yalta named a final figure of 20 billion dollars in reparations as a basis for discussion and, in recognition of the heavy war burden carried by the Soviet Union, declared that 50 percent of this total should go to that country. The Russians took this tentative figure of 10 billion dollars in reparations as a rock-solid commitment and never deviated from it. Considering that the country had suffered some 35 billion dollars in war damage, by conservative estimates, this was hardly unreasonable. The British and Americans, however, backed off from this figure at the Potsdam Conference in July 1945, thus causing an impasse. Secretary of State Byrnes finally finessed the issue by postponing a general reparations settlement but stipulating that in the meantime all the Allies should continue removing equipment from their own zones. In addition, a certain percentage of industrial equipment from the Western zones would be traded for agricultural goods from the Soviet zone. The reparations debate never advanced beyond this point, despite endless negotiations at the various conferences of foreign ministers over the next two years. In the end, the Russians wound up with about 4.25 billion dollars in reparations and the Western Allies about half a billion. This totaled far less than the 20 billion discussed at Yalta or the 9 billion that Germany paid in reparations after World War I.

The future of Germany divided the Allies even more sharply than the financial wrangling over reparations. The French, invaded by Germany three times in less than a century, adhered firmly to the same demands they had made after World War I: separation of the Rhineland and the Saar Province from Germany and their incorporation into France, international control of the industrial Ruhr Valley of Germany, heavy reparations, and a long occupation. France, however, was admitted to the councils of the great powers only by permission of the British and the Americans and it wielded little independent power. The other three Allies had abandoned their plans for partitioning Germany by the end of the war and agreed that a unified, but demilitarized, Germany would be best for the future of Europe. The Russians differed from the Anglo-Americans, however, on the nature of the German government that should be formed.

Each side in the developing struggle over the future of Germany wanted to reconstruct the defeated country in its own image. The Russians desired a strong central government, which they believed that local communists could dominate, and a command economy, whereas the Anglo-Americans preferred a looser, federal structure of government, a United States of Germany so to speak, and a free enterprise, capitalist economy. These were the maximum goals, but each side also had a fall-back plan, a set of minimum aims. In short, if neither side could control the reconstruction of a unified German state, each would settle for half a loaf, half a Germany. That is what eventually happened.

In playing this poker game over the future of Germany, the Russians held more cards than the Anglo-Americans. The Soviet occupation zone was far smaller than the Western zones, counting about 17 million people compared to 49 million in the other three areas, but it was largely self-sufficient, contained the best agricultural land, and encompassed the capital of the nation, Berlin. The Russian occupiers brought a group of German Communists, led by Walter Ulbricht, into their zone and introduced a disciplined, command economy. The Soviet-occupied territory of Germany, therefore, was swiftly up and running economically, self-sufficient in food and producing nearly as much coal as it had before the war. The Soviets could afford to wait, and stall, until they got their way on German reunification, for they had already attained their minimum goal. Soviet foreign minister Molotov proved to be truly gifted at stalling, wearing down his opposite numbers with untiring, monotonous repetitions of Stalin's line. Time was on his side.

The British, French, and Americans, on the other hand, faced a grimmer situation in western Germany. Their zones encompassed the center of German industrial might, the Ruhr River valley, and they found that German industry had been less damaged by Allied bombing than originally believed. Yet the Western zones lacked food for the urban population, and the Germans felt little incentive to work hard at reconstruction since their wages could buy very few goods and the future of their country seemed uncertain. Without the goad of military compulsion that restored production so swiftly in the Russian zone, West German workers spent more time scrounging for food in the countryside than working at their jobs in the cities. About half of all business exchanges in the West had been reduced to barter, with American cigarettes functioning as the major black market currency.

The British and the Americans, therefore, needed an agreement with the Russians, so that they could integrate the German economy and feed the population of their zones, more than the Russians needed an agreement with them. As a result, the Russians stuck to their maximum demands — 10 billion dollars in reparations and a centralized, demilitarized, neutral German state. The Anglo-Americans stopped sending reparations from their zones to the Russians in mid-1946 and they tentatively formulated plans to unite the British, American, and French zones into one economic entity. Then nature stepped in, forcing a firmer policy on the part of the Americans and precipitating a final break with the Russians.

The winter of 1946-47 in Europe was the harshest in seventy years. Temperatures across the Continent fell to twenty degrees below zero Fahrenheit for several weeks and snow lay on the ground until late March. Even in England food rations were reduced below wartime levels, but in devastated Germany famine prevailed, spreading malnutrition and death among the children and elderly of the urban centers. American leaders had hoped to get through the reconstruction period cheaply and not be played for "Uncle Sap," as they believed they had been after World War I; but the harsh winter of 1946-47 punctured these hopes.

European recovery, the Americans now realized, required a coordinated plan and substantial amounts of American aid, and it could not wait for an agreement with the Russians. A full-scale economic recovery in Western Europe would checkmate the efforts of communist parties and labor unions to take over in countries such as France and Italy. The ideas of George Kennan, who advocated a "containment" of communist influence through economic, political, and military action, reinforced the lessons of the harsh winter. In the first half of 1947, therefore, the American government gradually formulated two new, related policies known as the Truman Doctrine and the Marshall Plan.

General George C. Marshall, the American chief of staff during World War II, took office as secretary of state in January 1947, replacing James F. Byrnes, who had lost President Truman's confidence during his wrangles with the Russians. On February 21, 1947, the British ambassador delivered an urgent message to Marshall's office, informing the Americans that Great Britain could no longer afford the military and economic aid it had been extending to the Greek government fighting against a communist insurgency. Marshall and his under-secretary, Dean Acheson, swiftly decided that the United States should assume the burden of "containing" communism. At a White House meeting with prominent congressional leaders on February 27, Acheson argued the case for what would later be called the "domino theory." If Greece fell to communist insurgency, then Turkey would be next, then Iran and the whole oil-rich Middle East. The Russians might not stop until they reached the borders of India. Senator Arthur Vandenberg of Michigan, the leading Republican on the Senate Foreign Relations Committee, turned to President Truman and said, "If you will say that to the Congress and to the country, I will support you."

On March 12, 1947, Truman delivered a rousing address to a joint session of Congress, requesting 400 million dollars in aid to Greece and Turkey. More importantly, the president universalized his request into a general policy. He told Congress: "I believe that it must be the policy of the United States to support free peoples who are resisting attempted subjugation by armed minorities or by outside pressure. I believe that we must assist free peoples to work out their own destinies in their own way." This statement, the Truman Doctrine, was breathtaking in its lack of limits. Drawing directly on George Kennan's advice that "Soviet pressure against the free institutions of the Western world is something that can be contained by the adroit and vigilant application of counter-force at a series of constantly shifting geographical and political points," the containment policy became the basis for all of America's military interventions throughout the Cold War. Yet in its initial formulations, Kennan, Marshall, and Truman envisioned primarily economic assistance to other nations. The very next sentence in Truman's March 12 address, after those quoted above, reads: "I believe that our help should be primarily through economic and financial aid which is essential to economic stability and orderly political processes." In the war-ravaged, winter-blasted Europe of early 1947, the best way to fight communism was not with guns, but with coal and food. So the Truman Doctrine was swiftly followed by the Marshall Plan.

Secretary of State Marshall announced the new approach to European economic recovery in a commencement address at Harvard University on June 5, 1947. Marshall was a wooden speaker, and even on the printed page his words seem bland; but the British had been warned of the speech's significance beforehand and were primed to respond. Marshall stated the purpose of his plan succinctly: "Our policy is directed not against any country or doctrine but against hunger, poverty, desperation, and chaos. Its purpose should be the revival of a working economy in the world so as to permit the emergence of political and social conditions in which free institutions can exist." He then went right to the heart of the new approach: "The initiative, I think, must come from Europe. The role of this country should consist of friendly aid in drafting of a European program and of later support of such a program so far as it may be practical for us to do so."

The British foreign secretary, Ernest Bevin, a socialist but fiercely anticommunist labor leader, immediately took the initiative by arranging a meeting with his counterpart in Paris, Georges Bidault, for June 17. Following instructions from George Kennan to the British ambassador, they then invited the Russians to join the economic planning process, strictly for form's sake, since they did not expect much cooperation. Molotov arrived in Paris on June 27, but he denounced the Marshall Plan as anticipated the very next day and withdrew from the process on July 2. The Americans, British, and French breathed a sigh of relief. It seemed much simpler to pursue the minimum goal of reconstructing Western Europe than to reopen old arguments with the Russians.

Even without the Russians, planning for European recovery did not go smoothly. On July 12, 1947, representatives of fifteen European nations met in Paris, but instead of working out a coordinated recovery plan, they simply presented shopping lists, which they hoped the Americans would pay for. By the end of August, the Europeans were asking for 29 billion dollars. George Kennan and several other emissaries then arrived in Paris and extended what Secretary Marshall had euphemistically called "friendly aid" in working out the program. By the time President Truman presented the Economic Cooperation Act to Congress in November 1947, the total aid bill had been pared to 17 or 18 billion over five years. At the advice of Senator Vandenberg, Truman kept the dollar shock low by simply asking for a one-year first installment of 5 billion dollars. Congress passed the bill on April 3, 1948.

Altogether, the United States eventually contributed just over 13 billion dollars to European recovery through the Marshall Plan. Just the announcement of a plan, agreed to by all the Western European nations and underwritten by the United States, unleashed latent economic forces in Europe. George Kennan later concluded that "the psychological effect was four-fifths accomplished before the first supplies arrived." Europeans themselves plowed over one-fifth of their gross domestic product into new capital investment, and by the middle of 1951 industrial production had reached a level 43 percent above the prewar figure. U.S. financial aid did not rebuild Western Europe single-handedly, but it provided what several historians have called the "crucial margin."

In a bitter irony, the Marshall Plan, one of the most far-sighted, unselfish, and successful American policies of the twentieth century, precipitated the irrevocable split with the Russians, the division of Europe, and the onset of the Cold War.

The Marshall Plan posed daunting challenges to the Russians. If they joined the planning process, they would have to open up their economy to the scrutiny of others, providing facts and figures about production and consumption they preferred to keep secret. Though they desired American financial aid for reconstruction, they did not like the conditions. Furthermore, if Eastern European countries such as Poland and Czechoslovakia joined the plan, as they were eager to do, their economies would grow more closely integrated with those of Western Europe and would begin to escape Soviet control. This threatened even the minimum goal of the Soviet Union, a closed economic-political buffer zone between Germany and Russia. Stalin, therefore, bluntly forbade participation in the Marshall Plan by the East Europeans, and he called together their leaders in September 1947 for the formation of a new Communist International, the so-called Communist Information Bureau, or Cominform. The Soviet orchestrator of the Cominform conference, Andrei Zhdanov, confirmed what had become obvious to all by then: the world was divided into "two camps."

The Western Allies solidified their camp by constructing an anti-communist government in western Germany and an anti-Russian military alliance embracing most of Western Europe. Abandoning any pretense of four-power cooperation, the United States, France, and Britain conferred in London from February to June 1948 on the future of *West* Germany. On June 18 they introduced a new currency, the *Deutschmark,* in the three Western zones, and the following month they authorized representatives of the eleven German *Lander* (states) under their control to write a new federal constitution. At the same time, the British, Americans, and Canadians held joint military staff talks in Washington, then invited other Western European nations to join these exploratory negotiations for a military alliance.

The Russians reacted aggressively by pressuring their former allies in Berlin, which lay more than a hundred miles inside the Soviet zone of occupation but was jointly occupied and administered by the United States, Russia, Britain, and France. The four powers had never negotiated written agreements on road or rail access from the Western zones to Berlin, and the Russians had consistently limited the other powers to just one autobahn and one rail line. On June 24, 1948, the day after the Western powers extended their currency reform to West Berlin, the Russians stopped all rail and road traffic to the city and cut off electricity from the power stations in their sector. The Communists hoped that the Western powers would back down and leave Berlin, after which the whole city could be incorporated as the capital of the Soviet zone. The main goal of the blockade, however, was to halt the formation of a West German government and force an Allied return to negotiations for a united Germany. The Russians did not want to set off World War III. They just wanted a favorable ending to World War II.

Instead, the Berlin blockade boomeranged against the Russians. The Allies had secured written agreements in November 1945 designating three air corridors to Berlin from the West. Few people believed that significant amounts of supplies could be ferried to Berlin by air; but through a herculean effort the Americans and the British mounted the largest airlift in history, from the end of June 1948 until the Russians finally lifted the blockade in May 1949. Instead of dividing the Western Allies and demoralizing the Germans, the Berlin blockade created a tremendous feeling of solidarity among them. It became a self-fulfilling prophecy, hastening the consolidation of a divided Germany which it was designed to prevent.

Berlin, a city of about three million people in 1948, generally imported about 12,000 tons of supplies a day from the Western zones of Germany, including 2,000 tons of food. The British and American transport planes could only carry about two and a half tons apiece. Nevertheless, in the first full month of the blockade, the Anglo-Americans managed to airlift just over the required food minimum of 2,000 tons. Most of the imported food was nourishing but unpalatable, and mainly dehydrated. This led to endless jokes among Berliners. One cartoon showed a scrawny stork delivering a flat, two-dimensional baby

19

with an instruction label: "Dehydrated. Soak in warm water for twenty minutes." By the end of the year, the monthly airlift totals had exceeded 4,000 tons per day, but this fell far short of what would be needed to survive the winter. Coal could not be dehydrated.

Miraculously, the winter of 1948-49 proved as mild as the one two years before was severe. The temperatures in Berlin rarely fell below freezing and the transport pilots enjoyed near-summer flying conditions. By the time the winter ended, the Americans had brought in new transport planes and were ferrying over 7,000 tons per day. The Russians finally lifted the blockade on May 12, 1949, in exchange for new four-power talks on the status of Germany. These duly convened in Paris on May 23, droned on for about a month, then adjourned with nothing settled. On the very day the Paris talks began, May 23, the Western occupying powers signed the West German Basic Law. The Germans held elections in the Western zones on August 14, and on September 20 Konrad Adenauer, a conservative Catholic politician from Cologne, took office as chancellor of the German Federal Republic. In October, the communist-dominated Socialist Unity Party proclaimed the founding of the German Democratic Republic in the Russian zone. Germany was definitively broken in two, a division that would last for forty years.

Just as the Berlin blockade was winding down in April 1949, the United States, Canada, and the nations of Western Europe signed the North Atlantic Treaty,[3] which went into effect on August 24, 1949. A few days later, on August 29, the Russians announced their first successful atomic bomb test, much sooner than the Americans believed possible. The Cold War had begun in earnest, with Germany and Europe divided, and both sides armed and dangerous.

The Cold War in Europe had its origins in a process that some social scientists call "disjointed incrementalism," that is, neither side followed a master plan or blueprint but each took a series of small steps that seemed reasonable at the time but led to unforeseen consequences. The British journalist Martin Walker puts the same point more clearly and vividly: "In retrospect, the congealing of the Cold War in 1947-48 was oddly like a series of volleys in a tennis match." The Americans announced the Marshall Plan, Stalin countered with the Cominform. Britain and America introduced currency reforms in western Germany and took the first steps toward a West German state. Russia responded with the Berlin blockade. The Western Allies then countered with NATO and the creation of West Germany. This back-and-forth volleying began

3. Twelve states signed the original NATO Treaty: the United States, Canada, Iceland, Great Britain, France, Italy, Belgium, Netherlands, Luxembourg, Norway, Denmark, and Portugal. In the early 1950s, Greece, Turkey, and West Germany were admitted to the alliance.

during World War II and continued until the match stalemated in 1949. It is impossible to say who lobbed the first volley. A series of wild shots made the Grand Alliance fly apart.

Could it have turned out any differently? The experience of one small European country indicates that at least in some circumstances it might have. Finland, which fought alongside the Germans in a bitter border war with Russia, then was defeated and occupied by the Red Army, was not partitioned or reduced to satellite status as was the rest of Eastern Europe. The Russians ensured that Finland would remain "friendly"; indeed they signed a Treaty of Friendship, Cooperation, and Mutual Assistance in 1948 forbidding the Finns to join any alliance or coalition against the Soviet Union. Yet no communist government ever took power in Helsinki, and the Finns remained a constitutional democracy with a free-enterprise economy, just like their Scandinavian neighbors. In this case, a "friendly government" on the border of the Soviet Union was not compelled to become a satellite.

Finland escaped the Cold War for a number of reasons. First of all, the fierce resistance of the tiny Finnish army, up until their final surrender to the Russians in September 1944, impressed Stalin and laid the basis for a policy of mutual respect. Yet this could hardly have been the crucial factor. After all, the Germans fought even more effectively against Russia and Stalin felt no urge to act leniently towards them. A second reason why the Soviet Union adopted a flexible Finnish policy is that Finland lay on the periphery of Stalin's security concerns. Unlike Poland, it was not a classic invasion route into Russia. Nevertheless, the Finnish front was not unimportant. The Finns took part in the thousand-day siege of Leningrad that claimed the lives of over a million Russians; and the Finnish border, both before and after Finland's defeat by Russia, lay tantalizingly close to the former imperial capital.

Paradoxically, it seems that the major reason why Finland was treated so differently from the rest of Eastern Europe is that Stalin enjoyed a totally free hand there. The Western Allies never contested any of his moves in that country, and thus the ever-suspicious Stalin never had grounds to fear the worst. Great Britain clearly recognized that Finland formed part of the Soviet strategic sphere, and the British representative on the postwar Allied Control Commission acted merely as an observer. The United States never declared war against Finland so it did not sit on the ACC and did not protest any of the Soviet actions.

Indeed, all three powers agreed at the Teheran Conference, in December 1943, that Russia would exercise predominant interest in Finland so long as it guaranteed the postwar independence of the country. The fact that agreement was reached so early, at the height of Allied cooperation, aided the Finns, and Finland later proved so unimportant to Britain and the United States that they

Finland after World War II

lobbed no rhetorical protests toward the Kremlin. Free of any security threats on the Finnish frontier, Stalin permitted a Conservative Finnish politician, J. K. Paasikivi, to remain president of that country and did not encourage the Finnish Communist Party, which polled about a quarter of the votes in postwar elections, to overthrow the government. Benevolent neutrality on the part of the Finns suited Russian interests.

Finland's status vis-à-vis Russia turned out roughly equivalent to Canada's relationship with the United States. Neither Finland nor Canada could be altogether independent in their foreign policies, for their giant neighbors would never permit them to join a hostile alliance. Yet neither was a true satellite, lacking internal freedom and independent sovereignty. The Finnish or Canadian "model" may not represent the best of all possible worlds for a nation-state, but it does point the way to a happier fate than that suffered by Poland and its neighbors.

It seems unlikely that Stalin would ever have applied the Finnish model to Poland and East Germany, for that unhappy stretch of territory had proven too vital to Russian military defense. Nothing but a firm Communist hold on those regions would reassure him. It might have been applied in Czechoslovakia, which was governed by a genuine coalition government until it was overthrown by the Communist Party in 1948. Truman and his secretaries of state, however, vehemently protested Soviet actions, instead of simply conceding that all of Eastern Europe lay within the Soviet sphere. Less idealistic rhetoric but more realistic geopolitical policy on the part of the United States might have ensured a happier result.

American leaders could only have pursued such a realist policy if they possessed a clear vision of an alternative future for Europe, different from the hostile division that ensued, yet different too from the temporary cooperation of the Grand Alliance years. Such an alternative vision might have looked something like this: all of Eastern Europe would be conceded as a Soviet sphere of influence, whereas Western Europe, specifically France, the Low Countries, and the British Isles, would be considered firmly within the American sphere. In between, the center of Europe, from Sweden in the north, down through a united Germany, Austria, Switzerland, and Italy, would be neutralized and demilitarized as a buffer zone between the Russians and the Anglo-Americans. Perhaps, such a policy might have permitted Stalin, or at least his less rigid successors, to loosen up in Eastern Europe.[4]

4. After Stalin died in 1953, Nikita Khrushchev did sign the Austrian State Treaty of 1955, ending four-power occupation of that country and stipulating its neutrality. The Cold War had hardened too much by this time, however, for such a solution to be applied to Germany.

This is not just a hypothetical policy alternative, for something very similar actually took place in northern Europe. Sweden remained neutral throughout the Cold War. Finland on the east had a treaty of friendship and a limited military alliance with Russia, whereas Norway and Denmark on the west joined NATO but limited their commitments to the alliance, not permitting nuclear weapons or foreign bases on their territory. All the Nordic countries preserved their internal freedom, and the level of international tension remained relatively low in the region.

At the very moment when the Cold War was crystallizing, during the Berlin blockade, George Kennan began to re-think his previous hardline policies towards the Soviet Union and explore something akin to the northern European model for Central Europe. Kennan's policy planning staff delivered a wide-ranging memorandum, known as Plan A, to Secretary of State George Marshall in November 1948, shortly before Marshall relinquished his office to Dean Acheson. Plan A called for a halt to the construction of a separate West Germany and in its stead a new series of negotiations on German unification. In order to make this possible, Kennan advised that all four occupying powers should withdraw their troops to the borders of Germany, the British to Hamburg, the Americans to Bremen, the Russians to Stettin, and the French back to Alsace. The division of Europe, however, had proceeded too far for Kennan's revised plans to be accepted. When Plan A was leaked in the *New York Times* on May 12, 1949, the French and British protested sharply and Secretary of State Acheson ended any further discussion of a united Germany. By this stage in the emerging Cold War, both sides were content to settle for half of Germany, half of Europe, so long as that half were firmly embedded in their own political, economic, and military system. The Scandinavian, Finnish, Kennan solution was never attempted in the heart of Europe.

As a result, the United States and the Soviet Union confronted each other as hostile rivals for forty years, in Europe and then throughout the world (as we will see in later chapters). In retrospect, this may not seem such a disastrous development. After all, cold war is far more acceptable than hot war, and the second half of the twentieth century has proven less bloody than the first half. Since the Cold War finally ended in 1989-91, some politicians and strategists manifest a certain nostalgia for it. The rigid bipolar rivalry imparted stability to international relations and made most crises relatively predictable. The post–Cold War world seems messy and ill-defined by comparison. Historian John Lewis Gaddis, in a brilliant and provocative series of essays, has even renamed the Cold War the "Long Peace," pointing out that forty years without a great power war is longer than most such periods in recent history.

I believe it is a mistake to take too sanguine a view of the Cold War, however. There may not have been a direct military conflict between the Soviet

Union and the United States, but there were major, bloody wars between the United States and other communist countries in Korea and Vietnam, and the Soviet Union fought a large-scale, equally disastrous war in Afghanistan. On several occasions, notably during the Cuban missile crisis of 1962, the world came dangerously close to a nuclear holocaust.

Historian Walter LaFeber's viewpoint on the Cold War is more sobering, and, in my opinion, more accurate than Gaddis's notion of a long peace. LaFeber opens his widely used textbook on the history of the Cold War with this paragraph:

> The Cold War has dominated American life since 1945. It has cost Americans $8 trillion in defense expenditures, taken the lives of nearly 100,000 of their young men, ruined the careers of many others during the McCarthyite witch hunts, led the nation into the horrors of Southeast Asian conflicts, and in the 1980s triggered the worst economic depression in forty years. It has not been the most satisfying chapter in American diplomatic history.

In addition to the purely American consequences of the Cold War highlighted by LaFeber, this book will show how the Russian-American rivalry affected, and often poisoned, the history of the entire world in the second half of the twentieth century.

CHAPTER TWO

Cracks in the Iron Curtain

E ven as the Iron Curtain settled down over Europe, "from Stettin to Trieste" in Churchill's words, the solidarity of the two armed camps began to come apart at the seams. Just behind the city of Trieste, one of the most militant communist nations, Yugoslavia, broke away from Stalin's control in 1948 and charted an independent course in foreign policy. On the other side of the curtain, French leaders never felt comfortable deferring to the American superpower and admitting that their country's days of world leadership were finished. Though France did not break away from the Western alliance until several decades later, it did pioneer new relationships with other countries in Western Europe which eventually led to greater European unity, independent of the superpowers. In the first years after World War II, therefore, the very years when the Cold War froze solid, Europe was also beginning to come apart, and then find new ways of coming together.

Yugoslavia, the first "heretic" in the Communist bloc, had already endured immense stress and sheer terror before its traumatic break with Stalin's Russia. The "Kingdom of Serbs, Croats, and Slovenes," as it was officially called until the name "Yugoslavia" (land of the South Slavs) was adopted in 1929, first emerged out of the wreckage of the Austro-Hungarian Empire after World War I. King Alexander Karadjordjević of Serbia proclaimed himself ruler of the newly enlarged country on December 1, 1918. The Croats and Slovenes feared dominance by the more numerous Serbs, but they initially accepted the union of South Slavs as a better alternative than the revival of Austrian-German power or the expansion of Italian influence across the Adriatic.

Nationalist tensions divided the new state almost from its birth. The initials of royal Yugoslavia in the Serbo-Croatian language, SHS, were interpreted

26

by many Croats to mean "Serbs Want It All" *(Srbe Hoce Sve)*, and by Serbs in turn as "Only the Croats Spoil It" *(Samo Hrvati Smetaju)*. In fact, Serbs did dominate the officer corps of the army, the upper civil service, and the police. The constitution of the state symbolized Serbian preeminence, for it had been adopted on June 28, 1921, St. Vitus Day, the Serbian national holiday commemorating the medieval battle of Kosovo Plain. Croats and Slovenes called this governmental instrument the *Vidovdan* (Vitus Day) Constitution. Historian Aleksa Djilas has concluded that "many Croatian nationalists in the 1930s considered Croatia to be an occupied territory."

The moderate leader of the Croatian peasant party was assassinated in the halls of parliament on June 20, 1928, and the more extreme Croatian nationalists, led by Ante Pavelić, went into exile in Mussolini's Italy, forming a terrorist organization, named *Ustasha* (Uprising). In response, King Alexander proclaimed martial law on January 6, 1929, initiating a royal dictatorship that attempted to will divisive nationalism out of existence and impose a greater Yugoslav consciousness on all his subjects. He divided the country into nine new provinces, each named after geographical features, such as rivers or the seacoast, rather than ethnic groups. Under the new scheme, no piece of land was labeled Serbia, Croatia, or Slovenia (this is when the name of the kingdom was changed tô Yugoslavia).

On October 9, 1934, an Ustasha assassin struck down King Alexander while on a state visit to France. His brother, Prince Paul, acting as regent for the new king who was still a child, continued Alexander's oppressive, anti-Croatian policies, until it was too late. Shortly before Hitler sparked off World War II, the Yugoslav ruler conceded a large amount of internal autonomy to a newly designated Croatian province and forged a coalition government of moderate Serbian and Croatian leaders. This *Sporazum,* or agreement, did not placate Croatian extremists. When the Nazis invaded the Balkans in May 1941 and drove the Yugoslav king, regent, and government into exile in Britain, they partitioned the country and installed the Ustasha leader, Pavelić, as ruler of the puppet state of Croatia.

Ante Pavelić, a Catholic Croat from the mountains of Hercegovina, had been educated at a Jesuit prep school, then took a law degree at the University of Zagreb, in the main city of Croatia. During his Italian exile he began aping the mannerisms of Benito Mussolini, calling himself the *Poglavnik,* or Leader. When he took power in 1941, he proclaimed an Italian nobleman King Tomislav II of Croatia, but the new monarch prudently never set foot in his kingdom. Pavelić's Ustasha movement was not, perhaps, truly fascist, for it lacked the dynamism, expansionism, and economic control of either Mussolini's Fascists or Hitler's Nazis.[1] It was an old-fashioned nationalist movement,

---

1. In chapter 16 of volume 1, (p. 290)I developed a definition of fascism as "an authoritarian system of government based on the 'leader principle' (one-man rule), and

looking backward to an imagined medieval past rather than forward to a technocratic future. Yet the Ustasha shared one brutal feature with the Nazis: They committed genocide during World War II.

On June 22, 1941, Mile Budak, the minister of religion and deputy leader, announced his government's policy toward the two million Eastern Orthodox Serbs who lived within the Roman Catholic state of Croatia: they would "convert a third, expel a third, and kill a third." Within weeks, terrorist squads were murdering the inhabitants of whole villages and sending any survivors on a hasty trip to the nearest Catholic priest for re-baptism or else into pell-mell flight. The Ustasha also slaughtered any Jews or Gypsies they could find, but their main goal was to "cleanse" the country of the "Serbian oppressors." Serbs who escaped the terror committed atrocities in revenge. Tragically, the Slavic Muslims of Bosnia often found themselves caught in the middle.

The Croatian puppet state set up a number of concentration camps to facilitate its policy of genocide, most notably at Jasenovać in the marshes along the Sava River. At least seventy thousand Serbs, Jews, and Gypsies were killed at this camp alone. For the most part, however, the Croatian genocide was more haphazard than Hitler's Final Solution. The greatest numbers of Serbs were killed in their own villages or on the run, rather than in industrial killing factories. Eyewitnesses reported that Ustasha gangs would descend upon a village and order all the peasants to gather at the town hall. Then they would tie the victims' hands behind their backs (sometimes just the men, but more often the women and children also) and either march them out into the forest or load them onto trucks. At a suitably isolated spot, the terrorists would open fire with their rifles and push the dying victims over a cliff. In exceptionally brutal instances, the village populace would be locked in an Orthodox church which was then set on fire. The entire procedure resembles the Young Turk genocide against the Armenians more than the Nazi Holocaust. No one knows for sure how many people were slaughtered in Croatia during the war, but conservative historians who are not biased toward either side estimate about 330,000, roughly one-sixth of the Serbs living in the Ustasha state at the beginning of the war.

The decades-long strife between Croats and Serbs, culminating in genocide, played a major role in the Communist rise to power in Yugoslavia during and after World War II. Though Stalin's Communist International, the Comin-

---

marked by — extreme nationalism . . . ; central direction and mobilization of the economy; violence as an ordinary political practice; glorification of military values; and expansionist foreign policies." The Ustasha certainly fulfilled the requirements of authoritarian, violent, nationalist one-man rule, but they had relatively static, conservative goals and did not aspire towards either territorial expansion or control of the economy the way Mussolini did in Italy.

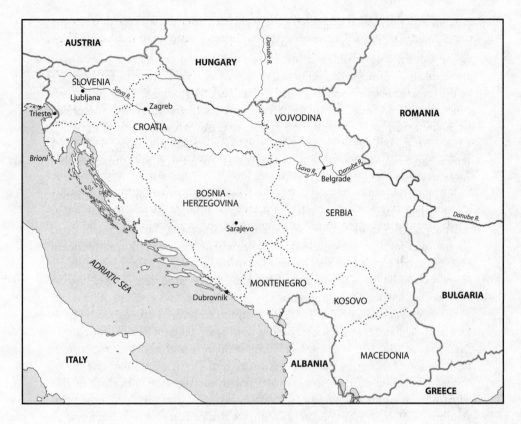

Yugoslavia, 1940-1990

tern, had actively promoted ethnic divisiveness in Yugoslavia and attacked the royal government as a capitalist tool of the French and British imperialists, the native Communists avoided ethnic wrangles. The Communist Party of Yugoslavia dutifully mouthed the Comintern line when required but in fact was one of the few all-Yugoslav organizations that included Croats, Slovenes, Serbs, and other ethnic minorities on an equal footing. Though the party was often riven by factional disputes, these quarrels rarely broke down along ethnic lines. When nationalist passions exploded with unprecedented violence during the Ustasha terror, the Communists were uniquely poised to transcend nationalism and furnish a unifying alternative.

The leader of the Yugoslav Communists, Joseph Broz (whose revolutionary nickname was "Tito"), embodied this transnationalism since his father was a Croat and his mother a Slovene. He was born on May 7, 1892, in the village of Kumroveć about twenty miles north of Zagreb, near the river border between Hungarian-ruled Croatia and Austrian-controlled Slovenia. He was baptized a Roman Catholic but apparently lost his faith by the time he left his village to seek work elsewhere. Broz apprenticed to a locksmith and became quite adept at tinkering with machinery. Later he liked to call himself an engineer, but in fact he took a variety of jobs, including waiting on tables. He was drafted into the army of the Austro-Hungarian Empire in 1913 and had become a non-commissioned officer by the time war broke out. Though indubitably a son of the working class, Joseph Broz showed few if any signs of radicalism at this early date. One of his biographers, Stefan Pavlowitch, sums up his youth in this fashion: "The impression one gets . . . during this period is of a young boy desperate to get away from the hard life of his native village. He dreams of appearances: waiters and non-commissioned officers wear smart clothes, and those occupations consequently appeal to him."

Broz was wounded and taken prisoner by Russian troops in 1915 and spent the next two years in prison camps until he was set free during the revolution of 1917. He was present in Petrograd during some of the events of that revolutionary year and was briefly imprisoned, but by his own account he did not do much during the Russian Revolution. He spent most of the time in far-off parts of Siberia, where he married a Russian woman (the first of five wives). He definitely joined the Communist Party upon his return to Yugoslavia after World War I but did not become an activist until 1925, at the age of thirty-three. He then became a full-time Communist union organizer, working his way up to general secretary of the Croatian Metalworkers Union, spending five years in King Alexander's prisons, and subsequently traveling across Europe for the Comintern. He survived Stalin's purges of the late 1930s and was finally confirmed as general secretary of the Yugoslav Communist Party in 1939. Somewhere along the way he adopted the nickname of "Tito." This held no special meaning but was simply a common name in the region where he grew up. It derives from *Titus* in Latin and is spelled the same in Italian.

Tito and the Yugoslav Communists mounted a partisan resistance against the German and Italian invaders during World War II, constantly shifting their camps within the natural fortress of the Bosnian mountains. They also fought a double civil war with the Croatian Ustasha and the non-communist Serbian resistance, nicknamed the *Chetniks* (bandits). The Chetniks wore long beards for they had sworn not to shave until they had driven out the foreigners, but the Partisans, like fanatical true believers everywhere, remained clean-shaven. More importantly, the Partisans numbered many women and a wide variety of ethnic groups among their followers, whereas the Chetniks were exclusively Serbian men. Women did not generally rise to high positions within the Communist resistance but representatives of the various Yugoslav nationalities did. Tito's closest lieutenants included Edward Kardelj, a Slovene; Alexander Ranković, a Serb; and Milovan Djilas from Montenegro (a formerly independent state closely allied with Serbia in language and culture).

The Partisans survived seven offensives by the Germans, including one that forced them into a long march along the mountain spine of Bosnia in the summer of 1942, another that resulted in a heroic withdrawal across the Sutjeska River with thousands of wounded in May of 1943, then the seventh and final offensive aimed at capturing Tito himself on his birthday in 1944. When the Nazi armies finally retreated under Allied onslaughts, Stalin's Red Army joined Tito's Partisans to liberate the Yugoslav capital of Belgrade on October 23, 1944. In the meantime, the British had been dropping supplies to the Partisans, judging that they showed more fight against the enemy than the Chetniks did. Tito met personally with both Churchill and Stalin during 1944, and emerged as uncontested ruler of Yugoslavia by the end of the war.

It has often been said that Tito's followers were the first Communist Party since the Russian Bolsheviks to win power on their own, rather than as a gift from the conquering Soviet army. In the most literal sense, this is not quite true. The Communist Party of Yugoslavia numbered only about twelve thousand members on the eve of World War II, and though it was united and well disciplined, it would not have come to power anytime soon if the war had not broken out. The Communist Partisans were the most active resistance fighters in the Balkans during the war, but they could not have defeated the Germans by themselves. The constant battering of Hitler's armies by both Western and Eastern Allies, then the final push on Belgrade by the Russians, were required to bring Tito to power. It is true, however, that by 1944 the Partisans had largely won the civil war against both Chetniks and Ustasha, becoming the strongest indigenous military power in Yugoslavia. Unlike the leaders of other Soviet satellites, who were imposed on their countries by the Russians, the Yugoslav

Communists spent the war fighting and winning on their native ground, not pushing paper in the Kremlin.

The most important reason why Tito was able to consolidate his power in Yugoslavia is the transnational appeal of his Communist movement. The Ustasha terrorists virtually drove the Serbian resistance into Tito's hands, and toward the end of the war, as it became clear that the Nazis and Ustashas would lose, many Croats saw joining the Partisans as a safe way out, for Tito's Communists welcomed them and did not take revenge against Croatians. The Communist Party was an all-Yugoslav movement with committed followers from every region and every nationality of the multinational state. It was able to transcend the fierce nationalist passions of wartime and square the circle of Balkan ethnicity. British journalist Richard West has concluded: "Ironically, Ante Pavelić's policy towards the Serbs led to the very two things he most feared and detested: a Communist government and a reunited Yugoslavia."

The first postwar elections, in early 1946, were clearly rigged, producing a 96 percent majority for the officially endorsed slate of candidates, but Tito was genuinely popular and could probably have won a fair election. War weariness and his party's multi-ethnic appeal would have ensured that. Yet it would be a mistake to consider Tito at this time (1945-48) as anything other than a committed Communist. In fact, American and British leaders considered Yugoslavia the model Soviet satellite, rigidly authoritarian in its internal policies and devoted to the cause of worldwide revolution and the expansion of Communist influence.

Tito himself was a Stalinist by background and conviction. After all, he survived the purges of the late 1930s, partly by the good luck of being absent from Moscow most of the time, but also because he fitted the Stalinist profile of a working-class leader, with no intellectual pretensions and a proven record of suppressing all factionalism within his party. If his biographers are to be believed, however, he might be characterized, somewhat whimsically, as a Stalinist with a heart of gold. He apparently lacked the paranoid suspiciousness of the Soviet dictator and possessed a remarkable ability to forgive past enemies, so long as they no longer posed a threat to him or his movement. He once commented on Stalin's purges (after he had broken with the Soviet leader): "They should have been hit over the head, but not beheaded." Though he imprisoned and executed numerous political enemies, he generally avoided torture and elaborate show trials.

Joseph Broz Tito, therefore, led a united party and country after World War II and was the second most important Communist in the world after Joseph Stalin. That, of course, soon proved to be a problem. Stalin always worried about number two, lest he possibly overshadow number one. In 1948, therefore, the Soviet dictator mounted a propaganda campaign against Tito and expelled him from the international communist movement. This caused the first crack in the Iron Curtain.

Even during the war, tensions had developed between Stalin and the Yugoslav Communist leaders. Stalin was waging coalition warfare with Britain and the United States, and he therefore instructed the subordinate communist parties of Europe to downplay their revolutionary goals and simply fight for "national liberation." The Yugoslavs, however, proclaimed a "Red Republic" at the village of Uzice in Serbia and ostentatiously organized "proletarian brigades" as the spearhead of their resistance forces. At the end of 1943 Tito and his lieutenants established a provisional government for the liberated portions of Yugoslavia, without consulting Stalin. While these hints of insubordination rankled the Soviet dictator, his meager aid to the Partisans, far inferior to what the British provided, frustrated the Yugoslavs.

None of these irritants, however, broke into the open, and at the end of the war Tito was filled with self-confidence and enjoyed immense prestige in the international communist movement. Furthermore, the Yugoslavs, considering themselves natural leaders of the Balkans, proved more zealous to spread communism than the Russians did. They explored the possibility of federation with the governments of Albania and Bulgaria, and aided communist revolutionaries fighting the British-backed government of Greece. Tito was constructing a Balkan solar system within Stalin's communist galaxy, with Belgrade as the sun around which the smaller planets revolved.

Stalin, however, continued his cautious, defensive foreign policies after the war, trying to avoid confrontation with the nuclear-armed American forces and their British allies. He had made a deal with Churchill in 1944 to stay out of the Greek civil war, in return for a free hand elsewhere in Eastern Europe, and he largely kept his promise. When Yugoslav aid to Greek rebels provoked the Truman Doctrine in March 1947, Stalin believed that Tito had gone too far and needed to be reined in.

The causes of the Tito-Stalin split, therefore, were twofold: a naked power conflict between two proud leaders and a disagreement over foreign policy. Tito did not rebel against Stalin because he disagreed with his dictatorial policies or because he wished to construct a different kind of communism, a communism with a human face. He did not rebel against Stalin at all. The Soviet leader precipitated the split, since he could abide no threats to his own authority, and because he viewed Tito's foreign policy as too adventurous and dangerous. He decided toward the end of 1947 that in a world polarizing into two hostile camps all communist parties must march to the same tune, under his direction.

Stalin invited the Yugoslav leaders to Moscow for consultations in January 1948. Tito, who had survived the purges of the 1930s by avoiding the Soviet capital, excused himself this time as well, sending Milovan Djilas and other subordinates. The Soviet dictator ordered the Yugoslavs to sign a treaty binding them to consult with the Soviet government on all foreign policy issues, and they dutifully complied. Then, in March, Stalin increased the pressure by withdrawing Soviet military and economic advisors from Yugoslavia and sending a long letter denouncing Tito's supposed deviations from orthodox Marxist ideology. Any other satellite leader would have sent back a fawning response, filled with self-criticism and repentance. Tito himself would have done so before World War II, but the wartime exploits of Yugoslav Communists had so increased his pride and prestige that he refused this time. An exchange of letters between Belgrade and Moscow ensued over the next several months, in which the Yugoslavs attempted to conciliate the Soviets without admitting any errors. They also refused to attend the second meeting of the Cominform in Bucharest in June. At Stalin's direction, therefore, the international communist organization expelled Yugoslavia on June 28, 1948, coincidentally the Serbian national holiday, St. Vitus Day.

The Soviets then applied every form of pressure short of outright invasion to eliminate Tito and bring more obedient Communists to power in Yugoslavia. All the other satellite leaders denounced Tito, and the press and radio in Russia and Eastern Europe called upon "healthy elements" in the Yugoslav party to overthrow him. The Soviets infiltrated Yugoslavia with secret agents who fanned the flames of ethnic divisiveness, particularly in the province of Macedonia, and hatched assassination plots. Finally, in 1949 Russia and all the Communist states of Eastern Europe imposed an economic blockade against Yugoslavia.

The Tito-Stalin split surprised the United States and its allies, but they saw in it an opportunity to pull back the Iron Curtain. So they supported Tito with economic and military aid, until Stalin's death in 1953 removed the overt pressure on Yugoslavia. During the three years of total Communist blockade, 1950-53, Yugoslavia's imports from the United States and five Western European nations soared from about 25 percent of its trade to 65 percent. All told, the Americans supplied 2.3 billion dollars in aid, including 719 million dollars worth of military supplies.

Considering how ruthlessly the Soviets crushed deviant communist movements in Hungary in 1956 and Czechoslovakia in 1968, it may seem odd that Stalin did not send the Red Army crashing into Yugoslavia in 1948. Yet a number of considerations made this always-cautious leader pause. First, Russia shared no common border with Yugoslavia, so military action would have to be coordinated with the satellite states of Romania, Hungary, and Bulgaria. This posed no insuperable obstacle, but did complicate the logistics, especially before the satellite state armies had been built up to full strength. Second, and more importantly, Tito and his Partisans had shown their ability to survive sustained assaults during World War II by withdrawing into the mountains of Bosnia. If Tito had defied Hitler and lived to tell the tale, he would probably do the same to Stalin and the Red Army. Finally, in 1948, the United States still enjoyed a nuclear monopoly, so Stalin avoided any moves that might provoke an American response. Even after the Soviets exploded their own atomic bomb in 1949, they remained behind America in the nuclear arms race and moved cautiously. Such caution was not misplaced, for the American military in the early 1950s advocated nuclear strikes on Bulgarian, Romanian, and Hungarian cities if these satellite countries attacked Yugoslavia. Though the Russians did hatch a detailed invasion plan in the summer of 1950, later revealed by a dissident Hungarian general, they never launched it.

Tito edged back toward the Soviet bloc after Stalin's death and then later carved out for himself a leadership role among the world's nonaligned nations (as we shall explore in parts 2 and 3). His top lieutenants, Edward Kardelj and Milovan Djilas, convinced him to support a new form of communist self-management in industry, whereby workers' councils took control of key factories without rigid party direction from Belgrade. In the 1960s, Minister of Tourism Milka Kufrin, one of the few female Partisans to attain an important role in government, opened up the country to Western visitors bringing hard cash. The Yugoslav government also permitted its own citizens to travel outside the Communist bloc. All these adaptations of the orthodox communist model were consequences, not causes, of the Tito-Stalin split. They do illustrate, however, that alternatives existed within the Communist bloc, even during the most frigid years of the Cold War.

Internal divisions and independent leaders were not unique to the Iron Curtain nations. On the other side of Europe, France produced its own "Tito" figure, General Charles de Gaulle, a heroic leader of wartime resistance against the Nazis who became a proud and prickly irritant to one of the superpowers after the war. De Gaulle and Tito were nearly the same age and both sat out World War I as prisoners of war, but otherwise their lives and careers unrolled quite differently.

Charles de Gaulle was born on November 22, 1890, to a provincial bourgeois family of Lille in northern France but was raised in Paris. He received a Jesuit education and remained a fervent Catholic all his life. He trained as a professional soldier, and after his POW years in Germany, worked his way up to brigadier general in both staff and line posts, espousing the new military doctrine of mobile, armored warfare which the Germans would use to such telling effect in their blitzkrieg. Whereas Joseph Broz came from peasant and working-class roots and toiled for the cause of international communism, de Gaulle was middle-class, religious, and fiercely nationalist.

When the French military and government capitulated to the Nazis after only a few weeks of fighting in 1940, de Gaulle felt profoundly humiliated and refused to accept the authority of the collaborationist regime at Vichy. Unlike Tito, however, who led the Partisans in person, the dissident general went into exile in Great Britain. Though hardly anyone had heard of him, he persuaded Churchill to let him broadcast an appeal for continued French resistance on the BBC. He then rallied the remnants of French forces in the imperial possessions of Africa, and in an audacious feat of political magic, transformed himself into a symbol of fighting French resistance. When the British asked him for a background biography, he replied: "I am a free Frenchman. I believe in God and in the future of my fatherland. I belong to no one." To anyone who would listen, he proclaimed, without a hint of humor or irony, "I am France."

Not many Allied leaders cared to listen. Franklin Roosevelt disliked the French in general, believing them unregenerate imperialists past their prime, and he loathed de Gaulle in particular. Stalin considered the French general amusing but irrelevant and simply ignored him. Churchill could be driven into towering rages by de Gaulle's arrogance and ingratitude, but he forced himself to deal with the general since he believed that France must play an important role in the postwar world in order to rebuild a balance of power in Europe. De Gaulle was not invited to any of the Big Three conferences during or after the war and was not even consulted before the Allies invaded French territory in North Africa. Churchill, however, convinced the other leaders to grant France an occupation zone in Germany and a permanent seat on the United Nations Security Council. Only de Gaulle's fellow general, Dwight D. Eisenhower, showed him much respect, graciously permitting him and his Free French forces to liberate Paris in person after the Normandy invasion of the Continent. De Gaulle made the most of the opportunity, swiftly co-opting the Resistance leaders who had remained in France and establishing himself at the head of a provisional government. He only avoided the kind of civil war that Tito fought in Yugoslavia because the collaborationists recognized they were defeated, the Communists followed Stalin's instructions and remained passive, and Eisenhower loaned de Gaulle two American divisions to overawe his opponents in Paris.

De Gaulle remained at the head of the French provisional government for only six months after the end of the war. All the old politicians of the defeated Third Republic flocked back to Paris to re-launch their careers, and the Constituent Assembly of the new Fourth Republic was deadlocked between Communists, Socialists, and Christian Democrats. De Gaulle viewed this political scene with disgust, believing that the party politics of revolving prime ministers was a recipe for national disaster. In his opinion, only a strong presidential form of government (with himself as president, of course) could save France from dominance by the American superpower. In a calculated political gamble, he resigned abruptly on January 20, 1946, expecting to be called back to power as a savior. Eventually he was proven right, but he had to wait twelve years.

Shortly before he resigned, however, General de Gaulle made one of the most important decisions of his life, one that held great significance for France and for all of Europe. In December 1945 he delegated Jean Monnet to establish a planning commission and supervise the reconstruction of the French economy. Monnet did more than that. He pursued an alternative vision of Europe and the world, pointing a way through and beyond the Cold War.

Omer Marie Gabriel Jean Monnet, born in the Cognac region of south-western France on November 9, 1888, was nearly the same age as de Gaulle but far different in temperament and outlook. Monnet possessed deeper local roots and, at the same time, a wider international field of vision than the nationalist general. He came from peasant stock in the vine-growing and brandy-making region of Cognac, and many of his friends and associates remarked upon his stubbornness and practicality, "like a peasant determined to sell his cow." Yet, in fact, he was two generations removed from the soil. His father had entered the ranks of the merchant class, managing a cooperative of small brandy distillers; and Jean had entered the family business as a globe-trotting salesman while still in his teens. His biographer, François Duchêne, points out that "if Cognac was in one way a narrow provincial community, it was also international, the min-iature world capital of brandy." Monnet, therefore, grew up with loyalties both narrower and wider than traditional nationalism.

He pursued international vocations all his life, and except for his father's brandy business, he claimed never to have applied for a job he did not invent. During World War I he worked with the French ministry of supply, coordinat-ing raw material purchases with the Allies. When his plans for continued eco-nomic cooperation were rejected at Versailles, he took a post as deputy secre-tary general of the new League of Nations. Returning briefly to the brandy business after his father's death, he then spent the rest of the 1920s and 1930s as an international merchant banker, arranging loans, making deals, and building up a network of influential friends all over the world.

Though he was already fifty years old when World War II broke out, that conflict proved to be the most formative and significant event of his life. In the years just before the war, Monnet worked again at the tasks of economic coop-eration, arranging French aircraft purchases in the United States. When his country was overrun by the Nazi blitzkrieg in 1940, he desperately proposed that Britain and France merge politically in order to continue resisting the in-vaders. Churchill agreed but the French government refused and capitulated to Hitler instead. Monnet fled to London, received a British passport signed per-sonally by Churchill, then spent most of the war in Washington cajoling aid out of Uncle Sam. Unlike de Gaulle, who irritated Franklin Roosevelt and most U.S.

leaders, Jean Monnet proved to be the Americans' favorite Frenchman. One of his co-workers during the war claims that Monnet would sometimes draft a message from Churchill to Roosevelt and then help the president compose the reply. Another remarks that he "thought in English and counted in dollars." Monnet saw the future in Washington. Impressed by the organizational energy and can-do spirit of the Americans, he realized that Europe's only hope lay in cooperation with the new superpower. As historian John Gillingham has concluded: "In the United States Monnet learned how to organize Europe."

Before Monnet, or any other French leader, could organize Europe, however, France needed to recover from its profound defeats in World War II. General de Gaulle revived the confidence and spirit of the French with his old-fashioned nationalist rhetoric. Monnet began the economic reconstruction of the country as director of the *Plan de Modernisation et d'Équipement* (Plan for Modernization and Investment). The Monnet Plan, as it is usually called, directed a substantial portion (18-20 percent of GNP annually) of French government spending and American Marshall Plan aid toward investment in key economic sectors, such as coal, power dams, railways, steel, and cement. Such an investment strategy was painful in the short run, short-changing consumer goods and housing, and fueling inflation that eroded workers' wages. It laid the foundations, however, for a long-range refurbishing of the French economy, making a particularly strong impact on the railway system and electrical grid. In the words of Monnet's biographer, "it encouraged an at least partial shift . . . from the pretensions of a moth-eaten great power to the realism of a medium-size but ambitious economic one."

Monnet's realism and practicality proved crucial when he began "organizing Europe" in 1950. The movement for European integration and unity was born less out of idealism than pragmatic considerations. To put the matter simply, France still feared Germany. In the immediate postwar years, the French representatives on the Allied occupation commissions resisted any attempts to reunite, reconstruct, or rearm Germany, often proving more disruptive and irritating than the Russians. Britain and the United States, as was discussed in the previous chapter, eventually decided to ignore the Russians, partition Germany, and rebuild their portion of the defeated enemy into a strong ally against communism. They ignored the objections of the French, too, correctly assuming that France had few if any independent options.

French fears of German revival centered upon a specific region, the heavily industrialized Ruhr River valley just over the border from France. The coal mines and steel mills of the Ruhr had provided the arms and energy for two disastrous invasions of France in the twentieth century. The French, however, did not just fear the Ruhr industrial barons; they also needed them economically. Northeastern France and portions of the Low Countries formed an economic unit with the German Ruhr. Indeed, a thousand years before, this region had been united in a single kingdom of Lotharingia (the origin of the French regional name Lorraine). In the twentieth century, the steel mills of Lorraine relied on coal and coke from the Ruhr. After World War II, therefore, the French wished to detach the Ruhr from the grasp of their enemy and either annex it or place it under international authority. The newly born German Federal Republic (West Germany), under its elderly but vigorous chancellor, Konrad Adenauer, resisted these threats as strongly as possible.

Jean Monnet found a way out of this political-economic tangle. On May 10, 1950, French foreign minister Robert Schuman, at Monnet's urging, proposed a pooling of the coal and steel resources of France, West Germany, and other democratic European nations into a single market area. Germany would retain sovereignty over the Ruhr and Lorraine would remain French, but coal and steel would pass back and forth as if there were no border. Monnet harbored long-range plans for a full-scale common market and perhaps a political merger into a "United States of Europe," but this initial step was a narrowly defined integration of just one economic sector, coal and steel. Monnet was content to label his proposal the "Schuman Plan," for he believed that "men in power are short of new ideas . . . [but] they want to do the right thing so long as they get the credit." In a classic example of turning lemons into lemonade, Monnet transformed the German Ruhr from a problem into an opportunity.

Both the German chancellor and the French foreign minister were predisposed to accept Monnet's coal-steel pool because of their geographically "Lotharingian" backgrounds. Schuman, as his German-sounding name suggests, was born in Lorraine when it was still ruled by the kaiser's Germany. Indeed, he served in the German army during World War I! Adenauer came from a heavily Catholic district of the Rhineland, quite close to the French border. These two leaders not only shared regional roots and a common religion but a Christian Democratic Party orientation. In fact, politicians from Christian Democratic parties held key posts in all six of the countries which joined the coal-steel pool and later formed the European Common Market. The extremes of left and right, the Communists and the followers of Charles de Gaulle, opposed European integration; but in a brief moment of creative influence, a centrist "Christian international," to coin a phrase, exercised decisive European leadership.

Despite their common backgrounds and worldviews, however, the leaders of France, Germany, and the other Western European countries would not have accepted the coal-steel pool unless national interests reinforced their predispositions. Germans longed for international acceptance and political rehabilitation, and feared that if they rejected the Schuman Plan the Allies would resume the dismantling of factories, which they had only stopped at the end of

1949. The French, on the other hand, viewed the integration of the Ruhr into a larger entity as a way of controlling and taming German industrial and arms-making capacity. They also desired secure access to coal from the Ruhr. In both Italy and France, enlargement of the political and economic sphere diluted the influence of large communist parties. Finally, the Low Countries saw integration as a guaranteed avenue into the huge German market. After much hard bargaining, therefore, representatives of six nations — France, West Germany, Italy, Belgium, Luxembourg, and the Netherlands — signed the Treaty of Paris on April 18, 1951. After ratification by the Six, the European Coal and Steel Community (ECSC) went into operation in August 1952. Jean Monnet took office as president of the nine-member High Authority of the ECSC, which proceeded to establish common markets for coal, iron ore, scrap iron, and steel. The "first government of Europe" had begun functioning.

It did not function very well. Monnet, who was neither economist nor industrialist, found himself consistently outmaneuvered by the coal and steel magnates of the various countries. The strong economic recovery that ensued in Europe in the 1950s owed little to the coal and steel community, but would have occurred in any case. Later, when problems did develop, such as a drastic overproduction of coal from 1959 onward or the challenge of new energy sources, such as oil and nuclear fission, the ECSC could find no solution. The economic impact of the Schuman Plan, therefore, was virtually negligible. Furthermore, the next steps toward European unity proved abortive. In response to the Korean War, Monnet spearheaded an effort to create the European Defense Community, with German, French, Italian, and other national armies melded into one force. At the same time, a number of legislators suggested an overarching European political community to which the new army and the coal and steel community would report. These plans proved too ambitious and threatening to the French National Assembly, which refused to ratify the European Defense Community in 1954. Attempts to unify Western Europe seemed destined for failure.

Yet as historian John Gillingham has emphasized, the Schuman Plan proved to be a political "triumph of failure." Such a paradox happens from time to time in the violent realm of revolutionary politics. For example, the 1916 Easter Rising in Ireland was a total fiasco, yet it stimulated nationalist resentments against England that resulted in independence less than a decade later. So, too, in the non-violent world of Monnet's politics. In the course of founding and operating the ECSC, European leaders became accustomed to dealing with each other as friendly rivals, not enemies. They slowly built confidence in the process of international cooperation and integration. Even half a Germany remained more powerful and potentially threatening than France or any of the other nations of Western Europe, but the Germans proved pragmatic and flexible in their dealings with Monnet and his followers. It is easy to be cynical, or even despairing, in such a violent time as the twentieth century, yet it appears that most European leaders learned something from the horrors of World War II. They did not let the rejection of the common defense community or the growing irrelevance of the coal and steel community discourage them, but pushed onward and established a wider common market.

Monnet himself played little direct role in the birth of the Common Market, for he was engrossed in another integration scheme, the formation of Euratom, a regional atomic energy agency. Instead, the foreign ministers of the Six met at Messina, Italy, to "relaunch Europe" in the summer of 1955. Under the leadership of the Belgian Paul-Henri Spaak, who shares the title of "Mr. Europe" with Monnet, a committee soon hammered out a proposal for a full-scale common market that would be phased in over a period of twelve years. The same six nations that composed the European Coal and Steel Community signed the Treaty of Rome on March 25, 1957, and the European Economic Community (EEC; usually called the Common Market) went into effect on New Year's Day 1958. This timing was fortunate, for General de Gaulle returned to power in France during 1958. Had the Treaty of Rome come up for ratification during his regime he might well have blocked it.

The Common Market was not an overnight success. Complete integration of the European national economies did not take place until 1992, instead of the original target date of 1970. During the decade of the 1960s, while General de Gaulle served as president of France, he twice vetoed the application of Great Britain for entry into the community.[2] Furthermore, the EEC did not develop exactly the way Monnet had envisioned. Instead of a strong supranational authority governing a United States of Europe, the Common Market proved to be a coalition or alliance of sovereign states that occasionally made economic concessions out of self-interest or necessity. Yet something significant had occurred in Europe. Though the Continent remained divided by the Cold War, and nation-states retained their jealous sovereignty, Western Europe became more and more of an economic unit, built around a French-German core. Gradually, it became an independent third force between the two superpowers. Jean Monnet, more than any other individual, was responsible.

In a century filled with mass murderers, such as Hitler, Stalin, and Pavelić, and dictators and demagogues, like Tito or de Gaulle, it is refreshing to encounter Jean Monnet. He never fought in an army or held elective office, yet he in-

2. In the immediate postwar years, Great Britain had held aloof from European integration, preferring to retain its close ties with the Commonwealth nations and to cultivate a "special relationship" with the United States. When both these schemes failed, the British belatedly applied for membership in Europe.

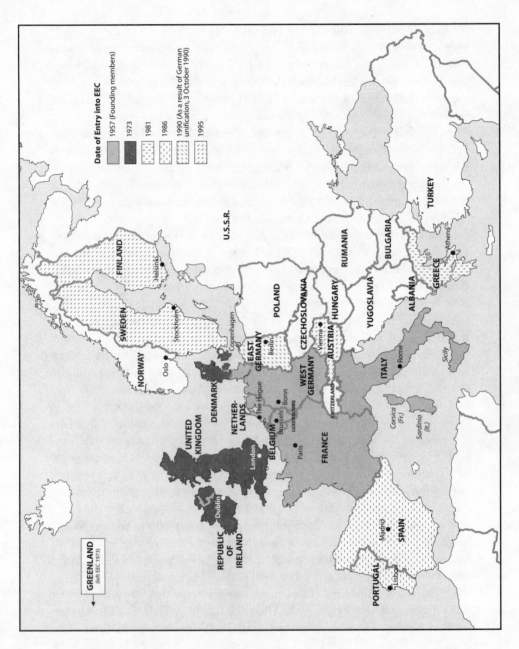

Date of Entry into EEC

1957 (Founding members)
1973
1981
1986
1990 (As a result of German unification, 3 October 1990)
1995

U.S.S.R.

TURKEY

FINLAND

Helsinki

SWEDEN

Stockholm

NORWAY

Oslo

Copenhagen

POLAND

CZECHOSLOVAKIA

EAST GERMANY

Berlin

HUNGARY

Vienna

AUSTRIA

RUMANIA

BULGARIA

YUGOSLAVIA

ALBANIA

GREECE

Athens

DENMARK

NETHER-LANDS

The Hague

Brussels Bonn

BELGIUM

LUXEMBOURG

WEST GERMANY

SWITZERLAND

ITALY

Rome

Sicily

UNITED KINGDOM

London

Paris

FRANCE

Corsica (Fr.)

Sardinia (It.)

REPUBLIC OF IRELAND

Dublin

SPAIN

Madrid

PORTUGAL

Lisbon

GREENLAND
(left EEC 1973)

Growth of the European Economic Community (Economic Union)

fluenced his country, Europe, and the world as profoundly as any politician or general. He employed the tools of intelligence and persuasion instead of violence or trickery, exercising influence behind the scenes rather than before the public. A recent English biographer of de Gaulle, Charles Williams, entitled his book about the imperious general *The Last Great Frenchman*. Monnet should be included in that company as one of the two greatest Frenchmen of the century. Indeed, I would argue that Monnet's talent was far more rare, and more valuable, than de Gaulle's, for it brought out the best in others. A French government official who knew both individuals once remarked: "With the General, you feel like the least intelligent of men. With Monnet, your intelligence seems to grow." Monnet's biographer, François Duchêne, calls him an "entrepreneur in the public interest."

Monnet's strongest weapon was his ability to change the context of an argument. When Germany and France were deadlocked over control of the Ruhr, he enlarged the field of vision, proposing a supranational authority and pointing to the more distant goal of a united Europe. Late in the century, it became fashionable to call this kind of change in the terms of debate a "paradigm shift." The American statesman George Ball, who worked with Monnet on the formation of the Coal and Steel Community, has proposed a more interesting analogy to explain the effectiveness of his technique. Monnet employed the strategy of sectoral integration, i.e., forging a supranational authority in just one area at first, the way Hitler's armies used the tanks of the Panzer Corps, as a spearhead of attack. In the blitzkriegs of World War II, tanks and planes would concentrate on one sector of the enemy defense, break through as rapidly as possible, then spread out behind the lines, changing the whole nature of the battlefield. So, too, in Monnet's politics. He concentrated his attack on one sector, then transformed the intellectual context of the argument. As John Gillingham has pointed out, after the announcement of the Schuman Plan "the word 'Europe' would never be spoken in quite the same way again."

The formation of a common market in Western Europe was not, strictly speaking, a crack in the Iron Curtain; indeed, in the short run, it reinforced the division of Europe. Unlike Tito's break with Stalin or de Gaulle's later attempts to withdraw from NATO, Monnet's efforts at European integration were encouraged by one of the superpowers, the United States. Monnet adopted much of his vision for a United States of Europe from the existing United States of America, which he came to know well. He built networks of influential American businessmen and politicians he could rely on for support and kept them well informed of his plans and schemes. At the end of World War II, American leaders encouraged the unification of Europe, as a way of strengthening the Western alliance against communism. The Marshall Plan had required the Europeans to organize themselves and write a recovery proposal of their own.

They failed to do this effectively, but Marshall Plan aid strengthened the hands of planners like Monnet. Before Schuman announced the proposal for a coal and steel community in 1950, he informed Secretary of State Dean Acheson, who convinced President Truman to respond favorably to the French initiative. Ironically, therefore, the United States encouraged a process that later in the century helped Europe become an economic rival.

Though the Cold War had polarized Europe into two hostile camps by mid-century, neither camp was ever completely monolithic. Yugoslavia's Joseph Broz Tito seemingly threatened the absolute control of Stalin over the Communist bloc, and so was expelled and threatened with invasion. The wily Yugoslav, however, managed to preserve his country's independence and carve out a separate role for himself in world politics. In France, General Charles de Gaulle tried to challenge the might of the other superpower, but was unable to exercise his personal authority until later in the Cold War. In the meantime, a more creative Frenchman, Jean Monnet, took the first steps toward overcoming nationalism and uniting Europe into an independent force. The deadly rivalry between the United States and the Soviet Union breathed a long frosty chill over Europe, but it never completely froze the forces of European political change. It never "stopped history," as it became fashionable to say at the end of the century. Though Europe, which had ruled the world in the late nineteenth and early twentieth centuries, was now overshadowed by the superpowers, Tito, de Gaulle, and Monnet still found ways of asserting European influence in the second half of the century.

PART TWO

INDEPENDENCE, REVOLUTION, AND CIVIL WAR IN ASIA

GK

World War II decisively altered the balance of power and, more importantly, the calculus of prestige in Asia. Japanese conquests in the Pacific and on the mainland of Southeast Asia shattered forever the myth of European invincibility, which had already been cracked and weakened by the First World War and various nationalist revolts in the interwar years. On the vast Asian subcontinent of India a non-violent protest movement, inspired by Mohandas K. Gandhi, paved the way for independence. At the same time in China, Mao Tse-tung captained a violent revolution that not only secured freedom from European domination but effected a massive social upheaval. The other countries of Southeast Asia also challenged the continuation of European colonial rule. The Philippines, Burma, and Ceylon (today's Sri Lanka) won independence relatively easily after World War II, as their colonial masters, the United States and Great Britain, simply gave up and relinquished power. However, in British Malaya, French Indochina, and Dutch Indonesia, revolutionary independence movements struggled against greater odds, with different results in each colony.

The Cold War between communism and capitalist democracy shadowed each of these Asian freedom movements. Though India had both socialist and communist parties, the Indian National Congress outmaneuvered or co-opted them at every step; and the end of British rule remained largely unaffected by the ideological struggle in Europe. In China, however, Mao's Communists overturned the Nationalists of Chiang Kai-shek in a bitter civil war that became intertwined with the Soviet-American rivalry. The other freedom movements in Southeast Asia fell somewhere between these two extremes, with communists gaining the upper hand in Indochina, but suffering defeat in Malaya and Indonesia. Finally, in the tiny Korean peninsula of northeastern Asia, the struggle between communism and capitalist democracy not only resulted in civil war, but sparked a large-scale shooting war between one of the superpowers, the United States, and the communist troops of North Korea and China. This first major armed conflict of the post–World War II era heated up the Cold War to the boiling point and nearly overflowed into World War III, but it was ultimately contained after three years of bitter fighting.

CHAPTER THREE

Soul Force versus the British Raj

The British established their *Raj* (which means reign or empire) in India through a policy of divide and rule. When the British left India after World War II, they could not devise a formula that would patch together all-India unity; instead, they partitioned the subcontinent into two states, Pakistan and India, then beat a retreat. Over a century of divide and rule gave way to a hasty and ignominious divide and quit. The freedom struggle led by Mohandas K. Gandhi and the Indian National Congress, however, did achieve a remarkable amount of unity through most of India and came to power with a greater sense of legitimacy and moral authority than many later anti-imperialist regimes. Gandhi's leadership by "soul force" marks one of the most amazing accomplishments of twentieth century nationalism.

The divisions which marked both the beginning and the end of the British Raj should hardly be surprising, for India is a country of great diversity in a land of continental size. The Asian subcontinent measures two thousand miles from north to south, and a little more at its widest point from east to west at the northern bulge — approximately the size of Europe without Russia or the United States east of the Mississippi River.[1] It encompasses a wide range of environments, from the snow-capped Himalayas in the north, to the fertile plain of the Indus and Ganges Rivers at the heartland, to coastal jungles and inland deserts further south. Different climates produced different staple foods, thus marking out one fundamental division of India, between wheat-eaters in the north and rice-eaters of the tropical south.

1. This description refers to undivided, pre-independence India, and thus includes the territory of the present-day states of Pakistan, Bangladesh, and India.

Despite its great size, geography makes India a natural unit, for it is enclosed by the highest mountains in the world on one side and the ocean on all the others. Over thousands of years, a certain cultural unity has enveloped the subcontinent, but the forces of division appear much stronger. Indians belong to three major racial groups — Aryan and Mongolian in the north and Dravidian in the south — and four linguistic groups, Indo-European, Dravidian, Tibeto-Chinese, and Austro-Asiatic. The people of modern India still speak in at least fourteen different tongues, though Hindi and English are the official languages. Climate, environment, and history have produced great diversity in India.

The fertile variety of the Indian subcontinent seems to have stimulated the religious imagination, for Indians have been prolific creators of religions. Both Hinduism and Buddhism developed in India long before the time of Jesus Christ. Today Hindus comprise the great majority of Indians and Buddhism has spread throughout Asia, but the latter has retained only a tiny minority of its native population. Two other minority faiths, Jainism and Sikhism, emerged as variants of Hindu beliefs and practices, and three religious groups (Muslims, Christians, and Parsis) arrived in India as conquerors. Along with religious creativity, Indians have also shown great aptitude for the rational logic of mathematics. Between about 500 and 800 A.D. Indians developed the concept of the zero and the style of numerals usually called "Arabic." In fact, Arab traders borrowed these ideas from the Indians and later transferred them to Europe.[2]

This ancient cultural exchange indicates that India was not isolated or unchanging before European "discovery" and rule. Arab and Indian merchants conducted a lively trade in spices and fine cotton cloth, and these commodities reached both Europe and China through intermediaries. The general level of material civilization was roughly similar in both Europe and India at the time of first contact about 1500. Indians used iron implements and explosive weapons, just as Europeans did, and had developed intricate trade and financial networks. Europeans enjoyed superior technology in just one aspect, the great range and mobility of their sailing ships. Not surprisingly, therefore, the first

2. This background section on India is meant to provide a means for evaluating cultural differences. In chapter 3 of volume 1, I developed a "roadmap" for navigating the contrasts between two cultures, which avoids ethnocentrism or a sense of cultural superiority on the one hand and cultural relativism on the other. This relatively neutral approach to different cultures includes four steps: (1) examine the nature of the climate and environment in a country; (2) analyze various functions that a particular society performs especially well; (3) judge a society primarily by its own standards; then (4) honestly assess the difference in outlook and beliefs, the "values gap," that still remains, between two different societies. Though I will not always apply these four criteria systematically in each chapter, the reader should keep them in mind.

European footholds in India were trading posts (usually called "factories") along the coast. What drew Europeans to these isolated outposts was the lure of profits from the spice trade. As a character in one of Salman Rushdie's novels remarks: "They came for the hot stuff, just like any man calling on a tart."

Beyond the spice-trading entrepots on the seacoast, the heart of India lay in its villages. In the nineteenth century over 700,000 villages dotted the countryside, each averaging about five hundred acres and between fifty and a hundred families. As long as the villagers could grow and eat their staple crops of wheat or rice and their customs were left undisturbed, they cared little what kind of traders plied the far-away sea routes or who ruled over them at higher levels of government.

From the perspective of modern-day nationalism, we tend to ask, "Who ruled at the center? What kind of government did India have?" In fact, when Europeans first arrived in India, they encountered one of the few successful, all-India central governments in history, the Mogul Empire centered at Delhi on the plain of the Ganges River. The Moguls were Islamic nomads who invaded India through the Khyber Pass in the late fifteenth century, then ruled over most of the subcontinent from about 1500 to 1750. After the mid-eighteenth century, Mogul rule became weaker and less effective, giving Europeans an opportunity to extend their influence. From an ethnocentric, European point of view, therefore, we might say that India was "declining" in the eighteenth and nineteenth centuries. Yet judging India by its own standards, much of this proves irrelevant. Historian Judith Brown has concluded: "India's political ecology raises basic problems for anyone attempting to exercise power on the subcontinent. . . . Sheer size and diversity mean that it will always be difficult to administer from an all-India centre." Mogul power was exceptional and transient. The decentralization and division which English conquerors took advantage of was the ordinary Indian condition.

Europeans found most of Indian society and culture repellent and made little effort to understand it. Even from a more neutral, twentieth-century viewpoint, some aspects of Indian society appear exotic at best or backward at worst, and Indian nationalists have tried to reform or abolish them. The feature of Indian society that most immediately struck Europeans was the caste system. Hindu scriptures divided the social structure into a hierarchy of four basic, functional groupings: the Priests (Brahmins), Warriors (Kshatriyas), Traders (Vaishyas), and Cultivators (Shudras). Those who performed the lowest, most polluting tasks of everyday life, such as cleaning latrines or picking up garbage, were outcasts or untouchables. This stylized hierarchy, however, did not adequately describe Indian society. In fact, dozens of castes subdivided villages and towns into smaller and more finely drawn social groups. Caste differs fundamentally from class in one respect: a person can never change from one caste to

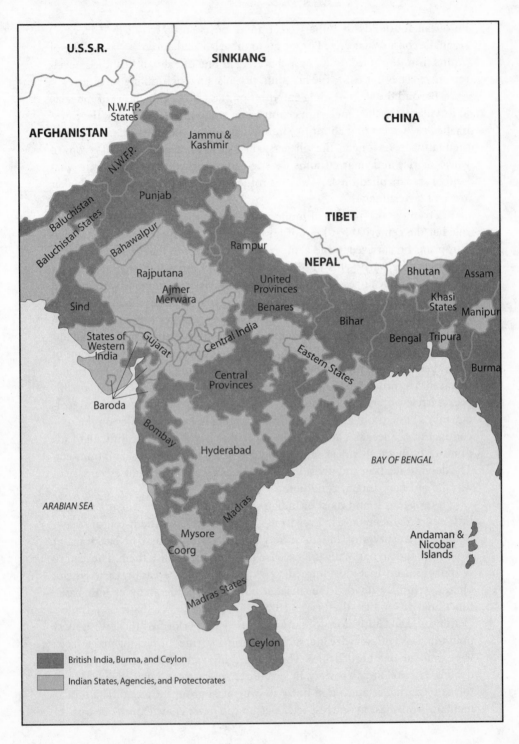

British India

another; he or she is born into it and must marry within it. Even if a Shudra somehow gains an education and earns a fortune, he or she cannot become a Brahmin. Caste society, therefore, seems unjust and non-dynamic to Europeans or Americans, but it makes for a stable society, where everyone has a place and remains content with it.

Several specific Indian customs offended Europeans, particularly the practice of child marriage and the inferior status of widows. Indian families generally arranged marriages for their children when they were very young, so that the union could be consummated as soon as the girl reached puberty. If her husband died at an early age, the young widow was forbidden to remarry and became a second-class citizen, without any economic or social function of her own. The most extreme version of female self-effacement, *suttee,* was practiced by some of the upper castes who required a widow to commit suicide by plunging herself into the flames of her husband's funeral pyre. The British attempted to ban *suttee* as early as 1829, but despite their revulsion at many Indian customs they adopted a generally "live and let live" attitude toward most of them. They had come to trade, and too much harping on cultural differences was bad for business. The British for the most part, therefore, slotted themselves into existing Indian society as yet another caste, the ruling caste, leaving the rest alone as much as possible.

The British Raj remained fragile and artificial throughout its entire history. Only a handful of English soldiers or traders were hardy enough to survive the climate and unfamiliar diseases of Asia, and few of them brought their wives and families with them until late in the nineteenth century. In 1837, when the British were just consolidating their hold over all of India, only 41,000 English lived in the country. Nearly a century later, in 1921, the entire European population, including women and children, still numbered only 156,500, in a country of 300 million Indians.

After suppressing a bloody revolt in 1857, the British deposed the last figurehead Mogul emperor in Delhi and assumed direct control over two-thirds of the land area and three-quarters of the population of India. Yet hundreds of principalities remained under the rule of Indian *rajahs* or *maharajahs*,[3] ranging from large, country-size principalities such as Hyderabad in south-central India to tiny city-states north of Bombay. Each principality remained technically independent, but a British resident at the rajah's court ensured that his policies did not conflict with British interests. In fact, the 562 Indian princely states were nothing more than British protectorates.

Small numbers of British rulers dominated Indian politics, either directly in the Raj or indirectly in the princely states. The British felt innately superior

3. *Rajah* means ruler or prince, whereas a *maharajah* is a "high ruler" or king.

to Asians, and no less a believer in racial superiority than Adolf Hitler much admired the British Raj, hoping to imitate it when he invaded Russia. Yet, little superiority was in evidence. Modern weapons were available to both antagonists, and native Indian soldiers did most of the fighting on both sides. Fundamentally, the British conquered India for two reasons. First of all, at the highest political level, they skillfully employed divide and rule tactics. Individual Indian princes fought each other more than they did the British and never united against the invaders. The British also recruited minority ethnic or religious groups, such as the Gurkhas of Nepal or the Sikhs of Punjab, as their shock troops, and when they scored a military victory over a particular prince they would enlist many of his defeated soldiers into their own ranks, thus co-opting them. The second reason that the British could successfully conquer and rule India lay at the village level. As mentioned earlier, the average villager did not care whether a Mogul emperor or an English empress held ultimate authority. The majority of Indians did not know they had been conquered or did not care. In short, the British Raj was largely irrelevant to the masses.

The Indian Crown Colony, however, did prove very relevant to its British rulers; indeed it was the linchpin of the whole empire, the jewel in the crown of Victorian England. Around the turn of the century, at the high noon of empire, India absorbed about one-fifth of Great Britain's exports and direct investments. India itself exported valuable commodities, such as tea, coffee, cotton, jute, rice, and animal hides, to Europe and the Americas, thus helping the British Empire balance its books. The Raj also taxed Indians to support their own army, and the British deployed these troops throughout their empire, not just in India itself. One English prime minister referred to India as the "English barrack in the Oriental Seas." In the late nineteenth century, Indian troops served as troubleshooters in China, Persia, Ethiopia, Singapore, Hong Kong, Afghanistan, Egypt, Burma, Nyasaland, Sudan, and Uganda; and Indians fought in the Boer War and both world wars of the twentieth century. Exploitation of India allowed the British to stretch their slender resources much further; but above all, the rule of a tiny island over a huge, very old, and continent-sized country provided enormous prestige. Much of Britain's imperial ego, so to speak, was invested in India.

Prestige, or *izzat*, also proved enormously important in retaining control over India. Though the masses hardly knew they had been conquered, the Indian elites felt it acutely. The upper castes skillfully accommodated themselves to British rule, with educated Brahmins acquiring bureaucratic posts in the administration or training as lawyers, and experienced merchants transferring their trade from the Arabs and Portuguese to the English. In the process, however, they lost a great deal of confidence and self-respect. The constantly asserted superiority of the English, backed by the threat of force, created a colonial mentality among Indian elites who internalized a sense of their own inferiority. When Mohandas Gandhi was a small child, a school chum convinced him that Englishmen were natural rulers because they ate a lot of meat. The impressionable Indian secretly gorged himself on red meat for a time, but soon became disgusted and returned to the customary Hindu vegetarianism. The tiny numbers of British rulers required numerous collaborators to continue their dominance. As long as their prestige and supposed superiority granted them legitimacy, they could continue to divide and rule, yet once enough Indians refused to collaborate, maintaining the Raj would become too expensive and the British would have to quit. Indians, therefore, pushed for and won independence when the educated elite, and then more gradually the village masses, discovered that they were not inferior to their rulers.

The British had never attempted to "uplift" the masses of Indians or spread literacy throughout the villages. As late as 1921 only 13 percent of Indian men and 1.8 percent of women could read and write. The Raj's educational efforts were concentrated at the higher levels, in order to produce the cadres of clerks their colonial bureaucracy required. An English-language Indian newspaper in 1853 described the Raj's government as "a despotism tempered by examination." Few Western-educated Indians, however, could rise very far. In 1909, only 60 Indians served in the elite Indian Civil Service, which employed a total of 1,142 administrators. The resulting "babu explosion" fed the first stirrings of nationalist resentment against the English. *Babu* was the term for an English-speaking, Indian clerk. Originally a neutral, or even affectionate, descriptive word, it gradually became a term of derision, connoting a bumbling, shuffling brown ignoramus who spoke imperfect English. In reality, the growing numbers of Western-educated individuals, the babu explosion, meant that a significant portion of the Indian elite was under-employed and frustrated. The intellectual proletariat, that is, over-educated and under-employed workers, have proven the most dangerous class of the twentieth century in many different countries. Such individuals flocked to various fascist movements between the world wars in Europe. Indeed, Mussolini and Hitler both belonged to this class. In India, and later in other colonized nations, the intellectual proletariat spearheaded the forces of nationalism.

The most significant nationalist organization, the Indian National Congress, first met in 1885. Convened by the Scotsman Allan Octavian Hume, a retired British civil servant with pro-Indian sympathies, the Congress was not yet a political party, but an annual gathering of the Indian elite. At the end of each year during the Christmas and New Year's season, when the weather was cooler and the schools and law courts were closed, teachers, lawyers, journalists, merchants, and landowners congregated in a major Indian city to socialize with their peers, share their frustrations, and articulate their grievances. Hume published a letter in the press in 1888 avowing that "we look forward to a time, say fifty or seventy years hence, when the Government of India will be precisely similar to that of the Dominion of Canada. . . ." In fact, India gained complete independence fifty-nine years later, but few besides Hume foresaw that. Congress limited itself to polite petitions requesting greater representation of Indians in the various organs of colonial government. After the turn of the century, however, a younger group of educated Indians, influenced in part by the Irish Home Rule movement, tried to push Congress toward more radical demands or even toward independence, but moderates remained firmly in control of the organization.

Congress attempted to represent all varieties of Indians, but it became increasingly identified with the Hindu majority. In 1906, therefore, leaders of the Muslim community, which comprised about 25 percent of India's population, organized the All-India Muslim League as their own political organization. The League and the Congress reached an accommodation during World War I, presenting a united front against the British and demanding some form of autonomous self-government as a minimum goal. In order to retain Indian loyalty for the war effort, the secretary of state for India, Edwin S. Montagu, announced on August 20, 1917, that the goal of British policy was "the progressive realization of responsible government in India as an integral part of the British Empire."

The Montagu Declaration promised, in effect, that India would be prepared for dominion status, that is, the self-governing state of the white colonies within the British Empire, but it laid down no timetable for home rule. The resultant governmental changes, passed by the British Parliament in 1919, granted authority over health, education, and public works to elected Indian councils at the provincial level, but reserved control over police and finance to the appointed English governors. The all-India central government remained largely unchanged and firmly under control of the English viceroy. Time still seemed to be on the side of the British Raj. However, an expatriate Indian lawyer, M. K. Gandhi, who had been out of the country for over twenty years, returned in 1915 and eventually transformed the Indian National Congress into a powerful nationalist movement.

Mohandas Karamchand Gandhi was born on October 2, 1869, in Porbandar, a small port city in one of the Gujarat-speaking princely states north of Bombay. He belonged to the *Modh Bania* caste of small tradesmen and moneylenders, but his recent ancestors, including his father, had held government positions at the princely court. Nevertheless, the family of six children was brought up in quite modest circumstances, sharing a large house with five other families. According to Hindu custom, Mohandas was married at age thirteen to a girl his own age named Kasturbai. The young bridegroom was no saint but rather a little tyrant. He later remarked that "I learned the lesson of nonviolence from my wife. Her determined resistance to my will on the one hand, and her quiet submission to the suffering of my stupidity on the other, ultimately made me ashamed. . . ."

After Mohandas's father died in 1888, the extended family pooled their resources and sent the nineteen-year-old to England for legal training, a momentous step for the Gandhi family since their caste customs forbade travel over the ocean and Mohandas was declared outcast when he sailed. Recognizing the gravity of the event, Putlibai, his devoutly Hindu mother, made him vow to abstain from wine, women, and meat while abroad. Mohandas earned his law degree in three years and was called to the bar on June 10, 1891, then sailed for Bombay two days later. Yet his English degree did not produce the fame and fortune his family had optimistically expected, for Gandhi's ineptness in public speaking made him an indifferent advocate. He barely earned a living during the first two years of his practice, so when a group of Indian Muslim merchants asked him to go to South Africa and settle a long-standing lawsuit for them, he jumped at the chance. One of his biographers, Judith Brown, sums up the prospects of the young Gandhi at this stage of his life: "In April 1893 he set sail once more from Bombay, an Indian nonentity, his once high hopes dashed on the rocks of reality, now bound for a routine legal job which seemed like an escape from failure rather than a challenging opportunity."

The province of Natal in South Africa, where Gandhi's boat landed, counted 43,000 Indians to only 40,000 white European settlers. Most had come over as indentured servants to work on sugar and coffee plantations and had stayed on as laborers or gardeners when their term of service expired; but the Indian community also included a fair number of wealthier Muslim traders, such as Gandhi's employers. Shortly after his arrival, the young lawyer bumped against the reality of South African life for anyone with a dark skin. He was tossed out of the first-class railway coach and spent the night on a small-town station platform. Though the Hollywood version of his life, Richard Attenborough's 1982 film *Gandhi*, ties his entire career to this incident, Gandhi's commitment to political struggle actually evolved slowly over a period of time. He spent about a year on his clients' lawsuit, working effectively as a brief-drafter though still terrified of speaking in public. As he prepared to return to India, however, Natal passed a law depriving Indian settlers of the right to vote. A group of merchants asked the lawyer to stay on and fight the legislation, guaranteeing him enough legal work to support himself. Gandhi agreed to try it for just a month, but eventually he brought over his family and remained for twenty more years.

South Africa was a rude school for Gandhi's personal, religious, and political growth. He started a newspaper to inform the Indian community of their rights and to protest government injustices, and eventually he conquered his shyness and became an effective public speaker and fundraiser. The publicity he drummed up reverberated back in England, revealing the nakedness of South African racial discrimination for the first time.

After several years in South Africa, around the turn of the century, Gandhi embarked on a personal quest for enlightenment, deepening and broadening his religious views and evolving an unusual ascetic lifestyle. He corresponded frequently with a Jain jeweler and poet in Bombay, Rajchandra Ravjibhai Mehta, known familiarly as Raychandbhai. The Jain religion is a small offshoot from Hinduism that stresses absolute non-violence and the "many-sidedness" of truth. Raychandbhai's influence proved crucial in the development of Gandhi's religious beliefs. It confirmed his growing pacifism, which he had taken from European sources such as the Christian Sermon on the Mount and the philosophical novelist Leo Tolstoy, and made him more tolerant of other religions. Gandhi believed that all faiths encompass aspects of truth, but that none embodies The Truth. He finally decided he could do the most good by working within his own Hindu tradition, which he hoped to reform and update. He often remarked that "it is good to swim in the waters of tradition, but to sink in them is suicide."

In the early years of this century, Gandhi radically simplified his lifestyle. He replaced the top hat and suit coat of an English lawyer with the loin cloth, loose robe, and cloth hat of a Hindu peasant, and moved his family to a rural commune he called Tolstoy Farm. Then, in 1906 he took a vow of *bramacharya*, or celibacy, and thereafter refrained from sexual intercourse the rest of his life. *Bramacharya* was a traditional practice of withdrawal that many Hindu men pursued at the end of their lives, in order to prepare for a new incarnation; and, of course, it is required for the unmarried clergy in Catholic Christianity. Yet Gandhi was in the prime of his life at age thirty-seven, with a wife and four children. He believed that celibacy was spiritually necessary to fortify himself for his life's work, which still lay ahead of him. There is no record of what his wife Kasturbai thought of his perfectionism, though she remained loyally by his side until her death nearly forty years later. His eldest son, however, felt starved for affection in Gandhi's ascetic household and eventually broke with his father. It could not have been easy living with a man on a quest for sainthood.

The South African years also helped Gandhi develop his distinctive political technique, which he later applied in the Indian struggle for independence. In 1906 the activist Gandhi called a mass meeting to protest the passage of an Indian Registration Act which required Indians to be fingerprinted and to carry a pass card at all times. He had been slowly developing a technique of non-violent resistance to unjust laws, but felt that the current term for such tactics, "passive resistance," was inadequate. There was nothing passive about the mass protests Gandhi was planning. Therefore he sponsored a newspaper contest for a new name. A cousin of Gandhi's won the prize for the word *sadagraha,* which meant "firmness in the truth." Gandhi refined this slightly to *satyagraha,* which had richer connotations and could be translated variously as "truth power" or "soul force."

Satyagraha took the practice of *ahimsa,* or non-violence, which was common to most Indian religions, out of the realm of personal, individual virtue and transformed it into a strategy of mass protest and collective action. A follower of Gandhi did not practice non-violence simply as a solitary witness against injustice or to make himself or herself feel good, but to effect social change. The practitioners of Gandhian pacifism were not passive or cowardly, but courageous and active. Since they believed that all truth is partial, they tried to engage opponents in dialogue, not overwhelm them. Most importantly, the means of protest were consistent with the ends or goals. Since Gandhi sought a society of peace and harmony, he carefully tailored the means to that end, calling *satyagraha* "the end in process and the ideal in the making." Typically, non-cooperation was the first step in a protest, including strikes, boycotts, and a refusal to accept honors or recognition from the government. Active civil disobedience, the direct breaking of unjust laws, would then follow. By way of example, two thousand Indians protested the Registration Act in Transvaal by tossing their registration pass cards into a huge bonfire. Along with Gandhi they were all arrested and served hard time in jail.

The techniques of *satyagraha* earned relatively meager returns during Gandhi's years in South Africa. The provincial and Union governments made a few concessions that were important to Indians, such as the abolition of a tax on former indentured laborers and the legalization of non-Christian marriages, but the overall pattern of discrimination against non-whites was barely affected. Gandhi finally returned to India, by way of England, just as the First World War broke out. Despite the modest nature of his political success in South Africa, he had earned a reputation as a leader and had forged a new technique of mass action. South African prime minister Jan Christian Smuts felt overjoyed to be rid of him: "The saint has left our shores," he wrote to a friend, "I sincerely hope forever."

Perhaps the most important characteristic of "the saint" as he left his South African training ground was the wholeness of his personality. He did not compartmentalize his life. Everything he did was political, and everything was religious. His public life was his private life, and vice versa. As one of his biographers, Calvin Kytle, has pointed out: "He not only mixed politics with religion; he mixed religions." Such wholeness of character has proven the most important resource for individuals resisting tyranny and oppression in the twentieth century.

There was also a more political aspect to Gandhi's character. In South Africa, the Gujarati Hindu lawyer became an all-India nationalist. Twentieth-century immigrants have frequently discovered their national identities outside of their home countries. Gandhi met and worked with a wider variety of Indians in South Africa than he would have had he stayed at home. His first clients and strongest financial supporters were Indian Muslim merchants, and the masses who followed him were mostly low caste, Tamil-speaking laborers, originally from the south of India. Gandhi also had extensive contacts with sympathetic Europeans and with Indian women, who became increasingly active in his protests. In sum, he left South Africa with a well-formed, if somewhat unorthodox, personality and a highly developed national consciousness.

When Gandhi returned to Bombay early in 1915, one of the leading moderate members of the Indian National Congress, Gopal Krishna Gokhale, immediately began to groom him as a possible successor. Gokhale advised him to take a year and look around "with his ears open and his mouth shut." Traveling through the dusty villages of his homeland, Gandhi planned to spend the rest of his life as a sort of social worker and spiritual director to the downtrodden, who had already begun to call him Mahatma, "Great Soul," and Bapu, "Father." With a bequest from Gokhale and other wealthy Indians he set up an *ashram* (hermitage) north of the city of Ahmedabad, living in a cell-like room in the midst of a communal farm. He spearheaded a few *satyagraha* campaigns during the years of the First World War, but these were aimed at local, economic grievances, without much broader political significance.

Both in South Africa and upon his return to India, Gandhi had remained a loyal British subject. He wished to reform abuses within the colonial system, but had not yet thought of abolishing it. During the Boer War and in the early weeks of World War I that he spent in England, he had organized Indian ambulance brigades to assist the war effort in a non-violent way, and he had even recruited soldiers for the Indian army after returning to his native land. A brutal English atrocity shortly after the war, however, shocked Gandhi out of his imperial loyalty and launched him and the Indian Congress on the road to independence.

On March 18, 1919, the British government of India passed the Rowlatt Acts, named for Sir Sidney Rowlatt, a special commissioner who had recommended that wartime restrictions on speech, assembly, and the press be continued. Gandhi, who naively believed the British would show their gratitude for Indian support of the war, felt betrayed, and he proposed a traditional Indian protest measure, the *hartal,* a day of fasting and mourning that was tantamount to a general strike. On April 6, 1919, shops closed in all the major cities and workers boycotted their jobs at the bureaus of the colonial government. The stoppage was far from total, but it affected every province to some extent. Congress followed up the one-day *hartal* with a campaign of selective civil disobedience, selling banned literature openly and convening forbidden public meetings. The *satyagraha* campaign turned violent, however, so Gandhi admitted his "Himalayan mistake" and called it off.

In the midst of the Rowlatt *satyagraha*, General Reginald Dyer banned all processions or meetings in the capital of Punjab Province, Amritsar. Disregarding the order, ten to twenty thousand people, including many women and children, gathered in the Jallianwalla Bagh, an enclosed garden with walls on three sides. Without further warning, Dyer's troops shot 1,650 rounds of rifle fire into the unarmed crowd, killing about 400 and leaving over 1,000 wounded unattended. The Amritsar massacre snapped the slender bonds of loyalty tying the Indian elite to Great Britain. Not only the killing itself, but also the clumsy way the British tried to cover it up, convinced the Indians that Englishmen were no longer trustworthy.

In the following year, Gandhi virtually took over the Indian National Congress, writing a new constitution that extended its organization down to the district level and prescribed direct election of delegates. At the December 1920 annual meeting, Congress formally adopted *swaraj* "by all legitimate and peaceful means" as its main goal. *Swaraj* literally means "self-rule," and it originally held a personal, ascetic connotation of self-discipline and control of the senses. Congress leaders had gradually begun to endow the term with a political charge, translating it variously as "self-government," "home rule," or even "independence." The ambiguity of the word made it a useful political slogan, drawing support from radicals and moderates alike. In 1920, Gandhi himself still aimed only at home rule, dominion status, within the British Empire, not complete independence, but the political meaning of *swaraj* was to him its least important aspect. For Gandhi, self-rule encompassed an entire way of life based on economic self-sufficiency instead of the consumption of imported goods, and a nearly anarchist belief in self-government by the 700,000 villages of India rather than a strong central government. He urged all his followers to learn how to ply a spinning wheel and to spend some time each day spinning *khadi,* or homespun cotton cloth.

The 1920 Congress, following Gandhi's lead, proclaimed a year-long push for *swaraj* by means of a massive non-cooperation campaign. The Indian elite, such as the Bengali poet Rabindranath Tagore, gave up their British honors and titles, lawyers refused to argue cases in the British courts, and ordinary citizens stopped paying taxes. Following the Irish model of Sinn Fein, Congress established alternative institutions of justice and government to replace those being boycotted, and Gandhi urged his followers to burn their British-made clothes and spin their own. Again violence broke out sporadically, and when a mob burned down a police station with twenty-two policemen still inside, Gandhi called off the campaign.

The Rowlatt *satyagraha* and non-cooperation campaigns of 1920-21 failed to achieve their goals. The British did not grant home rule nor did they relax the restrictions on speech and assembly. Furthermore, not all Gandhi's followers pursued non-violent means. Yet the soul force movement against the Raj made Gandhi a national figure and revitalized Congress, giving it a mass appeal. In 1919 60 percent of Congress delegates came from the major cities and towns of India, but by 1923 two-thirds were elected from rural districts. Gandhi's campaigns transformed Congress from an upper-class debating society to an activist political party with a mass base.

Still, the 1920s were lean years for the nationalist movement. The British saved Gandhi's reputation after the failure of non-cooperation by arresting him and keeping him in prison for almost two years. Upon release he withdrew to his ashram and devoted himself to social service, denouncing the injustice of untouchability and the degraded status of women, and spreading the gospel of homespun cloth. In the meantime, younger members of Congress, such as Jawaharlal Nehru, a Cambridge-trained lawyer and intellectual, were growing restless. At the end of 1929, Nehru was named president of Congress, which adopted *purna swaraj*, complete independence, as its formal goal.

Only Gandhi enjoyed the national prestige to lead an independence movement, but he shocked the Congress leaders by announcing instead a campaign of civil disobedience on a seemingly lesser issue, the tax on salt. Salt proved to be a brilliant symbolic focus for the new *satyagraha*, for it was a necessity of village life, a commodity which everyone used and which loomed far more important in the life of the poor than the rich. In 1930 Gandhi called on Indians not to pay the salt tax but rather to make their own salt illegally by boiling sea water. On March 12, 1930, the Mahatma led a group of disciples from his ashram on a march to the sea at Dandi. Their 240-mile pilgrimage took twenty-four days, gathering followers and publicity as it went along. On April 5 they reached the sea and Gandhi ceremonially broke the law by boiling a kettle of salt water. In the days to come, the salt *satyagraha* spread to other coastal regions and grew to encompass a complete boycott of foreign cloth as well. The British arrested Gandhi on May 4, but almost immediately the viceroy, Lord Irwin, released him and withdrew the ban on making salt for personal use.

Biographer Calvin Kytle has stated: "Though it was to be seventeen years before India became formally independent, freedom for India was inevitable from the moment Gandhi stooped on the beach at Dandi for a handful of salt." This probably overstates the case, for had World War II not mortally wounded British power, the Raj might have lingered on for decades more. Yet the salt *satyagraha* did show that Indians from all classes had overcome the colonial mentality and no longer deferred to their rulers. Nationalism eclipsed imperialism, and the Indian National Congress assumed the mantle of legitimacy that the British had lost.

Over the next ten years, the British made some significant governmental concessions but still held ultimate authority at New Delhi. A series of round-table conferences in London between government ministers and Indian leaders produced no consensus, but the British Parliament passed the massive Government of India Act in 1935, which granted nearly complete home rule to the provinces but not the central government. A socialist wing of Congress and an independent communist party scornfully rejected this compromise, but with Gandhi's blessing, local Congress politicians eagerly contested the 1937 elections held under the new act and took power in eight of the eleven provinces. "Working the reforms," as it was termed, gave Congress practical government experience, unusual for a nationalist independence movement. The outbreak of World War II in 1939, however, short-circuited this evolutionary process. The viceroy, Lord Linlithgow, declared India at war automatically along with the mother country, without consulting any Indian politicians. Such imperial arrogance outraged the Congress leaders, who immediately withdrew from the provincial governments in protest.

The British breathed a sigh of relief, declared emergency rule over the provinces for the duration of the war, and proceeded to deploy the Indian army wherever it was needed, just as always. Yet they also sent a sympathetic socialist politician, Sir Stafford Cripps, to placate the Indian leaders and negotiate with them. Cripps promised either full home rule or independence after the war, depending on the will of the people, but the Congress leaders did not believe him. Gandhi described Cripps's promise as "a postdated cheque on a failing bank." Behind Cripps stood Prime Minister Winston Churchill, who had once denounced Gandhi as a "half-naked Indian fakir" and who still hoped to keep the empire intact. Only an unequivocal promise of independence, an invitation to form a provisional government, and the convening of a constituent assembly during the war would have satisfied Congress. When the Cripps mission failed to produce this, Congress passed a "Quit India" resolution on August 8, 1942. In the midst of a total war, the British did not hesitate. They arrested Gandhi and most of the principal Congress leaders the very next day and kept them imprisoned throughout the war. British troops ruthlessly suppressed all attempts at protest, whether violent or non-violent.

At the end of the war, Winston Churchill's government fell from power in London and was replaced by the Labour Party of Clement Attlee, which was more receptive to the anti-imperial urgings of Britain's American ally. The war had depleted the confidence and resources of the British people who, rallying to the anti-communist cause of the Cold War in Europe, had little energy left over for imperial intransigence. Furthermore, England's economic interest in India had weakened over the first decades of the twentieth century. Indians took a lesser share of British exports and investment than they did previously, having developed local industries of their own as well as Gandhi's spinning wheels. England was not forced out of India by either violent revolution or non-violent Gandhian protest, but could have remained in control through the application of sufficient military force. War-weariness and a rational calculation that India was no longer worth the cost of retaining as a colony convinced the British to retire with as much speed and dignity as possible.

British determination to quit India, however, faced a serious obstacle. Indians were divided into two large religious communities, and if the English simply scuttled away they might leave behind them a civil war between Muslims and Hindus. In 1945 about 25 percent of Indians, 95 million people in all, were Muslims. They formed an overwhelming majority in the small northwestern provinces of Sind, Baluchistan, and the North West Frontier, and a narrower majority in the large, important provinces of Punjab in the northwest and Bengal in the northeast. Gandhi had always made concerted efforts to include Muslims in his movement, and the Congress and the Muslim League had cautiously collaborated for a time. Yet as the moment of independence grew closer, Muslim leaders increasingly viewed Congress as a Hindu organization bent on a tyranny of the majority. Ironically, the religious trappings of Gandhi's campaigns reinforced this image, however tolerant and broadminded the Mahatma might be personally. As a minority in a united India, Muslims realized they could never exercise much influence in a central government based on majority rule.

Mohammad Ali Jinnah, a Bombay lawyer from the small Khoja Muslim sect, became undisputed head of the Muslim League in 1934 and began hatching a "two-nations" strategy. If Muslims remained a communal social group they would always constitute a minority, but if they could gain recognition as a nation, they must be accorded equality of status, however few their numbers. The idea of a separate Muslim nation-state on the Indian subcontinent had been suggested by others as early as 1930, and in 1934 an Indian Muslim student in London coined the term "Pakistan" for this proposed entity. Pakistan was a compound word combining *P* for Punjab, *A* for Afghania (North West Frontier Province), *K* for Kashmir, *S* for Sind, and *stan* for Baluchistan. It could be translated as "land of the pure." Neither Jinnah nor other Muslim leaders adopted the aim of an independent Pakistan immediately, but by 1940 the Muslim League had pledged itself to that goal. Indian historian Ayesha Jalal has suggested that Jinnah did not really want a small, independent Pakistan, but was using it as a bargaining chip to extract concessions, particularly a loose federal system that would preserve Indian unity but protect Muslim interests. If this really was his strategy, it backfired. In their haste to quit India, the British seized upon the simple solution of partition into two states.

Actually, the Labour government made one last attempt to find a creative solution to the "great divide" of Indian politics. In March 1946 Sir Stafford Cripps and two colleagues from the British Cabinet arrived in India and began marathon negotiations with representatives of both Congress and the Muslim League. The British plenipotentiaries finally presented a three-tiered plan for a loose federation of Indian states with a weak central government, responsible only for defense and foreign affairs. Individual states would be allowed to group themselves in regional alliances, and thus the Muslim states could create Pakistan within an all-India framework. The Cabinet mission plan came close to Jinnah's real goal, but he was reluctant to jump at the offer too eagerly and thus lose his bargaining leverage. Eventually, the Muslim League gave its cautious approval, but Congress, which felt overconfident and smelled victory, rejected the plan. The League then swiftly withdrew its approval as well. Thus the last chance for an all-India solution was lost.

The Attlee government, therefore, sent India a new viceroy in March 1947, Lord Louis Mountbatten, a cousin of the king, armed with full powers and a firm deadline for British withdrawal by June 1948. "Dickie" Mountbatten was a self-confident soldier with royal blood in his veins and a rich and beautiful wife. Both Mountbattens charmed the Congress leaders, and Lady Edwina may even have become Jawaharlal Nehru's lover. More importantly, Mountbatten shortened the deadline even further to August 1947, and this concentrated the minds of both Hindus and Muslims. Gandhi resisted the breakup of India into two states until the very end, but in this final year of the British Raj his influence had waned, and the practical politicians, Nehru and Vallabhbhai Patel, convinced Congress to accept the British offer of divide and quit.

At the stroke of midnight on August 15, 1947, Pakistan and India celebrated independence. The newly created Muslim state was a two-winged monster, with East and West Pakistan divided by over a thousand miles of Indian territory, and it was greatly reduced in size by allowing non-Muslim areas of Punjab and Bengal to join India. It turned out to be, in a phrase Jinnah had used earlier, "a maimed, mutilated and moth-eaten Pakistan." India, in contrast, picked up more territory and population than it lost to Pakistan when nearly all of the princely states renounced their own theoretical independence and joined the new nation.

Gandhi did not attend the ceremonies in Delhi, for he considered the division of the country to be vivisection, the cutting up of a living body. Furthermore, he had more important work to do at the time. Partition, conceived in part as a means of preventing communal violence and civil war, did not deter bloody confrontations between Hindus and Muslims. Even before independence, thousands had been butchered in religious riots in Bengal, Bihar, and Punjab provinces. Then when Mountbatten announced the detailed boundaries of the two new states, right after the August 1947 celebrations, Hindu refugees began fleeing Muslim areas, and vice versa, often falling prey to vicious gangs of murderers. No one knows how many suffered in this vast upheaval, but conservative estimates run to about a million killed and two million left homeless. Gandhi spent the months before and after independence courageously walking through the regions of communal warfare, and sometimes succeeded in calming passions. On January 30, 1948, a young member of a Hindu fundamentalist group, Nathuram Vinayak Godse, fired three pistol shots into the Mahatma at a prayer meeting. He died instantly, invoking the name of the Hindu god Rama.

Mohandas Gandhi did not win Indian independence single-handedly; indeed his country would have broken away from the British Empire eventually had he never lived. The rising tide of nationalism throughout the world and the growing numbers of sophisticated, English-trained Indians pointed in that direction, and the exhaustion of Europe by the Second World War would have made it inevitable. Yet Gandhi decisively shaped the Indian freedom struggle and determined *how* independence would be won. Earlier revolutionaries, such as anarchists and socialists, had tripped over the means-ends problem. Though aiming at a harmonious, classless society, they had destroyed their dreams through violence. *Satyagraha* contained the desirable end within its means of operation. Soul force grabbed the moral high ground and pushed the British off balance; it kept Congress united and extended its reach down to the masses. It provided an alternative to violent revolution that has been widely imitated by anti-imperialists in other European colonies and by the American civil rights movement.

Nevertheless, the Mahatma died believing he had failed, and indeed he did not attain any of his wider goals. *Swaraj* did not inaugurate an anarchist utopia of self-reliant villages but a strong, centralized state which has not hesitated to use the emergency police powers it inherited from the British. Rather than relying on homespun cloth and handicrafts, modern India has become an industrial power and has recently entered the computer age. Salman Rushdie, with his usual irreverence, makes one of his fictional characters a devotee of "Not Ram [the Hindu god] but RAM [random access memory]." Indian customs that Gandhi believed were immoral accretions to Hinduism, such as untouchability and the degraded status of women, have been officially banned or discouraged but not thoroughly uprooted. In 1998 India and Pakistan both joined the ranks of nuclear military powers, by testing atomic bombs.

Yet Gandhi spoke with a powerful moral voice in the midst of the most bloody of centuries. In order to illustrate how important such moral leadership is, I would like to suggest an unusual, even bizarre, comparison between Mohandas Gandhi and Adolf Hitler. This is a comparison which highlights a *contrast,* I hasten to add, not an argument that the two were equivalent.

Both Gandhi and Hitler were outsiders to their own nations, for Hitler was born in Austria, not Germany, and Gandhi spent twenty-one formative years in South Africa; and both were nonentities in their youth and young adulthood. Each discovered an unexpected talent for speaking to and moving the masses, and each assumed leadership by playing on a sense of national humiliation. Their opponents did both Hitler and Gandhi a favor by putting them in jail and making them martyrs when early attempts to seize power had failed. Each leader played a lone-wolf role in relation to his own political party and led primarily through an intangible, almost mystical quality of attraction. Ultimately, both men failed to reach their goals, but they exercised an enormous impact on their times.

The point of this comparison is that values matter. It would not have been difficult to rouse the Indian people to violence against the century-long humiliations of the British Raj, just as Hitler spurred the Germans to violently overturn the ignominious Versailles Treaty. The superficial resemblances between Gandhi and Hitler suggest that they shared some of the psychological and sociological characteristics of successful nationalist leaders in the twentieth century. Yet the quality of their values and the content of their ideologies differed profoundly. Gandhi's moral leadership and his strategy of soul force left a positive legacy for the world and a powerful example for later anti-imperialist struggles.

CHAPTER FOUR

The World Turned Upside Down

The Chinese Communist leader Mao Tse-tung (Mao Zedong)[1] labeled the pre-revolutionary regime of his country "semi-feudal and semi-colonial." Unlike India, China had never become a colony in the formal political sense. Since the mid-nineteenth century, however, the European imperial powers had demanded trading concessions from the Chinese government, built up railroads between the major cities, and claimed the right of extraterritoriality, that is, exemption from Chinese law for their nationals living in the country. The coastal and river cities of China were indeed semi-colonial, dependent for their prosperity on foreigners and native *compradors,* or middlemen. The vast countryside, where over 70 percent of the people lived, remained largely untouched by foreign interests, except in the areas where Christian missionaries had penetrated, but it was semi-feudal. Serfdom had been abolished two thousand years previously, but large landowners still dominated and controlled the lives of the people as truly as medieval European lords or southern American slaveowners.

The governmental regime of Chiang Kai-shek (Jiang Jieshi), a military man who had taken power in the 1920s, trumpeted the "Three Principles of the People" — nationalism, democracy, and people's welfare — but only the nationalism proved genuine. Chiang's Nationalists were so corrupt and authoritarian that they made a mockery of democracy, and so dependent on the land-

1. I use the older and more familiar system of transliterating Chinese into English, which was in use at the time of the events I am narrating and is employed in most of the books I consulted. In the last two decades, a different, and somewhat awkward, new system of transliteration has been introduced. I place the new spelling in parentheses the first time a Chinese word appears in the text.

owners and compradors that they did nothing for the people's welfare. Though originally allied with the small Chinese Communist Party in the struggle to unify the country and resist foreign dominance, the Nationalist Kuomintang (Guomindang) Party of Chiang Kai-shek had tried to destroy the Communists in 1927 and had subsequently driven them underground and out into the countryside.[2]

After the heroic "Long March" to escape Chiang's troops, the Communists took refuge in the remote region around Yenan (Yan'an) in the far northwest of China and began plotting Chiang's overthrow. One of their slogans, *fanshen*, which literally means "to turn the body" or "to overturn," best sums up the goals of the Chinese Revolution. The Chinese Communists turned Marxist doctrine on its head, organizing the peasants as their revolutionary spearhead, something that no Russian Bolshevik believed possible. They beckoned the peasants to overturn their landlords, obtaining both land and justice in the process. They inspired the oft-beaten women of rural China to overturn the despotic authority of their husbands and assume new roles as equals. They urged individuals to overturn their thoughts and become committed to the welfare of the collective community, not pursue selfish ends of their own. Though few outside Mao's circle believed they would ever come to power in the world's most populous country, the Communists indeed turned the world upside down during and after World War II. Having come to power as liberators, however, the Communists stayed on as rulers; and Mao Tse-tung became emperor of a new dynasty, more ruthless and capricious than any in China's past.

When the Japanese had first begun encroaching on Chinese territory in the early 1930s, Chiang Kai-shek's government refused to recognize their conquests but did not actively resist, concentrating instead on the internal battle against the Communists. "The Japanese are like a disease of the skin," Chiang intoned, "but the Communists are like a disease of the heart." Eventually, Chiang's own military subordinates forced him to make peace with the Communists and turn his attention to the Japanese. In September 1937 the Kuomintang and the Chinese Communist Party formally announced the formation of a united front against foreign invasion. Mao's Communists pledged to give up armed rebellion against the government, cease their policy of confiscating land from the wealthy, rename the Workers' and Peasants' Democratic Government in Yenan the Government of the Special Region of the Republic of China, and subordinate the Red Army to the government as the renamed Eighth Route Army. Except for the temporary cessation of land confiscation,

2. A fuller account of the duel between the Communists and the Nationalists, plus background on Chiang Kai-shek and Mao Tse-tung, can be found in chapters 4 and 20 of volume 1.

these Communist concessions were cosmetic only. Mao preserved essential independence of action for his regional government and army.

The Japanese swept Chiang Kai-shek's troops from the cities and towns of coastal China, forcing him to trade space for time and withdraw into the interior province of Szechwan (Sichuan), where he established a temporary capital at Chungking (Chongqing). From the end of 1938 until the close of the war in 1945, the Nationalists remained holed up in the southwest of China, fitfully supplied by the British and Americans who flew in "over the hump" of the Himalayas from Burma and India. Exhausted from the losing struggle against Japan, Chiang and his followers waited for the Allies to win the war for them. This conceded initiative to the numerically inferior, but better organized Communists.

Mao's armed guerrillas moved out of their bases around Yenan and infiltrated behind the lines of the Japanese throughout northern China. The Japanese controlled the semi-colonial parts of the north while the Communists organized resistance in the semi-feudal backcountry. Since the invaders stayed close to the north-south and east-west railways criss-crossing the North China Plain, the Communists joked that the Japanese were "nailed to the cross." Becoming overconfident, the Communists mounted a full-scale attack, the Hundred Regiments Offensive, on the Japanese garrisons at the end of 1940, but were beaten back. The Japanese then moved major reinforcements up from the south of China. They dug moats and built walls and blockhouses along the railways they controlled, clamping an iron checkerboard over the Communist areas, then sent vast numbers of soldiers into the squares of the board to exterminate guerrillas and scorch the earth that supported them. The Japanese commanders called this campaign the "Three Clears" — clearing all grain, all draft animals, and all people from the resistance areas. The Chinese grimly labeled it the "Three Alls" — burn all, kill all, loot all.

Japanese sweeps continued in northern China through all of 1940 and 1941 and part of 1942, until military reverses elsewhere forced them to ease the pressure. Yet they never extinguished the resistance. Chinese spies warned the Communists of impending Japanese moves so the rural organizers would immediately "empty the house and clear up the field," moving peasants, cattle, grain, even furniture to safer areas or concealing them in caves and underground tunnels. Japanese troops would rage across a virtually empty countryside. Furthermore, the all-out nature of the Japanese attacks played into the hands of Mao's mobile guerrilla bands, which would swiftly attack the lightly garrisoned rear areas the Japanese had just evacuated. The Three Alls campaign, therefore, proved devastating but not fatal to the Communists. In the meantime, the united front between Communists and Nationalists had been marred by numerous clashes and misunderstandings. There seemed little doubt that if both Chinese forces survived World War II a civil war would likely break out.

When the Japanese surrendered in August 1945, Chiang Kai-shek's position appeared far stronger than that of Mao Tse-tung's Communists. During the war the United States had treated Chiang's Nationalist regime in Chungking as the legitimate government of China and sent General Joseph Stillwell to train his soldiers and General Claire Chennault to create a Chinese air force, the Flying Tigers. President Franklin Roosevelt consulted Chiang in person at the Cairo Conference of late 1943, and he tried to build up China's international prestige as one of the Big Four powers. The other two members of this elite, the Russians and the British, viewed the American backing of the Chinese Nationalists with amusement, as one of those inexplicable American peculiarities they had to tolerate. Nonetheless, at the end of the war, Chiang had an army of four million men, with thirty-nine divisions trained and equipped by the Americans, whereas the Communists commanded about a million soldiers, most of them ill-equipped with captured Japanese weapons.

The American government pursued a two-faced Chinese policy after the war. On the one hand, U.S. envoys brought Mao Tse-tung and Chiang Kai-shek together in person at Chungking and persuaded them to sign a new non-aggression pact and go through the motions of building a coalition government. For most of 1946, the eminent American general, George Marshall, stayed in China trying to make the united front policy work. Yet at the same time that Americans were acting as peace mediators, the U.S. military gave massive aid to one side in the struggle, Chiang's Nationalists. Immediately after the armistice in Asia, the American air force and navy had transported Chiang's troops from their stronghold in Chungking to the coastal regions of China so they, rather than the Communist Eighth Route Army, could accept the Japanese surrender. Chiang ordered the defeated Japanese commanders to continue fighting the Communists until Nationalist regiments arrived. The Americans also landed 53,000 of their own marines at the strategic ports of Tientsin (Tianjin) and Tsingtao (Qingdao) and the old capital of Peking (Beijing) to secure them for the Nationalists, and gave, loaned, or sold over a billion dollars worth of military supplies to Chiang Kai-shek.

Yet despite the American tilt towards the Kuomintang, the anti-Communist struggle in Asia had not yet become a great power confrontation, for ironically, the Soviet Union pursued an even more equivocal policy than the United States did. Russian troops occupied Manchuria at the very end of the war and accepted the Japanese surrender there, but the Soviets gave scant support to the Chinese Communists in the internal struggle for influence in that region. President Roosevelt had convinced Stalin at the Yalta Conference to recognize Chiang Kai-shek, not the Communists, as the legitimate ruler of China,

Old and New Names for the Provinces of China

and the Russians had duly signed a treaty of alliance and friendship with the Nationalist government. The Russian army dealt correctly with the Kuomintang officials that the Americans transported to Manchuria. Chiang himself asked the Russians to stay on a few months later than the agreed deadline for their withdrawal, because his troops were not yet ready to ensure law and order. When the Russians finally left Manchuria in May 1946, they hauled away a great deal of industrial equipment as reparations and left a great cache of captured Japanese weapons for the Communist insurgents in the countryside, but they otherwise stayed out of the emerging Chinese civil war. Stalin likely believed it safer to have a weak, divided China on his southern border than a strong country united behind either Chiang or Mao. If he could show the Americans how cooperative he was, so much the better.

When full-scale civil war finally broke out between the two Chinese factions in the summer of 1946, Chiang's forces controlled most of southern China. In northern China, however, they found themselves in the same strategic box as the Japanese, holding the cities and railways but not the country villages in between. Throughout the summer of 1946, the Nationalist forces advanced across the North China Plain, trying to link up their capital in Nanking (Nanjing) with the old capital of the north, Peking. The Communists retreated and preserved their own forces intact, organizing peasant resistance behind the lines as they had done against the Japanese. The following summer, however, the Communists went on the offensive against overextended Nationalist forces, both in Manchuria and on the North China Plain. Besieging Chiang's troops in the cities, they induced many soldiers to defect and their commanders to surrender, along with all their arms and supplies. When the Communists finally marched into Peking in January 1949, they rode in captured American trucks and tanks. In April of 1949, the People's Liberation Army, as the old Eighth Route Army had been renamed, crossed the Yangtze River into southern China and on April 24 entered the Nationalist capital of Nanking. By the end of the year, Chiang Kai-shek had fled with his remaining followers to the island stronghold of Taiwan, where his successors remain today.

The first and most obvious reason why the Communists triumphed in the Chinese civil war of 1946-49 is that Chiang Kai-shek's regime lost legitimacy in the eyes of the Chinese people and collapsed internally. The Nationalist soldiers had fought fiercely in the early years of the anti-Japanese war, and even while inactive in their Chungking redoubt they enjoyed great prestige as a battered remnant of unconquered China. Yet Chiang continued to view the Communists as the greater long-term threat than the Japanese, and thus he permitted collaboration between his followers and the foreign invaders in occupied areas. When the war ended, Nationalist commanders who had served as puppets of the Japanese claimed that they were following a "crooked path to national salvation" with the full approval of Chiang Kai-shek. Chiang welcomed such collaborators with open arms, alienating those who had suffered under Japanese occupation. Worse still, the Nationalist soldiers and officials acted more like an occupying than a liberating force, seizing commercial and industrial properties for their own profit and adopting a condescending attitude toward the general populace. Within a short time, the term "Chungking-ite" had taken on the same connotations as the American word "carpetbagger." In some areas, the people called Chiang's officials "blood-sucking devils."

Nationalist corruption and condescension was soon compounded by economic incompetence. In particular, a raging currency inflation wiped out all confidence in the Nationalist government. Confined to Chungking during the war, and thus cut off from the sources of its economic support in the coastal cities, Chiang's government had financed itself by printing paper money. After the war, it unwisely continued this practice, wiping out the savings of people on fixed incomes and setting off a wave of labor strikes. Inflation made the currency so worthless that a south China paper mill began recycling it as raw material. Historian John King Fairbank has summed up the situation perfectly: "Instead of learning to live off the countryside as the CCP [Chinese Communist Party] had to do, the GMD [Guomindang, or Kuomintang] lived off the printing press." When the government introduced a new gold yuan in August 1948 to curb inflation, it required all citizens to exchange any gold, silver, or foreign currency they had been hoarding. Since the new bills soon became nearly worthless, the entire exercise amounted to the confiscation of 179 million dollars worth of gold and silver assets.

Government corruption and incompetence decisively alienated China's intelligentsia. Inflation ate into the salaries of professors, reducing them to an intellectual proletariat, and students dropped out of school for lack of funds or future prospects. "Unemployment follows graduation" became the byword of the universities. The hard-pressed students and professors, therefore, staged four waves of anti–civil war demonstrations between December 1945 and June 1948. When two American marines were accused of assaulting a female student on Christmas Eve 1946 in Peking, the demonstrations took on a decidedly anti-American tone. By the time the Nationalist military effort had crumbled in 1948, the workers, students, professors, and even many of the businessmen of the cities had given up on Chiang Kai-shek and his American supporters. Many intellectuals openly defected to the Communist ranks and the rest waited in resignation.

A sentence from John Reed's famous book about the Russian Revolution, *Ten Days That Shook the World,* aptly describes the collapse of Chiang Kai-shek's Nationalists: "In the relations of a weak government and a rebellious people there comes a time when every act of the authorities exasperates the masses, and every refusal to act excites their contempt." A less famous but even better journalistic account of the Chinese Revolution, Jack Belden's *China Shakes the World,* makes virtually the same point: "In other words, that classic moment in the life of a dying regime had arrived when the leaders of the old society organize their own suicide."

Mao's Communists, however, did not wait passively for China to fall into their laps like a ripe persimmon. Instead, they organized the peasant masses in the countryside and engulfed the cities. This was the distinctive feature of the Chinese Revolution, what set it apart from the Russian Communist model: the peasantry, not the industrial proletariat, formed the spearhead of revolt. Land reform was the key to this peasant militance.

China's peasant masses, who comprised 70-80 percent of the population, were not serfs tied to the land, and the majority were not simply tenant farmers. More than half owned at least some land, though they might rent additional plots from a landlord as well. Nevertheless, landholdings were tiny and the farmers were desperately poor. When peasants met in the fields or village streets they commonly greeted each other with the question, "Have you eaten?" Rural hunger was caused by land erosion and natural disasters as much as by greedy landlords, but the peasants still bitterly resented the landowners, who "peeled and pared" them, in the homely rural term for exploitation.

As a social class, landlords had once formed an educated elite of classical degree holders who felt some paternalistic responsibility for the people's welfare, but in the twentieth century the degree examinations at the imperial court had been abolished, then the empire and emperor also disappeared. Many of the traditional gentry left the countryside for new opportunities in the cities, selling their land or becoming absentee landlords. The new, pushy landowners who took their place were collectively known by the peasants as "local bullies and oppressive gentry." All they cared about was making money, and they found many ways to extort grain or cash from the peasants. They charged their tenant farmers land rent, of course, which averaged about 45 percent of the total harvest; but they also raked in numerous fees, tips, and bribes as holders of local government offices. Their dominant economic position in the villages made them the primary money-lenders. The American journalist Jack Belden remarked that the largest, most solid building in many a village was the pawnshop. The peasants themselves sighed with resignation: "In good years, the landlord grows crops in the fields. In bad years, the landlord grows money in his house."

Peasant bitterness fed off political and social grievances as well as economic causes. Landowners controlled the machinery of local government, which levied taxes and conscripted manpower for public works or for service in the army. Most of the new landlords avoided manual labor themselves and practiced conspicuous leisure. They wore flowing gowns and let their finger-nails grow out to ridiculous lengths. With too much time on their hands, they smoked opium, gambled, and roamed the village, raping the wives of their ten-ants. *Fanshen,* the Communist slogan for land reform, meant the turning over of a whole rotten system of political, economic, and social relations.

When the Chinese Communists first organized their party in the early 1920s, they did not tap into this reservoir of peasant resentment; rather they fol-lowed the orthodox Marxist line by organizing the industrial proletariat. China's working class, however, was very small, and Chiang Kai-shek easily sup-pressed its revolutionary stirrings. In 1926, however, the party sent Mao Tse-tung to his native province of Hunan to investigate a series of spontaneous peasant uprisings, and there he found a new road to revolution. In his *Report on an Investigation into the Peasant Movement in Hunan,* he laid out for the first time what became known as the "mass line": listen to the grievances of the peasant masses, concentrate them into practical policies, then go back among the masses and lead them. From the masses to the masses, from the peasants to the peasants — this became Mao's strategy for the rest of his life.

The Chinese Communist Party leadership, the so-called Twenty-eight Bolsheviks, all young students trained in Moscow, did not immediately adopt the new mass line, but Mao found an opportunity to give it a practical test. Af-ter fleeing Chiang Kai-shek's suppression in Shanghai, he led a group of follow-ers into a mountainous border area between two provinces, where governmen-tal authority was weak. From 1931 to 1934, Mao presided over the grandly titled Chinese Soviet Republic, around the town of Juichin (Ruijin) in the province of Kiangsi (Jiangxi).

Chiang's ruthlessness had taught Mao the bitter lesson that "all power comes from the barrel of a gun," so he organized the border ruffians he found in Kiangsi into a formidable military force. Along with Chu Teh (Zhu De), a gifted general who defected from Chiang's army, he developed the guerrilla tac-tics that the Eighth Route Army would later use to such great effect. When the Nationalist army pursued the guerrillas, they retreated and waited patiently un-til they could fall upon an isolated column and wipe it out. More important than their tactics, however, was the behavior of the Communist soldiers. At Mao's urging, they paid for the supplies they took from the peasants, cleaned up the village huts they stayed in, left the farmers' daughters alone, and even helped out in the fields. Finally, the Communists seized the land of local land-lords and distributed it as equally as possible among the local tenant farmers. Thus they turned the peasantry into a friendly sea in which the guerrilla forces could swim like fish.

In 1934, Chiang Kai-shek brought such overwhelming military force to bear against the Kiangsi Soviet that the Communists had to flee for their lives

on the Long March to Yenan. Then, the Japanese war forced a united front between Communists and Kuomintang, and Mao promised to abandon his policy
of land confiscation. Throughout the united front period, the Communists
kept their pledge in form, but not in substance. In the areas they controlled behind the Japanese lines in northern China, they forced the landlords to offer a
double reduction to the peasants, lower rent and lower interest rates. At the
same time, they introduced a new, graduated tax system that bore down heavily
on the landlords but virtually excused the peasants from payment. The double
impact of higher taxes and lower income forced the landowning class to sell off
some of their land, often to their own tenants. Historian Tetsuya Kataoka has
accurately termed this double reduction policy "confiscation by installment."
The Communists, therefore, never abandoned their policy of "land to the tiller,"
but simply changed tactics during the wartime united front.

After the Japanese war, the peasants of northern China, whose consciousness had been raised by the Communist guerrillas and organizers, took matters
into their own hands and settled accounts with landlords who had collaborated
with the Japanese. This "anti-traitor movement" became extremely violent as
peasants unleashed centuries of pent-up frustration against their economic and
political masters. At Long Bow Village in Shansi (Shanxi) Province, where
American aid worker William Hinton worked and studied for almost a year,
about a dozen people were beaten to death and some average peasants were
wrongly denounced and thus lost their land. In a similar village that journalist
Jack Belden visited, a mob of seven hundred men and women seized a landlord,
tied him to a tree, then hacked him to death with knives, hoes, and sickles, leaving his mutilated body lying in a field.

These postwar peasant reactions were little better than lynchings, but the
Communist Party organizers soon channeled them into a more systematic attack on the entire rural ruling class. On May 4, 1946, the Communist Central
Committee officially abandoned the wartime double reduction policy and
openly advocated confiscation of large landholdings. A year later, on October
10, 1947, the Draft Agrarian Law confirmed the land confiscations and cancelled
all peasant debts. Article 6 of this law proclaimed the egalitarian goal of land reform: "In terms of quantity, land is to be taken from those with more and given
to those with less; and in terms of quality, it should be taken from those with
better and given to those with worse."

In the course of land reform Communist organizers developed, through
trial and error, innovative methods of mass struggle. They urged the poor peasants to speak out publicly and "Accuse, Speak Bitterness, and Struggle Against
Oppressors." This was revolutionary in itself, for long tradition held that "a
poor man has no right to talk." When a peasant stood up in a village meeting
and boldly denounced the large landowner who had charged him outrageous

interest or violated his daughter, it proved psychologically cathartic for the individual and built solidarity among the other peasants who shared similar experiences.

When it came time to divide up all the land seized from the large landowners, the organizers adopted the tactic of "self report, public appraisal." In long public meetings, each villager would classify himself or herself as either a poor, middle, or rich peasant and estimate how much his or her fields yielded. Then the whole village would be asked to comment and criticize, to accuse the informant of lying or to ratify his or her self-assessment. After many days of such meetings, a certain rough justice was worked out and the land was divided. Jack Belden asked the typically American question, "Do they live any better?" after land reform, in the village he visited. He concluded: "You could not find a poor peasant enjoying a great banquet over the New Year holidays, but neither could you find him cowering in the fields to avoid his creditors, nor could you find a peasant who gave his daughter as a slave to his landlord or as a sleeping companion. . . ." *Fanshen* caused a psychological revolution as much as an economic one.

The Communists used the techniques of mass psychological struggle for other purposes besides land reform. Party members were subject to mutual and self-criticism sessions at their local headquarters, to ensure that they followed the party line. When the Eighth Route Army captured Nationalist soldiers, they marched the prisoners of war out into a field and conducted a meeting. Communist veterans told their life stories, explaining how they had "turned over" against the landlords and improved the lot of their families. Then one after another, the prisoners would relate their tales of woe, telling how they had been conscripted into Chiang's army and their families were left facing starvation. Before long, the Nationalist soldiers defected en masse to the Communist army.

Women also "turned over" against their husbands. For centuries women had served as little more than servants or beasts of burden in the rural villages of China. They entered into arranged marriages at a very early age and were then expected to stay at home and cater to their husbands' every whim and need. Men routinely beat their wives, for even the smallest offenses. When the Communists secured an area, they not only started a Peasants' Association to supervise land reform but a Women's Association as well. Women were encouraged to work in the fields, particularly if their husbands were absent in the army, and to participate in village struggle meetings. In Long Bow Village, where William Hinton observed the process of *fanshen,* seven of the thirty local peasants recruited into the Communist Party were women. When a village congress was elected, women comprised nearly half, 16 out of 35, elected delegates.

The Women's Associations investigated reports of wife beating and took collective action to wreak revenge. A group of women would approach the astounded male offender with clubs and sticks, then bind his hands and drag him away for investigation. Often this turned into a kind of lynching, as the women fell upon the wife-beater and pummeled, kicked, or bit him. If such shock treatment failed and the man continued to beat his wife, the village authorities would grant the woman a divorce and possibly even drive the man out of the village. More than any other Communist action, the encouragement of women to stand up against their husbands turned the Chinese countryside upside down.

The techniques of mass struggle that Chinese Communists employed and perfected resemble Protestant camp meetings, psychiatric treatment sessions, or perhaps twelve-step programs. Yet Jack Belden has suggested an even more striking analogy: "The Communists took power by making love to the people of China. The rural proletarians and the rural women joined the revolution because they were given human sympathy . . . and one emotion that was lacking from [their] life — hope."

Stirred by both hatred and hope, a desire for revenge and a dream of a better life, the peasants of northern China swelled the ranks of the Communist forces and swept the Kuomintang off the mainland. In 1948 and 1949 the Communist Revolution returned to the cities, from which it had been violently driven two decades before. The Communists used a combination of social pressure and coercion to stamp out long-standing ills such as prostitution and opium smoking. For decades after the Communists came to power, foreign visitors always commented on the absence of beggars and riff-raff from Chinese cities. The Communists also suppressed inflation with equally direct measures. They banned the circulation of gold, silver, and foreign bills and strictly limited the note issue of native Chinese currency. When Shanghai financiers continued to speculate in precious metals, the People's Liberation Army surrounded the stock exchange and arrested over two thousand traders. A decade of war, inflation, and economic collapse had so demoralized China's urban dwellers that they welcomed a strong hand.

Despite the use of force and psychological pressure against undesirable urban elements, Mao laid down a relatively moderate line to restore economic activity in the cities. Only the largest industrial and commercial firms, those operated by Chiang's political cronies and with foreign connections, would be expropriated. The so-called national bourgeoisie would be left in possession of their property and encouraged to increase production. The long-suffering working class was asked to accept still more sacrifices and not push for large wage increases.

As of October 1, 1949, when the Communist Party officially proclaimed the founding of the People's Republic of China, the country had undergone a revolution but was not yet a socialist state. Small and middle-sized peasant holdings predominated in northern China, where *fanshen* had been completed, and the older pattern of large-scale landlord and tenant farming still prevailed in the south. The state had seized the "commanding heights" of the urban economy but had not abolished all private property and was encouraging entrepreneurs to invest their capital and create jobs. Mao Tse-tung summed up the essence of his revolution at mid-century when he proclaimed: "China has stood up." The Chinese overthrew the semi-feudal system of landlord control in the countryside and the semi-colonial foreign-dominated capitalism of the cities. Oppressed women and poor peasants stood up and asserted their rights and dignity as human beings. In a deep psychological sense, the whole Chinese population stood up, "turned over," and erased a century of national humiliation. As Jack Belden concluded: "The only way for China to rid herself of feudalism and Western domination was to build a strong power, but the only way to build this power was to raid the feudal manors and organize the released prisoners. This is what the Communists did and what Chiang failed to do."

If Mao Tse-tung had died at mid-century, he would be remembered as a great agrarian revolutionary, a strong Chinese nationalist, and a master psychologist of the masses. By analogy with the Russian Revolution, Mao could be considered both Marx, the philosopher, and Lenin, the organizer, of revolution. Unfortunately for his reputation and for the fate of the Chinese people, however, Mao lived on for another quarter-century and also became China's Stalin. The rebel turned into an emperor and the master psychologist changed into a purveyor of mass terror. The world turned upside down once again.

In the first two or three years after they took power, the Chinese Communists rapidly spread the *fanshen* process of land reform to the newly conquered regions of southern China. The gentry were humiliated and dispossessed with great violence, as anyone who opposed the revenge of the poor peasants was conveniently labeled a counterrevolutionary. At least two million opponents of the new regime were executed between 1950 and 1952 and perhaps an equal number were dispatched to labor camps.

Land reform completed one revolutionary process, the partition of agricultural property into small, relatively equal, self-sufficient farms, and it marked the beginning of another, the combination of these peasant plots into larger, more efficient, more socialized, collective farms. The Communists initially believed that establishing socialism in the countryside would be a slow, gradual process; and they began tentatively, by encouraging the formation of mutual aid teams and voluntary cooperatives for more efficient purchasing, marketing, and allocation of labor. Yet Mao, like Stalin before him, was in a hurry to catch up with the more productive countries of the world, so in 1955 and 1956 he accelerated the process of collectivization. Communist organizers, capitalizing on the local enthusiasm still percolating through the villages from the *fanshen* campaigns, convinced the peasants that pooling their resources would enhance their livelihood. By the end of 1956, 90 percent of peasant households had given up their land to the state and worked on one of 485,000 collective farms. Unlike in Russia, the Communists in China had put down deep roots in the countryside and the peasants still trusted the revolutionaries.

Stalin's drive for collectivization of agriculture in the 1930s had resulted in a virtual civil war against the peasants, and at least fourteen million Russians were exterminated; but the Chinese managed a similar feat with a minimum of violence. Its economic results, however, proved meager. As historian Maurice Meisner has summarized: "Collectivization brought neither the economic disaster some feared nor the economic growth its advocates anticipated." In order to force the pace of growth, therefore, Mao declared the "Great Leap Forward" in 1958, an attempt at social engineering that led to an economic and human catastrophe.

With an almost godlike detachment, Mao theorized that China's very backwardness could be used as a springboard for progress:

> China's 600 million people have two remarkable peculiarities: they are, first of all, poor, and secondly blank. That may seem like a bad thing, but it is really a good thing. Poor people want change, want to do things, want revolution. A clean sheet of paper has no blotches, and so the newest and most beautiful words can be written on it.

In the years 1958 to 1960, Mao imposed the Great Leap Forward upon the "poor and blank" rural masses, spurring them on to herculean production efforts. Enthusiastic young peasants worked nearly around the clock on collective farms and public works projects, and in the construction of new rural industries. Mao called this process "walking on two legs," that is, increasing *both* agricultural and industrial production at the same time. Instead of planning primarily for heavy industry, as Stalin did in Russia, Mao dreamed of both large, heavy industrial complexes in the cities and smaller, consumer-oriented factories in the countryside. He intended to use the huge pool of peasant labor, which often lay idle during slack seasons of the agricultural cycle, to overcome China's lack of capital and technology. Mao urged the masses to work "more, faster, better, and cheaper."

Besides setting economic goals for the Great Leap, Mao also hoped to refresh the revolutionary ardor of the Communist Party by forcing urban administrators out of their offices and into the fields, thus overcoming the gaps between city and countryside, party and the masses. To cram the necessary technical knowledge into the heads of party workers and keep them ideologically sound, he encouraged a proliferation of "half-work, half-study" programs that would make party members "Red and expert." In short, Mao wanted to have it all — agriculture, industry, education, indoctrination — and in a hurry.

Some of the Great Leap projects were fiascoes from the start, such as the "backyard" iron foundries into which untrained peasants tossed their cooking pots and other bits of metal flotsam in a vain attempt to create something from nothing. Other construction efforts, such as the building of dams and irrigation tunnels, produced more permanent, beneficial results. Yet the forced enthusiasm of the Great Leap eventually exhausted the energy of the peasants and disrupted the economy, with devastating results.

China's unpredictable weather and rampaging rivers have often produced terrible famines, but the deadly hunger of the late 1950s and early 1960s was primarily a man-made phenomenon. Trying to combine industrialization with agricultural production stretched the labor of China's masses too thin, often removing the peasants from the fields just when they were needed most. Urban Communists, with no agricultural experience, sometimes directed the farmers to plow and plant in ways that only produced soil erosion, not bumper crops. It was, however, the frenzied enthusiasm and competitive spirit of the Great Leap that produced the most deadly harvest. Local Communist leaders vied with each other to set the most unrealistic production targets and then felt obliged to meet them, no matter what. So even when bad weather in 1959 reduced the grain yield, the Great Leapers reported bumper crops to their superiors, who therefore kept upping the grain requisitions to feed industrial workers in the cities. As a result, peasants were left with less than subsistence rations on the collective farms. When the scale of the economic disruption became obvious to more technically trained Communist leaders, they attempted to rein in the disastrous experiment, but Mao stubbornly insisted on continuing into 1960, before finally admitting defeat. In the meantime, an estimated *20 to 30 million* Chinese died of starvation, disease, or overwork. Mao, unlike Stalin, was not a mass murderer by intent, but his ill-conceived flight of economic imagination, the Great Leap Forward, eclipsed the atrocities of the Soviet leader's collectivization and industrialization campaigns.

Mao Tse-tung lost power and influence due to the disasters of the Great Leap period. Though he remained chairman of the Chinese Communist Party, he gave up the governmental post of chairman of the Republic and relinquished control over day-to-day affairs to more sober managers. His status as symbolic leader of the Revolution remained undiminished, and the early 1960s saw a great increase in the myth-making of his personality cult. The little red book of *Quotations from Chairman Mao* was first published in 1964, and before long all of China and many university campuses in Europe and America were flooded with a billion copies of these "sacred writings." Yet Mao bitterly remarked that the Communist leaders already treated him "like a dead ancestor." Seventy years of age in 1963, Mao had come face to face with his own mortality.

Always a believer in a "permanent" or "uninterrupted" revolution, Chairman Mao recognized that any mass movement is likely to lose its drive, to become regularized and bureaucratized when it succeeds in grabbing power. Nor was he the first to make this discovery. The American revolutionary Thomas Jefferson once remarked that a country needs a revolution every twenty years or so, that is, once a generation. Anyone who believes in fundamental change is likely to feel frustrated when rebellious youth turns into cautious old age and revolutions yield to institutions. In China the veterans of the Long March would soon be leaving the scene, and Mao disliked the self-satisfied young Communists who were preparing to take over. Revolutionaries had become rulers and the party now attracted as many opportunists as rebels. Chairman Mao, therefore, felt a need to raise up "revolutionary successors," young men and women who would perpetuate the enthusiasm that he himself still felt. Endowed with a restless, reckless temperament, he considered life a process of constant change.

In the summer of 1966, therefore, Mao Tse-tung shook up China's Revolution one more time, calling on the youth of China to rebel against their elders in the Great Proletarian Cultural Revolution. On May 25, 1966, a philosophy professor and six students at Peking University hung up a massive wall poster attacking the president of the university and the local party administration of the city. The authorities quickly tore it down, but one of Mao's henchmen sent a copy of the text to the chairman, who approved the radical student manifesto. Encouraged by the "Great Helmsman" of the Revolution, the students opened a campaign on June 18, criticizing and humiliating professors and administrators, forcing them to wear dunces' caps on their heads and self-critical posters around their necks.

Students and other young Communists across the country imitated the rebellious youth of Peking. Born too late to take part in the revolution against the Kuomintang and the imperialists, Chinese youth of the 1960s relived those heady days vicariously, dressing up in military fatigues and calling themselves Red Guards. Like a retired general, an emperor, or a god, Mao Tse-tung reviewed about ten million of these Red Guards in a series of massive rallies staged in Peking's Tiananmen Square between August 18 and November 26, 1966. Mao never spoke at these rallies, but simply showed himself to the masses, dressed in military garb and accompanied by his radical fourth wife, Chiang Ch'ing (Jiang Qing). The students held aloft their little red books of Mao quotations while the chairman raised his arm in a revolutionary salute.

When the rallies ended, the Red Guards ran amok, in their home cities, on university campuses, and elsewhere across the country, for the state railways offered them free transportation anywhere they chose to travel. It was like spring break with weapons. They broke into government offices and private homes, dragging men, women, and children of bourgeois or intellectual backgrounds into the streets and forcing them to "confess" their counterrevolutionary sins and humiliate themselves publicly. As the frenzy grew, the radicals beat, tortured, or executed their hapless victims. In the remote southwestern province of Kwangsi (Guangxi), zealots buried people alive and sometimes ate their flesh.

Intellectuals were the most common victims of the ironically named Cultural Revolution. Though once a struggling student himself, a member of the intellectual proletariat, Mao Tse-tung had never trusted members of the intelligentsia. They seemed too privileged and remote from the masses. So he unleashed students against professors and the uneducated against the elite. Writers were forced to burn or tear up their manuscripts, then sent down to the countryside to dirty their hands by plowing fields or slopping hogs. Others spent years in prison labor camps. Sometimes the Red Guards paraded a large group of intellectuals to a killing ground for execution by firing squad but left some, chosen at random, still alive as bodies dropped around them. The novelist Zhang Xianliang, who apparently underwent this form of "Chinese roulette," has concluded: "Although the gun may never have been fired, the bullet of fear and repression has lodged inside the brain. Every intellectual in China lives with this kind of bullet in his brain." When it was all over, the survivors grimly joked that "the Cultural Revolution was about doing away with culture."

Besides watering the tree of revolution with human blood and making himself feel young again, Mao Tse-tung also used the Cultural Revolution to settle some political scores within the party and purge anyone suspected of less-than-total loyalty to himself. Liu Shao-ch'i (Liu Shaoqi), the vice chairman of the party and Mao's designated successor, disappeared from public view in November 1966, was placed under arrest and denied medical treatment for his diabetes, then finally died of pneumonia in 1969. Teng Hsiao-p'ing (Deng Xiaoping), the general secretary of the party, was sent off to the provinces to renew his proletarian credentials working in a factory, but was not otherwise harmed. Peking students verbally attacked Chou En-lai (Zhou Enlai), the prime minister, but he survived with his governmental power intact.

As the Red Guards increasingly threatened Communist Party rule, Mao finally authorized the regular soldiers of the People's Liberation Army to restore order and send the unruly students out into the countryside for their own "reeducation." This second phase of the Cultural Revolution, from fall 1967 until the Party Congress of April 1969, proved even bloodier than the period of Red Guard ascendancy, for the army was better armed and more ruthless than the radical students. Estimates of the death toll from three years of Cultural

Revolution range from a low of 400,000 to about 2.2 million. Yet like Stalin's party purges of the late 1930s, the significance of the Cultural Revolution extends far beyond the numbers killed. A whole generation of Chinese was scarred by the events of the late 1960s. Rather than renewing the revolutionary ardor of the young, the Cultural Revolution left them with a legacy of fear and repression, instilling in them an overwhelming urge to play it safe. Though the worst excesses ceased in 1969, the decade from the beginning of the Cultural Revolution until Mao's death in 1976 is now considered the "ten lost years" of the Chinese Revolution.

Zhang Xianliang, in his novel *Getting Used to Dying,* presents a haunting vignette of the elderly Mao sitting alone and bored in his palatial residence, instructing a bodyguard to bring in firecrackers and set them off one at a time. Perhaps no better image could be found for Mao's final attempt to turn the world upside down. Yet it would be inaccurate to ascribe the terrors of the Great Leap Forward and the Cultural Revolution only to the senility of the Chinese Communist leader. Mao was not a "good revolutionary" before 1950 and an "evil emperor" after that date. In fact, his beliefs and policies showed a remarkable consistency, and his revolutionary career was marked by constant attempts at cultural revolution or thought control. During the darkest days of the war against Japan, for example, in 1942 and 1943, Mao and his security chief K'ang Sheng (Kang Sheng) mounted the Rectification Movement which required party members to engage in public self-criticism and struggle sessions, subjecting many of them to imprisonment and torture. Few were executed, but at least 40,000 were expelled from the party and some were driven insane and committed suicide. Mao's quarter century of nearly absolute power, however, gave his penchant for mass manipulation a wider scope and resulted in much heavier casualties.

Unlike Mohandas Gandhi in India, Mao believed that the ends justified any means, no matter how extreme or deadly. He sometimes called off or moderated struggle campaigns, but only if they threatened his own authority, not out of moral or humanitarian concern. The Yugoslav Communist Milovan Djilas labeled Stalin "one of those rare terrible dogmatists capable of destroying nine tenths of the human race to 'make happy' the one tenth." This description applies almost literally to Mao Tse-tung. He once shocked Prime Minister Jawaharlal Nehru of India with a cavalier remark about nuclear war: "If the worst came to the worst and half of mankind died, the other half would remain while imperialism would be razed to the ground and the whole world would become socialist."

During an unsuccessful coup attempt in 1969, Chinese conspirators code-named Chairman Mao "B-52," the U.S. strategic bomber that carries nuclear weapons. Mao's biographer, Ross Terrill, underlines the appropriateness of "the image of Mao as a giant moving high above all else, striking suddenly." Flying above the masses with dogmatic certainty, Mao Tse-tung led one of the most successful revolutions of the twentieth century but left a deadly legacy of violence.

CHAPTER FIVE

Unity in Diversity

I n China after World War II, Mao Tse-tung's Communists overwhelmed a
decadent nationalist movement; the reverse took place on the islands of Indonesia. In the Indonesian revolution, nationalism triumphed over both European imperialism and Marxist communism, producing one of the most inspired, and inspiring, leaders of the twentieth century: Sukarno. Unfortunately,
Indonesia's history also illustrates the limits of a purely nationalist revolution.

The long string of East Indian islands between the continents of Asia and
Australia, which have become the fourth most populous country in the world,[1]
would seem to have few natural attributes of a nation-state. Over thirteen thousand islands, including Java, Sumatra, two-thirds of Borneo, and half of New
Guinea, as well as thousands of tiny uninhabited specks of land, sprawl over an
expanse as large as the territorial United States. More than three hundred distinct ethnic groups, speaking over fifty languages, inhabit these isles. Yet when
the Netherlands East Indies declared independence after World War II, the national revolutionaries surprised their Dutch masters with their unity and tenacity. The independent republic of Indonesia then adopted as its motto the phrase
Bhinneka Tunggal Ika, "diverse yet united."

Some elements of unity in diversity had existed for centuries. Most of the
islands are racially homogeneous, having been settled by migrants from the
Malay Peninsula of Asia; and the Malay tongue has long served as a common
language, a *lingua franca*, for traders throughout the archipelago. The sea di-
vides the Indies into separate islands, but it also unites them, or at least their

1. Indonesia today has a population of approximately 195 million people, ranking it
behind China, India, and the United States, but ahead of Russia.

coastal areas, into a common economic and linguistic region. This long-established system of coastal trading also brought a common religion, Islam, to the East Indies. The courts and rulers of Java and some other islands had long been dominated by a Hindu-Buddhist culture transplanted from India, but beginning in the thirteenth century Arab traders spread Islam widely throughout the islands. Today, Indonesia is 87 percent Islamic, the largest Muslim country in the world, with more believers in Allah than all of the Arab countries combined. Yet the Muslim community is divided between reformist and traditionalist believers, and many Indonesians are merely nominal adherents to Islam, melding it with older religious traditions. The Christian minority also has exercised influence disproportionate to its small numbers. Religion, therefore, has more frequently been a divisive than a unifying force.

The East Indies did not experience political unity until the twentieth century. At least two kingdoms based on Java had extended their power temporarily over neighboring islands in earlier centuries, but they never consolidated control over the whole island chain. When Europeans first arrived in the seas off Asia in the sixteenth century, they encountered numerous small kingdoms, sultanates, and trading cities. Europeans made no attempt to conquer the entire archipelago at this time, but simply grabbed the trade of the fabled "Spice Islands," the Moluccas (now called Maluku). Cloves, pepper, and nutmeg, essential to preserve and flavor the food of Europe, were the magnets drawing early imperialists to the East Indies.

European power and control grew slowly in this region, which from their point of view lay at the end of the earth. The Portuguese disrupted the established trading system of the islands by capturing the port city of Malacca across the straits from Sumatra in 1511, but their overall impact on the area remained slight. The Dutch sent their first mission eastward in 1595, and in 1619 they sacked and burned the town of Jayakerta on the north coast of Java. The Dutch East India Company established its headquarters among the ruins in a new city they named Batavia. For two centuries thereafter, Dutch traders ruthlessly managed a monopoly over the production and selling of cloves in the eastern spice-growing islands, chopping down whole groves of clove trees to constrict the supply and raise prices, and deporting entire populations from rebellious islands. They also extended their control over the northern coast of Java, the most populous island; but they did not dominate the powerful kingdoms of inland Java until the mid-eighteenth century. All in all, the Dutch followed a policy similar to that of the British in India. They dominated militarily by playing one indigenous kingdom against another, but they contented themselves for the most part with trading relations and indirect rule.

In the nineteenth century, however, the balance of economic and military force between Europe and the rest of the world tilted decisively towards Europe.

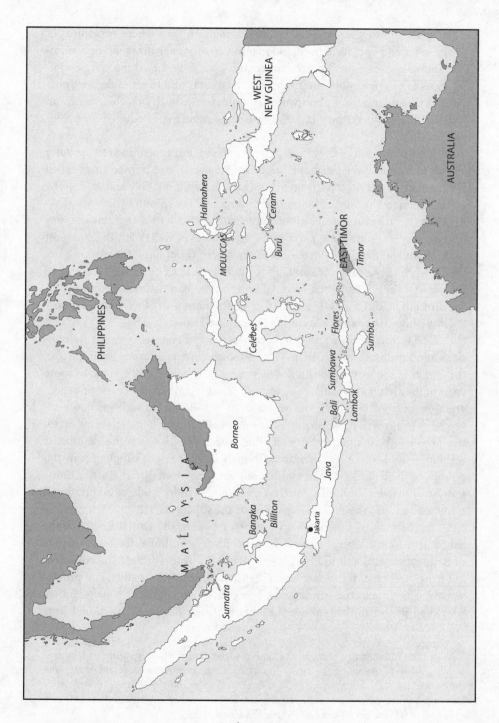

Indonesia

The Dutch imposed an effective colonial system on Java, where two-thirds of the Indonesian population lived, leaving four traditional rulers with only nominal authority over a small portion of central Java. They forced the Javanese villagers to pay 40 percent of their rice crop in land tax and to set aside large portions of village land for the cultivation of export crops such as coffee, sugar, and indigo. Nineteenth-century Holland prospered on the coerced profits of colonial produce.

Toward the end of the century the Dutch sent out expeditions to the outer islands of Sumatra, the Celebes (now called Sulawesi), and Borneo (now called Kalimantan) to suppress native rebellions and head off possible annexations by other imperialist powers. The European scramble for colonies that carved up Africa in the late nineteenth century impelled the Dutch to act quickly lest they find interlopers controlling parts of the East Indies as well. With the conquest of the Islamic kingdom of Aceh[2] on the northern tip of Sumatra around 1910, the Dutch finally brought nearly all of the islands under one political regime for the first time. The Dutch colonial government had defined the borders of the future state of Indonesia and had given the Indonesians a common enemy against whom they could develop their national consciousness.

The factors of time and distance shaped the encounter between Indonesians and European imperialism. Due to the enormous distance from Europe, the Dutch were tardy in consolidating their rule over the East Indies. In some parts of the archipelago, such as Aceh, the Dutch regime lasted for only a generation or so, from 1910 until the outbreak of World War II, and was never accepted as legitimate. As we shall see, it was difficult for the Dutch to bring effective power to bear upon Indonesia after World War II, when the nationalist revolution took place. Furthermore, though Indonesia got caught up in the politics of the Cold War, it lay sufficiently far away from Soviet Russia, Communist China, and capitalist America to secure its independence and national unity without too much interference from the superpowers.

At the turn of the twentieth century, however, the Dutch finally established firm control over their only major colony. As in India, the first stirrings of nationalism and a desire for independence developed among the educated, but frustrated, elite of Indonesian students, teachers, civil servants, and professionals. This intellectual proletariat, however, emerged about a half-century later than in India. Throughout the nineteenth century, the Dutch had pro-

---

2. The Indonesian government changed the system of transliterating its language into English in 1972. Among the most noticeable changes was the replacement of *Dj* (as in the capital city of Djakarta) with *J* (now Jakarta) and *Tj* (as in Atjeh) with *C* (now Aceh). I have adopted this new system since few English-speakers were familiar with the old Dutch system and the new forms generally make sense in English.

vided few educational opportunities. In 1900 only 265,940 Indonesians, out of a total population of 36 million, were receiving any education at all, and only 1,545 Indonesians and 325 "foreign Orientals" (Chinese, Arabs, and Indians) were attending the elite Dutch-language primary schools. A grand total of thirteen Indonesians and four foreign Orientals matriculated at the Dutch-language secondary schools at the turn of the century. No university education was available in the Netherlands East Indies until the 1920s, but a handful of professional schools had been organized to train teachers, doctors, and civil servants.

A feeling of frustrated nationalism crystallized for the first time at the single school for training native doctors, the Stovia (*School tot opleiding van indlandsche artsen*), in the western Javanese city of Bandung. At Stovia, sons of the lesser *priyayi,* or administrative officials, widened their horizons by studying with like-minded individuals from all over the islands. A number of Stovia graduates, finding their chances for upward mobility extremely slim, organized the first nationalist organization, *Budi Utomo* (Noble Endeavor) on May 20, 1908. This group expanded to a membership of about ten thousand, composed mainly of graduates from Stovia and the other professional institutes, but it never developed a mass base. The organization engaged in cultural and educational activities, but its political petitions were so tame that the Dutch colonial authorities never even bothered to ban it. *Budi Utomo* withered away, much as the Indian National Congress might have had it not been invigorated by Mohandas Gandhi.

. Other organizations soon sprang up which were either more radical or more deeply rooted among the populace. Religion was the surest vehicle for mobilizing the masses, so by 1916 the Muslim Association, *Sarekat Islam,* had enrolled members of the trading middle class and some of the more devout rural peasantry into an organization with eighty local branches and 357,000 members. In May 1914, a Dutch socialist, Hendrik Sneevliet, who later became a Comintern official in China, organized the first Social Democratic Party in the Indies. When most of the expatriate Dutch socialists were arrested or exiled immediately after World War I, Indonesian worker and peasant leaders reorganized the party on May 23, 1920. Soon renamed the *Partai Komunis Indonesia* (PKI), Communist Party of Indonesia, it was the oldest Marxist party in Asia and in later years the largest outside Russia or China.

In the first two decades of this century, therefore, Indonesian activists established three different kinds of organizations — secular nationalist, religious, and socialist. Despite many changes of names, countless jailings, and suppressions, these three ideological tendencies shaped political opinion in Indonesia for most of the century. They persisted so strongly because they tapped into the existing Indonesian social strata. The nationalists drew their support primarily from the old nobility and the administrative elite of the colony, whereas the religious parties mobilized the devout Muslim trading classes, who functioned much like the commercially minded Protestants of Europe. Finally, the socialists made their strongest appeal to the small working class of the cities and the oppressed peasant majority in the countryside. This three-fold division between *priyayi* — the educated elite; *santri* — pious Muslims of city and countryside; and *abangan* — nominally Muslim peasants who still retained many of their older, pre-Islamic customs, had both economic and cultural aspects and threatened the unity of Indonesian society even more than language, ethnicity, or geography.

In the early 1920s the nationalist *Budi Utomo* was very weak and the religious *Sarekat Islam* suffered a series of divisions. The Communist PKI prematurely launched an uprising in western Java and eastern Sumatra at the end of 1926, which the Dutch authorities savagely suppressed. The surviving Communist leaders were exiled, shot, or imprisoned at a concentration camp in the remote jungles of western New Guinea (now called Irian Jaya). The unsuccessful PKI uprising removed the Communist Party from Indonesian politics for nearly twenty years, leaving the field open to the nationalists, who finally organized an effective political party in 1927, the *Partai Nasional Indonesia* (PNI), Indonesian Nationalist Party.

A generation of Indonesian students born around the turn of the century and educated either in Holland or at the newly founded Universitas Indonesia in Bandung took over the nationalist movement from the ineffective *Budi Utomo* elite in the 1920s. The European-trained students, led by Mohammed Hatta from west Sumatra, founded a new political journal named *Indonesia Merdeka* (Independent Indonesia). Previously, "Indonesia" had been a purely geographical term devised by nineteenth-century European mapmakers to distinguish the Dutch Indies from British India, but the nationalist students now publicized the word as the name of their native country. At the same time, the new intelligentsia adopted the old trading lingo, Malay, as their national language, using it in their literary endeavors and political tracts. This new Indonesian language proved to be an inspired choice. One of the greatest threats to the unity of Indonesia was the fear of domination by populous Java. Had the nationalists tried to impose the Javanese language on the country, they would have provoked regional, ethnic revolts. By adopting a widely used language which was more prominent on the outer islands than in Java, however, they helped to build national unity out of diversity. Language never became a divisive issue as it had been in Europe or it later became in the newly emerging nations of Africa.

In October 1928 a youth congress in the capital of the Netherlands East Indies brought the first wave of nationalist agitation to a climax. The assembled students revived the ancient name of the capital city, Jakarta, refusing to use the

Dutch word Batavia. They adopted a banner with broad red and white stripes, still the Indonesian Republic's flag today, and sang an anthem entitled "Indonesia Raya," written by a native poet who died young. The congress finally ratified a revolutionary slogan of "Indonesia, one people, one language, one mother land."

The Dutch authorities soon nipped this flowering of nationalism in the bud by simultaneously arresting all the prominent leaders on a single day in December 1929. Throughout the 1930s, the East Indies remained economically crippled by the worldwide depression and politically repressed by a Dutch administration which believed Indonesian independence would come "perhaps a few centuries hence." Not until World War II was any further revolutionary activity possible.

In the meantime, the nationalist who would lead his country to independence had proclaimed an ideological manifesto uniting the many strands of Indonesian diversity into a new unity. In 1926 a technical student named Sukarno published an article in *Young Indonesia* entitled "Nationalism, Islam and Marxism." Relying on Ernst Renan's classic description of nationalism as "the will and desire to live as one" and the feeling that "we have done great things together in the past," Sukarno expressed the power of nationalism to blend with other ideologies. In a colonial society both Marxism and Islam naturally inclined to nationalist appeals. Nearly all capitalists in the colonial East Indies were foreign capitalists, so Marxists could combine their class consciousness with nationalism. Again, in colonized Indonesia the enemies of Islam, the Christians, formed the ruling class, so fervent Muslims could ally their religion with nationalism. In Sukarno's view, Marxism and Islam orbited nationalism like planets around the sun. At the end of his passionate plea for unity, Sukarno declared: "It only remains to look for an organizer who can make himself a Mahatma of this Unity. . . ." He probably had a candidate in mind.

Sukarno was no Mahatma Gandhi. He lacked the Indian leader's spirituality and in later life earned a notorious reputation as an international playboy. Yet he did have oratorical power to move the masses and deft political instincts that made him the indispensable leader of the Indonesian nationalist movement. Born on June 6, 1901, in the eastern Javanese city of Surabaya, he was originally named Kusno Sosro Sukarno, but like many Indonesians he used only the one name throughout his life. In fact, as soon as he entered politics, he adopted a populist stance by calling himself simply Bung Karno, Brother Karno. Sukarno came from the *priyayi*, or aristocratic-administrative class, yet his father stood at the low end of the colonial administration, working as a schoolteacher in a native primary school. His mother came from Bali, the only island where older Hindu traditions had been preserved intact, and his father was a free-thinking Muslim, so Sukarno was multicultural by birth. He shared a typical Javanese intellectual trait of trying to combine diverse religions and cultures into a new synthesis. Scholars sometimes categorize human personalities as either "lumpers" or "splitters." Splitters are the ideologues who chop logic and refine their thought with minute distinctions, whereas lumpers comfortably combine many diverse streams of thought into a more or less stable amalgam. As his essay on nationalism, Islam, and Marxism testifies, Sukarno was a super-lumper.

The schoolteacher's son was one of very few Indonesians who received a Dutch language education, and in 1921 he enrolled in the newly established technical college at the fledgling university in Bandung. He received the title of *Ingenieur* upon graduation in 1926 and worked briefly as an architect and technical designer, but he found his true vocation in politics. While a student he had founded the General Study Club which published the *Young Indonesia* journal, and a year after graduation he took the lead in organizing the PNI, the Indonesian Nationalist Party.

Sukarno followed Gandhi's policy of non-violent non-cooperation, but he and his fellow nationalists had not yet touched the masses. When the Dutch arrested him and his compatriots on December 29, 1929, few protests followed. Though Sukarno was released from prison after two years, he was re-arrested in August 1933. This time he snapped. Not an ascetic like Gandhi or a man of steel like some Communists, he could not face the prospect of long incarceration, so he wrote secret letters to the authorities recanting his political views and begging forgiveness. The Dutch remained adamant, however, so Sukarno was jailed again and later sent into internal exile in a remote part of Sumatra. He remained there until he and the Indonesian nationalist movement were rescued by the Japanese.

When the Japanese navy swiped at Pearl Harbor on December 7, 1941, they were heading for the Dutch East Indies, whose supplies of oil and rubber they coveted. After brief but furious naval battles, the colonial administration on Java surrendered on March 8, 1942. The Dutch had tried to evacuate Sukarno and other political prisoners to Australia but they moved too slowly, reaching the Sumatran port of Padang after the last Allied boat had left. The Japanese military transported Sukarno to the capital city of Jakarta where he and most of the nationalists willingly cooperated with the occupiers.

Collaboration did not bear the same stigma of treason in Indonesia that it did in Nazi-occupied Europe. The Japanese portrayed themselves as champions of all Asia against European imperialism, and many Asians, including Sukarno, believed them. At the very least, nearly every nationalist believed that "the enemy of my enemy is my friend." Sukarno and Mohammed Hatta fronted a number of Japanese-sponsored advisory councils during the war, and they even traveled to Tokyo for an audience with the emperor in November 1943. However, one leading nationalist, Sutan Sjahrir, feigned illness and remained quietly underground, in radio contact with the Allies. The Indonesian nationalists, therefore, enjoyed the best of both worlds. Yet the common people suffered severely during the Japanese occupation. The military authorities requisitioned large quantities of rice at low prices and conscripted over 250,000 men for labor duty throughout the Greater East Asia Co-Prosperity Sphere. Only 70,000 of these forced laborers returned alive. Widespread hunger and starvation stalked the land during the final, dying year of Japanese control.

Despite the brutality of their occupation, the Japanese gave Indonesian nationalism a new lease on life. Since the military banned the use of the Dutch language, the educated elite learned to communicate regularly and easily in Indonesian. The occupiers also distributed radios to villages throughout the archipelago so that their nationalist "advisors" could exhort the people, in Indonesian, to support the military. Peasants came to know Sukarno's voice as they gathered around the "singing trees" in the village squares. Unlike the Dutch, the Japanese authorities tried to mobilize and energize the common people in numerous organizations so that they would work willingly for the empire. The most important of these organizations was the paramilitary PETA, *Pembela Tanah Air* (Defenders of the Homeland). The Dutch had never dared arm the Indonesians, but the Japanese did. When the war ended, therefore, the previously docile Indonesians had been aroused, mobilized, and armed.

The Japanese did not originally plan on independence for Indonesia, but as the war turned against them they changed their minds and instructed the nationalist leaders to hold constitutional talks. The Investigating Committee for Preparatory Work for Indonesian Independence divided sharply between secular nationalists and those desiring an Islamic state. In a long speech on June 1, 1945, Sukarno proclaimed his idea of unity in diversity.

Sukarno called his political philosophy *Panca Sila,* or five principles — nationalism, internationalism, consensus through deliberation, social justice, and belief in one God. He linked the first two principles, nationalism and internationalism, as contrasting ideals that needed to co-exist in a healthy tension. Quoting Gandhi, he declared: "I am a nationalist, but my nationalism is humanity." The third principle, consensus through deliberation, could be translated as democracy or republicanism, but these English terms miss the nuances of the Indonesian word *musyawarah.* In thousands of Indonesian villages, local leaders would deliberate public issues for hours or even days, considering all sides of a question and letting every point of view be expressed, until a consensus was reached through compromise. Sukarno believed this principle of unanimity through deliberation and compromise was a better governmental ideal than the Western practice of majority rule. He further linked this Indonesian style of political democracy with his fourth principle, social justice, or economic democracy. Finally, the fifth principle of belief in one God constituted a typically Indonesian compromise. The state would not be dominated by Islamic law; rather all religions would be honored and citizens would be encouraged to live by their own religious beliefs.

Thus the five principles boiled down to three, which Sukarno called socio-nationalism, socio-democracy, and belief in God. He even proposed a single term to sum them all up: *gotong-royong,* or mutual cooperation. Though this statement of principles might sound like sloganeering to cynical Western observers, it was a genuine development of Sukarno's 1926 article and it touched a deep need for harmony and reconciliation in Indonesian culture. Sukarno remained committed to *Panca Sila* as a distinctive Indonesian ideology for the rest of his life. It is one of the first, and most eloquent, expressions of a now common Asian theme, the need for an alternative to both communism and parliamentary democracy. In the short run, it finessed the division in the Investigating Committee between religious and secular delegates, leading to adoption of a constitution in just two months.

The war ended more suddenly than anyone expected after the atomic bombings of Japan in August 1945. Sukarno, Hatta, Sjahrir and the other nationalist leaders felt uncertain whether they should proceed with a Japanese-sponsored independence declaration or wait for the Allies to make their postwar policy known. Before they could make up their minds, the revolutionary youth of the capital forced their hands. Sukarno's generation, the first Indonesians with a modern education, had reached middle age by the time of World War II. To the *pemuda,* or youths, who followed them into secondary and higher education, they appeared timid and hesitant. The Japanese had closed the university during the war, but the educated youth gathered in Jakarta youth hostels to exchange information and plan for the future. Their less educated counterparts in smaller towns and villages had been mobilized for service in the armed PETA or other youth organizations. Not having seen any real fighting during the war, they were itching for action, excitement, and change. To the *pemuda,* revolution was a matter of style or attitude as much as policy. Many wore their hair long and vowed not to cut it until independence was achieved. Others adopted foreign heroic models, such as the cowboy or the samurai, ostentatiously swaggering about with pistols or swords. Yet they fought for the cause of national independence with a tenacity that surprised their elders.

Early in the morning of August 16, 1945, two cars pulled up to the houses of Sukarno and Hatta, and six of the most radical *pemuda* kidnapped the nationalist leaders. They drove to a remote suburb of Jakarta and spent all day browbeating the two into issuing an immediate declaration of independence. About ten that night they all returned to the capital, consulted the Japanese authorities, who promised to look the other way, and then drafted a short statement. Sutan Sjahrir desired a declaration filled with anti-Japanese, pro-Allied statements, and the radical young kidnappers wanted to include ringing demands for social revolution and the confiscation of property. Sukarno typically stalled and compromised, finally writing a bland, simple declaration: "We, the people of Indonesia, hereby declare Indonesia's independence. Matters concerning the transfer of power and other matters will be executed in an orderly manner and in the shortest possible time." Only Sukarno and Hatta signed the declaration, which was read outside Sukarno's house at 10 A.M. on August 17 and then broadcast throughout the archipelago in the following days.

The curious manner in which Indonesians declared their independence illustrates a major split running through the nationalist revolution, a split between *diplomasi* (negotiation) and *perjuangan* (struggle). The older, recognized nationalist leaders tried to secure independence through negotiations, first with the Japanese, then with the Dutch and the Allied military occupation forces, then finally at the United Nations. The *pemuda,* and later the Communists, preferred to seize independence through violent struggle. The kidnapping of timid officials, which came to be called a *daulat* action (from the words *kedaulatan rakyat,* people's sovereignty), became the signature maneuver of the *pemuda* radicals. Most often these *daulats* proved non-violent and ended happily, as with the declaration of independence, but sometimes they turned to torture and murder.

The Dutch had few soldiers available at the end of the war to reclaim their colony and thus had to wait for their allies, the British and the Americans, to act. Lord Louis Mountbatten, the Allied commander in Southeast Asia, could not spare any troops for occupation of the far-flung East Indies until the end of September 1945. This allowed republican leaders to set up provisional governments and take control of the administrative apparatus while the remaining Japanese troops looked the other way. When the British, mostly Indian, troops finally arrived on Java, they interpreted their mission quite narrowly, to release European prisoners of war and repatriate the Japanese to their home islands. To the outrage of the Dutch, they often treated the Indonesian republicans as a de facto government. The situation unfolded differently on the outer islands, where mainly Australian troops met with little resistance from the republicans and soon ceded control back to the Dutch.

The months immediately after the independence declaration were turbulent and unsettled on the main island of Java. The radical youth held rallies in the cities, raised the republican flag on public buildings, and urged the Japanese to give them their weapons. Many of the Japanese commanders complied, showing open sympathy for the republicans. In the countryside, the *pemuda* attacked landlords and village leaders who had exploited the peasants. These rural purges were generally not so violent as the *fanshen* upheavals in Communist

China. Typically the *pemuda* would humiliate exploiters by parading them through the village to the sound of clanging pots and wooden clappers, rather than assassinate them. Sometimes a village headman simply abdicated in favor of another family member or a local rival.

The nationalist leaders in the capital tried to control the outbursts of radicalism and negotiate with the British. Sometimes they succeeded. On September 20, 1945, for example, the Jakarta *pemuda* turned out a massive crowd of 200,000 for a rally in Ikada Square opposite the government buildings. Sukarno gave a brief speech, then convinced the crowds to disperse in an orderly fashion. But in Surabaya, the second largest city on Java, the *pemuda* revolt led to tragedy. Urged on by a radical leader called Bung Tomo, young people poured into Surabaya in October 1945, threatening the four thousand Gurkha Indian troops with violence. The British flew Sukarno into the city on October 29 and he momentarily calmed the crowds, but soon after he left the British general was killed in a confused exchange of shots. He may have been hit accidentally by his own troops. Nevertheless, the British retaliated with a fury, unleashing sea and air attacks on the city. The *pemuda* resisted in three weeks of savage street fighting that convinced the British to cease military support of the Dutch.

The revolution continued for four more years, from 1945 through 1949, but fighting was not continuous and never reached the levels of the Surabaya battles again. The British finally evacuated towards the end of 1946, leaving the Indonesians to face the Netherlands Indies Civil Administration (NICA). The split between the strategies of *diplomasi* and *perjuangan* actually worked in favor of the Indonesians. The combination of moderate leaders who wished to negotiate backed by the threat of uncontrollable violence by the youth eventually resulted in a ratification of Indonesian independence. In this respect, the Indonesian revolution strongly resembles both the Irish and the Indian independence movements.

Sukarno, as first president of the republic, found himself in a difficult and vulnerable position. His oratory proved indispensable for rallying support to the revolution, and even the most radical youth realized they could not do without him. Yet he was a liability in negotiating with the Dutch, who considered him an arch-collaborator. During most of the revolution, therefore, Sukarno ceded diplomatic and governmental duties to other leaders, notably Hatta and Sjahrir, who had smoother, European-trained techniques, and limited himself to public appeals for unity. He remained, however, a master at bridging divisions in the populace, usually talking as militantly as the *pemuda* but backing the moderate leaders in their diplomatic negotiations.

For their part, the Dutch felt determined not to give up their only major colony without a fight. The Netherlands East Indies held far more economic importance to the Dutch than India did to the British; therefore, the NICA negotiated half-heartedly while building up military strength for reconquest. Since the Dutch controlled most of the outer islands, where the greatest mineral wealth was found, they were willing to recognize republican control of Java, which had the greatest number of people and the fewest natural resources. They promoted federalism in the territories under their control, eventually setting up fifteen puppet governments on the various islands of the archipelago. Then they dangled the prospect of something like British Commonwealth status, that is, autonomous self-government, for a federal Indonesia that would include the republic on Java and the many newly formed states on the outer islands.

Considered in the abstract, federalism might make a good deal of sense in a highly diverse territory such as Indonesia, but Dutch sincerity was suspect from the beginning. Their offers looked more like a divide-and-rule tactic than a serious plan for the future. Nonetheless, republican leaders on Java, knowing they could not match the growing military strength of the Dutch, negotiated reluctantly on the basis of a federal state, but held out tenaciously on crucial details of sovereignty for the republic.

The Dutch launched two offensives, which they called "police actions," during low points in the negotiations, the first on July 20, 1947, and the second on December 18, 1948. In both cases, they swiftly overran the cities and towns of Java, but the fledgling Indonesian republican army and the armed radicals simply retreated into the countryside and launched guerrilla campaigns against the occupiers. These police actions ultimately aided the Indonesian nationalist cause. As the armed refugees fled the cities, they lived among the peasants, spreading the gospel of national independence to countless isolated villages for the first time. Furthermore, the highhanded actions of the Dutch turned international public opinion against them.

Between the two Dutch police actions, in 1948, the beleaguered republic survived a Communist coup attempt. This dragged the Indonesian revolution into the Cold War but proved helpful in earning international support. The Communist PKI had revived swiftly during the exciting times following the declaration of independence, but its leaders were orthodox Marxists who followed Moscow's lead and initially cooperated with the moderate nationalist leaders. As the Cold War heated up halfway around the world in 1947 and 1948, Moscow's line changed. Now Stalin encouraged radical revolts in colonial territories to distract and embarrass the British, Americans, and Western Europeans.

On August 11, 1948, a hardline Stalinist named Musso, a veteran of the unsuccessful 1926 Communist revolt, returned to Indonesia for the first time in two decades. He forced all the left-wing political parties to merge with the PKI and urged a more militant social revolutionary policy upon urban workers and peasant organizers. Not even Musso was foolhardy enough to think he could mount a successful revolution immediately, but in September 1948 unruly radicals in the Indonesian military started fighting a rival, pro-government division of troops, and the PKI decided they could not stand idly by. Sukarno acted swiftly against the Communists. He broadcast an appeal to the nation on September 19, then sent loyal troops to wipe out the rebels around Madiun in east Java. Musso himself was killed in battle on October 31, 1948, and all resistance was crushed about a month later. Unlike Mao Tse-tung in China, Musso and his PKI colleagues had not put down deep roots in the countryside. They had no Long March legends to give them credibility but had spent their years of exile in Moscow. Thus the second Indonesian Communist uprising failed. Over 35,000 Communists and sympathizers were arrested and over 8,000 were killed in battle or executed.

The ruthless suppression of the Madiun revolt paid handsome dividends when the Dutch unleashed their second police action in December 1948. American public opinion opposed European colonialism and favored national independence movements in a vague and diffuse way, but fear of communism often overrode these unfocused anti-colonial emotions (as we will see frequently in future chapters). The decisive anti-communism of the Indonesian Republic in 1948, however, allayed the Cold War fears of the American government and earned crucial diplomatic support from the Americans.

When the Dutch overran Java in the second police action, Sukarno and his entire cabinet allowed themselves to be captured without a fight, counting on international support to reverse the Dutch victory. The army, meanwhile, melted into the countryside and continued guerrilla action. This combination of *diplomasi* and *perjuangan* worked perfectly. The United Nations, with American backing, demanded a Dutch cease-fire on December 31, 1948, and after six months of negotiations, the republican government leaders were released from captivity. A round-table conference then agreed upon a very loose union between the Netherlands and a federal Indonesia, composed of the republic and the fifteen states in the outer islands. On this basis, the Dutch transferred sovereignty to Indonesia on December 27, 1949. Once the Dutch departed, however, the hastily contrived federal system collapsed. Most of the puppet states readily dissolved themselves and joined the republic, and the few that proved recalcitrant were overwhelmed by Indonesian troops. On August 17, 1950, the fifth anniversary of its declaration of independence, Indonesia proclaimed itself a united, centralized, republican state. Only the western half of New Guinea remained in Dutch hands, but it was later acquired through a combination of threats and diplomacy.[3]

3. The Indonesian Republic made one further territorial acquisition, which was not recognized by the international community. In December 1975 Indonesian troops seized the newly independent, formerly Portuguese territory of East Timor. About 60,000 people, 10 percent of East Timor's population, died in the fighting. In 1996 a Roman Catholic

The Indonesian nationalist revolution reached a successful conclusion with less violence than the Chinese Communist revolution of Mao Tse-tung, but it did not pursue non-violence as a systematic policy the way the Indian National Congress did. The republican government, the radical youth, and the Dutch military all committed atrocities during the course of the conflict, but the overall level of violence remained relatively low. Inter-ethnic massacres took place on some of the outer islands, but their ferocity never rivaled the Hindu-Muslim bloodlettings which accompanied the India-Pakistan partition on the subcontinent. Probably the most numerous victims of the revolution were the Chinese and mixed-race Eurasian minorities, whose relative prosperity and close ties with the Dutch made them easy scapegoats.

The nationalists owed their triumph in part to the weakness of the Dutch, particularly in the months immediately after World War II, and to a sympathetic climate of world opinion. Had the Dutch or the British brought full military force against Indonesia right after the Japanese surrendered, the lightly armed and poorly organized revolutionaries would have been overwhelmed. If the nationalists had turned leftward and cooperated actively with the Communist PKI, they would have lost American and British support in the United Nations and might have been left to their fate. As it turned out, both the distance of Indonesia from the power centers of the world and a favorable turn in Cold War politics eased the way to Indonesian independence.

The nationalist cause also showed more appeal to a wide range of Indonesians than might have been expected. Nearly all the ethnic and religious groups hated the Dutch more than they feared dominance by the populous island of Java. The revolutionary leaders came from a variety of backgrounds. For example, Sukarno had been raised on Java but both Mohammed Hatta and Sutan Sjahrir belonged to the Minangkabau of west Sumatra, the largest ethnic group on the outer islands. In south Sulawesi, the four major republican leaders murdered by the Dutch belonged to four different ethnic groups. Though the main action of the revolution took place on Java, the leaders spoke Indonesian, not Javanese, and thanks to Sukarno they did not try to impose Islam on the entire populace. Sukarno's *Panca Sila* and his charismatic oratory smoothed the way toward unity in diversity. After independence was won, a number of regional revolts broke out in the 1950s, but by that time the government had consolidated power sufficiently to overcome

bishop who opposed the annexation of this largely Christian territory, Carlos Felipe Ximenes Belo, received the Nobel Peace Prize. In 1999 the United Nations held a plebiscite in which the citizens of East Timor voted for independence from Indonesia. In response, the Indonesian military and para-military militias unleashed a reign of terror in the territory, but a United Nations peacekeeping operation restored order and was preparing the territory for independence as the century ended.

them. Throughout the twentieth century, any nation-state with even minimal support has been able to mobilize formidable political and military force against dissenters.

Indonesia, however, remained a turbulent and poverty-stricken country throughout the early decades of its independence. The population grew explosively, from 77 million in 1950 to 97 million in 1961, and it has doubled by the end of the century. The government did make an enormous investment in education, raising the literacy rate to 46 percent by 1961 from only 7 percent near the end of Dutch rule. Economic development, however, did not keep pace, and the country was unable to provide suitable jobs for all the newly educated. Lest the intellectual proletariat turn against the republic, the government became the employer of last resort, swelling the size of the civil service from about 145,000 under the Dutch regime to over 800,000 in 1960.

Sukarno continued for a time as a ceremonial president, delivering inspirational speeches and traveling abroad. He soon staked out a position, along with Marshal Tito of Yugoslavia, as a spokesman for the non-aligned nations in the Cold War world. Politics in Indonesia degenerated into a confused tangle of party squabbles, and national elections were repeatedly postponed. When the long-awaited balloting took place in September 1955, over 90 percent of the adult population, both men and women, turned out for the freest and fairest vote in Indonesia's history. Yet the results did not provide a clear political direction for the nation. The leading parties represented the three major streams of ideology in the country — Islam, secular nationalism, and communism — but no party gained more than 22 percent of the vote, and a welter of minor parties still cluttered the legislature. Indonesia stood at a political crossroads much like Italy in the early 1920s. In both cases, parliamentary democracy seemingly failed and the economy lay in tatters, so people expressed a desire for a strong leader to take charge. Sukarno stepped in, as Mussolini had in Italy.

The president moved step by step to increase his authority. In a speech on October 28, 1956, he called for an end to party misrule and the building of a new system of government he called "guided democracy." The following year he declared martial law, and then in 1959 he dissolved the constituent assembly which had been laboring for years to write a more democratic constitution. Finally, on independence day, August 17, 1959, he orated for two hours, elaborating a new version of his unity in diversity theme which he called *Nasakom*, a blend of *Nasionalisme, Agama, Komunism* (Nationalism, Religion, Communism). In an increasingly heavy-handed manner, he proceeded to impose his thought on the nation as its official ideology, banning many of the opposition political parties and clamping censorship on the press.

Perhaps a different comparison, other than Mussolini and fascism, may help explain Sukarno's guided democracy, which ran from 1959 to 1965. Like

Chairman Mao in China at roughly the same time, Sukarno was getting old and feared both his personal and political powers might slip away. His private life became more scandalous as he combined the high life of drinking, gambling, and womanizing with his many international journeys. In politics, he believed that multiparty government had debased the unity and solidarity of the revolution, and he worked to recapture the old revolutionary energy. He therefore became a cheerleader for his people, developing a theme for each year of the guided democracy period, such as the "Year of Struggle" and the "Year of Triumph."

The slogan for 1963, the "Year of Living Dangerously," expresses Sukarno's mood most vividly. Like Mao, he feared becoming a "dead ancestor" while still alive. At the end of the Year of Living Dangerously, he proclaimed: "I do not like tranquility, which is frozen and dead; I do not like sluggishness. What I like is dynamism, vitality, militancy, activity, a revolutionary spirit!" The period of guided democracy in Indonesia, therefore, was a less violent counterpart of China's Cultural Revolution, a desperate attempt by an aging, charismatic leader to invigorate the revolutionary spirit of his people.

Sukarno ruled by decree more than by legislation and became increasingly sympathetic to the Communist Party of Indonesia and the Communist Chinese in international affairs. In the depths of the Cold War, the American government considered him a Communist dupe, and the CIA cultivated contacts with military officers and regional dissidents who might overthrow him. He survived five assassination attempts, including a spectacular strafing of the presidential palace by a renegade air force pilot in 1960. Yet he never enjoyed full dictatorial powers. Instead he maneuvered between the two most powerful forces in the country, the Communist Party and the army, trying to preserve a balance between them. Though he kept many political opponents under house arrest, he imprisoned few and murdered even fewer. Unlike Mao's China, Sukarno's Indonesia had no concentration camps or re-education centers. His tilt towards the Communists may have had more to do with overconfidence in his own balancing powers than ideological affinity. Since he had destroyed the Communists once before, in the Madiun revolt of 1948, he may have felt that he could do so again whenever necessary. So, in the meantime, he helped the PKI develop as a counterweight to the conservative military. His primary goals were to keep the country united and himself in power.

The major weakness of Sukarno's guided democracy was its lack of a firm, consistent economic policy. Inflation spiraled out of control during these years, and the population endured increasing poverty and even starvation. Sukarno was a super-nationalist, an inspired prophet of national unity, but his nationalism eventually proved empty. Slogans, speeches, and lofty ideas wore thin while the population grew and children went hungry. Sukarno's Australian biographer, John David Legge, has accurately summed up the failure of guided democracy: "Indonesia's problem was not that an authoritarian regime had emerged but rather that the new regime, like the old one, was unable to mobilize the power that was needed if government was to be effective and if the gigantic problems of the economy were to be tackled seriously."

In 1965 Sukarno's balancing act faltered. For the third time in the twentieth century, the Communists tried to increase their power through a premature and poorly organized uprising. On the morning of October 1, a junta of air force officers with close ties to the PKI arrested and killed six of the leading army generals in Jakarta. They then transported Sukarno to the air force base and invited him to front for a new revolutionary government. It is unclear whether this was a full-scale Communist coup or simply an attempt to tilt the balance of guided democracy toward the left and away from the army. As always, Sukarno played for time and waited for events to unfold. General Suharto, who had escaped arrest on the morning of October 1, mobilized the army and put down the revolt. A reign of terror then broke out with army encouragement. Communists throughout Indonesia were arrested or lynched and mobs attacked the Chinese minority again, as they had during the revolution. At least 200,000 people, and perhaps as many as 500,000, died in the army repression of 1965. General Suharto reduced President Sukarno to figurehead status, but he did not remove him altogether until March 12, 1967. Suharto then assumed the post of president and imposed a truly authoritarian regime on the country. He served as president for over thirty years, until he was overthrown by a new generation of *pemuda* in 1998.

An Indonesian scholar, Eka Darmaputera, has argued that the governments of new nations face three primary tasks: nation-building, order, and economic development. (It is significant that democracy is not on this list. Many Asians still are groping for an alternative to the unruliness of democracy.) Sukarno proved an inspired nation-builder, and his *Panca Sila* remained enshrined as national ideals, even under Suharto's military dictatorship. Yet he proved unable to keep order or promote economic development. The military regime of General Suharto kept order with a vengeance, but was unable to solve Indonesia's economic problems. His government tilted sharply toward the United States during the Cold War and encouraged foreign investment. A small stratum of newly prosperous business and professional people emerged in Indonesian cities, but the countryside and the urban slums remained mired in deep poverty. General Suharto did not have to engage in nation-building, however, for Sukarno's revolutionary generation accomplished that task amazingly well.

Perhaps the best definition of nationalism is "a feeling that we have done great things together in the past, are continuing to do great things together in the present, and shall do great things together in the future." Sukarno and his generation sensed that this feeling need not be based on a common ethnic origin or religion, but depends instead on common experiences, great deeds which make people swell with pride, and common enemies, deep hatreds that bind people together. The Indonesian national revolution produced the heroic deeds, myths, and enemies necessary for the emotion of nationalism as well as an unfinished agenda for the future. A national unity was forged out of diversity.

CHAPTER SIX

Tigers and Elephants

When Japan charged through Southeast Asia in 1941 and 1942, it broke forever the myth of invincibility surrounding the European colonial powers. Small Japanese forces landed in the remote jungles of Malaya and Thailand shortly after Pearl Harbor and soon fought their way into the British base of Singapore, showing that the countryside could engulf the city strongholds of the imperialists. Mao Tse-tung in China also overwhelmed the cities with armed guerrillas from the countryside, and many Asian revolutionaries followed his example. In Indonesia, the Dutch never recovered their legitimacy or power, and Sukarno's nationalists took over through a timely combination of urban revolt, guerrilla war, and international intervention. On the mainland of Southeast Asia, Britain and France brought more power to bear on their colonial dependencies of Malaya and Indochina, holding out longer than the Dutch. Yet ultimately they too left. The mystique of the guerrilla had replaced the myth of European imperialism.

Mao wrote the classic description of revolutionary insurgency: "The guerrillas are like fish, and the people are the sea in which they swim." The Vietnamese Communist Ho Chi Minh penned an even more striking analogy:

> It will be a war between a tiger and an elephant. If ever the tiger stops, the elephant will pierce him with his tusks. Only the tiger doesn't stop. He lurks in the jungle by day and emerges only at night. He will leap onto the elephant and rip his back to shreds before disappearing again into the shadows, and the elephant will die from exhaustion and loss of blood.

Yet the tigers did not always win. Ho Chi Minh's Communists vanquished

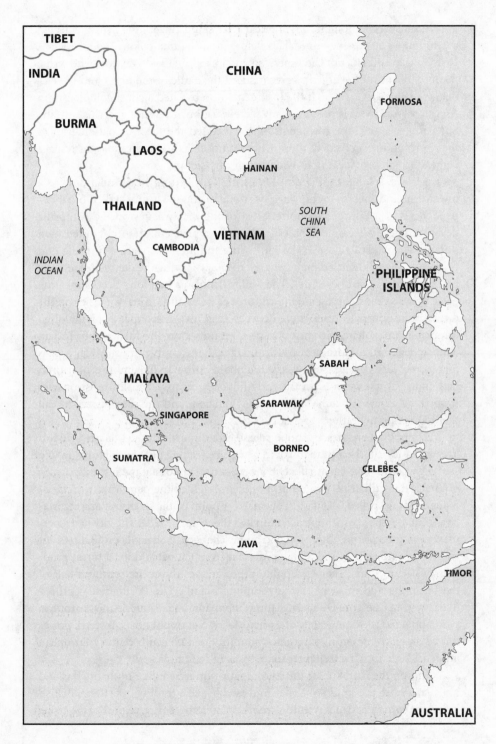

Southeast Asia

the French and later fought the Americans to a standstill, but the British defeated a Communist insurgency in Malaya before granting that colony independence. Neither Mao and Ho, nor the American and European Cold Warriors who wrote manuals of counterinsurgency, ever reduced the battle of the tigers and the elephants to an exact science. If the insurgents who revolted against colonialism in Asia after World War II possessed any secret weapon, it was not guerrilla warfare, but nationalism. Those insurgents who harnessed the force of nationalism to their revolutions succeeded; those who did not failed. The examples of Malaya and Indochina provide ample evidence for this dictum.

Malaya, a long, thin peninsula jutting south from the mainland of Asia toward the Indonesian archipelago, was one of the most unusual colonial dependencies of a European empire. Most of the Malay states on the peninsula never technically became colonies but remained protectorates under their own sultans. The Malays, close racial kin to the Indonesians, were a farming and fishing people who settled mainly in river valleys, leaving the dense, perpetually green jungles to the aborigines. The Malay Peninsula had long been a meeting place between the peoples and the cultures of India and China, for it lies on the direct, monsoon-driven sea route between these two Asian giants. China often claimed a benevolent, distant political suzerainty over the Malays, but Indian culture exercised a more pervasive influence. For example, most Malay words for abstract ideas derive from classic Indian literature. Indian culture, of course, had many diverse strands. In the early fifteenth century, Muslim missionaries from India converted the Malays to their religion, and the rulers came to call themselves sultans rather than rajahs.

For many centuries, the political and economic life of the Malay world followed a historical rhythm that would bring one trading port to the fore, only to see its predominance eventually ebb away as another coastal town stole its trade or attacked it militarily. When Europeans first sighted the peninsula, the city of Malacca (now spelled Melaka), at the narrow point of the straits separating Malaya from the island of Sumatra, dominated the region's trade. The city had a permanent population of about 100,000 and exchanged thousands of boatloads of spices for textiles from India, fine porcelain from China, and local forest products. Malacca's sultan exercised political power over the entire southern half of the peninsula and most of the surrounding islands. The Portuguese captured Malacca in 1511, and the Dutch later threw them out in 1640, but neither European power attained the dominance of earlier Malayan entrepôt ports. Instead, power flowed away to numerous tiny states, so until the nineteenth century European influence remained even slighter than it was in Indonesia.

In 1786 the British East India Company purchased the uninhabited island of Penang from the sultan of Kedah and established a trading base there. British influence spread gradually until a century later the entire region came to be called "British Malaya." Yet Malayan politics remained complex and decentralized. The British purchased another lightly populated island at the tip of the peninsula in 1819 and founded the city of Singapore. Then in 1824 they struck a treaty with the Dutch under which Britain relinquished any claim to islands in the Indonesian archipelago and the Dutch handed over Malacca to the British. Thus these two European powers drew a line down the middle of the Malacca Straits that still marks a political boundary today, between the states of Malaysia and Indonesia. Penang, Malacca, and Singapore eventually became a crown colony, known as the Straits Settlements, but the British did not control any other territory in the region until the latter part of the nineteenth century. The rest of Malaya was divided into the independent states of Kelantan, Trengganu, Pahang, Perlis, Kedah, Perak, Selangor, Negri Sembilan, and Johore.

To protect their trading interests and preempt the Germans and French, who had begun showing interest in the region, the British finally extended their influence over the states of Perak, Selangor, Negri Sembilan, and Pahang, beginning with a treaty of protection with Perak in 1874. This and subsequent protectorate treaties resembled those negotiated with Indian rajahs, providing for a British resident at the sultan's court whose advice "must be asked and acted upon on all questions other than those touching Malay religion and custom." For the time being, the state of Johore, whose English-educated sultan had established a stable regime, remained independent, and the northern Malay states of Kedah, Perlis, Kelantan, and Trengganu remained under the nominal protection of Thailand (Siam), an independent Asian kingdom with whom Britain enjoyed friendly relations. In 1909, however, the Thais transferred their treaty rights to the British, and in 1914 Johore was also brought under the British umbrella.

Earlier, in 1896, the British had induced Perak, Selangor, Negri Sembilan, and Pahang to form a federation with a new capital at Kuala Lumpur (the present-day capital of Malaysia). The more recently protected states, however, firmly refused to join this federation. So, during the first half of the twentieth century "British Malaya" comprised a complicated political alphabet soup: the SS, or Straits Settlements (Penang, Malacca, Singapore), which were directly ruled as a crown colony; the FMS, or Federated Malayan States (Pahang, Perak, Selangor, Negri Sembilan), with a centralized Malay government and a British resident general; and the UMS, or Unfederated Malay States of Perlis, Kedah, Kelantan, Trengganu, and Johore, which though under British protection remained separate from the central government of the federation.

Political decentralization marked just the beginning of Malaya's complexity. In the course of the nineteenth and early twentieth centuries, the Malays found themselves nearly swamped by immigrants from other Asian countries, particularly China and India. The river valleys of the peninsula contain the richest deposits of tin ore anywhere in the world, so masses of peasants from overpopulated China migrated to Malaya and began panning for tin, like the American Forty-niners panned for gold in California. Chinese also set up numerous small shops and cultivated pepper, tapioca, and gambier (a plant used for dyeing and tanning). Late in the nineteenth century, British capitalists began planting rubber trees, which were native to South America, and importing indentured laborers from south India to work the plantations. By 1921 the population of Malaya included 1,627,108 Malays (about 50 percent), 1,173,354 Chinese (roughly one-third), and 471,628 Indians (14 percent). Historians Barbara and Leonard Andaya aptly sum up the situation of British Malaya in the early twentieth century: "Put crudely, the European was to govern and administer, the immigrant Chinese and Indian to labor in the extractive industries and commerce, and the Malays to till the fields."

In both the Federated and Unfederated Malay States, the sultans continued to reign but not to rule. The British residents functioned like prime ministers for constitutional monarchs. Most of the civil servants in the federation governments were Europeans, Indians, or Chinese, but in the unfederated states the Malays held the majority of government posts. These Malay civil servants, however, were usually relatives of the sultans, and owed their primary allegiance to ruler, state, and social class, not to a Malayan nation.

Nationalism remained much less developed than in India or Indonesia. Only a handful of Malay commoners received an education beyond the primary level, so the critical mass of teachers, journalists, and lawyers who backed Gandhi's and Sukarno's nationalist movements did not develop in Malaya before the Second World War. In the eyes of the British, Malays were rice-growing peasants. The federation and state governments designated whole sections of the country as Malay reservations, where only rice could be grown and only Malays could grow it. A European serving on the Federal Council in Kuala Lumpur declared in 1915:

> The great object of education is to train a man to make his living. . . . You can teach Malays so that they do not lose their skill and craft in fishing and jungle work. Teach them the dignity of manual labor, so that they do not all become kranies [clerks] and I am sure you will not have the trouble which has arisen in India through overeducation.

To some extent Malay peasants internalized the feelings of inferiority that both their traditional rulers and the British encouraged. When asked after World War II why they had not taken a more active role in government before the war, many Malays replied "it wasn't fitting" or simply "afraid of the sultan."

After regaining control from the Japanese in 1945, the British had no in-

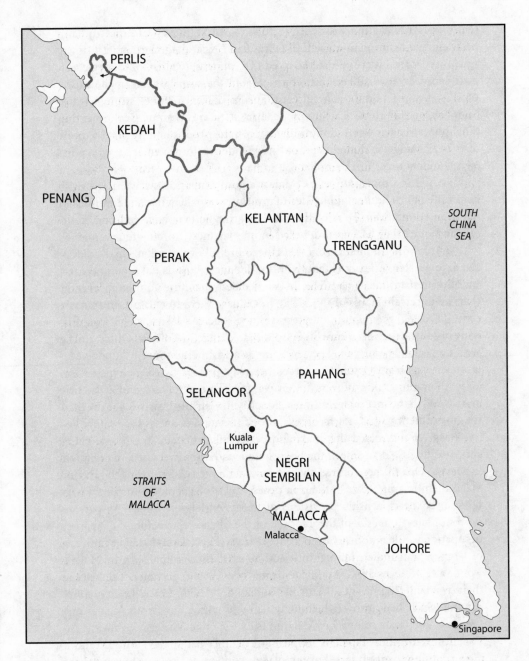

British Malaya

tention of granting independence to Malaya. Though they had quit India in haste, they did not plan on withdrawing from Asia altogether. Indeed, for at least two decades after the war, the Indian Ocean remained, in the strategic military sense, an English lake, far removed from the main spheres of the superpowers, the Soviets and the Americans. The Royal Navy retained strong bases at Simonstown, South Africa; Mombasa, East Africa; Colombo, Ceylon; and at Singapore. Malaya was economically more important to the British Empire than India had been on the eve of its independence, for tin and rubber exports were major sources of U.S. dollars.

While resuming control of Malaya's governments, however, the British committed a monumental blunder that unintentionally stimulated feelings of Malayan nationalism. Four of the nine Malayan sultans had died during the war and one other had been deposed by the Japanese, so only four remained with a firm hold on their thrones. Furthermore, all of the sultans had collaborated, to greater or lesser extent, with the Japanese, just as Sukarno and most Indonesian nationalists had. The British decided, therefore, to use the leverage that the uncertain status of the Malay rulers gave them to create a much more centralized Malayan Union, in effect a single state of Malaya which would finally become a British colony. Sir Harold MacMichael, a Colonial Office official with no previous Malayan experience, made a whirlwind tour of the nine Malayan capitals from October to December 1945, pressuring the sultans to sign away their remaining powers in return for some symbolic and monetary awards. When he met with resistance, MacMichael firmly insisted that the British government would not recognize any of the sultans unless they signed.

Malays considered this highhanded treatment of their traditional rulers very insulting. So did some of the Englishmen who had served most of their lives in Malaya. One of these retired civil servants remarked disapprovingly: "Having failed them in war, we rush them in peace." Yet a bigger storm of controversy broke over the citizenship provisions of the new Malayan Union. All persons born in Malaya or resident there for ten of the fifteen years before the Japanese occupation would automatically become citizens. This meant that large numbers of Chinese and Indian immigrants, and all of their children born in Malaya, would attain citizenship. The Malays feared they would become a minority in their own land. To prevent this, the British had decided to detach the city of Singapore, which had an overwhelmingly Chinese population, from Malaya and keep it as a separate colony, but Malayan fears were not assuaged. As always, nationalism grows most rapidly in opposition to other nations or ethnic groups.

Noting the groundswell of popular discontent, the sultans boycotted the installation of the first British governor of the Malayan Union on April 1, 1946, and called for renegotiation of union terms. More importantly, popular protests of nearly Gandhian proportions greeted all the arriving British officials, and in March 1946 a Pan-Malayan Malay Congress met and declared the MacMichael treaties "null and void." This Congress led to the founding of Malaya's first mass political organization, the United Malays National Organization (UMNO), led by Dato (an honorific term, equivalent to Sir) Onn bin Jaafar. The British backed down, striking a deal with UMNO and the sultans for a looser federation where the rulers retained some of their local rights and powers. The citizenship law was revised so that only those Chinese with both parents born in Malaya could become citizens, and thus a Malay political majority was guaranteed. By accident, the British had launched Malaya on the road to independence; but before the country reached that goal it had to survive a revolutionary guerrilla insurgency, a war of the tigers.

Throughout Southeast Asia between the two world wars, communism had appealed primarily to the uprooted overseas Chinese; the Malayan Communist Party (MCP), founded in 1930, was an almost exclusively Chinese organization. When the Japanese occupied the country they murdered Chinese leaders, Communist and non-Communist alike, driving the survivors into the jungle for shelter. As a result, the primary resistance organization, the Malayan Peoples Anti-Japanese Army (MPAJA), was primarily Chinese, with its core of leaders provided by the Communist Party. British commandos supported the MPAJA and air-lifted supplies to them. One of their leaders, Chin Peng, was awarded the Order of the British Empire. Immediately after the war ended, the MPAJA massacred those they considered collaborators, mainly Malays, setting off a race war as Malays retaliated. The British occupation troops restored order, disarming the MPAJA, but they allowed the Communists to organize labor unions and operate as a legal party.

The communist underground from which Asian revolutionaries emerged was a brutal and devious school. The chairman of the MCP's Central Committee before and during the war was a Vietnamese named Loi Tak. Unknown to his comrades, he had been a French intelligence agent in Indochina, and then, in succession, a servant of the British and the Japanese. Fearing discovery of his double life, Loi Tak fled Malaya in 1947 but was later gunned down by a Communist hit squad in Thailand. He was succeeded by Chin Peng, the anti-Japanese war hero, who remained a committed Communist despite his OBE award. The Malayan Communist Party blamed Loi Tak for following an overly passive policy after the war and decided on an armed insurrection instead. They sent a number of disciplined killer squads out into the jungle and on June 16, 1948, these assassins began murdering European plantation owners in the state of Perak. The Malayan government declared a state of emergency on June 18, which was to last for a full twelve years.

Because of the confused leadership situation and the ad hoc nature of the insurgency's origins, the Malayan Communists were not able to mount a coordinated, effective revolution all at once. Instead, the Emergency unrolled in three stages. From 1948 through 1949 the Communists mounted sporadic attacks on plantations, police stations, and military convoys, but devoted most of their efforts toward building up their forces and their supplies. In 1950 and 1951 the insurgency rose to the peak of its ferocity, with about eight thousand insurgents in arms and over five hundred terrorist incidents per month, including the spectacular ambush and assassination of the British high commissioner, Sir Henry Gurney, on October 6, 1951. Finally, from 1952 on the Communists withdrew deeper into the jungle and scaled down their attacks until the insurgency finally petered out at the end of the decade.

British counterinsurgency policy also advanced through three stages. At first, the army sent out battalions of soldiers to search for and destroy the Communist guerrillas, but the "elephants" advanced so slowly in the dense jungles that the "tigers" usually had time to elude them. The words of a Napoleonic officer serving in Spain 150 years previously, in a war where the word "guerrilla" was first coined, seem equally appropriate to the British in Malaya: "Wherever we arrived, they disappeared, whenever we left, they arrived — they were everywhere and nowhere. . . ."

In 1950 the British inaugurated a new, more realistic, phase of counterinsurgency with the appointment of General Harold Briggs as director of operations in Malaya. The so-called Briggs Plan concentrated on the denial of food and other essential supplies to the Communists. Guerrillas could live, move, and fight in the jungle, but they could not obtain the rice, weapons, and ammunition they needed there. Instead they relied on supplies from sympathetic Chinese squatters who had been eking out an existence on landholdings along the forest fringes.

Analysts have used many different analogies to describe the essentials of the Briggs Plan. One writer compared it to the systematic hunt of a man-eating tiger or leopard, but another, less romantically, found it more like pest control than grand strategy: "In order to destroy the enemy he [General Briggs] is breaking up the nesting places of the pests." Still others have likened guerrilla warfare on land to submarine attacks by sea. In both cases, it is more effective to destroy the bases that supply the raiders than try to hunt them in the vastness of the sea or the jungle. Whatever analogy one uses, the basic principle of the plan, pursued even more vigorously by Briggs's successor, General Gerald Templer, was the resettlement of nearly a half million Chinese squatters from their homes in guerrilla territory. A character in Han Suyin's novel, *And the Rain My Drink*, describes the experience of resettlement:

> He knew a village which had been twice razed to the ground. Once by the Japanese, and last year by the British. The first time the people had been warned

by the jungle guerrillas, and many had fled. . . . Those that could not escape the Japanese massacred. The second time the British had come at dawn, and surrounded the village. In six hours the whole population had been carted away in trucks . . . and the whole area destroyed by fire.

The half-million evicted Chinese squatters were resettled in over five hundred "new villages" where they were guarded behind barbed wire, but also given legal title to land and helped to build more secure lives for their families. This anti-Communist, ethnic cleansing program combined ruthlessness and humanitarianism in roughly equal measures. Many Chinese considered the new villages little more than concentration camps, but ironically a great number of Malay peasants also resented them as undeserved welfare handouts to the Chinese. In any case, the resettlement program fulfilled its primary purpose by denying essential supplies to the guerrillas.

Finally, in the third phase of the Emergency, from 1952 on, large numbers of guerrillas surrendered or were captured while trying to infiltrate the heavily defended new villages. The hard core retreated deeper into the jungle-clad mountains of the interior and finally to the Thai border. In such remote retreats, supported meagerly by aborigines or Thai sympathizers over the border, the guerrillas remained relatively safe but ineffective and irrelevant. Chin Peng and his inner circle of Communist officials never did surrender when the Emergency ended on July 31, 1960.

The Malayan Emergency was thoroughly studied in the 1950s and 1960s by military experts seeking a formula to defeat guerrilla tigers elsewhere. The British, in particular, trumpeted the success of Briggs and Templer in Malaya and offered unsolicited advice to their American Cold War allies when they were later fighting in Vietnam. Many analysts emphasized the importance of high anti-guerrilla force ratios. At the beginning of the Emergency, government army and police forces outnumbered the Communists by about 5 to 1; this ratio approached nearly 12 to 1 during the critical second period of fighting. A ratio of 10 or 12 to 1, therefore, came to be considered a magic number.

Such purely military factors, however, proved less important in defeating the guerrillas than two more basic weaknesses of the Communists. First, they were isolated from any effective aid. The British Navy sealed off the Malay Peninsula on three sides, so neither Russia nor China could transport aid to the Malayan Communist Party; and although the land border with Thailand offered sanctuary, the Thais were officially neutral and did not furnish arms or supplies to the Communists. The second reason why the Malayan Communists failed was that they could not draw on the power of nationalism to buttress their cause. Put simply, the Malayan Communist Party was not

113

composed of Malays, but rather of an immigrant minority, disliked and feared by the native Malays.

Both the rebels and the government appeared foreign to the Malays, but the British eventually took steps to harness the forces of Malay nationalism to their side. General Templer, when he succeeded Briggs as director of operations in January 1952, convinced the British government to schedule elections and gradually move the country toward independence. The main Malay political organization, UMNO, made his task easier by forging an alliance with moderate Chinese leaders and with the small Indian National Congress in Malaya. The British believed, rightly as it turned out, that they could avoid the inter-ethnic bloodletting that marred their exit from India, once they got past the Emergency with the Chinese Communists.

Onn bin Jaafar's successor as head of UMNO was Tunku (a royal term, the equivalent of prince) Abdul Rahman, son of the sultan of Kedah, whose great-great-great grandfather had ceded Penang to the British in 1786. Abdul Rahman led his Alliance Party to an overwhelming victory in the first national elections in July 1955, winning all but one of the fifty-two popularly elected seats in the legislature. Though Templer's political reforms had further en-larged the Chinese electorate, most of the Chinese did not register or vote, and over 80 percent of the electors in 1955 were Malays. At the leadership level, how-ever, the multi-ethnic alliance held firm. Thirty-five of the successful Alliance candidates were Malays, fifteen were Chinese, and two were Indians. The Ma-lays and the Chinese then struck a bargain, whereby citizenship would finally be granted to all persons born in Malaya, but in return Malay would be de-clared the national language. With these terms written into a new constitution, Malaya became an independent member of the British Commonwealth on Au-gust 31, 1957. The new country signed a defense treaty with Great Britain, and British officers stayed on to help mop up the Communist terrorists. The British had won the war of the Emergency in Malaya, but in the process they lost their colony.

Malaya began its independent existence with a robust export economy based on rubber, tin, timber, and oil, and a healthy spirit of ethnic and politi-cal compromise. These assets, along with its relatively small population (6,278,758 at the time of independence), spared it many of the troubles of other Asian nations. The traditional sultans of the nine Malay states shared a unique, rotating constitutional monarchy for the country. The Alliance con-tinued to dominate the government and Tunku Abdul Rahman remained prime minister until 1970, but free elections were held every four years. Re-newed rioting between Chinese and Malays in 1969 resulted in the declaration of another emergency, but the country did not become a dictatorship and the emergency was lifted in less than two years. Malaya, therefore, has survived both Communist insurgency and inter-ethnic rivalries that have destroyed other post-colonial societies.[1]

Vietnam's experience with French imperialism ran roughly parallel to that of Malaya with the British, but its precolonial history had been quite different. The French called the Asiatic region they colonized Indochina, the land between India and China, and this can serve as a general descriptive phrase for all of Southeast Asia. In Malaya the influence of India proved stronger, whereas Vietnam fell under the cultural spell of China. Malays adhere to the religion of Islam, which they inherited both from India and directly from Arabia, whereas the Vietnamese are predominantly Buddhists with a strong Confucian tradition among the elite. The name of the country, Vietnam, means "land of the south," that is, south of China. Indeed China conquered and ruled Vietnam for over a thousand years, from 111 B.C. to 939 A.D. Thereafter, it was an independent kingdom ruled by a series of dynasties. Though its culture was patterned on a Chinese model, Vietnam's politics was shaped by resistance to Chinese attempts at recapturing its dominance.

The Vietnamese were a rice-growing lowland people, settling primarily in river valleys and along the seacoast, just like the Malays. Their heartland lay in the delta of the Red River, which empties into the Tonkin Gulf just south of the border with China. They remained separate from and antagonistic to the Indian-influenced kingdoms of Laos and Cambodia, westward over the mountains, and the aborigines in the jungles and highlands.

Vietnam differed from Malaya in several important respects. First, Vietnam's population was much larger, with about 23 million inhabitants early in the twentieth century as compared with only 3 million on the Malay Peninsula. As early as 1000 A.D. population pressure in the Red River valley had set off an expansionist movement among the Vietnamese peasantry, who slowly migrated southwards seeking more land. The Vietnamese discovered the Mekong River delta to the south around 1500, and finally reached the limit of their expansion at the Ca Mau Peninsula on the Gulf of Siam about 1750. Vietnamese sometimes describe the shape of their country, with its two large river deltas at either end connected by a long thin coastal strip, as two baskets of rice dangling from the ends of a bamboo pole.

Vietnam was also more centralized politically than Malaya. This was due in part to the influence of the Chinese model, but also to the strong central

1. In September 1963 the country was renamed Malaysia with the reunion of Singapore to the Malay Peninsula and the addition of two former British colonies on the northern coast of Borneo, Sabah and Sarawak. This new federation proved only partially successful. Singapore again seceded in August 1965, and is now an independent city-state. The north Borneo territories remain in Malaysia.

leadership required to administer the river works which made the deltas habitable. Vietnam provides an example of what some world historians call a "hydraulic civilization," that is, one dependent on the management of water resources for its survival. Such civilizations typically were more centralized and authoritarian than others. In the Red River valley heartland of Vietnam, the river is canalized between a gigantic system of dikes, which extend over 1,600 miles.

Unlike Malaya, with its string of tiny, independent sultanates, Vietnam was one country, enjoying a strong feeling of ethnic consciousness best described as incipient nationalism. There were important regional differences between north, center, and south, which gave rise to periods of civil war between competing dynasties. Yet in 1802, before the French conquest, Vietnam was reunited under the Nguyen dynasty ruling at Hue. Later divisions of the country were due to colonial and then Cold War politics. The Vietnamese, therefore, on the eve of their colonization, were a populous, self-conscious people with a strong tradition of central rule.

The French conquered Vietnam much as the British did Malaya, slowly, gradually, almost absentmindedly. From 1535 onward the Portuguese, the Dutch, the English, and the French had all established trading posts along the Vietnamese coast, but their impact was slight and all but the Portuguese had pulled out by 1700. The English and French were too consumed by their rivalries elsewhere — in Europe, North America, and India — to pay any attention to Indochina. In Malaya, local traders from the British East India Company had finally aroused the interest of their government in the Southeast Asian region; Catholic missionaries provided a similar impetus to the French in Vietnam. In 1858, therefore, a French fleet, using the protection of the missionaries as a pretext, captured the major port city of Tourane (later called Danang) and the following year occupied Saigon in the Mekong Delta. The real reason for French intervention lay elsewhere. Like the English, the French were increasing their trade with China so were looking for a base somewhere on the way to that country. Also like the English in Malaya, the French feared that some other European power would seize Vietnam if they did not.

In 1862 the French forced the Vietnamese emperor to sign a treaty ceding Saigon and the surrounding three provinces to France. Five years later, in July 1867, the French proclaimed a protectorate over Cambodia, thus securing for themselves control over the entire lower Mekong and its fertile delta. This area remained the primary focus of French economic interest, for they improved the local canal system, quadrupled the amount of land available for cultivation, and turned the Mekong Delta into one of the great rice bowls of Asia. They did not conquer the rest of Vietnam until 1882, when a French captain stormed Hanoi on his own initiative and the government in Paris confirmed his actions

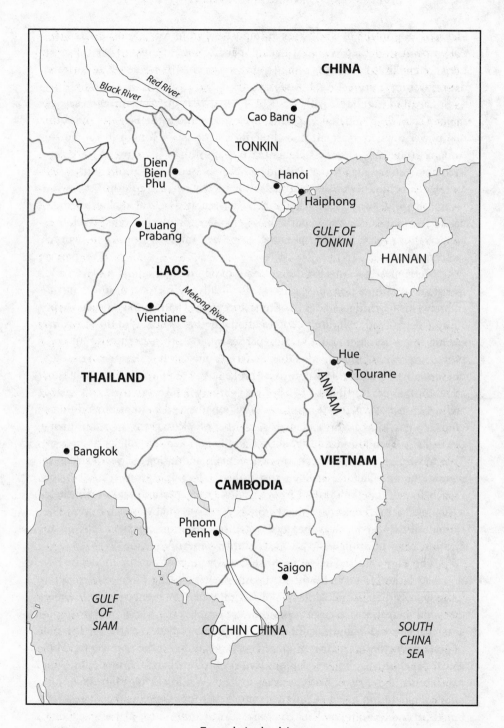

French Indochina

and sent reinforcements. The French imposed a protectorate on the Vietnamese emperor and then waged a brutal "pacification" campaign for the next twelve years. In the meantime, they rounded out their conquest of Indochina, declaring Laos a protectorate in 1893.

Laos and Cambodia had always been separate from Vietnam, and they remained sparsely populated, neglected backwaters under the French. The colonial power divided Vietnam into three jurisdictions — Tonkin in the north, Annam in the center, and Cochinchina in the south — expunging the name Vietnam from the map just as Poland had been erased from Europe shortly before. Cochinchina was directly ruled by France, whereas the other two were technically protectorates, but the French thoroughly dominated all of them. A nationalist journalist aptly remarked: "Vietnamese mandarins were just clothes hangers for multicolored robes, the emperor simply a 'mannequin dore' [golden dummy]."

Vietnamese nationalism did not have to be invented, as did Malayan and Indonesian national self-consciousness, for it already had strong roots in the country's history and its tradition of resistance to the Chinese. Yet it needed to be cultivated and made relevant to the twentieth-century concerns of the Vietnamese masses. A number of nationalist parties sprang up in the 1920s, but they proved weaker and more divided than Sukarno's movement in Indonesia or Gandhi's in India. An anti-colonial uprising broke out at Yen Bay, a military garrison about thirty miles northwest of Hanoi, on February 9, 1930, but the revolt fizzled and the French condemned hundreds of nationalist leaders to death and thousands more to long prison sentences. A number of Vietnamese communist parties had also been founded in the 1920s and then unified into one party in 1930. They too capitalized on depression-era discontent, mounting a series of strikes at plantations and factories, which snowballed into mass protests against the French. In the Nghe Anh Province of central Vietnam, peasants and workers held a "liberated area" for almost a year before being dispersed by French troops. The Communist leadership was then decimated by execution or exile to the Poulo Condore concentration camp off the coast of southern Vietnam.

The Communists, however, possessed advantages that the moderate nationalists lacked. The Vietnamese peasantry felt the sting of colonial rule far more sharply than the peasants of Malaya did. When the French planted rubber trees and increased rice cultivation, they conscripted the Vietnamese peasants as virtually forced laborers, rather than bringing in outsiders as the English did in Malaya. Furthermore, they imposed heavy taxation on the populace and organized the salt, alcohol, and opium trades as colonial state monopolies, with ridiculously high prices. As a character in Regis Wargnier's 1993 film *Indochine* said to a plantation owner: "You treat people as if they were [rubber] trees. You buy them and drain them. You're vultures." The Communists also enjoyed outside support, both from France, where an active Communist Party was the darling of the intellectuals, and from Moscow's Comintern, which hand-picked Asian cadres for intensive training. In sum, the Vietnamese Communists possessed deeper roots and a greater revolutionary potential than any other communist party in Asia. As historian William Duiker has remarked, when World War II broke out, "the movement, the man, and the moment converged."

The man, of course, was Ho Chi Minh. Born in 1890 in Nghe Anh Province, a hotbed of resistance to French rule in central Vietnam, he took on many aliases during his lifetime and it remains uncertain what his real name was. American journalist David Halberstam has remarked: "It is indicative of the many shadows in Ho's career that there is a difference of opinion on almost every fact in his life: his date of birth, his father's name, his own name, whether he ever married, etc." Most probably his family name was Nguyen, and the revolutionary nickname he used most often before World War II was Nguyen Ai Quoc (Nguyen the patriot).[2]

The future revolutionary came from a family of the traditional scholar-gentry, but his father had refused to serve in government under the French, working instead as a schoolteacher. Ho received a reasonably good education in French and Vietnamese, then worked his way to Europe as a cook on a steamer sometime before the First World War. He became a founding member of the French Communist Party in 1920, then went to Moscow for study in 1923. For the rest of the 1920s, he organized Vietnamese exiles in China. Ho and his associates helped finance their underground movement by selling out an older Vietnamese nationalist to the authorities in Shanghai, from where he was extradited to Saigon. (Like everything else in Ho's life, the details of this incident are disputed.)

Ho himself was arrested in Hong Kong in 1931. He dropped out of sight for nearly a decade, and many thought him dead; but in fact he had escaped from prison, then lived in Russia and China. When the Second World War broke out, he made his way back to the border between China and Vietnam and began calling himself Ho Chi Minh (He Who Brings Enlightenment). A founder of both the French and the Vietnamese Communist parties, trained in Stalin's Moscow and Mao Tse-tung's Yenan, Ho was the best-equipped Asian communist after Mao himself.

2. Vietnamese names cause much confusion for Americans and Europeans. The family name comes first, as in China or Japan. However, unlike the Chinese or the Japanese, Vietnamese usually call a person by the given name. So, for example, the Communist military leader, Vo Nguyen Giap, was generally called General Giap and the American-sponsored president of South Vietnam, Ngo Dinh Diem, was called President Diem. To add to the confusion, especially prominent people may be referred to by their family names. Thus Ho Chi Minh was always called Comrade Ho or President Ho.

In May 1941, Ho and the Communist Central Committee set up an umbrella organization for all anti-Japanese, anti-French nationalists, called *Viet Nam Doc Lap Dong Minh Hoi* (the League for the Independence of Vietnam), or Viet Minh for short. Unlike the Chinese Communists in Malaya, the Viet Minh lay low for most of the Second World War, building up a base area in the mountainous region between Hanoi and the Chinese border, but fighting relatively little. Nonetheless, they received supplies from the Nationalist Chinese, the British, and the Americans. The U.S. Office of Strategic Services (the wartime equivalent of the CIA) even established a code name for Ho Chi Minh, calling him "Lucius."

Shortly before their surrender to the Allies, the Japanese allowed the Vietnamese puppet emperor, Bao Dai, to declare independence, and the rulers of Laos and Cambodia followed suit. In fact, Ho Chi Minh's Communists possessed the strongest fighting force and the most popular support in Vietnam as the war came to a close. The Viet Minh, therefore, marched into the cities of Hanoi and Hue unopposed in August 1945, and Bao Dai prudently abdicated. On September 2, 1945, Ho Chi Minh proclaimed the independence of the Democratic Republic of Vietnam (DRV), in a declaration which closely followed Thomas Jefferson's American declaration. This represented more than a rhetorical flourish. During the war, President Franklin Roosevelt had often stated his opposition to French colonialism, so Ho had every reason to expect American support, or at least recognition. He was soon disappointed.

British and French troops occupied southern Vietnam and Cambodia in late September 1945, while the Nationalist Chinese performed the same service for the Allies in northern Vietnam and Laos. The British soon chased the representatives of the DRV out of their zones, handing Saigon and the rubber plantations back to the French. The Chinese gave Ho's government in Hanoi a freer rein, allowing the Communists to consolidate their authority before the Chinese left in the summer of 1946. At that point, the French did not have sufficient military force to re-occupy the north, so a stalemate ensued, with both sides engaging in negotiations, but really stalling for time to build up their forces. On November 23, 1946, the French exploited a minor incident with Vietnamese customs agents in the northern port of Haiphong, bombarding the port from air and sea. Over six thousand Vietnamese civilians were killed. The Viet Minh then retaliated against the French on December 19, 1946, and full-scale war broke out. The First Indochinese War would rage for seven and a half years.

The French controlled Saigon and most of southern Vietnam, and they built a defense perimeter around Hanoi and the Red River delta in the North. The Vietnamese, however, held their base area north of Hanoi and kept the French confined primarily to the cities and towns throughout the rest of the country. Communist forces commanded by Vo Nguyen Giap followed the clas-

sic strategy of "protracted war" laid out by Mao — first withdrawal, then equilibrium, followed by a general offensive. The first stage of the war, from 1946 to
1950, resembled the Malayan Emergency, with the Communist "tigers" mounting hit-and-run attacks in the jungles, while the French "elephants" lumbered
after them futilely.

After 1950, however, the nature of the war changed. Mao's Communists in
China, fresh from their defeat of Chiang Kai-shek, started supplying the Vietnamese Communists on a large scale, often with American weapons they had
captured from Chiang's soldiers. The Russians also contributed some equipment, particularly motorized transport. Escalating beyond guerrilla tactics,
General Giap swiftly cleared all the French posts along the Chinese-Vietnamese
border, then attacked the French strongholds in the Red River delta. The French
managed to repel the attacks, with great loss of life, by using armored gunboats
on the rivers and dropping napalm from the air. The two sides had reached a
rough equilibrium of military force. Giap still avoided set-piece battles for the
next few years, but slowly built up and trained a large, formidable conventional
army.

Ho Chi Minh and General Giap had hoped for American support, but the
French were the ones who received it. After the Communist victory in China
and the outbreak of the Korean War in 1950 (see chapter 7), the war in Vietnam
became politically redefined. Instead of a nationalist, anti-colonial revolt, the
French portrayed it as a war between the Free World and the Communist
World. Lines were being drawn all over in the early years of the Cold War, and
the Americans decided to help the French draw one in Southeast Asia. Between
1950 and 1954, American aid averaged about a half billion dollars annually, and
by the end of the war the United States was paying 80 percent of the French ex-
penses in Vietnam. Large-scale aid to both sides ensured a stalemate in the First
Indochinese War, unlike the steady progress the British were making at the
same time against the Communists in Malaya.

The Vietnamese Communists finally broke the deadlock in 1954 due to a
massive miscalculation by the French military. General Giap, still not wishing
to risk everything on a major battle, marched his forces across the top of Vietnam and threatened to overrun lightly garrisoned Laos. In an attempt to divert
and slow down his advance, the French built up a strong force in the valley of
Dien Bien Phu near the Laotian-Vietnamese border. This proved to be a mistake for two reasons. First, Dien Bien Phu lay at the extreme range of French air
support, about two hundred miles from Hanoi. Planes dropping paratroopers,
supplies, or napalm had to take on extra fuel and could only remain over their
targets for about twenty minutes. Second, the French military position was a
classic geographic trap.

Dien Bien Phu lay in a huge mountain valley, shaped something like an oak-leaf with small rivers running through the "veins." Eleven miles long and three to six miles wide, it was surrounded by peaks and ridges averaging about two thousand feet in height. French pilots called this valley the "chamber pot," and one French journalist got himself in trouble by comparing it to a Roman stadium, or lion pit. Ho Chi Minh, when he was briefed on the French position, turned a military helmet upside down and plunged his hand into it, saying, "The French are there." Then he ran his finger gleefully around the rim and exclaimed: "We are here." General Giap moved three full infantry divisions and a heavy artillery division, with all their equipment, from the Chinese border to the remote rim of Dien Bien Phu. Thousands of laborers carried rice, ammunition, and parts of artillery pieces on their shoulders or on heavily laden bicycles along jungle tracks, taking cover whenever French planes appeared in the sky.

All military defeats appear stupid with hindsight, but Dien Bien Phu still seems stupider than most. The French fell into a trap due to overconfidence in their own technological superiority. They believed they were still fighting an ill-equipped band of jungle guerrillas, like the British in Malaya. When top-ranking brass visited the valley and questioned whether the soldiers needed more artillery, the chief gunnery officer bragged that he had more than enough. The French did not realize that Giap's troops possessed Chinese guns comparable to, if not better than, their own. They further misjudged how the Vietnamese would use their artillery. Normally, a twentieth-century military force would set up its artillery *behind* the mountains and lob the shells over in precise geometric patterns, but the French believed that the size and shape of the valley would not permit this. General Giap, however, installed his artillery batteries in deep caves on the *front* side of the hills, directly facing Dien Bien Phu. Heavy camouflage and smoke from burning underbrush obscured the flashes of the guns and prevented the French from getting a precise fix on their locations. After just a day of deadly bombardment, which began on March 13, 1954, the boastful French gunnery officer committed suicide.

Along with the artillery barrages, the Vietnamese launched nearly daily infantry attacks on the beleaguered garrison of Dien Bien Phu. They dug an elaborate network of trenches that brought their troops closer and closer to the fortified French posts. The best-known French historian of the war, Bernard Fall, concluded that "all this was pure, orthodox, eighteenth-century siege technique." The siege lasted nearly two months, with the French parachuting fresh troops into the meat grinder whenever weather conditions permitted. The garrison had started with about 11,000 men, and almost 4,000 more had reinforced them, but when Dien Bien Phu finally surrendered on May 7, 1954, only 10,000 were left to march into prisoner of war camps. The rest had died or deserted.

As the Dien Bien Phu garrison entered its final agony, peace negotiations began in Geneva, Switzerland, with the four big powers (the Soviet Union, the

United States, Great Britain, and France), plus Communist China and all the states of Indochina represented. The French stalled for time and urgently begged the Americans for either a nuclear strike around Dien Bien Phu or else troop reinforcements. After some confused arguments in Washington, President Dwight Eisenhower finally refused both requests. The French government in Paris fell shortly after Dien Bien Phu did, and the new prime minister, Pierre Mendes-France, promised that he would either make peace at Geneva or resign within thirty days. Right on deadline, July 21, 1954, the Geneva accords ended the First Indochinese War. France and the Democratic Republic of Vietnam signed a cease-fire and began repatriating prisoners. A second document, called the Final Declaration, was hammered out by all parties but not formally signed by any of them. It divided Vietnam at the seventeenth parallel and called for all French troops to withdraw south and all Communist forces to regroup to the north. The French breathed a sigh of relief and packed up for home.

The separation of Vietnam was supposed to be temporary, with free elections held nationwide within two years. In the depths of the Cold War, however, the Americans did not wish to relinquish the entire country to the Communists, so they hastily built up a separate South Vietnamese government under President Ngo Dinh Diem, a Catholic Vietnamese who had been living in exile in the United States. The reunification elections were never held.

The Geneva accords did not mark the end of war in Vietnam, but simply an uneasy truce. Nevertheless, the Vietnamese Communists had succeeded in winning at least half a country by 1954, when the Communist insurgency in Malaya was already petering out. There were many reasons for the different results. The insurgents in Malaya were far fewer, numbering no more than 8,000 at any one time and never advancing beyond pure guerrilla warfare. General Giap, on the other hand, concentrated 40,000 soldiers around Dien Bien Phu and brought his own big guns to bear against his opponents. The Malay Peninsula was smaller than Vietnam, giving the guerrillas less room to maneuver, and was also more prosperous and better governed, thus producing fewer grievances for the Communists to exploit. The British under Generals Briggs and Templer took the guerrillas more seriously than the French did in Vietnam and hammered out logical and consistent counterinsurgency policies.

Two other reasons, however, proved more important in explaining the greater success of the Vietnamese revolutionaries. First, on a purely military level, the Viet Minh enjoyed the advantage of what Bernard Fall has called an "active sanctuary" across the border in China. Beginning in 1950, the Chinese Communists actively aided the Vietnamese revolt with arms, advisors, munitions, and heavy weapons. In contrast, the Malayan Communists could only seek a passive sanctuary across their northern border in Thailand. The rebels remained relatively safe, but the Thais gave them little effective assistance.

Beyond force levels, sanctuaries, and battle tactics, however, the broad nationalist appeal of the Vietnamese Communists provided the key ingredient to their success. Ho Chi Minh and his followers, though dedicated and ruthless Communists, never ceased being nationalists. The 1930 founding platform of the Vietnamese Communist Party included a mix of nationalist, Marxist, and moderate reformist proposals, appealing to a wide range of dissidents. Then in 1940, when the party established the united front called the Viet Minh, it proclaimed that "the problem of class struggle will continue to exist. But in the present stage, nation is above all." Historian Joseph Buttinger has rightly concluded: "nationalism was an integral part of the Vietnamese cause, not merely a cover for their real aims." Ho's socialist beliefs were real enough, but he became the most successful insurgent leader in Southeast Asia by recognizing that socialism *plus* nationalism was the most powerful force in the postwar world. Socio-nationalism, more than the strategy and tactics of the "tiger" against the "elephant," proved decisive.

CHAPTER SEVEN

Drawing a Line

The first place in Asia where the Cold War superpowers drew a line and made a stand was on the Korean peninsula. The Cold War began in Europe, when the Soviet Union and the United States rushed to fill the vacuum left by Germany's defeat, yet the lines of confrontation swiftly stabilized and Europe did not erupt into open warfare. The ambitions and interests of the Cold War adversaries at first seemed less clearcut in Asia than they were in Europe. Neither Russia nor America became fully engaged in Mao's revolution or the ensuing civil war against Chiang Kai-shek's Nationalists. The British fought the internal Communist insurgency in Malaya largely on their own, and neither the French nor the Viet Minh in Indochina received much assistance before the Korean War broke out in 1950. The conflict in Korea, therefore, brought the full force of the Cold War to Asia, thus globalizing the conflict. Indeed, it served as a kind of Third World War by proxy. As British journalist-historian Martin Walker has remarked: "People with brown and black and yellow skins paid the price of what had begun in Europe as a white man's quarrel."

It is ironic that Korea became a Cold War hot spot, for no one except its immediate neighbors had shown much interest in the country previously. A mountainous peninsula thrusting from the mainland of northeast Asia toward Japan, Korea is about the size of England. Yet an old saying relates that if Korea's rugged terrain were flattened with an iron, the country would be as big as China. The peninsula has clearly defined natural boundaries, the ocean on three sides and the Yalu River in the north, and a homogeneous population that combined Buddhist religion with Confucian values. Korea's Yi dynasty, ruling from 1392 to 1910, gave the name *Choson* (or *Chosen*) to their country, which means "land of the morning calm." The present-day term "Korea" harks back to

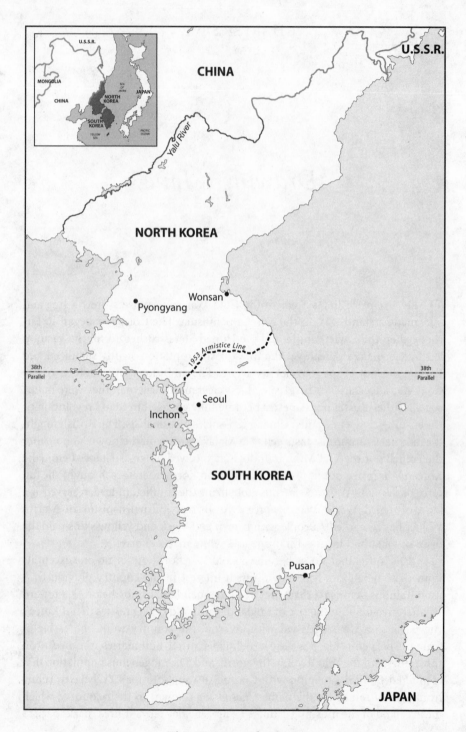

The Division of Korea

an older dynasty, the Koryo (918 to 1392). The translation of this word, "high mountains and sparkling waters," aptly describes the country.

Like Vietnam, Korea traditionally paid tribute to China, and its ruling class adopted Chinese language and culture. Chinese influence, however, did not produce such a violent reaction in Korea as it did in Vietnam. For much of its history, the Koreans held China in high regard as a benign elder brother. Other neighbors proved less friendly. Mongols invaded in the thirteenth century and the Japanese in the sixteenth. After about 1600 both Japan and Korea adopted stringent isolationist policies, closing off their realms from all foreign influences. Indeed, Korea became known as the "Hermit Kingdom," with a foreign policy that historian Bruce Cumings sums up as "no treaties, no trade, no Catholics, no West, and no Japan."

French and American gunboats tried to blast their way into this closed kingdom in the late nineteenth century, but Koreans fought them both off. Then on February 27, 1876, Japan, acting as a proxy for the European imperialists, forced an unequal treaty on the Korean king, opening up the country for trade and granting extraterritorial status to Japanese nationals in the country. In 1882 the United States, Great Britain, and Germany all signed similar treaties with Korea. A sharp anti-foreign movement, named *Tonghak,* or Eastern Learning, festered in the countryside, adopting as its slogan: "Drive out the Japanese dwarfs and the Western barbarians, and praise righteousness." Yet there was little the Korean elite or the Tonghak rebels could do to fend off domination by other nations. Koreans felt that they were "shrimps among whales" in East Asia.

Three whales in particular, Korea's immediate neighbors of China, Japan, and Russia, contended for predominant influence on the peninsula in the late nineteenth century. Japan, emerging as a modern imperialist power in its own right, eliminated China's centuries-old overlordship of Korea in the Sino-Japanese War of 1895. This left Russia and Japan contending for economic and strategic advantage on the peninsula. The Japanese offered a deal that would trade off Russian dominance in Manchuria and the northern part of Korea for a preponderant Japanese influence in the south. They offered to divide the peninsula into spheres of influence, roughly at the thirty-eighth parallel, a line that took on immense importance later in the twentieth century. The Russians arrogantly refused to bargain with Asians, so the Japanese attacked a Russian naval base, initiating the Russo-Japanese War of 1904-1905. As a result of their victory in this war, the Japanese imposed a protectorate over all of Korea, with the blessing of the British and the Americans.[1]

On August 22, 1910, the Korean king abdicated and his prime minister

1. These events are analyzed in greater detail in chapters 4 and 5 of volume 1.

ceded the country to Japan in a formal treaty of annexation. Japan had originally grabbed Korea for strategic reasons, to give it a defense in depth against Asian rivals, particularly Russia; but the colony soon took on great economic importance. The Japanese cultivated Korea as a rice bowl to feed their own burgeoning urban population. Then in the 1930s they developed steel and chemical industries, powered by hydroelectric energy, primarily in the northern part of the peninsula. Such industrial development was unusual in a colony. Ultimately it provided about 25 percent of Japan's World War II industrial capacity.

The Japanese kept a tight political rein on Korea. The closeness of the colony to the imperial ruling power permitted constant oversight by Japanese soldiers and bureaucrats, and the swift repression of any dissent. The funeral of the last Korean king on March 1, 1919, turned into a mass protest against Japanese rule in over six hundred towns and cities; but the Japanese army crushed the demonstrators, killing somewhere between 2,000 and 7,500 Koreans, and arresting tens of thousands more. Thereafter, most Korean nationalists or radicals went into exile in China, Russia, or the United States.

Collaboration became a bitter issue in Korea. Unlike Indonesia, Malaya, or Vietnam, where Japanese rule lasted only as long as the Second World War and where it served to drive out the European colonizers, Japanese conquest of Korea lasted a generation and had no redeeming side effects in the eyes of Koreans. Exile became an essential badge of honor for Korean nationalists. The two leaders who took their country into the Korean War of 1950-53 spent their exiles in the emerging superpowers. Yi Sungman (1875-1965) spent much of his adult life in the United States, where he took a Ph.D. in international law at Princeton and became known as Syngman Rhee.[2] Kim Il Sung (1912-1994) fought the Japanese as a guerrilla leader in China and Manchuria and spent most of the Second World War in a Russian military camp. Neither of them trusted any leaders who had remained in Korea under the Japanese occupation.

The forced industrialization of Korea by the Japanese disrupted ancient customs and uprooted much of the population; and World War II devastated the country even more. After the war, the squabbles of competing exile leaders were superimposed on a demoralized and disgruntled people. Even if the Cold War had never happened, Korea would have erupted into some sort of civil war after 1945. The involvement of the superpowers, however, magnified the conflict.

The division of the Korean peninsula came about casually, almost accidentally, at the end of World War II. The disposition of liberated Korea rated a very low priority among the Allied powers. At his December 1943 meeting with

---

2. Korean names, like Japanese and Chinese names, place the family name first. However, Americanized or Europeanized Koreans will often reverse the order.

Winston Churchill and Chiang Kai-shek at Cairo, Egypt, President Franklin D. Roosevelt unveiled a vague plan for a long multipower trusteeship over the country, and a few weeks later, Joseph Stalin approved the idea without much discussion at the Teheran Conference. There the matter rested until 1945. The Soviet Union did not declare war against Japan until the closing days of the world conflict, but in August 1945 the Russian armies rapidly occupied Manchuria and marched into Korea. When the atomic bomb compelled Japanese surrender, the Americans suddenly became worried about leaving Soviet troops alone in Korea.

Around midnight on August 10-11, 1945, the head of the State-War-Navy Coordinating Committee in Washington, D.C., instructed two young army officers, Dean Rusk and Charles H. Bonesteel, to find a map of Korea and draw a demarcation line between American and Soviet troops on the peninsula. The two picked the thirty-eighth parallel because it was easy to make out on the map and because it included the capital of Seoul within the American zone. U.S. troops would not actually arrive in Korea for almost a month, so if Stalin wanted to occupy all of Korea he could have done so. However, he agreed to the thirty-eighth parallel and halted his troops at that line. Korea seemed relatively unimportant to Stalin, and the thirty-eighth parallel coincided with old tsarist claims in the peninsula, so the Soviet leader remained satisfied for the moment.

General John R. Hodge arrived in Korea with about 25,000 American troops from Okinawa on September 8, 1945, and his occupation policies immediately aggravated a delicate situation. Coalitions of leftist nationalists, including communists but not necessarily dominated by them, had formed people's committees as de facto governing bodies throughout the country in the final days of Japanese rule. Hodge instinctively distrusted these radical bodies and relied instead on Japanese troops and conservative Koreans who had collaborated with the Japanese. This unfortunate decision alienated many Koreans and increased the ideological polarization and rampant factionalism of the local political scene. Hodge convinced his superiors that the exiled nationalist Syngman Rhee would lend legitimacy to the occupation authority. So Rhee arrived in Seoul on October 16, 1945, about the same time that Kim Il Sung returned to the Soviet zone in the North.

Over the next three years, these two leaders built up separate regimes, with the not-so-subtle encouragement of their superpower patrons. Officially, both the Russians and the Americans remained committed to a unified Korea under a multipower trusteeship, but as the Cold War developed in Europe during 1946 and 1947 neither side trusted the other sufficiently to establish a unified Korean regime. Nevertheless, both sides still viewed the Korean standoff as more of a nuisance than a major arena of conflict. In 1947 President Truman, preoccupied with the status of Berlin and Germany and the defense of non-communist regimes in Turkey and Greece, dumped the Korean problem in the lap of the United Nations. UN consideration of Korea's status seemed like a win/win situation for Truman. If the Soviet Union cooperated with a UN plan to reunify Korea and hold elections throughout the country, Communist influence might prove strong enough to win the elections, but at least the process would be fair and democratic, and the United States would be rid of a troublesome problem. If, as seemed more likely, the Russians refused to cooperate, then the U.S. could sponsor separate elections in South Korea and build up a client state with a relatively clean conscience.

As expected, the Russians refused to allow UN supervision of all-Korea elections. So on May 10, 1948, Koreans south of the thirty-eighth parallel voted for members of a South Korean National Assembly. Since Syngman Rhee's major opponents boycotted the elections in protest against partition of their country, Rhee's supporters won overwhelmingly and voted him first president of the Republic of Korea (ROK). General Douglas MacArthur, the supreme commander for the Allied powers in Japan, flew over from Tokyo for Rhee's inauguration on August 15, 1948. In the meantime, the North Korean Workers Party (the Communists), which had rapidly consolidated its control in the North, held its own elections for a Supreme People's Assembly, which met on September 3, 1948. A year before the similar division of Germany was finalized, Korea had been partitioned into two separate states, each claiming to speak for all Koreans.

The Soviet Union withdrew its occupation forces from its zone of Korea at the end of 1948, and the United States followed suit during the summer of 1949. Both Kim Il Sung in the North and Syngman Rhee in the South wanted to cross the thirty-eighth parallel and unify the country, but neither Korean government possessed sufficient military force to accomplish this by itself. Kim's Communist Party, though faced with factional disputes, was firmly in control of North Korea, but Rhee's regime in the South looked shaky.

A major rebellion against the South's separate elections broke out on the large island of Cheju, off the southern coast of Korea. Islanders had a long history of independence from the mainland and were still governed by people's committees that opposed Syngman Rhee. A guerrilla force of 3,000 to 4,000 controlled the rugged interior of the island for over a year, until ROK army forces finally subdued them in mid-1949 with a loss of about 30,000 lives, or 10 percent of the island's population. On October 19, 1948, two regiments of army troops about to embark for duty on Cheju Island revolted in the port city of Yosu. The rebels held the city and a neighboring rail junction for several days before being driven out and taking refuge in the surrounding mountains. Both the Cheju and Yosu rebellions were led by indigenous rebels and not directed from the North. Indeed, they may have disrupted a more extensive plan that

Kim's Communists were hatching to overthrow Syngman Rhee. In any case, the two failed rebellions set off a wave of repression and turned South Korea into a police state.

Throughout 1949 numerous border incidents broke out along the thirty-eighth parallel between the armies of the two states. Most of these were provoked by Rhee and his generals, who were eager to march north against the Communists. American and United Nations observers did their best to limit these engagements, but some of them turned into major battles. At the same time, Kim Il Sung's Communists began infiltrating trained guerrillas into the South to join up with indigenous rebels and undermine Rhee's regime. In the year *before* full-scale war finally broke out in June 1950, over 100,000 Koreans were killed in border clashes and guerrilla engagements. The civil war started long before the international war did.

Rhee had been the more belligerent Korean leader before 1950, but the balance of military force on the peninsula changed drastically in that year. Forty to fifty thousand Korean Communist veterans of the Chinese civil war filtered back home after Mao Tse-tung's victory in China. These battle-hardened soldiers formed the spearhead for Kim Il Sung's invasion of the South. Just as importantly, Kim finally managed to persuade both Joseph Stalin and Mao Tse-tung to support his bid for reunification of Korea.

Until recently, Americans could only guess who initiated the Korean War on the Communist side, but since the end of the Cold War Chinese and Russian documents and historical studies have cleared up much of the mystery. Briefly put, Kim Il Sung initiated the war with the permission of both Stalin and Mao. In a secret visit to Moscow from March 30 to April 25, 1950, Kim convinced Stalin that a decisive surprise attack by North Korean forces could win the war within a matter of days, since the people of the South would rise up against Syngman Rhee as soon as Northern forces crossed the parallel.

Neither Kim nor Stalin thought the United States would intervene to save Rhee's regime. The American government had been sending mixed signals for over a year. Both General MacArthur in March 1949 and Secretary of State Dean Acheson on January 12, 1950, had publicly declared that the U.S. defense perimeter in the Pacific ran through the Aleutian Islands, Japan, the Ryukyus (including Okinawa), and the Philippines, but did not include mainland areas such as Korea. Yet Acheson had also reaffirmed American support for South Korea on a number of other occasions. American policymakers were hedging their bets in South Korea, afraid that Syngman Rhee might turn out to be a "little Chiang Kai-shek."

The ambiguity of American policy misled Stalin. He believed that Kim's proposed military action would win a cheap Cold War victory and draw American attention away from Europe. Three international scholars, Sergei N.

Goncharov, John W. Lewis, and Xue Litai, drawing on previously closed documents, conclude:

> The Soviet dictator would be pursuing his goals on several levels — to expand the buffer zone along his border, to create a springboard against Japan that could be used during a future global conflict, to test the American resolve, to intensify the hostility between Beijing and Washington, and, finally and foremost, to draw U.S. power away from Europe.

Nevertheless, Stalin remained cautious and did not plan to support the North Korean invasion openly or commit Soviet troops. He told Kim to ask Mao for his permission and for more direct assistance, if necessary. Stalin had been impressed by Mao's victory in China and was willing to concede him a leading role in Asia, but he also distrusted the Chinese leader and nurtured an old grudge against him. In the depths of World War II, when Hitler's armies penetrated deep into Russia, Stalin had asked Mao to mount an attack against Japan, thus preventing Japanese assaults on the Soviet Union in Asia. Mao refused, husbanding his resources for his own struggle. Now in 1950, Stalin made Chinese participation a stringent condition for Kim's adventure. The Soviet dictator was playing a devious game with his Asian allies, ensuring that he remained in control but not running any direct risk. Like President Truman he was trying to create a win/win situation on the Korean peninsula. With his usual brutal directness, Stalin instructed Kim Il Sung: "If you should get kicked in the teeth, I shall not lift a finger. You have to ask Mao for all the help."

Accordingly, Kim made a pilgrimage to China in May 1950. Mao thought the Korean action inconvenient, for he was planning his own invasion of Taiwan to complete the unification of China under Communist rule. Yet Mao felt gratitude for the staunch North Korean aid in his own civil war and harbored deep suspicions that he would have to confront American might in Asia sooner or later, so he gave a general pledge of support. Yet he did not ask about the details of the Korean invasion and was probably not consulted about its starting date.

In sum, American carelessness, indecision, and ambiguity, plus Soviet and Chinese recklessness, caused the Korean War. A simmering civil war turned into an international conflict because of miscalculations on both sides.

The North Koreans launched their attack across the thirty-eighth parallel at 4:00 A.M. on Sunday, June 25, 1950 (Korean time). Seven infantry divisions, about 135,000 soldiers, poured across the line at four different points, supported by up-to-date Soviet tanks, artillery, and aircraft. The 95,000 soldiers guarding South Korea were much more lightly equipped and therefore fell back before the onslaught. The North Koreans captured Seoul four days later, on

June 29, and their headlong drive south was slowed more by the terrain than by opposing forces. Then the other superpower intervened.

Despite the previous uncertainty of its Korean policy, the Truman administration in Washington reacted with unusual speed and decisiveness. Washington was thirteen hours behind Korean time, so news of the invasion reached the American capital on Saturday, June 24. By the next evening, the president and his top diplomatic and military advisers had reassembled from various vacation spots and decided to ask the United Nations for a resolution condemning the North Korean action. Over the next few days, the United States enjoyed a relatively free hand at the United Nations, since the Soviet Union had been boycotting the Security Council for most of the year. On June 27 President Truman committed American troops to the struggle and the same day the UN called on all its members to do likewise. Due to the absence of the Soviet Union, the United Nations, for the only time in its history, played the role it was originally designed for: collective action against aggression. Eventually a dozen nations contributed soldiers or equipment to the war, though the United States and South Korea bore the brunt of the fighting.

The Soviet boycott of the Security Council in 1950 has long been considered a major blunder by Stalin. Yet recent research in Soviet sources shows that the boycott was no oversight or accident. Russian delegates walked out of the UN to protest that body's refusal to seat Communist China and throw out the Nationalist Chinese regime of Chiang Kai-shek; but some scholars believe Stalin may actually have wanted to keep Mao's Chinese out of the UN. In this view, the Russian boycott of the Security Council was the first step toward total withdrawal from the UN and the establishment of an exclusively Communist international organization, directly under Moscow's control. Less conspiratorially, other scholars believe Stalin simply miscalculated and bought Kim Il Sung's assurances that the war would be short and the United States and UN would do nothing. In any case, the UN actions in June 1950 gave the war in Korea international legitimacy.

The United States clearly would have intervened on its own if it had not received UN backing. During the frantic debates in Washington in late June 1950, the president and State Department officials proved more militant and decisive than the military leaders. The Joint Chiefs of Staff still argued that Korea held little strategic significance. At best it was a backwater and at worst it could become a trap. Yet the political leaders viewed the North Korean military action as an important challenge to American leadership in the Cold War and a test of American credibility.

Drawing a line across the Korean peninsula had obscured the internal nature of the conflict and raised it to an issue of international concern. Once a line was drawn, it had to be defended or the United States would lose face in the

international competition against the Communists. Domestic political considerations reinforced the decision to respond with force. Republicans had been
battering the Democratic administration for months over the "loss" of China to
Mao Tse-tung. Truman did not think his party could afford any more such
losses to the Communists.[3]

The Korean War lasted for three bloody years. Though the fighting remained limited to the Korean peninsula, it involved one of the superpowers directly and the other covertly. Both sides worked hard to signal the limited nature of their actions in Korea. Soviet pilots flew fighter planes in the war, but
they disguised their uniforms and their equipment with Korean and Chinese
markings and kept primarily to the northern reaches of the peninsula. American intelligence knew of this Russian involvement but kept it secret and did not
challenge it. Nevertheless, on a number of occasions the war threatened to
break out of its peninsular straitjacket and expand into World War III.

The battlefield history of the Korean War falls into four stages: (1) from
June through August of 1950 North Korean forces pushed the South Korean and
American defenders back to a small perimeter at the southeastern end of the
peninsula, threatening to push them off the mainland altogether; (2) in September 1950 the American army under General MacArthur launched a daring
amphibious landing at Inchon, behind the North Korean lines, which turned
the tide of battle and sent the North Koreans fleeing northward across the
thirty-eighth parallel and almost to the Yalu River; (3) in November 1950 the
Chinese Communists intervened and prevented a North Korean defeat, pushing the Americans and South Koreans back across the thirty-eighth parallel;
(4) from June 1951 until the final armistice in July 1953 the war stalemated near
the thirty-eighth parallel, with bloody but inconclusive fighting and long, frustrating peace talks.

Some Americans believed that the mere appearance of white soldiers in
Korea, fresh from winning the greatest war in human history against Japan and
Germany, would stop Kim Il Sung's forces in their tracks. Military historian
Max Hastings quotes an American soldier who "figured to be a week in Korea,
settle the gook thing, then back to Japan." He was sorely mistaken. The only
American forces immediately available for duty in Korea were untested occupa-
tion troops in Japan, with little heavy equipment and limited ammunition. The
North Koreans pushed them back relentlessly until they made their final stand
behind the broad Naktong River, in a perimeter fifty miles wide by a hundred

---

3. One of my earliest childhood memories concerns a map of Korea printed in the
Chicago Tribune, then a leading Republican newspaper that much concerned Truman. Apparently the *Tribune* had painted North Korea in brilliant red ink, so I asked my mother
why North Korea was colored red. "Because that's where the Reds are," she replied.

miles deep surrounding the port city of Pusan. By the time Americans and South Koreans took refuge in the Pusan perimeter, they had inflicted heavy casualties on the North Koreans and had been reinforced by additional American divisions. United Nations forces actually outnumbered North Koreans at this point but were so demoralized they did not realize it. Nevertheless, they managed to blunt the final North Korean assaults across the Naktong in the first few days of September 1950.

General MacArthur, still supreme commander of Allied occupation forces in Japan but now also the UN commander in Korea, immediately began planning a counterstroke. He and his tightly knit group of subordinates had mastered the art of amphibious warfare in the Pacific during World War II, and they now conceived a daring landing well behind the North Korean lines. Rather than waste lives in a frontal assault out of the Pusan perimeter, MacArthur planned to land his forces at Inchon, the port city for Seoul, then swiftly seize the capital.

Inchon posed difficult operational problems for an amphibious landing. The harbor had an enormous thirty-two-foot tidal range and at low tide became a quagmire of mud. Landing forces could not attain tactical surprise since they first had to seize an island commanding the approaches to the harbor, then wait for another high tide before landing at Inchon itself. Unbeknown to MacArthur, the Chinese military had guessed his plans and warned Kim Il Sung of a possible landing at Inchon. Kim apparently disregarded these warnings, either out of arrogance or because his troops were exhausted after the headlong dash south. On September 15, 1950, under cover of a massive air and sea bombardment, MacArthur's troops successfully landed at Inchon and quickly took the city. What happened next illustrates the political and symbolic nature of the Korean War.

MacArthur's chief of staff, General Edward Almond, planned to capture Seoul by September 25, the three months' anniversary of the war's outbreak, as a gift for his commander. After the easy landing at Inchon, however, North Korean resistance stiffened considerably. American troops reached the capital on September 25, and MacArthur's headquarters back in Japan announced the capture of Seoul; but it took three more days of deadly hand-to-hand street fighting to secure the city. Not until September 29 was it safe enough for the supreme commander and South Korean president Syngman Rhee to fly into Seoul for a ceremony at the devastated capitol building. Had Almond and MacArthur not been in such a rush, American forces could have surrounded Seoul and eventually captured it with less destruction and loss of life.

The swift successes at Inchon and Seoul had other unfortunate ramifications as well. They made MacArthur, Truman, and the American public overconfident, and eager to exploit their military success. At the same time, events happened so fast that international diplomacy was unable to keep up. The re-capture of Seoul and the driving of North Korean forces back across the thirty-eighth parallel marked a logical time and place for the Korean War to end. UN collective action had repelled aggression and restored the status quo on the peninsula. Yet the Americans now over-reached themselves. After limited de-bate, the Truman administration decided to carry the war north over the thirty-eighth parallel and reunify Korea by force. On September 27 the Defense De-partment instructed MacArthur to pursue and destroy Kim Il Sung's forces, so long as neither Russian nor Chinese troops intervened. Only South Korean troops, not Americans or Europeans, were permitted to operate in the extreme north near the Chinese and Russian borders, so as not to provoke such inter-vention.

ROK troops crossed the parallel on October 1, followed by the Americans on October 9. Combined forces captured Pyongyang, the North Korean capital, on October 19. In the meantime, another attempt at symbolic warfare went awry. The Inchon operation had so inflated MacArthur's reputation that he de-cided to duplicate it on the other side of the peninsula. Accordingly, he ordered a marine landing at the North Korean port of Wonsan. However, the troop transports had to wait offshore for two weeks while minesweepers cleared the coast and the harbor. In the meantime, South Korean troops had raced over-land and were waiting to greet the U.S. Marines when they finally landed on October 25.

Militarily, it seemed that the war was nearly over. MacArthur planned to have the troops home by Christmas. North Korean forces retreated north nearly as fast as they had raced south four months earlier. Yet they were probably not so shattered as it seemed. Following Maoist strategy of withdrawal when the enemy is strong, Kim's forces had melted away into the mountains and were preparing a prolonged guerrilla resistance. Yet before they could put this plan into operation, they received massive reinforcements from the Chinese.

Mao Tse-tung feared that the overconfident Americans would not stop with the destruction of North Korea but might attack China itself. So on Octo-ber 2, 1950, as the first South Korean forces were crossing the thirty-eighth par-allel, Mao called the Chinese Communist Politburo into session and proposed the sending of "volunteers" to aid North Korea. The Chinese leader met consid-erable resistance. After all, China faced an enormous task of political consolida-tion and physical rebuilding from its own civil war and revolution. Yet the Po-litburo made a preliminary decision to intervene on October 2 and informed Stalin by cable the same day. Chou En-lai flew off to Russia to ask Stalin for as-sistance, but true to his word the Soviet leader offered none. He even reneged, temporarily, on a promise of air support for Chinese troops.

Mao, therefore, planned a limited intervention, followed by a defensive posture, in order to settle the war by diplomacy or at least allow time to build up Chinese forces. He informed Kim of his intentions on October 8 and signaled his commitment by assigning his eldest son to serve as an interpreter with the Chinese troops. Large numbers of Chinese began filtering across the Yalu River, and they encountered South Koreans in battle for the first time on October 25. In the last days of October and the first few days of November, the Chinese fought pitched battles with Americans and South Koreans, halting their advance north. Then from about November 5 onward, a lull settled over the battlefields. Stalin had finally sent fighters to cover the Chinese troops but he still refused to dispatch bombers. Mao rested on the defensive, as planned, and waited for an American response.

MacArthur misinterpreted this first Chinese intervention as a mere feint, rather than a dire warning; so he launched his so-called final offensive toward the Yalu on the day after Thanksgiving, November 25. The Chinese now attacked in full force and drove the UN armies back. MacArthur's troops were poorly prepared to blunt the Chinese onslaught. The American general had divided his forces into two columns, each operating separately on either side of the central mountain chain. The Communists attacked primarily at nighttime, when American airpower proved less useful and when the frigid winter cold was at its most intense. The American retreat became a rout. Marines along the east coast of the peninsula managed a disciplined withdrawal to the port of Wonsan from which they were evacuated by ship on December 9. Yet the rest of the American soldiers simply fled southward in what became known as "the big bugout." This three-hundred-mile retreat marked one of the greatest military disasters in American history. Max Hastings, the British military historian, compares it to the French defeat by Hitler in the spring of 1940 or the British capitulation to Japan at Singapore in 1942.

The next few months marked the low point of American fortunes in Korea, and one of the most dangerous periods of the entire Cold War. At a press conference on November 30, 1950, President Truman declared that he would take "whatever steps are necessary to meet the military situation." When a reporter asked if that included the atomic bomb, the president replied: "That includes every weapon we have." This statement so alarmed the British that Prime Minister Clement Attlee flew across the ocean for a consultation. From this time on, America's allies, who had followed U.S. leadership almost automatically in the Korean War, became less deferential and more diligent in trying to keep the war from expanding beyond Korea.

Truman may have blundered with his atomic bomb reference, or perhaps he was sending a warning to the Chinese and the Russians. Military planners were considering use of the atomic bomb in late 1950. At the request of the Joint Chiefs, MacArthur listed twenty-six possible "retaliation targets" in North Korea and

China. If UN allies had not calmed down the American leaders in their moment of panic, and if the Chinese forces had succeeded in annihilating the American troops rather than just pushing them back, the United States might well have resorted to atomic warfare. Historian William Stueck has concluded that "events from late November through the second week of January had pushed the world closer to global conflict than at any time since 1945." Only the Cuban missile crisis of 1963 matches this moment as a danger point in the Cold War.

American and South Korean forces did not stop running until after they had crossed the thirty-eighth parallel and then evacuated Seoul on January 4, 1951. Thereafter, a new field commander, General Matthew Ridgway, managed to stop the panic, re-instill discipline, and even mount a counteroffensive that recovered Seoul and again crossed the parallel in March 1951. This time the American government decided not to over-reach and called a halt to operations near the demarcation line of the peninsula.

General MacArthur, who still retained overall command of the Korean theater, chafed at these new restrictions. He publicly declared on March 24, 1951, that China was beaten and should lay down its arms. He then sent a letter to a conservative Republican congressman, Joseph Martin of Massachusetts, implicitly criticizing the policy of his superiors in Washington. "There is no substitute for victory," MacArthur's statement concluded. This proved too much for Truman, who then asked the Joint Chiefs of Staff whether MacArthur should be relieved of command for insubordination. On April 8, 1951, the military chiefs so recommended, and Truman recalled MacArthur in a hastily convened news conference in the early morning of April 11. Officials in Washington feared a news leak and thus rushed to release a statement. The general heard the news of his recall on a radio broadcast.

MacArthur had long been a difficult subordinate for two presidents. During World War II, a British officer, Lieutenant Colonel Gerald Wilkinson, described the general's character:

> He is shrewd, selfish, proud, remote, highly strung and vastly vain. He has imagination, self-confidence, physical courage and charm, but no humor about himself, no regard for truth, and is unaware of these defects. . . . With moral depth he would be a great man.

Harry Truman summed up MacArthur more briefly as a "supreme egotist who regarded himself as something of a god." Yet Truman had an extra reason for finally reining in the general. The Washington military brass were about to give the theater commander in Korea added leeway to mount air strikes across the Yalu into Chinese territory, if necessary to protect American soldiers. In addition, they were sending an air force squadron armed with atomic weapons to

138

bases in the western Pacific. Simply put, neither the president nor the Joint Chiefs trusted MacArthur with these awesome responsibilities, which could lead to world war or even nuclear war. Therefore, they recalled him; and after a noisy political reception, the general, in his own words, "just faded away."

The military situation in Korea stalemated near, but slightly to the north of, the thirty-eighth parallel. That mythical line never represented a militarily defensible position. So from mid-1951 until mid-1953 both sides chose more easily fortified positions along the hilltops north of the parallel and dug in. Though much bloody fighting ensued in the remaining two years of war, it resembled the trench warfare of World War I more than the mobile warfare of World War II. A British officer at the front later recalled: "Everyone could see that we had reached stalemate, unless someone started chucking atom bombs."

Fortunately, no one chucked any nukes, but negotiating an end to the deadlocked war proved difficult and prolonged. Neither side felt eager to call it quits. Both General Ridgway, who succeeded MacArthur as supreme commander, and his successor, General Mark Clark, still thought the war could be won with troop reinforcements and a looser rein on American bombing missions. Mao and Stalin thought they might outlast the Americans and eventually convince them to go away. Nearly all Koreans, North and South, wished to fight on and reunify the peninsula. However, the military commanders in the field began negotiations for a cease-fire after the battlefield stabilized in the summer of 1951. At the very least, this would allow time for regrouping and resupply of the troops. Yet neither side showed any sense of urgency in the truce negotiations which began at the ancient Korean capital of Kaesong on July 10, 1951, then relocated to the military camp of Panmunjom on October 25. Both sides postured, stalled, and tried to score propaganda victories.

Eventually the truce negotiations at Panmunjom deadlocked over a single issue: repatriation of prisoners. A recently adopted Geneva convention stipulated that all prisoners should be returned promptly at the end of a conflict, even if they did not wish to go back to their home country. However, American leaders remembered that after World War II Stalin had imprisoned or executed many of the Russian POWs liberated from Germany and returned to the Soviet Union. President Truman, in particular, who felt Stalin had betrayed him in that instance, remained adamant against any forced repatriation of prisoners. When the Americans interviewed Chinese and North Korean POWs they discovered that great numbers feared returning home. The Americans realized that this gave them a tremendous propaganda advantage in the Cold War.

With no end of the Korean War in sight and the president's personal popularity at a low ebb, Truman declined to run for reelection in 1952. General Dwight D. Eisenhower, the popular hero of the World War II Normandy invasion, easily defeated Democrat Adlai Stevenson. In the course of his campaign,

Eisenhower promised "I shall go to Korea," presumably to break the stalemate. The president-elect kept his promise in December, but the visit was largely cosmetic and settled nothing.

The Chinese and Russians, however, feared that the new administration might be less restrained than its predecessor and possibly extend the air war to cities and military targets in China or the Soviet Union. Then on March 5, 1953, Joseph Stalin died. The collective leadership that succeeded him wanted to end the Korean War and consolidate its own position within Russia and in Eastern Europe. Therefore, serious negotiations resumed at Panmunjom on April 26, 1953. Negotiators struck a compromise on the prisoner of war issue. All POWs who wished to return would be repatriated immediately. Those who did not want to go home would be turned over to a neutral nations committee for screening and interrogation. If they remained adamant, they would not be forcibly repatriated. Syngman Rhee almost torpedoed the final truce, for he did not want the war to end with the partition of Korea. On June 18, 1953, South Korean guards opened the gates of the POW compounds and allowed over 25,000 Korean prisoners to escape. This embarrassed the U.S. military, but by this time the United States, China, and Russia wanted out of Korea, so they ignored the overwhelming wishes of Koreans on both sides to fight on. On July 27, 1953, military delegates signed a truce agreement at Panmunjom and the fighting stopped that evening. The war never officially ended. Korea remains partitioned today and 37,000 American troops still remain at the cease-fire line in the center of the peninsula.

The Korean War could have been prevented altogether by better leadership on either side or at least halted sooner than it was. If the American government had chosen not to occupy the southern half of the peninsula at the end of World War II, the country never would have been divided. Though much internal conflict would have troubled a united Korea and the country would have remained under Soviet influence, the major international struggle would have been prevented. Or, after the division of the peninsula, if the United States government had firmly signaled its intention to defend the South, Stalin never would have permitted Kim's forces to attack. The United States chose a bad combination of two options — drawing a line through Korea, but a wavy line. As for the Communist side, Sergei Goncharov and his colleagues conclude summarily that "it was reckless war-making of the worst kind." Stalin brutally discounted his Asian allies, the North Koreans, who "lost nothing, except for their men."

Once the war began, it could logically have ended at three points in 1950: when the United Nations forces reached the thirty-eighth parallel in September; after the North Koreans were pushed back and Chinese forces first appeared in October and November; or when the Chinese and North Koreans regained the thirty-eighth parallel at the end of the year. In all three instances, however, the attacking force, the one with momentum, felt reluctant to pause for a diplomatic solution. Both sides over-reached and tried to win a total victory. Finally, even after a stalemate was reached, neither side wished to lose face with the other, and so the war dragged on, with increasing casualties.

This war of miscalculations remained a limited war fought with conventional weapons, but its effects reached far beyond the Korean peninsula. Korea changed the tone and the scope of Cold War politics. In short, it spread the Cold War to Asia, thus globalizing the superpower confrontation.

Almost immediately after Kim Il Sung's forces crossed the thirty-eighth parallel, the ramifications of the North Korean invasion were felt elsewhere. President Truman ordered the American Seventh Fleet to patrol the straits between Taiwan and the mainland of China. In the short run, this was a defensive measure, intended to limit the war by preventing either Mao's Communists or Chiang's Nationalists from attacking the other. Yet in the long run it became a commitment to preserve and defend Chiang Kai-shek's regime on Taiwan. Similarly, in the wake of the North Korean invasion, the American government sharply increased its military aid to the French in Indochina. Thus Truman's decision to resist the North Korean onslaught in June 1950 eventually led to two wars, not one, on the Asian mainland.

The Korean War militarized the American government in startling new ways. Shortly after the war began, generals took charge of both the Defense Department and the Central Intelligence Agency. Though George Marshall, the new defense secretary, and Walter Bedell Smith, the director of intelligence, were prudent, honorable men, their appointments bent a long-standing tradition of civilian control over the military. More importantly, the American government gave the military immense new resources to deploy. Before the Korean War broke out, the National Security Council had issued a far-ranging policy paper, NSC-68, envisioning a rapid buildup of conventional forces and a large increase of taxes to pay for them. NSC-68 was just a piece of paper with little chance of implementation before the Korean conflict, but thereafter it became a blueprint for Cold War mobilization. Secretary of State Dean Acheson remarked that "Korea saved us." The American military budget tripled, reaching 50 billion dollars in the year after the Korean War broke out. The CIA also grew enormously. In 1949 this fledgling agency, established just the year before, had a staff of 302 people with a budget of 4.7 million dollars. By 1952 the spy contingent had grown to 2,812, assigned to 47 stations, with a budget of 82 million dollars.

The Korean War also had significant effects on other nations. The United States committed large numbers of troops to the defense of Western Europe and accelerated the rearmament of West Germany as part of NATO. Thus Stalin's bid for a cheap and easy victory in the Cold War backfired, as Russia became more tightly surrounded and contained than before. Mao's China, on the other hand, greatly increased its confidence and prestige by successfully fighting the strongest nation on earth to a draw. Though in the short run, the war made Communist China more dependent on Soviet aid and assistance, in the long run it probably rendered a Chinese split from the Soviet Union more likely.

Japan, ravaged by conventional and atomic bombing during World War II, had not yet recovered or rebuilt by 1950; but the Korean War jumpstarted its economy. Manufacturing output in Japan increased 50 percent in the year immediately following Kim's invasion. During the three-year conflict, the U.S. military purchased much of its "non-lethal" equipment, such as clothing, vehicles, and electronic devices, from the revived Japanese factories, with procurement averaging about 800 million dollars per year. The Toyota Motor Company, for example, received a vital infusion of orders for army trucks. All in all, this war-induced purchasing functioned like a Marshall Plan for Japan, rebuilding its economy, restoring its confidence, and launching the nation on a remarkable trading career in the second half of the twentieth century.[4]

In this torrent of international consequences flowing from the Korean War, it is easy to forget about Korea itself and the Korean people. The war may have been limited in American and Russian eyes, but there was nothing limited about its devastating effects on Korea. Americans counted relatively few casualties, compared to other wars — 33,629 American dead and 105,785 wounded. The British Commonwealth troops had 1,263 killed and 4,817 wounded. The other UN members who sent soldiers — Turkey, Belgium, France, Greece, the Netherlands, Ethiopia, Colombia, and the Philippines — suffered a total of 1,800 dead and 7,000 wounded.

The South Korean army, however, reported almost a million casualties — 415,000 dead and 429,000 wounded. There are no accurate figures for Communist losses in battle, but the American military estimated that about 1.5 million Chinese and North Koreans died. Thus the "limited war" in Korea was responsible for 2 million dead, on the battlefield alone.

The war wreaked even greater havoc behind the lines. The U.S. administration forbade bombing in China or Russia, but the aerial campaign against North Korea was virtually unlimited. American planes pounded cities, towns, factories, and hydroelectric dams in the North. One particularly devastating air raid, on June 20, 1953, just a month before the armistice, sent a torrent of water rushing twenty-seven miles downstream, wiping out six miles of railway, five

---

4. The United States signed a peace treaty with Japan in September 1951, which officially ended the Second World War in the Pacific and restored full sovereignty to the Japanese government in April 1952.

bridges, two miles of highway, and five square miles of rice paddies. All told, both parts of Korea lost over a million homes and 25,000 industrial plants. Since the Korean struggle was a civil war first and foremost, Koreans did much of the damage to each other. Both sides massacred tens of thousands of suspect civilians during their brief months of occupation on the other side of the thirty-eighth parallel. Out of a population of 30 million, nearly 2 million Koreans died, 5 million became refugees, and 10 million saw their families divided between North and South.

Of all the upheavals in Asia after World War II, the Korean War proved the most deadly and the least decisive. When the killing finally stopped, the war ended where it began, near an imaginary line on a map. Alone of the countries partitioned by the Cold War, Korea still remains divided today.

PART THREE

THE MEDITERRANEAN ROAD TO NATIONHOOD

GK

In East Asia, revolts against European imperialism came suddenly, dramatically, and usually violently at the end of the Second World War. Social revolutions, civil war, and in the unique case of India, a non-violent mass movement, brought national independence in their wake. In southwestern Asia and northern Africa, however, around the Mediterranean Sea, the road to national independence followed a more winding course.

The Arab peoples had already mounted a dramatic revolt against the Ottoman Turkish Empire during the *First* World War. In conjunction with the British and French, Arab armies swept out of the Arabian Peninsula, through Palestine and Syria to the ancient Arab capital of Damascus. When the First War ended, however, the Arabs found that they had merely traded one set of imperial masters for another. The British and French divided up the territories at the eastern end of the Mediterranean between themselves and decided that the Arabs were not yet ready for complete autonomy. The two European powers, therefore, held the Arab lands, not as outright colonies, but as mandates for the League of Nations. In the short run, this legal fiction made little difference, but in the longer term it pointed Arab countries in the direction of nationhood. They arrived at that destination more quickly than the British and French expected, but more slowly than they themselves hoped. Several Arab nations took steps along the road to independence between the wars, but the Second World War accelerated the process. By mid-century, the major Arab nations had asserted their independent sovereignty.

In the meantime, another nation was growing in the heartland of the Arabs. The British had reserved a small portion of the Mediterranean basin, the biblical lands of Israel, as a national homeland for Jews fleeing persecution in Europe. Between the world wars, the Jewish population swelled, leading to sharp conflicts between Jews and Arabs who were uncomfortably sharing the same homeland. Hitler's fanatic attempts to exterminate Europe's Jews made a refuge desperately necessary, and shortly after World War II the world's great powers finally recognized Israel as an independent state, setting off the first of many wars between Israel and the Arabs.

Egypt rose to preeminence among the new Arab states. A group of nationalist army officers, led by Gamal Abdul Nasser, overthrew the Egyptian government in 1952 and thereafter pursued a more revolutionary, and fiercely anti-Israeli, policy. The Cold War rivalry between Russia and the United States, as well as the final dying gasps of European imperialism, complicated the attempts of Nasser and his followers to pursue their own independent, neutralist policies.

Finally, at the western edge of the Arab world, in France's North African colony of Algeria, one of the bloodiest wars of national liberation broke out in the late 1950s. The war in Algeria brought one of France's greatest twentieth century leaders, General Charles de Gaulle, back to power in the mother country, but even he could not prevent the Algerians from forcing their way down the twists and turns of the road to independence. After de Gaulle settled with the Algerians in 1962, the Mediterranean Sea was finally surrounded by an unbroken string of independent states.

CHAPTER EIGHT

Family, Religion, and Nation in the Arab Heartland

The defeat and dismemberment of the Ottoman Empire during World War I left Arab nationalism politically and intellectually dominant in the Arab heartland. Upper-class notables and middle-class intellectuals in the urban centers of the Middle East[1] had developed the notion of nationalism in the late nineteenth century. The rapid progress of European nation-states provided a powerful example, but developments within the empire proved more impor-

---

1. The term "Middle East" is, of course, Eurocentric. Looking out from Europe, geographers and politicians called eastern Asia the "Far East," western Asia the "Middle East," and the Anatolian and Balkan peninsulas the "Near East." Confusingly, "Near East" and "Middle East" were often used synonymously for all the lands surrounding the Eastern Mediterranean. I shall continue to use "Middle East" as a widely inclusive geographic term, including more than just Arab lands. According to the American Historical Association's *Guide to Historical Literature*: "The Middle East is commonly understood to consist, in terms of late twentieth century political geography, of Turkey, Iran, Israel, the Arab countries of Southwest Asia, and Egypt. North Africa includes Morocco, Algeria, and Tunisia; Libya is assigned to either the Middle East or North Africa." The more neutral phrase, Southwest Asia, has never caught on the way East Asia has. In this chapter, however, I am focusing exclusively on the Arab lands east of Egypt. Arabs often employ the term *mashriq* to describe this area, distinguishing it from Arab North Africa, known as the *maghrib*. Neither of these words are well known, however, to Americans or Europeans. In this chapter, therefore, I will use a variety of terms — Arab Asia, the Arab East, the Arab rectangle, or the Arab heartland — to refer to the modern-day countries of Saudi Arabia, Yemen, Oman, Qatar, Bahrain, United Arab Emirates, Kuwait, Iraq, Syria, Lebanon, and Jordan, and the Arab portions of Israel.

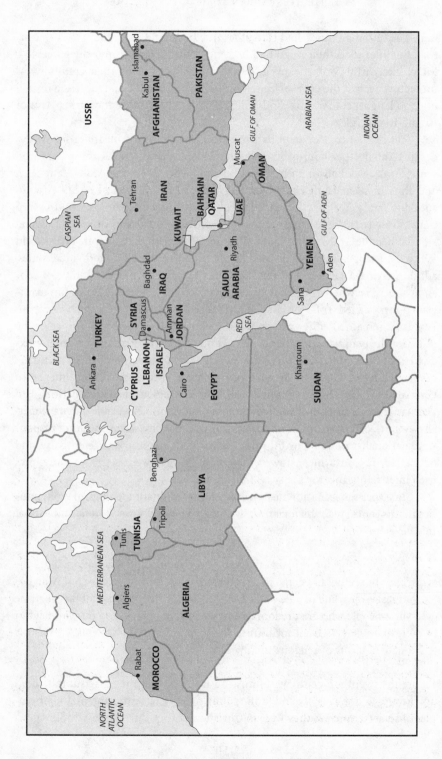

The Middle East and North Africa

tant. The Ottoman Turks had ruled the Arab heartland since the sixteenth century, but after 1800 their reign had become politically and militarily enfeebled. Many thoughtful Arabs believed the Ottomans were losing their credibility as protectors against the encroachments of "infidels," and thus advocated a revival of Arab language, literature, and political activity to restore the earlier days of Arabic-Islamic glory.

Yet the concept of nationalism held more than one meaning for Arabs, causing intellectual confusion and political problems. In its most common sense, Arab nationalism embraced all people who spoke the Arabic language, and thus many nationalists advocated a single state to rule over all Arabic-speaking lands. Yet practical politics ruled out this tantalizing vision of Arab unity, so alternative meanings for nationalism grew up alongside pan-Arabism.

When the Arabs found themselves free of the Ottoman Empire after World War I, the European powers divided up the Arab heartland into individual states, administered as League of Nations mandates. France controlled the states of Lebanon and Syria, whereas Great Britain supervised Iraq, Palestine, and a tiny artificial country called Transjordan. The tribal and religious rulers of the Arabian Peninsula remained either wholly independent, such as the Saudi prince in the center of the peninsula, or at least autonomous under British protection, for example, the emir of Kuwait. Over the years, loyalty to these local states gradually developed, particularly on the part of politicians who had a vested interest in their survival. Thus Syrian, Iraqi, or Saudi local-state nationalism constituted an alternative to an all-embracing pan-Arab nationalism. The Arabic language usually employed the word *umma*, community or people, when speaking of pan-Arab nationalism, and the word *watan*, homeland or country, to refer to the land of one's birth. Confusingly, however, *umma* and *watan* were (and are) sometimes used interchangeably for the two kinds of nation.

In either sense, nationalism has been the dominant ideology of Arab politics in this century. Yet historian C. Ernest Dawn has pointed out the novelty of this development:

> Since 1918 the doctrine that the Arabs are a nation and that nationality is the basis of politics has come to be accepted by a very large majority of Arab political leaders and of at least the lay intellectuals. The espousal of this doctrine by a people who are predominantly Moslem in religion is a development of revolutionary significance, since for many centuries Moslems viewed the state in terms of religion and dynasty.

Before the twentieth century, submission to God (Islam means "submission") and loyalty to one's family and to the ruling dynasty were the organizing principles of society, much as they were in Christian Europe during the Middle Ages.

Even after the appearance of modern nationalism, older loyalties to family dynasties and to the religious realm of Islam remained potent. So Arab politics in the twentieth century has presented a complicated mix of family, religion, and nation. In the two decades after World War I, nearly all the political leaders of Arab Asia spoke in strident pan-Arab tones, calling for the creation of one Arab nation-state; but they acted primarily as local-state politicians, advancing gradually toward the full independence and sovereignty of their own homelands. While doing so, they often drew on the older forces of dynastic loyalty and Islamic religion.

Two dynasties, the Hashemites and the Saudis, vied for preeminence in the Arab heartland. The prophet Muhammad himself had belonged to the clan of Hashim in the city of Mecca, and those Hashemites who can trace their ancestry directly back to the Prophet bear the honorary title *sherif*. A Hashemite sherif has ruled as emir of Mecca in the region of Hejaz since 1073 A.D.; at the time of the First World War, the incumbent emir was Hussein ibn Ali, who had obtained the post in 1908. Hussein's family tree and his position as guardian of the Muslim holy places gave him enormous religious prestige, but the poverty of the Hejaz made him economically dependent on the pilgrim trade to Mecca. Therefore, Hussein's fixed goals after becoming emir were to win as much autonomy from the Ottoman Empire as possible and to expand his rule over the surrounding principalities.

When World War I broke out, Hussein assessed his position carefully before choosing sides. He finally decided that a Turkish defeat and a British victory would best serve the interests of himself and his four sons, so he instigated the Arab revolt in 1916,[2] and his son Feisal eventually led Arab armies all the way to Damascus. Hussein won from the British a promise of an independent state, or a confederation of states, in the Arab rectangle of Asia, and he adopted the rhetoric of Arab nationalism to buttress his cause. Yet his primary goals remained quite traditional — to protect Islam and the holy places and to extend the influence of his family in the surrounding areas. The British reneged on most of their promises after the war, but they did recognize Hussein as king of the Hejaz and admitted his tiny state to the League of Nations as one of its founding members.

Hussein's most dangerous rival in the Arab heartland was the emir of Nejd from the House of Saud in the desert center of the peninsula. Abdul Aziz bin Abdul Rahman al Saud (often called Ibn Saud, or son of Saud, by Europeans and Americans) was a generation younger than Hussein, born in either 1876 or 1880, depending on the source. After his family was expelled from its traditional center of power, the oasis town of Riyadh, young Abdul Aziz recaptured

2. For a detailed narrative of the Arab revolt, see chapter 12 in volume 1.

the city with a daring surprise attack in 1902. For the rest of his life, the Saudi prince loved to retell the story of his return from exile, through the desert with a stalwart band of warriors and on to the storming of Riyadh. Abdul Aziz's odyssey serves as Saudi Arabia's Long March, its founding myth; yet the real source of Saudi power lies in religion. Ibn Saud's kingdom was founded "in the name of God."

A Muslim holy man named Muhammad ibn Abdul Wahhab caught the attention of an earlier Saudi emir in the 1740s and thereafter the House of Saud was dedicated to the spread of the Wahhabi version of Islam. The Wahhabis are puritans, fundamentalists, true believers, who brook no compromise with pagans or infidels, and preach an undiluted monotheism without any glorification of men or saints. They rigidly enforce the Islamic prohibitions against alcohol and tobacco and look with suspicion on most modern inventions. Their faith gives them a missionary zeal that has, over the past two centuries, often driven the Saudi family to spread its rule over much of Arabia.

Abdul Aziz had already conquered the province of al Hasa on the east coast of Arabia and begun negotiations with the British for the recognition of his conquests, when he discovered a new source of power, the religious sect called the *Ikhwan,* or Brotherhood. The *Ikhwan* were a group of bedouin nomads who, under the influence of a revived Wahhabi puritanism, had decided to form settled communities, the better to practice their faith away from the superstitions of the desert. They combined their bedouin warrior mentality with missionary fervor, and by 1917 had founded two hundred settlements with over sixty thousand fighting men. Abdul Aziz placed himself at the head of the *Ikhwan,* using them as his shock troops. In order to demonstrate his conversion to their uncompromising faith, he publicly destroyed his beloved gramophone.

Great Britain recognized the Saudi state in a treaty of December 1915; but in the maelstrom of World War I, the British largely forgot the desert ruler. Instead, they concentrated their attentions upon Hussein, who possessed a more prominent religious position as keeper of the holy places and a strategic location on the Red Sea. Saudi troops, therefore, took no part in the Arab revolt and spent most of the war years consolidating Ibn Saud's rule in Arabia.

When the war ended, the Saudis and the *Ikhwan* immediately threatened Hussein's position in Hejaz. Hussein's second son, Abdullah, was trying to extend Hejazi influence to the interior when his army was attacked by the *Ikhwan* at the town of Turaba, about sixty miles southeast of Mecca. The Muslim Brothers surprised Abdullah's camp at dawn on May 26, 1919, slaughtering most of the Hashemite forces. Abdullah narrowly escaped in only his nightshirt.

The Battle of Turaba revealed the underlying balance of power in the Arab rectangle. The Hashemites had earned great prestige in the world of Arab nationalism, but they were weaker on their home ground than the Saudis. Nei-

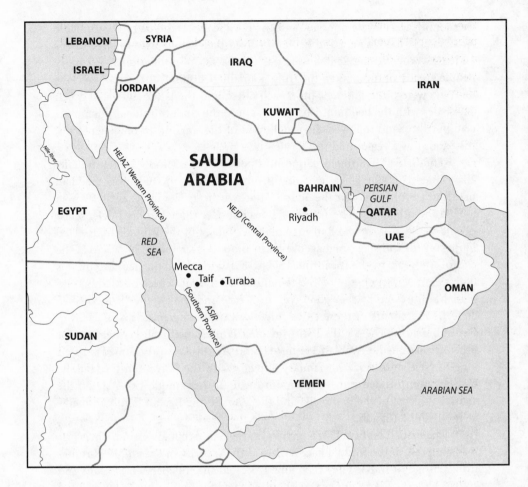

Saudi Arabia

ther family, Hashemite nor Saudi, fit the European stereotype of the nomadic Arab sheikh, for Hussein and his family lived their whole lives in large towns and cities whereas the Saudis were oasis dwellers. In all of Arabia, sedentary people greatly outnumbered the truly nomadic bedouin. Yet Hussein and Abdul Aziz were quite different from each other, and the latter cultivated much closer ties with the bedouin. Hussein practiced the smooth trade of the politician but Ibn Saud followed the rough road of the warrior. In religious terms, the Saudi was a zealot and the Hashemite a prelate.

The British, who held paramount power in the Middle East, gradually abandoned Hussein, since he clung inconveniently to the promises they had made and broken. When the Saudis attacked the Hejaz in 1924, the British looked the other way. The *Ikhwan* massacred over three hundred defenseless people at the hill town of Taif in September 1924, but then Ibn Saud asserted more control and stage-managed a nearly bloodless surrender of Mecca at the end of the year. In the meantime, Sherif Hussein had abdicated, leaving his oldest son, Ali, in charge of the remaining Hashemite cities of Medina and Jeddah. Impressed by the "good cop" of Mecca and fearing the "bad cops" of Taif, the merchants of these cities convinced Ali to surrender a year later, in December 1925. The Saudis had won their contest with the Hashemites for preeminence in the Arabian Peninsula, and Abdul Aziz proclaimed himself king of Nejd and Hejaz on January 8, 1926. With the *Ikhwan* in the lead, he had already rounded out his kingdom through the conquest of Asir on the southwest coast of the peninsula and the lands of the Rashid family immediately north of Riyadh.

The British set firm limits on how far the Saudis could expand. Their primary interest in the Middle East remained the security of sea and land routes from Europe to India. They therefore protected the independent sheikhs and sultans along the Persian Gulf coast and warned the Saudis not to expand too far north and threaten the land route from the Mediterranean to the Tigris and Euphrates valleys. In November 1922, at a conference in the port town of Uqair on the Persian Gulf coast, the British high commissioner, Sir Percy Cox, drew red lines on a map, marking the northern and eastern borders of the Saudi lands. In the rest of the peninsula, however, the Saudis could conquer at will. No one suspected that a huge pool of oil lay under the sands of the Arabian Peninsula, so the British did not care who ruled in the interior. They had already decided to abandon Sherif Hussein.

Once his conquests had reached the limits permitted by the British, Abdul Aziz found the fanatical Brotherhood warriors an embarrassment and a threat. So when the *Ikhwan* rebelled against his authority in 1929, he assembled a large army with a cavalcade of armored cars to crush them. The last of the *Ikhwan* surrendered the following year; and in September 1932, Ibn Saud proclaimed the unification of all his principalities into the Kingdom of Saudi Arabia, within the same borders it still retains today.

Unlike the other territories of Arab Asia, Saudi Arabia was independent in fact as well as in name. It remained desperately poor, however, for oil would not be discovered beneath its sands until 1938. The king relied on the revenue of the pilgrim trade in Mecca, as Hussein had before him, and on meager grants and loans from the British. Ibn Saud often pledged his commitment to the pan-Arab cause, but in practice he preferred to build up his own state before signing on to grandiose schemes of Arab unity. He was a cautious local-state nationalist and a religious zealot with a sense of limits.

The British torpedoed the Hashemite Sherif Hussein's plans for a single Arab state or grand confederation of states throughout Arab Asia and refused to let him live on Arab soil when he went into exile in 1924, confining him instead to the island of Cyprus. However, they did try to conciliate Arab nationalists by doing something for his family. Hussein's oldest son, Ali, was sickly and his youngest son, Zaid, still just a boy; but Abdullah and Feisal, his second and third sons respectively, had played major roles in the Arab revolt. While Abdullah fought the Turks and the Saudis close to home, Feisal led the Arab armies into Damascus and served as his father's major spokesman to the European Allies. A Syrian national congress named him king in Damascus after the war, but the French swiftly deposed him when they took over the Syrian mandate in July 1919. Two years later, the British offered him the throne of Iraq, which lay within their mandate, and Feisal accepted.

In the meantime, Abdullah, who had expected to rule over most of the Arabian Peninsula until the Saudis defeated him at Turaba, turned his attention northward. In September 1920 he traveled up the Hejaz Railway from Medina to the small Jordan valley town of Maan in what was still considered southern Syria at the time. Many nationalist refugees from Damascus had fled there when the French took over, because this southern sliver of desert and river valley had become part of the British mandate. Abdullah's presence was welcomed by the emigré nationalists and created a fait accompli for the British. The colonial secretary, Winston Churchill, decided in 1921 to recognize Abdullah's authority "temporarily for six months" in what historian Elizabeth Monroe has called "the vacant lot which the British christened the Amirate of Transjordan." The Hashemite's temporary stay soon became permanent.

When Europeans label a piece of real estate a "vacant lot" one should normally feel suspicious. After all, the English and Americans dispossessed the North American Indians by proclaiming their lands empty and thus open to colonization. Yet in the case of Transjordan, the adjective "vacant" came quite close to the truth. Abdullah's new domain contained a few small towns and a strip of fertile land along the Jordan River on the west, but the rest of his territory consisted of desert wilderness without any natural boundaries. The British drew some straight lines on a map defining Transjordan's frontiers, primarily to reserve a corridor for an oil pipeline from Iraq to the Mediterranean. In 1921 the new emirate within these artificial borders counted only about 230,000 inhabitants, almost evenly divided between sedentary people and nomads. The capital, Amman, was merely a village of two or three thousand. By the Second World War the country's total population had risen to just 300,000.

The territory across the Jordan River from Palestine, which is what Transjordan means, had never been considered a political or administrative unit before, and its people felt no sense of local-state loyalty. This proved both an advantage and a disadvantage to Abdullah. Lack of local nationalist leadership gave him a free hand, but it also meant he had little to work with. His personal goal remained clear and simple — to get out of Transjordan as soon as possible, back onto the wider Arab stage. In particular, he hoped to win the throne in Damascus that his brother had lost. Yet the weakness of his mini-state and his lack of leverage on the great powers made this goal impossible to attain. In contrast to the Saudis on his southern border, who were warlike and independent, occasionally threatening to overrun his little territory, Abdullah of the Hashemites was totally dependent on the British. Many in the Arab world considered him simply a stooge of the imperialists.

Abdullah's loyalty during World War II did convince the British to declare Transjordan (which now became known simply as Jordan) an independent kingdom, and Abdullah was crowned on May 25, 1946. Yet the treaty confirming Jordan's sovereignty contained a military annex which bound the kingdom very closely to Great Britain. Abdullah still depended heavily on a British monetary subsidy and on the British-controlled Arab Legion for military protection.

While Abdullah simmered in Transjordan, his brother, Feisal, whom he had come to envy, faced a difficult task of nation building in his own new kingdom. The land between the Tigris and Euphrates Rivers, called Mesopotamia by the Greeks and al-Iraq by the Arabs, had been a cradle of civilization centuries and millennia before the time of Christ. Sumerians and Akkadians, Assyrians and Babylonians all built empires in the fertile, irrigated lands between the rivers. Twentieth-century inhabitants of Iraq generally retain little memory of these ancient civilizations, better known to archeologists than to the Islamic masses, but their histories do suggest a rhythm which governs events in the region. Historian Phebe Marr explains:

> The rise and fall of the Akkadian Empire [2400 B.C. to 2200 B.C.] followed a pattern that was to persist in the river valley right up to modern times. Rapid expansion was followed by incomplete assimilation of diverse peoples; inter-

nal rebellions and palace revolutions broke out; and wars on the frontiers and invasions by highlanders finally destroyed the empire.

This historical rhythm of conquest, empire, division, and decline was governed by a historical dilemma. Iraq's agricultural lands required extensive irrigation systems; therefore, the country needed firm and stable government to build, maintain, and protect the dams and canals. Iraq provides a classic example of what historians call a "hydraulic society." Yet the diversity of peoples within the country and its lack of defensible natural boundaries made it unlikely that firm and stable government would persist. Phebe Marr again sums up: "Iraq acquired a reputation that it retains today, of a country difficult to govern."

Feisal faced several specific problems when he was crowned king of Iraq on August 27, 1921. The British had extended the traditional borders of the land between the rivers northward to encompass the desert expanses of al-Jazirah and the mountain highlands bordering on Turkey. Though this territory originally fell within the French mandate, the British insisted on including it for two reasons: oil was suspected in the region around Mosul and Kirkuk in the north, and the mountains would form a more defensible military barrier against Turks and Russians. However logical from the imperial point of view, this expansion of Iraq exposed the new country to the full force of the ancient historical rhythm by adding Kurdish highlanders, Assyrian Christians, and Arab nomads to the Sunni and Shiite Arabs of the cities and more settled agricultural regions.

The Kurds were the most numerous and independent of the non-Arab groups brought under British-Iraqi rule, representing about 20 percent of the mandate's population. An ancient people who lived in the mountains separating the modern states of Turkey, Iraq, and Iran, the Kurds had fought for thousands of years to preserve some sort of autonomy within the empires of more powerful peoples. Primarily Sunni Muslims, they spoke several distinct but related languages, and their society was organized on family and clan lines. At the time of the First World War there were few urban professionals or intellectuals among the Kurds, so they had not yet developed cadres of nationalists as the Arabs had. The Kurds, therefore, were disunited and unable to present a forceful case for national self-determination, so they were parceled out to the various successor states that arose from the wreckage of the Ottoman Empire, including Iraq.

In short, the newly created Iraqi state was divided religiously between Sunnis, Shiites, and Christians; ethnically between Arabs and Kurds; and socioeconomically between tribal nomads and sedentary people. The country had little coherence either geographically or demographically.

Though Feisal was a renowned leader of the Arab revolt, in Iraq he was an outsider, fighting the force of local-state nationalism and subject to the same suspicions of subservience to Great Britain that dogged his brother Abdullah. The British mandate was intensely unpopular in Iraq. Both Arab nomads in the Euphrates Valley and Kurdish villagers around the hill town of Suleimaniya had raised rebellions before Feisal even arrived, and the British spent more money suppressing them than they had provided to Hussein, Feisal, and Lawrence of Arabia during the war. They then imposed Feisal upon the nationalists in Baghdad, spiriting away at least one local leader to exile in far-off Ceylon. The British realized, however, that persistence in such heavy-handed policy would prove far too costly, so they avoided speaking the word "mandate" in Iraq and struck a treaty with Feisal's government to veil their power in the country. The 1922 Anglo-Iraqi Treaty required the king to follow British advice on foreign policy and financial matters and to install British advisors in all major government departments. The treaty was scheduled to remain in effect for twenty years, and at the end of that time nationalists hoped to win their independence.

In fact, a semblance of independence came even sooner. Feisal proved adept at striking a balance between his British masters and the local nationalists in Baghdad. Then in 1927 the Iraq Petroleum Company discovered oil in commercial quantities near Kirkuk, providing a small, but dependable, revenue stream for the government. Meanwhile, the worldwide depression forced the British to cut back their commitments wherever they could. So in 1930 they signed a new Anglo-Iraqi treaty, which formally relinquished the League of Nations mandate, declared Iraq independent, and called for its admission into the League in 1932. This treaty, however, still tied Iraq closely to the British on military and foreign policy matters and granted the Royal Air Force the rent-free use of two air bases in Iraq.

These air bases were crucial parts of the deal, for throughout Asia and Africa between the world wars, British security policy relied heavily on airpower as a cheap and terror-inspiring means for suppressing native rebellions. In Iraq British airpower fell primarily on Kurdish highlanders. RAF bombing destroyed over half the dwellings in seventy-nine Kurdish villages in the early 1930s, illustrating the full horror of air war half a decade before the Nazis leveled Guernica in the Spanish civil war.

Iraq became the first of the Arab mandated states to gain independence, yet after 1932 the country could best be described as an independent state restricted by a British protectorate. The country's internal divisions remained as sharp as ever. The British had used the time-honored tactics of divide and rule, relying heavily on small minority communities, such as the Assyrian Christians, to staff their police force. So shortly after independence, many Assyrians, fearing retribution, tried to flee the country, were turned back at the borders, and then massacred by the Iraqi military. The Kurds had begun developing a

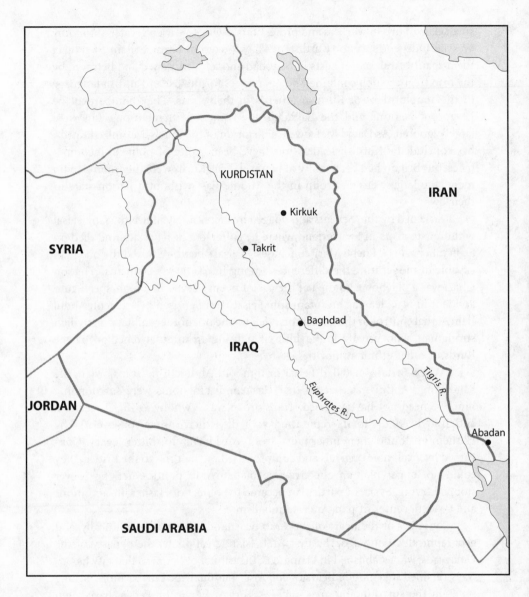

Iraq

small class of urban workers and professionals who espoused greater autonomy or even independence for Kurdistan. They looked to Great Britain to protect them against Arab nationalists in Baghdad and felt threatened and betrayed by the 1930 treaty, which contained no guarantees for the use of Kurdish language or the appointment of Kurdish officials in their areas. They bombarded the League of Nations and the Baghdad government with petitions, but were largely ignored. As David McDowell, a historian of the much-victimized Kurds, has concluded: "Kurdish leaders may have been guilty of political incompetence, but Britain had been guilty of betrayal." The Kurds were then, and remain today, the largest ethnic group in the Middle East without a nation-state of their own.

Sickened by these events and dogged by increasingly ill health, King Feisal withdrew to a spa in Switzerland where he suffered a heart attack and died on September 7, 1933. Phebe Marr concludes: "Feisal's death removed the one man capable of moderating the differences among Iraq's diverse elements." His son Ghazi was a playboy who died at the age of twenty-seven in a high-speed auto accident in 1939, leaving an infant son, Feisal II, supervised by a regent, Abdul Ilah. Actual control of the government fell to one or another military or civilian strongman, who usually found himself fighting an internal rebellion by the Kurds or other ethnic minorities.

When Britain installed Feisal in Iraq and Abdullah in Transjordan, the Saudi king, Abdul Aziz, feared that Hashemite kingdoms were surrounding him. He need not have worried. Transjordan was a wholly artificial creation, and Iraq lived up to its reputation as a difficult country to govern. The Hashemites found their inheritance from World War I a bitter legacy. Consumed by local-state quarrels and compromised by their ties to the British, they could no longer play an effective role in pan-Arab politics. Yet they never stopped trying. Syria, in particular, became the object of Hashemite ambitions and a storm center of pan-Arab nationalism.

Syria lies at the heart of the Arab heartland, historically, politically, and geographically. Long ago, the first Arab-Islamic caliphate, the dynasty of the Umayyads, was established in Damascus, the capital of Syria; so that city has always retained a symbolic primacy for Arab nationalists. Furthermore, strong states in the surrounding area, such as Turkey, Egypt, or Persia, have often struggled to control Syria. As historian Patrick Seale points out: "Syria lies at the center. . . . Whoever would lead the Middle East must control her."

Syria's four major cities, Aleppo, Damascus, Homs, and Hama, gave birth to the leading Arab nationalist associations before World War I, and a sense of pan-Arab unity animated most nationalists when Feisal and the British captured Damascus in 1918. Yet, local-state nationalism developed in the area as well, just as it did in the other Arab states carved out of the Ottoman Empire. This sense of a specifically Syrian nationalism, however, was complicated by uncertainty over how much territory Syria encompassed. Under the Ottomans, the province of Syria embraced the whole region east of the Mediterranean Sea, including the present-day states of Lebanon, Israel, and Jordan. Many Syrian nationalists advocated single statehood for this entire region, a "Greater Syria." The British and the French, however, divided the territory between themselves as separate mandates. The French then proceeded to carve up their mandate even further.

France's primary interest in the Middle East was the Christian minority clustered around the Lebanon mountain range. These snow-clad peaks rise just a few miles back from the Mediterranean seashore, extending for about ninety miles north to south and soaring to heights of over ten thousand feet. They have always served as a refuge for minorities in the Middle East, not only the Maronite Christians but the unorthodox Muslim sect called the Druze. The French had considered themselves protectors of the Christians as far back as the Crusades, but this general interest became more narrowly focused on the Lebanon region of Syria in the nineteenth century when France developed extensive trade and investment networks there. When the French claimed their mandate in the Middle East after World War I, they separated Mount Lebanon from the rest of Syria and then added a larger hinterland to it, creating "Greater Lebanon" with a Christian majority of just 51 percent.[3]

France's invention of a Christian-dominated Lebanese state and its open favoritism toward Christians and other minorities in Syria outraged Arab nationalists, who considered the French mandate even more illegitimate than British rule in Arab Asia. Resentment against the French in Syria came to a head in the Great Revolt of 1925-26, the largest Arab uprising between the world wars. Druze highlanders in their mountain strongholds south of Damascus linked up with urban nationalist leaders to attack the French in the summer of 1925, and by September of that year they had set up a provisional government. The French retaliated savagely, bringing in troops from their African colonies of Morocco and Senegal and arming irregular bands of local minorities. They shelled rebel quarters in Damascus on two different occasions, killing at least a thousand civilians each time and leaving much of the city in ruins. They then surrounded the city with barbed wire and ventured out on "search and destroy" missions into rebel strongholds. The revolt finally petered out at the end of 1926, after 6,000 Syrians had been killed and 100,000 left homeless.

3. At various times during their twenty-year mandate over Syria, the French attempted further administrative divisions, trying to create separate states for other religious minorities such as the Muslim Druze and Alawite sects. Thus, at one time between the world wars, French Syria consisted of five administratively separate states. But by World War II only Lebanon remained separate and the coastal region of Alexandretta had been ceded to Turkey.

Following the failure of the Great Revolt in Syria, moderate nationalists from the upper classes of urban merchants and rural landowners formed a National Bloc and pursued a policy of "honorable cooperation" with the French. They hoped to earn the trust of the mandatory power and gradually assume greater governmental autonomy and self-government. To show their moderation, they abandoned pan-Arab dreams, rebuffed the various overtures from Abdullah of Jordan or Feisal of Iraq to join forces with the Hashemites, and focused their attention on developing a local-state nationalism. However, they nurtured hopes of a Greater Syria, more extensive than the French mandate.

After Iraq gained its limited independence through the Anglo-Iraqi Treaty of 1930, the Syrian National Bloc embarked on a quest for a similar treaty with France. Negotiations during 1933 failed to produce an agreement, primarily due to nationalist claims for a Greater Syria. As the worldwide depression spread misery throughout Syria, as in so many other countries, the National Bloc leaders saw more radical nationalists stir the masses to a new revolt. In January 1936, a general strike of workers, shopkeepers, students, and government employees broke out in Damascus, and the National Bloc swiftly assumed its leadership. Finally, in April 1936 the French ended the strike by reopening treaty negotiations with both Lebanese and Syrian leaders.

Both treaties were completed by the autumn, calling for independence and admission of the new states to the League of Nations, but firmly tying them to France militarily and economically. The French parliament ratified the treaty with Lebanon in November 1936, granting it restricted independence, like Iraq. The Lebanese then worked out a precarious ethno-religious compromise they called their National Pact. Under its unwritten terms, the president of the state of Lebanon would always be a Maronite Christian, the prime minister a Sunni Muslim, and the Speaker of the House a Shiite Muslim. All government offices would be divided in a ratio of six Christians to five Muslims. This pact held the country of Lebanon together for over thirty years until a series of civil wars began to tear it apart in the 1970s.

French hardliners, however, forced a rejection of the Syrian treaty. Unrepentant imperialists in France considered Arab nationalism an artificial creation, stirred up by the British and their stooges the Hashemites during World War I. They judged the proposed treaty a British plot to undermine French interests. Thus, on the eve of World War II, Syrian nationalists had been thwarted and their country remained an unhappy French mandate.

The Second World War, like the First, fundamentally altered the landscape of the Middle East. It threatened the very existence of the two mandatory powers, France and England, pushing them to adopt desperate measures in the Arab rectangle. Hitler's armies overwhelmed France in the spring of 1940 and installed the collaborationist Vichy regime of Marshal Pétain. The Allies could not alter the regime in France until the Normandy invasion of 1944, but elsewhere in the world the British expelled pro-Nazi Vichyites from French colonies. In June and July of 1941, British soldiers combined with a small group of General Charles de Gaulle's Free French forces to take control of Syria and Lebanon. De Gaulle's representative promised independence to both states, but the French stalled and consolidated military control over the region. From the Arab point of view, the Free French proved just as repressive as their pro-Nazi countrymen.

The Syrians and Lebanese eventually attained full independence at the end of the war. In May 1945, as the war wound down in Europe, the French landed colonial Senegalese troops in Beirut, then shelled Damascus one more time, leaving four hundred dead. This outraged the British, who had already recognized Syria and Lebanon as independent states. The British forced the French soldiers back to their barracks in Damascus and virtually compelled the French government to withdraw from the Middle East. At the end of August 1946, all French troops left Syria and Lebanon, ending the French presence at the eastern end of the Mediterranean.

During the war, the British did not tolerate neutral or pro-German Arabs any more than they did the Vichy French. Iraq was the only Arab mandatory state to become independent before the war, but the treaty of 1930 still bound it to British foreign policy. So when Rashid Ali al-Gailani, who wished to remain neutral in the war, was named prime minister at the end of March 1940, British ambassador Kinahan Cornwallis delivered a virtual ultimatum to the Iraqis — dismiss Rashid Ali and join the war effort against Germany or face the consequences. Cornwallis, who had served as advisor to Iraq's Ministry of the Interior for fifteen years under the mandate, still retained the manners and attitudes of an imperial pro-consul.

Cornwallis's ultimatum so inflamed Arab nationalists in Iraq that the regent Abdul Ilah had to flee Baghdad in April 1941 hidden under a pile of Oriental rugs in the back seat of the American ambassador's car. With the constitutional head of state absent, Rashid Ali and his military backers were technically acting outside the constitution by remaining in power. Therefore, the British dubbed their actions the "Rashid Ali coup" and landed troops from India at the port of Basra on April 17 and 18. It was not truly a coup, however, but an attempt to pursue an independent, neutralist foreign policy by a legally appointed government.

With the war going badly elsewhere and the Germans driving east through the Soviet Union towards the Middle East, the British military did not hesitate or worry about diplomatic niceties. On May 2, 1941, without any preliminary negotiations, the Royal Air Force launched a preemptive strike on the Habbaniyyah air base near Baghdad, destroying 60 percent of the Iraqi airplanes on the ground. Such preemptive attacks were common in World War II: Churchill had previously ordered the British navy to bombard a French fleet in Algeria and to torpedo Italian warships lying at anchor in Taranto. All three of these sneak attacks, including the strike on Iraq, occurred before the Japanese raid on Pearl Harbor.

As soon as the fighting began in Iraq, Emir Abdullah of Transjordan ordered the Mechanized Brigade of his Arab Legion to guide a second phalanx of British troops across the desert towards Baghdad. The Legion then cut the major railway north of Baghdad and remained on duty until Rashid Ali's government was toppled. Abdullah hoped that this proof of loyalty to Britain would finally win him a throne in Syria after the war, but neither the Syrians nor the British wanted him in Damascus. Abdullah received his consolation prize in 1946 when Jordan was granted independence and he was crowned king in Amman.

In the short term, Abdullah in Jordan and his Hashemite relatives in Iraq came out on top. The Iraqi regent returned to Baghdad on the heels of the British troops, with the leading pro-British politician, Nuri al-Said, in tow. They chased Rashid Ali into exile, executed many of his followers, and pursued a firmly pro-Allied policy for the rest of the war. Yet in the long run, the suppression of Rashid Ali's government and Hashemite collaboration with the British invasion and occupation of Iraq marked the beginning of the end for the descendants of Sherif Hussein. A disgruntled Palestinian assassinated Abdullah of Jordan on July 20, 1951, but his dynasty survived. His son Talal proved mentally incompetent, so his grandson Hussein became king in 1952 and reigned in Jordan until his death in 1999. His son Abdullah succeeded him as the last of the Hashemite rulers of the Arab world. King Feisal II of Iraq reached his majority in 1953, with the regent still scheming in the background and Prime Minister Nuri al-Said remaining firmly pro-British. Eventually, a 1958 revolution toppled the monarchy, and Feisal II, Abdul Ilah, and Nuri were all murdered.

The British and French presence in the Arab rectangle was quite brief, as imperialist ventures go, and left little behind. The French had never been trusted or respected outside the Christian community of Mount Lebanon, and their departure in 1946 was complete and decisive. The British remained the paramount power in the region for another decade after World War II, despite the independence of their formerly mandated territories, tied closely to Jordan and Iraq by defense treaties. Yet eventually their influence waned and the Cold War rivals, the United States and the Soviet Union, replaced them as the dominant outside influences in the region (see chapter 10).

Considering the importance of oil in the second half of the twentieth century, it is worth emphasizing the minor role petroleum politics played during the mandatory years between the world wars. The first Middle Eastern oil had been discovered in the non-Arab country of Persia (Iran) in 1908, and the British strongly suspected the presence of a large oil field in northern Iraq when they first took up the mandate there after World War I. The drilling company finally brought in a gusher near Kirkuk on October 15, 1927, but the extent of petroleum deposits throughout the Arab lands was unknown. In fact, British geologists felt so certain that no oil would be found on the Arabian Peninsula that they allowed American companies to negotiate exploration rights with King Ibn Saud. Standard Oil of California struck oil on the island of Bahrain, an independent sultanate off the coast of Arabia, in 1932, and finally discovered an immense oil field in the al-Hasa region of Saudi Arabia in 1938.

When the Saudi wells first began flowing, the Middle East as a whole still accounted for only one-twentieth of the world's oil output. The United States remained the largest producer, pumping nearly two-thirds of the world's supply and refining most of the fuel that won the war against Germany and Japan. Great Britain relied on the Western Hemisphere, mainly the United States and Venezuela, for 57 percent of its oil imports in 1938. Only 22 percent came from the Middle East, almost all of it from Iran, not from the Arab states. World War II further slowed the pace of exploration in the Middle East and forced the closure of many wells, lest they fall into the hands of the Germans. When the British suggested in July 1941 that the American government extend Lend-Lease aid to Saudi Arabia until oil production could resume, President Franklin Roosevelt simply scribbled on a memo to an aide: "Will you tell the British, I hope they can take care of the King of Saudi Arabia. This is a little far afield for us."

Attitudes toward Middle Eastern oil changed rapidly, however. Even before the war ended, Roosevelt reversed himself and authorized Lend-Lease shipments to Saudi Arabia, though it was not an ally and was not fighting in the war. Then on February 18, 1944, in a scene reminiscent of Churchill's and Stalin's casual deal dividing up the Balkans into spheres of influence, President Roosevelt told the British ambassador in Washington: "Persian oil is yours. We share the oil of Iraq and Kuwait. As for Saudi Arabian oil, it's ours." No formal oil agreement was ever concluded between the English and Americans and the Arabs soon asserted their own ideas about who really owned the black gold lying under their countries, but Roosevelt's attempted division of spoils indicates the new significance of Middle Eastern oil in world politics. A pioneering American oil engineer accurately predicted in 1944: "The center of gravity of world oil production is shifting from the Gulf-Caribbean area to the Middle East. . . ."

The gravitational shift in oil production held immense consequences for the future, but it played little role in hastening or retarding Arab independence. The oil fields were mainly concentrated around the Persian Gulf in Iran, Iraq, the east coast of Saudi Arabia, and the tiny independent emirates. No oil has ever been discovered in Syria, Lebanon, or Jordan. The British took up mandates in the Middle East, not because of oil, which they could obtain through leases and concessions from independent states, but because they wished to protect the land, sea, and air routes to India, their premier colony in Asia. When India became independent, the British lingered in the Middle East mainly from force of habit. The French remained in Syria and Lebanon as long as they could, also out of habitual, knee-jerk imperialism, and to checkmate the British.

The Arabs did not win their independence from the French and English mandatory powers all at once in a spectacular revolution. Rather they earned it with a series of small revolts, general strikes, and nearly endless negotiations. England and France would have preferred to delay the inevitable as long as possible, but the depression and the Second World War hastened the process.

Though all the Arab states of Asia, except for the tiny emirates along the Persian Gulf, had gained independence by mid-century, only Saudi Arabia's prospects looked attractive. The kingdom was a stable religious autocracy with immense untapped oil wealth. The Saudi monarchy had captured the attention of the United States and proceeded to play the Americans off against the British, in the process winning monetary benefits and the freedom to maneuver. Lebanon preserved its tenuous ethnic and religious balance and enjoyed a measure of prosperity for several decades after the war, but eventually succumbed to its own internal divisions. Syria and Iraq experienced a long series of military coups, counter-coups, and dictatorships. Little Jordan under the last Hashemite remained generally stable, but unimportant.

In the years immediately after the Second World War, two major historical events mobilized a new generation of Arab nationalists. The creation of a Jewish state in the Arab heartland enraged Arabs in all the states surrounding it (see chapter 9), and the seizure of power by a radical clique of army officers in Egypt (see chapter 10) inspired hopes for a transformed social order throughout the region. The moderate, accommodationist politics of the first generation of Arab nationalists largely ended with independence. The older style of religious and family leadership persisted in Saudi Arabia and the small emirates but not elsewhere in the Arab rectangle. The Hashemites and their contemporaries proved to be transitional figures, between the traditional politics of family and religion and the new style of secular, militant nationalism. The new nationalists, like the old, spoke in pan-Arab terms, but even they acted primarily as local-state leaders. All the Arab states shared a fear of Zionism and a hatred for Israel, the settler state that had grown up in their midst, but even these powerful negative forces could not unite them politically.

CHAPTER NINE

A Settler Colony with a Difference

The colonies claimed by European powers over the past few centuries fell into two fundamentally different categories. Most, such as British India, the Dutch East Indies, or French Indochina, were conquered primarily for their natural resources and cheap labor, and were ruled by a mere handful of European soldiers and administrators. Few Europeans settled permanently, or for very long, in these extractive colonies. Yet in a number of cases, impoverished or persecuted settlers from the imperial mother country found a colony attractive for permanent settlement and emigrated in substantial numbers. British North America, which became the United States and Canada, furnishes the classic examples of settler colonies, where the immigrants eventually outnumbered and displaced the indigenous inhabitants. In Africa and Asia, where the climate seemed less congenial to Europeans, settler colonies were fewer in number and more sparsely settled, but they did exist. Algeria, South Africa, and Kenya are notable examples; and in a tiny corner of southwestern Asia called Palestine, a settler colony with a difference, *Eretz Israel* (the land of Israel), grew up alongside the native Arab population.

In all settler colonies, the European immigrants tried to create new lives for themselves with little thought for the indigenous inhabitants. Encounters with the natives, when not openly hostile, were steeped in ethnocentrism. European settlers believed they were actually doing the natives a favor by cultivating the land more intensively, introducing new methods of agriculture and industry, and creating more wealth. Yet historian Ann Moseley Lesch astutely points out:

> In practice, however, the settlers tended to be less benevolent than acquisitive, exerting pressure on the home government to grant them valuable land and

mineral resources and to obtain a predominant role in government. The economic advance of the local population was often delayed, and their economic
requirements were subordinated to those of the settlers.

An analogy with contemporary American life may help clarify the immi-
grant/native conflict in settler colonies. In the late twentieth century, young
white suburbanites have begun moving back to selected neighborhoods in cities such as New York or Chicago. These so-called yuppies, young urban professionals, often buy old two- or three-family dwellings from absentee landlords
who had been renting them to African-American, Latino, or working-class
white families. The newcomers are not hostile to the existing tenants, yet inevitably they displace the poorer inhabitants by renovating their buildings, raising
rents, or moving their own extended families into the dwellings. Eventually,
they "gentrify" the neighborhood, raising its socioeconomic profile. City governments benefit from the increases in their property tax rolls, but low-income
city dwellers are forced to compete for a dwindling stock of affordable housing.
Much the same processes are at work in settler colonies but on a larger scale.
The imperial government favors the "gentrifying" of its colonies, which makes
them more economically productive and less of a burden on the mother country. The natives are left to look after themselves and are presumed to benefit
from the trickle-down economic effects of the settler society.

Such a gentrification took place in Palestine in the late nineteenth and
early twentieth centuries, but with several significant differences from other
settler colonies. First, the settlers were not immigrants from the imperial
mother country (Great Britain), but Jews from Central and Eastern Europe.
Furthermore, these immigrants were not entering what they considered a new
land, but rather a very old, very hallowed territory their ancestors had inhabited
thousands of years before. The Jews were not just looking for real estate, but
were reclaiming what they believed to be the Holy Land. The Arabs who lived in
Palestine also considered parts of it holy. Al-Aqsa Mosque in Jerusalem was the
third most revered site in the world of Islam, the place from which the prophet
Muhammad ascended to heaven. Finally, the settlers were encouraged, not just
by the imperial ruler, but also by a mandate from the League of Nations. Under
British and international protection, therefore, the state of Israel gradually took
shape as Jews from Europe gentrified a holy neighborhood they considered
their own, but which already had an Arab population. The result was one of the
most intractable conflicts of the twentieth century.

Though expelled from Israel by the Romans nearly two thousand years
ago and dispersed throughout Europe and the Mediterranean world, Jews never
completely disappeared from their original homeland. Tolerated by the Arabs
and the Ottoman Turks, about five or six thousand Jews remained in Palestine

in 1800, most of them highly orthodox religionists who lived near the holy places of Jerusalem. In the late nineteenth century, however, the rise of European nationalism revealed to the persecuted Jews of Eastern Europe that they could regain their dignity and status as a people if they built a nation-state of their own. The Austrian journalist Theodor Herzl launched the Zionist movement with his book *Der Judenstaat* (The Jewish State) in 1896, and a series of congresses beginning the following year gave the movement political momentum. Not all Zionists insisted that the Jewish nation-state be in the ancient land of Israel. In fact, the British government in 1903 offered Herzl some land in present-day Kenya as a possible Jewish colony, but the Zionist organization finally turned down the offer. If Jews had accepted the Kenyan solution, they would have confronted all the usual conflicts of any settler colony, but by holding out for Israel/Palestine, they created a settler colony with a difference, one that was considered holy ground.

Between 1882 and 1903, 25,000 Jews fled the increasingly frequent pogroms of Russia and emigrated to Palestine. The Ottoman Empire did not officially permit such immigration, but government corruption and inefficiency made it easy to evade restrictions. By 1914, about 85,000 Jews lived in Palestine, more than 10 percent of the area's total population of 790,000, representing a higher proportion of Jews than in any other country of the world.

Great Britain assumed responsibility for the Jewish settlements of the Middle East with the issuance of the Balfour Declaration on November 2, 1917, in the midst of World War I.[1] Motivated by both a strong sympathy for Zionism and by hardheaded strategic considerations, Britain's wartime leaders decided to retain control of Palestine after liberating it from the Ottoman Empire. The Balfour Declaration stated: "His Majesty's Government view with favour the establishment in Palestine of a national home for the Jewish people . . . , it being clearly understood that nothing shall be done which may prejudice the civil and religious rights of existing non-Jewish communities in Palestine. . . ." The dual obligation implied by this statement, to foster and protect both Jews and non-Jews (the statement did not use the word "Arabs") in the same country, ultimately proved impossible.

Some Jews and Englishmen believed that Palestine was a virtually empty land, a kind of Wild West they could settle, but most knew better. A census in 1922 revealed that the territory had an Arabic-speaking population of 668,000 people, mostly Muslims but including about 71,000 Christians as well. Jews numbered 83,000, about 11 percent of the population. Palestine was far from uninhabited, but it appeared politically empty to Great Britain. Never a self-

1. See chapter 12 of volume 1 for a fuller description of early Zionism and the Balfour Declaration.

governing political entity, Palestine had been divided by the Ottoman Turks into two provinces, one ruled from Beirut and the other from Jerusalem. Many Arabs still considered it a part of Greater Syria, with its metropolis in Damascus. To Europeans, it looked like Palestine had fallen through the cracks of the Ottoman Empire and was ripe for reorganization. As historian Christopher Sykes has pointed out: "One reason why the authors of the [Balfour] Declaration went ahead with their policy was that they believed . . . that Palestine was one of the only places in the world where it could safely be put into operation." They were wrong. In the twentieth century, the world was already too crowded for the insertion of one national group into the territory of another.

Having assumed an impossible and contradictory task, the British strove to pursue an "equality of obligation" toward both the embryonic Jewish national home and the indigenous Palestinian Arab population. Sir Herbert Samuel, an English Jew, took office as the first British high commissioner for Palestine on July 1, 1920. This might seem to favor the Jews, but in fact Samuel disappointed the Zionist leadership with his evenhandedness. His successor in 1925, Field Marshall Lord Plumer, was one of the few English generals who had gained in reputation during the First World War, and he adopted an even more Olympian, above-the-fray attitude toward Arabs and Jews.

Yet for all their attempts at fairness, the British felt closer to the European Jews than they did to the Arabs, and the politics of the mandate were steeped in ethnocentrism. Theodor Herzl had described his proposed Jewish state as "part of a wall of defense for Europe in Asia, an outpost of civilization against barbarism." Much later, at a time of Arab violence against Jews, the English Zionist leader Chaim Weizmann declaimed: "On one side, the forces of destruction, the forces of the desert, have risen, and on the other stand firm the forces of civilization and building. It is the old war of the desert against civilization." Most British Gentiles put a slightly different twist on the contrast. Like Lawrence of Arabia, many English citizens viewed the nomadic Arabs of the desert as "clean," but the "levantine" Arabs of Palestine and other Mediterranean coastal areas as corrupt and oily. Both the British and the Jews characterized the Palestinians as a mass of ignorant *fellaheen* (peasants) exploited by a tiny landowning class of *effendis* (honorable gentlemen). They believed the masses of Arabs would be better off in the long run through contact with progressive European settlers, such as the Jews.

The Palestinian Arabs, for their part, felt convinced that Jewish money and English cunning had hatched a gigantic conspiracy encircling the globe. On a more personal level, many Muslim Arabs found the Jewish women who worked in agricultural communes and strolled arm-in-arm with their husbands in the streets of the cities, profoundly shocking and immoral.

These ethnocentric stereotypes had some basis in reality. A landowning and officeholding class of urban notables had developed in Palestine, just as in other regions of the Ottoman Empire, but the mass of Arab peasants were illiterate and poverty stricken. In 1931, for example, 93.4 percent of Jewish males could read and write, compared to 25.1 percent of Muslim males. Jews enjoyed a further linguistic advantage, for over two thousand of them could speak Arabic in 1931 whereas only twenty-one Arabs in Palestine could speak Hebrew. Jews were not all wealthy, as anti-Semitic myth proclaimed, but Zionism was a worldwide movement that collected donations, large and small, from Jewish philanthropists and workers alike. Historian Kenneth Stein summarizes the contrast between the Arabs and Jews in Palestine quite accurately: "The Zionists did not have vast resources at their command, but they were skilled, schooled, and able to purchase a nucleus for a state. The Palestinian Arabs, in contrast, suffered from severe deprivation, a lack of capital, and less-clear-cut goals."

During the three decades that Great Britain administered Palestine as a mandate, the conflict between Arabs and Jews revolved around three major issues: immigration, land, and political power. Immigration always remained the most explosive, for shiploads of Jews unloading in the port cities of Haifa and Jaffa were highly visible. Sir Herbert Samuel first showed that he would not overly favor the Jews when he temporarily suspended Jewish immigration after some Arab-Jewish riots in Jaffa in May 1921. Even when immigration resumed, however, it did not overwhelm the country's absorptive capacity during the decade of the 1920s. Jewish arrivals averaged about 8,000 per year from 1920 to 1923, then rose to a sharp peak of 34,000 in 1925 due to anti-Semitic policies in Poland that forced many Jews out. The numbers swiftly fell, however, averaging fewer than 5,000 a year from 1928 to 1931. In one year, 1927, more Jews left Palestine than entered it. The 1931 census found that both Arab and Jewish populations had grown, with the Jews then numbering 174,000 (17 percent).

The overwhelming majority of Jewish immigrants settled in cities and towns. In fact, they created a whole new city, Tel Aviv, out of a garden suburb of Jaffa. Nevertheless, some of the most idealistic Zionists believed it important for Jews to settle upon and work the land. Jews had been barred from land ownership in Russia, eking out their livings primarily as craftsmen, shopkeepers, and peddlers. Even the poorest Russian or Polish peasants ridiculed Jewish men, looking down on them since they did not till the soil. Zionists, therefore, determined to earn new respect and dignity by becoming farmers in Israel. Much of the philanthropic money gathered by Zionists went into the Jewish National Fund for land purchases. Like modern-day yuppies moving into a rundown neighborhood, they usually found willing sellers, either absentee landlords living in Beirut or Damascus, or else local notables who owned extensive estates outside their towns or cities. Right at the beginning of the mandate period, in 1919, the Jewish National Fund purchased a huge tract of land in the Jezreel Valley of Galilee, running about forty miles from the coastal mountains through the hill country of the interior. Settlers drained swamps and built roads in the valley, establishing numerous collective farms, or *kibbutzim.*

For convenience, the Jewish land-purchase agencies preferred to buy large tracts of land from small numbers of sellers. They also made every effort to have the existing Arab tenant farmers evicted from the land before purchase, usually providing compensation payments that were difficult to refuse but quickly spent once the former tenants became landless. Masses of Arabs, therefore, were displaced from the land, either migrating to the outskirts of cities to work as casual laborers or else doubling up with relatives in the less fertile hill country of Judea and Samaria. A gradual internal partition of Palestine took place in the 1920s and 1930s through the operation of the economic marketplace. Jews became more concentrated in the cities, the agricultural areas of the coastal plain, and the Jezreel Valley, whereas Arabs were pushed back into what later became known as the West Bank of the Jordan.

Two parallel societies developed in Palestine, competing for the attention of the mandatory authority and aiming at a monopoly of political power. Zionists organized a quasi-government, the Jewish Agency Executive, to manage their own affairs; and they founded their own labor union, Histadrut, a system of Hebrew-language schools, and a Hebrew university on Mount Scopus in Jerusalem. Histadrut even mobilized a self-defense militia, the Haganah, which the British officially deplored but privately tolerated. Historian Ann Moseley Lesch has summed up the growth of the Jewish *Yishuv* (settlement) in Palestine: "As the Jewish community grew from 11 percent of the population in 1922, to 16 percent in 1931, and to 28 percent in 1936, an immigrant could live entirely within a Jewish area, dependent in no respect on the Arab majority and coming into only incidental contact with Arabs." Sociologists of immigration call this phenomenon "institutional completeness."

The Arabs, on the other hand, relied on the traditional leadership of the urban notables, who reorganized administrative mechanisms they had inherited from the Ottoman Empire and established new, nationalist associations. Muslim-Christian associations sprang up immediately after the First World War to protest the growing Jewish immigration and establish liaisons with the British. At first they followed a Greater Syria policy, advocating union with King Feisal's regime in Damascus, but after the French expelled Feisal and took over in Syria, the Arabs of Palestine largely abandoned the Greater Syria ideal and focused on local concerns. The Muslim-Christian associations held periodic congresses and established the Arab Executive to negotiate with the British, but they were hampered by sharp rivalries between the leading families of notables and did not forge as united a political community as the Jews did.

Just as important as these Arab nationalist associations were the religious office of mufti and the Supreme Muslim Council, reestablished by the British in January 1922 to oversee the spending of Muslim charitable funds and control the religious courts. Following an old Ottoman procedure, a college of notables held an election for mufti of Jerusalem in April 1921. This post had generally been held by a member of the Husseini family, but Amin al-Husseini, the scion of the family, came in fourth in the balloting. The British high commissioner was supposed to choose from among the top three candidates, but through deft manipulation, Sir Herbert Samuel convinced one candidate to withdraw and then selected al-Husseini.

Muhammad Amin al-Husseini was born in Jerusalem in 1895, and when he made the pilgrimage to Mecca with his mother in 1913 he acquired the customary title *Hajj* or *al-Hajj.* Both his father and his older brother served as mufti, but rivalry with the Nashashibi family produced the contested election of 1921 and British intervention. Amin was an Arab nationalist who took part in the violent religious demonstrations of April 1920 and escaped into exile with bedouin tribes across the Jordan. He and a number of other Arab and Jewish agitators were pardoned, and during the May 1921 riots in Jaffa, the Husseini family conspicuously kept the peace in Jerusalem. This probably influenced Herbert Samuel to come down on their side in the mufti elections, held contemporaneously with the riots.

Throughout the 1920s inter-communal rivalry between Arabs and Jews halted political development in Palestine but remained relatively muted and peaceful. No further rioting or violence broke out for seven years after the disturbances of May 1921. The mufti of Jerusalem devoted himself to religious works, establishing a Muslim orphanage, repairing schools, and opening a library and museum in the Haram al-Sharif, the holy precinct surrounding al-Aqsa Mosque and the Dome of the Rock. He launched a fundraising drive throughout the Muslim world, gathering enough money to restore al-Aqsa and gold-plate the impressive Dome of the Rock.

The mufti was a believer in the pan-Arab cause who verbally denounced the Zionists and championed Palestinian independence, but throughout the 1920s he remained preoccupied with his religious duties and observed a tacit truce with the British. The Arab Executive, under the presidency of an older relative of the mufti's, Musa Kazim al-Husseini, took the lead in political agitation and negotiation. In a December 1920 congress, the Palestinian Arabs laid out the basic demands to which they adhered for the next two decades: a renunciation of the Balfour Declaration by Britain; independence for Palestine; an end to Jewish immigration until the independent state could set its own immigration policy; and federation of Palestine with the neighboring Arab states. When the British mandatory authorities tried to set up a more normal government for the territory, proposing an elected legislative council to advise the high commissioner, the Arab Executive rejected the proposal and refused to take part in elections. The British high commissioner therefore scrapped the council plan in 1923 and ruled by decree for the rest of the mandate. In this, as in so many other ways, Palestine remained a colony with a difference.

Arab rejection of the legislative council may seem puzzling and short-sighted, for the Arabs formed an overwhelming majority of the population and would dominate any elected body. However, participation in a British-sponsored government would bestow legitimacy on the mandatory regime and the Balfour Declaration, and the Arab leadership refused to do this. The non-cooperation strategy illustrates a political dilemma facing the Palestinian Arabs. If they joined a council with only advisory powers, they would recognize the regime while gaining little in return. If they refused participation, they would seem intransigent and the British would naturally rely more heavily on the Jewish community.

In the 1930s, the Arab leadership judged it had made a tactical blunder and signaled its willingness to join a legislative council, but this time the Jewish Agency torpedoed the scheme. Though still a minority in Palestine, the Jews demanded "parity" on any elected council, claiming that their economic strength equaled that of the Arabs, even if their numbers did not. Gandhi's strategy of boycott and non-participation worked in India because the British eventually became exhausted and went home. Such a strategy failed in Palestine because it was a settler colony, and an unusual one at that. The Jewish settlers had no intention of leaving, for they had no mother country to which to return. Instead, they hoped to stall political development until they became a majority and could dominate the state.

Given the political stalemate in Palestine, it was only a matter of time before violence erupted. Religious disagreements finally lit the fuse in 1928 and 1929. The Western Wall of the Muslim shrine in Jerusalem, the Haram al-Sharif, is also the only surviving portion of the Jewish Temple of Herod, destroyed by the Romans. The area surrounding the wall was a residential quarter, owned by a Muslim charitable trust or *waqf*. Traditionally, pious Jews would come to the Western Wall (also called the Wailing Wall by Gentiles) to pray and lament the unhappy fate of their people. Over the centuries, the Arabs had permitted this Jewish devotion, but disputes often broke out over such trifles as the bringing of benches or chairs for Jews to sit on while praying. Christopher Sykes has sarcastically summed up the explosiveness of Jerusalem: "In one city of three great religions . . . almost invariably the disputants fly to arms because someone has placed a venerable lamp on an unagreed lampstand, or has moved a venerable stone, or has opened a venerable door, or has said his prayers in some venerable place where someone else claimed exclusive rights." On September 24, 1928, the Jewish Day of Atonement (Yom Kippur), such a dispute touched off a protracted conflict in Jerusalem.

Jewish worshipers erected a screen in the street next to the Western Wall, in order to separate men from women as was customary in orthodox synagogues. The Arabs protested this deviation from the usual routine at the wall, and the British police ordered the screen removed. Over the next six days, the Zionists organized protests and demonstrations against the insult to Jewish worshipers. The mufti of Jerusalem became alarmed, fearing the Jewish protests signaled a campaign to assert ownership of the Western Wall. He therefore launched a propaganda assault against the Jews lasting almost a year after the Yom Kippur incident. With British approval, he stepped up the renovation work on the Haram al-Sharif, disrupting Jewish prayers next to the Western Wall.

The Wailing Wall war of nerves finally erupted into violence in August 1929, when a corps of tough-looking bodyguards carrying sticks accompanied Jewish worshipers to the wall. Rumors spread through the Arab quarters that the Jews were planning to seize the Haram al-Sharif by force. A letter with the forged signature of the mufti circulated through the countryside, calling Arabs into Jerusalem to protect the holy places. Then on August 23, 1929, Arabs began attacking and killing Jews in Jerusalem; the Jews fought back, and the violence spread to other cities. A total of 133 Jews and 116 Arabs were killed in the rioting.

A petty religious dispute prompted the 1929 riots, but if it had not been a screen in the street, something else would eventually have sparked a conflagration. The Arab and Jewish communities were jostling for space in the same narrow confines and were bound to bump into each other. The mufti, Hajj Amin al-Husseini, was widely blamed for inciting the violence, but a British investigatory commission found no direct evidence to indict him. In fact, he was scrambling to keep up with popular outrage more than he was leading it. For the next decade, Palestinian Arabs faced another political dilemma, just as intractable as the participation-versus-boycott dilemma of the previous decade. If the Arabs engaged in violence, as they increasingly did in the 1930s, they could gain attention from the British and possibly force concessions. Yet the more they attacked the Jews with force, the more they stimulated the Jewish community to consolidate its institutional power and build up the Haganah as a clandestine army. Violence proved as self-defeating as non-cooperation in the long run. The Arabs found themselves in a no-win situation. A settler community enjoys decisive advantages that neither violence nor non-violence can easily overcome.

Throughout the violent decade of the 1930s, British policy became less evenhanded and began to oscillate like a pendulum, from pro-Arab to pro-Jewish and back again. Christopher Sykes has detected a pattern underlying the oscillations. After a disturbance in Palestine, the British government sent out a royal commission to study the problem. The commission's recommendations led to more studies and then finally a "White Paper" (a public statement of official policy). If the policy appeared too pro-Arab, Zionist lobbying in London prompted modifications; if it favored the Jews, Arab violence forced a reassessment. The British never did settle on a consistent policy, but the various commissions did explore nearly the full range of possible solutions to Arab-Jewish conflict. Their failure to satisfy the two sides illustrates how impossible the problem was.

The first royal commission, chaired by Walter Shaw, a retired colonial official, followed the Wailing Wall riots. The Shaw Commission report of March 31, 1930, concluded, unsurprisingly, that the fundamental cause of the disturbances was the "Arab feeling of animosity and hostility towards the Jews." To the distress of the Zionists, however, it recommended that immigration and land purchase policies be restricted in order to lessen Arab hostility. An intensive study of the land problem by another retired civil servant concluded that 29.4 percent of Arab families had become landless since the beginning of the mandate. This led to the publication of a White Paper on October 21, 1930, implementing restrictions on land purchase by Jews. Lobbying by Chaim Weizmann and other English Zionists proved so intense, however, that the government backed down within a few months. On February 13, 1931, Prime Minister Ramsay MacDonald issued a public letter to Weizmann, largely written by the Zionists themselves, officially "clarifying," but actually repudiating, the policy of the White Paper. It reaffirmed the Balfour Declaration and encouraged further Jewish immigration and settlement in Palestine. The Arabs immediately branded MacDonald's statement the "black letter."

In the next few years, external forces exacerbated relations between Arabs and Jews in Palestine. Hitler became chancellor of Germany in 1933, and his rabid anti-Semitism imparted a new urgency to Jewish immigration plans. From just 4,075 immigrants in 1931, the numbers rose swiftly to 42,359 in 1934. By 1936, the Jewish population of Palestine numbered 370,000, about 28 percent of the total. After the 1930 White Paper scare, the Zionists had started planning their land purchases with strategic goals in mind, consolidating control over contiguous tracts and purchasing marginal land that could act as buffers for Jewish settlements. At the same time, the worldwide economic depression combined with severe droughts and insect plagues to devastate Palestinian Arab agriculture. A fall in wheat prices increased the landlessness and indebtedness of the peasantry, and the increasing Jewish presence in Palestine made for a convenient scapegoat. Ironically, the one agricultural sector where prices held firm was the citrus industry, largely controlled by Jewish farmers on the coastal plain.

Arab youth groups and secret societies proclaimed a general strike on April 19, 1936, just as a similar strike was winding down in neighboring Syria. This caught the mufti and the other urban notables off guard, for the Arab Executive had ceased to exist and numerous competing political parties had sprung up in its wake. The older leadership immediately gathered and, temporarily shelving their personal and party differences, formed the Arab Higher Committee to channel the largely spontaneous general strike. Hajj Amin al-Husseini was elected president. After a summer of violence, the committee arranged a face-saving termination of the strike. The kings of neighboring Arab countries publicly called for another royal commission to study the situation, and in return the Arab Higher Committee called off the strike on October 12, 1936.

The commission, chaired by Lord Robert Peel, arrived in Palestine in November of 1936 and the following July produced the most thorough study of Arab-Jewish relations ever conducted under the British mandate. The six commissioners recommended a reduction in Jewish immigration to twelve thousand annually over the next five years and the prohibition of land sales in certain parts of the country. They candidly admitted, however, that such palliatives would probably do little to reduce tensions. Therefore, at the prompting of one of its members, Professor Reginald Coupland of Oxford, the Peel Commission laid out a radical alternative — an end to the British mandate and a partition of Palestine into two states, one Arab and one Jewish. Coupland theorized that two peoples with a well-developed national consciousness could not live peaceably together in one state. Unfortunately, the history of the twentieth century amply supports his thesis.

The Peel Commission produced detailed maps defining a Jewish state encompassing most of Galilee and the coastal plain, and an Arab state on the West Bank of the Jordan and in the Negev Desert. They recommended that Great Britain retain control of Jerusalem and a few other strategic enclaves, in order to protect the holy places and ensure peace in the region. The proposed partition closely followed the demographic shape of Palestine as determined by Jewish land purchases and internal migration of Arabs over the previous decades. However, population movements never prove as tidy as mapmakers would like them to be. Over 200,000 Arabs would remain as a minority in the proposed Jewish state. The Peel Commission suggested that they be removed to the Arab state, by force if necessary. This draconian recommendation followed the example of the forced Greek-Turkish population exchange imposed by Kemal Ataturk after World War I.

Zionists disagreed about the implications of the Peel Report. A majority probably felt disappointed at the tiny size of the proposed Jewish state, but Chaim Weizmann and the important labor leader in Palestine, David Ben-Gurion, judged that official recognition of a Jewish state, no matter how small, was worth seizing. Looking into the future, they believed that Zionists could later expand the nucleus of the Jewish state. When someone complained to Ben-Gurion at the "loss" of the Negev in the Peel Report, the labor leader replied: "It's not going anywhere." The Zionist Congress in 1937, therefore, ex-tended cautious approval to the Peel Report.

The Arab Higher Committee, however, totally rejected the scheme. Pales-tinian Arab leaders had never admitted the legitimacy of the Balfour Declara-tion and the fostering of a Jewish national home, and they were appalled at the idea of a Jewish state in their midst. The British attempted to arrest Amin al-Husseini for his intemperate denunciations of the report, but they bungled the job and the mufti took refuge in the Haram al-Sharif. In October 1937 he es-caped into exile in neighboring Lebanon, where the French were happy to em-barrass the British by keeping him under house arrest but allowing him to lead the Higher Committee in absentia.

In the meantime, a full-scale Arab revolt had broken out in Palestine. Par-tition, though seeming equitable to the British and other outsiders, meant the permanent loss of nearly half of Palestine to alien settlers. Arab nationalists in Galilee took the lead, for they faced the most drastic consequences if the Peel Report's deportation scheme were implemented. On September 26, 1937, Arabs murdered the British district commissioner in Nazareth. The British govern-ment immediately declared a state of emergency and outlawed the Arab Higher Committee. Though the mufti escaped, several of his colleagues were deported to the remote Seychelles Islands in the Indian Ocean. Nevertheless, Arab guer-rilla bands roamed unchecked over large parts of the country in the spring and summer of 1938. Rebels occupied the Old City of Jerusalem and the largely Arab city of Jaffa, cutting the road between Jerusalem and the Mediterranean. The British brought in reinforcements and finally regained control by the end of 1938, ruthlessly demolishing Arab houses, detaining thousands of suspects without trial, and hanging over a hundred rebels. They also armed thousands of Jewish auxiliaries to aid in the pacification of the country.

Nevertheless, British confidence had been shaken by the violence and the government now backed off from its partition scheme. Yet another White Paper was issued in May 1939, promising independence to a single state of Palestine within ten years. Jewish immigration would be limited to 10,000 per year for the next five years, plus an extraordinary admission of 25,000 Jewish refugees for humanitarian reasons. After five years, no further Jewish immigration would be permitted unless the Arabs consented. The White Paper's immigra-tion policy ensured that the independent Palestine which would emerge in the future would have an Arab majority. The Arab revolt had succeeded in its major aim of halting the creation of a Jewish state. Yet the Arab victory proved tempo-rary, as historian Ann Moseley Lesch explains: "Violence proved to be a double-edged weapon: although useful to pressure the colonial power, it accelerated the mobilization of the rival national movement and thus further undermined the position of the indigenous group."

World War II hit the Middle East with cataclysmic force, even though the area east of the Suez Canal saw little fighting. The Holocaust destroyed two-thirds of the Jews of Europe and impelled the survivors to seek places of refuge. Tragically, the United States, Great Britain, and other opponents of Nazi Germany refused to take in large numbers of Jewish refugees, so they inevitably looked to Palestine. In retrospect, the enormity of the Holocaust would seem to create a moral presumption in favor of the Zionist enterprise in Palestine. Yet the Arabs responded with an unanswerable argument of their own. Christian Europeans had committed genocide against the Jews, yet other Christian nations were unwilling to take in the survivors, insisting instead that Muslim Arabs provide a safe haven. Christopher Sykes, a British historian with strong sympathies for Zionism, nevertheless concludes: "The Arab case against Palestine as the answer to Hitler was strong. It should be remembered."

Neither Arab objections nor British attempts to control immigration could stop the final exodus of Jews to Palestine and the creation of the state of Israel. In 1935 the international Zionist Congress had elected the militant labor unionist David Ben-Gurion chairman of the Jewish Agency Executive, relegating the more moderate English Zionist Chaim Weizmann to the largely honorary post of president. Symbolically and realistically Zionist power had passed from the Diaspora to the Yishuv. The leaders of the settler colony had outgrown their overseas sponsors.

David Ben-Gurion was born David Grin on October 16, 1886, to a moderately prosperous but politically radical family in a small town of Russia. Just short of his twentieth birthday, in August 1906, he emigrated to Palestine on a Russian cargo ship; soon afterward he adopted a new name, taken from one of the last defenders of Israel against the Romans. He spent much of World War I in exile in the United States but immediately after the war helped found the Jewish labor union, Histadrut. This organization was more of a political party than a labor union, and in fact it created an all-embracing way of life for Jewish workers, with a complete roster of social, intellectual, welfare, and even military groups. Ben-Gurion was well versed in Marxism and admired Lenin for his ruthless decisiveness, but he always put his Zionist political aims ahead of class consciousness. He lived by the motto: "We must make a nation of the class we represent."

When World War II broke out, Ben-Gurion proclaimed a two-fold policy for the Jews of Palestine: "We will make war [with the British, against Hitler] as though there were no White Paper, and we will fight the White Paper as though there were no war." Unlike the Middle Eastern Arabs, who remained largely neutral during the war or even tilted toward the German side out of hatred for the English, Jews needed no urging from Ben-Gurion to oppose Hitler. Zionists tried to organize their own Jewish brigade, but lack of supplies and resistance within the British government stalled this plan until the war's final year. In the meantime, ten to fifteen thousand Jews simply joined the British army.

The second half of Ben-Gurion's dictum, fighting the White Paper as if there were no other war going on, proved more significant in the long run. Even before World War II, the Jewish Agency had approved Ben-Gurion's plan for an "immigration rebellion," that is, mass illegal immigration to Palestine in defiance of British policy. Ben-Gurion planned open, not clandestine, immigration as a political act of resistance against the British, even more than a humanitarian activity. Relatively few Jews were saved by the "immigration rebellion" but the operation admirably served its political purpose. After the war, when Britain still continued immigration restrictions, the Jews sent Holocaust survivors to Palestine on old leaky scows, defying the British ban. A former American cruise ship, renamed *Exodus 1947*, was rammed and boarded by British naval vessels in July 1947, and the 4,500 refugees on board were returned to an internment camp in Hamburg, Germany. This particular incident, and the whole immigration rebellion, rallied world public opinion much as Gandhi's nonviolent marches in India had. European settlers in most colonies were considered symbols of imperialism, but the Holocaust and the *Exodus 1947* made Jewish settlers into Davids fighting Goliath.

At the same time, Jewish terrorist organizations, the *Irgun Zvai Leumi* (National Military Organization), led by future prime minister Menachem Begin, and the even more fanatical Stern Gang, founded by Abraham Stern and led by another future prime minister, Yitzhak Shamir, broke away from the semi-official Haganah defense forces in Jewish Palestine. In 1944 they began a terror campaign to drive the British out of the country. Ben-Gurion at first dissociated the Jewish Agency from the terrorists and even helped the British hunt down members of the Irgun and the Stern Gang, but after the war he struck a secret deal with the terrorists and declared an all-out Hebrew revolt against the British mandate. On October 31, 1945 the revolt began in spectacular fashion, with a coordinated attack that severed the railway system of Palestine in 163 places. A second elegant coup, in June, 1946, blew up all the land bridges connecting Palestine with the outside world. In reprisal, the British staged a nationwide search for terrorists and arrested nearly the entire Jewish Agency Executive. Ben-Gurion, who avoided arrest since he was in Europe at the time, called off the Hebrew revolt. Yet the Irgun mounted one more attack on July 22, 1946, blowing up an entire wing of the King David Hotel housing the British military headquarters. Like the Irish after World War I, the Jews of Palestine defeated the British with a combination of violence and non-violence.

British policy in Palestine, which had oscillated uncertainly since the early 1930s, lost all direction in the postwar years. Ernest Bevin, the foreign minister in Britain's Labour government, believed the Balfour Declaration had

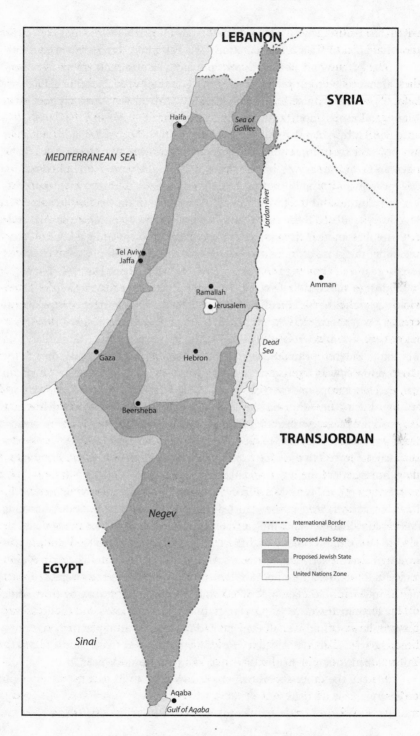

The United Nations Partition Plan for Palestine, 1947-48

been a mistake and vowed not to alienate Arab allies by allowing more Jews into Palestine. Local British officers stationed in Palestine were sickened and outraged by the Irgun and Sternist terror campaigns against their troops. One general, when recalled to Britain, literally pissed on the soil of Palestine before embarking. Yet the Zionists still retained many sympathizers and supporters in Britain, and more importantly, in the United States.

Ben-Gurion had shrewdly realized during the war that England, and all of Europe, was a spent force and that the United States was the rising power. So he called an extraordinary Zionist conference at the Biltmore Hotel in New York City for May 1942. The Biltmore Declaration demanded unrestricted immigration to Palestine and the formation of a Jewish commonwealth. After the war, Ben-Gurion enlisted the aid of wealthy American Jews to purchase surplus military supplies and arms-making machinery, which were smuggled into Palestine under the guise of industrial equipment. American Zionists also mounted a well-organized campaign to win support from President Harry Truman.

Most of the Middle East experts in the U.S. State and War Departments, acutely aware of the oil potential of the Arab lands, tried to steer American policy in a pro-Arab direction. President Truman sometimes resisted this trend, but not consistently. Truman was primarily interested in the Middle East as a solution to the European refugee problem. Truman's humanitarian concern for Jewish refugees was also buttressed by political considerations, for American Jews were numerous in three key states — New York, Pennsylvania, and Illinois. In August 1945, he endorsed the Jewish Agency demand for resettlement of 100,000 European Jewish refugees in Palestine. Had British foreign secretary Bevin gone along with this request, he might have defused the displaced persons issue and averted the later *Exodus 1947* fiasco. He resented American meddling, however, and held firm against immigration to Palestine.

Events moved rapidly to a conclusion in Palestine. Following their withdrawal from India in 1947, the British admitted the failure of their decades-long attempt to rule impartially in Palestine. They had already asked the United Nations to study the problem, and the UN Special Committee on Palestine had produced a new partition plan for an Arab and a Jewish state. The British government, therefore, announced on December 11, 1947, that they were renouncing the international mandate in Palestine and would withdraw by the middle of May 1948. Just two weeks previously, both the Americans and the Russians, in a rare show of Cold War agreement, had voted in favor of partition and pressured their UN allies to do likewise. Both the United States and the Soviet Union hoped to supplant the British as the paramount power in the Middle East and keep the other superpower out. Each tried to forge a friendship with the emerging Jewish state.

Fighting broke out almost immediately in Palestine after the UN partition vote and the British renunciation of the mandate. The Palestinian Arabs had been leaderless and demoralized since the failure of the 1936-39 Arab revolt. Hajj Amin al-Husseini had spent the war years in Berlin, broadcasting anti-British propaganda, and had not been allowed back to Palestine after the war. Most of his former colleagues on the Arab Higher Committee were dead, in jail, or in exile. The surrounding independent or soon-to-be-independent Arab states denounced the UN partition plan, but they were not so united as their anti-Zionist rhetoric suggested. King Abdullah of Transjordan, like all his Hashemite family, was willing to live with the Jews in Palestine, so long as he advanced his own ambitions of greater influence in the Arab world. He conducted secret negotiations with both the British and the Jews, explaining his desire to annex the Arab portions of Palestine but promising not to attack the Jewish community. He largely kept his promise and subsequently did annex the West Bank of the Jordan. The Syrians and Egyptians were militantly anti-Zionist, but they faced internal political problems and could not mobilize all their forces against the Jews. Furthermore, they distrusted Abdullah.

The Arab states could not openly declare war on the Jews until after the British withdrawal from Palestine in May 1948, for they still depended heavily on Great Britain militarily and politically. So from December 1947 until the end of the British mandate, the fighting consisted mainly of small-scale guerrilla engagements between the Jewish Haganah, which now openly cooperated with the terrorist Irgun and Stern Gang, and bands of Arab irregulars sent in from Syria or organized within Palestine. During this first stage of the Arab-Jewish war, the civil war within Palestine, both sides were poorly armed, but the Jews were much better organized and highly motivated. Much of the local Arab population simply wanted to be left alone, and numerous Arab villages struck nonaggression pacts with neighboring Jewish villages so that the populations of both could concentrate on sowing and reaping their crops. Ben-Gurion himself reported to a colleague on March 17, 1948: "It is now clear, without the slightest doubt, that were we to face the Palestinians alone, everything would be all right."

Yet Ben-Gurion realized that the Arab states would intervene as soon as British troops left, so he prepared the Haganah for larger battles to come. March 1948 marked a turning point in the balance of forces within Palestine. Ben-Gurion authorized the military to pursue Plan D, a move from defense to offense aimed at opening the road between Tel Aviv and Jerusalem. That same month the first shipment of arms that Jewish agents had purchased from the Soviet bloc in Czechoslovakia began arriving. By the time the British withdrew and the Jews declared an independent state of Israel on May 14, 1948, the Haganah was better armed and better placed strategically to resist the Arab invasion, which occurred the next day.

On paper, the Arab and Jewish forces seemed about evenly matched. Egypt committed 10,000 soldiers and Transjordan's King Abdullah contributed the 4,500-man Arab Legion. Iraq, Syria, and Lebanon sent in smaller numbers, for an Arab total of about 21,000 to 23,000. The Jewish forces numbered about 30,000, but not all of them were adequately armed, so their effectives totaled about the same as the Arabs. The Arab states, however, did not coordinate their plans, but simply invaded the territory closest to their own borders. The Jewish forces were able to defeat them piecemeal. Israeli historian Simha Flapan has concluded: "The Arab states invaded Israel not as united armies determined to defeat a common enemy but as reluctant partners in an intrigue-ridden and uncoordinated coalition, whose members were motivated by mutual suspicion and mistrust. . . . The invasion was dictated as much by the aspirations of the Arab states to stop each other as by their undoubted hatred of the new Jewish state."

The Israelis not only defended their newly proclaimed state, but expanded its borders substantially over the UN partition plan. They won their victory not primarily through conventional military strength, but in highly political campaigns for immigration and land. Ben-Gurion's immigration rebellion earned much sympathy for Jews across the world and undoubtedly influenced the United Nations vote for partition in 1947. In a more direct sense, immigration helped the Israeli military resist Arab invasion. Between March and July 1948, at the peak of the fighting, 12,939 able-bodied Jewish men arrived from Europe; most were immediately armed and pressed into service.

The Israelis also won the demographic and territorial war. Plan D called for a systematic clearing of Arab villages along strategic roads. Villagers were expelled and their houses leveled. This limited forced migration was soon supplemented by a terror-stricken mass exodus of hundreds of thousands of Arabs from Jewish-held territory. The Jewish authorities never proclaimed a clearcut, definitive policy of expulsion, though some local commanders did make sure that all Arabs left their zones. However, Ben-Gurion and other leaders clearly wanted an Israeli state with as few Arabs as possible, so they saw the largely spontaneous flight of terrified Arabs as a blessing and steadfastly refused to let them return after the war. All in all, between 600,000 and 760,000 Palestinian Arabs became refugees in the 1947-48 war. The Israelis cleared 350 villages of Arabs, blowing up their homes, confiscating their lands, and resettling Jewish immigrants from Europe in them.

The Jewish Yishuv in Palestine was a settler colony with a difference. Since no other country of the world would take them in before, during, or after World War II, Jews fought for their own homeland with their backs to the wall. Unlike any other settler colony in the twentieth century, they not only defeated the indigenous population politically and militarily, but drove them out of the country. The Arab population of the Jewish areas in Palestine fell from approximately 700,000 before the 1947-48 war to 167,000 (less than 20 percent) immediately afterward. Israel began its independent existence as a relatively homogenous Jewish state, but the hundreds of thousands of Palestinian Arab refugees just outside its borders seriously threatened its long-range stability and ensured future conflict.

CHAPTER TEN

The Life-Line of Imperialism

European imperialism retreated slowly but steadily during the first half of the twentieth century, as two world wars hammered at European power and a rising tide of nationalism eroded the basis of European confidence and supposed superiority. The Irish war of independence after World War I signaled the beginning of the end for the British Empire, and the hasty departure from India and Palestine after World War II marked another decisive turning point. Similarly, the French abandonment of the mandate in Syria and Lebanon and their forced withdrawal from Indochina threw France's empire into crisis. Yet at mid-century neither power admitted that the end of imperial glory had arrived. Both Britain and France held firmly to their colonies and protectorates on the continent of Africa, and the two new superpowers, the Soviet Union and the United States, had not yet spread their influence very far into either Africa or southern Asia. Indeed, Great Britain still considered the Indian Ocean a "British lake," exercised predominant influence in the Middle East, and shared control of black Africa with France. Both the British and French believed they could co-opt moderate nationalist leaders and maintain a refurbished imperialism.

In the mid-1950s, however, the president of the newly independent state of Egypt, Gamal Abdul Nasser, nationalized the Suez Canal, a key artery on the life-line of imperialism. The aging imperial powers of France and England clumsily applied nineteenth-century gunboat diplomacy against Egypt, with humiliating results. The Suez crisis of 1956 symbolized the end of European imperialism.

It seems appropriate that the empires foundered in the Egyptian sands, for Egypt had always been the most curious and atypical of colonies. Indeed, it

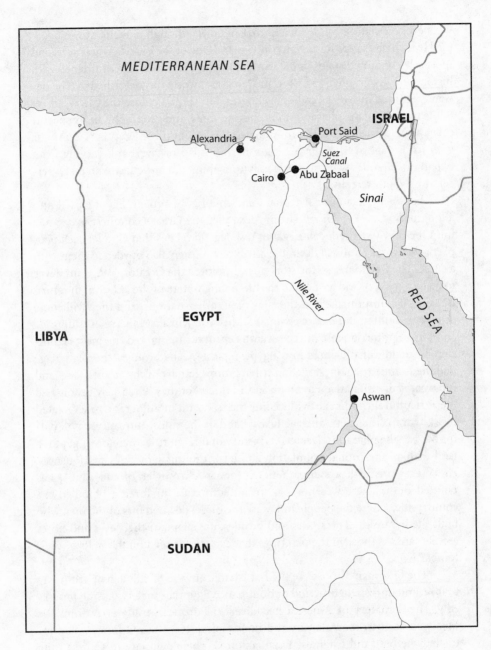

Egypt

was never officially a colony of a European power, though in reality it was occupied by British troops for seventy-four years. One of the oldest civilizations and
most self-contained states in the world, Egypt is a country "overburdened with
history and geography," as historian Derek Hopwood has described it. The nation's recorded history stretches back several millennia before the Christian era
to the time when the pharaohs built the pyramids, and geography, more specifically the Nile River, has always dominated the livelihood of Egyptians. The Nile,
with its annual overflow irrigating a narrow strip of riverbank varying from
two to fifteen miles wide, makes possible an abundant agriculture on just 5 percent of Egypt's terrain.

Following its impressive pharaonic era of government, Egypt lapsed into
a long period of foreign rule from Alexander the Great's conquest in 332 B.C.
until the mid-twentieth century. An Arab legend relates that God let each people of the world choose a desirable attribute but then also burdened them with
a curse. The Egyptians, so the story goes, implored the Creator: "We want never
to go hungry." So God gave them the life-giving waters of the Nile, but in return
he said: "This will make you the envy of all other nations, and they will come
into your country and rule over you. For this, you will always serve outsiders."

The Arab conquest in the seventh century A.D. marked the most significant incursion of outsiders into Egypt, for the Arabs brought their language
and the Islamic religion, settled in tribal groups in part of the countryside, and
intermarried with native Egyptians in the cities. Yet they left largely untouched
the agricultural rhythms of village life, the tradition of autocratic rule dictated
by a "hydraulic" society, and the heavy hand of the ruling bureaucracy, all dat-
ing back to the pharaohs. Despite its history of foreign rule, therefore, Egypt is a
land with a long-rooted population and a continuous national consciousness.
As Peter Mansfield, a sympathetic European chronicler of the Arabs, has
pointed out: "There was never a strong admixture of foreign blood in the
countryside, where the people today are the direct descendants of the men who
built the pyramids. Their faces and profiles, the shape of their eyes and noses
are the same as those in the paintings that can still be seen on the walls of their
tombs."

The Ottoman Turks were the last Islamic empire to rule Egypt, from 1517
to 1914, and during their period of dominance Egyptian society declined markedly. The discovery of America had diverted European trade away from the
Mediterranean to the Atlantic, and the dominance of the Ottomans had attracted the best and brightest Egyptians from their own city of Cairo to the
Turkish imperial capital of Constantinople. Egypt's population had fallen from
a high of about ten million to only four million by 1798, when Napoleon briefly
conquered the land of the Nile. An Ottoman soldier named Muhammad Ali,
who helped drive the French troops out in 1801, established himself as perma-

nent governor from 1805 until 1848. He passed on his rule as *khedive*, a Persian-derived term meaning "prince," to his descendants. Though Egypt was not fully independent, a member of the Muhammad Ali family presided over its government until 1953.

One of Ali's descendants invited the French entrepreneur Ferdinand de Lesseps to dig the Suez Canal, connecting the Mediterranean with the Red Sea and drastically shortening the water route from Europe to India and the rest of Asia. The canal, which opened with elaborate ceremonies in 1869, legally belonged to Egypt, which was a semi-autonomous province of the Ottoman Empire. In actual fact, however, it was operated by Europeans for the benefit of Europe. French investors owned a preponderance of shares in the Universal Suez Canal Company, which enjoyed a long-term lease to operate the canal for ninety-nine years, until November 1968. Though the Egyptian government originally owned 44 percent of the company, the khedive's over-ambitious development schemes plunged the country into debt, forcing him to sell the Egyptian shares to the British government in 1875. This made European influence predominant in Egypt and marked the effective end of the Muhammad Ali dynasty's autonomy.

When an Egyptian army officer, Colonel Ahmad Arabi, revolted against European dominance, the British fleet bombarded the port of Alexandria, landed an expeditionary force, defeated Arabi's troops, and occupied Cairo in September 1882. The French government had entered a period of retrenchment at this time so they declined to support the British in Egypt. British troops and administrators, therefore, occupied Egypt alone, on a "temporary" basis, in order to protect the canal route to India and safeguard European investments in the canal company. The British never annexed Egypt formally as a colony. Indeed, they did not even declare it a protectorate until the First World War, and from 1882 to 1922 they publicly promised sixty-six times that they would soon withdraw. They never did. Egypt still legally belonged to the Ottoman Empire, with self-government under its own khedive or ruler, but it was actually a "veiled protectorate," one of the most curious colonies in the history of European imperialism.

With centuries-old roots, Egyptian nationalism spread rapidly among the urban notables and prominent landowners, the same classes that led the nationalist revolt in other Arab countries. After World War I, a group of nationalists, including the prominent Egyptian lawyer and judge Saad Zaghlul, formed a delegation (*wafd* in Arabic) to present the case for Egyptian independence at the Paris Peace Conference. The British arrested Zaghlul and his colleagues, imprisoning them on the island of Malta, and the country erupted in protests. Eventually the Wafd leaders were released and journeyed to Paris, but their petitions were ignored. The British repressed the popular discontent in Egypt, then in 1922 they tried to defuse it further by unilaterally declaring Egypt an independent state. This grant of independence, however, was a sham, for the British government reserved jurisdiction over four matters: security of communications through Egypt (that is, control of the Suez Canal), Egypt's defense (continued military occupation), protection of foreign interests and minorities in Egypt (extraterritorial rights), and the status of the Sudan (which had been jointly administered by Britain and Egypt since the nineteenth century). In reality, Egypt enjoyed less autonomy as a supposedly independent state than it did under Muhammad Ali when it remained part of the Ottoman Empire.

During the interwar years, Egypt's politics were dominated by a power struggle between the nationalist Wafd, which had transformed itself into a political party; the Egyptian ruler, whose title had been upgraded from khedive, to sultan, and then to king; and the British military. Whenever a free election was held, the Wafd would sweep to victory, but the nationalist politicians would inevitably offend either the king or the British occupiers, prompting a dissolution of parliament and an appointed government of stooges with no popular following.

In frustration, the younger generation of educated urbanites turned to radical organizations such as Young Egypt or the Muslim Brotherhood. Both groups were led by members of the intellectual proletariat. A British adviser to the Egyptian government, Alex Keown-Boyd, accurately described the radical students in 1936:

> The primary causes of their discontent . . . can be summarized under . . . [3] headings: (a) the difficulty of graduates of university and other government schools in obtaining employment, and the low salaries offered; (b) the rivalry amongst different political parties . . . ; (c) Italian [Fascist] propaganda.

Young Egypt *(Misr al-Fatat),* founded by the lawyer Ahmad Hussein in 1933, had fascist trappings, such as a paramilitary band of Green Shirts, but its fundamental goal was to resurrect the civilization of the pharaohs. Ahmad Hussein taught his followers, including the young Gamal Abdul Nasser, that "life was meaningless without dignity, patriotism, and self-respect." The Muslim Brotherhood, as its name implied, drew more specifically on religious sources, but it too opposed British influence and the continuous affronts to national dignity.

Prompted by student demonstrations and persistent pressure from Wafd politicians, the British finally struck a treaty with Egypt in 1936 that recognized a more substantial independence for the country and admitted it into the League of Nations. The British promised to withdraw their troops from most of Egypt and limit them to only ten thousand soldiers, based in the Suez Canal

Zone. The following year a further agreement began phasing out the extraterritorial rights that Europeans had long enjoyed.

Egypt had attained roughly the same status as Iraq, but the 1936 Anglo-Egyptian Treaty still granted Britain the duty of defending Egypt and permitted a renewed occupation in time of war. This swiftly became a reality when Italian and German forces threatened the canal during World War II. The British declared martial law and poured hundreds of thousands of troops into Egypt. A notorious incident in 1942 underlined how dependent Egypt's government still remained. The British ambassador, Miles Lampson, demanded that the young King Farouk appoint a pro-British prime minister in February 1942. After two days of unsuccessful negotiations, Lampson sent Farouk an ultimatum on February 4: "Unless I hear by 6:00 P.M. today that al-Nahhas has been asked to form a government, His Majesty . . . must accept the consequences." Since Farouk did not comply by the deadline, Lampson ordered British tanks to surround the palace, then presented the king with a choice between abdication or compliance with British orders. The king complied. Ironically, Musatafa al-Nahhas, whom the British imposed as prime minister, was a member of the nationalist Wafd Party. This humiliating incident eventually doomed the Wafd, the monarchy, and the British in Egypt.

After World War II neither king, nationalist politicians, nor British occupiers could control the fury of the Egyptian masses. In the spring of 1946 radical students and workers staged a general strike which resulted in a violent clash with the British, leaving twenty-three dead "Canal Martyrs." One of the freest elections in Egyptian history swept the Wafd back into power in 1950, and in October 1951 Prime Minister al-Nahhas, no longer a British client, unilaterally annulled the 1936 Anglo-Egyptian Treaty. Young Egypt, the Muslim Brothers, and other radical groups mounted both an employee boycott and a guerrilla war against the Suez Canal Company. This goaded the British into retaliation. On January 25, 1952, British troops surrounded the police station at the canal city of Ismailia, bombarding it into submission with the loss of more than fifty Egyptian police defenders. The next day, thereafter known as Black Saturday, hundreds of policemen marched in protest through downtown Cairo. They were soon joined by radical mobs who systematically torched buildings owned by the British or other foreigners. Black Saturday plunged the country into chaos. Four different governments rose and fell during the first half of 1952, before a military coup finally toppled the regime on July 23, 1952.

A small coterie of young soldiers, calling themselves the Free Officers, took over army headquarters in downtown Cairo shortly after midnight on July 23. The senior officers did not resist and only two soldiers were killed in the operation. The coup plotters then seized the Cairo radio station, broadcasting news of the revolution to the populace at 7 A.M. On July 26 the army rebels surrounded the king's summer palace at Alexandria and forced him to abdicate. King Farouk, who had lost the respect of Egyptians, sailed away on his yacht and lived out his life as an international playboy. Farouk's infant son was briefly considered his successor, but in 1953 the Free Officers abolished the monarchy completely, ending the Muhammad Ali dynasty and declaring Egypt a republic.

Egypt did not have a strong military tradition, for during the centuries of foreign domination most army officers had been outsiders, directly responsible to the ruler. However, the 1936 Anglo-Egyptian Treaty opened up military careers to native Egyptians, for the Wafd government liberalized the entrance requirements of the military academy, allowing young men of any social class to take a competitive examination for admission. The Free Officers all belonged to the first few graduating classes from the liberalized academy in the late 1930s. They included both Gamal Abdul Nasser and his successor as Egypt's president, Anwar al-Sadat.

The average age of the coup leaders when they took power in 1952 was thirty-three years. Most came from humble backgrounds, the first of their families to receive professional training. They had joined radical student demonstrations in the 1930s, chafed under British officers during World War II, and taken part in the disastrous invasion of Palestine in 1948. The inadequate preparations of their generals and the corrupt profiteering of leading politicians shocked and humiliated the junior officers. Arab historian P. J. Vatikiotis has summed up the background of the Free Officers: "Nasser's generation sought an army career for very practical reasons of material security, social prestige, and possible political involvement — in that order." They were members of the intellectual proletariat seeking careers in the military.

Gamal Abdul Nasser was typical of his generation. He was born in the city of Alexandria on January 15, 1918, but his father, a postal clerk, had recently come from a small town in Upper Egypt (the far south of the country, up the Nile River). Historian Derek Hopwood comments: "His family belonged to the middle layer of small proprietors and tenants. . . . This class gave Nasser both his roots in the Egyptian countryside and his escape into another world." Gamal enjoyed a comfortable childhood, but his father moved frequently from one post office job to another, and the son often lived with relatives. The death of his mother at an early age and his father's swift remarriage reportedly shocked and humiliated Gamal. Without endorsing any particular psychological diagnosis, his biographers assert that this experience proved traumatic, intensifying his natural seriousness and his suspicious personality.

Nasser belonged briefly to Young Egypt and took part in street brawls and protests during his years at secondary school in Cairo; then he entered the military academy in the second class after the entrance requirements were liberalized. As early as 1939, he and a group of classmates began meeting secretly to discuss Egypt's problems and prospects, but no formal organization was established until after the 1948 Palestine War. Nasser himself wrote a possibly apocryphal account of how the Palestinian fiasco affected him. "One day, Kamal al-Din Hussein was sitting near me in Palestine, looking distracted, with nervous darting eyes. 'Do you know what Ahmed Abdul Aziz [a colonel who belonged to the Muslim Brethren] said to me before he was killed? . . . Listen, Kamal, the real battlefield is in Egypt.'"

Returned from the humiliating defeats in Palestine, Nasser put his natural talent for secrecy and conspiracy to use by organizing the Executive of the Free Officers in 1949. Several of his colleagues, including Sadat, had flirted with the Germans and Italians during World War II, mounting assassination and bomb plots against British and Egyptian politicians, all to no avail. Nasser now decided on a different strategy, a secret, tightly organized conspiracy of like-minded officers who would bide their time until the opportunity of a takeover presented itself. Between 1949 and 1952 the Egyptian government of king and corrupt ministers slowly destroyed itself. The old regime finally fell to Nasser's coup nearly bloodlessly, without a struggle.

The young officers originally put forward a sympathetic older soldier, General Muhammad Naguib, as their leader and called on a traditional politician to serve as prime minister. Yet within a few months they decided to take control themselves, transforming the Executive of the Free Officers into the Revolutionary Command Council (RCC). The prime minister resigned, and less than two years later General Naguib was shunted aside and placed under house arrest. Within the RCC Nasser held undisputed authority, and Egypt's revolutionary regime evolved into an authoritarian dictatorship.

Though radical in his determination to overthrow the political order and expel the British, Nasser had no well-formed ideology when he took power. His colleagues among the Free Officers espoused a wide variety of political views, from conservative Islamic principles to left-wing Marxism. In its first few years, the revolutionary government implemented just one important economic reform, land redistribution. In September 1952 the RCC decreed a limitation of land holdings to two hundred *feddans* (a little more than two hundred acres) and ordered the distribution of excess land to small farmers and the landless. The decree also fixed rents paid by tenant farmers at seven times the land tax. Since many landlords had corruptly reduced their taxes, they now found that their tenants' rent was accordingly minimal. The land reform did not prove all that radical in practice, with only about 10 percent of Egypt's land redistributed. Yet the rent reduction earned the gratitude of the masses, and the elimination of large estates destroyed the political power of the landlord class.

Aside from land reform, Nasser and his colleagues concentrated their efforts on ending the British occupation. The Free Officers immediately engaged in negotiations with the British, and they removed one obstacle in January 1953 by allowing a referendum on Sudanese independence. To the surprise of the Egyptians, who considered the unity of the Nile Valley self-evident, the Sudanese chose separation and became an independent state on January 1, 1956.

England's Conservative government, however, with Winston Churchill back as prime minister again, dragged its heels in the negotiations. Churchill himself was spoiling for a fight. He half hoped that Nasser would try to seize the Suez Canal by force so the British could "give the Egyptians a military thump." Nasser did not oblige him, however, and Churchill's own ministers convinced him that Great Britain could no longer afford to maintain soldiers at Suez. In October 1954 the British signed a new treaty with Egypt providing for a gradual withdrawal of all troops from the Suez Canal Zone over a period of twenty months. Civilian technicians would maintain the military base in a ready condition, and the British would retain the right to reoccupy it if Egypt, its Arab allies, or Turkey were attacked by an outside force. This latter provision indirectly drew Egypt into a Cold War alliance, for the expected aggressor was Soviet Russia, but the defense provisions would expire after only seven years. Nasser considered this a small price to pay for total British evacuation. The last contingent of British soldiers left Egyptian soil shortly after midnight on June 13, 1956, after seventy-four years of "temporary occupation." Egypt was finally independent in fact as well as in name.

During the four years between the Free Officers' coup of 1952 and the British evacuation in 1956, Gamal Abdul Nasser consolidated his control of the government and developed a public persona both in Egypt and on the international stage. Inexperienced in public affairs, he was at first a wooden orator, reading a prepared speech in formal Arabic. Then in October 1954, while defending the treaty with Britain to a skeptical audience in Alexandria, he survived an assassination attempt by one of the Muslim Brethren. He smashed the Brotherhood, arresting and executing its leaders, but he also emerged with greater self-confidence and evolved a colloquial style of speechmaking. For the rest of his life, his speeches were extremely long, but the crowds loved them. One Egyptian writer referred to Nasser's regime as the "eighteen-year-long monologue."

On the international scene, Nasser cultivated friendships with Marshal Tito of Yugoslavia and Prime Minister Nehru of India. Together, these three developed a doctrine of "positive neutralism" or "non-alignment," trying to steer an independent course between the two Cold War superpowers. The non-aligned states of what was beginning to be called the Third World held a coming-out party at Bandung, Indonesia in April 1955. The leaders of twenty-nine Asian and African countries, representing more than half the human race, denounced colonialism, the Cold War, and the threat of nuclear annihilation.

Sukarno, the president of Indonesia and host of the conference, gave a rousing keynote speech describing the "life-line of imperialism" running "from the Straits of Gibraltar, through the Mediterranean, the Suez Canal, the Red Sea, the Indian Ocean, the South China Sea, and the Sea of Japan. For most of that enormous distance," he continued, "the territories on both sides of this life-line . . . are no longer the victims of colonialism."

Nasser was deeply affected by the symbolism of Bandung, and with his country standing astride the "life-line of imperialism" he soon found an opportunity to strike a blow against the pretensions of the European imperialists. The key to Nasser's actions had always been the quest for personal and national dignity. The Young Egypt movement of Ahmad Hussein taught him the necessity of overcoming colonial humiliations with dignity and self-respect. In the words of his biographer, Peter Mansfield, "the idea that the descendants of the men who built the pyramids will once again astonish the world is fundamental to his thinking."

In short order, Nasser did astonish the world, proving that his words about national dignity were not just empty rhetoric. In September 1955, he broke the arms embargo that England, France, and the United States had imposed on the Middle East after the 1948 Palestine War, purchasing 200 million dollars' worth of weapons from the Soviet Union through intermediaries in Czechoslovakia. Playing both sides of the Cold War, he then struck a deal in December 1955 with the United States, Great Britain, and the World Bank to finance the High Dam on the Nile River at Aswan. This 365-foot-high dam, running over three miles across, would collect the waters of the Nile in a vast reservoir, permitting year-round irrigation for agriculture and providing electricity for new industries.

On July 19, 1956, however, Secretary of State John Foster Dulles told the Egyptian ambassador that the United States was withdrawing its financial support for the Aswan Dam. Anti-Communist congressmen and newspapers had agitated against the Egyptian loan because of the Czech arms deal and Egypt's recent recognition of Communist China. Dulles was also beginning to think that the massive loan might actually alienate Egyptians since great sacrifices would be required to pay it back. He thought he was letting his clients down easy when he announced that the Egyptian economy was too weak and underdeveloped to sustain such a massive project, but this only added to the humiliation. Nasser himself, who was flying home from a summit conference with Tito and Nehru in Yugoslavia when he heard the news, felt the rebuff as an insult to Egypt's honor and his own pride.

Within one week Nasser retaliated in spectacular fashion. He celebrated the fourth anniversary of King Farouk's abdication, July 26, 1956, with the crowds in Manshiya Square, Alexandria, the same location where he had narrowly escaped assassination two years before. Launching into one of his patented harangues, he narrated the history of Egypt's humiliation by Great Britain, the recent triumphs of the Free Officers' revolution, and the country's glorious future prospects. Then, explaining the complicated financial negotiations for the High Dam he uttered an unusual sentence: "I started to look at Mr. Black [Eugene Black, president of the World Bank], who was sitting in a chair, and I saw him in my imagination as Ferdinand de Lesseps." This was more than an anti-imperialist historical analogy; "de Lesseps" was a pre-arranged codeword. When the radio carried this word across Egypt, Mahmoud Yunis, a military engineer, sprang into action and directed a lightning-quick seizure of the Suez Canal. Nasser kept speaking into the night, repeating the codeword fourteen times to make sure.

Egypt already owned the Suez Canal; Nasser's action on July 26 simply nationalized the operating company, whose franchise would expire in another twelve years in any case. One of the fundamental attributes of sovereign states is the power of eminent domain, the authority to buy out private property if it is needed for the public interest. Both Britain and France had exercised this authority extensively after World War II, nationalizing most of their heavy industries. Mexico had taken over the oil companies within its boundaries in the 1930s, and though this became an international incident, the companies eventually accepted Mexico's offer of monetary compensation. Since Nasser was offering to compensate the owners of the Suez Canal Company, nationalization was legal under international law and custom. Even the British Cabinet conceded that "from the strictly legal point of view, his action amounts to no more than a decision to buy out shareholders."

Yet the British government did not let the matter rest. Sukarno's phrase uttered at Bandung, "the life-line of imperialism," literally described the English attitude toward the Suez Canal. Anthony Eden, who had succeeded Churchill as prime minister in April 1955, decided on the very evening of the canal nationalization that Nasser "must not be allowed to get away with it." In public, the British said they were seeking an international authority to run the canal, but in private the Cabinet also decided to overthrow Nasser's government.

President Dwight Eisenhower and Secretary of State John Foster Dulles shared the British irritation at Nasser but did not feel it as urgently. They therefore promoted several international conferences to negotiate a settlement. The British played along, but at the same time they quietly conspired with the French and the Israelis for a joint attack upon Egypt. At an ultra-secret conference in the Paris suburb of Sèvres between October 22 and 24, leaders of the three countries hatched an elaborate plot, which they executed at the end of that month.

At 5:00 P.M. on October 29, Israeli paratroopers dropped into the Sinai

Desert about forty-five miles from Suez. This maneuver was intended to look like a full-scale attack on the Suez Canal, though in fact the Israelis had no intention of advancing that far. Their actual goal lay far to the south, at the Straits of Tiran, where Egypt had been blockading Israel's outlet to the Red Sea. Feigning surprise at the supposed Israeli threat to the canal, the English and French governments presented an ultimatum the next day, demanding that *both* Israel and Egypt withdraw ten miles from the Suez Canal. Israel was not that close, and Egypt had forces on both sides of the canal since it ran right through the country. The English and French then informed the Egyptians that they would temporarily occupy the Canal Zone in order to ensure the safety of shipping.

This ultimatum, like that delivered to the Serbian government by Austria-Hungary in 1914, was made to be rejected. The English and French hoped it would provide a modicum of legal cover for the recapture of the Suez Canal that they had already planned. Egypt, of course, rejected the ultimatum, and Nasser, sounding much like Winston Churchill, told the Cairo crowds: "We shall fight to the last drop of our blood. We shall never surrender."

The British and French could not follow up the ultimatum with swift military action. Their expeditionary force had assembled almost a thousand miles away, on the island of Malta; and because of the elaborate cover story, they could not embark until October 31, after the Egyptians rejected the ultimatum. Steaming at the slow speed of the troop transports and landing craft, they would not arrive off Suez until six days later. In the meantime, British and French bombers destroyed the Egyptian air force on the ground, and psychological warfare broadcasts urged the overthrow of Nasser. This simply stiffened resistance and solidified Nasser's position. Egyptians remembered that the last "temporary occupation" lasted for seventy-four years.

While the Anglo-French flotilla steamed across the Mediterranean, the U.S. government denounced the planned invasion and took the matter to the United Nations. England and France vetoed a Security Council resolution demanding a cease-fire. Turning then to the General Assembly, where the veto did not apply, the Americans carried a cease-fire resolution in the early morning of November 2 by a vote of 64 to 5, with 6 abstentions. Only the Commonwealth stalwarts of Australia and New Zealand supported England, France, and Israel in this vote. The Canadian minister for external affairs, Lester Pearson, then presented a plan for a UN emergency force to separate the combatants and buy time for an overall settlement of the Suez Canal dispute. The General Assembly adopted the Canadian resolution on November 4, the first time the United Nations had ever authorized a peacekeeping force. Secretary General Dag Hammarskjöld accepted the offer of a Canadian general to command the force and recruited soldiers from eight nations.

Despite the flurry of activity at the United Nations, England and France went ahead with their punitive invasion of Egypt. Early in the morning of November 5, British and French paratroopers dropped near Port Said, at the Mediterranean end of the Suez Canal. Nasser had distributed weapons to the populace, and the disorganized resistance in Port Said prevented the paratroopers from taking the city on their own. The next morning, the main invasion force came ashore and captured the port city, then began moving up the canal. If their mission was to protect international shipping, as their governments maintained, they had already failed. Throughout the three months of the gathering crisis, Egyptian pilots had surprised the world by operating the canal efficiently; but as soon as the Europeans invaded, the Egyptian military sunk fifty-two ships in the canal, effectively blocking all traffic.

The Suez invasion halted abruptly at midnight Greenwich Mean Time, November 6/7, before the commandos had captured the whole length of the canal. The United States backed up the moral suasion of the UN resolutions with economic pressure, preventing the International Monetary Fund from supporting the pound sterling in currency markets and refusing emergency shipments of American oil to replace the supplies no longer flowing through the Suez Canal. The Soviets had also made threatening statements, and a London newspaper editorialized, "we had not realized that our Government was capable of such folly and such crookedness." The American economic measures proved decisive; in the mid-twentieth century, England and France could no longer afford an imperial adventure without the backing of a superpower.

In retrospect, the Suez invasion seems almost inexplicable. Anthony Eden himself had once stated that "in the second half of the twentieth century we cannot hope to maintain our position in the Middle East by the methods of the last century." Yet that is precisely what England and France attempted at Suez. It might be useful, therefore, to ask of each participant, "What was he thinking?"

Given his obsession with national pride and dignity, Gamal Abdul Nasser's motivation is easy to surmise. He must have been thinking, "Why are these imperialists doing this to me?" He had nationalized the Suez Canal in retaliation for the rejection of Aswan Dam financing and in hopes that canal revenue would provide an alternative source of funds to build the dam. Cognizant of the risks, he estimated the probability of an armed intervention as high as 80 percent in the first week after nationalization. He believed the odds would drop, however, to around 20 percent by October, so he was taken by surprise when the blow finally fell. He even received a warning from his military attaché in Paris the day before the ultimatum was delivered but did not believe it.

When Israeli paratroopers dropped into Sinai, Nasser was bewildered, for he recognized that it was not a full-scale attack. Telephoning an aide, he exclaimed: "The Israelis are in Sinai and they seem to be fighting the sands, because they are occupying one empty position after another." Once the ultimatum was delivered and he realized that the major threat would come from England and France, he ordered Egyptian troops out of the Sinai Desert so they would not be cut off on the east side of the Suez Canal. He then coolly mobilized Egyptian resistance, defying the air raids by going about in an open car and showing himself to the crowds. With neither superpower supporting the invaders, Nasser correctly predicted that although he might lose the battle, he would ultimately win the war of international public opinion.

Anthony Eden's reasoning is more perplexing, for he was an experienced foreign minister who had long understudied Churchill for the role of prime minister. Prior to Suez he was considered something of an expert on Arab affairs since he had taken his Oxford degree in Oriental languages and had successfully handled the Anglo-Egyptian treaty negotiations of the mid-1950s. On the only occasion when Eden had met Nasser face to face, February 20, 1955, at the British embassy in Cairo, he startled the Egyptian colonel by addressing him in fluent Arabic.

On the most personal level, in the summer and autumn of 1956 Anthony Eden was thinking about how lousy he felt. He had endured two operations for gallstones in 1953 and the surgeons had botched the job, damaging a bile duct and leaving him subject to frequent fevers and attacks of jaundice. During the months of the Suez crisis he was visibly exhausted, living primarily on stimulant drugs to counteract the depressive effects of his primary medications. While it is impossible to know exactly how much his physical condition affected his judgment, it certainly cannot have improved it.

Eden was also thinking a lot about Hitler, Mussolini, and World War II. He had first made his political reputation by resigning from Neville Chamberlain's Cabinet in February 1938, in protest against the policy of appeasement. Eden judged that the greatest mistake the British and French had made before World War II was not resisting Hitler early in the game, when he reoccupied the Rhineland in 1936. It therefore became an *idée fixe* for him that dictators must be nipped in the bud, before they can threaten the world. In his lucid moments, he realized that Nasser was no Hitler, but he wrote President Eisenhower in August 1956 that "the parallel with Mussolini is close."

Prime Minister Guy Mollet of France did consider Nasser another Hitler. He told Eden that the Egyptian's plan for conquest was written down in a book called *The Philosophy of the Revolution,* and he likened that ghost-written volume of Nasser's to *Mein Kampf.* Mollet and his closest colleagues in the Socialist government of France were all veterans of the World War II Resistance, and, like Eden, they were fighting the previous war all over again. So too was Australian prime minister Robert Menzies, who had first supported Chamberlain's appeasement policy in the 1930s only to be proven wrong. For the rest of his career he tried to live down that mistake. During the Suez crisis, he steadfastly supported the British by voting against UN condemnations.

Aside from these personal considerations of physical health and collective historical memory, the leaders of Britain and France were focusing on deeper matters of national interest. Much of the oil pumped in Iran, Saudi Arabia, and other Persian Gulf states was transported through the Suez Canal to European markets; petroleum accounted for about two-thirds of the canal's traffic in the mid-1950s. The permanent under-secretary of Great Britain's Foreign Affairs Ministry, Ivone Kirkpatrick, wrote a memo in September 1956 summing up Britain's primary concerns in Egypt:

> If we sit back while Nasser consolidates his position and gradually acquires control of the oil-bearing countries, he can and is, according to our information, resolved to wreck us. If Middle Eastern oil is denied to us for a year or two, our gold reserves will disappear . . . [and] I doubt whether we shall be able to pay for the bare minimum necessary for our defense. And a country that cannot provide for its defense is finished.

For the first, but not the last, time in the twentieth century, a world power attacked a Middle Eastern dictator out of concern for its oil supply.

The French had another interest at stake. After being forced to abandon their mandate in Syria and Lebanon, France had only one major colony in the Arab world, the North African territory of Algeria. However, Algerians had started an anti-colonial revolt against French rule (see chapter 11) which was aided and encouraged by Nasser's regime in Egypt. If Nasser were overthrown, the Algerian revolt might be ended or at least weakened.

The motives of the Israelis were also quite simple. David Ben-Gurion, who had guided Israel to independence and victory over the Arab states in 1948, had returned to power as prime minister and defense minister in 1955. A committed hardliner, Ben-Gurion believed the Arabs would never allow the Jews to live in peace unless they experienced the military might of the Israeli defense forces. He also welcomed the opportunity to deal with England and France as an equal and an ally. The day he signed the Protocol of Sèvres, committing Israel to provide the pretext for the Suez farce, he wrote in his diary: "This is a unique opportunity that two 'not so small' powers will try to topple Nasser, and we shall not remain alone against him while he becomes stronger and conquers all Arab countries."

That leaves only the superpowers' motives unaccounted for. The British later alleged that Secretary of State Dulles misled them into expecting American support. Dulles was an enthusiastic Cold Warrior, prone to seeing threats where none existed, and he had a disconcerting habit of telling his allies what he thought they wanted to hear. In particular, on August 1, he told Eden in person that "a way had to be found to make Nasser *disgorge* what he was attempting to swallow." However, on that same occasion, Dulles brought Eden a letter from President Eisenhower warning against the use of military force. This was Eisenhower's, and the U.S. government's, consistent position throughout the crisis. In fact, Eisenhower was one of the few world leaders who understood what Nasser was doing. He wrote Eden on September 3 that "Nasser thrives on drama," so the best policy would be one which drained the situation of drama. In other words, the American president counseled a quiet, negotiated solution, rather than a military intervention, at least until after his presidential reelection, scheduled for the first week of November. Eden may have felt he was receiving mixed signals, but this was self-deception or wishful thinking on his part. Eisenhower made his position clear and backed it up with economic pressure. Ultimately, the British were the ones who had to disgorge what they had swallowed.

The Soviets played a relatively small role in the Suez crisis, for they were preoccupied with a colonial adventure of their own, the suppression of the Hungarian revolt (see chapter 18). The bid by Hungary's native communists to escape from Russian domination came to a head the same day that Eden's flotilla set sail from Malta to Suez. By November 4, Russian tanks had crushed the Hungarian rebels, and the Soviet government then, hypocritically, sent off threatening notes to the British, French, and Israeli "aggressors." In this instance, the Americans did back their European allies, informing them confidentially that the Russian threats were all bluff, and publicly warning the Russians to stay out of the Middle East.

The motivations of the various actors in the Suez drama, therefore, can be summarized this way: Anthony Eden of England was thinking about Mussolini and oil; Guy Mollet of France was contemplating Hitler and Algeria; the Russians were concentrating on Hungary; the Israelis were thinking about survival; and the Americans focused on negotiations and elections. Finally, Nasser might have thought, "How did I get this lucky?"

Egypt lost the military battles of Suez. Two to three thousand Egyptian soldiers were killed or captured by the Israelis in the Sinai Desert, and the fierce resistance to the European landing at Port Said resulted in 2,700 Egyptian casualties. Egypt's entire air force was destroyed and its major economic asset, the Suez Canal, was temporarily closed to traffic. Yet the country bounced back swiftly and Nasser emerged as a hero to the Arab world, as if he were the victor of Suez. Continuous American and international pressure forced the French and English to pull out their troops from the Canal Zone on December 23, 1956. The next day, Egyptians celebrated by pulling down the monumental statue of Ferdinand de Lesseps from its pedestal overlooking Port Said harbor. The Israelis evacuated all their occupied positions in Egypt on March 6-7, 1957. The Egyptians then reopened the Suez Canal to all nations except Israel. United Nations peacekeeping forces took up posts on the Egyptian side of the border with Israel, since Ben-Gurion denied them permission to patrol on Israeli territory. They kept the region peaceful for a decade, giving both Egypt and Israel valuable time to concentrate on economic development.

Ironically, the Suez invasion produced some of the effects it was designed to prevent. Anthony Eden feared that Nasser harbored expansionist aims in the Arab world, but the dramatic events of 1956 greatly magnified his influence in the Middle East, for the Arab masses idolized him as the hero who had stared down the European empires. Thereafter he meddled more in pan-Arab agitation, undermining neighboring governments through propaganda and internal subversion, not military threats. Largely against his better judgment, Nasser consented to a union of Egypt and Syria in 1958, proposed by the pan-Arab *Baath* (Resurrection) Party of Syria. The United Arab Republic that was forged from this union proved uncomfortable for both countries and only lasted three years. In the meantime, a pro-Nasser junta of military officers overthrew the Hashemite monarchy of Iraq in 1958. The Egyptian president was no Hitler, but as historian Henry S. Wilson has written, "Suez transformed Nasser from a little-known colonel behind the 1952 coup into a colossus bestriding both non-aligned and anti-colonialist movements."

Nasser's economic policy, dubbed "Arab socialism," also became more radical. After nationalizing the Suez Canal, he expropriated the property of major European-owned banks and industries. The Soviets stepped in with financing for the Aswan High Dam, which was begun in 1960 and completed shortly after Nasser's death in 1970. The Egyptian government refined its land reform legislation and launched a five-year plan emphasizing the growth of new industries.

Yet despite his dependence on Soviet aid and his dedication to state economic planning, Nasser was not a communist. Indeed, before the Suez crisis he and the Free Officers had close ties with the American CIA and would have preferred to buy arms and accept financial aid from the United States. The cancellation of the Aswan Dam financing virtually threw Nasser into the arms of the Russians. Thereafter he relied on the Soviet Union for military, economic, and diplomatic assistance, yet ruthlessly jailed local Egyptian communists. He explained to a *London Times* interviewer in 1962 that "Communism is in its essence atheistic. . . . It is quite impossible to be a good Moslem and a good communist." Like Sukarno in Indonesia, Gamal Abdul Nasser pursued a policy of socio-nationalism — a vigorous assertion of national pride and dignity coupled with ambitious plans for economic development. Perhaps Anthony Eden was partially right all along. Nasser did resemble Mussolini more than Hitler or Stalin: he was an authoritarian nationalist and a developmental dictator.

The Suez crisis brought the Cold War to the Middle East, with the Soviet Union and the United States replacing England and France as the outside powers vying for influence in the region. The United States did not earn much gratitude for forcing an end to the Anglo-French invasion, for Arabs remembered the clumsy cancellation of the Aswan Dam loan and resented the so-called Eisenhower Doctrine, which asserted an American right of intervention if communists threatened to take over any Middle Eastern government. Therefore, the Soviet Union, without doing much of anything during the Suez crisis, became one of its major beneficiaries, exercising influence on Middle Eastern politics for the first time. Egypt, Syria, and Iraq leaned to the Russian side in the Cold War, whereas conservative monarchies such as Jordan and Saudi Arabia tilted towards the United States. Yet Nasser constantly maneuvered between the two superpowers and remained as non-aligned as possible. During some years of the 1960s he accepted substantial aid and trade from both sides.

The Suez crisis also had enormous consequences outside the Arab world. International organizations, such as the United Nations, the World Bank, and the International Monetary Fund, proved themselves effective, but under American direction. American clout at the World Bank precipitated the Suez crisis by canceling the Aswan Dam loan, and similar pressure on the IMF helped bring it to an end. UN peacekeepers, organized by America's neighbors, the Canadians, cooled the region for a decade afterward.

Britain and France re-evaluated their declining international positions and accelerated plans for decolonization of their remaining possessions in Africa (see part 4). After 1956, England even turned away from its ties with the Commonwealth nations and began building new links to the European Common Market. The French, too, became more committed to the cause of European unity. Allegedly, German chancellor Konrad Adenauer remarked to Guy Mollet at the end of the Suez invasion, "Europe will be your revenge." The French also took another lesson from Suez. They blamed the failure of the expedition on the clumsy joint military command in which French generals served under British superiors, and also on the British readiness to cave in to American pressure. Therefore, after General Charles de Gaulle took power in France, he pulled French troops out of the joint NATO command, developed an independent nuclear strike force, and kept a cool distance from the American superpower in international diplomacy. Yet before all this took place, France fought one more colonial war along the life-line of imperialism, a far more devastating struggle in Algeria than the botched Suez invasion.

CHAPTER ELEVEN

Terror and Torture

I f Palestine could be characterized as a settler colony with a difference (see chapter 9), French Algeria was the archetype of a true settler colony. In the mid-twentieth century Algerians of European origin numbered just under one million in a total population of about ten million. This 9 to 1 ratio of natives to settlers was the lowest of any colony in Africa. In neighboring Morocco, for instance, natives outnumbered colonists 22 to 1. The French did not even consider Algeria, legally speaking, a colony, but rather a part of metropolitan France. The territory was divided into three French *departements* (provinces) whose European population sent delegates to the National Assembly in Paris, just like citizens of Bordeaux or Marseilles.

The settler population was rooted in Algeria. The ancestors of some had come as early as the 1840s, and by the twentieth century most were Algerian-born and had never set foot in France. Some settlers became wealthy capitalists, like Henri Borgeaud, who owned vineyards, banks, and cigarette factories; but many more resembled the novelist Albert Camus, a working-class, street-smart punk with many Arab friends. So when Muslim Algerians bid for independence in 1954, the eight-year conflict that ensued had many characteristics of a civil war and was marked by terror and torture. At least a half-million Muslim Algerians died, and nearly all of the million European settlers fled into exile.

French Algeria had been founded on violence from the very beginning. In 1827 Hussein Dey, the semi-independent ruler of Algiers (*dey* was his title) who owed nominal allegiance to the Ottoman Empire, insulted the French consul, striking him on the arm with a peacock-feather fly swatter. French gunboats demanded an apology but the dey refused, so the consul and his retinue departed and the Algerian government expelled the French trading community. Three years later, on June 14, 1830, a French fleet landed troops just west of Algiers, and by July 5 the dey had capitulated. That same day the foreign soldiers sacked the city in an orgy of rape and looting. Much deeper motives lay behind this episode of gunboat diplomacy than a mere insult. The French had lost their North American and Indian empires to the British and were looking for new fields to colonize, and the tottering monarchy of the Bourbons needed a popular foreign adventure to dazzle the populace. So the French seized the opportunity in North Africa, just across the Mediterranean.

The territory surrounding the port city of Algiers is vast and diverse. A narrow band of beaches, mountains, valleys, and high plains runs about 600 miles along the coast of the Mediterranean, extending no more than 200 miles inland. Five ranges of the Saharan Atlas Mountains, some soaring as high as 8,000 feet, separate the coastal strip from the Sahara Desert. Each segment of the environment supports a different kind of economy, from grain and fruit growing near the coast, to olive trees along the hilltops and cattle grazing on the high plains.

The inhabitants of Algeria, called Berbers by the Greeks (from the word for barbarian), were a fiercely independent people whose own word for themselves means free or noble men. The coastal strip has often been colonized by other Mediterranean powers, such as the Carthaginians and the Romans, but the Berbers long remained unconquered in the interior. They resisted the waves of Arab invasions longer than any other people in Asia or Africa. Although they accepted the Muslim religion quite swiftly, they did not adopt the Arabic language until the twelfth century. By the time of the French conquest, Algeria had a population of three million people, about three-quarters Arabic-speaking with the rest still speaking a Berber dialect. Approximately 45 percent of Algerians were nomadic, whereas half worked as sedentary farmers and about 5 percent lived in cities. Historian John Ruedy sums up the political situation of this highly segmented society on the eve of the conquest: "For a sizeable minority of Algeria's population, the dey was ruler in a direct sense. For others he was suzerain; for others, he was ally; and for still others, he was irrelevant."

The Amir Abdel Kader mounted a rebellion against the incoming French that united almost two-thirds of Algeria under his authority for nearly a decade, but divisions among the rebels weakened his position. Then, General Thomas Robert Bugeaud, appointed French governor general in November 1840, scorched the earth and starved the populace of Algeria until they submitted. Civilians who sought refuge in caves were burned out or asphyxiated. Still, it took forty years before the French had conquered and "pacified" all of present-day Algeria. Even before Bugeaud's massacres, a French parliamentary commission of inquiry had written that "we have outdone in barbarity the barbarians we have come to civilize." Bugeaud's repression and that of his successors caused a drastic population crash in Algeria, from about 3 million Muslims in 1830 to only 2,134,000 in 1872. The French entered Algeria amidst a million corpses and exited it over a century later in a similar bloodbath.

European colonists fleeing poverty poured into the cities of Algiers, Constantine, and Oran and took up some of the most fertile land on the plains near the seacoast. In 1872 they numbered 279,691 and by the turn of the century 633,850. Not all of the settlers were French; in fact, the great majority came from Spain, Portugal, Italy, or the island of Malta. Collectively, they became known as *pieds noirs* (black feet), either from the black shoes they wore or from their sun-darkened skins. The Spanish-born were often called *pataouètes* (potato-eaters), and in the cities of Algeria a popular *pataouète* dialect mingled French and Spanish words.

The *pieds noirs* looked upon themselves as pioneers in a savage land. A fictional character in Jean Lartéguy's novel *The Centurions* sums up this attitude:

> We want to hold on to this land because we were born here and made it what it is. We've got as much right to it as the settlers of the Far West who drew up in their covered wagons on a river bank where there was nothing but a handful of Indians.

Yet most of the colonists did not settle on the land, but rather in the cities, where they became shopkeepers or laborers. From a high of about 40 percent in the early years, the percentage of settlers engaged in farming declined to just 21 percent by the mid-twentieth century. Most European landholdings consisted of huge estates, often planted with grapevines and worked by the labor of natives. The cities of Algiers, Constantine, and Oran were overwhelmingly European at the turn of the century, but they became less so as Muslims migrated from the countryside during the first half of the twentieth century.

If the *pieds noirs* were not quite the homesteaders they fancied themselves, the natives were not all that savage either. In fact there is evidence that colonization, far from bringing progress to a backward land, actually *de*developed Algeria and other colonies. Due to the Muslim emphasis on reading the Koran, literacy was relatively widespread before the French conquest. Algerian nationalists today claim that the literacy rate in Algeria in 1830 exceeded that of France. Historians have been unable to confirm whether this was actually true, but it is undeniable that the literacy rate declined in Algeria during the years of French rule. In 1954, when the colonial revolt broke out, 86 percent of men and 95 percent of women were illiterate, a statistic which historian John Ruedy calls "a monumental indictment of a system that for more than a century had claimed to be civilizing the uncivilized." At this same time, about 600,000 Muslims lived in Algerian cities without any visible regular means of support, and nearly half that number had emigrated to France in order to make a living.

Though Algeria was legally part of France and all its inhabitants were French subjects, only those of European origin were considered citizens. In order to become citizens, native Algerians had to renounce the laws of Islam and live under French legal codes. Since this was tantamount to apostasy from their religion, only about 2,500 Muslims became French citizens by the 1930s. Muslims could not vote for delegates to the French parliament until after World War II, and they only began electing delegates to local councils in 1919. Though they outnumbered the Europeans 9 to 1, their representation in such councils was limited to one-quarter or one-third of the delegates. An early Algerian nationalist, Messali Hadj, commented: "The achievement of France is self-evident. It leaps to the eyes, and it would be unjust to deny it; but if the French have done a lot, they did it for themselves."

Messali Hadj belonged to a small group of North Africans who had discovered their Algerian national identity while working as immigrants in France. In 1926, with the aid of French Communists and union leaders, Messali formed the *Étoile Nord-Africaine* (North African Star), the first organization openly calling for Algerian independence. Most native leaders back in Algeria, however, were not yet thinking along these lines. A reform Muslim movement headed by Abd al-Hamid Ben Badis promoted the slogan "Islam is my religion; Arabic is my language; Algeria is my fatherland," which later became the motto of independent Algeria. Yet Ben Badis's Association of Reformist Ulama focused more on the protection and reformation of religious institutions than the advocacy of nationalism. Middle-class professionals, called *evolués* (evolved ones) by the French, accepted the French promise of assimilation in language and culture but wanted to advance toward full citizenship without giving up their Muslim religion and customs.

Ferhat Abbas, born in 1899 to a Muslim judge who had been awarded the French Legion of Honor, typified the liberal, assimilated Algerian Muslims. Abbas had studied in French-speaking schools and trained as a pharmacist. He became active in the federation of local elected officials and pushed for full equality of rights for Muslims so that Algeria could become a province of France in fact as well as in name. In 1936 he published an article in a French newspaper rejecting nationalism:

> Had I discovered the Algerian nation, I would have become a nationalist. . . . However, I will not die for the Algerian nation, because it does not exist. I have not found it. I have examined history, I questioned the living and the dead, I visited the cemeteries; nobody spoke to me about it.

207

Despite a common language and common religion, Algeria did not possess, in Abbas's opinion, the great deeds, the feeling "we have done great things together in the past," required by the classic definition of nationalism. Yet ironically, the French provided the occasion for such "great deeds." A Muslim character in Lartéguy's novel *The Centurions* comments: "Like Ferhat Abbas I've looked for Algeria in books and cemeteries and never found her. But since then you've filled our cemeteries sufficiently to create a history for us."

The French could have satisfied moderate leaders such as Ferhat Abbas with prudent, timely reforms consistent with their own alleged aims of assimilating and civilizing Algerians. The best opportunity came in 1936, when Léon Blum's Socialists formed a Popular Front government in France and his minister responsible for Algerian affairs, Maurice Viollette, introduced a reform bill. The Blum-Viollette bill would have granted immediate citizenship and full voting rights to Muslims who had served in the French army or administration and to all high school graduates. Such persons would be permitted to retain their rights and customs under Islamic law and thus would enjoy the advantages of dual citizenship. Only about 25,000 Algerians fit these criteria at the time, but once the principle of equal-dual citizenship was established, it could be expanded further. However, the French settler community opposed the bill fiercely, lobbying successfully against it in the French National Assembly. The Blum-Viollette bill never passed. It represented the last, best chance to retain the loyalty of Algerian moderates such as Ferhat Abbas.

The defeat of France by Germany at the beginning of World War II and the establishment of a Nazi puppet regime further damaged France's prestige. When the Americans landed in North Africa in 1942, speaking of democracy and driving shiny new mechanized vehicles, Algerians felt even more contempt for the French. The moderate Ferhat Abbas united temporarily with radicals such as Messali Hadj to issue the Manifesto of the Algerian People in February 1943, calling for a separate, autonomous Algerian state. General de Gaulle's Free French government, which resided in Algiers for a time during the war, offered to grant French citizenship to an even larger category of people than the rejected Blum-Viollette bill would have, but Algerian expectations had been raised and this concession came too late.

At the end of the war, Messali and other radicals plotted to transform French victory celebrations into Algerian protest demonstrations. In most cases, these remained peaceful, but at the town of Setif, near the city of Constantine, a Muslim mob ran wild on VE Day, May 8, 1945, slaughtering a hundred European settlers. The French military mounted massive reprisals, summarily executing large numbers of Muslims in Setif and the surrounding area, and bombing and shelling remote villages in the mountains. The French government reported about 1,300 Muslim deaths but more impartial estimates

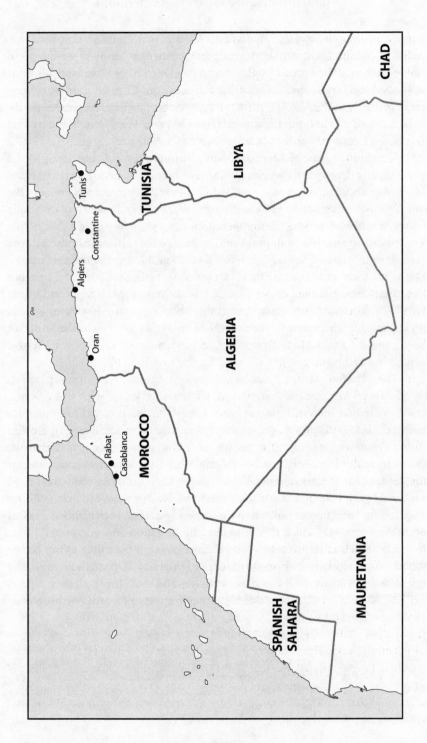

Algeria

range from 6,000 to 45,000. A pattern of violence was established at Setif that would predominate during the war for independence. Muslims would begin the violence, and the French would overreact with counter-terror. Yet Muslims could, and did, argue that colonialism was a system of institutionalized violence, so the French were the primary aggressors. The argument became increasingly circular, but one thing is certain. The cemeteries were filling up and convincing Ferhat Abbas that the Algerian nation did exist.

The constitution of France's Fourth Republic, established after World War II, finally declared all Algerians citizens of France. The two kinds of Algerians, Europeans and Muslims, would vote in separate electorates, choosing the same number of delegates. However, such "equality" remained fundamentally unfair, for Muslims greatly outnumbered Europeans. Even such grudging concessions came to very little in practice. The *pieds noirs* committed massive vote fraud in the national, local, and provincial elections held under the new constitution, resulting in the choice of very moderate, assimilated Muslims. Settler intransigence barred the road of peaceful, legal reform for Algeria; and at the same time, a paramilitary group called the OS (*Organisation Speciale*, Special Organization), which had splintered off from Messali Hadj's leadership, was suppressed by the French authorities. Both moderate and radical change seemed blocked.[1]

The Algerian war for independence was born out of frustration, defeat, and despair. The hopes of nationalists after World War II had been beaten down, but in 1954 the French too suffered a crushing defeat — at Dien Bien Phu in Indochina (see chapter 6). Aware that France had been humiliated by Ho Chi Minh's Communists, a group of young Algerian nationalists decided to strike while their colonial masters were still demoralized. An executive committee of nine leaders, who became known as the *neufs historiques* (nine historical ones), chose the name *Front de Libération Nationale* — National Liberation Front (FLN) — for their new organization on October 10. Then they planned a revolt for November 1, 1954, All Saints' Day in Catholic France and Algeria.

The revolutionaries of 1954 were a generation younger than either Ferhat Abbas or Messali Hadj, with an average age of thirty-two, about the same as the Free Officers in Egypt. They came from villages and small towns all over Algeria and had relatively limited educations, though all were literate. With no out-

---

1. France proved less intransigent toward Algeria's two North African neighbors, Tunisia and Morocco. After the French defeat in Vietnam, Prime Minister Pierre Mendes-France began negotiations with the popular Tunisian nationalist leader Habib Bourguiba and with the sultan of Morocco. Both countries became fully independent in March 1956. The smaller size of the settler communities in Tunisia and Morocco and the fact that they were only protectorates, not a part of metropolitan France, made these two decolonizations easier than in Algeria.

standing chieftain such as Ho Chi Minh, they established a collective leadership and resisted the cult of personality throughout the ensuing eight-year war. Most had served in the French army, and the fighting in France and Italy during World War II revealed to them that they were the equal of any French soldier. Yet when they returned home to the news of the Setif massacre they suffered a profound disillusionment. Most joined Messali Hadj's independence movement, and many were arrested as members of the OS. Nearly everything they had done in life had failed, but they knew how to fight and they believed in themselves and their cause, which was simple nationalism. Their lack of professional training makes it difficult to apply the "intellectual proletariat" label to them or compare them directly with the Free Officers in Egypt. If they resembled any group from earlier in the twentieth century, it might be the "primitive rebels" of Young Bosnia who sparked off the First World War.

Much had changed, however, since the days of Gavrilo Princip, and the FLN had a wider range of strategy and tactics available than the Young Bosnians. The *neuf historiques* adhered to no sophisticated ideology, but they had studied the methods of guerrilla warfare espoused by Mao Tse-tung and Ho Chi Minh. After dividing the country into six *wilayas,* or regions, they planned a coordinated series of attacks against symbolic targets in each area, such as police stations or power plants. These lightning strikes were intended to announce their existence as a movement and rally the Algerian populace to their side. The collective leadership of the plot strictly forbade attacks on civilians, for they hoped to avoid the horrors of the Setif massacre. The revolutionaries would mount their main effort in the remote Aurès Mountains, which could serve as a revolutionary base, like Mao's strongholds in Kiangsi or Yenan.

Not much happened in the early morning hours of All Saints' Day 1954. Few of the terrorist strikes went according to schedule, and the populace remained indifferent. Even the plan to keep civilians immune from violence went awry when a vacationing French schoolteacher was killed and his wife seriously wounded in a bus ambush. The rebels retreated into the hills, fragmenting their organization into operational groups of only four or five so that few conspirators would be betrayed if anyone were captured. They tried to both inspire and frighten the Algerian masses by assassinating Muslims who held positions of authority in the French regime. The terrorists slit the throats of such "collaborators," leaving them with a wound from ear to ear that the French began calling *le grand sourire* (the big smile).

Declaring a policy of "collective responsibility," the French army fanned out into the countryside executing suspected terrorists and leveling whole villages merely on the suspicion they may have harbored rebels. When they bombed rebel hideouts, they rarely warned surrounding villages first. In a sense, the French lost Algeria much the way the British lost Ireland: by over-

reacting and responding to terror with counter-terror. The collective responsibility raids of late 1954 and 1955 crippled the FLN rebels militarily and prevented them from establishing secure base camps, but they also converted
many other Algerians to their cause. In particular, the followers of Messali Hadj
and the members of the small Algerian Communist Party came over to the
FLN. In a major propaganda coup, Ferhat Abbas, the leading assimilationist
who had earlier been unable to find the Algerian nation, announced his adherence to the FLN in April 1956 over Cairo radio.

In August 1955, the FLN leaders of the Constantine *wilaya* changed the
nature of the revolt by abandoning the policy of civilian immunity and intentionally creating a new Setif massacre. On August 20 armed bands inflamed
mobs of overheated, unemployed workers and peasants to attack both *pieds
noirs* and Muslim collaborators in Constantine, Philippeville, and surrounding
villages. One hundred and twenty-three men, women, and children were
hacked to death and mutilated. Pregnant women had babies ripped from their
wombs and men's sexual organs were cut off and stuffed in their mouths. Just as
at Setif, the French authorities mounted massive retaliations against Muslims,
killing 1,273 according to official figures, but possibly as many as 12,000. The
Philippeville massacres, as these events came to be called, decisively escalated
the cycle of violence in Algeria. As the FLN leaders had hoped, they polarized
the European settler and native Muslim communities so severely that compromise solutions would henceforth be extremely unlikely.

With the guerrilla war still going badly in the countryside, the FLN leadership decided to duplicate the Philippeville terrorism in the capital of Algiers.
Saadi Yacef, the commander of the region, orchestrated a series of random
bombings reminiscent of the anarchist outrages at the turn of the century. On
September 30, 1956, three middle-class Muslim women, light-skinned enough
to pass for Europeans and dressed in stylish European clothes, planted bombs
in the downtown Air France terminal and in two popular watering-holes, the
Milk Bar and the Cafeteria. Only the latter two bombs exploded, killing several
women and children and injuring dozens. Though the military cordoned off
the Casbah, the Muslim quarter of Algiers where Yacef operated his bomb factories, searching everyone who came in or out, the bombings continued on a
regular but unpredictable schedule. The FLN practiced collective responsibility
just as the French army did. They did not believe there were any innocent *pieds
noirs.*

The Battle of Algiers was above all a cruel publicity stunt. The FLN realized that they could fight and die for years in the Aurès without doing any damage to French colonialism or gaining attention for their cause. Algiers, however,
swarmed with foreign journalists and consular officials, who instantly took
note of the bombings. The terrorists believed the old adage, "there is no such

thing as bad publicity." One of the FLN leaders, Ramdane Abane, stated grimly: "One corpse in a jacket is always worth more than twenty in uniform." The United Nations began holding debates on the "Algerian question," and in July 1957 a young American senator named John F. Kennedy delivered a speech asking his government "to place the influence of the United States behind efforts . . . to achieve a solution which will recognize the independent personality of Algeria." The Battle of Algiers internationalized the independence movement.

The terror of Algiers increased, however, as the French counterattacked. Despairing of any conventional police solution to the bombing campaign, the governor general on January 7, 1957, turned over full civil and military authority to General Raoul Salan, who delegated operational responsibility to General Jacques Massu and the elite Tenth Paratroop Division. The paratroopers marched into Algiers like conquering heroes, threw away the rulebook, and smashed the FLN network of terrorists. They began by breaking a general strike that the FLN called on January 28. The paratroopers pulled down the bars from the shuttered shops of the cities and dragged their proprietors to work kicking and screaming. They then set out to find Yacef and his cohorts in the Casbah by systematically torturing all suspects. Though the FLN had carefully organized their networks in tight pyramids so that each operative knew only his or her superior and two immediate subordinates, the torture chambers slowly churned out more and more names.

Victims were beaten, dunked in barrels of water, and injected with high-pressure hoses up the rectum. Many were hooked to electrodes and jolted with high voltages. Nearly all eventually talked. As many as three thousand died under torture. Most of the FLN high command abandoned the city; then Yacef was captured and the last high-ranking terrorist, the legendary Ali la Pointe, was killed in September 1957. The French won the Battle of Algiers, but the grisly drama of terror and torture had put the Algerian struggle on the map. From then on, the whole world was watching.[2]

In France, protests against the use of torture rocked the weak governments of the Fourth Republic from both the left and the right of the political spectrum. The French military had increased their garrison in Algeria to half a million men, but most of these were reluctant draftees whose service time had been extended to twenty-seven months or reservists grudgingly called up from civilian life. Nearly everyone in France knew someone serving in Algeria, and when one of these citizen soldiers was killed, their relatives asked what the war

2. The publicity value of this urban conflict continued even after the war was over. An Italian filmmaker, with the assistance of Saadi Yacef, who played himself in the film, made a fascinating propaganda movie called *The Battle of Algiers* in 1967. It swiftly became a cult classic for radicals in the United States and elsewhere.

was accomplishing. Many of the soldiers themselves suffered nightmares and depression when they returned home, particularly if they had participated in or witnessed torture.

The elite paratroopers felt disgust at the squeamishness of the conscripts and the general public in France. These military professionals had suffered the humiliation of defeat and surrender in 1940, then joined de Gaulle's resistance forces, risking capture and torture by the Gestapo. They had tasted defeat and captivity again in Indochina and finally had been pulled away from Suez with victory seemingly in reach. The paratroopers felt as frustrated in 1957 and 1958 as the FLN founders had in 1954. So did the *pieds noirs,* who feared that the Fourth Republic might negotiate away their rights in Algeria.

In the spring of 1958, France went thirty-seven days without a government, as political parties and factions tried to cobble together yet another coalition. Politics, like nature, abhors a vacuum, so the paratroopers and settlers joined hands in Algiers to fill it. On May 9, 1958, the Algerian rebels executed three French soldiers who had been taken prisoner. This prompted General Salan, the commander in chief, to lay a wreath in their honor at the war monument in downtown Algiers on May 13. As soon as he had finished the ceremony, a mob of *pieds noirs* went on a rampage, sacking the Government General offices and demanding that the military form a committee of public safety, a tried and true device for a coup d'etat. The paratrooper commander, General Massu, responded positively, more to keep order than to overthrow the government; but General Salan boldly put himself at the head of a movement to change the regime in France, preserve a French Algeria with all available means, and bring General Charles de Gaulle back to power.

De Gaulle, leader of the Free French during World War II, had resigned as prime minister shortly after the war in disgust at the partisanship of the politicians. He had expected to be called back soon by a desperate nation, but instead had been relegated to writing his memoirs. Now he was sixty-seven years old, visibly aging, and eager to save France for a second time. His coterie of supporters were actively encouraging the military rebels in Algiers, but de Gaulle himself played a waiting game at his country home of Colombey-les-Deux-Églises.

On May 15 General Salan, after some prompting from a de Gaulle emissary, shouted *"Vive la France! Vive l'Algérie Française!"* and *"Vive de Gaulle!"* from the balcony of the Algiers Government General. The next day, thirty thousand Muslims, encouraged by the paratroopers, joined the *pieds noirs* in demanding de Gaulle's return. Then on May 24, the paratroopers launched the first phase of "Operation Resurrection," seizing power on the French island of Corsica, a stepping-stone toward mainland France. The rest of the plan called for a parachute drop at an airfield outside Paris, followed by swift capture of the city's key points. The French public braced for either a bloodless coup or civil war.

De Gaulle finally made his move on June 1, 1958, addressing the National Assembly with his terms for taking over the government. He demanded the power to rule by decree for six months while the Assembly went on "a holiday" and authority to write a new constitution and submit it to the voters in a referendum. The Assembly granted his requests, voting him in as prime minister by a margin of 329 to 224. The paratroopers called off Operation Resurrection. Charles de Gaulle took power much like Mussolini did in 1922, legally but under the threat of force. Unlike Mussolini, however, he did not create a dictatorship, but a parliamentary system with a strong president. On September 28, 1958, the French voters overwhelmingly approved his constitution for the Fifth Republic, which remains in effect today. De Gaulle was elected first president of the Fifth Republic on December 21.

The Algerian crowds and the military returned de Gaulle to power in order to crush the nationalist revolt, but he himself considered Algeria a sideshow. He nurtured larger plans to restore France's greatness by renovating its economy and playing a dominant role in Europe. Yet first he had to do something about Algeria. De Gaulle flew across the Mediterranean to the troubled colony just four days after taking over. On the evening of June 4, 1958, he appeared in full military dress on the balcony of the Government General in Algiers, proclaiming to the crowd of *pieds noirs,* "I have understood you!" Just what he understood, however, was not immediately clear, probably not even to himself. Most likely he would have preferred a negotiated settlement with a moderate Algerian leader, someone like the Ferhat Abbas of the 1930s, who had attended good schools and spoke excellent French. By this time, however, Abbas had become titular president of the FLN's provisional government and most other moderates had either been converted or murdered by the revolutionaries.

To strengthen his bargaining position, President de Gaulle unleashed General Maurice Challe against the rebels. Using tactics that had become familiar in the twentieth century, Challe's troops cleared large areas of Algeria by resettling over a million villagers in "regroupment camps." Then the paratroopers, guided by Muslim auxiliaries, smashed any guerrillas found in the free-fire zones. Believing resistance was futile, the FLN withdrew the main body of their administrative and military cadres to havens in newly independent Tunisia. The French built a two-hundred-mile-long electrified fence sealing off the Tunisian border, and unlike the ill-fated Maginot line of World War II, this barrier actually worked. After losing 6,000 fighters and 4,300 weapons testing the fence, the army of the FLN, under a new chief of staff, Colonel Houari Boumedienne, decided to regroup in the Tunisian sanctuary. When General Challe was posted back to France in the spring of 1960, Algeria had been largely pacified in the military sense, but the FLN rightly judged that time was on their side and they could afford to wait.

On September 16, 1959, de Gaulle delivered a major speech laying out the political options for Algeria. He pledged that four years after peace had been concluded he would offer Algerians three choices: complete independence and separation from France, complete integration into France, or a federal association with the mother country. "I deem it necessary," de Gaulle asserted, "that recourse to self-determination be here and now proclaimed." Though they had not gained a victory on the field of battle, the Algerian nationalists had essentially won when de Gaulle conceded the notion of self-determination. The general himself hoped that Algerians would choose the third option, loose association with France, but this would never satisfy the FLN. A first attempt at peace talks in June 1960 failed utterly when the Algerians refused even to consider a cease-fire until the French conceded independence.

In the meantime, the settlers and the military, who had summoned de Gaulle from retirement to preserve a French Algeria, felt betrayed. The most hotheaded of the *pieds noirs* believed they could break the general as easily as they had made him. So on January 24, 1960, the "ultras" proclaimed a general strike and set up barricades in the center of Algiers. The police, who were largely sympathetic to the settlers, tried herding them back to their residential quarters with unloaded weapons, but the ultras started sniping at them, so the police finally loaded and fired back. The paratroopers looked on from a distance and did not intervene. The *pieds noirs* controlled the city for nearly a week behind their barricades, but finally an emotional televised speech by de Gaulle in Paris and a torrential rainstorm in Algiers ended "Barricades Week." Yet the *pieds noirs* still pledged resistance to Muslim self-determination, openly vowing they would leave Algeria, either with "a suitcase or a coffin," rather than give in.

De Gaulle had little respect for the *pieds noirs*, and he now wanted to get out of Algeria at any cost so that he could focus French pride upon himself and his leadership of a new Europe. He was a maddeningly egotistical military man, who had sanctioned draconian repression in the countryside of Algeria and silently condoned the continuation of torture. Yet he possessed the wisdom to know when it was time to quit. So he scheduled a referendum to give himself a free hand in negotiating with the FLN. When he visited Algeria in December 1960 to canvass support for his position, he met fierce hostility from the settlers and would have been assassinated if he had set foot in Algiers, which he carefully avoided.

De Gaulle won his referendum on January 8, 1961, approving his moves toward Algerian self-determination, but three months later the military moved against him. General Challe, disgusted that pacification efforts had been slackened after his reassignment, joined General Salan and two other disgruntled generals in a revolt on April 20, 1961. With one paratroop regiment wholeheartedly behind them, the generals easily took over Algiers, and the officers of most other military formations throughout the colony were sympathetic. Yet the plotters had underestimated de Gaulle and overlooked the war-weariness and common sense of the ordinary soldiers. De Gaulle broadcast one of his greatest speeches on Sunday, April 23, appealing to the patriotism, loyalty, and obedience of the troops. He specifically absolved the soldiers of any obligation to obey their superior officers. The draftees and reservists, huddled around their transistor radios, heard de Gaulle's message loud and clear, and frustrated the revolt by their passive resistance. Generals cannot march without privates, and the privates refused to fight their own government. After four days and five nights, the revolt collapsed and General Challe surrendered on April 26.

Diehard settlers and military officers went underground after the revolt, constructing a clandestine network called the *Organisation Armée Secrète* — Secret Army Organization (OAS) — which unleashed a wave of terrorism in Algeria and in France itself. Using sophisticated plastic explosives, they assassinated government and military officials and created a state of anarchy in the city of Algiers. Comparing the reign of terror to the machine-gun era of Al Capone, the overwhelmed Algerian police dubbed every radio notice of a new atrocity a "Chicago alert." In just six months of 1961 and 1962, the OAS killed more people in Algiers than the FLN had during the entire war, including the notorious "Battle of Algiers." If the purpose of such terrorism was to preserve French Algeria, however, it backfired. The bombings, particularly those close to home in metropolitan France, outraged public opinion and gave de Gaulle the leeway he needed to quit Algeria.

Secret talks between French government representatives and FLN delegates prepared the way for public talks at Evian, France, in March 1962. De Gaulle eventually gave way on the final sticking point, the status of the Sahara Desert. Historical Algeria had been limited to the mountains and plains near the Mediterranean, so the French believed they had a right to keep the Sahara, which had never been ruled from Algiers before they themselves conquered it. The desert held both economic and military importance for France since oil had started flowing from Saharan wells in January 1958 and the French military had exploded their first atomic bomb in the desert vastness on April 25, 1961. The FLN, accurately gauging French war-weariness, remained intransigent throughout the negotiations: no cease-fire until full independence was conceded to Algeria *including the Sahara*.

On March 18, 1962, the French gave up and signed a peace agreement on the FLN's terms. The cease-fire went into effect the following day, and two months later even the OAS admitted defeat and stopped fighting. Both countries, France and Algeria, held referenda confirming the agreement, and on July 5, 1963, 132 years after the dey of Algiers had capitulated to the French, Algerians celebrated independence.

Two scrambles ensued, as French settlers hustled into exile and Algerian revolutionaries fought and schemed for power. Even before the referendum confirming independence, 350,000 *pieds noirs* had departed in June 1962. By the end of the year, only 30,000 remained of the million or so French Algerians. About 50,000 settled in Spain and a few thousand more in Canada or South America, but most flooded into Marseilles and the south of France, where they remain a disgruntled and bitter minority, often supporting extremist French politicians. Unlike the Arab-Israeli war, where the settlers stayed and the natives went into exile, the Algerian settlers abandoned their homes.

In the meantime, the solidarity of the FLN's collective leadership cracked as several factions struggled for power. Perhaps 15,000 died in the internal fighting after independence, and even larger numbers of Algerians who had cooperated with the French were massacred. Finally, the army that Colonel Boumedienne had carefully preserved across the border in Tunisia restored order and imposed a government under Ahmed Ben Bella at the end of September 1962.

Ben Bella was one of the original revolutionaries, the *neuf historiques*. Born in 1918, he had fought with the French army in World War II and been profoundly disillusioned by the Setif massacre. Joining Messali's underground *Organisation Speciale*, he pledged to fight colonialism "by all means." In exile when the revolt broke out, Ben Bella was one of a handful of "outside leaders" of the FLN who negotiated, not too successfully, for weapons and economic support in Cairo and other North African capitals. While flying from Morocco to Tunisia in October 1956, his plane was hijacked in international air space by the French air force, and Ben Bella, along with other FLN members, spent the rest of the war in a French prison. His release was one of many prickly issues that delayed a peace settlement.

Ben Bella read much left-wing literature in prison and emerged as a committed socialist. A vain and ambitious man, he envisioned himself as an Algerian Nasser who would transform his country and play a major role in Third World politics. Opposition to the cult of personality was so ingrained in the FLN's political culture, however, that Ben Bella soon alienated most of his colleagues. On June 19, 1965, Colonel Boumedienne's army staged a bloodless coup, deposing President Ben Bella, who was imprisoned for the next fourteen years. A government composed of military officers, intellectuals, and technically trained bureaucrats took over, with Boumedienne as president.

Born in 1927, Houari Boumedienne was a bit younger than the other revolutionaries. His real name was Mohammed Ben Brahim Boukharouba, but he adopted the names of a local mountain range and a Muslim saint popular near his birthplace as his revolutionary nicknames. He was a stern, puritanical, nononsense military officer who shunned the limelight and was content to rule behind the scenes. He presided over a directorate that governed the country until his death in 1979, pursuing policies of economic self-sufficiency and diplomatic independence from both superpowers in the Cold War. The president rarely appeared in public and did not build up a personal following like Nasser, Tito, or Ben Bella. Independent Algeria under Boumedienne remained poor but proud, stable, austere, and authoritarian. Its various constitutions proclaimed it a socialist state, with Arabic as its national language and Islam its official religion.

Algerians claim that a million people died in their war of independence, just as the Spanish have also appropriated that round figure for their civil war dead. The actual number of deaths was probably lower than that. The French counted only 17,456 dead among their troops[3] and claimed to have killed 141,000 Algerians in battle. However, greater numbers died as a result of torture and terror than on the battlefield. Estimates of total deaths, therefore, run from a low of 300,000 up to the official one million. An additional million, the *pieds noirs*, went into permanent exile, and more than three million Algerians had been settled in regroupment camps or otherwise displaced. Only about half these refugees ever returned home. So in round numbers, the Algerian war of independence resulted in a half million deaths, a million exiles, and a million and a half displaced persons.

Algeria represents the nightmare scenario of decolonization. Individuals of honor and integrity made attempts to stop, or at least limit, the terror and torture, but to no avail. Albert Camus, for example, the Algerian-born French writer who received the Nobel Prize for literature, proposed a "civil truce" after the Philippeville massacres in 1955. He told a mixed group of Muslims and Europeans in Algiers that his appeal "is addressed to both camps in the hope that they will accept a truce insofar as innocent civilians are concerned. . . . Whatever the ancient and deep origins of the Algerian tragedy, one fact remains: no cause justifies the death of the innocent." Neither side abandoned the use of terror, however, and Camus later discovered that two Muslim friends on whom he had relied to promote his civil truce were FLN agents.

The FLN defended its use of terror as a just reprisal for previous French violence. For example, the Philippeville massacres were justified as a response to the collective responsibility raids of the French military, and the Battle of Algiers was supposedly prompted by the execution of captured revolutionaries and the French bombing of houses where suspected rebels lived. At a deeper level, all acts of terror could be considered retaliation for the institutionalized violence of colonialism.

The most influential justification of revolutionary violence was presented

---

3. By way of comparison, the United States, with roughly the same number of troops in Vietnam, suffered nearly 58,000 deaths.

by Frantz Fanon, a black man born in the French Caribbean island of Martinique and trained as a doctor and a psychiatrist. He lived and worked in Algeria until his death from leukemia at a young age in 1961. His book *The Wretched of the Earth* became a cult classic for radicals in the 1960s, both in the United States and in Europe. Fanon emphasized the atmosphere of institutionalized violence that both European imperialism and the Cold War created. Cynically and bitterly, he commented: "the colonized peoples are well adapted to this atmosphere; for once, they are up to date."

Fanon the psychiatrist then argued that violence was not only inevitable in a colonial situation, but beneficial and therapeutic:

> But it so happens that for the colonized people this violence, because it constitutes their only work, invests their characters with positive and creative qualities. . . . At the level of individuals, violence is a cleansing force. It frees the native from his inferiority complex and from his despair and inaction.

This argument may be at least partially valid, but when one strips away the rhetoric it reduces itself simply to the dictum "revenge is sweet." Furthermore, it is difficult to square Fanon's description of violence as therapeutic with his own evidence. Later in his book, he presents haunting case studies of both Europeans and Muslims who had committed acts of terror or torture and were mentally ill as a result. He even identified a form of catatonic muscle stiffness in patients that he could not find in the medical literature and which he therefore concluded was unique to the Algerian war. Violence may feel good at the time, but it leaves scars. A French Catholic magazine surveyed returning soldiers from Algeria, asking them for their worst memory of the war. A larger number singled out participation in torture or atrocities than the death of their comrades.

Terrorism is often described and justified as the "weapon of the weak," the last resort of those resisting tyranny. Political scientist Martha Crenshaw Hutchinson has concluded: "Terrorism, a low cost and easily implemented strategy, was the only feasible alternative for the new nationalist organization because the FLN lacked *both* the necessary material resources (money, arms, soldiers) *and* active popular support." The strategy proved effective in both coercing and inspiring popular support, instilling fear in the European settlers, provoking military over-reaction, and gaining international publicity. Such a utilitarian argument is compelling. Since the French considered Algeria part of France itself, they would not depart without a strong push. However, the international climate of opinion was running against colonialism after World War II. The French themselves would soon cut loose all their colonies in sub-Saharan Africa without a struggle. Therefore, it may not have been necessary for the conflict in Algeria to take on violent forms. A massive, well-organized campaign of non-cooperation and non-violent resistance, such as that mounted by Gandhi in India, may have sufficed, if carried on as persistently as the FLN pursued its war. One should not conclude that revolutionary terrorism was the *only* alternative.

On the other side of the struggle in Algeria, the use of torture elicited a strong response of protest in France. Predictably, intellectuals on the left, such as Jean Paul Sartre and Simone de Beauvoir, issued manifestoes against torture, but even Catholic periodicals, which had traditionally supported the army and the right, condemned it. The military defended the torture of suspects on two grounds: it was an efficient way of obtaining vital information, and it countered the terror of the rebels by making the populace fear the French more than they did the FLN.

These pragmatic rationalizations for torture could be quite elaborate and at least superficially convincing. Soldiers argued that the suffering, and even the death, of one or two suspects was justified if it obtained information about future bombings, thus saving the lives of dozens or hundreds of innocent civilians. General Jacques Massu, one of the few officers who openly and publicly defended torture, pointed out, correctly, that more Muslims than Europeans suffered from FLN terrorism. He thus considered the war in Algeria, and its concomitant tortures, part of France's responsibility to protect its Muslim subjects. He and his wife Suzanne showed that they were not hypocrites by adopting two orphaned Muslim children. Massu's Catholic chaplain, Pere Delarue, blessed the use of torture, prescribing its use "without joy, but also without shame, done only because of concern with duty." The journalist Bernard Fall presented the most concise utilitarian argument: "Torture is the particular bane of the terrorist."

The French paratroopers won the Battle of Algiers by wringing information from suspects and eventually eliminating the leaders of the revolt; but in the long run, the use of torture backfired. It outraged both Muslim Algerians and the citizens of metropolitan France, persuading many of the former to join the FLN and prompting the latter to push for evacuation of Algeria. The counter-productiveness of the OAS's terror campaign within France itself is so obvious as to require no additional comment.

In sum, then, FLN terror was effective as a weapon of the weak, but it is possible that non-violent alternatives might have proven just as effective. The use of torture by the French military, though useful in the short run, ultimately aided the cause of Algerian independence.

Aside from such pragmatic arguments, the violence of the Algerian war seems repugnant to all religious and moral sentiments. Furthermore, torture was specifically prohibited by Article 5 of the United Nations' Universal Declaration of Human Rights, adopted in 1948 and signed by France: "No one shall be subjected to torture or to cruel, inhuman, or degrading treatment or punishment." In conclusion, it seems impossible to disagree with the words that Albert Camus put in the mouth of a fictional character, modeled after his own father. In *The First Man,* a novel Camus was working on when he died and which was published posthumously thirty-five years later, Lucien Cormery, discovering a mutilated body with its sexual organs cut off and stuffed in the victim's mouth, cries out: "A man doesn't do that." His companion chides him: "There are Frenchmen who do it too." Cormery replies: "Then they too, they aren't men."

PART FOUR

THE SCRAMBLE
OUT OF AFRICA

The European imperial powers scrambled out of Africa almost as quickly and mindlessly as they had tumbled in. The Englishman Lord Derby coined the phrase "Scramble for Africa" in 1884 to describe the unseemly haste with which England, France, Belgium, and Germany carved up the African continent in the late nineteenth century. Economic greed, a thirst for national prestige, and a fear that someone else would preempt prime real estate impelled the colonialists. A half century later, however, the world had changed profoundly. First the Great Depression then the Second World War weakened the European powers economically, politically, and morally. The colonies in Africa had never paid off as handsomely as the first colonizers hoped, so they appeared increasingly as expensive luxuries. Furthermore, the excesses of Hitler and Mussolini had fatally damaged the legitimacy of imperialism. Finally, the two new superpowers, the Soviet Union and the United States, were committed ideologically and rhetorically, if not always in actual fact, to anti-colonialism. So England and France hustled out of their imperial commitments in order to get right with the world. Ideas change over time, and ideas do have consequences.

Africans were not just passive victims of imperialism and then unwitting beneficiaries of decolonization. They cooperated in and profited from the slave trade for centuries; they actively shaped the nature of colonial society, for European settlers always remained few in numbers; and their protests finally hastened the end of European domination. Most African nations south of the Sahara did not have to fight wars of liberation, as the Vietnamese, Indonesians, and Algerians did; but they did mount effective, and sometimes violent, protest movements against colonial rule which accelerated the timetable of decolonization. From the mid-1950s until the mid-1960s, therefore, England, France, and Belgium cut loose nearly all their African colonies (Germany had been stripped of its possessions after World War I). Only the Spanish and Portuguese colonies and the Republic of South Africa remained under white rule. This intensive wave of decolonization was caused by forces at three levels: the international — a changing balance of power and changes in prevailing ways of thinking; the metropolitan — European powers found themselves economically weakened and dangerously overextended; and the local — Africans took matters into their own hands and demanded independence.

African nationalists inherited a continent damaged even before Europeans assumed formal political control in the late nineteenth century. Slavery and the slave trade, beginning in West Africa in the late fifteenth century and reaching their peak in the two centuries from 1650 to 1850, profoundly disrupted African life. Roughly eighteen million Africans were exported as slaves from 1500 until the late nineteenth century, about two-thirds of them to the Americas and the rest to Asia and the Middle East. Perhaps another eight million were captured, transported, and enslaved within Africa itself. Altogether, the African slave trade represented the largest human migration in history until the great waves of European immigration to the New World in the late nineteenth and early twentieth centuries.

Yet unlike the European migrations, the African population movements were involuntary. They led to demographic declines in West Africa and some other localities, and Africa as a whole experienced no population growth from 1750 to 1850, a time when Europe was increasing in numbers and economic strength. The slave trade also skewed the male-female population ratios, since young, healthy males were the prime candidates for American slavery. An increase in political tyranny, incessant warfare, and great insecurity in society also followed as Africans scrambled to capture potential slaves and sell them for a profit to the Europeans. Historian Patrick Manning has chillingly summed up the psychological ramifications of this insecurity: "To consider Africa at the time of the greatest extent of slavery and the slave trade, we must imagine a situation in which everybody knew the value, as a captive, of everyone he or she met. . . . The commoditization of humanity . . . [forced] Africans to take a short-range view of economic conditions. . . . I am left with the impression that they had to live each day as if it were their last."

Formal colonialism increased the economic and psychological damage in Africa. Most of the European possessions were "extractive colonies," deemed unfit for white habitation but potentially valuable for their mineral and agricultural resources and cheap labor. Therefore, the imperial powers invested little in the health and welfare of the population, limiting their development expenditures to transportation lines linking the mines and plantations to ports on the seacoast. The colonies, therefore, were gigantic funnels that drained manpower (slaves), natural resources, and profits from the African interior to the coast and onward to Europe and America. Furthermore, the racial superiority and condescension of the Europeans often induced feelings of inferiority in Africans.

African independence came swiftly as Europeans scrambled away in the mid-twentieth century, but the departing colonialists left a lethal legacy behind them.

CHAPTER TWELVE

Tribes, Nations, and States

W est Africa is the region with the longest history of European-African interaction, for most of the slaves transported to the Americas came from
this area. Just north of the equator, its climate poses great challenges to human
habitation, and it was long considered a graveyard for white residents. The indigenous black inhabitants suffered high rates of infant mortality from malaria
and other tropical diseases, but those who survived infancy built up at least
partial immunity, making them convenient candidates for slavery in the tropical climes of the Western Hemisphere.

The region can be subdivided into three or four geographic belts, running east and west from the Gulf of Guinea in the south to the Sahara Desert in
the north. The coastal belt consisted of swamps and mangrove forests, lightly
populated by fishermen, subsistence farmers, and traders. Just beyond the
coastal swamps lay a fifty- to one-hundred-mile-wide belt of tropical rain forest. The tse-tse fly infected this region, making the raising of horses or large
herds of cattle impossible. Despite the lush vegetation, the soil was relatively
thin and poor, suitable mainly for root crops, including the yam, the staff of life
in much of West Africa. This entire stretch of rain forest was often referred to as
Guinea, from which the modern state of Guinea takes its name. Beyond the rain
forest, a much wider region of scrubby bush, grassy savannahs, and occasional
hills, called *bilad as-Sudan*, or land of the blacks, by the North African Arabs,
rolled on to the fringes of the Sahara. The savannahs of West Africa remained
free of the tse-tse fly infestations and thus the rulers and traders of the region
depended heavily on horses for transportation and warfare.

Generally speaking, West Africa turned its back on the sea, and its larger
states and most important trade routes developed in the interior. The savannah

region gave birth to large-scale empires such as Ghana, Mali, and Songhai in medieval times; later, powerful kingdoms such as Asante and Dahomey developed in the rain forest. The coastal regions remained sparsely populated, divided, and decentralized. West Africa was not isolated from world trade and outside influences, however. Rather than sailing the ocean, as Europeans did, West African merchants organized great caravans to cross the Sahara Desert and trade with North Africa and the Middle East. They brought back the Islamic religion, and eventually at least one-third of West Africans became adherents of the Muslim faith, particularly in the northern savannah regions.

The arrival of European ships along the coast — first the Portuguese, then the Dutch, English, and French — slowly reoriented this international trade from the north, across the desert, to the south and west, across the ocean. For more than three centuries, from about 1500 to 1850, Europeans bartered textiles, liquor, and firearms for slaves and commodities along the coast, but rarely penetrated into the interior. The names they gave the coastal regions indicate what they hoped to acquire — the Gold Coast (Ghana), the Slave Coast (Nigeria), and the Ivory Coast (as it is still called today). When slavery was abolished and the slave trade suppressed in the nineteenth century, Africans turned to what was called "legitimate trade," producing mainly palm oil and peanuts, which were valued as raw materials for soap, lubricants, and margarine. This set a pattern that continued under European rule — Africans produced bulk commodities, often through forced labor of one kind or another, and exported them to Europe in exchange for manufactured goods. Many countries grew dependent on one or just a few export crops, no longer growing enough food to feed their populations. This economic pattern underdeveloped the continent, proving just as deadly to African welfare as political colonization.

The British had established one small colony, Sierra Leone, early in the nineteenth century, as a haven for freed slaves, and the French secured a tiny foothold on the continent's western tip at Senegal. The full conquest of West Africa, however, took place in the latter part of the nineteenth century. The British seized the small island of Lagos in 1861; and as one of their officials perceptively commented, the British presence in the Niger Delta was like soap in a sponge. Once in, it could never be rinsed out. By 1899 Great Britain had consolidated authority over the entire delta of the Niger River and extended "protection" over a vast region to the north as well. Similarly, to the west the British began influencing the Gold Coast from the coastal regions around Accra, then toward the end of the century they defeated the powerful Asante empire inland and extended a protectorate over it. In the meantime, French adventurers had penetrated inland from their foothold in Senegal and had landed along the Ivory Coast.

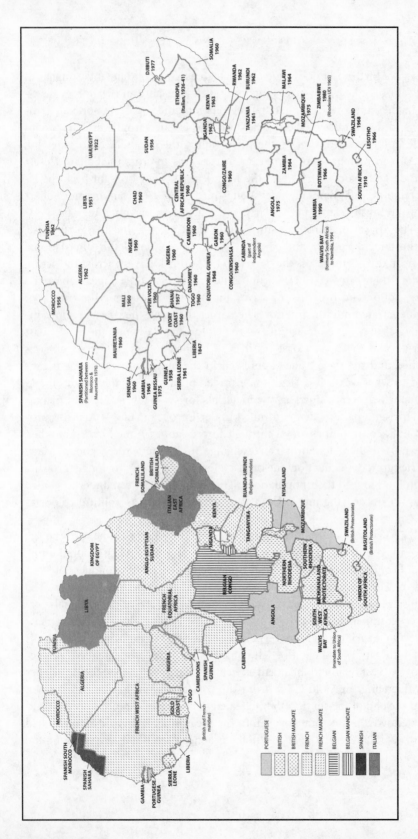

Africa before and after Independence

By the turn of the century, England ruled four colonies in West Africa — Gambia, Sierra Leone, Gold Coast, and Nigeria; whereas France controlled a larger, but more sparsely populated, area of eight colonies — Senegal, Mauritania, Soudan (Mali), Niger, Guinea, Ivory Coast, Upper Volta (Burkina Faso), and Dahomey (Benin). France and Britain divided up the German colonies of Togo and Cameroon between themselves after World War I.[1]

One of the most obvious and most detrimental legacies of European colonialism, both in West Africa and throughout the continent, is the artificial nature of political boundaries, what historian Basil Davidson has called "the black man's burden." European colonialists grabbed and claimed whatever they could through force of arms or hastily composed treaties with African kings, then their governments back in Europe sorted out the claims, most notably at the Congress of Berlin in 1885. The result is sometimes referred to as the "partition of Africa," but it was more like an amalgamation. Precolonial Africa had known a number of large, multi-ethnic empires and a few compact principalities closely akin to European nation-states, but most African kingdoms were quite small, and a large number of Africans lived in "stateless societies" composed of village groups loosely connected by kinship ties. The Europeans amalgamated these states and societies, large and small, into larger, wholly artificial political entities.

The borders of the colonial states often cut across natural geographic features, well-worn trade routes, or preexisting political boundaries. Frequently, they also divided members of a single ethnic group from their brothers and sisters on the other side of a border. A prime example of this mindless statecraft is the British colony of Gambia. Traders staked out a narrow strip of land on either side of the Gambia River, averaging about fifteen miles in width; but this tiny enclave was surrounded by French Senegal, which controlled the headwaters of the Gambia River as well as its natural trading hinterland. Even in European imperialist terms, these boundaries made no sense, yet they still exist today.

Each colonial state embraced numerous African ethnic groups which the colonialists routinely labeled "tribes," a misleading, demeaning, and loaded term. The word "tribe" conjures up images of primitive people gathered in the forest or roaming over the plains in small hunter or warrior bands. In this sense, perhaps, the word is simply a synonym for a group of nomads or hunter-gatherers. Such people did exist, on every continent, at earlier points in human history, and a few still exist today. The word "tribal" is used, apparently without

---

1. West Africa also included the tiny Portuguese colony of Guinea-Bissau, a slice of Spanish Sahara, and the independent state of Liberia, originally founded as a home for freed American slaves.

much of a pejorative connotation, in studies of the Islamic Middle East and North Africa to distinguish nomadic people whose societies are organized primarily on kinship lines from city dwellers and agriculturalists who live sedentary lives. In sub-Saharan Africa, however, the word "tribe" obscures more than it enlightens, and it nearly always implies inferiority. Only a minority of Africans at the time of European conquest lived as nomads or hunter-gatherers. Most were peasant farmers, like most Europeans.

What used to be called a tribe can more neutrally be described as an ethnic group, a group of people with a common sense of identity, based on language, customs, historical memories, and descent from real or mythical ancestors. African ethnic groups were usually small and local, such as the people of Umuofia, a collection of nine villages in eastern Nigeria immortalized by the novelist Chinua Achebe. These people spoke a language, Ibo,[2] in common with many other villagers and later were incorporated into a much larger political entity called Nigeria; but originally the people of Achebe's novels, and most real Africans, took their identity primarily from their families, clans, and groups of villages.

The British and French colonizers, noting the linguistic similarities between neighboring villages, lumped them all together into one "tribe" (e.g., the Ibo) and sought out or created one or a handful of "chiefs" who would speak for the "tribe." The Africans caught on to this game quickly and soon many individuals were competing for the prestigious and lucrative job of chief, that is, intermediary between the tribe and the colonial government. In this sense, then, the imperial power created both tribes and chiefs for their administrative convenience.

As time passed, these artificial tribal groupings became more real, building up a sense of loyalty and identity in their members, particularly when individuals migrated from the countryside to the cities. In the strange environments of Lagos, Nigeria, or Accra, Gold Coast, migrants sought out people who spoke their language or came from their own or neighboring villages for mutual help, protection, and companionship. Eventually these tribal associations evolved into political lobbies and pressure groups. Modern tribal or ethnic groups in Africa, therefore, were more often special interest groups than primordial, ancient identities from the precolonial past. Most of these ethnic groups remained relatively small, and African colonies often contained quite a number of them. Others, however, were large enough to be considered nations

2. I transliterate the names of African language and ethnic groups in the form commonly used during the time period described. Therefore, I use "Ibo" instead of the contemporary term "Igbo," and in chapter 13 I use "Kikuyu" rather than "Gikuyu." Nearly all historical sources use the older forms.

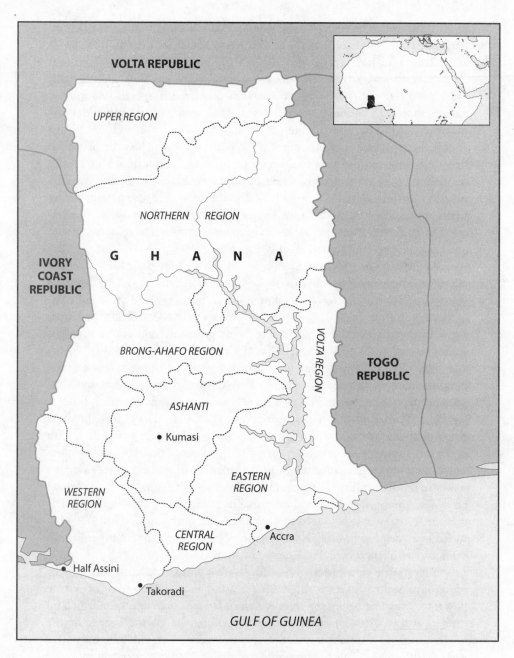

Ghana (Gold Coast)

unto themselves. The Irish journalist and politician Conor Cruise O'Brien often pointed out that the Ibo of Nigeria are more numerous than his own nation and inhabit a region larger than Ireland.

Nevertheless, artificial and divided though African colonies were, many did foster a sense of loyalty and national self-consciousness, at least among an educated minority. Students often discovered this sense of identity while studying overseas. The narrator of one Achebe novel states: "It was in England that Nigeria first became more than just a name to him. That was the first great thing that England did for him." Returned from their education abroad, this nationalist elite led the protests against colonial rule after 1945, winning independence within the same boundaries as the old colonies. These nationalists, as rulers and administrators of the newly emerged states, developed a vested interest in their preservation and resisted both fragmentation into smaller states or amalgamation into larger federations.

West Africa provides two good case studies of nation-state formation and ethnic group rivalry. The Gold Coast, or Ghana, was long considered a model colony, and its progress toward nationhood can be considered an "ideal type" of decolonization, useful for comparisons elsewhere. Nigeria, on the other hand, diverged from the ideal because of its great size and ethnic diversity, which ultimately led to a destructive civil war.

The Gold Coast was the oldest British possession in West Africa, and it became a relatively prosperous and peaceful colony. An African blacksmith imported a few cocoa beans into the country in 1879 and enterprising farmers swiftly recognized their value as a cash crop. The Gold Coast exported its first batch of cocoa in 1885 and by 1911 it was the world's leading producer, with much of its rain forest cleared for the planting of cocoa beans. Cocoa production bound the country together by linking inland farmers to traders along the seacoast, but it also forged an economy dangerously dependent on one export crop. The Gold Coast possessed many of the attributes of a nation-state. The majority of its people belonged to Akan linguistic groups which had settled in the country nearly a thousand years previously, and they had recently enjoyed a unified state of their own, the Asante kingdom.

The Asante (often spelled Ashanti) were a group of Akan-speaking ethnic groups united under a single king around 1695. The symbol of Asante power was a golden stool, supposedly descended from heaven, upon which no human ever sat. In common with most African kings, the keeper of the golden stool, or *Asantahene*, was not an absolute monarch. Rather, his power was carefully hedged in by numerous councilors and advisors and by other members of the royal family. If his rule became misguided or oppressive, he was "de-stooled," usually by the young men of the community. Asante reached the high point of its power around 1800, when it encompassed nearly all the modern state of Ghana. Basil Davidson and other African nationalist historians argue convincingly that Asante was a nation-state, comparable to European nation-states, with recognized boundaries, a central government, a national language, and historical memories that bound the populace together. Asante armies defeated the British on several occasions in the early nineteenth century, but the British mobilized their forces for two final assaults on the kingdom in 1874 and 1895.

Thereafter, in the Gold Coast and throughout their African and Asian empires, the British practiced what has come to be known as "indirect rule." Since few English men or women were willing to settle in tropical climes and the British government remained reluctant to spend much money on the empire, colonial governors had to rely on the local power structure they found in each colony. Therefore, they propped up the authority of the Asante kings and nobles, and either discovered or invented chiefs in other parts of the Gold Coast as intermediaries between the mass of people and the colonial state. The political outcome was paradoxical. Chiefs were ultimately puppets, dependent on the British for their power, but within their recognized spheres of authority they could act as petty despots, without the checks and balances that had accompanied traditional kingship. Rather than training the natives for democracy, the colonialists imposed a more authoritarian system than the one they had previously lived under.

This state of affairs enraged the small minority of Africans who had received an English-language education in missionary schools and who considered themselves an elite. This class of frustrated professionals formed the intellectual proletariat, whom we have seen in other countries and other contexts — overeducated and underemployed individuals whose ambitions and dreams were blocked by a political system of dubious legitimacy. Many of them were journalists or lawyers, and Nigerian historian Elizabeth Isichei has noted that both those professions thrive on grievances. In 1920, they founded the National Congress of British West Africa, an organization modeled on the Indian National Congress, but without a leader with the charisma of a Gandhi. Its Gold Coast branch was known as the United Gold Coast Convention (UGCC), a tame and well-mannered organization advocating greater opportunities for the professional elite.

After World War II, however, more raucous voices drowned out the polite protests of the UGCC. Returning servicemen, who had fought side by side with white soldiers and proved themselves the equals of anyone, found the colonial Gold Coast humiliating and frustrating. Those who had stayed at home faced severe economic difficulties, for the war had driven up prices and forced commodity shortages. The intellectual proletariat was joined by a more volatile, less-educated bunch of "verandah boys." These youths had received an elementary school education but could neither afford more schooling nor find jobs that used their literacy, so they hung around the streets and slept on verandahs. Just as returning soldiers from the trenches of World War I had fueled the fascist movements of Europe, so the disillusioned veterans of Africa found hope and excitement in the anti-colonial independence movements after World War II. These African nationalists were not fascists in any ideological sense, but they came from the same social stratum, a sort of lower middle class.

Unwittingly, the UGCC provided the ideal leader for this explosive but unfocused group of anti-colonialists when they hired Kwame Nkrumah, then studying in England, as their general secretary in November 1947. Nkrumah was a typical member of the intellectual proletariat. He was born in September 1909 in a village of the Nzima, a small Akan-speaking ethnic group at the far southwestern corner of the Gold Coast. His father was a prosperous goldsmith and his mother a trader who sold rice and sugar throughout the region. He was baptized a Roman Catholic and educated at missionary schools, but he later described himself as a "non-denominational Christian and a Marxian Socialist," not too unusual a combination for African nationalists. He taught in a small-town school for a few years, then attended the colony's first teachers' college at Achimota, just outside the colonial capital of Accra. After more teaching duties at various mission schools, he decided to seek higher education in the United States.

Nkrumah studied economics, sociology, philosophy, and theology at Lincoln University and the University of Pennsylvania, supplementing a meager scholarship with menial labor of all kinds. After World War II he sailed for England, where he mixed more study at the London School of Economics with political activism among the growing African student population. A friend who had studied with him in America suggested his name to the UGCC for the new post of general secretary, so at the beginning of 1948 he arrived in his own country for the first time in twelve years.

A local leader, unconnected with either Nkrumah or the UGCC, had mobilized economic discontent in the Gold Coast by proclaiming a consumers' boycott of European-made goods until the government and the large trading companies reduced prices. Then on February 28, 1948, the war veterans of the colony marched on the governor's castle in Accra to protest the meagerness of their pensions. A nervous policeman fired on the marchers, setting off days of riots by the veterans and the verandah boys. The Accra riots inflamed Africa the same way that the Amritsar massacre had ignited Indian nationalism. The British blamed Nkrumah and the other leaders of the Convention, labeling them communists and holding them in jail for eight weeks until the truth of their non-involvement became obvious.

After the Accra riots, Nkrumah realized that the younger and more radical protesters showed more potential than the UGCC. Without formally breaking from the Convention, he organized a parallel youth organization and an unofficial national college where youths who had been expelled from school could be educated and mobilized. Consciously distinguishing themselves from the UGCC, which advocated "Self-Government within the shortest possible time," Nkrumah's youth movement yelled for "Self-Government Now." In June 1949 they broke off from the older organization, forming the Convention People's Party (CPP).

Borrowing liberally from Gandhi, Nkrumah launched a movement of "positive action," that is, non-violent protest, on January 8, 1950. As often happened in India, the movement escaped the leader's control and occasionally became violent; but the British, just as they did in India, saved the leader's reputation by arresting him and making him a hero. The British decided to hasten the tempo of decolonization and hold elections for a colonial legislature in February 1951. Though still in jail, Nkrumah ran for office and his Convention People's Party swept 34 of the 38 contested seats. The British governor released Nkrumah and offered to appoint him leader of government business in the legislature (essentially, the prime minister) if he traded in self-government now for self-government soon. Nkrumah accepted, rationalizing his move as a shift from positive action to tactical action. He and his followers wore their "prison graduate" caps into the legislature on the first day of business; the only African minister who had not served jail time fashioned his own distinctive headgear with the label DVB, "Defender of the Verandah Boys." The British stalled a bit, insisting on two further elections so Nkrumah could prove his support throughout the country, but his party swept the polls both times. On March 6, 1957, Britain granted independence to the Gold Coast, which Nkrumah's government renamed Ghana in recollection of the ancient West African empire.

The Convention People's Party had united the verandah boys with ambitious traders and merchants to build a movement, and then had earned mass support with Nkrumah's biblical-sounding injunction, "seek ye first the political kingdom and all things will be added unto you." Of course, it was not that simple. Regional political parties grew up in the northern savannah region, which was loosely connected to the rest of Ghana; among a minority ethnic group across the Volta River in the eastern part of the country; and especially in the heartland of the old Asante kingdom. The nobles of Asante, favored by the British under indirect rule, resented the upstart Nkrumah's ascension to power; and the king of Asante ostentatiously absented himself from Ghana's independence celebrations.

Nkrumah attacked this regional, "tribal" discord with both carrots and sticks. He rewarded supporters throughout the various regions with jobs and development projects, classic pork-barrel politics as practiced the world over.

The CPP became more of a political patronage machine than an ideological mass movement. He took care of the intellectual proletariat and their younger siblings, the verandah boys, by increasing government employment. By 1965 70 percent of all salaried employees in Ghana worked for the state. Nkrumah also repressed the opposition severely. First he banned all regional parties, but when his opponents united in a new national party to continue their agitation, he eventually obtained a constitutional amendment declaring Ghana a one-party state. He did not execute his opponents, like many one-party dictators, but he did arrest them in large numbers under a series of preventive detention, treason, and sedition laws. Finally, he was declared president for life and began building a cult of personality, giving himself the title *Osagyefo,* or "redeemer."

Besides pork-barrel politics and police repression, Nkrumah also sought a larger solution to the problem of national unity. He hoped to enlarge the vision of Ghanaians by building a pan-African movement and uniting all the newly independent states into a huge, powerful federation. Nkrumah had been converted to pan-Africanism while studying in the United States. American blacks, far removed from specific ethnic groups or countries of Africa, tended to consider the whole continent when they started searching for their roots, and some African leaders, like Nkrumah, saw the wisdom of this. If all or most African countries could coordinate their economies and concert their diplomatic efforts, they would develop more rapidly and exercise more influence on world politics. Nkrumah believed so strongly in pan-Africanism that he secured a clause in the Ghanaian constitution granting the government power "to provide for the surrender of the whole or any part of the sovereignty of Ghana." However, the rulers of independent African states generally preferred remaining big fish in small ponds rather than merging their ponds into the ocean of pan-Africanism. Though the Organization of African Unity was organized in 1963, no state was willing to surrender any of its hard-earned sovereignty.

Four years after independence, Nkrumah took a sharp turn toward a socialist economy in Ghana, but he was unable to change the capitalist ways of his followers and he alienated potential allies in Britain and the United States. Then, as cocoa prices plummeted in the mid-1960s, Ghana's economy plunged into debt and depression. Finally, on February 24, 1966, while Nkrumah was out of the country, the military seized the key points of Accra and overthrew his regime with a minimum of bloodshed. Kwame Nkrumah died in exile six years later, his dreams of African socialism and pan-African unity in tatters. He had been a flawed visionary, more like Sukarno than Gandhi.

Ghana's experience of one-man, one-party rule proved typical of many African colonies as they burst into independence. Dictatorship, however, did not reflect ancient African traditions, as both its supporters and its critics often argued. Rather, it was the product of authoritarian government under Euro-

Nigeria

pean colonialism and a response to regional, tribal divisions. Put simply, Nkrumah and his contemporaries gathered power into their own hands because they had observed the British doing it and because they feared the country would fly apart if they did not. Democracy, pluralism, and political opposition appeared as expensive luxuries that new states could not afford.

Ghana's example proved infectious. Other African countries hastened into independence sooner than their colonial rulers or even they themselves had expected. Many of them became one-party dictatorships with either charismatic leaders, such as Nkrumah, or military rulers. When General de Gaulle returned to power in France during the Algerian crisis, he offered a "package deal" to all the remaining French colonies: increased autonomy and continuing development aid within a French community of nations, or else complete independence. Only Guinea, ruled by Nkrumah's friend and supporter Sékou Touré, chose independence in 1958, and the French immediately cut off all aid, even ripping out the government telephones when they departed. Nkrumah then proved his commitment to pan-Africanism by bailing out Guinea with a 28-million-dollar loan from Ghana.

Two years later, however, with the Algerian war still dragging on and the British colonies hurtling toward independence, de Gaulle finally decided that maintenance of the empire was more trouble than it was worth. The colonies of French West Africa had been joined administratively in a loose federation, and some pan-African advocates, particularly Senegal's Léopold Sédar Senghor, wished to maintain and even strengthen this federation. However, both the French and the most influential African leader, Ivory Coast's Felix Houphouet-Boigny, preferred separate independence for each colony. So in 1960, Senegal, Mali, Niger, Dahomey, Togo, Upper Volta, and the Ivory Coast all became independent states. The artificial lines that European colonialists had drawn on the map of Africa proved amazingly durable, as neither pan-African federation nor tribal divisiveness could erase them.

In Africa's largest state, however, such divisiveness came very close to tearing the country apart. Nigeria has a larger population than all the rest of West Africa combined, about 30 million at mid-century, 108 million now; and with the smallest proportion of Europeans to Africans anywhere on the continent, it did not have to wrestle with a white settler problem like Algeria did. The country produces abundant agricultural products for export, including cocoa, peanuts, palm oil, and rubber, and possesses a wealth of coal, tin, and other minerals. Oil was discovered in the 1950s, and Nigeria is now Africa's largest producer of "liquid gold." Such a large country, however, was purely a British creation and had never enjoyed political unity before colonial times.

The Niger River and its major tributary the Benue neatly divide present-day Nigeria into three regions: north, west, and east. Though the river eventually gave the British colony its name, it has never unified and dominated the life of the area's people the way the Nile does in Egypt, for each region has developed quite separately. A single ethnic group is predominant in each region, though many minorities coexist with them. In fact, almost 250 distinct languages have been identified within Nigeria.

The north is the largest region, including about 75 percent of the land area and more than half the people. Islamic empires have dominated the savannah grasslands of the north for centuries, giving it a political and cultural aspect more akin to the Middle East than to the rest of sub-Saharan Africa. About 40 percent of the northerners speak the Hausa language, but the dominant political group was the nomadic Fulani, who conquered most of the north around 1800 and then intermarried with the Hausa. The British found a long-established and stable political system in the northern region, with an Islamic caliphate at Sokoto recognized as overlord by local emirs throughout the savannah grasslands.

By contrast, the western region experienced a century of turmoil before colonization. The Yoruba were the dominant ethnic group in the west, and they had long enjoyed political unity under the Oyo empire, a rainforest principality similar in many ways to Asante. Around 1800, however, Oyo fell apart under pressure from the Fulani nomads in the north. The Yoruba fell into a series of civil wars and political struggles between smaller successor states to Oyo. This made it relatively easy for British missionaries and traders to penetrate the region and eventually colonize it from the British beachhead at Lagos.

The Ibo of the eastern region lived quite differently from both the Yoruba and the Hausa/Fulani. Grouped in self-governing villages without an overarching political state, their society approximated the ideal sought by European anarchists in the nineteenth century. Their stateless existence, however, was not chaotic. Though they had no kings they did have priests, oracles, and well-understood cultural traditions that prescribed codes of conduct for everyday life. Each village convened a council of elders to decide matters of common interest, and all the males of the village would assemble on particularly grave occasions. As described in Chinua Achebe's classic novel *Things Fall Apart*, traditional Iboland seemed stable and prosperous, but it was no utopia. Slavery was common, rival villages frequently went to war, captives were often murdered as human sacrifices, and the region was one of the most heavily populated in Africa, so tardy rains or other natural disasters could cause famine and starvation.

The experience of the Ibo suggests that the anarchist ideal of stateless societies, long admired by many European intellectuals, is suited primarily for people who employ a low level of technology. The very "primitiveness" and political decentralization of the Ibo, however, made their society durable and hard to conquer. When the British defeated a Fulani emir or a Yoruba king, the people rapidly submitted; but the European invaders had to "pacify" each Ibo village, one by one. They did not fully complete the task until the First World War. Even then, the proud Ibo chafed under British rule. In 1929-30 women from the eastern villages rioted repeatedly against the imposition of new taxes, an event remembered in Iboland as the "Women's War."

The British took full control of the Niger region in 1899. At first only Lagos and its vicinity were governed as a crown colony, and the rest of the territory was grouped into northern and southern protectorates. In 1906 the entire south was unified administratively as the Colony and Protectorate of Southern Nigeria. Finally in 1914, both north and south came under control of a single governor-general and the borders of modern-day Nigeria were finalized. Still the different regions continued to be administered separately.

In the north, Lord Frederick Lugard practiced a pure form of indirect rule. Since the emirs and their caliph were already recognized as legitimate rulers by the people, the British simply installed residents at their courts and took a portion of the existing taxes levied on the masses. This system closely resembled Britain's approach in Malaya and much of India. The handful of English officials who manipulated the northern government grew very fond of "their" emirs, enjoyed playing polo with them, and fancied themselves "Lawrences of the Savannah." They cherished the exotic separateness of northern Nigeria, and many outside observers joked that if all the Africans evacuated the British administrators in the north and the south would go to war with each other.

The British also tried to practice indirect rule in the western and eastern regions, but they had a harder time identifying legitimate chiefs to support. Particularly in Iboland, the whole notion of chieftainship was completely alien. The colonial government established native courts in the east, whose African functionaries were granted warrants of authority and thus were labeled "warrant chiefs." These local officers often became corrupt, and they were always resented by the Ibo. The warrant chiefs were the primary targets during the Women's War.

In sum, British administrative practices reinforced and exaggerated differences between north and south, east and west in Nigeria. The Africans themselves further aggravated regional tensions. The Yoruba had been dealing with the British far longer than the inhabitants of the other two regions, so in the early days of the colony they held the majority of posts in the federal administration. The competitive Ibo, however, who valued individual achievement more highly than some other African cultures, worked hard to catch up. They took advantage of mission schools and many converted to Christianity. Both individual ambition and heavy population pressure in Iboland drove them to seek work and opportunity in cities of the north and the west. Such migration, rather than leading to increased understanding between groups, usually produced friction. Ibos "abroad" in the other two regions of Nigeria stuck together and became more ethnically conscious than they had been back home. In a very real sense, it was these internal migrants who invented Ibo nationalism. Pushing, ambitious, and successful, they were resented by the indigenous groups of the west and north, much as Jews in Europe or the overseas Chinese in Southeast Asia have been resented.

Nigeria moved toward independence in the same way and on much the same schedule as the Gold Coast, but regional and ethnic loyalties undercut the emerging sense of Nigerian nationalism. Nationalist parties developed among the educated elite between the two world wars, primarily in Lagos and a few other cities. Then at mid-century, these parties became mass movements. The "Standard VI boys," so-called since they had completed the British Standard VI (roughly equivalent to eighth grade in the United States) but then dropped out, pushed the parties into more radical stances, just like the verandah boys did in the Gold Coast. However, the major parties were regionally based and no one leader, like Nkrumah, emerged to overcome this divisiveness.

Nnamdi Azikiwe, a Christian Ibo, was the outstanding Nigerian nationalist at mid-century. Five years older than Nkrumah, he had preceded him to college in America and exercised a decisive influence on the future Gold Coast leader during a stint as a newspaper editor in Accra. First in the Gold Coast and then in Nigeria, "Zik" introduced a form of sensationalist, American-style journalism that proved highly popular but often aggravated group tensions. He founded the Nigerian Youth Movement in the late 1930s, but it fractured along ethnic lines, and a Yoruba leader from the western region, Obafemi Awolowo, took control of it. After the Second World War, each of these men established a regionally based political party, Awolowo's Action Group in the west and Azikiwe's National Congress of Nigeria and the Cameroons (NCNC) in the east. Later a handful of English-educated schoolteachers started the National People's Congress in the north.

None of these three parties could govern the Federation of Nigeria alone, so Nkrumah's one-party solution to the problem of national unity was not available in Nigeria. When the British declared it independent in October 1960, the country was governed by a coalition between the Northern People's Congress and the NCNC, with the Action Group in opposition. The federal prime minister was an English-educated, Muslim Hausa, Abubakar Tafawa Balewa, but the real powers in the country were the regional leaders: Awolowo; the northerner Ahmadu Bello, usually called the Sardauna of Sokoto (a religious title); and Azikiwe.

Though federalism, in theory, would seem an appropriate solution for a multi-ethnic state such as Nigeria, and indeed it was the only possible political form for the central government, in practice it did not work. The Federation of

Nigeria was weak and unstable, like Yugoslavia in this century or the United States before the civil war. In particular, the Muslim north, though the most populous region, felt at a disadvantage because both the Yoruba and the Ibo had taken greater advantage of English-language education. Before World War II only one northerner had gone overseas for higher education, and in 1947 a mere 251 northern students were attending secondary school. So if positions in government were based on merit, that is, on civil service examinations in English, northerners could not compete. In fact, the Ibo alone held a majority of positions in both the army and the federal government. Furthermore, the main oilfields discovered in the 1950s lay in the eastern regions, dominated by Ibos. The three regions, therefore, engaged in a competitive scramble for jobs and development funds, corruption proliferated at all levels of government, and the north frequently threatened to secede.

Things fell apart in 1966. Early in the morning on Saturday, January 15, a cabal of mid-level army officers seized and assassinated Prime Minister Balewa in Lagos, the Sardauna of Sokoto in the north, and a prominent western regional leader, Samuel Akintola. The conspirators also eliminated a number of senior army officers. The coup succeeded completely in the northern capital of Kaduna, but an alert major general, John Aguiyi Ironsi, swiftly regained control in Lagos. Nothing much happened in Iboland. Historian Elizabeth Isichei has astutely argued that most military coups in Africa are motivated by two major factors: an idealistic urge to end the corruption of civilian politics and more self-interested matters of internal army politics. Both these motives impelled the "January boys" of Nigeria in 1966: a slowing of promotions in the post-independence army after the first wave of Nigerian officers had replaced the British, and disgust with the rampant corruption.

General Ironsi skillfully negotiated the surrender of the coup leaders in Kaduna, jailing them but procrastinating over their ultimate fate. Then after consultation with terrified civilian politicians, he decided to take power himself, at least temporarily. Most Nigerians, particularly in the eastern and western regions, welcomed the Ironsi regime as a necessary stabilization measure, but the coup and its aftermath ultimately caused further division in the country. More by force of circumstances than by design, most of the January coup leaders had been Ibos. Ironsi himself was also an Ibo, and though he bent over backwards to include officers from other regions in his regime, northerners began to view the whole business as an Ibo conspiracy to take over the country. The general's failure to execute or otherwise punish the ringleaders of the coup fed this suspicion. Then when Ironsi, in May 1966, decreed a more centralized, less federal, form of administration for the country, the north broke out in riots and anti-Ibo pogroms that killed hundreds. Finally, on the evening of July 28, 1966, northern army officers won the "return-match," a counter-coup that toppled and killed Ironsi.

Nigeria remained poised between northern secession and complete chaos in the three days following the second coup, but finally a thirty-one-year-old staff officer, Yakubu "Jack" Gowon, emerged as compromise choice for head of state. Gowon was a northerner, but from a minority ethnic group, the Angas, and was a Christian as well. His choice thus met the minimum demand of northerners for one of their own to rule, but allayed southern fears of Muslim domination. The threat of northern secession was averted and the country held together a bit longer.

In September 1966, northerners began killing Ibos resident in northern cities. Between six and eight thousand men, women, and children were slaughtered. The September massacres set off an exodus of about one million Ibos from the north, and perhaps another half million from the western region as well. This mass of terrified humanity crowded into the already overpopulated Ibo eastern region, where another military leader, Colonel Emeka Ojukwu, had taken command. Even before the massacres, however, a smaller migration of Ibo intellectuals, determined to build their own nation-state separate from Nigeria, had begun resigning their posts at universities in Ibadan and Lagos and returning home. Nigeria had effectively split in two by the end of 1966.

Ojukwu and Gowon remained personally cordial and attempted to negotiate a reconciliation, but their room for maneuver was limited by nationalist firebrands on both sides. On March 31, 1967, Ojukwu appropriated all federal revenues and federal property in the east, and in retaliation Gowon's government slapped an economic blockade on Iboland. Finally on May 26, an eastern consultative assembly packed with Ojukwu's supporters authorized secession, and on May 30, 1967, the colonel proclaimed "the territory and region known as Eastern Nigeria . . . an independent sovereign state of the name and title the Republic of Biafra." Biafra had been an ancient kingdom to the east of Iboland and the Bight of Biafra was the body of water immediately south of the new country.

Nigeria's descent into secession and civil war paralleled the experience of the United States a century before. In both cases, one region of the country, the southern United States and the Ibo east, had previously dominated the federal government but had seen its position suddenly and traumatically erode. In each case, the region that had fallen from power felt isolated and threatened, and therefore sought safety in secession. Just as the Confederate capture of Fort Sumter in South Carolina sparked a civil war, so too Biafra's seizure of federal property prompted two and a half years of bloodshed. War strategy was also roughly similar in both civil wars. The federal government attempted to isolate, blockade, and strangle the upstart region, whereas the secessionists merely sought to survive. Neither Biafra nor the southern Confederacy had to win their struggles; they simply had to avoid losing. Both failed, after a gallant, nearly suicidal struggle.

Nigerian forces began the war tentatively by nibbling away at Biafra's frontiers, but the secessionist regime mounted a surprise counterattack deep into western Nigeria. Had they succeeded in reaching Ibadan or Lagos, General Gowon's government might have collapsed and Biafra would have won its independence, but the attack fell short by about a hundred miles. Two months after it started, the Biafran thrust across the Niger River ended, and the war settled into a pattern of action-stalemate-action, as Nigeria mounted a number of offensives that repeatedly failed to end the war.

Meanwhile, overpopulated Biafra suffered intense famine. Ultimately many more people died of starvation than from gunshot wounds. European and American humanitarian agencies, stimulated by skillful Biafran propaganda and charges of genocide against Nigeria, airlifted immense amounts of food and medicine into the beleaguered Ibo strongholds. Yet only a handful of African nations recognized Biafra. Great Britain and the Soviet Union supplied the Nigerian army with weapons and ammunition, whereas the United States stayed neutral. France tilted towards Biafra but did not recognize it or supply enough aid to tip the balance. Finally, after yet another "final offensive" cut the dwindling territory of Biafra in two around Christmastime 1969, the Biafran military convinced Ojukwu to leave the country. His replacement, Colonel Philip Effiong, sued for peace and surrendered to Gowon, his classmate at the British military academy of Sandhurst, on January 15, 1970. The Nigerian civil war had lasted two and a half years and taken at least 600,000 lives. This tally of fatalities just about matches the numbers for the American civil war and exceeds the total in the Spanish civil war of the 1930s.

The Biafran charge of genocide does not stand up. Although the initial massacres of Ibos in September 1966 were genocidal in intent, designed to kill or expel the minority group from the north, the war itself was fought along conventional lines. The federal blockade produced mass starvation, just as the Allied blockade of Germany in World War I had done. Yet this action was intended to end the war and bring the Ibos back, not exterminate them. During the fighting, civilians and some Nigerian soldiers slaughtered Ibos at the cities of Asaba and Onitsha, but these massacres were exceptional and were not ordered by the Nigerian commanders. Unfortunately, these atrocities convinced most Ibos that the threat of genocide was real. Not until Nigeria had reconquered substantial territory without a mass murder of Ibos did the remaining secessionists realize they could safely surrender. Fear of genocide played a major role in prolonging the war.

One final parallel with the American civil war marked the Nigerian struggle — the aftermath of war in both cases proved remarkably mild and nonvindictive. General Gowon quoted Abraham Lincoln's phrase about "binding up the nation's wounds" and promised that there would be no "Nuremberg trials" and no reprisals. He kept his word. No Biafran leaders were executed and most were imprisoned for only a few months' time. As in the American South after the civil war, the major punishment imposed was disqualification from holding political office. This policy of leniency contrasts strongly with the Spanish civil war, after which General Franco's regime executed at least thirty thousand prisoners.

The U.S., Spanish, and Nigerian civil wars decisively discredited secession, and none of these states has been threatened with a break-up since then. Gowon's regime divided the three big regions of the country into smaller provinces, thus giving minority ethnic groups influence in some of the smaller provinces and reducing the temptation of secession that country-sized regions had posed. Nigerian politics have continued to be rocky, however. General Gowon was himself overthrown in 1975 by another military faction and went into exile in England for a time. He later returned safely to Nigeria and still lives there. Military regimes have governed the nation for all but a few years since the civil war, and despite its mineral riches, the country still suffers from unequal distribution of wealth.

The words of a British journalist, John de St. Jorre, written in 1972 still ring true today: "Nigeria has a new unity but many old problems." Both Ghana and Nigeria, in quite different ways, have sought first the political kingdom, but all else has not been added unto them.

CHAPTER THIRTEEN

Land and Freedom

Paleontologists have dug the oldest human fossil remains out of the gorges of East Africa; yet in the ages since these early ancestors lived, the climate and environment of this region has proven inhospitable to human life.[1] In historic times, thin soil and uncertain rainfall made East Africa a sparsely populated frontier region, the last part of Africa intensively settled. Ironically, however, a few patches of this challenging territory looked more congenial to white settlement than other parts of Africa. In the colonial period, European settlers grabbed the cool, fertile East African highlands, reserving them for their exclusive use. As in all settler colonies, therefore, the drive for freedom also became a struggle for land, breaking out into the violent Mau Mau movement of the 1950s. After the British colonies of Kenya and Tanganyika won their independence in the early 1960s, they experimented with two very different ways of owning and working the land. Struggles for land and freedom, therefore, provide the twin themes of East Africa's modern history.

The terrain of East Africa generally lies higher in altitude than the jungles, savannahs, and coastal swamps elsewhere on the continent, with plains or steppes between 3,000 and 4,500 feet above sea level, the ruggedly beautiful highlands beyond 4,500 feet, and Africa's tallest mountain, Kilimanjaro, soaring to 19,340 feet. Karen Blixen, a European settler who wrote a memoir called *Out*

---

1. Conventionally, the term "East Africa" applies to the former British colonies of Uganda, Kenya, Tanganyika, and Zanzibar. The latter two merged into one state called Tanzania in 1964. Geographically, East Africa might also include Rwanda and Burundi, former Belgian territories just south of Uganda. In this chapter, I concentrate primarily on the twentieth-century history of Kenya and Tanganyika.

246

of Africa under the pseudonym Isak Dinesen, claimed that "the chief feature of the landscape . . . was the air. Looking back on a sojourn in the African highlands, you are struck by your feeling of having lived for a time up in the air." Much of the landscape is either desert or semi-arid grassland, loaded with wild game and punctuated by fantastically shaped thorn trees, but only about 15 to 25 percent of the land is suited to agriculture. The monsoons off the Indian Ocean arrive on a regular yearly schedule, but sometimes they are late or fail entirely, leading to drought and famine.

These same monsoons, which blow from the northeast in the winter months then shift to southwest in April, blew seafarers from India and Arabia to the African coast of the Indian Ocean many centuries ago. East Africa, therefore, developed ports and trading posts along the ocean, unlike West Africa, which turned its back on the empty Atlantic. Arabs brought Islam with them, intermarried with Africans, and eventually developed a hybrid language, Swahili, combining Arabic and Bantu. Swahili towns such as Kilwa and Mombasa were built on islands just off the coast or else on narrow peninsulas and sandspits surrounded by natural moats formed by creeks and swamps. They traded exotic products from the interior, such as elephant ivory and rhino horns, for the products of India and Arabia, but they remained quite isolated from the African interior in most aspects of day-to-day life. Neither Islam, nor literacy, nor even the coastal building techniques in stone and lime mortar penetrated more than a few miles inland.

The earliest effective imperialism in East Africa came not from Europe but from Asia. The Portuguese had bombarded and subjugated several of the coastal cities in the fifteenth and sixteenth centuries, but their rule remained superficial and sporadic, allowing the East African coast substantial autonomy as long as the towns paid tribute. Arabized Africans expelled the Portuguese from their last stronghold, Mombasa, in 1698. At the beginning of the nineteenth century, however, a vigorous ruler of Oman, a principality at the southern tip of Arabia, began conquering the offshore islands and coastal towns along the Indian Ocean shore of Africa. The Omani sultan Sayyid Said finally moved his capital from the Arabian Peninsula to the African island of Zanzibar in 1832, and a successor, Sultan Majid, founded a new town on the mainland, which he named Dar es Salaam (Haven of Peace), in 1866.

Under Omani rule, Arab traders penetrated far into the interior, all the way to the great lakes of central Africa, organizing caravans of ivory and slaves. East Africa had not been touched by the earlier European trade in slaves for the Americas, and although slavery did exist, it did not pervade society. After 1800, however, the demand for slaves in Arabia, India, and the Indian Ocean plantation islands of Reunion and Mauritius brought all the horrors of the slave trade to the region with concentrated force. Sultan Sayyid created a local venue for slaves by transforming Zanzibar island into a one-crop plantation economy, based on the growing of cloves for export. Swahili spread as a *lingua franca,* or trader's lingo, wherever the influence of the Arabs and Arabized Africans extended in the interior. The Omani sultan did not possess the military power to conquer and occupy all of East Africa. Arab traders formed small settlements at the intersections of interior trade routes, and the sultan could concentrate sufficient numbers of armed soldiers to protect them, keeping open the vital trade in tusks and humans. Nevertheless, the Africans of the interior remained largely self-governing, their societies disrupted but not destroyed.

The interior of East Africa was home to the most diverse group of African peoples anywhere on the continent, with all four major language groups — Bantu, Nilotic, Cushitic, and Khoisan — represented. The majority of East Africans spoke a Bantu language and were descended from agriculturists who brought intensive farming techniques and the use of iron from their original homeland in the Congo River basin around the year 1000. Pastoral, cattle-herding peoples, such as the Luo and the Masai, had also pioneered portions of East Africa, particularly around Lake Victoria and in the great Rift Valley which bisects the region. The Masai were an unusually tall, nomadic people who built their entire culture and economy around their cattle. They rarely ate meat, but subsisted on a diet of milk, cheese, and dried cow's blood. Though they often came into conflict with agricultural people, they also interacted with them, trading cattle for grain and haggling over bride prices for the daughters from settled communities. Most East Africans, whether herders or farmers, lived in stateless societies, like the Ibo of West Africa. The mingling of these small-scale societies was not always peaceful, but it was rarely accompanied by all-out war. Settlement of the harsh frontier lands proceeded slowly, over many generations, and was more often marked by intermarriage and assimilation than warfare. East Africans battled nature more fiercely than they did each other.

Europeans came to East Africa only late in the nineteenth century. The British had long kept a watchful eye on the Omani sultans, as they did over all maritime powers on the road to India, but they did not make Zanzibar a formal protectorate until 1890, when the British government realized that Germany was interested in the region. That same year they also established a protectorate at the very center of the continent in Uganda, since they feared that either France or Germany might seize the headwaters of the Nile and threaten Egypt. Such a fear was wholly fanciful but at the tail end of the scramble for Africa, all the great powers were acting more out of paranoia than policy. The Germans did establish a colony in East Africa in 1891, replacing the inefficient rule of a German trading company along the coast north and south of Dar es Salaam (present-day Tanzania). Over the next decade and a half they ruthlessly extended their rule into the interior. In the meantime, when the Omani sultan protested the growing European incursions into his domain, the British navy bombarded his palace in 1896 and installed a compliant stooge on the throne. East Africa's future lay in the hands of Europeans as the twentieth century opened.

The British were not quite sure why they were in East Africa, but they decided to create something economically useful by building a railway from the Indian Ocean coast into the interior. The Uganda Railway, which some English cynics dubbed the "lunatic express," started at Mombasa and ran 580 miles to Kisumu, on Africa's largest lake, which the British named Lake Victoria. Imported Indian laborers built the railway, and many stayed on in Africa after the road was completed. The British used overwhelming military force to guard the East African Protectorate, as the narrow strip of land from the sea to the lakes was called. The nomadic Masai allied with the British to defeat the Kikuyu and other ethnic groups along the right of way, but when the wars were over the British rewarded their allies by removing them from their traditional herding pastures in the Rift Valley. The rail builders founded the town of Nairobi halfway up the line as their administrative headquarters, and this later grew to be the colony's capital and largest city.

Conquest of East Africa was greatly eased by a series of catastrophes which the region suffered in the 1890s. European incursions had upset the delicate environmental balance of this fragile ecosystem. Rinderpest, a cattle disease, spread from Indian cows imported by the Italian army into Ethiopia, decimating the priceless herds of the Masai and other pastoral peoples. Smallpox spread throughout the region, and the rains failed repeatedly that decade, bringing widespread starvation. Both British and German East Africa (later Kenya and Tanganyika, respectively) suffered catastrophic population losses of about a million people each, and many parts of the land reverted to bush, becoming reinfested with tse-tse flies. The Germans and the English, therefore, assumed control of a devastated and partially empty land.

In order to fill it up, both colonial governments encouraged Europeans to settle in the temperate highland regions and grow cash crops for market. By the time of the First World War, about 5,000 whites had settled in German East Africa. Their plantations, which grew coffee, cotton, rubber, and sisal (a hemplike plant used in making rope), occupied just 1 percent of the land but employed about 100,000 Africans, 10 percent of the colony's labor force. The British Colonial Office first tried to convince the Zionist Organization to direct Jewish settlers to East Africa, rather than Palestine, but after investigating the region the Zionists declined. Had they accepted, the present-day Arab-Jewish conflict of the Middle East might instead have been an African-Jewish conflict. Indians who built the rail line were reinforced by more immigrants from the subcontinent, and for a time it looked as if East Africa might become "India's

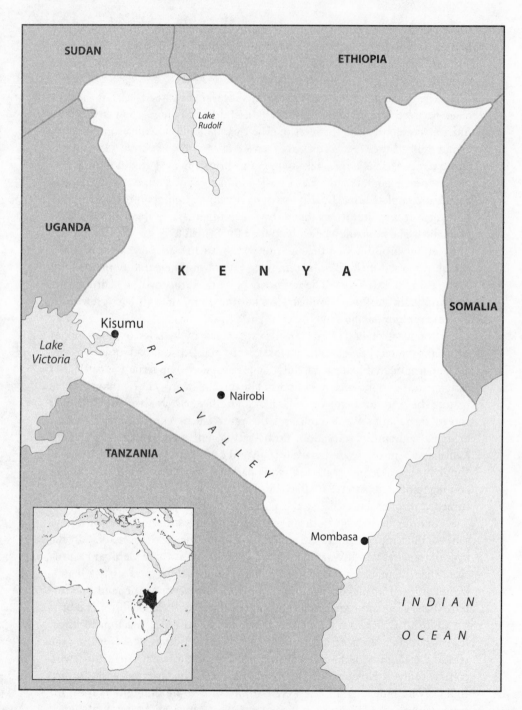

Kenya

America." However, enough English men and women emigrated so that the British commissioner could unofficially declare the area "a white man's country" in 1904.

The British settled in the highlands and the Rift Valley of central Kenya on land previously grazed by the Masai or farmed by the Kikuyu. The government declared all land in the protectorate crown land and then granted enormous estates to the white settlers. Lord Delamere, the leader of the settlers, received 176,768 acres. Since they could not farm all this land themselves, they encouraged African families, mainly from the Kikuyu people, to live as tenant farmers on their estates. The tenants could grow grain for their own consumption, but were also obligated to work at least half the year tending coffee, tea, or other cash crops. The settlers called their African tenants "squatters," emphasizing their lack of legal tenure on the land.

Meanwhile, the whites lived a fantasy life, like feudal lords and ladies. Karen Blixen (Isak Dinesen) wrote that her two best friends were both men from another age: "If Berkeley [Cole] were a cavalier of the Stuarts' day, Denys [Finch-Hatton] should be set in an earlier English landscape, in the days of Queen Elizabeth." What she neglected to mention, and probably did not realize, was that she herself had stepped back into the Middle Ages. She loved and cared for her "squatters" as she did her domestic animals, writing extravagant prose about both, but she never considered the Africans as human beings capable of rational thought and action. It is fortunate for Blixen that her farm went bankrupt and she left Kenya in the 1930s, for she probably would have been hacked to death by the Mau Mau had she remained.

During World War I, the British fought a long, frustrating war against African guerrillas led by Colonel Paul von Lettow-Vorbeck in German East Africa. They enlisted over 200,000 African troops and nearly a million porters and laborers. Perhaps 10 percent of these conscripted Africans died of disease or exhaustion before the war ended with Great Britain in possession of all East Africa. The former British East African Protectorate became the Colony of Kenya, and the British retained German East Africa as a League of Nations mandate. A civil servant devised the name "Tanganyika" for the mandated territory, from two Swahili words meaning "sail" and "bright arid plain." The mandatory authorities sent the German colonists packing but did not encourage English settlers to replace them, so Tanganyika never became a settler colony like Kenya.

Nationalism developed in East Africa according to the standard model that has already been described for West Africa and the colonial societies of Asia. In the period between the two world wars, the intellectual proletariat, mission-educated clerks, teachers, and civil servants, founded organizations that mirrored the Indian National Congress before Gandhi. In Tanganyika, the African Association (TAA) came into existence in 1929, evolving out of an earlier group of civil servants; but historian John Iliffe has characterized its activities as "tea-party" politics, stunted and underdeveloped, in part because of the uncertain status of the territory. Great Britain flirted with the idea of trading the mandate for Tanganyika to Germany as part of its appeasement policy. Tanganyika remained at the bottom of the priority list among all of England's African colonies.

Makerere College, a professional and liberal arts school founded by the British in Kampala, Uganda, in 1922, trained the leading edge of the intellectual proletariat — teachers, civil servants, and future agitators — for all the British East African colonies. Tanganyikans, however, remained at a disadvantage since the mandatory government discouraged their attendance. By 1939 only about fifty students from Tanganyika had enrolled at Makerere and only one had gone on to higher education in Europe. John Iliffe has summed up the status of mid-century Tanganyikan nationalism succinctly:

> By 1947 the African Association possessed all the elements of nationalism except the determination, the techniques, and the popular support to seize power. Its politics were only ideas and resolutions. Yet ideas matter.

In Kenya, the ideas of nationalism were greatly complicated by ethnic rivalries and the struggle for land with the white settlers. The Kikuyu, who had felt the full impact of settler land policies and missionary education in their homeland just northeast of Nairobi, played the leading role in nationalist politics. Like the Ibo of Nigeria, they also became a lightning rod for the resentment of other African ethnic groups. The first Kenyan nationalist organization, the Young Kikuyu Association, was founded by Harry Thuku in June of 1921. Thuku soon changed its name to the East African Association, yet it remained a largely Kikuyu group. A protest march in Nairobi on March 15, 1922, prompted the British to fire upon the crowd, imprison Thuku for nine years, and ban his organization.

Another group of educated Kikuyu launched the Kikuyu Central Association (KCA) in 1924; then in 1928 they engaged a young municipal meter-reader with the Christian name of Johnstone as their general secretary. Under the African name of Jomo Kenyatta, he eventually became the colony's premier revolutionary and the first president of independent Kenya. Born sometime between 1890 and 1894 as Kamau wa Ngengi, the future leader received an English-language education at the Church of Scotland (Presbyterian) mission in Fort Hall and was baptized as Johnstone Kamau in 1914. When he moved to Nairobi to work in the city water department, he adopted the word for his Kikuyu beaded belt, *kenyatta*, as his surname.

General Secretary Kenyatta energized the KCA by leading it on a crusade against the cultural imperialism and ethnocentrism of his former mission teachers. In the 1920s, the Protestant missionaries strongly condemned the continuation of "pagan" practices by any of their students. In particular, they singled out the custom of "female circumcision." This rite of passage for young women, common to many societies in Africa and the Middle East, requires the cutting of the woman's clitoris. Europeans and Americans, then as now, considered the practice barbaric, painful, and demeaning. They did not condemn the comparable custom of male circumcision, however, probably because it was also practiced by some Europeans. The Kikuyu, with Kenyatta in the lead, rallied behind their initiation customs, male and female, as cornerstones of their culture. Many Christians seceded from the mission churches to start their own independent African churches and schools, and the KCA greatly increased its membership.

At the crest of its popularity in 1929, KCA sent Kenyatta to London with a list of grievances for the Colonial Office. He received a cool reception and came back to Kenya the following year empty-handed. He then returned to England and remained for fifteen years, studying, traveling, and agitating. Under the influence of a noted anthropologist, Bronisław Malinowski at the London School of Economics, Kenyatta published a book entitled *Facing Mount Kenya,* which defended Kikuyu customs, including female circumcision. For the book cover, he changed his name from Johnstone to "Jomo," a word of his own invention, and posed in an animal skin while clutching a spear. When Jomo Kenyatta returned to Kenya in September 1946, with a reputation as *Mzee,* the old man of the nationalist movement, he headed the Kenya African Union (KAU, pronounced "cow"), organized in 1944 as the first attempt at a colony-wide political party. Yet before KAU and Kenyatta could apply pressure on the British for an end to colonial rule, they found themselves enmeshed in a deepening land crisis.

Kenya's struggles for the land went back to the earliest days of settler dominance, for the colonial government had elaborated a system of segregation and discrimination much like South Africa's. The Crown Lands Ordinance of 1915 extended the land leases of the white settlers from 99 to 999 years, effectively forever, and empowered the British governor to expand the size of the "white highlands," those lands set aside exclusively for Europeans. Then the government set aside "native reserves" for the various African ethnic groups, much like Indian reservations in North America. The white highlands and native reserves policies not only deprived Africans of the best land, they effectively kept the African ethnic groups separate and disunited.

The loss of land was felt most sharply by the pastoral Masai and the agricultural Kikuyu of central Kenya. Deprived of their traditional grazing lands and their right to wander, the Masai fell into a sharp demographic and cultural decline. The Kikuyu at first found an escape from the crowded native reserves by taking up land as tenants (squatters) on the estates of the white highlands. A government land commission in 1934 found that 110,000 Kikuyu were living outside their reserves. By 1948 the number had swelled to 194,146, nearly a quarter of the total Kikuyu population. Most were squatters in the highlands or urban drifters in Nairobi.

The Resident Native Laborers Ordinance of 1937 began pressuring squatters to return to their native reserves. The law increased the labor requirement for squatters from 180 days per year to 270, reduced the number of cattle they could own, and authorized white settlers to evict them at will. Increased mechanization of the large white farms during and after World War II induced the settlers to use this authority liberally.

Jomo Kenyatta, therefore, found Kikuyuland bursting at the seams when he returned after World War II. Dispossessed squatters had no place to live in the already crowded reserves, so many of them drifted to Nairobi where they formed an underworld of petty crime based on family and clan, like the European Mafia. In both towns and reserves the disinherited competed with demobilized soldiers and their families for land and employment. Both groups pushed Kenyatta and the KAU into more militant postures, much as the verandah boys of the Gold Coast nudged Nkrumah at the same time. Meanwhile, the white settlers were enjoying unprecedented prosperity, as war veterans increased their numbers and worldwide demand for coffee, tea, wheat, and sisal boomed. The settlers of Kenya accounted for less than 1 percent of the population, but they owned 20 percent of the land and produced 85 percent of the colony's export crops. Three thousand white families owned more land, about seven and a half million acres, than the one million Kikuyu in their native reserves. Like the *pieds noirs* of Algeria or the Israelis of British Palestine, Kenya's white settlers were arrogant, organized, and aggressive at mid-century, unaware that their comfortable world was about to explode.

Within five years of his return from England, Kenyatta lost control of KAU and the nationalist movement. He and his lieutenants had organized an unofficial "parliament" in the town of Kiambu, at the Banana Hill mansion of a Kikuyu chief, and had invited Nairobi radicals Fred Kubai, Bildad Kaggia, and others to form an action group. In order to cement the unity of all nationalists, the parliament began administering oaths, modeled on traditional Kikuyu male initiation ceremonies, to the militants. A typical oath required a series of statements such as this: "If you ever disagree with your nation or sell it out, may you die of this oath." This strategy backfired, for the urban radicals launched a mass campaign to persuade the underclass of Nairobi and the Kikuyu reserves to take the oath, stealthily pushing the movement towards revolutionary violence. They also made it an exclusively Kikuyu affair, and by September 1952 over three-quarters of the Kikuyu population had taken the Oath of Unity. The campaign proved both too narrow and too comprehensive. Its narrowness limited it to one Kenyan ethnic group, the Kikuyu, but its comprehensiveness opened it to all sorts of opportunists, fellow-travelers, and even government spies. Both features contributed to the ultimate failure of the movement.

By the fall of 1952, the radicals had taken control of KAU activities and had begun terrorist attacks against isolated white settlers and pro-government Kikuyu leaders, but they were far from prepared for a full-scale insurrection. The militants called themselves by many names, such as *muhimu* (Swahili for "important") or *muingi* (the community), but the title which stuck was "Mau Mau." No one knows who coined this name or what precisely it means. It may have been a play on words with KAU, in Kikuyu, meaning "little" and Mau signifying "greater." Or it may simply have been a free-flowing war cry. Even today, the noun "Mau Mau" and its verb form "Mau Mauing" are used all over the world as expressions of terrorism. In any case, the actual terrorists in Kenya preferred to call themselves the Land and Freedom Army, a title which accurately captured the goals of their movement.

A new British governor, Sir Evelyn Baring, son of the longtime proconsul in British Egypt, surprised the Kikuyu militants by declaring a state of emergency the night of October 19/20, 1952. Shortly after midnight, colonial troops arrested 187 suspected agitators, including Kenyatta and the more radical leaders Kubai and Kaggia. Kenyatta was tried and convicted of "managing Mau Mau," a verdict which gave him altogether too much credit but resulted in a decade-long imprisonment. Most of the real leaders of Mau Mau also served long prison terms, but their followers retreated to the forests surrounding the Kikuyu reserves and carried on a ferocious guerrilla war. Unlike many revolutionary movements, Mau Mau was a true peasant revolt, without the leadership of intellectuals or ideologists. Only three of the rebels had as much as a high school education; most were illiterate and spoke no English.

The Mau Mau kept the initiative for almost three years, concentrating most of their attacks on wealthy African farmers and government collaborators in the Kikuyu reserves but sometimes brutally murdering a white settler family. Without educated leaders, however, they rapidly lost the public relations war. The British skillfully played up the handful of massacres against whites and succeeded in typing the Mau Mau movement as a barbaric throwback to pagan rituals. They portrayed the oath ceremonies as a kind of black mass of bestiality.

Given the religious aura of the Kikuyu oaths, it is tempting, but misleading, to characterize Mau Mau as a kind of religious revitalization movement. Anthropologists have identified many such revitalization movements among people who are colonized by stronger nations. In many instances, a religious prophet has appeared among the disinherited, denouncing foreigners and claiming magic powers that will protect devotees against foreign bullets. The Ghost Dance religion of the Sioux Indians and the Boxer Rebellion in China were notable examples of revitalization movements.

East Africa also experienced such a revitalization, but it occurred fifty years earlier than Mau Mau, in German East Africa. In 1904 a prophet began distributing *maji* (water) as a medicine to protect believers from foreign attacks. In July 1905 a full-scale Maji Maji rebellion broke out, which the Germans crushed brutally with a scorched earth policy. Perhaps a quarter million Africans died. Maji Maji was a true revitalization movement; but Mau Mau was a largely secular struggle for land and freedom, with the Kikuyu oaths as the only overtly religious trappings.

Eventually the British crushed the Mau Mau, drawing heavily on their experiences with Communist guerrillas in the Malayan Emergency of 1948. They cracked Kikuyu unity by organizing and arming a Home Guard, drawn largely from the more prosperous, landed Kikuyu in the reserves. Nearly 100,000 Kikuyu, about 10 percent of the group's population, served in the Home Guards. The Mau Mau Emergency, therefore, took on the aspect of a civil war, with landed Kikuyu battling the landless. Most of the soldiers in the British army were also Africans, drawn from other ethnic groups in Kenya and from surrounding African colonies such as Uganda and Tanganyika.

In April 1955 the British gained the upper hand by mounting Operation Anvil in the African slums of Nairobi. Throwing a cordon of troops around the whole city, the soldiers systematically combed through the African districts, arresting 24,000 Kikuyu as suspected Mau Mau sympathizers. Then the British turned their attention to the native reserves, resettling virtually the whole Kikuyu ethnic group, about a million people, in 854 strategic villages, just as they herded the suspect Chinese population into fortified villages in Malaya. The military forced these captive villagers to dig a fifty-mile-long ditch around the Mau Mau's main forest redoubt, separating the rebels from their sources of food. With the Mau Mau isolated physically and politically, soldiers, police, and Home Guards systematically swept the forest hideouts until by the end of 1955 only about 1,500 rebels remained on the run.

British troops withdrew from Kenya in November 1956, but the emergency remained in force until 1960 to reassure the white settlers and give the authorities a free hand in stamping out the remnants of Mau Mau. The government supplied the following official casualty figures: about 200 soldiers of all races died on the British side, but the Mau Mau also murdered 1,819 African, 26 Indian, and 32 white civilians. The latter number, 32 white civilians killed, is worth noting, considering the extensive publicity given to atrocities against whites. Historian Robert Edgerton asserts that "more white Kenyans were killed in traffic accidents in Nairobi alone than were killed by the Mau Mau rebels."

The government forces, for their part, reported 11,503 rebels killed in action, but Edgerton concludes "there can be little doubt that this figure is a substantial and intentional underestimate." In addition, more than 80,000 "suspects" were sent to rehabilitation camps, where the British authorities, believing their own propaganda about the pagan revivalism of Mau Mau, subjected the detainees to extensive doses of Christian evangelization. Many died under brutal conditions, until the beating deaths of eleven inmates on March 3, 1959, led to the dismantling of the rehabilitation camps.

Shorter and less deadly than either the Algerian revolution or the Malayan Emergency, the Mau Mau movement ended in a complete and humiliating defeat at the hands of British colonial forces and their favored Kikuyu and other African allies. Yet it succeeded in changing the political environment. The British government had not planned to grant independence to its East African colonies as swiftly as it had in West Africa. They deemed Tanganyika too underdeveloped, and they were committed to maintaining settler supremacy in Kenya, just as they were in the Rhodesias. Wherever white settlers were present, such as the French in Algeria or the English in Kenya, Europeans acted far more intransigently than they did in purely extractive colonies such as the Gold Coast or Nigeria. Yet Mau Mau demonstrated that the white settlers of Kenya could not protect themselves, and therefore the British government had to take over, declare an emergency, and pour in troops. Great Britain lacked the money and manpower to bear such a burden for very long. Therefore, after crushing Mau Mau, the government ignored the settlers and accelerated the process of decolonization throughout East Africa. Historian Wunyabari O. Maloba has concluded: "The Mau Mau revolt did not alone lead Kenya to independence . . . [but it] made settler colonialism no longer feasible in Kenya and raised the price of colonial control for Britain to an intolerable level."

Thus *both* the Mau Mau forest fighters and the intransigent white settlers lost. Ironically, the main winners were the imprisoned leadership of KAU, who played no part in the emergency, and the loyalist Kikuyu Home Guards, who actively resisted the revolutionary movement. Jomo Kenyatta emerged from prison in August 1961 a national hero, a father figure, and a symbol of unity transcending ethnic groups and political factions, much like Nelson Mandela a generation later in South Africa. In October of that same year he assumed the presidency of a newly formed political party, the Kenya African National Union (KANU). In his absence, the British had tried and failed to contain African nationalism by pushing a policy they called "multiracialism," which sounded progressive but would actually perpetuate white settler dominance. A new generation of nationalists, such as the Nairobi labor union official Tom Mboya and the Luo leader from western Kenya, Oginga Odinga, rejected multiracial quotas in government, demanding simple majority rule instead. At a series of constitutional conferences in London, the British capitulated and set a timetable for self-government. Kenya became an independent nation on December 12, 1963, with Jomo Kenyatta as prime minister. A constitutional amendment passed one year later declared the country a republic, under Kenyatta's presidency.

The independent government of Kenya inherited, and continued, a British policy that settled the long-standing struggle for land among the Kikuyu. In 1954-55 a British civil servant, Roger Swynnerton, had drafted a land consolidation scheme giving Kikuyu loyalists firm title to farms large enough for both food crops and cash crops. As a result of the independence negotiations, the British government provided loans to implement the Swynnerton Plan. The so-called million-acre scheme transferred 200,000 acres a year over a period of five years from white settlers in the highlands to African peasants. About 50,000 families took advantage of this policy, primarily the families of Home Guards and other Kikuyu loyalists. At the same time, President Kenyatta assured whites that Kenya still welcomed them, stemming the exodus of settlers which had been running at about 6,000 a year since the end of the emergency. Unlike Algeria, therefore, Kenya retained an influential white population which stabilized at about 40,000 in 1965. Whites retained control of the largest plantations and ranches, whereas African peasants received more marginal lands in the highlands.

Meanwhile in Tanganyika, a newly formed nationalist association, the Tanganyika African National Union (TANU), moved peacefully toward independence while the Mau Mau Emergency raged across its northern border. A Christian schoolteacher named Julius Nyerere founded TANU as the country's first effective political party at a meeting on July 7, 1954, afterward commemorated as the *Saba Saba* meeting ("seventh day of the seventh month" in Swahili). Nyerere had been born in 1922 near Musoma on Lake Victoria to one of eighteen wives of a chief, whose ethnic group, the Zanaki, numbered only about 40,000 persons. Julius attended mission schools and was baptized a Catholic in 1943, the year his father died. He then attended Makerere College, the training ground for most of East Africa's leaders, and studied further at Edinburgh University in Scotland. Upon his return to Tanganyika he married a Christian convert from another ethnic group of the lakes district, took a teaching post at a Catholic secondary school near the capital of Dar es Salaam, then dedicated himself to transforming TANU into a mass nationalist party.

Nyerere skillfully manipulated Tanganyika's status as a United Nations trust territory (successor to the League of Nations mandate) to further his goal of self-government. Under the League of Nations, mandatory authorities wielded virtually unrestricted control over their territories; and any complaints against their rule had to be routed through their own government bureaucracy. With the establishment of the United Nations after World War II, however, in-

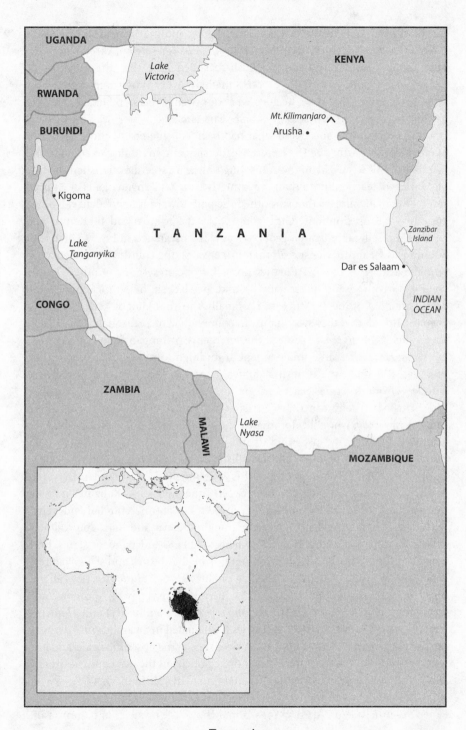

Tanzania

habitants of trust territories acquired the right to mount complaints directly to the UN Trusteeship Council. In March 1955, Julius Nyerere appeared before the Trusteeship Council and made a well-reasoned case that the Africans of Tanganyika should eventually exercise majority rule. When questioned how long "eventually" should be, he guessed about twenty years. In fact, Tanganyika became independent just six and a half years later.

TANU's speedy success in what had been considered the most backward of colonies was partly due to Nyerere's leadership and his ability to educate and inspire his followers. Throughout his long political career he cherished the title of *Mwalimu,* teacher, more than any other honor. Yet Tanganyika also enjoyed several other advantages that smoothed the path toward independence. No single ethnic group dominated the country, as the Kikuyu did in Kenya, and Nyerere himself came from a group so small it threatened nobody. The use of Swahili was far more widespread than in Kenya, so the country possessed a potential national language. Furthermore, European settlers numbered only about twenty thousand in Tanganyika, and they lacked the political power and economic clout of the Kenyan settlers. Finally, the Mau Mau of Kenya so frightened the British that they were happy to cooperate with a reasonable, intelligent leader such as Nyerere and prevent the emergence of Tanganyikan radicalism.

Tanganyika became independent at midnight on December 9, 1961. Two years later, at the same time that Kenya gained its freedom, the British also withdrew from its earliest East African possession, the island state of Zanzibar. The British left behind a sharp division on Zanzibar between the Arabized Muslim minority, who still dominated the government and economy, and the black African majority. Just a month after independence, on January 11-12, 1964, Zanzibar's Africans revolted and established a socialist regime. Acting out of fear that a similar revolt might topple his government on the mainland, Nyerere in April 1964 engineered a merger between Tanganyika and Zanzibar into the renamed state of Tanzania. The union proved rocky at times, but has endured.

The neighboring East African nations of Kenya and Tanzania followed drastically different land and development policies as independent states. Both employed similar slogans in Swahili, emphasizing hard work and struggle. President Jomo Kenyatta of Kenya enlisted an old logger's cry, *Harambee* (let's all pull together) as his inaugural theme, and President Julius Nyerere of Tanzania countered with the mantras of *Uhuru na umoja* (freedom and unity) and *Uhuru na Kazi* (freedom and work). Both countries participated in an ambitious East African common market, with common services such as the post office, rails and harbors, and airlines. Yet, the different economic policies of the two countries gradually drove them apart, destroying this attempt at federalism in 1977.

Kenyatta's government set the direction of Kenya's economy in Sessional Paper No. 10, issued on April 27, 1965. Tom Mboya, the minister of planning and economic development, entitled the document *African Socialism and Its Application to Planning in Kenya,* thereby granting a rhetorical sop to radicals within the nationalist ranks; but the paper's policies came down firmly on the side of a mixed economy and a guided capitalism. The Kenya government rejected nationalization of land or industry and encouraged foreign investment, guaranteeing that the profits of multinational corporations could be freely expatriated. Since the British had already developed a certain amount of industry in Kenya's capital of Nairobi and her major port of Mombasa, independent Kenya continued to function as a manufacturing and distribution center for all of East Africa. Though the country suffered from an imbalance of trade with Europe, buying more than it sold, it compensated by selling much more to Tanzania and Uganda than it bought from them. Thus Kenya became a link in the chain of multinational economic imperialism.

Sessional Paper No. 10 cut more sharply with its Africanization policies. Though the government embraced capitalism and foreign investment, it wanted Africans to profit from the newly created wealth. Development assistance, therefore, was targeted toward companies that hired Africans for middle- and upper-level managerial positions; and restrictive immigration laws made it increasingly difficult for non-citizens to trade or work in Kenya. These laws exercised their greatest impact on the resident Asians, who had dominated the retail trade and small industry in colonial times. As a result Kenya's Asian population (mainly Muslims from India or Pakistan) was more than cut in half, from 176,613 in 1962 to 78,600 in 1979. In practice, Kenya's "African socialism" encouraged a few rich Europeans and Americans with capital, whittled away the numbers of Asian traders, and created a whole new class of African capitalists. Many of the African "big men" who profited from these policies were "double-dipping" civil servants, for after 1971 the government authorized its employees to participate in private business in addition to their public jobs. Kenyatta and his relatives set such an extravagant example that they were widely referred to as "the royal family."

Though Kenya's encouragement of foreign investment and inclination toward the West in Cold War politics pleased European and American leaders, the country's economic record is mixed at best. Kenya enjoyed steady economic growth, but the fruits of this growth were very unequally distributed. Kenyan historian William R. Ochieng has explained his country's post-independence experience as a classic case of neo-colonialism displaying "characteristics typical of an underdeveloped economy at the periphery: the preponderance of foreign capital, the dominance of agriculture, the limited development of industry, and heavy reliance on export of primary products and imports of capital and manufactured consumer goods." Most important of all, Ochieng concludes, "Kenya continues to remain a land of a few rich people and millions of poor folk."

In neighboring Tanzania, on the other hand, Julius Nyerere piloted a unique egalitarian experiment in agrarian socialism. Nyerere, a fervent practicing Catholic, drew his socialism more from Christian than Marxist sources, but in a country whose main religions were Islam and traditional African beliefs, he carefully couched his preaching in secular terms. Above all, he argued that agrarian socialism was based on traditional African customs. According to Nyerere, everyone in precolonial Africa had worked for a living, except for the old, the young, and the sick. No one became very rich or very poor, for land was held in common by the clan or village and the extended family supplied aid to any of its members in need. Nyerere, therefore, coined the word *Ujamaa* (Familyhood) as the descriptive term for his variety of African socialism.

Tanganyika's colonial rulers had introduced the concept of private property but had not gone very far towards developing industry or creating a landed middle class, such as the Kikuyu under Kenya's Swynnerton Plan. Therefore, the very poverty and underdevelopment of Tanganyika at the time of independence gave Nyerere his opportunity to follow a socialist path. The independent government immediately declared that all land belonged to the state and would be leased to farmers rather than sold to them outright, and it encouraged the populace to reside in villages, where common services could be provided, rather than on isolated farms. Nyerere's most fervent followers mocked the *nouveaux riches* landowners and civil servants of neighboring Kenya as members of the tribe of "Wa Benzi" (those driving Mercedes Benz or Porsche automobiles). In order to prevent the formation of such a tribe in Tanzania, Nyerere's government issued the Arusha Declaration on February 5, 1967, outlining a policy of economic self-reliance based on communal ownership of land and de-emphasizing industry and foreign investment.

Immediately after the issuance of the Arusha Declaration, the government nationalized all foreign banks in the country as well as firms engaged in food processing or the import-export trade. Nyerere accepted the reality of scarce resources in Tanzania but set out a goal of equality and sharing among all the people. In order to set a good example, the Arusha Declaration prescribed a stringent code of ethics for government employees, forbidding ownership of shares in corporations or the purchase of urban property for rental to others. No civil servant was allowed to hold more than one salaried position. In contrast to Kenya, therefore, Tanzania's civil servants did not become a class of privileged capitalists. The ratio between the top civil servant's income and the minimum wage of a worker fell from a high of 50 to 1 in colonial times to a more egalitarian 9 to 1 by 1977.

The cornerstone of Tanzanian socialism was laid in the countryside, with the foundation of *Ujamaa* villages. The government encouraged peasants to relocate in villages initially for practical reasons, since it would be impossible to provide schools and other modern services to a population lightly scattered across East Africa's inhospitable landscape; but the Arusha Declaration added a socialist purpose to the growth of villages. Tanzania, therefore, pursued a policy much like the British during the Mau Mau Emergency in Kenya, but for ideological rather than security purposes.

Nyerere explained his agrarian policy most fully in a booklet entitled "Socialism and Rural Development," issued about six months after Arusha. Nyerere's pamphlet provided an elegant, possibly idealized, basis for *Ujamaa* in traditional African family life:

> This pattern of living was made possible because of three basic assumptions of traditional life. . . . The first of these basic assumptions . . . I have sometimes described as "love". . . . A better word is perhaps "respect". . . . [A second assumption is that] all the basic goods were held in common, and shared among all members of the unit. . . . Finally, and as a necessary third principle was the fact that everyone had an obligation to work.

Next, the *Mwalimu*, or teacher, as Nyerere liked to call himself, frankly admitted that traditional African familyhood was not perfect. In particular he singled out the fact that men were more equal than women. "It is impossible to deny that the women did, and still do, more than their fair share of the work in the fields and in the homes," he wrote. Finally, he outlined a three-stage process toward agrarian socialism in Tanzanian villages: the first, and essential, step is movement to the villages, where peasants must cluster together for self-help and self-reliance; second, a small number of villagers should be persuaded to farm a communal plot of land as a demonstration project, in addition to their own leaseholds; then, finally, when all are convinced of the value of communal work, all farming will be done on the common land.

The Tanzanian version of agrarian socialism more closely resembled the *Kibbutzim* of Israel or the self-reliant villages of Gandhi's India than the forced labor of Chinese communes or Soviet collective farms. Nyerere summed up his vision:

> This means that most of our farming would be done by groups of people who live as a community and work as a community. They would live together in a village; they would farm together; market together; and undertake the provision of local services and small local requirements as a community.

Unfortunately, *Ujamaa* proved less attractive in practice than in theory. The government found it impossible to persuade all the people to cluster in villages, so in the mid-1970s they resorted to compulsion. By 1977 13 million out of

Tanzania's 14 million people resided in 7,684 villages with an average population of 1700. The majority of these villages, however, had not advanced beyond stage two of Nyerere's socialization process. The forced relocation of peasants plus a devastating drought in the mid-seventies disrupted agricultural production, necessitating the importation of food to prevent starvation. The consequences of *Ujamaa* proved much less deadly than Mao's suicidal Great Leap Forward in China; however, the inadequacies of the policy led Nyerere's government to allow a greater role for individual capitalist farming.

Both Kenya's guided capitalism and Tanzania's *Ujamaa* socialism succeeded in their own terms, but failed when considered in a wider context. Kenya achieved impressive figures for economic growth throughout the 1960s and 1970s, creating wealth for individual Africans, but the result was an unequal society badly divided along class lines. A character in James Ngugi's epic novel *A Grain of Wheat* exclaims: "But now, whom do we see riding in long cars and changing them daily as if motor cars were clothes? It is those who did not take part in the movement...." Tanzania, on the other hand, produced an admirable philosophy of community and achieved a relatively equal distribution of resources, but these resources remained meager and inadequate.

Tanzania's disappointing experience with *Ujamaa* mirrors a frustration felt by many who worked for social justice in this century. Nyerere's essays on socialism are humane, elegant expressions of ideals that still seem fresh and readable thirty years later. However, they are essentially *moral* essays, lacking the hard statistics and detailed plans of economic blueprints. Most idealists and reformers who grew up in the middle decades of this century felt more at home with such political and moral discussions than with economic planning. Yet the hard facts of economics have defeated many an idealistic scheme. The dilemmas facing world leaders at the end of the century are less dramatic and deadly than those of the mid-century, but harder to solve. Fighting Hitler and fascism or struggling for freedom against colonialism were physically dangerous and required great courage, but they were intellectually and morally easy, with the issues clearly outlined in black and white. Balancing the individual economic incentives that produce greater wealth against the need for a just distribution of resources is intellectually challenging and difficult to accomplish. In East Africa, as in the rest of the world, it has proved easier to win freedom than to conquer the land and create an abundant, egalitarian economy.

CHAPTER FOURTEEN

Chaos and Cold War

T he drama of colonial liberation in Africa played on a separate stage from the Cold War throughout the 1950s. Neither superpower had ever possessed colonies in Africa, nor did the continent hold the same significance as Berlin or Korea. Russian and American rivalry helped precipitate the Suez crisis, but once Nasser nationalized the canal all his antagonists stood on the same side of the Cold War divide. The Algerian revolutionaries espoused a Marxist philosophy but they received little aid from the Soviet Union. Black African leaders such as Kwame Nkrumah of Ghana routinely invoked Marxist platitudes and played both superpowers against each other in an attempt to increase foreign aid, but neither the Russians nor the Americans became heavily involved. In 1960, however, the independence of the Belgian Congo touched off a series of chaotic events that escalated into the first full-scale Cold War confrontation in Africa. The two major themes of the century's second half, decolonization and the superpower Cold War, collided during the Congo crisis.

The Belgian Congo was one of the largest and most curious of all the European possessions in Africa. Belgium itself was not an expansionist power, or even a power at all in European terms. The nation owed its sole venture in colonialism to its ambitious king, Leopold II. His father had belonged to a minor German royal family, the House of Saxe-Coburg-Gotha, and had been placed on the throne of Belgium when that tiny state was created out of French- and Flemish-speaking provinces in 1831. Leopold II ascended the throne in 1865 and immediately found his kingdom too small for his ambitions. Constitutional monarchs had little to do in nineteenth-century Europe, so the king became obsessed by a search for colonies as an outlet for his vast fortune and boundless energy. The frugal Belgian government made it clear that the nation was not thirsting for empire; therefore, Leopold ventured out on his own personal entrepreneurial quest.

Like many other Europeans, Leopold was captivated by the saga of the English explorer-journalist Henry Morton Stanley's search for the missionary David Livingstone. When Stanley completed Livingstone's explorations in the years 1874-77, descending the Congo River to its outlet at the Atlantic Ocean and bringing back tales of fabulous wealth, the Belgian king hired him as his agent. Leopold convened a geographical congress and organized the International Association of the Congo, ostensibly for the purpose of spreading European knowledge and stamping out the slave trade in Africa, but actually as cover for his colonial ambitions. An international consortium of bankers backed the king, who sent Stanley to negotiate treaties with the local chiefs of the Congo basin. Treaties in hand, Leopold convinced the European powers at the Congress of Berlin (1884-85) to recognize an entity called the Congo Free State. The Congo was *not* at first a colony of the Belgian state, but a personal possession of King Leopold. Since the enterprising king was posing as an advocate of free trade and an opponent of slavery, France, Germany, and England felt content to let him manage the heart of central Africa, thus ensuring that none of the great powers would control it. As historian Thomas Pakenham has concluded, "in effect the self-styled philanthropic king had been chosen to act in Africa as a trustee for the whole of Europe."

The king eventually found such an implicit trusteeship inhibiting. He had poured his own personal fortune into the search for ivory, gold, or other riches in the Congo, only to see it all disappear. Fortified by new loans from the bankers and the Belgian government in the 1890s, he finally struck it rich in the rubber trade. The invention of pneumatic tires for bicycles and automobiles created an insatiable demand for the latex of rubber trees, which grew wild in the Congo River valley. The king's soldiers did stamp out the slave trade, which Swahili merchants from East Africa had spread to the eastern reaches of the Congo, but his own traders and merchants replaced it with a vicious system of forced labor which proved just as bad. Whole villages were depopulated when the Belgians descended upon them, impressing the males as rubber tappers or porters and scaring the women and children into the forest, where many were killed by wild beasts. As word of these atrocities filtered back to Europe, the Congo Reform Association was founded in Great Britain by Edmund D. Morel in 1904. Finally international pressure forced Leopold to cede control of the Congo to the Belgian government, with orders to act as Europe's trustee in cleaning up the mess. Thus in 1908, the Congo Free State was replaced by the Belgian Congo, and the *London Daily News* remarked: "Never before was greatness forced by circumstances upon a more reluctant people."

The Belgians' colonial acquisition was the second largest in all of Africa,[1] eighty times larger than Belgium itself and roughly equivalent to the eastern half of the United States. It included the Congo River valley with its lush rain forests, plus grassy savannah lands to the north and south of the river basin. Thanks to Leopold's military campaigns against local African peoples and Swahili traders in the 1890s, it also embraced the more temperate upland plateau of Katanga, which had more in common geographically with East Africa than with the rest of the Belgian Congo. Due to the poor soil of most areas and the ravages of slave trade and forced labor, this vast territory was relatively underpopulated, numbering only about eight million inhabitants at the time of the Belgian annexation. The Congolese included over 250 distinct ethnic groups, most speaking a variant of the Bantu language. A majority lived in small-scale, stateless societies, especially in the rain forest, but several large kingdoms had been created in the savannahs and the uplands.

The Kongo kingdom, which ultimately gave its name to the river and the modern nation, had controlled the river mouth when Portuguese explorers first sighted the area in the fifteenth century, but their state finally disintegrated under the impact of the Atlantic slave trade four centuries later. Other numerous groups, particularly the Luba and the Lunda, ruled over powerful states in the upland regions of the eastern Congo. The Swahili from the east and the Belgians from the west smashed them in turn. The Luba in the Kasai region made a smooth transition to Belgian rule, hiring themselves out for railroad construction and mining jobs and becoming the most urbanized of the colony's people. They were frequently referred to as the "Jews of the Congo." A final "tribe" or ethnic group was created by the perceptions of the Belgians. Any of the people who lived upstream from their new capital of Leopoldville (Kinshasa)[2] were called Bangala, though in fact they belonged to many different small-scale societies. Over the first half of the twentieth century, the Africans themselves began to adopt this identification as Bangala. The trader's lingo that they spoke on the docks of Leopoldville, dubbed Lingala, became the most widely used in the river valley, even though it was entirely synthetic and not native to any of the ethnic groups in the colony.

The Belgian government created three "pillars," three powerful administrative structures — church, colonial government, and business corporations — to rule the diverse peoples of the Congo. The colonial administration was

---

1. Sudan is the largest in land area.

2. About a decade after independence the former Belgian Congo changed its name to Zaire and also renamed most of the cities with African titles. In this chapter, I will use the European names primarily but will cite the African name in parenthesis the first time the city is mentioned.

more pervasive than anywhere else in Africa, with local agricultural officers enforcing the sixty days per year of compulsory labor required of most males. The Catholic Church, the established church of Belgium, sent out numerous missionaries who built mission posts in nearly every village. By mid-century, almost half the population was Christian and over five hundred native Africans had been ordained as priests. The Belgian government left nearly all schooling to the missionaries, and many Congolese were attracted to the church for its educational opportunities as much as its spiritual appeal. Finally, the economy of the colony was dominated by a handful of giant corporations, all controlled by an interlocking directorate in Belgium. These corporations maintained the vital rail link from Leopoldville to the Atlantic Ocean that King Leopold's Free State had built in the 1890s, and they gradually extended the rails to bring far-off Katanga into communication with the coast. The *Union Minière du Haut Katanga* dominated the mines of that province, which by the 1920s had become the world's third largest source of copper. Cobalt, uranium, diamonds, and gold were also mined in Katanga and other provinces of the eastern Congo.

Historian Crawford Young has aptly summed up the impact of this dense administrative structure on ordinary Africans:

> The administrator came to count the villager, collect his head tax, perhaps inoculate him, and certainly to put him to work building roads and tilling the fields. The missionary, Catholic or Protestant, came to evangelize him; no village was likely to be very far from a mission station. . . . And company agents would come to the village to recruit him. . . . Worker and peasant . . . sought an end to the process of being dragged, wrenched, and tugged into a modern society. . . . No more taxes, no more cotton, no more census-takers, no more vaccinators, no more identity cards, no more army recruiters.

The final sentence of Young's analysis echoes the cries of Proudhon and the European anarchists who rejected the intrusiveness of the modern state. Africans who had lived in stateless societies for centuries were naturally anarchic in their response to Belgium's heavy-handed colonialism. They used the words *Bula Matari,* meaning "he who breaks rocks" in the language of the Kongo people, as their collective term for the colonial government.

The Belgians considered their solid and profitable trusteeship of the Congo permanent, and made no long-range plans for handing over authority to Africans. Consequently, when both Great Britain and France decided to cut loose their African colonies after the Second World War, neither the Belgians nor the Congolese were prepared to follow suit. In 1953, only twenty-one African students were studying in European-language schools, and in the previous year, Thomas Kanza had become the first Congolese student to matriculate at a

Belgian university. Three of the four categories in the civil service were reserved for university degree holders, which meant in effect that all Africans were barred. Housing was as segregated as government service and education, with the Africans living in native quarters on the fringes of Leopoldville and other Belgian cities. The European settler population had increased after World War II, especially in the prosperous mining province of Katanga, and whites routinely insulted and humiliated Africans. Society in the Belgian Congo in the mid-twentieth century resembled that of South Africa or the Rhodesias, where a white supremacist culture had developed.

The intellectual proletariat nurtured a nationalist movement in the 1950s, but this class was significantly smaller than elsewhere in Africa, so the development of Congolese nationalism was greatly retarded. In 1956 a group of Catholic Africans published a cautious statement calling for greater educational and employment opportunities within the colonial system; but an ethnic association of Kongo-speaking groups, the ABAKO *(Alliance des Ba-Kongo)*, countered with a more vigorous riposte, which mentioned the word "independence" for the first time. The ABAKO had originated as a cultural association in 1950, but with the appointment of Joseph Kasavubu as president in 1955 it had become more overtly political. Still it was merely a regional, ethnic grouping. In October 1958, the Congo's first truly national political party, the MNC *(Mouvement National Congolais)* was founded by Patrice Lumumba.

Kasavubu and Lumumba were the odd couple of the Congo, and within two years they would be thrust together into leadership of an independent nation. Unlike other Africans leaders, neither had received a university education or studied overseas. Joseph Kasavubu was born in 1913 and had prepared for the priesthood in a Catholic seminary, but he eventually changed his mind and became a schoolteacher. Cautious, suspicious, and almost sphinx-like in his silences, he contrasted sharply with the charismatic and impulsive leader of the MNC.

Patrice Lumumba, born in 1925, did not complete high school but dropped out to work as a postal clerk in Stanleyville (Kisangani), Orientale Province. All his teachers and associates recognized in him a special intensity and brilliance. While working in Stanleyville, he became the leader of no less than seven professional, cultural, and political associations. During his first visit to Belgium in 1955, on a government-sponsored tour for young Congolese *evolués* ("evolved ones," potential leaders), Lumumba caught the attention of the Belgian colonial minister, who planned to appoint him to a job in his ministry. However, upon his return to the Congo Lumumba was charged with embezzling post office funds and sentenced to two years' imprisonment. When he was released he moved to Leopoldville and honed his persuasive skills as the sales manager for a local brewery. "Charismatic" is an overworked adjective, but apparently it applied fully to Lumumba. It was often said that if he walked into a room dressed as a waiter with a platter of food on his head, he would emerge as prime minister. Opponents also applied less flattering adjectives, such as "impulsive" and "unstable." His friend and only biographer, Thomas Kanza, concedes that Lumumba was impulsive, a man in a hurry, adding an even more ominous adjective, "fatalistic," to his description:

> Close friends declared that he was predestined not to live long. He was con-
> vinced of his mission to free the Congo, but he also firmly believed that he
> had only a short time at his disposal. . . . This would certainly explain his im-
> patience, his impulsive behavior. . . .

Because Kasavubu had been the first to call for independence and at the same time was flirting with separatism for his Kongo ethnic group, the Belgians initially considered him the more radical of the two leaders. Accordingly, they denied him a visa for the Pan-African Conference that Kwame Nkrumah had called in Accra, Ghana for December 1958, but they let Lumumba attend. The thirty-three-year-old Congolese was enthralled by Ghana's president, who had secured his country's independence the previous year. Nkrumah, for his part, recognized Lumumba as a promising protégé and encouraged him to give free rein to his oratorical gifts. Lumumba did just that upon his return to Leopoldville, scoring his first triumph with a mass audience on December 18, 1958.

Less than a week later riots in Leopoldville spurred the Belgians into des-
perate action, much as the Accra riots a decade earlier had pushed the British onto a course of decolonization. An ABAKO local branch was scheduled to meet at the YMCA on Sunday, January 4, 1959, but the mayor canceled the meeting permit. When some association members insisted on gathering, police blocked their entrance to the building and rioting broke out. The authorities temporarily lost control of the African districts, where mobs ran wild, looting shops and attacking visible symbols of church and government. According to the official casualty figures, forty-nine Congolese were killed in the rioting. In October 1959, similar disturbances broke out in Stanleyville and thirty Africans died. Kasavubu and the ABAKO leaders were jailed for two months after the Leopoldville riots, and Lumumba was arrested after the Stanleyville disorders. Thomas Kanza wrote prophetically in a Belgian newspaper: "The Belgians have committed one of the most serious of all errors — an unfortunately common one among colonizers. Prison, as everyone knows, is the waiting room where the political man sits until he receives his popular mandate."

With most of the French and British colonies hurrying toward independence and their Congolese subjects increasingly restive, the Belgians decided on

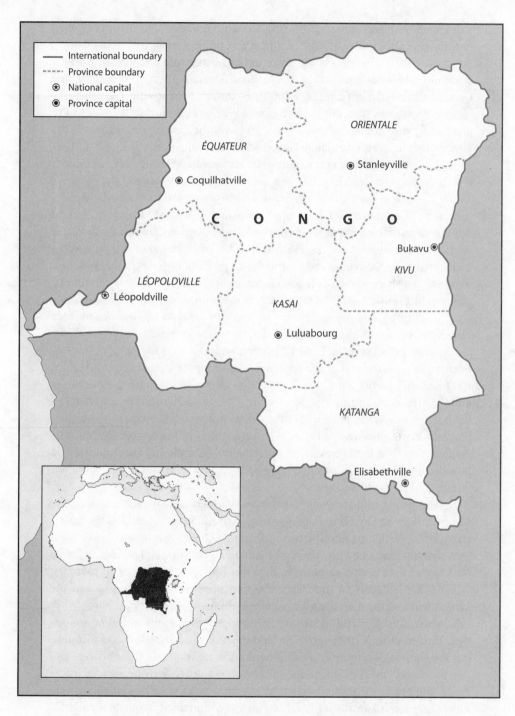

The Congo and Its Provinces at Independence

a desperate gamble (they called it the "Congolese wager"). Knowing they had not trained enough Africans for technical and professional posts in the Congo, they were betting that they could grant independence in name, allowing politicians to preen and strut on the stage, but still retain effective control of the Congo's three pillars of church, administration, and corporation. On January 13, 1959, right after the Leopoldville riots, Belgium announced its intention to grant independence in the near future; and over the next eighteen months the government hurriedly conducted a round-table conference in Brussels and organized elections in the Congo. Lumumba was released from prison in order to attend the conference in January 1960, and much to the surprise of the Belgians, all the Congolese leaders and parties united in a demand for immediate independence. The date was set for June 30, 1960. Lumumba's MNC won the largest number of parliamentary seats in the spring 1960 elections, but his party fell far short of an absolute majority. Eventually it became clear that only a government with both Kasavubu and Lumumba in prominent posts had any chance of building a successful coalition, so Kasavubu accepted the largely ceremonial position of president with Lumumba as prime minister.

Belgium's Congolese wager failed right from the start. On Independence Day, June 30, 1960, King Baudouin of Belgium and President Kasavubu of the Congo gave polite speeches, but Lumumba let loose with his flaming oratory. Forty years later, the text of the speech does not appear all that remarkable, for it is filled with pieties about the "struggle for liberty" and the people's desire to build a "free, rich, and prosperous country." However, Lumumba also detailed the horrors of "eighty years under the colonialist regime," including forced labor, humiliating insults, and the "profound suffering" of discrimination. The Belgian king, like his famous ancestor Leopold II, truly believed that he had presided over a model colony in a benevolent, paternalist fashion and could not understand Lumumba's rage.

The prime minister was not the only Congolese who felt angry in the summer of 1960. The *Force Publique,* or Congo military, watched as the politicians took prestigious and lucrative jobs in the new government, while their own mobility remained blocked by Belgian officers. Not a single African held a rank higher than master sergeant in the *Force Publique*. Adding insult to injury, General Émile Janssens, the Belgian commander of the army, lectured the Leopoldville garrison on the night of July 5. He wrote on the blackboard: "After Independence = Before Independence." Enraged, the troops mutinied against their foreign officers in Leopoldville and most of the other garrisons throughout the Congo. The rampaging soldiers sought to humiliate their officers and any white civilians they encountered. About two dozen Europeans were murdered, and nearly three hundred white women were raped. The Congolese were unleashing the frustrations of eighty years of colonialism upon their rulers.

Lumumba and Kasavubu acted swiftly to quell the mutiny. They immediately dismissed the Belgian officers and promoted all soldiers at least one rank, naming a civilian with scant military experience the new commander in chief and a former army corporal, Joseph Mobutu, as his chief of staff, with the rank of colonel. Then the president and prime minister toured the country together to calm the troops and the populace. When the Belgians offered to send in their own troops to protect foreign civilians, the Congolese government seemed ready to accept this assistance. Two events on July 11, however, changed their minds. The Belgian navy bombarded the port of Matadi in the lower reaches of the Congo River, causing many unnecessary casualties; and on the same day, at the opposite end of the country, the provincial president of Katanga declared his province independent of the Congo. Moise Tshombe, Katanga's leader, was encouraged in his secessionist stance by the Belgian mining companies and was immediately assisted by Belgian troops. When Kasavubu and Lumumba attempted to visit Elisabethville (Lubumbashi), the capital of Katanga, their plane was refused permission to land.

The intervention of Belgian troops in the Congo in mid-July, less than two weeks after the grant of formal independence, transformed the political chaos of the former colony into an international crisis. Such a blatant act of neo-colonialism flew in the face of world opinion, not only in Africa and Asia but in much of Europe and America as well. Kasavubu and Lumumba appealed to the United Nations for military assistance and technical aid to restore law and order, and the Security Council responded on July 14, 1960, with a resolution authorizing the secretary-general to comply. The first contingents of soldiers from Ethiopia, Ghana, Morocco, and Tunisia landed in the Congo within two days of the Security Council's decision. Eventually their numbers would grow to 19,828 soldiers from over twenty nations.

The United Nations acted promptly and vigorously in the Congo crisis because of the leadership of Secretary-General Dag Hammarskjöld. A Swedish civil servant with a doctorate in economics, Hammarskjöld was elected the second secretary-general of the UN in 1953 as a compromise candidate acceptable to both the Russians and the Americans. During his two terms of office he raised the prestige of the world body to the highest point it has enjoyed, either before or since. He once half-jokingly remarked that he was a secular pope, trying to lead the world without any battalions but only with moral authority.

Hammarskjöld was a very private, aloof individual with both intellectual and spiritual depth. The writer Conor Cruise O'Brien, who served under the secretary-general in the Congo crisis, compared him to a Belgian priest of his acquaintance: "What he enjoyed most in the world, I think, was being cunning in the service of God." Hammarskjöld's book of personal meditations, *Markings*, became a best-seller throughout the world after his death. One entry from this book illustrates how he viewed his role as world leader: "You are merely the lens in the beam. . . . You will know life and be acknowledged by it according to your degree of transparency, your capacity, that is, to vanish as an end, and remain purely as a means." He was too practical and realistic to believe that the United Nations could become a world government in his lifetime, but he sought to enhance its authority as a mediator in times of international crisis. During his tenure as secretary-general, he openly championed the newly independent nations of Asia and Africa and the "decent" middle powers, such as his own Sweden and its Scandinavian neighbors. One Asian leader acknowledged Hammarskjöld's success in this endeavor by calling the United Nations under his leadership "the summit meeting of the small nations."

The secretary-general had toured Africa early in 1960, and recognizing the signs of potential conflict in the Congo, he sent his under-secretary, the African-American diplomat Ralph Bunche, to attend the independence ceremonies in June. The UN's best troubleshooter was therefore on the spot when the Congo crisis first flared up. Bunche and Hammarskjöld's blue-helmeted peacekeepers nearly completed their mission during the first month of engagement, restoring order in the major cities and convincing the Belgians to begin withdrawing troops from all of the Congo except the breakaway province of Katanga. After meeting with Prime Minister Lumumba and his entourage at the United Nations in New York, Hammarskjöld went to the Congo for a first-hand look. On August 12 he and his military advisor, Indian general Indar Jit Rikhye, flew from Leopoldville to Elisabethville with a few hundred Swedish UN soldiers. As the transports circled the airport, Tshombe told Hammarskjöld that he could land but the troops could not. The secretary-general insisted, and Tshombe backed down. Other UN troops followed, and the Belgian military finally pulled out the next month. By the end of August, therefore, it looked as if Hammarskjöld and the United Nations had scored a great triumph. Only the reentry of Tshombe's Katanga into the Republic of the Congo remained to be negotiated. Yet managing the Congo crisis would not prove so easy, for events both inside and outside the country soon complicated the situation.

Since the story now becomes increasingly complex, it might be best to pause and survey the aims of all parties to the struggle, both Congolese and international. Prime Minister Patrice Lumumba was the key figure, a lightning rod for the whole crisis. Many considered him a communist and acted accordingly, but in fact he was a classic socio-nationalist in the mold of Sukarno, Nasser, or Nkrumah. Like those other Third World leaders, he believed in a strong central government to lead his people toward social and economic progress, and like them he was neutralist and opportunist in foreign relations, willing to accept assistance from both sides in the Cold War. Lumumba treated the United Nations peacekeepers like his own national army, trying to use them to end the Katanga secession and suppress his other political enemies. When

Bunche and Hammarskjöld asserted their independence from his direction, he denounced them and turned elsewhere for help. In late August he received a shipment of trucks and ten heavy transport planes from the Soviet Union, which he used to transport troops through Kasai Province for a drive on Katanga. This military foray proved disastrous, turning into a wild massacre of dissident ethnic groups that further alienated him from potential supporters at the UN and within the Congo itself.

President Kasavubu kept his usual silence and, after his initial tour of the country with Lumumba at the time of the army mutiny, was hardly seen in public. He remained less dedicated to national unity than the prime minister and would have been satisfied with a loose federal system allowing cultural autonomy for the Kongo people around Leopoldville. He enjoyed an immense political advantage over Lumumba since his own ethnic group predominated in the capital whereas Lumumba's personal supporters lived in faraway Stanleyville. The prime minister badly underestimated the cautious president of the Congo, believing him a lazy nonentity, but Thomas Kanza more accurately sized up Kasavubu as a "crocodile sleeping open-eyed beside the river."

The third major actor on the Leopoldville scene, Colonel Joseph Mobutu, was genuinely undecided about the extent of his role. The youngest of the three Congolese principals, he was just twenty-nine at the time of independence, a former army sergeant who had then gone into journalism. He had helped Lumumba organize his national political party, the MNC, and served as his private secretary, but somewhere along the line he began accepting money from the Belgian secret service as a police informer. After his appointment as army chief of staff, he began calling on the friendships he had made during six years of army service and quietly building a personal following among the troops. Hammarskjöld's military advisor, General Rikhye, saw Mobutu almost daily during the first months of independence and he later wrote that the colonel had few political ambitions at the time but merely wanted to end the gathering chaos in the capital city.

At the far end of the country, the province of Katanga had all the makings of a viable independent state: a history of political unity under a powerful king in the nineteenth century, only a handful of different ethnic groups, and most of all a prosperous economy based on mining. Geographically, the province shared the extensive copper belt with its colonial neighbor, Northern Rhodesia, and enjoyed good rail links to the sea through Rhodesia and Angola. Its healthy upland climate made it congenial to white settlers, who formed about 2 percent of the population, the same proportion as in Kenya. Moise Tshombe, the president of this breakaway province, differed from other Congolese leaders since he did not belong to the intellectual proletariat. Rather he was a member of a wealthy business family that had built a profitable chain of grocery stores. A genial, talkative, but indecisive individual, he made the perfect front man for the Belgian interests that wanted to keep Katanga under their control. In brief, Katanga was a version of Kenya's white highlands, with its wealth and power based on copper mining rather than ranching or farming. The very fact that it could survive as a separate nation is what made its secession so threatening to Lumumba and other Congo nationalists.

The Congo's size, strategic location, and mineral wealth made the country a natural site for superpower rivalry. Both sides in the Cold War knew that the uranium for the first atomic bombs had been mined in Katanga. In the late 1950s and early 1960s, the Soviet Union had a new and more adventurous leader in Nikita Khrushchev (see chapter 15), who hoped to establish a second front in the Cold War by recruiting the newly independent states of Africa to his side. The Soviet Union did not possess the air or sea transport capacity to send combat troops to central Africa, but Khrushchev believed he could buy Lumumba's support cheaply with some flamboyant words at the United Nations and a few planes, trucks, and guns. Khrushchev was willing to run risks in the Third World that the cautious Joseph Stalin never would have. Like nineteenth-century European imperialists, the Soviet leader gambled on a maximum political impact with a minimum investment.

The American administration of Dwight Eisenhower, on the other hand, was determined to prevent any Soviet gains in Africa. Just two weeks after independence, the American ambassador in Belgium warned his superiors of Lumumba's communist leanings; and CIA Director Allen Dulles concluded that the Congolese prime minister was "a Castro or worse." (See chapter 15 on the American obsession with Fidel Castro.) On August 25, 1960, after Lumumba had asked for unilateral Soviet aid, the CIA began plotting the prime minister's assassination. They sent a deadly poison that would mimic a tropical disease to the station chief in Leopoldville, but before this operative could succeed in his task the prime minister's political enemies did the job for him.

The Belgian government wanted to protect its citizens from the chaos of the Congo, but since nearly 100,000 of them had fled the atrocities of the army mutiny, significant numbers remained only in Katanga. Belgium's policy, therefore, aimed at protecting human and economic interests in the breakaway province, but the Brussels government stopped short of recognizing Katanga's independence so as not to offend its NATO ally, the United States. Great Britain pursued a similarly equivocal policy, backing Belgian economic interests in Katanga but trying not to irritate the United States. France, under General de Gaulle, haughtily ignored the entire crisis, but some individual French soldiers, defeated in the Algerian revolution, hired themselves out as mercenaries in Katanga. It became fashionable to blame most atrocities in that province on *les affreux* (the frightful ones), as the French mercenaries were called.

Dag Hammarskjöld tried to navigate a genuinely neutral course between the Cold War rivals. In the Congo he hoped to fill a political and military vacuum, while concentrating on his double mission to restore law and order and expel the last survivors of colonialism, Belgian advisors and mercenaries in Katanga. Yet he also tried to accomplish this mission with a minimum of force and without interfering in the internal politics of the Congo, a task which ultimately proved impossible. Though neutral in intent, Hammarskjöld's actions tilted toward the American side in practice, since his closest advisors at the UN were American citizens and he relied heavily on American financial and logistical aid to support the peacekeepers. If the planet was divided into three worlds during the Cold War, Hammarskjöld's UN policies created a tacit alliance between the First and Third worlds, the Americans and the Afro-Asian neutralist bloc. As Conor Cruise O'Brien has concluded: "Nobody said out loud: 'Keep communism out of Africa' . . . yet ineluctably, that was the spirit of the unspoken bargain . . . on which the continuance of the Congo operation had come to depend." It is not surprising, therefore, that Khrushchev became a noisy critic of Hammarskjöld. The Soviet leader attended the UN General Assembly session in person during the autumn of 1960, angrily demanding the secretary-general's resignation and his replacement by a three-man body, or "troika." At one unforgettable Assembly session in New York, Khrushchev removed a shoe and banged it on the table for emphasis.

Back in the Congo, President Kasavubu, the "sleeping crocodile," destroyed the uneasy calm that the United Nations had created with a surprise radio broadcast on September 5, 1960, dismissing Patrice Lumumba from his post as prime minister. Two days later the Congolese Chamber of Representatives delivered Lumumba a resounding vote of confidence, thus creating a governmental impasse. Then on September 14, Colonel Mobutu declared both the president and the prime minister "neutralized" and called back a group of students and professors from their studies to form a "College of Commissioners," with Kasavubu remaining as nominal president. This confusing series of coups thrust the Congo fully into the Cold War, with the Russians backing Lumumba and the Americans Kasavubu and Mobutu. Hammarskjöld and his advisors judged that Kasavubu had the best legal case, for the provisional constitution allowed the president to dismiss the government under extraordinary circumstances; and they also worked closely with Mobutu to keep order, even paying his troops on one occasion. Nevertheless, UN peacekeepers protected Lumumba in the prime minister's residence, with a second cordon of Congolese troops ringing them in order to prevent the prime minister's escape.

Patrice Lumumba broke free from this double house arrest during a tremendous thunderstorm on the night of November 27, attempting to reach Stanleyville, where his supporters had already set up an alternative government.

He might have made good his escape had he not stopped frequently along the way to address the crowds of peasants and workers who still idolized him. Mobutu's troops overtook him as he was crossing a river into friendly territory, beat him severely, and confined him to a military prison outside Leopoldville. Lumumba had foreseen this outcome when he told Thomas Kanza just before his breakout: "My dear Thomas, I shall probably be arrested, tortured, and killed. One of us must sacrifice himself if the Congolese people are to understand and accept the ideal we are fighting for."

A mutiny of troops guarding Lumumba in January 1961 convinced Kasavubu and Mobutu that their antagonist might yet make a comeback, and they also feared that the incoming Kennedy administration would revise American policy and demand Lumumba's release and inclusion in a coalition government. So on January 17 they flew him and two other political prisoners to Katanga, delivering them to their worst enemy, Moise Tshombe. Lumumba and his associates were beaten severely en route and died soon after arrival, under circumstances that have never been fully determined. Most observers believe that Tshombe and several members of his government were present at their death. The Americans were not directly involved in the murder of Lumumba, but they were clearly overjoyed at his elimination. A CIA operative in Elisabethville cabled his station chief in the capital: "Thanks for Patrice. If we had known he was coming we would have baked a snake."

At the time of Lumumba's assassination, the former Belgian Congo was divided into four parts. The central government under Kasavubu, Mobutu, and their commissioners controlled about half the country, whereas Lumumba's supporters ruled in Orientale Province around Stanleyville. Katanga still went its own way as a de facto separate state, and a portion of diamond-rich Kasai had also seceded. During the first eight months of 1961, the United Nations made herculean efforts to reconcile the various parties and create a unified Congo government. In July 1961 UN and American diplomats convinced the elected parliament to create a compromise government under Cyrille Adoula, a moderate labor leader, with all factions in the country represented except Katanga. For a second time, it appeared that the United Nations stood on the brink of success. Hammarskjöld determined to visit the Congo personally in September and negotiate the final reunion of Katanga with the central government, but miscalculations by his representatives in Africa torpedoed his plans and cost him his life.

Hammarskjöld had appointed the Irish writer and diplomat Conor Cruise O'Brien as his representative in Elisabethville during the summer of 1961, and O'Brien repeatedly asked Moise Tshombe to dismiss the white mercenary soldiers and technical advisers who were propping up his regime. When Tshombe refused, O'Brien and several other UN envoys decided to act more forcefully and present Hammarskjöld with a *fait accompli* in Katanga. On August 27, with the secretary-general's permission, they surrounded the post office, radio station, and interior minister's house, and demanded that Tshombe send the mercenaries packing. He agreed, but the European consuls in Elisabethville convinced O'Brien to call off the UN siege and let them take charge of their own nationals.

A few weeks later over a hundred mercenaries remained at large; so Mahmoud Khiary, a Tunisian serving in the UN Secretariat, flew to Katanga and ordered O'Brien and the Indian general commanding the peacekeepers to finish the job. He gave the impression that Hammarskjöld concurred and departed with a final admonition: "Above all, no half measures." On September 13, UN troops repeated the earlier operation, but this time Katangan soldiers and white mercenaries were ready for them and offered stiff resistance. Tshombe escaped to Northern Rhodesia, and when Hammarskjöld landed in Leopoldville later that day he was confronted with a major embarrassment. Apparently he had issued fairly ambiguous instructions to Khiary and O'Brien, which the two envoys interpreted in the most aggressive manner possible. Had the operation succeeded, he probably would have congratulated them and shared in the credit for a job well done, but since the operation had failed he was faced with the last crucial decision of his life.

Dag Hammarskjöld determined to make a final, personal effort at reconciling Tshombe with the central Congolese government. One of his aides, Brian Urquhart, believes the secretary-general intended to resign his post and retire if he were successful. He arranged to meet Tshombe at Ndola in Northern Rhodesia, pointedly instructing Conor Cruise O'Brien not to come along. His plane took off from Leopoldville on September 17, then flew a circuitous route that avoided Katangan airspace in complete radio silence. Shortly after midnight on September 18, the pilot radioed Ndola that he could see the airfield lights and was coming in. However, the plane descended too steeply, skimming the treetops and crashing. All thirteen people aboard died, including the secretary-general. Many conspiracy theories have been hatched about Hammarskjöld's death, but several investigations proved inconclusive, and his death was probably an accident.

Hammarskjöld was awarded the Nobel Peace Prize posthumously, but his death did not bring peace in the Congo. For the next year and a half, Hammarskjöld's successor, U Thant of Burma, and his representatives continued the thankless task of negotiating with Tshombe, whose own troops and mercenaries were slipping out of his control and increasingly harassing the UN peacekeepers. In December 1961, UN forces, reinforced with jet fighters and bombers from India, Sweden, and Ethiopia, engaged in a second, more destructive round of fighting in Katanga. The Kennedy administration brokered a truce between Tshombe and Cyrille Adoula, but the Katangan leader soon broke the agreement.

Finally, a year later a third round of UN attacks dislodged the secessionist forces from Elisabethville and the mining regions. The Americans provided full transport facilities for UN troops, but as in the previous two rounds their policy proved ambiguous. As journalist Madeleine Kalb describes it: "The U.S. government . . . gave the United Nations public support and encouragement, but in private it urged the secretary-general to pull back before his forces went too far." The Indian troops in Katanga, however, ignored orders to cease firing and utterly defeated the Katanga rebels. On January 14, 1963, Moise Tshombe capitulated and declared the secession at an end. UN forces stayed on for over a year more at the request of the Adoula government, but under severe financial pressures they finally withdrew from the Congo on June 30, 1964.

The United Nations mission in the Congo proved a qualified success at best. It short-circuited the Belgian attempt at recolonization and helped preserve the territorial integrity of the state by defeating the Katanga secession. It blocked any direct military intervention by superpower forces, but it could not prevent the Cold War rivalries from spilling over into Africa. The most obviously negative consequence of the UN operation was the death of Dag Hammarskjöld. None of his successors has ever enjoyed the same level of international prestige and support that the martyred Swede did. Yet an equally important result was the discrediting of such aggressive UN interventions in world trouble spots. The Congo mission crossed an ill-defined, invisible line between peace*keeping* and peace*making*. UN peacekeepers have often patrolled a truce line between antagonistic states *after both sides ceased firing and invited them in*. In the Congo, however, the UN forces actively sought to *impose* a peace settlement on Katanga. The world body did not undertake such an aggressive, controversial, and difficult peacemaking mission for thirty years after the Congo crisis, and when they did, in Somalia and Bosnia, the results proved equally questionable. Dag Hammarskjöld, for all his vision and international esteem, may have been overly ambitious. Without American support, the Congo operation would have come to nothing, but this tacit alliance simply exacerbated the Cold War, rather than mitigating it.

In retrospect, it might be asked why ending the secession of Katanga seemed so important. The mineral-rich province was thoroughly capable of standing alone and might have made a more successful independent nation than many others in Africa. Or perhaps a loose federalism might have solved the crisis. However, for progressive forces in Africa, Europe, and America, Katanga represented everything evil in the twentieth-century world — white settler dominance, neo-colonial economic exploitation, white mercenaries killing black people for fun and profit, and the maddening indifference of black stooges like Tshombe. Nationalist leaders in all the African countries inherited a vested interest in preserving the boundaries of their states laid out by the colonial powers, but this obsession with territorial integrity made more political and ideological sense in Katanga than elsewhere. Another consequence of the Congo crisis, therefore, was a thorough discrediting of all secessionist activity in Africa. It is important to recall that the secession of Biafra and the Nigerian civil war that followed took place *after* the Congo crisis. A major reason why most African leaders opposed the Ibo bid for separate statehood in Biafra is that they suspected white imperialist interests were backing it, just as in Katanga.

As a final tragic irony, the end of the UN mission in the Congo did not terminate the crisis. Adoula's government proved powerless to deal with the remaining supporters of Patrice Lumumba, who used both Soviet and Chinese aid to mount new rebellions, particularly in Orientale Province. These 1964 revolts were more truly communist-inspired than Lumumba's own movement had been. In desperation, Adoula resigned shortly after the UN troops left in 1964 and Moise Tshombe (of all people) came out of exile as a new compromise candidate for prime minister of the Congo. Both Hammarskjöld and Lumumba must have stirred uneasily in their graves. Tshombe rehired some white mercenaries to suppress the new revolts; and the American military, without any UN cover this time, assisted the central government. One planned operation called for Green Berets to parachute upstream from Stanleyville, then float by raft into the capital. This ingenious plan, however, had to be shelved when it was discovered that massive waterfalls separated the drop point from the provincial capital. In a more successful operation, the CIA hired Cuban refugees from the Castro revolution to fly modified, armed jet trainers in support of the government. Much later, the United States accused the Communists of introducing Cuban troops into liberation struggles in Angola and Mozambique, but the Americans had hired their own Cuban mercenaries first, in the Congo.

At the beginning of November 1964, a former Belgian secret service officer organized the European mercenaries into an effective fighting force, along with a unit of anti-communist Cuban exiles. On November 24, as the mercenaries approached Stanleyville, the U.S. air force dropped Belgian paratroopers into the city, allegedly on a humanitarian mission to rescue European and American hostages. The Lumumbist government was holding many whites hostages, but this precipitate action actually led to their execution rather than their rescue. Twenty-seven people were killed in Stanleyville and twenty-eight missionaries slaughtered out in the hinterlands before the paratroops restored order. In the aftermath of the siege of Stanleyville, the white mercenaries and Congolese troops ran amok, murdering and looting.

A year later, in October 1965, President Kasavubu dismissed Tshombe, and the parliament deadlocked once again in trying to choose a successor. Joseph Mobutu, who had remained in control of the Congo army throughout all the governmental changes, finally stepped in. With the encouragement of the CIA, he overthrew Kasavubu on November 25 and brought all semblance of parliamentary government to an end. He remained in power as a military dictator until his own overthrow, just before his death from cancer over thirty years later, in 1997. During all those decades of autocracy he enjoyed American political, economic, and military aid as a staunch bulwark against communism.

The Congo crisis began as a tragically belated movement for decolonization and national liberation, but it soon degenerated into a chaotic mixture of ethnic massacres, civil war, assassinations, and military coups. It witnessed a unique but ultimately unsuccessful international peacemaking mission by the United Nations. The ultimate legacy of the Belgian Congo's independence struggle, however, was the creation of an American Cold War bastion in the heart of Africa.

PART FIVE

NEW COMPLEXITIES, OLD RESPONSES

Now that it is possible to view the Cold War in its entirety, the conflict appears a great deal simpler than it did at the time. When I was teaching decades ago, I meticulously parceled out the history of the Cold War into various stages, for analytical purposes. By the time I left teaching, I had subdivided it into no less than six stages. Now I believe that the forty-year-long episode can best be comprehended as a drama with a beginning, a middle, and an end. The long middle period, from the death of Joseph Stalin in 1953 until the selection of Mikhail Gorbachev as head of the Communist Party in 1985, stands out as an era of lost opportunities. As the world became more complex and less bipolar, each superpower remained locked into stereotypical actions toward the other — new complexities, but old responses.

The Soviet sphere of influence had begun to fragment early on in the Cold War, when Yugoslavia broke away in 1948 (see chapter 2); but the major rift in the bloc came with the estrangement of Mao's China from the Soviet Union. By 1960, the rivalry between China and Russia had become clear to all the other communist nations, and it was revealed to the rest of the world in 1963. Yet the United States continued to treat the communist nations as a monolithic whole. American leaders also tragically misunderstood the newly emerging nations of Asia and Africa and the long-independent but economically underdeveloped countries of Latin America, equating assertions of militant nationalism with communism. Such misunderstandings led to the long American involvement in Vietnam's war of national liberation and to many interventions against radical regimes in Latin America. The Soviet Union, for its part, misjudged the capitalist nations of Europe and North America, missing many opportunities for constructive engagement and easing tensions. When countries that the Soviet Union considered its client states attempted to establish more independent policies, such as Hungary in the 1950s or Afghanistan in the 1980s, the Russians intervened to suppress such stirrings of nationalism. Both superpowers remained locked into intransigent policies as long as the Cold War lasted, and their reckless attempts to break the stalemate in the late 1950s and early 1960s brought the world to the brink of nuclear war.

Elsewhere in the world, away from the superpower rivalry, other countries showed an equally unimaginative approach to their foreign policies. In the Middle East, Arabs and Jews continued denying each other's legitimate aspirations, resulting in two disastrous wars in the 1960s and 1970s. The Cold War seemed contagious, freezing the mental powers of leaders around the world so that they forced new complexities into old responses.

CHAPTER FIFTEEN

Khrushchev, Kennedy, and Castro at the Brink

Nikita Khrushchev should have been an American. A self-made man with an earthy, common touch, a gambler and risk-taker who played politics for very high stakes, he shared many of the supposed traits of the typical American. Not a deep or profound thinker, he often failed to look far enough ahead to assess the consequences of his impulsive actions. A British diplomat summed up his style of leadership well: "He started with a brainwave, calling for rapid action alien to the thought processes of his more plodding colleagues and running risks of failure and even humiliation, but which, if successful, could bring big dividends. . . ." One can imagine that if he had been born in the United States he might have become a wealthy entrepreneur in commerce or industry. A short, fat, round-headed man, he shared the informality and boorishness ascribed to many self-made millionaires. In one of his most famous episodes, he removed his shoe at the United Nations in 1960, pounding his desk with it for emphasis. Khrushchev's personality and temperament recall the title character of the 1958 novel *The Ugly American*.

Yet Khrushchev was not an American, but a dedicated Russian Communist. Though he became famous worldwide for his 1956 denunciation of Joseph Stalin and his moderately reformist policies in the Soviet Union, predating by thirty years the more thoroughgoing reforms of Gorbachev, he actually was a true believer in the Communist system of politics and economy. He retained a naïve and idealistic belief in the superiority of communism, aiming not to destroy the system but rather to make it more efficient and effective. When he angrily remarked to a group of diplomats in November 1956, "We will bury you," he was expressing his faith in the ultimate triumph of communism over the decadent, capitalist West.

Nikita Sergeyevich Khrushchev was born on April 17, 1894, in the peasant village of Kalinovka in southern Russia, near the border with Ukraine. His father could not make a living off the land so he became a migrant worker in the mines of Ukraine's Donets Basin, about 275 miles away from home. The family moved permanently to the Donbass region in 1908, and the fifteen-year-old Nikita apprenticed as a pipefitter. All his life he retained a fascination with machines and an avid desire to tinker with them. The rawness of foreign-owned capitalist enterprises in tsarist Russia impressed itself powerfully on the future leader (the town of Yuzhovka where the Khrushchevs lived was named for a Welsh capitalist, John Hughes). By the time of the Bolshevik Revolution, Nikita had engaged in radical politics and union activities for many years, but he did not join the party until the spring of 1918. Thereafter, he served as a political commissar with the army during the civil war against the Whites, and then began a steady climb through the ranks of the party. His first wife had died during the civil war, leaving him with a young son and daughter. In 1924 he began living with a Ukrainian party organizer named Nina Petrovna Kuharchuk, though they did not officially marry until decades later.

Khrushchev decisively advanced his career by moving to Moscow in 1929, engaging in fierce inter-party rivalries while pursuing technical studies. Throughout the decade of the purges, he consistently toed a pro-Stalinist line, later admitting he was awestruck and frightened by the dictator. In 1938, Stalin appointed him Ukrainian party chief, with orders to clean house by eliminating suspect party members. During his later de-Stalinization campaign, Khrushchev downplayed his activities in Ukraine, but his biographer, William Tompson, emphasizes that "Khrushchev was sent to Ukraine not to liquidate the purge but to extend it." Another historian, Martin McCauley, concludes: "Khrushchev was wallowing in blood." He remained in Ukraine during World War II, acting as liaison between the civilian and military authorities fighting Hitler's invasion, then undertook another bloody purge of anti-Communist elements after the war. Stalin finally recalled him to Moscow in 1949 as a counterweight against Georgi Malenkov and Laurenty Beria, ambitious politicians who were maneuvering to succeed the aging dictator. Khrushchev himself had survived the purges primarily because Stalin and everybody else underestimated him.

When Joseph Stalin died of a stroke on March 5, 1953, a three-man collective leadership replaced him, with Malenkov as prime minister, Khrushchev the Communist Party chief, and Beria in charge of the secret police. Khrushchev soon out-maneuvered the other two. Beria, the long-time head of the KGB who had personally tortured many of Stalin's victims, was arrested while attending a meeting of the Party Presidium in June 1953. He and five close supporters were tried in secret and executed in December 1953, the last members of the Soviet elite to pay with their lives for choosing the wrong side. Their deaths marked the end of the Stalinist era. Georgi Malenkov appeared to have come out on top after Beria's death, but Khrushchev, relying on his deep support among the party rank and file, edged him out of his post as Soviet prime minister in February 1955 and replaced him with a loyal follower, Nikolai Bulganin. Malenkov remained a member of the Party Presidium (previously called the Politburo, or Political Bureau, under Stalin) for another two years.

Once established as the number-one man in the collective leadership, Khrushchev planned to reverse Stalin's priorities and raise the Soviet standard of living. He redirected government spending from the military and heavy industry towards agriculture and consumer industries. Furthermore, he took the audacious step of denouncing Stalin's atrocities. At the Twentieth Party Congress in Moscow, he electrified the delegates with his "Secret Speech," a four-hour monologue delivered early in the morning of February 25, 1956. As an idealistic, committed Communist, Khrushchev was appalled that Stalin had wiped out the "best and the brightest" of his generation, and thus he branded Stalin's purges as crimes against the party. He had experienced the shortsightedness of the purges firsthand during World War II, when the Soviet Union proved woefully short of imaginative and skillful leadership. Yet he stopped well short of attacking one-party rule. Neither did he mention the horrors of collectivization and forced industrialization in the 1930s, nor his own role in the Stalinist purges.

Nevertheless, the Secret Speech, which did not remain secret for long, changed the Soviet Union for good. The cultural and intellectual thaw that followed the Twentieth Party Congress proved short-lived, and Khrushchev himself was later overthrown by hardliners, but his de-Stalinization campaign eroded Communist rule. Gorbachev and his reformist followers grew up and apprenticed during the "first spring" of the Khrushchev era. William Tompson concludes, "had he [Khrushchev] known what those words would unleash he would likely have remained silent, but speak he did."

Shaken by Khrushchev's innovations and by the uprising of Hungarian nationalists against Soviet rule in 1956, a majority of Presidium members attempted to remove their leader in June 1957 and replace him with the old-line Stalinist, Vyacheshlav Molotov. A vote of 7 to 3 called for Khrushchev's resignation, but he successfully stalled until the assembly of the full Central Committee of the party, where he knew his support was solid. A Party Plenum, meeting from June 22 to 29, 1957, therefore, ratified Khrushchev's leadership of the party. Malenkov and Molotov were both removed from the Presidium, yet none of Khrushchev's rivals were killed or jailed. He had already changed the party that much. The following year, in March 1958, the party secretary eased out his friend Bulganin from the premiership and assumed office as head of government himself. Five years after Stalin's death, Nikita Khrushchev had solidified his position as undisputed head of the Soviet Union, but without the terror and absolute authority of his predecessor.

Khrushchev was driven by a personal and professional sense of inferiority in relation to the United States. Like most self-made men, he believed passionately in the system that had nurtured his own success, but he felt painfully aware that American prosperity remained greater than Russia's. He believed, however, that possession of atomic weapons and the missiles to deliver them created a situation of rough parity between the two superpowers, which would allow him to reduce spending for conventional weapons and divert resources to raising the standard of living. Therefore, Khrushchev pursued four broad foreign policy goals: to keep the bloc of Communist nations united, to demonstrate the equality of the Soviet bloc with the Americans, to increase Soviet influence in the Third World, and to ease tensions with the Americans. He called these often contradictory policies "peaceful coexistence," a highly dynamic state of worldwide competition between two rival systems which would not, however, lead to war. He was not defending the status quo in the Cold War but striving for victory. When he told Americans, "we will bury you," he sincerely believed that Russia would surpass the United States economically by 1970. He was not threatening nuclear annihilation, but it is hardly surprising that most Americans misunderstood him.

In order to convince the Soviet military and other internal skeptics that his reliance on nuclear deterrence had truly won the respect of the Americans, Khrushchev needed a foreign policy triumph. Not surprisingly, he turned to ground zero of the Cold War, Berlin. Since the victors of World War II had never agreed on a peace treaty with Germany after Hitler's defeat, the divided halves of both the German nation and its capital remained in a legal limbo. The Americans had recognized the Federal Republic of Germany in the West, incorporating its revived armed forces into the NATO alliance, but neither West Germany nor the United States officially recognized the German Democratic Republic in the East. The Soviets had responded with the formation of the Warsaw Pact in 1955, with East Germany as a member. Berlin remained occupied by the four victorious allies — France, England, the United States, and the Soviet Union — and loosely divided into eastern and western zones, but movement between the zones and between West Berlin and East Germany remained relatively free. As a result, many East Germans voted with their feet by slipping into West Berlin and then often moving on to West Germany. Both the Americans and the Russians had unofficially accepted the division of Germany, and only the Germans themselves retained any real interest in reunification, but the status of Berlin remained a sore point and a source of instability in Europe. Whenever the Russians wanted to get the Americans' attention, they applied pressure to West Berlin.

On November 27, 1958, Khrushchev sent an ultimatum to the Western powers, informing them that if West Berlin were not formally established as a "free city" within six months, he would sign a separate peace treaty with East Germany granting it control over the access routes to West Berlin. It appears that both the Soviet leader and the Russian public were genuinely worried about the possibility of West Germany acquiring nuclear weapons, but Khrushchev was also employing his deadline strategy to show both his internal opponents and the Communist Chinese that he was capable of saber rattling. He later called West Berlin the "sore blister on the foot of imperialism," and he undoubtedly enjoyed tromping on it.

The American government had no intention of abandoning West Berlin, but the Eisenhower administration prudently began a long series of negotiations to defuse the crisis. Khrushchev obligingly removed the six-month deadline, and in July 1959 he eagerly leapt at an American invitation to visit the United States for personal talks. This series of events indicates that Khrushchev was using the Berlin crisis simply as a tool and did not care too much about the actual status of the city. His main goal remained acceptance by the Americans as an equal. His first visit to the United States, during the last two weeks of September 1959, proved a personal triumph. Ordinary Americans, such as the Iowa farmer whose acres he inspected, found him down to earth and amusing, and the media portrayed his wife Nina as a devoted, 1950s-style housewife, much like Mamie Eisenhower. The Russian first couple never seemed more "American" than during this false spring of the Cold War. When the Communist first secretary and the American president finally met at Camp David at the end of the tour, they did not reach any decision over Berlin but they agreed to keep talking at a four-power summit. Khrushchev then invited Eisenhower for a return visit to Russia.

"The spirit of Camp David," as this thaw in East-West relations was dubbed, prompted Khrushchev to cut the Red Army's troop strength by 1.2 million men in January 1960 and to place even greater reliance on the Strategic Rocket Forces, which he had recently established as a separate branch of service. Yet the Russian leader paid a high price for his peaceful coexistence with the Americans. Immediately after his return to Moscow from the Camp David meetings, he left again for China, where Mao denounced the Russian's policy of détente with the United States. A year later, at an international conference of communist parties in November 1960, the Soviet bloc split down the middle, with at least a dozen parties backing China.

The easing of tensions between Russia and America, however, did not last long. The American government unwisely began aerial reconnaissance over the Soviet Union with high-flying U-2s on the eve of the summit conference, scheduled for Paris in May 1960. On May 5, Khrushchev announced that the Russian military had shot down one of the spy planes. American spokesmen attempted a clumsy deception, claiming that the plane was flying an innocent weather observation mission and had mistakenly strayed into Soviet airspace. Khrushchev then triumphantly revealed that the American pilot, Francis Gary Powers, remained alive and had admitted he was a spy. On May 11 Eisenhower confirmed the truth and took personal responsibility for authorizing the mission. When the summit conference opened in Paris four days later, Khrushchev insisted on delivering the first speech, in which he denounced the Americans and effectively torpedoed the conference.

Khrushchev's attempt to force the Americans into treating him as an equal had backfired. The U-2 incident personally humiliated the Russian leader and ended the brief thaw in the Cold War. Khrushchev refused any further dealings with the American administration until after the presidential elections of 1960, and he made it perfectly clear that he hoped Eisenhower's vice president, Richard Nixon, would lose to the Democratic challenger, John F. Kennedy. When Khrushchev returned to the United States at the end of 1960, he attended the discussions on the Belgian Congo crisis at the United Nations but did not meet with American officials. On his second American visit, he proved just as offensive and boorish as he had been charming the first time. It was during these debates that he pounded his shoe on the desk.

When John F. Kennedy took office, his personal style contrasted sharply with both that of his predecessor and his Cold War adversary, each of whom was old enough to be his father. The forty-three-year-old Kennedy cut a stylish figure of youthful energy and vigor, proclaiming that it was time to "get this country moving again." Yet in some ways, he was more like Khrushchev than appeared at the time. Though Kennedy was born to privilege and wealth, unlike the Soviet leader, he too felt insecure and therefore overcompensated by a posture of toughness. John Kennedy had been a sickly child, born with an unstable back and subject to numerous allergies and ailments. He almost died of diphtheria at age ten and in his teen years he developed Addison's disease, a rare ailment of the adrenal glands. Like Patrice Lumumba of the Congo, JFK rightly believed that he would die young; and this premonition imparted a fatalistic attitude toward life. Kennedy viewed life, politics, and foreign policy as a competition, a deadly serious game which one always played to win. Historian Thomas G. Paterson has pointed out that in the Kennedy administration "box scores proliferated for everything from the arms race to the space race." Like Khrushchev, the new president felt a need to prove himself the equal of anyone.

The president's eloquent inaugural address, delivered on January 20, 1961, set the tone for his administration. Ninety percent of the speech dealt with foreign policy, which was set in the coldest of Cold War contexts. Kennedy proclaimed provocatively: "Let every nation know, whether it wishes us well or ill, that we shall pay any price, bear any burden, meet any hardship, support any friend, oppose any foe to assure the survival and success of liberty." Both leaders were willing to risk war, but neither wished to wage one in the age of nuclear weapons. Kennedy summed up the policy followed by both in these words: "Let us never negotiate out of fear. But let us never fear to negotiate."

Kennedy began the contest by announcing large increases in military expenditures shortly after his inauguration. His father, Joseph Kennedy, had served as ambassador to Great Britain during the late 1930s, and JFK had imbibed the "lesson of history" that "only when our arms are sufficient beyond doubt can we be certain beyond doubt that they will never be employed." What seemed reasonable and prudent to Kennedy disturbed Khrushchev, who was still trying to whittle down his own military spending, so he pushed for an early summit conference. The two leaders met for the first and only time in Vienna on June 3-4, 1961. Khrushchev pushed for a settlement of the Berlin crisis, but Kennedy refused to make any concessions. So the Soviet leader issued a new ultimatum, vowing to settle the status of Berlin by the end of 1961. Kennedy spent the rest of the summer completely engrossed in the Berlin crisis. He ordered a partial mobilization of military reserves and accelerated the defense spending increases. In a nationally televised address on July 25, 1961, the president scared the public by calling for a crash program of civil defense, urging Americans to build air raid and fallout shelters so they might survive a nuclear war.

Khrushchev, on his side, felt a greater sense of urgency in this second deadline crisis than he had in the first. The U-2 incident had strengthened the hands of his domestic political opponents, so he needed a victory even more than in 1958-59. More importantly, East Germany was approaching a state of crisis that demanded a solution. Walter Ulbricht, the hardline Stalinist leader of the German Democratic Republic, had launched a major campaign to collectivize agriculture and mobilize labor, so hordes of young East Germans began fleeing the country. In July 1961, over thirty thousand left through the escape hatch provided by West Berlin, and the flight accelerated even more in the early days of August. Khrushchev needed to stop the hemorrhaging of personnel from his German satellite.

The Kennedy administration finally provided the Soviets and East Germans a way out of their Berlin problem. Though officially committed to the reunification of Germany into a united, non-communist state, the American government had long before reconciled itself to a two-Germanys policy. A communist East and capitalist West in Germany and Europe served American interests perfectly well, so long as the situation remained stable. Yet the mass flight from Ulbricht's socialist state was destabilizing the heart of Europe. So a number of public speeches by American politicians hinted that East Germany had a perfect right to close its own borders if it so chose. Khrushchev picked up the signal and decided, along with his Warsaw Pact allies, to seal off East Berlin from West Berlin, thus closing the escape route. Shortly after midnight on August 13, 1961, the first elements of what came to be known as the Berlin Wall went up. At first it was just some barbed wire, and the East Germans constructed it gradually and tentatively to make sure the Americans would not challenge it. Over the next few weeks, cement blocks were assembled into a wall extending a length of twenty-five miles, with watchtowers and free-fire zones backing it up on the East Berlin side.

Kennedy publicly denounced the wall, which soon became the prime symbol of the Cold War's division of Europe, but privately he felt satisfied. The wall provided the United States a public relations victory, for its very presence proclaimed that Germans would not freely choose communism. Khrushchev recognized this only too well. In the memoirs he published outside Russia after being removed from office, he reflected: "Paradise is a place where people want to end up, not a place they run from! . . . What kind of shit is that when you have to keep people in chains?" Yet he felt he had no choice but to throw up the wall. At least he solved one short-range problem by preserving the economic viability of East Germany.

Both sides made belligerent noises and gestures after the wall went up. Kennedy reinforced the troops guarding West Berlin and sent General Lucius Clay, the hero of the Berlin airlift of 1948, to show the flag on the ramparts. Khrushchev ostentatiously fired a new round of nuclear tests in the fall of 1961. Yet after the posturing — to show they were not negotiating out of fear — they began to negotiate again. Inconclusive meetings between Russian and American diplomats dragged on in both Moscow and Geneva through the early months of 1962. A State Department official aptly summed up these parleys: "They really just keep going around in circles." The Berlin crisis finally faded away without any formal decision. Since the wall stabilized the situation, the Russians stopped restricting Allied access to West Berlin and the Americans signaled they would not arm West Germany with nuclear weapons.

Chairman Khrushchev had gotten the worst of the contest in the second Berlin deadline crisis, but he had not abandoned his deadly game with President Kennedy. In October 1962, Americans discovered that the Russians had installed ballistic missiles with nuclear warheads right next door to the United States, in Cuba. The Cuban missile crisis proved even more dangerous than the two Berlin crises, bringing the world as close to a nuclear holocaust as it ever got during the entire Cold War.

President Kennedy had been obsessed with Cuba since before his own in-

Cuba

auguration, but American interest in the Caribbean island went back to the Spanish-American War of 1898. After U.S. military forces expelled Spain from its last New World colony in that brief war, they occupied Cuba for four years, finally granting it independence in 1902. Yet Cuban independence came with a compromising reservation, the Platt Amendment, which the United States imbedded in the first Cuban constitution. Under this provision, Americans reserved the right to intervene in Cuba to protect the island and their own interests, and the U.S. government was not shy about invoking this privilege. Franklin Roosevelt finally cancelled the Platt Amendment in 1934 as part of his "good neighbor policy" in Latin America, but American economic interests remained dominant. It is no exaggeration to state that Cuba was a colony of the United States in all but name for the first sixty years of the twentieth century.

General Fulgencio Batista short-circuited Cuba's fragile political system in 1952 by staging a bloodless coup a few weeks before a scheduled presidential election. Batista was no stranger to Cuban politics. In 1933, as a mere army sergeant, he had helped overthrow a previous dictator and had functioned as the power behind the throne of several weak governments during the 1930s. He won the presidency in his own right in 1940, but resigned voluntarily after serving out his term and retired to Daytona Beach, Florida. An attractive and charming man, he had once possessed a social conscience and had earned the backing of both the communist labor unions and the conservative armed forces during his one legal term of office. Yet as historian Hugh Thomas states, "in 1952 he wished to return to the presidency mainly for ignoble motives — the accumulation of money and the enjoyment of comfort in grand style." He must have been one of the weakest strongmen in history, a classic example of "violence without energy": enough repression to alienate nearly the entire population but not enough to prevent revolt. Thomas again concludes: "Batista clearly was a dictator who wished always to be loved . . . less himself a torturer than a weak man surrounded by cruel ones whom he could not control."

Batista never consolidated his dictatorship, and every ambitious politician in Cuba worked either to defeat him or overthrow him. One reckless revolutionary succeeded. Fidel Castro Ruz was born on August 13, 1926, to Angel Castro, a wealthy, self-made landowner who had emigrated from Spain as an orphan boy, and his second wife, Lina Ruz Gonzalez. A high-strung, rebellious boy, Fidel was sent to several religious schools before the Jesuits of Belen College in Havana partially tamed him. At Havana University from 1945 to 1950, he spent more time in political agitation than on his law studies, but after marrying in October 1948 he knuckled under and compressed about two years of study into just six months. A fellow university student later described Castro's intense seriousness: "I have never seen Fidel dance, and I don't know anybody who has seen him dance." This was highly unusual in a culture suffused by dance music. After graduating from law school in 1950, Castro planned a political career with the major opposition party, but when Batista cancelled the 1952 elections, he decided to mount a revolutionary challenge.

Fidel Castro belonged to the familiar class of the intellectual proletariat whose restless energy and ability seemed blocked by an oppressive political system. Similar to many other revolutionaries of the century, he was driven by socio-nationalism, a desire to win real independence for his nation and to improve the lives of ordinary people. He did not belong to the Communist Party and he had little understanding of Marx's writings, but he was radical by temperament and had already decided to pursue what he called "the vocation of revolution." On July 26, 1953, Fidel and his youngest brother, Raul, led about 150 poorly armed men in a desperate attack on two military barracks in his native Oriente Province. He hoped the attacks might spur a popular uprising, or at the very least would net his band of men a good supply of arms. Both attacks failed miserably, and the army then hunted down the rebels, torturing and killing any they managed to corral. About half of Castro's followers were killed, while thirty-two survived to stand trial and forty-eight escaped. Fidel eluded capture for a few days, but was finally taken alive, tried, and imprisoned on the remote Isle of Pines. The savage repression after the July 26 attack and Castro's defiant speech at his trial turned the reckless rebel into a national hero. Castro also used his time in prison to formulate his thoughts more clearly in a pamphlet titled *History Will Absolve Me*, which his friends smuggled out of jail for publication in June 1954. Like Hitler in Germany, Gandhi in India, or Nkrumah in Ghana, prison proved a crucially formative period for Castro and his revolution.

After Batista amnestied political prisoners in 1955, Castro fled to Mexico; but before he left, he launched his Twenty-sixth of July Movement at a clandestine meeting in Havana. Shortly after his arrival in Mexico in July 1955, Fidel encountered another would-be revolutionary, an Argentine named Ernesto Guevara de la Serna. Born in 1928 to a downwardly mobile middle-class family, Guevara had trained as a doctor; but since his graduation from medical school he had been wandering around Latin America as an "adventurer-observer," in the phrase used by his biographer, Paco Ignacio Taibo. The Cuban Twenty-sixth of July Movement gave Guevara a focus for his revolutionary energy, and he soon became an intellectual soul-mate of Fidel Castro. Like Fidel, he considered dancing "a waste of time," preferring to argue all night about points of ideology or revolutionary strategy. After months of continuous contact with Castro and his Cuban followers, Guevara was given a revolutionary nickname. Apparently, "che" is a common interjection in Argentine Spanish, much like "man" in American slang or "eh" in Canadian parlance. So the Cubans dubbed him Che Guevara. Over the next four years, Fidel and Che provided the inspiration for the Twenty-sixth of July Movement; but the Cuban Revolution was not a one or two man show. Urban workers and cane field laborers throughout Cuba suffered from a stagnant, one-crop economy and felt humiliated by the arrogance of Batista and his American business backers. Fidel, his brother Raul, and Che Guevara were members of the intellectual proletariat, but most of their followers came from humbler backgrounds.

Castro managed to scrape together twenty thousand dollars to buy an old yacht named *Granma* from an American resident of Mexico; and on November 25, 1956, he crammed eighty-two men onto this boat designed for twenty-five. The *Granma* was supposed to arrive off Cuba on November 30, in time to participate in a revolt that one of Castro's followers touched off in Santiago, Cuba's second largest city. Bad weather and poor seamanship, however, delayed the ship, so the revolt fizzled and the seasick rebels landed two days late on December 2. Everything went wrong. The boat ran aground about a hundred yards offshore, prompting Che Guevara to quip that "this wasn't a landing, it was a shipwreck." When the men reached shore, they found themselves in a mangrove swamp. After finally reaching firm ground two hours later, they were relentlessly pursued by Batista's waiting soldiers. Fidel himself was nearly killed in a cane field before he and fourteen of his followers escaped to the rugged Sierra Maestre Mountains. The landing of the *Granma* proved just as amateurish and disastrous as the later Bay of Pigs invasion that tried to topple Castro, but unlike that later fiasco, a few men survived to become mountain guerrillas.

Castro followed Mao's strategy of building a remote base supported by sympathetic peasants, but he had not learned it from the Chinese leader's writings. Rather, a Spanish Republican exile, Alberto Bayo, trained Castro and his men in Mexico, proudly reminding them that the word and the concept of *guerrilla* were originally Spanish. The rebels endured privation and hardships in the Sierra Maestre, and after one year they still numbered only about three hundred; yet their rebellion ultimately proved unusually easy. The Twenty-sixth of July Movement kept Batista's government in a state of turmoil with urban strikes and uprisings. The Cuban military mounted only one concentrated attack on the mountain guerrillas, in May and June 1958, but this failed due to poor planning and a total lack of intelligence. Eventually, like tsarist Russia, the Batista regime simply collapsed.

American support had been crucial to Batista's dictatorship, as it had been to all Cuban regimes of the twentieth century. In a memorable phrase, a State Department official once remarked: "I know Batista is considered by many as a son of a bitch . . . but . . . at least he is our son of a bitch, he is not playing ball with the Communists." Yet as Castro's revolt exploded into a full-scale civil war in Cuba, American business interests became worried. They did not care what kind of political system ruled, as long as it was stable and predictable. Once Batista's regime became unsteady, American businesses, and the Republican government they influenced in Washington, withdrew unquestioned support from their "son of a bitch." In March 1958, the United States slapped an arms embargo on Cuba. This was a correct, neutral diplomatic stance in a civil war, but it hurt Batista's army and the general's image more than it bothered Castro's guerrillas. Finally, on December 17, 1958, the American ambassador in Havana privately suggested to Batista that the dictator should step down. In the early hours of New Year's Day, January 1, 1959, after greeting his military supporters at the usual festive holiday party, Batista resigned and flew into exile in the Dominican Republic. Che Guevara marched into Havana with a band of guerrillas the next day, then Fidel Castro slowly and triumphantly made his way to the capital over the following week. Cubans hailed him as a liberator.

American observers of the Cuban Revolution, then and now, have always seemed obsessed with one question: When did Castro become a Communist? He did not officially announce his adherence to communism until late in 1961, well after he came to power; but historian Hugh Thomas believes Castro had made up his mind to ally with the Communists in the summer of 1959. Castro's American biographer Tad Szulc dates the decision even earlier, to a series of meetings in the Sierra during the spring of 1958. On the other hand, many Americans historians and political scientists, including myself, have often argued that Castro might never have become a Communist if the Americans had not opposed his revolution and pushed him into the arms of the Soviets. Even Nikita Khrushchev said as much to President Kennedy at the Vienna summit conference in June 1961.

However, the dynamics of revolution in any economically underdeveloped country would naturally push a rebel chieftain in a radical direction, and Fidel's closest confidants, Raul Castro and Che Guevara, were both Marxists. Certainly agrarian reform and nationalization of foreign properties were nearly inevitable policies for the Cuban revolutionaries to adopt. Furthermore, Fidel himself had an authoritarian personality streak that predisposed him toward dictatorship. One can also argue that a left-leaning dictator recently come to power in a semi-colony of the United States, only ninety miles from American shores, had little choice but to seek help from the Soviet Union. In those circumstances, to whom else would he turn? Yet even the Soviets were none too eager to offer assistance, since Cuba lay so far outside their sphere of influence. The American ambassador to Cuba, Philip Bonsal, has advanced the interesting hypothesis that American animosity may have pushed the "Soviet Union into Castro's arms," rather than vice versa. If the United States had not made Cuba a test case, Russia may have left it alone.

I would conclude that Castro was likely to become a Communist dictator no matter what attitude the American government adopted toward him. Nevertheless, it was not inevitable that Cuba become a virtual satellite of the Soviet Union. Castro would undoubtedly have preferred a more neutralist stance, playing both sides of the Cold War against each other to increase his own influence and obtain more aid. Tito in Yugoslavia and Nasser in Egypt successfully played this game. The United States, however, never gave Castro a chance to develop an independent Communist regime. In this sense, American policy helped produce the very outcome it was trying to avoid.

The Eisenhower administration first greeted Castro's regime cautiously. When Fidel visited the United States in April 1959 as a guest of American newspaper editors, his bearded face and cascading oratory made quite a splash in the media. Vice President Richard Nixon, however, spoke privately with him and concluded: "I was convinced Castro was either incredibly naïve about Communism or under Communist discipline. . . ." Nixon became an early advocate of a military attempt to overthrow the Cuban dictator. Not until after Castro nationalized foreign businesses and signed a trade treaty with Moscow, however, did the American administration commit itself to such a venture. On March 17, 1960, President Eisenhower authorized the CIA to plan an invasion of Cuba by anti-Communist Cuban exiles. John F. Kennedy was briefed about this operation in general terms during the election campaign and in greater detail right after the election. He inherited the CIA plans but eagerly accepted and elaborated them.

JFK was a great admirer of Ian Fleming's James Bond novels, and he often approached foreign policy in the spirit of 007. He personally designed the green beret for Special Forces troops in the U.S. Army, and his administration increased the number of Special Forces from about one thousand to over twelve thousand. The CIA hatched at least eight plots to assassinate Fidel Castro after he came to power, including a scheme involving a poison cigar. Kennedy personally authorized Operation Mongoose, a program of covert operations to weaken Castro's regime and ultimately topple him. He placed General Edward G. Lansdale, who was often reputed to be the American James Bond, in overall command of the operation. When Lansdale protested to Kennedy that he was not really James Bond, but that a low-level CIA officer held this real-life distinction, Kennedy insisted on meeting the individual, William Harvey, and appointing him chief of operations under Lansdale.

In the meantime, planning for the Cuban exiles' invasion had gone forward. The CIA was training disgruntled Cubans at a camp in the jungles of Guatemala, aiming to provide them with an invasion fleet and limited air cover. The Americans assumed that a Cuban underground would rise up in revolt against Castro when the invasion ensued. It was a mirror image of Castro's audacious attacks on the barracks and the landing of the *Granma*. The CIA plan, however, suffered from two dilemmas, one inherent in all amphibious landings and the other unique to this plan. First, any seaborne landing requires a preliminary air or naval bombardment to soften up defenses and attain the maximum chance of success; yet such a barrage often destroys the element of surprise. In this particular case, not surprise but maximum publicity might be necessary to touch off a Cuban uprising on the island. Such publicity, of course, like a preliminary bombardment, would make the military task of the invasion force more dangerous.

The final invasion plan created the worst of both worlds. Kennedy insisted on a secret landing in an out-of-the-way spot during the dark of night. Thus the CIA changed the landing point from the large city of Trinidad to the remote Bay of Pigs on the south coast of Cuba. This location minimized the possibility of help from indigenous Cuban sources and also made it impossible for the invaders to reach the mountains for a guerrilla campaign if their initial invasion failed. The Sierra Escambray Mountains lay a full eighty miles away from the Bay of Pigs, across impassable swamps. The Americans decided to risk a preliminary aerial bombardment with old B-26 bombers piloted by Cuban exiles pretending to be defectors from Castro's own air force. The bombing run on April 15, 1961, destroyed about half the Cuban planes on the ground, but it alerted Castro to the imminence of the invasion. Since no one believed the defector cover story, President Kennedy cancelled a second air strike the morning of the invasion.

When about 1,400 Cuban exiles waded ashore at the Bay of Pigs in the early morning hours of April 17, 1961, Castro's army of 25,000, backed by a militia of 200,000 reservists, was waiting for them. The surviving jets of the Cuban air force established complete control of the airspace over the landing point and scared away the support ships of the invasion force. Castro took personal charge of the defense and moved in tanks to oppose the invaders. President Kennedy, when informed of the fiasco, refused to commit American air power or troops to rescue the unfortunate exiles. Castro's forces rounded up 1,189 prisoners after killing 107 in battle. The fighting had been brief but fierce, and the defending Cubans lost 161 soldiers. The Americans eventually succeeded in exchanging food and medicine for the prisoners of war.

Kennedy's vendetta against Castro, apparently due not to personalities but to a simple, reflex anti-communism, provides the necessary background to, and a partial explanation of, the Cuban missile crisis. If Castro had not come to power in Cuba, the Soviets would have had no opportunity to place missiles close to the American borders. If Kennedy had not harassed Castro incessantly, invading his nation and attempting to assassinate him, Khrushchev might not have felt the urge to threaten the United States. Khrushchev and other Soviet leaders always contended that they placed ballistic missiles in Cuba simply to defend Castro from another American invasion. This is not a far-fetched or impossible rationalization, for the Kennedy administration was indeed considering another invasion plan, none too subtly code-named "Ortsac," or Castro spelled backward. However, the protection of Cuba was not the only reason for Khrushchev's decision to install missiles in the Caribbean. The Cuban missile incident formed another round in his ongoing battle to demonstrate equality with the United States, a continuation of the Berlin crisis in a new, tropical venue. Khrushchev was gambling that he could affect the balance of power cheaply, finally allowing him to concentrate on domestic economic growth.

Khrushchev conceived the idea of placing missiles in Cuba while walking along the Black Sea coast one day in May 1962 with Soviet Defense Minister Rodion Malinovsky. The Soviet marshal pointed out that American missiles looming on the opposite shore in Turkey could reach Kiev or Moscow. Seized by one of his typical "brainwaves," Khrushchev instructed Malinovsky to explore the possibility of aiming missiles at Washington from nearby Cuba. The Soviet military wrongly judged that medium- and intermediate-range missiles could be installed secretly under Cuba's palm trees, so with Castro's permission the installation began in the summer of 1962. The final tally of Russian weaponry in Cuba included forty missile launchers, with two missiles but just one nuclear warhead apiece, in addition to smaller tactical nuclear rockets and cruise missiles. Nearly 42,000 Soviet soldiers and technicians worked feverishly on the island.

A fierce hurricane season in the Caribbean prevented American reconnaissance from discovering the missile construction sites until the middle of October. Finally, on October 14 a high-flying U-2 produced conclusive photographic evidence that the Russians were installing surface-to-surface missiles in Cuba. President Kennedy convened his closest advisors on October 15 as an ad hoc executive committee of the National Security Council, called the ExComm for short; and over the next thirteen days, these dozen or so men met daily. General Maxwell Taylor, the chairman of the Joint Chiefs of Staff, succinctly summed up the three possible responses to the Cuban missiles — "talk them out, squeeze them out, or shoot them out." Initially, President Kennedy resisted all suggestions of talking them out. Aware that Republicans would accuse of him of being "soft on communism" if he attempted a diplomatic solution, JFK immediately demanded a tough response, probably an air strike on the missile sites with an invasion as a possible follow up. The military consistently advised this option throughout the entire crisis period.

Defense Secretary Robert McNamara, however, convinced Kennedy to start with the "squeeze them out" option. Correctly assessing that the new missile emplacements did not decisively change the balance of power, for the United States still possessed far more nuclear warheads capable of reaching Russian soil, McNamara proposed a naval blockade to stop further military shipments from reaching Cuba. Persuaded by McNamara and by Robert Kennedy, the president's alter ego at ExComm sessions, JFK adopted the blockade strategy as his first response to the missile crisis. On October 22 he told the American public and the world about the Cuban missiles, announcing his strategy to "quarantine" Cuba until they were removed. The Soviets were informed only an hour before the president's public speech.

The decisive test of the quarantine strategy came two days later when Soviet cargo ships approached the invisible line the American navy had drawn around Cuba. At the last minute, the ships stopped dead, then turned around. Reflecting the "Gunfight at the OK Corral atmosphere" of the crisis, Secretary of State Dean Rusk remarked with relief: "We're eyeball to eyeball, and I think the other fellow just blinked." Khrushchev had approached the brink, then pulled back. Yet the missiles still remained in Cuba and the Soviets were rushing to get them operational. Kennedy finally realized that he would have to talk them out after all. So did Khrushchev. On October 26, a long personal letter from the Soviet chairman arrived at the State Department by teletype over a three-hour period. Khrushchev insisted that the missiles were purely defensive in nature, and he suggested that an American pledge not to invade Cuba "would change everything." The next day, while the ExComm was still assessing Khrushchev's plea, another, more formal message was broadcast over Moscow radio. This communiqué of October 27 seemingly upped the ante by demanding not just a non-invasion pledge but also the removal of the American missiles from Turkey. Robert Kennedy and other members of the ExComm finally urged President Kennedy to ignore the second message for the moment, and respond positively to the more conciliatory first letter. Khrushchev jumped at Kennedy's offer, and on October 28 he broadcast a promise to withdraw the missiles in return for an American pledge not to attack Cuba. Privately, the president's brother Robert also told the Soviet ambassador that the United States would soon remove the missiles from Turkey.

The world probably did *not* stand quite on the brink of war in October 1962. Kennedy and Khrushchev had both become more prudent and careful as the crisis progressed, and neither was likely to unleash nuclear missiles. Though the military still urged an air strike and invasion of Cuba, JFK moved away from this option by the end of the thirteen days. Even if Khrushchev had not ended the crisis on October 28, Kennedy probably would have stalled for more time by extending the blockade to non-military items and continuing negotiations. Yet Khrushchev did not know this. It seems that he was prompted to settle by urgent messages from both the Cuban authorities and the Soviet embassy in the United States that the Americans were about to launch an invasion. Ultimately the two leaders proved more skillful at managing and ending the crisis than they had been in preventing it. Historian James Giglio concludes: "Both in effect blinked."

Yet the Cuban missile crisis did present a real possibility that a mistake would lead to nuclear war. The Americans had lost contact with the CIA's Operation Mongoose team that was running loose in Cuba and might commit some provocation. Also during the last days of the crisis, the American military had conducted a routine test launch of an ICBM, and a U-2 had wandered off course, briefly penetrating Siberian air space. Similarly, on October 27 a Russian officer in Cuba exceeded his orders and shot down a U-2 flying over the island. Had either Kennedy or Khrushchev been more trigger-happy, or had their militaries gotten out of control, these incidents could have led to a nuclear exchange.

The three gamblers — Khrushchev, Kennedy, and Castro — deserved each other, but the world deserved better. Many years later a Soviet general, Anatoli Gribkov, reflected: "I am profoundly convinced that the missiles should not have been brought to Cuba. . . . Soviet, U.S., and Cuban leaders should have sat down at the negotiating table with the secretary-general of the United Nations to find an agreement that would leave Cuba in peace." What a novel idea! Even without hindsight, American ambassador to the United Nations Adlai Stevenson had given similar advice before the missile crisis. At the beginning of the Kennedy administration, Stevenson argued against any invasion or subversion plans in Cuba and counseled the president to take Khrushchev's challenge of an economic competition seriously. If both countries avoided risky military adventures and competed openly for the hearts and minds of the world's peoples, Stevenson felt little doubt that the United States would win the competition. President Kennedy should have listened to him. Once the crisis broke out, Stevenson argued consistently in the ExComm for the "talk them out" option, suggesting on October 20 the outlines of the solution which the president eventually adopted a week later. Historian Mark White, who has written the best recent account of the thirteen-day ordeal, asserts that "the former governor of Illinois was the unsung hero of the missile crisis."

The October 1962 confrontation proved to be something of a "last hurrah" for two of the three leaders. The Central Committee of the Communist Party forced Nikita Khrushchev to resign two years later, on October 14, 1964. His fall from power did not flow directly from his lost gamble in Cuba, but was due more to domestic policy opposition. Khrushchev, as a true believer in the potential of communism, had kept the Russian party in a state of constant turmoil, trying to wring more dedication and hard work out of reluctant party comrades. Finally, he was overthrown by cautious gray men who wanted to enjoy their sinecures in peace and be done with all his "hare-brained schemes." Yet the Cuban missile crisis obviously did not improve his political stature in the Soviet Union. John Kennedy was assassinated on November 22, 1963, and at least some of the conspiracy theories surrounding his death allege that Cuban

302

agents may have killed him in reprisal for the Bay of Pigs, the Castro assassination plots, and the missile crisis. We will probably never know the truth. Only Castro endured. Indeed, he still rules Cuba forty years later, the longest-lasting head of government in the world.

Both good and bad consequences flowed from the Berlin and Cuban superpower confrontations. Before their early exits from the scene, Kennedy and Khrushchev took some tentative steps to avoid future crises. They installed a hotline for instant communications between the White House and the Kremlin and signed a treaty in 1963 banning nuclear tests in the atmosphere. Just as importantly, both governments tacitly accepted the fact of orbiting satellite photoreconnaissance, abandoning attempts to shoot down spy satellites. Neither side wanted more U-2 incidents destabilizing their foreign policies. As historian John Lewis Gaddis has argued, this ability of the superpowers to "live with transparency" was an important factor in keeping the Cold War under control.

Yet the Cuban missile crisis also killed all hope of ending the arms race. Khrushchev's successors rightly concluded that his attempt to reach military parity on the cheap, by relying on a few missiles hastily installed in Cuba, had failed. Therefore, they committed themselves to a large increase of ICBMs on Soviet soil and to a conventional arms buildup as well. Finally, in the 1970s the Russians reached a rough equality in arms with the United States, and they felt secure enough to pursue a policy of détente. Yet a decade or more was added to the length of the Cold War.

Above all, both sides failed to learn the major lesson of the Cuban crisis: that new situations in unfamiliar parts of the world demand new, imaginative, peaceful responses, not a military buildup or a threatening gamble. The United States government, buoyed by its seeming victory in the Cuban missile incident, arrogantly continued on its course of opposing communism everywhere in the world, most disastrously in Southeast Asia.

CHAPTER SIXTEEN

The War of Illusions

American intervention in Vietnam was grounded on two fundamental illusions: a belief that Mao's China was engaged in a relentless march to conquer all of Asia, and a conviction that the Asian nations would "fall like dominoes" unless the United States made a stand somewhere. These illusions were understandable in the 1950s, when the United States took over the task of fighting Indochinese communism from the French. Mao Tse-tung's forces had won a stunning victory over Chiang Kai-shek in China, unifying that Asian giant under Communist rule in 1949. Then from 1950 to 1953, American troops had fought a bitter war in Asia against Korean Communists and Chinese "volunteers." Korea convinced Americans that only a firm, military response could contain the march of communism. President Dwight Eisenhower gave the so-called domino theory its classic formulation in a 1954 speech: "You have a row of dominoes set up, and you knock over the first one, and what will happen to the last one is the certainty that it will go over very quickly." Another Republican, Henry Cabot Lodge, applied this theory to Southeast Asia with a slightly different image: "If you take a piece of string and put one end of it in Saigon on the map and measure off a thousand miles and make a circle, you'll find that within that circle are 240 million people. . . . Loss of this area would be a catastrophe."

Southeast Asia, however, differed from Korea. The Indochinese Communist Party had decisively linked nationalism and revolution at a party congress in 1941, thus harnessing the century's most powerful force, socio-nationalism, to their cause. They consistently opposed all foreign invaders or rulers, first the Japanese during World War II, then the French colonialists, and finally the American Cold War crusaders. (See chapter 6 for the earlier phases of the struggle, the First Indochinese War.) Though Chinese military aid had proven crucial to Ho's victory over the French in 1954, the two sides still tended to keep each other at arm's length. China had ruled Vietnam for more than a thousand years, and the two nations remained bitter enemies. International communism was not a monolith, and Ho Chi Minh was a Vietnamese nationalist, not a Chinese puppet. He would not likely call for Chinese troop reinforcements as Kim Il Sung of North Korea did. The Chinese Communists were not on the march in the mid-1950s, but had pulled back to consolidate their own revolution after the Korean War. They were absorbed in their internal Great Leap Forward. The only territory they planned to invade was the island of Taiwan, which they considered a constituent part of China.

The domino theory had a certain superficial logic to it, drawn primarily from the example of Hitler's piecemeal conquest of Europe in the 1930s. The nations of Southeast Asia, however, were not so interdependent as Europe was, and the Chinese were not as aggressive as Hitler had been. When, after twenty years of drawing a line against communism in Southeast Asia, the United States eventually did withdraw in the 1970s, none of the dominoes outside Indochina fell. Instead, just the opposite happened. Countries such as Indonesia, Malaysia, Singapore, and Thailand became aggressive capitalist "tigers" rather than helpless victims of communist aggression. The American struggle against Vietnamese Communists proved largely irrelevant to the rest of Southeast Asia, since it was based on illusions.

When the French were defeated at Dien Bien Phu in 1954, they convinced the great powers to cobble together a compromise peace agreement at Geneva in June and July of that year. The United States, however, intended to salvage at least half of Vietnam from Communist rule. The Geneva Accords divided Vietnam at the seventeenth parallel, but this line was intended merely as a temporary cease-fire marker. Internationally supervised elections for reunification of the country were mandated within two years of the cease-fire. Ho Chi Minh's forces could have won uncontested control over more territory south of the parallel, but their Communist allies, the Soviet Union and China, pressured them to accept the Geneva compromise. The Russians were concentrating on the division of Europe at this time and were trying not to offend the French and push them into closer cooperation with the Americans. The Chinese, for their part, wanted a friendly buffer zone in northern Vietnam, along their own border, but did not care whether Ho's Communists reunited the whole country or not. With their allies focused on other areas of the world, the Vietnamese Communists reluctantly accepted the Geneva Accords, confident they could win the upcoming elections. Most outside observers, including American government officials, agreed they would win such elections easily. Non-Communist national movements in Vietnam had long been weak and divided, unable to mount a serious challenge to the intellectual rigor and nationalist appeal of the Vietnamese Communists. Vietnam did not produce a Sukarno or a Gandhi to rally nationalists to a different banner.

The American government of Dwight Eisenhower, however, did not accept the Geneva Accords. Instead the Americans transformed the southern half of Vietnam into a separate, non-Communist state, propping up a staunchly anti-Communist Vietnamese, Ngo Dinh Diem, as president of this newly created country. Diem was a Vietnamese patriot from the traditional scholar-gentry class who had refused to cooperate with either Japanese or French puppet governments and had spent most of the previous decade in exile in the United States. A practicing Catholic and an ascetic bachelor, he was supported by prominent American Catholics such as Cardinal Francis Spellman of New York and the Kennedy family of Massachusetts. Diem returned to Saigon in June 1954, while the Geneva conference was in session, and with the backing of American CIA agents he soon established a government in the south. He based his regime primarily on the Catholic minority, which formed about 10 percent of the southern region's population, and on his large extended family, including his brothers Ngo Dinh Thuc, the archbishop of Hue, and Ngo Dinh Nhu, his right-hand man in Saigon. Between 1955 and 1961, the Eisenhower administration provided Diem's government with almost one and a half billion dollars worth of economic aid and over a half billion dollars in military equipment.

Diem refused to discuss unification elections with Ho Chi Minh's government north of the seventeenth parallel, and no such elections were ever held. None of the great powers on either side of the line cared about this violation of the Geneva agreements. With the Cold War crystallizing into a stable configuration in the late 1950s, Vietnam became just another partitioned country, along with Germany and Korea. The Vietnamese people experienced a brief respite from warfare, but they suffered severe repression on both sides of the parallel. In the north, the Communists tried to force collective agriculture on the peasants, and in the south President Diem discriminated against the Buddhist majority and crushed any signs of political dissent. Yet Ho's government clearly remained more popular, for it still relied heavily on the power of nationalism whereas Diem's regime was a foreign-born creation.

Gradually, in fits and starts, opposition to Ngo Dinh Diem burgeoned. Communist leaders in the countryside armed themselves for self-defense, occasionally taking the offensive by assassinating vulnerable government officials. The North Vietnamese government, absorbed in its own domestic problems, at first restrained the indigenous southern Communists, but eventually realized that they would have to lead the struggle or else lose control over it. A party plenum in Hanoi in January 1959 authorized an active policy of opposition to Diem, and then nearly two years later, on December 20, 1960, the National Liberation Front of South Vietnam (NLF) was organized as a broad umbrella group for the opposition, including both Communist and non-Communist elements.

In subsequent years, Americans debated endlessly whether the Vietnam War was an invasion of one sovereign nation by another or a civil war between two Vietnamese factions. In fact, the conflict was neither of these, but rather a national liberation struggle against a foreign-created regime. The NLF was dominated by the Communists, but this was due to the leading role that Ho's Communists had taken in the national struggle against the French. A team of American social scientists interviewing prisoners captured by Diem's troops concluded: "They certainly do not regard the present war as a struggle between North and South Vietnam, or between Communists and anti-Communists, but as a struggle between the legitimate leaders of an independent Vietnam and the usurpers protected by a foreign power." The South Vietnam of Ngo Dinh Diem was a Cold War illusion, a phantom state with scant indigenous support or substance.

Nevertheless, when John F. Kennedy replaced Eisenhower as president in 1961, he continued support for the Diem regime; indeed he greatly increased it. Kennedy and his advisors formed a self-confident team, a group of men who had served as junior officers in World War II and believed they could do anything. Robert S. McNamara, Kennedy's choice for secretary of defense, typified the "best and the brightest" whom JFK recruited. McNamara had served as a statistical control officer for the air force during World War II. Then Henry Ford II hired him and a group of systems analysts as high-level managers for his automobile company right after the war. The so-called Whiz Kids reinvigorated Ford, and McNamara finally rose to the post of company president just before Kennedy asked him to join his administration. Even thirty years later, in a somewhat penitent memoir, McNamara could not resist bragging: "I had no patience with the myth that the Defense Department could not be managed. . . . I had spent fifteen years as a manager identifying problems and forcing organizations — often against their will — to think deeply and realistically about alternative courses of action and their consequences." Men such as McNamara set out to save the Vietnamese from communism, "often against their will."

Kennedy and his men were confident, but not reckless. The president rejected requests from the military to send American combat troops into Vietnam in the early 1960s, but he increased monetary aid to Diem and approved a request for thousands of American military advisors. Eisenhower had kept American personnel under the limit of eight hundred advisors prescribed by the Geneva Accords but Kennedy gradually increased their numbers to sixteen thousand. This illustrates another important illusion that dogged American policymakers, the illusion of limited war and the middle way. Kennedy spent so much time and energy rejecting what he viewed as policy extremes, either a cutoff of American aid or the injection of full-scale combat troops, that he barely realized how significant an escalation his "middle course" represented. Small, incremental increases added up to a sizeable commitment, difficult to reverse.

Back in Vietnam, Diem's heavy-handed repression finally caught up with him. The Buddhist leaders of South Vietnam, without any Communist urging, began a campaign for fairer treatment of their co-religionists. A number of Buddhist monks shocked the world by publicly burning themselves to death in Saigon. Then on August 21, 1963, Diem's brother Ngo Dinh Nhu unleashed his secret police on a string of Buddhist pagodas. At the same time, however, Diem and Nhu, realizing how unpopular their regime had become, began exploring the possibility of negotiations with the National Liberation Front for the formation of a neutral government that would cut ties with the Americans. When the Kennedy administration discovered these peace initiatives, they informed some of Diem's generals that they would welcome the president's removal. The U.S. government did not initiate or formally authorize the coup, but it did send a message via CIA agent Lucien Conein that the United States would not prevent it. Conein posted himself at the insurgent generals' headquarters when they finally launched their coup on November 1, 1963, and he kept the American ambassador fully informed of the revolt's progress. Diem and Nhu initially escaped from the presidential palace, but they gave themselves up the next day and were immediately murdered. The American ambassador, Henry Cabot Lodge, announced recognition of the new regime in South Vietnam, then flew home for consultations. Yet he consulted with a different president than the one who had appointed him, for John F. Kennedy himself was assassinated on November 22, 1963.

One of the enduring myths of the Vietnam War, enshrined in Oliver Stone's film *JFK*, holds that President Kennedy was planning to withdraw American assistance from Vietnam at the time he died. This interpretation makes Kennedy's successor, Lyndon Johnson, the villain of the American tragedy in Vietnam. The evidence, however, reads the other way. Kennedy escalated American involvement and frowned on any South Vietnamese government that would even talk with the Communists. The death of Diem in November 1963 marked one of the crucial opportunities when the American government might have reassessed its policy and concluded that South Vietnam was too unstable to support. However, there are no indications that Kennedy was considering this before his own death. According to his aide Kenny O'Donnell, JFK thought he might be able to pull out of Vietnam a few years later if he were triumphantly reelected in 1964. That, of course, is possible, but completely unknowable. The important point is that Lyndon Johnson believed Kennedy had made

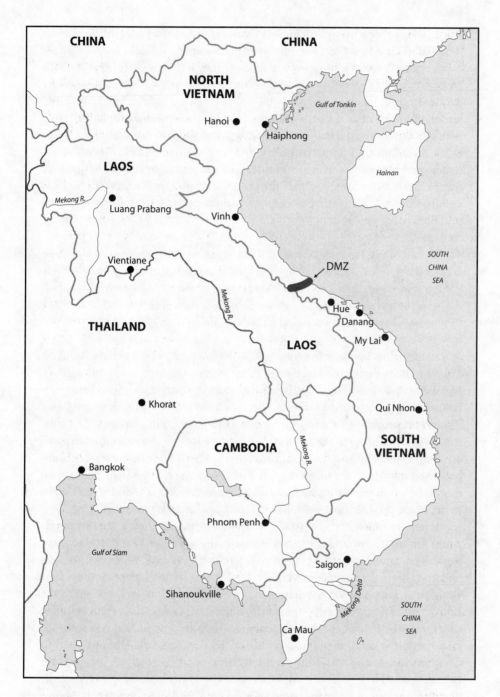

Vietnam, Laos, and Cambodia at the Time of the American War

a firm, unbreakable commitment in Vietnam. His decisions to escalate the war were based on a belief in *continuity* with the Kennedy policy.

Lyndon Baines Johnson was a Texan whom Kennedy had defeated in the Democratic primaries of 1960 and then recruited to serve as his vice president. An enormously skilled congressional politician who had served as majority leader of the Senate in the 1950s, Johnson still felt insecure around the glittering Kennedy Whiz Kids, particularly while discussing foreign policy. His own interests centered around domestic policy, and he hoped to create a Great Society that would extend government entitlement programs and civil rights to all Americans. Johnson realized that the growing American involvement in Vietnam could derail his plans, but he plunged in anyway. After his retirement, he told historian Doris Kearns:

> I knew from the start that . . . if I left the woman I really loved — the Great Society — in order to get involved with that bitch of a war on the other side of the world, then I would lose everything at home. . . . But if I left that war and let the Communists take over South Vietnam, then I would be seen as a coward and my nation would be seen as an appeaser.

During his first year in office, 1964, Johnson made two major decisions on Vietnam: he ordered an increase in covert warfare against North Vietnam, in particular, a series of South Vietnamese commando raids launched from PT boats; and he authorized a bombing strike against North Vietnam when one of these raids resulted in a naval incident. On August 2, 1964, the U.S. destroyer *Maddox* was cruising in the Tonkin Gulf, observing one of the South Vietnamese commando raids on Communist territory. North Vietnamese PT boats approached the *Maddox* and fired a few torpedoes that missed their target. Two days later, in the middle of the night on August 4, the *Maddox* and an accompanying destroyer, the *Turner Joy,* began firing in the dark at what they believed was a renewed torpedo boat attack. American airplanes from a nearby carrier could not locate any attackers, and it seems almost certain that the Americans were nervously firing at porpoises or seagulls. In any case, President Johnson and his inherited advisors seized upon the Tonkin Gulf incident to launch a furious air attack on North Vietnamese targets. Johnson, however, refused to authorize continuous bombing raids at this time. The more important result of the Tonkin Gulf incident was the congressional resolution that Johnson obtained in the wake of the attack. Overcome by patriotic fervor, both houses of Congress voted support for the president "to take all necessary measures to repel any armed attack against the forces of the United States." This virtually blank check served as the functional equivalent of a declaration of war against Vietnam.

After his reelection in November 1964, President Johnson finally made the decisions that transformed the struggle in Vietnam into a full-scale war. For over a year, Defense Secretary McNamara and other advisors had been urging the president to mount a sustained bombing campaign against North Vietnam. They calculated that Ho Chi Minh would rein in the Communist guerrillas in the South if the war hit closer to home. At the very least, a strong bombing campaign would increase the morale of the South Vietnamese governments, which were wracked by nearly continual coups after the fall of Diem. On February 7, 1965, a Communist attack on a helicopter base at Pleiku killed 8 Americans, wounded 126 more, and destroyed 10 U.S. aircraft. Johnson authorized a retaliatory air strike against North Vietnam. This bombing raid, and similar air sorties launched in the following days, were still simply tit-for-tat reactions, like the American response to the Tonkin Gulf incident. However, at the end of the month, Johnson finally authorized Operation Rolling Thunder, a series of sustained, systematic bombing attacks on North Vietnam, beginning on March 2. · This marked the first major escalation of the year, but even Rolling Thunder proceeded under the illusion of limited war and a middle way. Johnson forbade any bombing attacks on the North Vietnamese capital of Hanoi, its port city of Haiphong, or the border region with China. He didn't want to give the Communist Chinese any excuse to intervene as they did in Korea. When some military leaders assured him the Chinese would stay out, Johnson barked back: "That's what MacArthur thought."

The decision to bomb the North was taken before American ground troops were sent to Vietnam. Indeed, Clark Clifford, a high-powered Washington lawyer who was advising President Johnson as a private citizen at that time, has written in his memoirs that "the connection between bombing the North and sending American ground troops was not much discussed before the bombing began." Yet once the Americans began bombing systematically, their air bases in the South became obvious targets for NLF attacks. On March 6, 1965, 3,500 U.S. Marines came ashore to guard the Danang airbase. To protect the base effectively, the marines patrolled for miles around its perimeter. In this fashion, therefore, the American ground war began.

The rational calculus that bombing North Vietnam would force the Communists to ease pressure on the South proved to be another illusion. In fact, the northern government now began sending whole divisions of regular troops into South Vietnam to intensify what had been primarily a guerrilla war. On the other hand, the revolving door of coups in Saigon finally came to an end when a firm military government came to power in June 1965, presided over by General Nguyen Van Thieu and his prime minister, Nguyen Cao Ky. Immediately thereafter, Defense Secretary McNamara and the Joint Chiefs of Staff pressed President Johnson to commit large numbers of American troops and finally end the war with a military victory. Johnson debated the proposals for over a week at the end of July. Only George Ball, a Chicago lawyer serving as under-secretary of state, and Johnson's private adviser Clark Clifford argued against the sending of U.S. soldiers. Johnson agonized in a series of meetings at the White House and at Camp David, finally deciding to commit troops but to compromise on the numbers. Instead of following McNamara's recommendation to send 104,000 soldiers immediately and call up the reserves, Johnson sent 50,000 troops and increased the draft levees for the year, but did not activate the reserves. He tried to preserve the illusion of limited war and the middle way. Yet by the end of 1965, he was persuaded to raise the numbers of American troops in Vietnam to 180,000. The following year the numbers grew to 380,000, and in 1968 they topped out at around 540,000. Each increment was matched by North Vietnamese regulars or NLF recruits in the South.

The confidence of the Kennedy years had given way to a quiet desperation among American policymakers by 1965. One of Robert McNamara's deputies in the Defense Department, John McNaughton, summed up the administration's motivations in a memorandum written in March 1965. With the kind of quantitative precision his boss loved, McNaughton assessed American aims in Vietnam as "70% To avoid a humiliating U.S. defeat (to our reputation as guarantor), 20% To keep SVN (and the adjacent) territory from Chinese hands, 10% To permit the people of SVN to enjoy a better, freer way of life." Just as in the Cuban missile crisis, the American policymakers remained determined not to blink first. They believed that in every thatched-roof hut of the Third World, a family of peasants was attentively watching to see if the United States was strong enough to keep its commitments.

None of Johnson's advisors dissented from this reasoning or the decisions based upon it, even those such as Ball and Clifford who privately disagreed with it. Clark Clifford has unwittingly revealed yet another illusion surrounding the war, the "effectiveness illusion." Rather than resign noisily in protest, or in Clifford's case (since he held no office) speak out against the war, he and other silent dissenters chose to remain intimates of the president in the hope they would be more effective by working within the administration. This is the same dilemma that Pope Pius XII faced during World War II. Should he speak out against the Nazi Holocaust and thus exercise his moral leadership, or quietly work behind the scenes to save individual Jews? Should George Ball and Clark Clifford have become anti-war protesters, or should they have preserved their effectiveness to exercise a moderating influence in the administration? They chose the illusion of effectiveness. Eventually even Robert McNamara became uncertain about American policy; he and others departed the Johnson administration "for personal reasons." No major U.S. government official ever used his resignation as a platform to criticize the war policy.

The war on the ground in Vietnam unfolded as a confused, bloody affair halfway between a purely guerrilla struggle, such as in Malaya, and a conventional war with a moving front, as in Korea. Like most guerrilla wars, the insurgents controlled much of the countryside whereas the more heavily armed Americans and South Vietnamese held the cities and some major communications routes between them. American General William Westmoreland employed his growing troop strength and firepower in "search and destroy" missions, seeking out enemy troops, forcing them to stand and fight, and then annihilating them. The Communists did not always avoid such confrontations in pure guerrilla fashion, for Hanoi's leaders calculated that a high level of fighting with heavy casualties would eventually render the war unacceptable to the Americans. As the war raged on in 1965, 1966, and 1967, the killing became something of an end in itself to both sides. To the quantitative-minded Americans, a high body count after a battle equaled a victory. For the Communists, however, heavy casualties meant newspaper headlines and television footage in the United States that might weaken American determination to carry on.

The Communists won their bloody gamble by mounting a massive series of attacks on South Vietnamese cities and towns during the holiday of Tet, the Vietnamese New Year, in January 1968. The Americans were preoccupied with the defense of Khe Sanh, a firebase in the central highlands just below the seventeenth parallel. Knowing that this isolated outpost could turn into another Dien Bien Phu, General Westmoreland committed substantial resources to its defense, seemingly daring the Communists to give battle. The North Vietnamese did make a diversionary feint at Khe Sanh, but then on January 30, 1968, nearly 80,000 troops mounted surprise attacks in the center of Saigon, on the old imperial capital of Hue, and in thirty-six of the forty-four provincial capitals. Massive American firepower eventually blunted the attacks, but it took over three weeks to recapture Hue, with bitter house-to-house fighting that destroyed over half the city's residences. After one American officer had shelled the city of Ben Tre into submission, he told reporters: "We had to destroy the city in order to save it."

In purely military terms, the Tet Offensive was a defeat for the Vietnamese Communists. At least 32,000 attackers were killed and 5,800 more were captured. Perhaps 40 percent of the Communists' political operatives in the South were eliminated. The Americans regained control of all the towns and cities attacked. Yet politically speaking, Tet marked a shocking reverse for the Americans. As U.S. troop strength had mounted and the body count grew larger, American military leaders had confidently predicted that they could see "light at the end of the tunnel." Yet the massiveness of the Tet attacks indicated that the tunnel remained long and endlessly dark. The Vietnamese Communists were willing to fight as long as necessary to force an American withdrawal. This changed the political calculus in Washington.

President Johnson asked Clark Clifford to take over from Robert McNamara as secretary of defense. In Clifford's case, perhaps, the "effectiveness illusion" proved not so illusory after all, for by refusing to speak out against the war he was still available to help wind it down. Clifford swiftly convened a group of elder statesmen, "the Wise Men," who counseled that the war could not be won. Following their advice, President Johnson went on television the evening of March 31, 1968, and announced a drastic curtailment of the bombing campaign as a signal to the North Vietnamese that the United States desired negotiations. Then, springing his own surprise on his advisers, Johnson announced he would not seek reelection that year but would devote the remainder of his term to seeking peace in Vietnam. In May, North Vietnam responded to the bombing pause with a call for peace talks in Paris. The dramatic events of 1968 marked the beginning of the end for the Vietnam War. The American government no longer looked for ways to win the war, but for a means of withdrawing with a minimum of embarrassment.

Yet the war did not end in 1968. The Paris peace talks degenerated into meaningless wrangles over symbolic trivia, such as the size and shape of the negotiating table. Clark Clifford believes that President Johnson "was torn between a search for an honorable exit and his desire not to be the first president to lose a foreign war." The North Vietnamese, for their part, saw no need to hurry as time was on their side. They had waited thirty years for independence, they could hold out a few months or years more if necessary. South Vietnamese president Thieu also stalled, fearing that his government would not survive if its American protectors withdrew. Nothing had been settled by the time Richard Nixon replaced Lyndon Johnson as president in January 1969.

Richard Nixon, a conservative Republican from California, had served as Dwight Eisenhower's vice president then narrowly lost the 1960 presidential election to John F. Kennedy. In 1968 he finally won the presidency with an equally narrow victory over Johnson's vice president, Hubert Humphrey. Nixon fancied himself a master of foreign policy, and he recruited an equally confident individual, Harvard professor Henry Kissinger, as his national security advisor (secretary of state after 1973). Had they chosen to, Nixon and Kissinger could have abruptly ended the war as soon as they took office, building on the war-weariness that had set in after the Tet Offensive and blaming the whole debacle on their predecessors, the Democrats. Nixon had a firm reputation as an anti-communist that would have allowed him to weather any complaints from conservatives.

Nixon and Kissinger, however, pursued a subtler strategy that they believed would end the war during their first year in office. They called the strategy "Vietnamization," that is, the gradual withdrawal of American troops and the building up of South Vietnamese forces to take their place. At the same

314

time, Nixon exploited his own right-wing reputation with a ploy he called his "madman theory." Remembering how Dwight Eisenhower had ended the stalemate in Korea by threatening nuclear strikes, Nixon put out rumors that he was so insanely anti-communist he might do anything. He gave substance to these rumors by greatly intensifying the American bombing campaign. These bombing sorties did not target North Vietnam, but rather the infiltration and supply routes running through neighboring Laos, Cambodia, and South Vietnam itself. Nixon and Kissinger were bombing neutral nations and the country they were supposedly saving.

To some extent, Nixon's policy worked. By the end of 1970 he had reduced the number of U.S. soldiers in Vietnam from 540,000 to 340,000, and the war had begun to recede from the front pages of American newspapers. Yet the South Vietnamese troops still did not seem capable of handling the war on their own, and the North Vietnamese made no new concessions at the peace talks. The body count continued to mount. During the four years of President Nixon's first term in office, 15,315 Americans, 107,504 South Vietnamese, and an estimated 400,000 North Vietnamese died in the fighting. Finally, with his own reelection campaign in view, Nixon unleashed his madman theory with a vengeance, reinstating the bombing raids on North Vietnam that Johnson had halted four years previously. In addition, he clamped down a naval blockade on North Vietnam, even mining Haiphong harbor. The Russians and the Chinese, who were both moving toward détente with the United States and were nearly as sick of the Vietnam War as Americans were, pressured Hanoi to make a deal with the Americans and let them withdraw. Henry Kissinger and Le Duc Tho, who later received Nobel Peace Prizes for their efforts, made a breakthrough at the Paris peace talks in October 1972. The United States agreed to let North Vietnamese troops remain in the South after the American withdrawal, and the North Vietnamese dropped their demands that President Thieu be removed before the war ended.

Thieu stalled, however, as he had four years earlier, and Nixon remained reluctant to sign the peace agreement unilaterally, without the South Vietnamese allies. Not knowing what else to do, "madman" Nixon then unleashed the Christmas bombing of North Vietnam, authorizing American B-52s to attack Hanoi and Haiphong, which had previously remained off limits. Entire neighborhoods were obliterated and about two thousand civilians killed, but many more had been evacuated before the attacks took place. Russian-supplied missiles shot down somewhere between fifteen and thirty-four American bombers (the exact numbers are disputed) and over thirty pilots became prisoners of war. Unwilling to accept such politically sensitive losses, Nixon and Kissinger ended the bombing and on January 27, 1973, signed the same peace agreement that was available the previous October. Nixon bluntly informed President

Thieu he would sign it without him if he continued stalling. In effect, the Americans bombed themselves back to the peace table.

The South Vietnamese government held out for two more years after the last American troops withdrew in March 1973. Yet when the North Vietnamese army launched a major campaign in the spring of 1975, it smashed forward at a rate of speed that even surprised the attackers. The artificial South Vietnamese regime crumbled. President Thieu resigned on April 21, and when his successors tried to negotiate a truce the North Vietnamese refused. At 2:00 A.M. on April 30 the American ambassador and the last American civilians evacuated Saigon by helicopter, with desperate South Vietnamese fighting to climb aboard. By early afternoon of the same day, North Vietnamese soldiers controlled Saigon and the South Vietnamese government surrendered. The Communists swiftly reunified the country, renamed Saigon Ho Chi Minh City (Ho had died in September 1969), and arrested many former South Vietnamese officials for reeducation and indoctrination. No major bloodbath ensued, however. The thirty-year Vietnam War was finally over. It was the longest war in American history and the most intense liberation struggle of the twentieth century. Nearly 58,000 Americans and at least a million Vietnamese died in the conflict.

The Vietnam War, however, was not the only devastating struggle raging in Southeast Asia. The domino theory, as articulated by American policymakers, was an illusion, but it was also illusory to expect that a major war would not harm any innocent bystanders. The major "dominoes" that the United States feared would fall — Thailand, Malaysia, Indonesia, and Singapore — remained largely insulated from the catastrophe, but the small states of Laos and Cambodia, which had been joined with Vietnam in French Indochina, were less fortunate. The tiny landlocked kingdom of Laos had been declared neutral by international agreement during the Kennedy administration, before the United States became heavily involved in Southeast Asia. As the Vietnam War heated up in the mid- to late 1960s, the country was unofficially partitioned by the two contenders in Vietnam. The Communist Pathet Lao, always under direct control from Hanoi, dominated much of the Laotian countryside, whereas the royal government was manipulated directly by the CIA working out of the American embassy in Laos's capital, Vientiane. Since the Ho Chi Minh Trail, the major supply route between North Vietnam and Communist forces in the South, ran right through Laos, the Americans treated the country as a virtual free-fire zone. After the bombing halt of 1968, both the Johnson and the Nixon administrations shifted the preponderance of American airpower to these supply routes through Laos. By 1970 the country's forests and villages had been pulverized and over a quarter of the population was classified as refugees. Laos remained a helpless pawn in the struggle of greater powers until it was neutralized once again, with a Communist-dominated coalition government, by the Paris peace agreements of 1973.

Cambodia suffered even more severely than Laos in the fallout from the Vietnam War. The small kingdom of Cambodia, about the size of the state of Missouri, had once been the dominant power in Southeast Asia. The massive ruins at Angkor Wat, a major tourist attraction when the country is at peace, testify to the magnificence of the nation during its golden age from 802 to 1431. In the centuries afterward, however, the country was increasingly squeezed by the Siamese (or Thais) on the west and the Vietnamese on the east. Though Cambodia had once controlled the entire delta of the Mekong River, the Vietnamese gradually took over the region and pushed the Cambodians back toward their capital at Phnom Penh. Cambodia's survival as a nation had become so threatened that the king actually welcomed French protection in the nineteenth century. The French then unwittingly stimulated Cambodian national feeling by discovering the long-forgotten ruins of Angkor Wat and commissioning French scholars to translate and publish the Cambodian royal chronicle, detailing the glory years of the golden age.

Prince Norodom Sihanouk, crowned in 1941 at the age of eighteen, peacefully secured his country's independence in 1953 shortly before the French defeat in neighboring Vietnam. He then maneuvered for more than a decade to preserve his country's neutrality, leaning sometimes toward the Communist side in the Cold War and at other times toward the Americans. British journalist William Shawcross has described Sihanouk as "Chief of State, Prince, Prime Minister, head of the main political movement, jazz-band leader, magazine editor, film director, and gambling concessionaire. . . . He was a vain, petulant showman who enjoyed boasting about his sexual successes. . . . At the same time he had enormous political skill, charm, tenacity and, intelligence." He surely ranks as one of the top survivors of the twentieth century. Most writers use the metaphor of a tightrope walker to describe Sihanouk. At this writing, he is still titular head of Cambodia, though much horror has ensued since the date of independence, and he has long been powerless to control events.

In the late 1960s Sihanouk's tightrope act became increasingly perilous. The North Vietnamese not only ran the Ho Chi Minh Trail through the eastern provinces of his country but also established semi-permanent base camps and sanctuaries there which functioned as headquarters for the war effort in neighboring Vietnam. Sihanouk knew about these camps, resented them as typical Vietnamese meddling, but could do nothing about them. The Chinese also persuaded the prince to allow the passage of military supplies from the Cambodian port of Sihanoukville over an American-built highway to Phnom Penh, and then on to the Communist guerrillas in Vietnam. Sihanouk's military and civilian officials made handsome profits transporting these supplies. The Americans and South Vietnamese occasionally sent reconnaissance teams into Cambodia, seeking out the Communist sanctuaries, and sometimes engaged in hot pursuit of guerrillas across the border, but for the most part the Kennedy and Johnson administrations respected Cambodian neutrality. President Nixon, however, changed the policy and eventually became obsessed with the Cambodian sanctuaries, which he imagined were a kind of Communist Pentagon.

Just two months after his inauguration, on March 18, 1969, Nixon granted the long-standing military request to bomb the border areas of Cambodia. B-52 bombers rumbled off runways in far-off Guam or nearby Thailand to drop their loads in the jungle. The Americans kept these bombing sorties secret, even falsifying the official military reports by recording bogus targets within the borders of Vietnam. Sihanouk resented the air raids, as he resented the Vietnamese penetration of his country, but he did not protest publicly. The following year, on March 17, 1970, Cambodian general Lon Nol and Sihanouk's cousin, Prince Sirik Matak, overthrew the ruler while he was vacationing in France. Sihanouk had often followed a retreat-and-return political strategy, withdrawing to a spa in France while rival politicians quarreled in Phnom Penh, then triumphantly returning to clean up the mess they made. This time he miscalculated, stayed abroad too long, and was overturned by a unanimous vote of the Cambodian legislature. The officer class of the military and the small urban middle class had chafed under Sihanouk's sometimes clownish, old-fashioned authoritarianism, and therefore spearheaded the coup against him. Many suspicious Americans assumed that the CIA had helped overturn Sihanouk, but apparently the American spy agency was unaware of plans for this coup. American military officers fighting in Vietnam, however, undoubtedly encouraged some of the plotters, assuming that a military government in Phnom Penh would give them free rein to cross the border. One of Lon Nol's new ministers later pointed out that it was irrelevant whether the coup had official American backing or not: "We all just knew that the United States would help us. . . ."

The coup plotters' reasoning proved correct. An American journalist quipped that the only thing Nixon and Kissinger knew about Lon Nol was that his name formed a palindrome, reading the same backwards as forwards. Nonetheless, the Americans swiftly recognized his regime and began funneling military aid to his troops. Then on April 30, 1970, Nixon's madman theory kicked into gear again. American and South Vietnamese troops poured across the Cambodian border into two oddly shaped salients, christened the Parrot's Beak and the Fishhook, in search of the elusive Communist Pentagon. Lon Nol was not consulted but, like Sihanouk before him, there was nothing he could do about this invasion which President Nixon insisted on calling an "incursion." The Cambodian incursion had fateful consequences. In the United States it ignited the last flare-up of anti-war demonstrations, including a rally at Kent State University that was broken up by rifle fire from the Ohio National Guard. The Democratic majorities in Congress passed restrictive legislation banning the use of any American troops in Cambodia after June 30. Accordingly, the Americans withdrew, leaving behind thousands of South Vietnamese. On the ground in Cambodia, the incursion did not locate the elusive Communist headquarters, but it did disperse the Communists deeper into Cambodia and convince the North Vietnamese to support a bid for the takeover of the country.

The Cambodian Communist Party, which Sihanouk had dubbed the Khmer Rouge, was a tiny and extremely radical bunch of French-trained intellectuals. Their tightly knit collective leadership under the secretaryship of Saloth Sar, who used the revolutionary name of Pol Pot, drew on the most paranoid version of Cambodian nationalism, seeing threats not only from their surrounding neighbors but from capitalist forces of economic imperialism. One of the leaders, Khieu Samphan, had written a doctoral thesis in Paris arguing that Cambodian cities were parasites draining the strength of the people away from the villages. In 1970, however, the Khmer Rouge did not possess the power or popular appeal to put their ideological visions into effect. Pol Pot claimed the support of four thousand regular troops and fifty thousand guerrillas, but no one believed his forces numbered anywhere near those totals. The Vietnamese Communists had been concentrating on their own war and giving little or no assistance to the Khmer Rouge.

The overthrow of Sihanouk and the American invasion of Cambodia, however, changed the strategy of the Vietnamese Communists. Fearing that an alliance between Lon Nol and the Americans would squeeze them out of their sanctuaries and jeopardize their position in southern Vietnam, the North Vietnamese Communists threw their support to Pol Pot's Khmer Rouge and assisted their attempt to capture Phnom Penh. Prince Sihanouk, having taken refuge in China after the coup that deposed him, also lent his support to the Khmer Rouge as titular head of the revolutionary movement. His action represents one of the most severe examples of the "effectiveness illusion." By backing the Khmer Rouge he preserved his status as a player in the Cambodian political game, but he also bestowed legitimacy on a brutal movement that would later devastate his people. The Americans supported Lon Nol with military equipment and massive bombing support. After the Paris peace agreement and the withdrawal of all American troops from Vietnam, the U.S. Congress forbade any further bombing in Cambodia after August 15, 1973. Yet from the beginning of the Nixon administration in 1969 until that date, American aircraft had unloaded 539,129 tons of explosives on that small country, more than three times the tonnage dropped on Japan during World War II.

Lon Nol's regime held on to Phnom Penh, but not much else of the country, for two years after it lost American bombing assistance. The Khmer Rouge finally captured the city on April 17, 1975, two weeks before the North Vietnamese took over in Saigon. The very day that Phnom Penh fell Pol Pot's troops ordered the entire population of two million people to evacuate. They panicked the populace with rumors that the Americans were about to bomb the city — not a completely unreasonable fear given Nixon's "madman" stratagems — but this was not the real reason for the forced exodus. At a congress the preceding February, the party had voted to act upon Khieu Samphan's fears of urban contamination by emptying the nation's cities back into the countryside. Perhaps there has never been a clearer example of John Maynard Keynes's dictum that "madmen in authority . . . are distilling their frenzy from some academic scribbler of a few years back." The Cambodian Communists hoped to emulate Mao's Great Leap Forward, driving the people out of the cities and increasing rice production in the countryside, even though the Chinese themselves advised against it. They felt enormous confidence based on their exalted version of Cambodian nationalism. Pol Pot once remarked: "If our people can build Angkor, they are capable of anything."

The Khmer Rouge followed an ideology that was not only anti-urban, but also anti-foreign and anti-middle class. They swiftly killed or drove into exile the Chinese, Vietnamese, and other minority races living in Cambodia, and tried to seal off the nation completely from foreign contact. Not since Japan and Korea in the nineteenth century had any country followed so purely isolationist a policy. The Khmer Rouge also divided the native population into three classes: party members and revolutionaries; candidates for full revolutionary status; and a despised class of landowners, army officers, bureaucrats, teachers, and merchants, who were deprived of all rights. The top two classes enjoyed first call on rice rations, but the despised class was worked to exhaustion on a starvation diet. Eventually even the privileged class turned upon itself. After an unsuccessful coup attempt against Pol Pot, the Communist leader engineered a savage purge that would have made Joseph Stalin proud. Torture and execution centers were established in Phnom Penh and other areas of the country where tens of thousands of suspect party members, along with their families and close acquaintances, were eliminated and then buried in mass graves. Finally the Vietnamese put an end to Pol Pot's murderous regime with a lightning military attack that took Phnom Penh in January 1979. They installed a Communist, but non-genocidal, government in the country.

Estimates of those murdered in the Cambodian killing fields from 1975 to 1979 range from a low of 400,000 to a high of 3 million, out of a 1975 population of about 7 million. Journalists generally have accepted the round figure of 1 million dead, but recent estimates seem to be trending even higher. A U.S. State Department investigation has unearthed 10-20,000 mass graves, each holding between 100 to 250 corpses. The Cambodian genocide combined the racial holocaust of Hitler, the class murders and party purges of Stalin, and the insanely misguided economic policies of Mao. Political scientist Karl D. Jackson has concluded: "Seldom has any regime sought so much change so quickly, from so many. . . . In sharp contrast with their Vietnamese Communist contemporaries, the Khmer Rouge ruled almost exclusively with the sword rather than the pen, the loudspeaker, or the school."

Cambodian genocide was also the most horrifying consequence of the Vietnam War. Pol Pot and his associates were directly and solely responsible for perpetrating the atrocities, but the Vietnam War provided a unique opportunity for these literal-minded, murderous ideologues to come to power. Had the North Vietnamese not established bases in neutral Cambodia and had the Americans not bombed and invaded these bases, the Khmer Rouge would never have succeeded. Sihanouk would undoubtedly have faced internal opposition and perhaps been overthrown in any case. Given the power of Vietnam in the region it is likely that a pro-Vietnamese Communist government would eventually have taken over in Cambodia as it did in Laos. Yet it is difficult to conceive any scenario that would bring such a hard-core group as the Khmer Rouge to power, unless both Vietnam and the United States violated the country's neutrality the way they did in the early 1970s.

Political scientist Robert Melson has provided a compelling interpretation of the roots of genocide (which I have relied upon heavily in the first volume of this work). Melson argues that revolution in time of war provides the most fertile soil for genocide, citing the Armenian massacre of World War I and the Jewish Holocaust of World War II as prime examples. When a revolutionary regime, such as the Young Turks or the Nazis, comes to power in the midst of a war, they often feel threatened enough to eliminate their internal enemies. In Cambodia, the Khmer Rouge provided the revolutionary ideologues but the Vietnam War, spilling over into a country that was enjoying an illusion of peace and neutrality, gave them their opportunity. Cambodia was sideswiped into genocide.

CHAPTER SEVENTEEN

The Shark and the Sardines

American intervention in Southeast Asia stretched the previous limits of Cold War foreign policy, as was clearly understood at the time. Successive American presidents who intervened in Vietnam made the crucial decisions only after agonized soul-searching. When the United States fought communism in the Americas, however, the government's actions drew on long-standing traditions and seemed nearly thoughtless and automatic. A former president of Guatemala, Juan José Arevalo, once wrote a political fable whose title, *The Shark and the Sardines,* aptly characterizes relations between the United States and Latin America. Throughout the twentieth century, the United States has treated the twenty-six nations south of the Rio Grande as an exclusive sphere of influence and has rarely exercised much subtlety in asserting its predominance. In particular, the American shark considered the Caribbean Sea as its backyard swimming pool. Early in the century, the United States forcibly separated the province of Panama from its parent country of Colombia, in order to dig a canal linking the Caribbean to the Pacific. Then over the next three decades the U.S. Marines invaded and occupied three small nations in or around the Caribbean — Haiti, the Dominican Republic, and Nicaragua. They remained in the latter country from 1909 to 1933. In the bitter words of Uruguayan journalist Eduardo Galeano, "the Marines landed in Nicaragua for a while, *to protect the lives and properties of United States citizens,* and forgot to leave."

Most South and Central American nations have long been locked into an export-import pattern of dependency on just one or two main crops or minerals. As late as 1959, for example, 62 percent of Brazil's foreign earnings came from coffee and 71 percent of Chile's exports were copper ore. The Central

American nations have been contemptuously labeled "banana republics," since, as Galeano phrases it, they were "condemned to produce cheap desserts — bananas, coffee, and sugar." After World War I the United States replaced Great Britain as the main market for these products. In 1948, for instance, 45 million dollars' worth of Guatemala's 50 million dollars in exports (mainly coffee and bananas) were shipped to the United States.

Yet economics does not fully explain the American interest in the Western Hemisphere. Historians have isolated three primary motives for U.S. interventions in Latin America, identifying each with a particular American president from the early decades of the twentieth century. Teddy Roosevelt practiced "big stick" politics, intervening for transparent motives of national security; William Howard Taft was an exponent of "dollar diplomacy," protecting American economic interests; and Woodrow Wilson pursued an idealistic policy of "missionary diplomacy," trying to spread democracy and, in his own words, teach Latin Americans "to elect good men." Though each of these presidents did indeed accent a different aspect of American policy, it is important not to overemphasize the distinctions. Latin Americans, on the receiving end of U.S. intervention in their internal affairs, perceived little difference; and, in fact, one motive has tended to predominate, a desire to keep other great powers out of the Western Hemisphere. Historian Piero Gleijeses has well summarized the commonality of interest between various American administrations:

> Presidents Roosevelt, Taft, and Wilson shared the same aim: to control the political lives of the countries in the region and to bar any possibility, however remote or absurd, of European "interference," all in the name of that special "right to security" the United States has always claimed for itself and denied to others. Security and economic expansion were intimately linked in the minds and deeds of these three presidents. To this reality Woodrow Wilson added a new dimension: his intolerant dogmatism.

All three motives — economic, strategic, and ideological — melded together in the minds of American policymakers, with the strategic goal of preventing "foreign meddling" from outside the hemisphere usually predominant. Before World War II the foreign threat which the United States feared most came from Germany. As war approached, President Franklin Roosevelt abandoned the American policy of direct intervention and inaugurated the "good neighbor policy," trying to unite the Americas in a solid front against Nazi German penetration. He replaced naked intervention with a more subtle policy of political conciliation, economic cooperation, and military collaboration. In the year before Pearl Harbor, the U.S. government spent a half-billion dollars establishing military training missions in every Latin American country. Only two

Latin countries, Brazil and Mexico, contributed fighting troops to the war effort, but most of the other nations provided strategic bases for the Americans and denied assistance to the enemy. The war closed off commerce with most of the rest of the world, forcing the Latin nations to trade almost exclusively with the United States. World War II, therefore, marked the high point of American predominance in the Western Hemisphere.

In the postwar world the Soviet threat loomed large in the minds of American policymakers and public. The Truman administration pressured Latin American governments to break diplomatic relations with the Soviet Union, and all but Mexico, Argentina, and Uruguay did so. Most nations also outlawed their internal communist parties. In 1947 the shark and the sardines formed a mutual defense pact, the Treaty of Rio, which formalized the long-standing U.S. policy that an attack on any country in the Western Hemisphere should be considered an attack on all. The following year at Bogotá, Colombia, the Organization of American States (the OAS) was organized as an institutional embodiment of hemispheric solidarity and cooperation. Arevalo's fable satirized the sardines' role in this pact:

> You will proclaim to the four winds his [the shark's] good will. . . . You will learn by memory his fourteen points and the four freedoms. . . . And if by force of habit, the Shark should again take to his old ways, your spirit of loyalty will be shown by saying that this is a lie, that it is a slander of his enemies, that it is the echo of their constant envy of him.

The Military Assistance Act of 1951 intensified the cooperation between North, South, and Central American military services. Over the next two decades, the United States trained 54,270 Latin American officers, either at the School of the Americas in the Panama Canal Zone or at bases in the United States itself. The American military redirected the mission of Latin American armies away from external defense toward the fighting of internal, communist subversion. An unfortunate side effect of this military pan-Americanism was the encouragement of dictatorships. A Mexican politician once observed that if he had a list of the officers training in the Canal Zone, he could identify the next generation of dictators in Latin America. President John Kennedy reluctantly admitted this result of American policy when he was considering intervention in the Dominican Republic. There were "only three possibilities," he remarked, "in descending order of preference: a decent democratic regime, a continuation of the Trujillo [dictatorial] regime or a Castro [Communist] regime. We ought to aim at the first, but we really can't renounce the second until we are sure that we can avoid the third." In the midst of the Cold War, preventing communist parties from coming to power in Latin America overrode all other considerations.

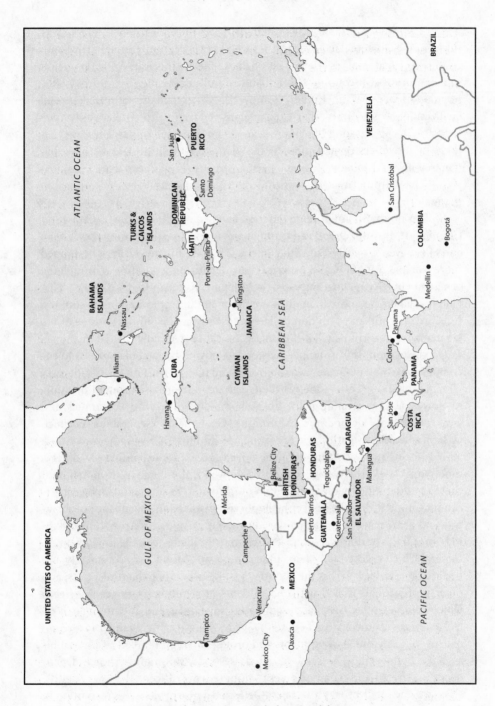

Central America and the Caribbean

The primacy of Cold War thinking appears most clearly in the 1954 over-throw of the Guatemalan government by CIA covert action. Immediately south of Mexico, Guatemala is the largest of the Central American countries, yet at mid-century it still counted fewer than five million people. Two-thirds of the population were Mayan Indians, impoverished descendants of a once-proud civilization. Most of the other Guatemalans referred to themselves as *ladinos* (or Latins), emphasizing their European origin and non-Indian language. *Ladinos* or foreigners owned most of the plantations that grew coffee and ba-nanas, with the Indians forming a permanent supply of cheap labor. As histo-rian Richard Immerman has concluded: "Guatemala itself was not poor, but the majority of its people were."

The predominant foreign interest in Guatemala was the United Fruit Company of Boston. Organized through a merger of smaller companies in 1899 and taken over in 1929 by Sam "the Banana Man" Zemurray, *La Frutera* shipped more bananas out of Central America than any other corporation. Through the generosity of corrupt governments, the company had acquired 550,000 acres of land in Guatemala, more than one-seventh of all the arable land in the country. It recorded profits of 65 million dollars in 1950, twice the annual revenue of the Guatemalan government. Latin Americans called United Fruit Company *El Pulpo*, the octopus, for its tentacles extended beyond banana plantations to en-compass nearly all of Guatemala's railroads and its only port on the Caribbean.

Throughout Latin America the Great Depression had brought dictators to power, as catastrophic price drops hammered one-crop economies and weakened fragile democratic institutions. Guatemala's General Jorge Ubico Castañeda ruled his nation with an iron hand and forged a sweetheart contract with United Fruit, granting it valuable legal privileges extending for ninety-nine years. As World War II progressed, however, the democratic, anti-fascist rhetoric of the Allies made the position of the dictators anomalous. The Ameri-can government did not notice the hypocrisy involved in the alliance of dicta-tors and democracy against totalitarianism, but many Latin Americans did. In May 1944, El Salvador overthrew its dictator, who fled into exile in Guatemala. General Ubico cracked down on student protestors in his own capital city and declared martial law across the country, but the urban merchants, lawyers, and other professionals joined with the students in a middle-class general strike. Ubico made a strategic retreat, resigning on July 1, 1944, and attempting to con-trol a new government from behind the scenes. However, on October 19 a group of army officers joined the students and professionals and forced Ubico and his associates into exile. The same social classes that were fighting for indepen-dence in African and Asian colonies — junior army officers, the lower middle class, and the intellectual proletariat — effected a nearly bloodless revolution in Guatemala in 1944.

The revolutionaries called a college professor, Juan José Arevalo Bermejo, back from exile in Argentina, where he had been teaching throughout most of the Ubico era. Arevalo defeated several conservative candidates for president in December 1944 and was inaugurated on March 15, 1945. He called himself a "spiritual socialist," for he resented the rampant individualism of North American society, but he also rejected Marxism as godless and materialistic. In practice, Arevalo was a radical nationalist who tried to engineer economic and social reforms in Guatemala and help overthrow the remaining dictators in neighboring Central American countries. His government passed a new labor code to protect workers and made some weak attempts to regulate land rents for tenant farmers, but Arevalo put his greatest energy into extending the educational system. Though he was not a communist, his labor reforms worried the United Fruit Company and his attempts to topple neighboring dictators offended the American government, which was still pursuing the democracy-dictator alliance against totalitarianism. In 1949 the Truman administration slapped an arms embargo on Guatemala and soon cut off nearly all economic aid as well. There is also evidence that Nicaragua's dictator, Anastasio Somoza, a particularly close U.S. ally, offered to invade Guatemala and overthrow Arevalo, but President Truman refused to authorize the coup.

In 1950 Colonel Jacobo Arbenz Guzman succeeded Arevalo as president in one of the freest elections the country had ever known. Born in 1913 to a Swiss immigrant father and a Guatemalan mother, Arbenz had light skin and Nordic features. Though originally well off, his pharmacist father became addicted to morphine and eventually committed suicide, leaving Jacobo without the means to attend university. He therefore chose the military as an alternative career path, graduating from the academy in 1935. Shortly thereafter he met and married a beautiful Salvadoran woman, Maria Villanova, who became a major intellectual influence on his life. Together they read and discussed the classics of literature and social science, eventually delving into the writings of Karl Marx and other revolutionaries. Arbenz took a leading role in the overthrow of General Ubico in 1944 and defended President Arevalo against numerous coup attempts during his term of office.

As president, Arbenz pushed the Guatemalan revolution farther than Arevalo had. He was not a member of the Communist Party, but he was drawn to communism by his reading and his social conscience. He also made friends with a number of young Guatemalan labor leaders who organized an underground Communist Party in 1949. In particular, José Manuel Fortuny, the secretary-general of the party, became like a brother to him. Arbenz and Fortuny drafted an agrarian reform law as the centerpiece of the new president's administration. This measure, which was passed into law on June 17, 1952, cleverly mixed radicalism with moderation. The law nationalized only the idle, uncultivated fields of United Fruit and other large landowners and provided compensation in government bonds paying 3 percent interest over a period of twenty-five years. Three percent was a reasonable interest rate in the low-inflation decade of the 1950s, but the value of the compensation was based on the property-owners' tax declarations. Since United Fruit and the Guatemalan native elite drastically understated the worth of their lands, Arbenz's agrarian reform caught them in their own lies. Over the next two years, over 100,000 peasants, mainly Mayan Indian families, settled on nationalized land. Though written by Communists, the reform did not mandate collective farms on the Soviet model but allowed the new owners to form cooperatives or hold the land as family farms. Arbenz and Fortuny were emphasizing nationalism, social justice, and economic development, with communization of society foreseen only for the distant future.

Agrarian reform in Guatemala precipitated an American reaction. In the late summer of 1953, about a year after the reform went into effect, the Eisenhower administration authorized the CIA to begin planning Operation PBSUCCESS, a covert conspiracy to assist disgruntled Guatemalans in overthrowing the Arbenz government. It is easy to ascribe economic motivation to the American plot, for Secretary of State John Foster Dulles had formerly worked at a law firm, Sullivan & Cromwell, that represented the United Fruit Company, and a number of other influential Republicans had close ties to the Octopus as well. Yet if only the property of United Fruit were at stake, the Eisenhower administration would probably have just continued the Truman administration arms and aid embargoes and pressured the Guatemalans to increase their compensation offer. Eisenhower and Dulles moved to overthrow Arbenz because they believed he was a Communist and because they wanted to stop any Communist penetration of Latin America. José Fortuny later remarked that the Americans would have overthrown Arbenz even if Guatemala grew no bananas. Eisenhower had campaigned on a platform that promised "liberation" of captive nations from communism, rather than mere "containment" of communism, as practiced by the Democrats. Though Eisenhower and Dulles were too prudent to challenge the Soviets in their own backyard of Eastern Europe, they believed they could successfully throw the Communists out of America's own backyard pool, the Caribbean basin.

Jacobo Arbenz considered himself a Communist, though he was not a party member. The Communists exercised intellectual influence over the Guatemalan president but they did not control his government, and their closeness to Arbenz was not generally known in Guatemala. Neither the president nor the Guatemalan party members were Soviet lackeys. A few Guatemalan Communists had attended meetings in Eastern Europe, usually at their own expense, and they admired the Soviet experiment, but the Russians paid little attention to them and had no plans to establish a beachhead in the Americas. Khrushchev's gambits in Cuba came almost a decade later and were products of a different era in Soviet history (see chapter 15). In a daring gamble to break the American embargo, Arbenz's government did negotiate an arms deal with the Communist government of Czechoslovakia in May 1954. This gave the Americans a good excuse for their conspiracy to overthrow him, but the plans had been authorized long before the arms purchase. In short, Arbenz in Guatemala posed no threat to American security, yet Dulles and Eisenhower wished to make an example of him.

Frank Wisner and Richard Bissell of the CIA organized a training camp for Guatemalan exiles, led by Colonel Carlos Castillo Armas, who had tried to overthrow President Arevalo's regime shortly before Arbenz's election. The plan called for psychological warfare more than a military assault. PBSUCCESS recruited only about 150 fighters, who would be no match for the small but disciplined Guatemalan army. The CIA hoped, however, that the Guatemalan commanders would consider the tiny exile brigade the vanguard of a much larger American force. Aided by the terror bombing of Guatemala City by American mercenary pilots and propaganda broadcasts from neighboring Nicaragua, the CIA plot worked. Castillo Armas led his band of rebels across the border on June 17, 1954, and promptly lost two battles to the Guatemalan military; but American psychological pressure and the growing radicalism of Arbenz's government caused the military commanders to demand the president's resignation. In order to avoid further bloodshed, Jacobo Arbenz complied, stepping down from the presidency on June 27, 1954. The American ambassador brokered a new government dominated by Castillo Armas. Nationalized estates were handed back to United Fruit and the peasants were expelled. Guatemala suffered from corrupt government, intense repression, and ferocious guerrilla battles for the next forty years. Only in 1997 was a tense peace agreement reached in the class warfare that followed the overthrow of Jacobo Arbenz.

Historian Piero Gleijeses, who discovered Arbenz's communist beliefs by the obvious but previously overlooked expedient of asking his wife and his surviving associates, has provided a balanced conclusion to the Guatemalan tragedy:

> Jacobo Arbenz is not one of history's giants. He made serious mistakes; he was naïve . . . [and] needlessly provocative. . . . He underestimated the threat from the United States. . . . [Yet] Jacobo Arbenz provided Guatemala with the best government it has ever had . . . and he presided over the most successful agrarian reform in the history of Central America.

The Cold War so warped American perceptions, however, that neither the policymakers nor the public could see these realities.

The American attempt to overthrow Fidel Castro in 1961 (see chapter 15) is more easily understood in light of the successful Guatemalan coup of 1954. President Eisenhower, who authorized the Bay of Pigs invasion, and President Kennedy, who gave the order to execute it, both believed that the CIA could topple a Communist-inspired government with a handful of exile troops because the CIA had done just that once before. Richard Bissell and many other operatives who had worked on PBSUCCESS guided the Bay of Pigs operation. Fidel Castro, however, had discussed the Guatemalan coup with Che Guevara while both were in exile in Mexico. Guevara had actually been present as an unknown adventurer in Guatemala City at the time Arbenz was overthrown, and he believed that the Guatemalan president should have withdrawn to the hills with his followers and waged a guerrilla struggle. Fidel learned the more practical lesson that he could not leave an uncommitted military establishment in place after the revolution. So when he came to power in Cuba in 1959, he swiftly dismantled Batista's professional army and replaced it with a revolutionary militia under his personal control. The CIA's fighters at the Bay of Pigs, therefore, met determined resistance from a disciplined force inspired by socio-nationalism. A risky plan that worked in Guatemala failed in Cuba.

Avenging the failure of the Cuban operation became an obsession for American Cold Warriors, and successive American presidents vowed to prevent any more Cubas from taking root in Latin America. When, for example, a group of progressive military officers in the Dominican Republic tried to bring the constitutionally elected president, Juan Bosch, back from exile in April 1965, the Johnson administration sent in marines to prop up a right-wing military junta that had earlier deposed Bosch. These events took place just as the Johnson administration was making its irrevocable commitments in Vietnam, and, presumably, the president did not want any left-wing distractions in America's backyard swimming pool. Political scientist Abraham Lowenthal has remarked that "the single most striking fact about the Dominican intervention of 1965 is that it could occur without any (known) prior objection being raised within the U.S. government." At the height of the Cold War, snuffing out any hint of communism in Latin America became an automatic American response.

A wave of communist challenges to the status quo was washing over Latin America in the 1960s, but it was inspired by Fidel Castro and the example of the Cuban Revolution, not by the Soviet Union. The old-line communist parties that were loyal to Moscow recruited a dedicated band of lifelong militants, usually from the labor movement; but they were small, weak, and generally less effective than communist parties in such European nations as France or Italy. They followed a conservative party line aimed at building up the power of the proletariat and gradually taking over from the bourgeoisie. On only two occasions before the Cuban Revolution, in El Salvador in 1932 and Brazil in 1935, did

Latin American Communists attempt insurrections, and both were swiftly crushed by the military. Castro came to power in Cuba despite the Communists, not because of them. He showed more audacity and understood the revolutionary situation of his native land more clearly than the Communists did.

After his success in Cuba, Fidel Castro felt eager to export the revolution to the rest of Latin America. The Soviet Union became very cautious on the international stage after the Cuban missile crisis and the dismissal of Khrushchev; but Castro was not merely a Soviet stooge, indeed he considered himself a model revolutionary with world historical significance. Though heavily dependent on Russia economically, Cuba followed independent policies both at home and abroad, at least through the 1960s. In both internal and international policy, Castro's closest follower, Che Guevara, played a crucial role.

Ernesto "Che" Guevara was born in 1928 and trained as a doctor in his native Argentina. He fought a lifelong battle with asthma that frequently took his breath away and laid him low. Rather than settling down to a comfortable medical practice, however, Guevara set off on a voyage of discovery throughout Latin America. Drifting from country to country and odd job to odd job, he occasionally practiced medicine or conducted research when the opportunity presented itself, but primarily he studied how "the other half lived." From 1950 to 1955, Guevara was, in the words of his biographer, Paco Ignacio Taibo, "a street photographer, poorly paid medical researcher, permanent exile, no-great shakes husband [he married for the first of two times in Mexico in 1955], letter writer, poet, and diarist." In July of 1955 Guevara met Fidel Castro, who had recently arrived in Mexico City after his release from Batista's prison, and this encounter gave his life direction and purpose. The two men were intellectual equals and both liked to talk, and talk, and talk. Yet unlike other dreamers Guevara had met in his wanderings, Fidel planned to do more than talk. He had a strategy for revolution in his home country. Guevara signed up as medical officer on the *Granma* when it sailed for Cuba in 1956 and from that time on he linked his fate to that of Fidel Castro.

Following the success of the guerrilla struggle against Batista in the Sierra Maestre Mountains, Che Guevara wrote a manual for revolutionaries, whose English edition, *Guerrilla Warfare,* hit the best-seller lists in the United States after its publication in July 1960. Yet Che became more than a guerrilla fighter. He held unglamorous bureaucratic positions in the Cuban government, such as minister of industry and chairman of the Cuban National Bank. When his father heard about his bank appointment, he exclaimed: "Fidel's crazy. Every time a Guevara starts a business, it goes bust." Che also served as Castro's most trusted roving ambassador, negotiating with governments on five continents.

In the early 1960s, Guevara waged an internal ideological battle within the Cuban Revolution. He championed an "idealistic strategy" at home and

331

abroad, whereas his more orthodox Communist opponents argued for a "materialist strategy." Economically, the debate boiled down to a choice between moral incentives for the building of socialism versus bread-and-butter, material incentives. Che the idealist hoped to create a "new man" in Cuba who would work for sheer love of humanity and occasional public praise by the authorities. Old-line Stalinists laughed at him and called him a romantic. Overseas, Guevara aimed to stimulate revolutions throughout the Third World, "one, two, three, many Vietnams," in his own words. Drawing on his and Fidel's experience in the Sierra Maestre, he urged the foundation of revolutionary *focos,* or hot spots, in mountains and jungles, believing that the flames of revolution would then spread quickly. Orthodox Communists urged caution and careful preparation before any revolutionary actions should be launched. Che initially won the debate, and Fidel Castro launched an all-out struggle to mobilize labor and produce an epic harvest in Cuba, 10 million tons of sugar. Despite his asthma, Che frequently left his office for weeks at a time and cut cane with the peasants. Cuba also provided arms and supplies to guerrillas in a handful of countries. In 1965 Che Guevara left his government duties and took personal charge of Cuba's guerrilla offensive. He fought first in the Congo in the dying days of the resistance against Moise Tshombe and Joseph Mobutu (see chapter 14). His main ally in that struggle was a little-known guerrilla named Laurent Kabila, who thirty years later would finally topple Mobutu and become president of Congo. After the failure of his Congo expedition, however, Guevara turned his attention to Latin America.

Che Guevara was obviously not a sardine but a big fish in the Latin American ocean. Compared to Jacobo Arbenz he *was* a historical giant, or at least a darling of history, with a remarkable resemblance to the Spanish movie actor Cantinflas and a worldwide following among youth and leftists. Yet the American shark did not leave him unopposed. In the 1960s, President John F. Kennedy launched a more sophisticated offensive against communism in Latin America. Drawing on the work of Latin American economists and reformist politicians, he proposed the Alliance for Progress in 1961, pledging 20 billion dollars of economic aid over the next ten years. JFK's Alliance pursued four goals, three of them publicly and one in secret: long-term economic development, structural reform of Latin American economies, political democratization, and counterinsurgency military action. With a romanticism and naïvete that matched Guevara's, Kennedy and his advisors trumpeted a peaceful revolution, avowing that if Latin Americans became more prosperous they would automatically become democratic. In fact, the number of Latin American dictatorships drastically increased during the 1960s, due in part to the secret, fourth aspect of the Alliance, military counterinsurgency. When choices had to be made between anti-communist dictatorships and messy democracies, the United States chose dictators.

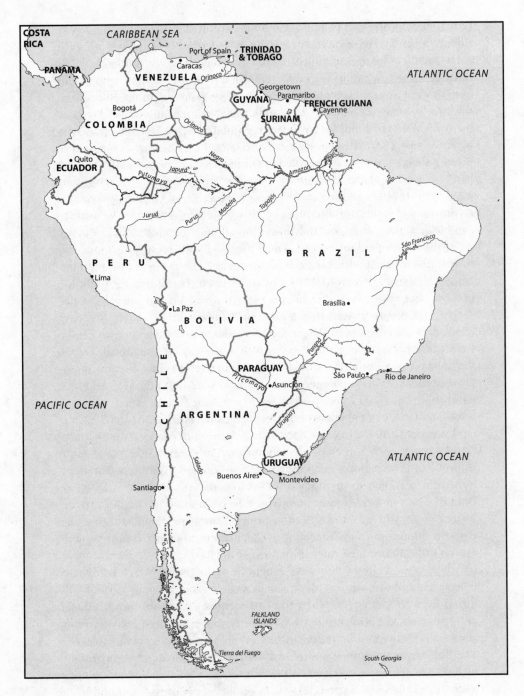

COSTA
RICA

CARIBBEAN SEA

Port of Spain **TRINIDAD**
& TOBAGO

PANAMA

Caracas

ATLANTIC OCEAN

VENEZUELA *Orinoco*

Georgetown
GUYANA Paramaribo
FRENCH GUIANA
Cayenne
SURINAM

Bogotá

COLOMBIA

Orinoco

Negro

Japurá

Amazon

Putumayo

Quito
ECUADOR

Juruá

Purus

Madeira

Tapajós

B R A Z I L

São Francisco

P E R U

Lima

Brasília

B O L I V I A

La Paz

C H I L E

Paraná

PARAGUAY

São Paulo
Rio de Janeiro

Pilcomayo

Asunción

Uruguay

PACIFIC OCEAN

ARGENTINA

Salado

URUGUAY

ATLANTIC OCEAN

Buenos Aires
Montevideo

Santiago

*FALKLAND
ISLANDS*

Tierra del Fuego

South Georgia

South America

The Kennedy and Guevara plans for Latin America collided head on in Bolivia, a landlocked, mountain republic in the center of South America. Che chose Bolivia as his main *foco* because of its strategic location, bordering on five other countries including his native Argentina, where he hoped to lead the revolution in person. Bolivia had already experienced a revolution in 1952, when the *Movimiento Nacionalista Revolucionario* (National Revolutionary Movement, or MNR) had toppled a military regime. The MNR government, headed by economist Victor Paz Estenssoro, nationalized the tin mines which dominated Bolivia's economy but paid compensation to the companies and worked hard to reassure the United States and other foreign investors. In the early 1960s, Paz's Bolivia became one of Kennedy's favorite Alliance for Progress countries, and Bolivia received more U.S. aid per capita than any other Latin American nation. However, the tough miners and urban workers who had made the 1952 revolution felt cheated by the MNR's moderate policies and began arming for a new struggle. So President Paz rebuilt the discredited military, with American assistance. In gratitude, General René Barrientos overthrew him in November 1964. American military and economic aid continued unabated.

Che Guevara arrived in the jungles of Bolivia in November 1966 with about fifty volunteer guerrillas, mainly from Cuba and Bolivia but a handful from other Latin American nations as well. Although he had literally written the book on guerrilla warfare, he did just about everything wrong. The remote farm he chose for his *foco* lay too far away from the radical mining districts in a lightly populated area whose peasants were apathetic and suspicious of strangers. He undervalued the importance of urban contacts and alienated the Bolivian Communist Party. In Cuba, Castro and Guevara had tapped into both nationalism and socialism as driving forces of revolution, but the peasants of Bolivia had little national consciousness. The Bolivian Communists were nationalistic, so much so that they resented Che the outsider. Historian Henry Butterfield Ryan perceptively compares Che's blunders in Bolivia with the American Bay of Pigs fiasco: "Both leapt into complicated military operations with ridiculous optimism, expecting popular support but all the time knowing far too little about the feelings of the people. . . ."

Guevara's Bolivian *foco* never caught fire. Che constantly eluded the Bolivian army and won a few battles through sheer ingenuity, but by July 1967, historian Ryan concludes, "his guerrillas had become a vagabond band . . . wandering pointlessly through the rugged countryside of southern Bolivia with no strategic objective and no means to make their revolutionary dreams prevail." The Bolivian military then put their American counterinsurgency instruction to good use. The Second Ranger Battalion, trained by a Green Beret team under Major Ralph "Pappy" Shelton, closed in on Guevara's dwindling band at the end of September 1967. On October 8, they trapped Che in the Yuro ravine near the town of La Higuera, wounding him and taking him prisoner. Of the seventeen guerrillas who remained with Che, only five escaped. The military executed Guevara about 1:00 P.M. on October 9, 1967. He was just short of forty years old.

Che Guevara was a man of violence who believed, like Mao, that power came from the barrel of a gun. Yet he was neither a torturer nor a mass murderer, like so many twentieth-century revolutionaries, and he lived utterly free of hypocrisy. Rather than enjoy the perquisites of the "new class," as other communists have in the Soviet Union and elsewhere, he lived an ascetic life and pushed himself physically in field labor and forced marches, despite medical disabilities that would have provided a ready excuse to take it easy. His admirers considered Che a secular saint. Eduardo Galeano eulogized him in these words: "He never kept anything for himself, nor ever asked for anything. Living is giving oneself, he thought, and he gave himself." Even his critics, such as historian Henry Ryan, acknowledge that his dedication to a cause was "inspirational, regardless of what one feels about his beliefs."

Yet ultimately Guevara's strategy failed, as did the competing plans of John F. Kennedy and the Alliance for Progress. Romantic leadership by individuals often bumps against limits of social structure and historical traditions, and history is not always made by heroes. Latin America's nations are plagued by dual societies, in which a thin elite and a small middle class, together comprising about 15 to 25 percent of the population, live comfortably alongside the impoverished three-quarters of the populace. The elite and the middle class resisted Guevara and took Kennedy's money, but they did not change. In the process, armies got larger, democratic governments gave way to dictators, and people were tortured and killed. Both the American shark and the big fish from Cuba might well have done better if they practiced the first principle of the ethical code that Che Guevara presumably learned at medical school: "First do no harm."

Another Latin American leader, Salvador Allende Gossens of Chile, tried to effect social and political change by a less violent method than guerrilla warfare. Born in 1908, Allende was a full generation older than Che, but his background bears many similarities to Guevara's. Both were raised in upper-middle-class families that had experienced some downward mobility, and each became a medical doctor. Allende, however, chose the road of conventional, electoral politics rather than the revolutionary path of Guevara. He was a founder of Chile's Socialist Party in 1933, won election to the Senate later in that decade, then served briefly as a cabinet minister in a coalition government during the 1940s. He ran for president three times, in 1952, 1958, and 1964, before finally winning the office on his fourth try in 1970. By then he was the grand old man of Chilean politics, a lover of good art and fine wines, married to a beautiful and politically active wife, Hortensia Bussi de Allende, but with a weakness for other women, especially his private secretary and mistress, Miria Contreras. Yet Allende was not a dilettante or a mere time-serving politician, but a committed socialist, and many who knew him believed that he secretly envied the romantic adventures of Guevara. Allende met the Cuban guerrilla leader on at least a half-dozen occasions, and, according to his friend and biographer, Fernando Alegria, he "would have liked to be that young doctor, a dreamer and fighter who abandoned his career, his family, his golden cage and went off to fight in the cities, plazas, and mountains of America." After Guevara was killed in Bolivia and three of his companions made their away across the Andes to Chile, Allende personally greeted the survivors and accompanied them back to Cuba. Nevertheless, despite his secret dreams of guerrilla struggle, Salvador Allende remained the leading proponent of the "Chilean way to socialism," the path of free elections.

Chile, a long, narrow strip of land between the Pacific Ocean and the Andes Mountains, had a long heritage of relatively stable, constitutional politics. Yet it was not quite the peaceful South American Switzerland its apologists have tried to portray. The country had seized the seacoast of Bolivia in the 1879 War of the Pacific, leaving that neighboring nation landlocked, then experienced a civil war later in the nineteenth century and a period of military rule in the 1920s. An unusually cohesive upper class of landowners and urban businessmen dominated society, and the economy was heavily dependent on a single industry, copper mining. The Communist Party of Chile, founded in the early 1920s, was the continent's oldest and largest, and Allende's Socialist Party championed more militant policies than the Communists. The nation's politics revolved around three groups of class-based parties: the elite Liberals and Conservatives, Christian and anti-clerical parties of the middle class, and the Socialists and Communists supported by the workers and peasants.

In 1964, Allende ran a strong race for president, gaining 39 percent of the vote, but the right wing buried its differences with the middle class that year, backing a relatively new centrist party called the Christian Democrats. In this essentially two-man race, the Christian Democratic candidate, Eduardo Frei Montalva, won a 56 percent majority. The United States provided substantial covert support to the Christian Democrats, with the CIA funneling somewhere between 3 million and 20 million dollars to their 1964 campaign. Frei became a darling of the Alliance for Progress, and the Americans continued to support him both openly and covertly. Yet Frei was not just an American stooge but a committed, non-socialist reformer in his own right. He attempted a halfway nationalization of the copper industry, with the government purchasing large shares of the three largest, American-owned mining corporations, and presented an ambitious agrarian reform law that limited the size of landholdings while compensating landowners for expropriated property. The Christian Democrats' centrist reforms, however, proved too conservative for the workers and peasants of Chile yet too risky and adventurous for the Americans. When Richard Nixon took office as president in 1969, he began winding down the Alliance for Progress. He particularly resented Frei and the Chilean Christian Democrats, whom he associated with the hated Kennedys. Henry Kissinger gave the Chilean foreign minister a tongue-lashing in June 1969, contemptuously dismissing his country with these words: "Nothing important can come from the South. History has never been produced in the South. . . . What happens in the South is of no importance."

By law a Chilean president could not serve more than one term, so in 1970 the Christian Democrats backed Radomiro Tomic as Frei's successor. They were unable, however, to continue their alliance with the upper-class elite, who presented their own candidate, a former president named Jorge Alessandri. Allende ran as the standard-bearer of a new five-party coalition called *Unidad Popular* (Popular Unity), which included his own Socialists, the Communists, and several splinter factions of the left wing. The U.S. government did not directly support any candidate or party, as they had in 1964, but concentrated on defeating Allende. Between March 1970 and the election in September, the CIA spent over $400,000 on anti-Allende propaganda in Chile. American corporations, led by International Telephone and Telegraph (ITT), which operated Chile's phone system, donated about $700,000 directly to Alessandri's campaign. Both Cuba and the Soviet Union contributed comparable amounts of money to Allende's Popular Unity coalition. Fractured along class lines, Chile had become a cockpit of the Cold War.

Allende's coalition won the three-way 1970 election, even though it garnered only 36.1 percent of the vote, edging Alessandri by only 39,000 votes out of 3 million cast. He actually gained a lower percentage of the vote than he had six years previously in the two-way contest with Frei. According to the Chilean constitution, if no candidate received a majority, the Chamber of Deputies would decide the election. Tradition dictated that the congressmen should choose the frontrunner, but the Nixon administration and the Chilean right wing worked hard to prevent Allende's selection. In the six weeks between the popular election on September 4, 1970, and the decisive congressional vote on October 24, the CIA not only continued its covert funding of anti-Allende propaganda but also bribed Chilean congressmen to vote against him. American agents established contact with Chilean military officers who were plotting a coup to short-circuit the electoral process altogether. Nixon and Kissinger personally authorized the scheme, which they called Track II to distinguish it from the long-standing covert funding activities; but their plans backfired. On October 22 a small group of officers attempted to kidnap General René Schneider, the Chilean chief of staff, but wounded him fatally in the process. This act so shocked the Chilean nation that Christian Democrats closed ranks with Popular Unity and peacefully elected Allende president in the congressional vote, after securing a constitutional statute of guarantees for basic liberties that the new Communist-backed government pledged to respect. Outgoing president Frei stood side by side with Allende at General Schneider's funeral.

President Salvador Allende, the first freely elected Marxist president anywhere in the world (Arbenz's Marxist convictions were not known to the voters when he was elected in Guatemala in 1950), enjoyed a brief honeymoon. His government stimulated the economy by mandating higher wages for workers and borrowing heavily for investment in industry. Such pump-priming, however, soon led to runaway inflation and a shortage of basic consumer goods. Allende confronted the vested interests of capital by completing Frei's half-hearted nationalization of the copper mines and pushing agrarian reform more thoroughly than the preceding government. Nationalization of copper proved so popular that it passed the Chilean congress unanimously on July 11, 1971. Allende, however, courted confrontation with the American-owned companies by refusing to pay any compensation for their property, alleging that they had enjoyed "excessive" profits on their operations since 1955. Even before the nationalization decree, the Nixon administration had decided to squeeze Allende's government by ending most American economic aid and voting against loans and grants in international agencies such as the World Bank. Allende termed this hostile American policy an "invisible blockade."

In the second and third years of Allende's presidency, Chile polarized sharply between left and right. The Socialist president headed a coalition government and was often powerless to control the activities of the far-left factions. For example, in January 1973, his minister of education, a member of the anti-clerical Radical Party, proposed a unified national school curriculum that would require the teaching of "socialist humanism" in all schools, public and private. Although the measure was swiftly withdrawn, it helped alienate the Christian Democrats. More importantly, perhaps, some of the Socialist and Communist ministers in the government pushed for nationalization of all industries and the collectivization of agriculture, even if these measures caused economic disruption in the short run. Both on the left and the right, paramilitary groups armed themselves and committed spectacular atrocities.

The nation's small-business entrepreneurs, especially the fiercely independent truckers who feared the expropriation of their vehicles, spearheaded the opposition to the Popular Unity government. A national truckers' strike in October 1972 turned into a virtual civil war as the military escorted strikebreakers and the strikers strewed bent nails along the highways and shot at the scab drivers. Allende earned a breathing space for himself by conceding most of the

338

truckers' demands and bringing several military officers into his cabinet to calm the country. He took advantage of this lull in November 1972 to leave the country, seeking political support at the United Nations and economic aid in Cuba and the Soviet Union. The Russians offered loans and credits, but not as much as Allende wanted or Chile needed. The Soviet Union did not wish to create another Cuba, which was a heavy drag on the Soviet economy.

In July 1973 the truckers mounted another strike, which was soon joined by the nation's shopkeepers and many of its lawyers, doctors, and other professionals. Allende faced a middle-class general strike that largely halted the economy. He began negotiations with the Christian Democrats in a last-ditch attempt to save his government, but most Christian Democrats had already concluded that Allende was a threat to democracy, and the president himself remained unwilling to make significant concessions. Tragically, the two major forces in Chile working for social justice, the Christian center and the Socialist left, failed to reconcile their differences.

Finally, on September 11, 1973, the military overthrew the Popular Unity government. The navy seized the country's major port of Valparaiso at 7 A.M., then army tanks and infantry converged upon the capital of Santiago. Allende was alerted at his residence shortly after the coup began and headed immediately to the La Moneda presidential palace, where he and about forty followers, including his mistress and two of his daughters, made a last stand. The president broadcast to the nation for the last time about 9:30 A.M., calling on the workers to defend themselves but not to commit suicidal sacrifices. Two jet fighters fired rockets into the presidential palace about noon, setting the building ablaze, then the air force also bombed Allende's home, where his wife narrowly escaped. After refusing a military offer of a safe conduct and a plane to take him into exile, the president sent his remaining loyalists out of the palace with a white flag and then shot himself. He died sometime between 1:50 and 2:20 P.M.

Chile's Christian Democrats believed that a military coup was necessary to end the Socialist experiment and stabilize the economy. They probably assumed that the soldiers would hand power over to them after a short period of time, but in this respect they miscalculated. The military government of General Augusto Pinochet Ugarte remained in power for seventeen years, until it finally relinquished control in 1990. The Pinochet regime, a right-wing dictatorship loosely modeled on Franco's Spain, made impressive free-market experiments, diversifying the economy and lessening its reliance on copper, but it increased the social and economic polarization of society and repressed all dissent. The regime ran a series of torture centers and concentration camps; by conservative estimates about 10,000 persons died. Somewhere between 600 and 1,000 prisoners simply disappeared.

The American government was not directly involved in the coup plotting as it had been in 1970. Sensing that the Allende government was doomed, Henry Kissinger and the American ambassador, Nathaniel Davis, concentrated on avoiding responsibility for its downfall. Still, the many acts of overt and covert opposition to Allende from 1964 to 1973 made the American position abundantly clear, and the Chilean military knew that their coup would be welcomed in the United States. Ambassador Davis has defended American actions in Chile, asserting that they were aimed at preserving democracy, not overthrowing Allende. According to Davis, the Popular Unity government had violated constitutional liberties, threatening the rights of free speech and private property, and it might have cancelled the next presidential election scheduled for 1976. Therefore, it was important to prevent the democratic opposition from being "asphyxiated." This argument is plausible and might have been convincing if it coincided with the facts. However, when the military took over in 1973 and established a dictatorship, the United States immediately terminated its support for the Christian Democrats and other opposition parties. The U.S. government only objected to communist authoritarianism, not right-wing authoritarianism. Anti-communism, not devotion to democracy, explains America's policy toward Allende's Chile.

American actions to protect its sphere of influence in the Western Hemisphere against communist penetration appear shameful and hypocritical. American policymakers trumpeted their defense of freedom and democracy against godless tyranny, yet they were unwilling to accept elections in Latin America that did not produce the "correct" solution. As Henry Kissinger once remarked, "I don't see why we need to stand by and watch a country go communist due to the irresponsibility of its own people." This pattern repeated itself elsewhere at the end of the century when the U.S. government encouraged Algeria to cancel free elections after it became evident that Islamic fundamentalists would win them. Yet the essence of democracy is the freedom to make mistakes, to be "irresponsible." Thomas Jefferson's first inaugural address provides the answer to Kissinger: "Sometimes it is said that man cannot be trusted with the government of himself. Can he, then, be trusted with the government of others?"

In retrospect, the government of Jacobo Arbenz would have been far better for Guatemala than the forty years of terror and civil war that followed its overthrow. Allende's government, for all its flaws, probably would have produced a more just and certainly a less murderous society than the dictatorship of Pinochet. It is far less certain that a successful guerrilla campaign by Che Guevara would have resulted in a better life for Bolivians and other Latin Americans. Guevara's "one, two, three, many Vietnams" would undoubtedly have reproduced the Cuban model of communism, which has been egalitarian but authoritarian. Yet these should be matters for Latin Americans themselves to decide. Does the shark know better what is good for the sardines? North Americans have long believed they had a duty to instruct Latin Americans in political and economic affairs. The Cold War accentuated this tendency, transforming it into an obsession.

CHAPTER EIGHTEEN

The Bear and Her Cubs

As the American shark patrolled the waters of the Western Hemisphere during the Cold War, so the Russian bear roughly shepherded her cubs, the satellite states of Eastern Europe and other border areas. When the Communist government of Hungary attempted to chart a neutral, independent foreign policy in 1956, or the Communist leaders of Czechoslovakia experimented with a more open, pluralist society in 1968, the Soviet mother bear slapped them down. Similarly, when a newly established Marxist regime in Afghanistan seemed on the verge of either self-destruction or overthrow in 1978, the Russians occupied the country for ten years in an invasion often compared to America's war in Vietnam.

At the height of the Cold War, comparing the American interventions in Latin America and Asia with the Soviet incursions into the Communist satellite states would be considered highly inflammatory, if not downright treasonous. Even today, such a suggestion remains controversial. Americans believe they are the "good guys"; they reject the notion that Soviet actions might have been morally equivalent to their own. Of course, the first and most obvious point of similarity between Americans and Russians is that the Communists also believed they were the "good guys" and that their system represented the "progressive" forces in the world. Yet the comparison should be explored further.

I certainly do not believe the Communist system of government was morally equivalent to the American. Soviet Russia was a thoroughly repressive, authoritarian, and totalitarian society, and even in functional terms it proved unsuccessful at providing a better life for its own citizens and perpetuating itself in power. Furthermore, when the Soviets intervened in the satellite states around their borders they tended to be more systematic and ruthless in their military actions than the Americans were in Latin America, and their political control remained more pervasive and total. For example, once the U.S. government had secured the deposition of Jacobo Arbenz in Guatemala in 1954, it largely left the country alone, oblivious to forty years of civil war and terrorism, and content that the Guatemalans did not have a communist government. When the Soviet Union invaded Czechoslovakia in 1968, however, their troops remained and they guided the indigenous Communist government in a heavy-handed fashion.

Yet the act of military intervention itself represents a striking parallelism between the two superpowers. Their political systems were different, but they often acted in similar fashion. Both the Soviet Union and the United States — from a combination of ideological, economic, and strategic motives — believed they had the right, and even the duty, to police their own spheres of influence. It is useful to make distinctions between the two forms of government and their means of exercising power, but from the point of view of the smaller nations they interfered with — the sardines and the bear cubs — these distinctions seemed unimportant. A diplomatic anecdote underlines this point. The Turkish ambassador to Mexico once congratulated Mexican officials on their good fortune in living next to a friendly, non-threatening superpower. The Turk was greeted by a prolonged and embarrassing silence then subjected to a long harangue about the evils of Yankee imperialism. Military or political intervention always appears unfriendly from the receiving end. One of the tragedies of the Cold War is that both sides ran roughshod over their natural allies.

The Soviet Union possessed a stronger motive for imposing uniformity upon its allies since it had suffered so severely during World War II. Historian Karen Dawisha emphasizes the importance of historical memory in Communist Russia: "As with the Jewish attitude to the Holocaust, so with the Russian attitude to the war: The loss will not, and must not, be forgotten, and the gains made as a result of the war will never be surrendered, especially in Eastern Europe." The American fear of a communist government in Chile, on the other hand, appears inexplicable and irrational compared to the Russian fear of an unfriendly government in Poland or Czechoslovakia. Enemies have repeatedly invaded Russia through the plains of Eastern Europe, so the Soviet Union did not tolerate any slack in the system of control and security in that region. Both the Soviet invasion of Afghanistan and the American involvement with Vietnam, however, do seem far removed from any obvious superpower security interest.

For a short time after the death of Stalin in 1953, it appeared that Moscow might tolerate a looser hold over Eastern Europe. Stalin's final years had witnessed the rise of "little Stalins" in the satellites, and these brutal dictators, such as Mátyás Rákosi in Hungary, had staged show trials and executed their rivals

343

Eastern Europe during the Era of Soviet Domination

just like their mentor in the Kremlin. The collective leadership that took over after Stalin's death demanded that the "little Stalins" relinquish some of their power and ease up on police terror. Uncertainty about who was actually in charge in Moscow and how far de-Stalinization might go introduced confusion into the politics of the Communist bloc. Then when Nikita Khrushchev consolidated his authority and delivered his "Secret Speech" denouncing Stalin in the early days of 1956, the opportunity for Communist governments to pursue "separate paths to socialism" seemed available.

In Poland, always the most sensitive of the satellites due to its size, strategic location, and the independent-mindedness of its people, the local Communists finessed this moment of opportunity by securing limited concessions from Russia but retaining firm control. Polish workers had pressured their government with explosive strikes and demonstrations in the industrial city of Poznań on June 28, 1956; then the country's religious leaders and intellectuals joined in, demanding greater personal freedoms. The situation looked critical enough for the top Soviet leaders, including Khrushchev and Molotov, to fly into Warsaw unannounced while the Polish Communist Party was meeting in October 1956. They finally agreed to let a Polish party leader, Władysław Gomułka, who had been eased out years before by Stalin, to take over again. Gomułka then released the Catholic primate, Cardinal Stefan Wysyński, from prison along with other political prisoners and persuaded the Soviets to take their military advisors back home with them. He also secured permission to ease up on collectivization of agriculture, which Polish farmers had fiercely resisted. Despite these concessions, however, Gomułka's Poland remained a one-party state and a faithful acolyte of Soviet foreign policy. As it turned out, any leader of a communist state would have to follow Gomułka's "realist" example if he wanted to avoid punishment from the Russian bear.

The reform leader in Hungary, Imre Nagy, attempted to go farther than the Poles, and he eventually paid with his life. Nagy was an unlikely hero, a life-long party bureaucrat who spent much of his life in the Soviet Union. Born in 1896 to poor peasant parents, he was drafted by the Austro-Hungarian government to fight in World War I, but after being taken prisoner by the Russians he became a Bolshevik and spent much of the next quarter century in Moscow. He survived Stalin's purges of the 1930s mainly due to his unimportance, and he stayed out of prison during Mátyás Rákosi's Hungarian purges in the early 1950s because the Russian bear protected him. The Hungarian Communist Party had an unusually large number of Jews from bourgeois origins on its Central Committee, and apparently Moscow valued Nagy as a token Christian with a humble background. A short man with a bushy beard and pince-nez eyepiece, Nagy looked like a professor or the bureaucrat that he was. By the time he had reached his fifties, his colleagues had begun calling him "the old man."

Yet despite his harmless and inoffensive appearance, Imre Nagy pursued the ideals of communism with the fierceness and consistency of a true believer. Nothing like Khrushchev in physical appearance or temperament, he resembled the Soviet first secretary in his sincere dedication to the potential of communism, believing that the communist system could and should become more humane and responsive to human needs. Miklós Molnár, a former Communist official in Hungary, remarked that "party work was unable to kill the human being in him, party policies did not make him forget the 'idea.'" The most important idea, or set of ideas, that Nagy pursued could be characterized as a variety of Marxist revisionism, the notion that socialism is a flexible, adaptable theory. In Hungary, he believed that the economy should remain socialized but that the government should be more democratic and the country should pursue a neutral course between the superpowers.

In June 1953, after Stalin's death, the collective leadership in the Kremlin summoned the Hungarian party leaders to Moscow, stripped Rákosi of half his power and perquisites, and designated Imre Nagy as the new prime minister. In a parliamentary speech of July 1953, Nagy proclaimed the Kremlin's new course, which changed the economic emphasis from heavy industry to consumer goods and food production. He also hoped to reinvigorate the party by allowing more popular participation in decision making but was unable to make any progress along these lines before Rákosi staged a comeback and dismissed him from office in the spring of 1955. As a private citizen, Nagy retired to his study and began formulating his ideas more fully in a document entitled "On Communism." In the words of historian Ben Fowkes: "the program of the revolution [as outlined by Nagy] was neutralism, a multiparty system, and the retention of the socialist foundations of economy and society, with the exception of collective farms." Gradually he attracted a following of intellectuals and like-minded political reformers, for as one of his colleagues noted, "Nagy liked to philosophize and these people liked to talk and talk." On Nagy's sixtieth birthday, in June 1956, a procession of Hungarian notables defied the party by publicly paying their respects to "the old man."

Shortly thereafter, Khrushchev finally dismissed the Hungarian strongman Mátyás Rákosi from all his party positions, but he replaced him with another hardliner, Ernő Gerő. Nagy remained outside the government. However, as word of Khrushchev's de-Stalinization speech spread and the Polish riots in Poznań became known, Hungarian writers, students, and workers agitated for changes in their own country. Most of the opposition leaders in the universities and the factories were committed Marxists, generally younger party members who had once been loyal Stalinists but became disillusioned by the purges and show trials under Rákosi. They did not want to overthrow socialism, but rather to get it back on track as a system dedicated to human welfare. The activities of students at the provincial university in Szeged illustrate how the demands of the intellectual proletariat started with matters of self-interest then snowballed into more explosive political demands. In early October the Szeged students demonstrated against the compulsory study of Russian language and the excessive amount of time spent on military training. By the time the government got around to making concessions on these matters, the students had begun demanding wholesale changes in party leadership and the withdrawal of all Russian troops from Hungarian soil. Elsewhere students made similar demands, and on October 21 and 22 the workers at several factories established independent workers' councils as instruments of proletarian self-management. A revolution was in the making, needing only a spark to set it off.

On the night of October 22, 1956, a group of students at the Technological University of Budapest planned a march to show solidarity with the Polish reformers under Gomułka, who were still meeting in Warsaw at that time. The next day, two bands of students took to the streets, one group demonstrating in front of parliament and another at the Stalin statue on the outskirts of the city. Young high school students and working-class toughs from the slums joined in and pulled down the statue of the Soviet dictator by brute force. The crowd tried to seize the radio station to broadcast their demands, but fighting broke out and the police fired into the crowd. Nearly the whole population of Budapest roamed the streets that night, October 23-24, and the crowds in Parliament Square yelled for Imre Nagy. Finally, Nagy, who had been on vacation and had taken no part in organizing the demonstrations, addressed the masses. "Comrades," he began tentatively. "We're not comrades any more," the crowd bellowed back. A revolution had begun.

Soviet troops, permanently stationed in Hungary according to the Potsdam agreements after World War II, moved into Budapest on the morning of October 24, but they did not fire unless fired upon. Many of the Russian soldiers fraternized in friendly fashion with the citizens of the Hungarian capital. This uneasy state of coexistence, however, evaporated after the so-called Parliament Square massacre of October 25, when panicky Hungarian secret policemen opened fire from the rooftops for over ten minutes, leaving about a hundred dead. Over the next few days, the Budapest crowds hunted down and lynched members of the secret police and engaged in running battles with the Russians, bravely tossing Molotov cocktails at Soviet tanks. On October 30 the Hungarian masses retaliated for the Parliament Square massacre by storming the municipal party headquarters on Republic Square and executing as many Communists as they could lay their hands on. A famous photograph published in *Life* magazine captured the fear on the faces of two Communists as they were about to be shot in Republic Square. Amazingly, these two were among those who survived the massacre.

347

Throughout this first week of the Hungarian revolt, neither the Soviets nor the Hungarian Communists knew quite what to do. Khrushchev himself recalled in his memoirs, "I don't know how many times we changed our minds back and forth." The Russians sent two high level officials, Anastas Mikoyan and Mikhail Suslov, to Budapest where they stayed for most of the last week in October. The Hungarian party called Nagy back to office, hoping to satisfy the crowds, but the new prime minister had a hard time keeping up with the escalating demands in the streets, which now included the removal of all Soviet troops and the establishment of multi-party government and workers' councils in all industries. On October 30, Nagy made a historic radio speech, announcing the end of one-party government and the formation of a multi-party coalition. He also promised to negotiate the withdrawal of Soviet troops and to explore a more neutralist stance in foreign policy.

That night, or the next day, the Soviet leadership, over the objections of their two men on the spot in Budapest, made the decision to crush rather than accommodate the Hungarian revolution. Khrushchev flew around Eastern Europe informing the other satellite leaders of the decision. Even Tito of Yugoslavia, who had long ago carved out his own semi-independent position, consented to the Soviet invasion, for in his own country he was a one-party dictator and he could not stomach such an open challenge to party dominance in Hungary. Khrushchev gave Tito five reasons for invading Hungary, but probably only two of them mattered: the shocking fact that Communist policemen were being murdered in Hungary, "strung up from lampposts and hanged by their feet"; and the political reality that if he did not act forcefully he might lose his own power in Moscow and the Russians might lose control over the satellites. Khrushchev cut to the heart of the matter when he told Tito, "If we let things take their course the West would say we are either stupid or weak, and that's one and the same thing." Even the two most "liberal" Communist leaders, Tito and Khrushchev, adhered to a form of the domino theory. If Hungary escaped from party control, others might follow suit.

On the morning of November 1, Soviet troops crossed the Hungarian border to reinforce those already within the country. Conveniently for the Russians, their invasion of Hungary took place at the same time that the British, French, and Israelis were assaulting Suez (see chapter 10). The United States, which would not have opposed the Soviets with force in any case, was so distracted by the folly of its allies that even its protests proved mild and inconsequential. In despair, Imre Nagy went on the radio again that evening, declaring Hungary's unilateral withdrawal from the Warsaw Pact and his intention to pursue a neutral course in the Cold War. The Soviet troops, however, reached Budapest at dawn on November 4 and swiftly put down all signs of revolt. Nagy and his government colleagues took refuge in the Yugoslav embassy, and a new government under János Kádár, who until November 1 had been one of Nagy's allies, was installed by the Russians. With promises of safe conduct, Nagy and his followers were lured out of the embassy for negotiations, but Soviet agents kidnapped them and took them away for trial. On June 16, 1958, Nagy and seven compatriots were executed. In the previous two years, twenty thousand Hungarians had been arrested, two thousand executed, and several thousand more deported to the Soviet Union.

Imre Nagy was betrayed and condemned by a reformer in the Kremlin, Nikita Khrushchev, a man whose views on communism were not dissimilar from his own. The Hungarian revolution was avowedly socialist and would probably not have brought back capitalism. Nagy and his followers wanted to pursue a neutral but friendly pro-Soviet foreign policy, much like Finland; they had no intention of joining the other side in the Cold War. However, unlike the Poles, the Hungarian reformers threatened the one-party monopoly of power, and the Soviet Union would not tolerate this deviation. The Hungarian crisis of 1956 set the limits of dissent in the Soviet empire for the next thirty years. Separate paths to socialism were sharply limited, and neither multi-party politics nor neutralism in foreign policy was permitted. Ironically, the collaborationist government of János Kádár eventually managed to stake out a slightly less rigid economic policy that resulted in "goulash communism," with a more comfortable level of consumer goods for average Hungarians in the late 1960s and throughout the 1970s. Yet Kádár paid for this deviation with a rigid adherence to Moscow's foreign policy line and a firm policy against dissent in Hungary.

Twelve years after the crushing of the Hungarian revolt, Communist leaders in Czechoslovakia attempted an even more thoroughgoing reform program, endeavoring to construct a system of "socialism with a human face." The "Prague Spring," as the Czechoslovak reform movement of 1968 came to be called, was actually preceded by a "Bratislava Spring" when Alexander Dubček was named leader of the Communist Party in the Slovak half of the country in 1963.

Dubček resembled Hungary's Imre Nagy in many ways, for he too was a lifelong Communist who spent most of his early years in Russia and rose through the party ranks as a cautious bureaucrat. Alexander was conceived in Chicago but born in his father's native village of Uhrovec on November 27, 1921, after his parents re-emigrated from America to Slovakia. The Dubček family soon set off for an idealistic socialist settlement, imaginatively named Interhelpo, in the wilds of Soviet Kirghizia. After eight years there, they moved to the large city of Gorky in European Russia, then finally returned to Slovakia in 1938. Dubček thus spent all but three of his first seventeen years in the Soviet Union, and he never lost a nostalgic pro-Soviet attitude. After fighting the Nazis with Slovak partisan forces during World War II, he worked his way up through the Communist Party bureaucracy in Czechoslovakia. His English biographer, William Shawcross, concluded that most people who knew the young Dubček "recall him as an unexceptionable, quiet, diligent, rather uninspiring but quite attractive, convinced Communist, who was noticeable only for his lack of pomp and authoritarianism." Like Nagy he was dedicated to the principles of communism, not its power and perquisites.

When he became first secretary in Bratislava he allowed an unprecedented amount of free speech to journalists and creative writers that slowly spread throughout the country, despite the fears and suspicions of the top Czech leader, Antonin Novotny. Many of the artists who first appeared during the Bratislava and Prague Springs later became famous in exile, such as the novelist Milan Kundera and the filmmaker Miloš Forman. Others remained in Czechoslovakia through all the ups and downs of the regime and finally surfaced after the collapse of communism. Most notable among the latter is the playwright Václav Havel, currently president of the non-communist Czech Republic.

The Czechoslovak Communist Party deposed Novotny, the last surviving "little Stalin" of Eastern Europe, in January 1968, choosing Dubček as his replacement. For the next six months the Czechs and Slovaks explored the limits of independence within the Communist bloc. The party replaced most of the remaining hardline Stalinists in the regime, permitted almost complete freedom of speech, and began laying the foundations for a society ruled by law, not party decrees. Activist pressure groups sprang up outside the Communist Party and demanded admission into a broader government coalition. At the same time, Dubček and his colleagues remained committed to socialism and a firm alliance with the Soviet Union. They did not even discuss a neutralist foreign policy such as the Hungarians had attempted in 1956. Historian Kieran Williams has provided a balanced assessment of the Prague Spring:

> For all their many virtues, the reforms of 1968, in intention and execution, amounted to only the liberalization of a Leninist regime, the gradual widening by the ruling elite of the non-prohibited zone, the sphere of things permitted, the space where people can feel themselves more or less free.

Dubček himself summed up the essence of his policies: "We began to trust the people and they began to trust us."

Even this limited reformism, however, threatened the Soviet Union's control over Eastern Europe. Though friendly to Dubček at first, the Russian leaders became alarmed as early as March 1968, when they summoned him to a meeting of all the satellite leaders in Dresden, East Germany. Dubček thought the Dresden meeting would be a routine discussion of mutual economic concerns, but he later told his biographer: "I sat down and saw that I was facing a ready synod . . . like when Jan Hus [a late medieval religious reformer] arrived at Constance [a church council that condemned him to death]." For the next five months the Prague reforms unrolled in an atmosphere of constant crisis. Dubček tried to keep abreast of the popular clamor for more freedom while re-assuring the Soviet leaders that his reforms did not threaten the security of the Communist bloc. Unfortunately, his actions sent the Soviets mixed signals, for he constantly promised to rein in the exuberance of his countrymen and then failed to do so. A stormy four-day meeting with Brezhnev in the small village of Cierna nad Tisou at the beginning of August produced a gentleman's agree-ment whereby the Soviets promised to withdraw the troops they had sent into Czechoslovakia for maneuvers earlier in the year. In return, the Czechs would re-impose censorship and curb the independence of non-party pressure groups. Dubček apparently did not realize that the Cierna conclave represented his last chance to avoid Soviet intervention. Brezhnev and other Russians tele-phoned Prague repeatedly throughout August, and János Kádár, the Hungarian leader who had taken over after the Soviet invasion of his country in 1956, asked Dubček face to face on August 17: "Do you *really* not know the kind of people you're dealing with?"

The Russians made up their minds that same day, August 17, at a Polit-buro meeting in Moscow. As in 1956, they believed that the introduction of free speech and the admission of non-Communist groups and individuals into the government would undermine one-party control and could not be tolerated. They also feared a domino effect that would undermine the stability of the Warsaw Pact and the inviolability of the post–World War II borders. Brezhnev captured the essence of Soviet fears when he remarked: "For us, the results of the Second World War are inviolable, and we will defend them even at the cost of risking a new war."

Overnight on August 20-21, 1968, 165,000 soldiers and 4,600 tanks poured into Czechoslovakia, both overland and by air. Unlike 1956, Russian troops were joined by soldiers from four other Eastern bloc nations — Poland, East Ger-many, Hungary, and Bulgaria. Within a week the combined armies totaled half a million men. Alexander Dubček could still not believe he had been betrayed by his lifelong friends, the Russian Communists. When the meeting of the Czechoslovak Party Presidium was interrupted by news of the Soviet invasion around midnight on August 20-21, Dubček exclaimed: "That they should have done this to me, after I have dedicated my whole life to co-operation with the Soviet Union, is the great tragedy of my life." The Czechs and Slovaks discov-ered what many Latin Americans already knew — with superpower friends one doesn't need enemies.

Having made this discovery, the people of Czechoslovakia responded with a remarkable, unplanned, and unexpected campaign of non-violent resistance. Dubček's Presidium managed to broadcast a statement to the nation affirming that the invasion forces had not been "invited" in to keep order, as the Soviet Union claimed, and the figurehead president of the country, Ludwig Svoboda, firmly refused to assemble a new collaborationist regime. Clandestine radio stations took to the air, encouraging non-cooperation and non-violent resistance, and the people of Prague, other cities, and occasionally even in the countryside, responded enthusiastically and creatively. The compulsory Russian language courses long imposed in Czechoslovakia rebounded on the invaders, for citizens argued vehemently and cursed at the soldiers in their native tongue. Then when the soldiers were off duty, they found themselves shunned as pariahs. If a single Soviet officer entered a movie theater or a restaurant, it emptied in a matter of minutes. The Czechs and Slovaks also delayed and disrupted the invaders by removing or changing street signs, blocking train traffic with obstacles on the rails, and mounting short-lived but precisely targeted strikes against critical support facilities.

Non-violent resistance continued for a week, throwing the Soviet plans completely off track. The Russians had expected a short, unopposed invasion that would be legitimized by a new government of collaborationists who would depose Dubček and welcome their Russian brethren with open arms. They had formulated no alternate plan, and thus had to improvise one. Dubček and his colleagues were arrested on the morning of August 21, but they were held inside armored cars most of that day while the Russians decided what to do with them. They were first flown to various locations around Eastern Europe then finally summoned to Moscow for negotiations. Dubček firmly insisted that he would not negotiate unless all his government members were present, then he bravely tried not to concede too much. He was hampered, however, by lack of knowledge about the state of resistance in Czechoslovakia. Had he known how successful it was proving, he might not have signed the compromise agreement of August 26 promising to "normalize" the situation in his country.

He and his colleagues returned home as heroes, and Dubček himself remained first secretary of the party during a long, frustrating "Prague Autumn" that stretched into the following year, but the citizenry soon became disillusioned when they realized that their government had essentially capitulated to the Soviets. The spontaneous non-violent resistance of August 1968 ceased as swiftly as it had begun, replaced by fitful individual gestures, such as the self-immolation of a student, Jan Palach, in January 1969. When the Czechoslovak hockey team defeated the Russians at a world championship match in March 1969, the populace of Prague descended upon Wenceslas Square in a nasty demonstration that proved little more than a lynching party for Russians and other foreigners in town. The Russians used this incident as their excuse for terminating the "Prague Autumn" as they had already ended the Spring. Alexander Dubček was replaced as party leader on April 17, 1969 by a hardline Slovak, Gustáv Husák, who finally "normalized" the situation. A year later Husák and Brezhnev signed a friendship treaty regularizing the presence of Soviet troops in Czechoslovakia.

The non-violent resistance of Czechs and Slovaks to the Warsaw Pact invasion failed primarily because it was spontaneous, unplanned, and disorganized. Dubček and other government leaders remained unaware of their fellow citizens' heroism and therefore did not try to evade arrest or refuse to sign the capitulation to the Russians. The Czech army, which might have done much more to disrupt the invasion, remained on the sidelines for the most part. Some of the most obvious measures of disruption, such as removing road and street signs, were taken several days too late for full effectiveness. Nevertheless, non-violent resistance did slow down the Soviet timetable significantly. Dubček was not removed until eight months after the invasion, instead of immediately, and the intervention was denied any credibility or legitimacy. Furthermore, fewer than one hundred people were killed during the invasion, whereas armed resistance would have produced far more casualties, as it did in Hungary in 1956. Though ultimately unsuccessful, the Czech resistance of 1968 represents, in the words of peace activist Gene Sharp, "the most significant attempt thus far to improvise civilian struggle for national defense purposes."

Nevertheless, the Soviets shrugged off any embarrassment that the non-violent resistance may have caused them. In the months after the crisis in Prague, Soviet ideologues defended intervention in the satellite states as a sacred doctrine of the Communist faith, the so-called Brezhnev Doctrine. There was nothing really new in this doctrine, which the Russians called "proletarian internationalism," for it merely codified past practice. Soviet leaders have always believed that Russia was the fatherland of socialism and that they therefore had a right and a duty to defend socialist regimes wherever they existed. Khrushchev acted out of this same belief in 1956, just as Brezhnev did in 1968. The Russians gave Dubček plenty of warnings that they thought this way. A letter agreed upon by the Warsaw Pact countries at a meeting in July 1968 ominously pointed out to the Czechs that "it is no longer your affair alone." The agreement reached at the Cierna meeting at the beginning of August also contained the key phrase of the Brezhnev Doctrine: "It is the common international *duty* of all socialist countries to support, strengthen and defend these gains, which were achieved at the cost of every people's heroic efforts and selfless labor." The Czech delegates themselves signed this document.

Finally, after the invasion, on September 25, 1968, *Pravda* carried an official statement entitled "Sovereignty and the International Obligations of the Socialist Countries." This document asserted:

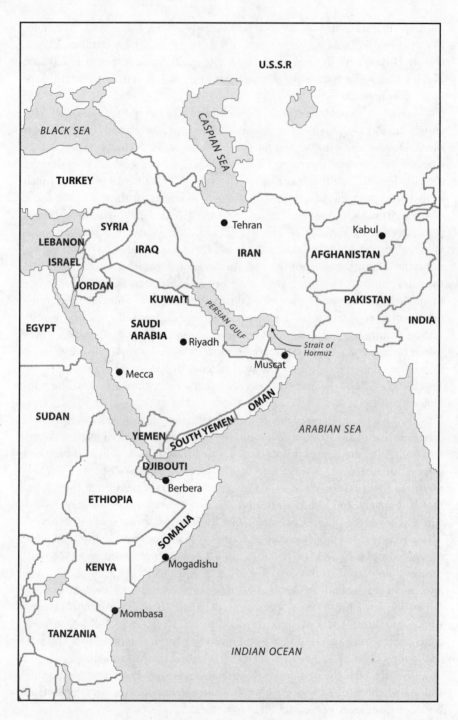

Afghanistan and the Middle East

The peoples of the socialist countries and Communist parties certainly do have and should have freedom for determining the ways of advance of their respective countries [a ritual bow to the idea of separate paths to socialism]. However, none of their decisions should damage either socialism in their country or the fundamental interests of other socialist countries. . . . Naturally the Communists of the fraternal countries could not allow the socialist states to be inactive in the name of an abstractly understood sovereignty, when they saw that the country stood in peril of anti-socialist degeneration [Big Brother knows best after all].

The *New York Times* published the complete text of this statement, which was swiftly dubbed the Brezhnev Doctrine or the Doctrine of Limited Sovereignty by American commentators. It remained the official party line until just before the fall of the Soviet Union in 1991.

The Czech invasion and the Brezhnev Doctrine froze the status quo in Eastern Europe. As historians Geoffrey and Nigel Swain have remarked, "the period from 1968 to the early 1980s was a 'long decade' during which East European society was held in aspic and change seemed inconceivable." American policy recognized this reality and quietly acquiesced in it, ushering in a period of détente between the superpowers. Disillusioned activists in both Latin America and Eastern Europe often suspected that the Americans and the Russians had made a deal at their expense, trading American silence over Czechoslovakia, for example, against Soviet inactivity when Chile's Allende was overthrown. There probably was no explicit deal, but both sides in the Cold War did find it expedient to respect the other's exclusive sphere of influence.

The American government eventually raised this practical restraint to the level of official policy, the little-known Sonnenfeldt Doctrine. In December 1975, Secretary of State Henry Kissinger's chief advisor on Soviet policy, Helmut Sonnenfeldt, told U.S. ambassadors in Europe that a greater "organic unity" between Eastern Europe and the Soviet Union worked in America's strategic interest by promoting stability. When this speech was leaked to the *New York Times* the following year it caused a furor, but it accurately reflected the policy of both superpowers towards the end of the Cold War. Stability in the two superpowers' spheres of influence was more important than trying to "win" the ideological and strategic battle. The Cold War had frozen hostility into cynicism and hypocrisy.

The final Soviet intervention within its sphere of influence, in the central Asian republic of Afghanistan, stretched the Brezhnev Doctrine to cover a situation far removed from Eastern Europe and involved the Soviet Union in a protracted and vicious war. Afghanistan is so remote from Europe or North America that its very name has become a journalistic shorthand for something far away that no one is interested in. The average Russian must have shared this perception as well, yet Afghanistan was not far away from the Asian portion of the Soviet Union. Indeed, it lay along its southern border, adjacent to the Soviet republics (now independent states) of Turkmenistan, Uzbekistan, and Tajikistan.

The Russians had been projecting their influence into this region since early in the nineteenth century, when their interests in central Asia clashed with the British who were probing northward from India. Jockeying for predominance over the various nomadic ethnic groups that lived in Afghanistan, the British and the Russians pursued what they called the "Great Game." Political scientist Milan Hauner has aptly summed up the rules:

> Russian ambitions in Afghanistan and adjacent areas were checked by British imperial power, and British ambitions were checked by Russian power. The competition for tactical advantage at the margins of this strategic standoff was the Great Game. The chance of a major strategic breakthrough for either side was never high, but neither was it impossible. . . . That is what made it so exciting.

The stalemate of the Great Game meant that neither Russians nor British occupied Afghanistan, but they determined its borders, constantly skirmished with its people, and ultimately neutralized the country as a buffer zone between their two empires.

During the Cold War the game continued, but with the Afghans as more active participants and the Americans halfheartedly replacing the British. A vigorous member of the Afghan royal family, Mohammed Daoud Khan, became prime minister in 1953 in an alliance with his cousin King Zahir Shah. He fell from power in 1963, but then after another ten years he overthrew the king and declared his country a republic, under his own presidency. During both of his administrations, Daoud guided Afghanistan along a non-aligned, neutralist path, much like Nasser in Egypt or Sukarno in Indonesia, playing off both sides in the Cold War to maximize economic and military aid. The Americans, however, remained largely uninterested, refusing most requests for military aid and sinking the lion's share of their economic assistance in a disastrously unsuccessful irrigation project. The Soviets, on the other hand, concentrated on small-scale, tangible aid projects, such as paving streets in the capital of Kabul and building bakeries in small towns. They also provided most of the arms and training for the Afghan military. By 1970, about seven thousand Afghan officers had trained either in Russia or Czechoslovakia, whereas only six hundred had received their education in the United States, Britain, or other countries. These military ties made Afghanistan a client state of the Soviet Union, though not quite a satellite, just as American military assistance bound the Latin American republics to the United States.

A small Marxist political party, the People's Democratic Party of Afghanistan (PDPA), was founded on January 1, 1965, by Nur Mohammed Taraki, the son of a small merchant who translated documents for a living and wrote realistic novels in his native Pashto language. This party soon split, however, when Babrak Karmal, a well-born Afghan related to the royal family, broke away from Taraki's *Khalq* (meaning "the people") faction to form the *Parcham* (Banner) Party. Both parties remained small during the Daoud years, and Karmal's Parcham was so moderate and respectable that it was nicknamed "the royal Afghan communist party."

Much to everyone's surprise, including the Russians', Khalq and Parcham temporarily patched up their differences, then overthrew Daoud in April 1978, the month of Saur (for Taurus the bull) in the Islamic calendar. The Saur Revolution was supported by only a few thousand members of the intellectual proletariat in the capital of Kabul who were as isolated from the masses as the Russian Bolsheviks of St. Petersburg had been in 1917. Afghanistan had never been a consolidated nation-state but was composed of at least ten major ethnic groups, mutually hostile to each other and owing their allegiance more to local, traditional leaders than to the central government in Kabul. National politics consisted of faction fighting in the capital, followed by attempts to buy the loyalty of the major ethnic groups in the countryside with economic assistance or outright bribes. Rather than try to win over the people, however, the Saur revolutionaries of the PDPA followed the Bolshevik example, compensating for their lack of popular support with utter ruthlessness. They offended the conservative peasants by trying to "liberate" women from Islamic customs and imposing a heavyhanded land reform scheme that alienated the very farmers it was intended to assist. They enlisted the aid of the East Germans to organize a secret police and crush all opposition to the regime. Then the revolutionaries turned on each other. Within just six weeks of the Saur Revolution, Taraki's Khalq faction began arresting, exiling, or murdering Parcham leaders. Babrak Karmal was one of the lucky ones, put out to pasture as ambassador to Czechoslovakia.

The Soviet Union recognized the revolutionary regime immediately after the Saur coup and increased its already heavy military support for the Afghan government. In December 1978 the Russians signed a friendship treaty that pledged "fraternal assistance" against any threats to the regime. The Soviet leaders, however, actually preferred the more moderate Parcham faction, and they began to cultivate Karmal and other deported Afghan communists as a kind of government-in-exile. Meanwhile in Kabul, the regime became even more radical and murderous, when the Khalq leader Hafizullah Amin overthrew his colleague Taraki, killing him in a pistol shootout in September 1979.

Resistance to the Saur regime had appeared immediately throughout Afghanistan and a great number of political parties and factions, ranging from Islamic fundamentalists to moderate liberals, organized just across the border in Peshawar, Pakistan. Within the country, traditional leaders attacked the regime from the right, and more radical, Maoist guerrillas struck from the left. The most significant opposition to the Khalq government was the popular uprising in the city of Herat on March 15, 1979. Mobs lynched fifty Soviet military advisors and their families, publicly torturing them before killing them all. The government retaliated by attacking the city with Soviet-made bombers, slaughtering at least five thousand civilians.

Appalled by the carnage and chaos along their southern border, the Soviet leaders began planning a military intervention like the one they had mounted in Czechoslovakia a decade earlier. The Russian intervention had a two-fold purpose: to impose a more moderate Marxist regime that would be subservient to them, and then to crush the opposition within Afghanistan. The Russians saw Afghanistan as both a threat and an opportunity. In accord with the Brezhnev Doctrine, they believed they could not, for reasons of prestige and security, allow a Marxist regime to be overthrown by non-communists. At the same time, the instability in Afghanistan presented an opportunity to consolidate their long-standing interests in that country and transform it into a full satellite, as in Eastern Europe.

On Christmas Eve 1979, Soviet transports convoyed about four thousand rapid-deployment troops to Kabul airport. Soviet military aid had become so massive by this time that Hafizullah Amin and his government did not realize these troops had come to depose them. Three days later, on December 27, a special team of commandos assassinated Amin; then Soviet troops and tanks poured across the Amu Darya River (more commonly called the Oxus by Europeans) on pontoon bridges and rumbled down the single, Soviet-built highway to Kabul. After consolidating their hold on the capital, the Russians flew in Babrak Karmal from Eastern Europe, imposing him as head of the new regime. By early 1980, Soviet troop strength had grown to about seven full divisions, roughly 85,000 soldiers. This number finally rose to 115,000, assisted by 30-40,000 rapid-deployment troops flown in on special missions from bases in the Soviet republics of central Asia.

Shock, surprise, and the icy winter of the Hindu Kush Mountains prevented any significant resistance in the opening months of the Soviet invasion; but with the spring thaw guerrillas began harassing the Soviet troops, and workers and students mounted a non-violent resistance in the capital and other cities. A strike of Kabul shopkeepers in February turned into a general strike; then in April the "children's revolt" broke out when female high school students, timidly followed by their male compatriots, demonstrated against the regime on the second anniversary of the Saur Revolution. Soviet soldiers gunned down fifty students (thirty of them female), and beat or arrested many more. Eventually the occupying army suppressed all non-violent demonstrations by closing down the high schools and arresting known student leaders several days before each significant revolutionary anniversary. Guerrilla warfare continued in the countryside, however, supported by guns and money from the United States and conservative Muslim countries, smuggled in by way of Pakistan. Eventually the war in Afghanistan cost the Soviet Union about 3 billion dollars per year in the mid-1980s, with the Americans and others pumping in about a half billion each year to the resistance and the United Nations spending another half billion in relief aid.

From the beginning, American observers often compared the Soviet invasion of Afghanistan to the Vietnam War. Neither the terrain nor the geographical situation were similar. Afghanistan is a landlocked country of mountains and deserts, populated by Muslim peasants — more like Algeria, where the French fought a long counterinsurgency campaign, than Vietnam. Yet Russia was sucked into a quagmire in Afghanistan much like the Americans were in Indochina, first offering military aid to an indigenous but unpopular regime, then invading the country, and finally running the show almost completely by themselves. In both cases, resistance proved more tenacious and resourceful than the invaders expected, and the warfare was marked by atrocities. Soviet military strategists cleared large portions of Afghanistan of civilians by repeatedly bombarding strategic regions from helicopter gunships, a policy scholars and journalists termed "migratory genocide." Both interventions lasted about the same period of time, ten years, for the Soviets did not finally withdraw from Afghanistan until February 1989. In neither instance were the invaders defeated militarily, but they made a political decision to cut their losses and attend to more important political matters at home. The Americans in Vietnam and the Russians in Afghanistan were fighting primarily for prestige, trying not to lose face in the seemingly endless round of Cold War skirmishes; but each suffered a devastating defeat in the court of public opinion.

The Russians admitted to 13,833 battlefield deaths in Afghanistan, far fewer than the 58,000 Americans lost in Vietnam. Afghan deaths, however, are estimated anywhere from a half million to a million, and several million more became refugees. Even after the Soviet Union withdrew its troops, the country remained ravaged by civil war, which still continues as I write these words in 1998. The Afghan invasion provides a final, devastating indictment of the Cold War. The Soviets called their armed interventions in other Marxist states "fraternal assistance"; yet they really constituted a smothering and dangerous form of maternal embrace. Anyone who stepped between the Russian bear and her cubs got mauled.

CHAPTER NINETEEN

War on a Small Planet

During the long middle period of the Cold War, as the two superpowers glowered at each other and chastised their own client states, regional conflicts continued to flare up throughout the world. In the Middle East, in particular, Israel and the Arab states fought two full-scale wars in the 1960s and 1970s. The causes of these wars were largely unrelated to the Cold War confrontation, but inevitably the conflicts became entangled in superpower rivalry.

It might be helpful to consider the Arab-Israeli wars through the use of a metaphor. Think of the Middle East as a small neighboring planet, where two hostile groups of people struggle for existence in close quarters and a harsh environment. After winning its independence, the state of Israel stretched from the mountains of Lebanon to the Gulf of Aqaba, which leads out to the Red Sea; but most of its population was wedged into a narrow coastal plain measuring only fourteen kilometers (nine miles) in width at its narrowest point. Artillery could easily lob shells back and forth across the borders, right into the middle of farm communities, and jet fighters could fly over neighboring capital cities in a matter of minutes. Egypt, though the largest of the Arab states, consists mainly of desert, with its population concentrated in the narrow Nile valley. If hostile troops should cross the Suez Canal, separating the Sinai Peninsula from Egypt proper, they would find themselves only about sixty miles from Cairo. On such a small, forbidding planet, wars were fought for high stakes, indeed for survival itself. The Arab-Israeli conflict of the 1960s and 1970s began in a struggle over water resources and ended with an epic battle for oil. Yet the fundamental cause of the conflict was not competition for natural resources, but the coexistence of two powerful nationalisms on a single small planet. Historian Miriam Lowi, in the course of a long study of water resources in the Middle

East, cuts right to the essence of the problem: "It was not simply that the Arab states felt threatened by the presence of Israel on their borders, but more importantly, they did not recognize the legitimacy of a Jewish state in Palestine. . . . The government of Israel, in turn, did not recognize the existence of a Palestinian people with rights to nationhood." (See chapter 9 for background on these competing nationalisms.)

Though small and poor, the Middle Eastern planet was not isolated, but uncomfortably near to the larger planet, Euromerica. The hostile inhabitants of the small planet would have battled each other frequently even if the Cold War had never existed, with sticks and stones if necessary, but their more powerful neighbors aided and abetted them with the most modern and deadly weapons. Furthermore, the lesser planet's battles aggravated the rivalry on the larger world, which even threatened to break into nuclear war at one point. Despite the complexities of this planetary interaction, the responses of all parties proved very simple, elemental, even instinctual. They threatened, bluffed, and blustered, then went to war.

In 1959 Israel began construction of a national water carrier, tapping the fresh water of the Sea of Galilee at the headwaters of the Jordan River, to irrigate the coastal plain and even the distant Negev Desert. Israel, Syria, and Jordan had long wrangled over Jordan River water, and both Arabs and Israelis had used the river for irrigation; but Israel's ambitious project marked the first diversion away from the Jordan Valley itself. This natural resource challenge caught the Arab nations at a moment of deep division. The union between Egypt and Syria in the United Arab Republic fell apart in 1961, and a series of radical regimes linking the military with the pan-Arab Baath (Resurrection) Party seized control in Syria, challenging Egypt's Nasser for leadership of the Arab world. The Hashemite monarchy in Iraq had also fallen to a radical wing of the Baath Party, which feuded with both Syria and Egypt. (See chapters 8 and 10.) Nevertheless, these pan-Arab, socialist regimes often joined, at least verbally, in a cold war of their own against the remaining conservative monarchies in the Arab world — Jordan, Saudi Arabia, and the small Persian Gulf states. The Soviet Union armed and aided the radical Arabs whereas the Americans backed Israel and the conservative Arab monarchies. When a civil war broke out during the early 1960s in Yemen, a desert state at the foot of the Arabian Peninsula, the radical and conservative Arab states took opposing sides.

As the Israeli national water carrier neared completion, President Gamal Abdul Nasser of Egypt called an Arab summit conference to discuss the water diversion. Thirteen kings, emirs, and presidents met in Cairo from January 13 to 17, 1964. The Syrians wanted to go to war over the water issue, but Nasser knew the Arabs were militarily unprepared. Instead, he won conference approval for a competing water diversion plan which would provide irrigation water to Syria and Jordan and slowly salt up the Sea of Galilee, depriving Israel of its use. The summit leaders also proposed a joint Arab military command and pledged to end their discords and meet frequently in the future. Arab divisions remained, however, and the protracted civil war in Yemen continued, exacerbating the inter-Arab tensions. Israel's water carrier reached the Negev in the summer of 1964, and the Arab water projects languished for lack of capital and equipment. Nasser's summitry had kept the Arab initiative in his own hands and had diverted Syria and the Palestinians from hasty actions, but it had not accomplished anything practical for the Arabs or detrimental to Israel.

At a summit conference in Alexandria, Egypt, in September 1964, the Arab states established the Palestine Liberation Organization (PLO) to give the dispossessed Palestinians a voice in their deliberations. The nearly one million Palestinians displaced from their homes at the birth of Israel, whose numbers doubled in the refugee camps over the next few decades, stood at the center of the Mideast conflict; but the Arab states generally pursued their own interests and agendas and did little for them. The founding of the PLO represented an attempt to control the Palestinians more than assist them, and in its early years it was a relatively tame organization. A more independent Palestinian organization, however, existed side by side with the PLO and eventually took it over. In 1959 a group of well-educated exiles founded *Fatah*, whose name is a reverse acronym for Palestine Liberation Movement. The word also means "victory" in Arabic. The early spokesman and eventual undisputed leader of Fatah was Yasser Arafat, born Abdel-Rahman Abdel-Raouf Arafat al-Qudwa al-Husseini, either in Jerusalem or Gaza in 1929. He was educated as an engineer in Cairo and worked briefly for Kuwait's Ministry of Public Works before devoting himself to national liberation activities.

Largely ignoring the Arab summits and the PLO, Fatah launched a series of commando raids against Israel on January 1, 1965, striking primarily against facilities of the national water carrier from bases in either Syria or Jordan. A year later, in February 1966, another coup in Syria brought an even more radical military regime to power, which afforded full support to Fatah's terrorist campaign. The Israelis, for their part, continued a policy inaugurated by David Ben-Gurion of deliberately overreacting to terrorism with massive reprisal raids of their own. One such reprisal, against a Jordanian village on November 13, 1966, backfired when it led to a condemnation of Israel by the United Nations Security Council. In April 1967, Syrian artillery shelled farm kibbutzes near the border, and Israeli Mirage jets battled Syrian MiG's over the outskirts of Damascus. The Arabs interpreted several strong Israeli statements in May 1967 as a threat to launch a preemptive attack upon Syria. A general regional war was becoming likely.

Unwilling to be upstaged by the militant Syrians and Palestinians, or to appear insensitive to their danger, Egypt's Nasser again stepped forward. On May 16, 1967, he demanded that the United Nations peacekeeping force that had separated Egypt's Sinai Peninsula from Israel since the Suez crisis of 1956 be withdrawn so that he could move his troops right up to the border. Most evidence suggests that Nasser was just bluffing, trying to scare the Israelis into stopping their reprisal raids against Syria and Jordan, and that he would have welcomed a compromise allowing some UN troops to remain. However, U Thant, the UN secretary-general, surprised him by acceding to his withdrawal request. The Israelis had complicated U Thant's position by refusing permission for UN troops to patrol on their side of the border, so when the secretary-general granted Nasser's request no peacekeepers remained between the two opposing sides. Having come so far, Nasser then upped the ante by establishing a blockade of the Strait of Tiran, at the entrance from the Gulf of Aqaba to the Red Sea. A pro-Israeli historian, Eric Hammel, has noted: "It is a virtual certainty that Nasser did not *intend* to go to war ... but he *did* intend to seize back from Syria the moral leadership of the Arab nation." On the small planet of the Middle East, the Arabs were engaged in two cold wars of their own, one against the Israelis and the other among themselves.

In such close quarters, the Israelis did not believe they could wait out Nasser's bluff. Their population was small, so if they mobilized all their reserves for defense the country's economy would grind to a halt in little over a week. Furthermore, their territory was so constricted that they enjoyed no strategic depth. Unlike the Russians in the world wars, they could not absorb an attack by withdrawing and fighting a war of attrition. Finally, the memory of the Holocaust made every Israeli life precious and turned every battle into a war for survival. For all these reasons, therefore, Israeli military doctrine dictated taking the battle to their opponents. The U.S. government understood the Israeli position. Preoccupied with Vietnam, President Lyndon Johnson tried to dissuade them from attacking the Arabs, but eventually he signaled a "yellow light" which meant, in effect, "go ahead, but don't count on us if you get in trouble." As political scientist William Quandt has noted, "for most motorists, the yellow light was tantamount to a green one." On June 5, 1967, the Israeli air force launched preemptive attacks that set off the third Arab-Israeli war.

The Egyptians were not caught sleeping, but they were surprised. Every morning for weeks, Israeli jets had taken off from the Negev Desert, then disappeared over the Mediterranean Sea for maneuvers. Just as regularly, the Egyptians scrambled their fighter squadrons at dawn. On June 5, this aerial two-step was repeated, and by 8:30 A.M. Cairo time (7:30 in Israel) all the Egyptian jets had returned to their bases and the pilots headed in for breakfast. However, the Israeli pilots were not flying maneuvers that day. At 8:45 the first wave of attackers swept in low from the Mediterranean, under the Egyptian radar coverage. Diving in pairs onto the airfields, fighter-bombers gouged the runways with explosives on their first pass then unleashed missile salvos and machine-gun fire against the parked airplanes on subsequent runs. Each wave of jets remained over their targets for seven minutes before returning to their bases. Flying time was so short on this small planet that the attackers could make a round trip, including a stop for rearming and refueling, in about an hour. Within just three hours of the opening attack, thirteen of the eighteen Egyptian airfields were inoperative. The Israelis destroyed the rest of the bases before midnight. More than 250 Egyptian planes were destroyed and over 100 pilots killed, whereas the Israelis lost only 19 of their own planes. Similar, though smaller-scale, raids destroyed the tiny force of 20 Jordanian jet fighters and at least 50 Syrian MiGs. Though hard ground fighting continued over the next six days, the outcome of the war was settled in these first few hours when the Israelis won absolute control of the skies.

With air supremacy assured, Israel's military enjoyed the luxury of picking off its enemies one at a time. Jordan's army was well trained and professional but very small, whereas Syria's was large but ill disciplined and undependable. The Syrians, moreover, were dug into defensive positions along the Golan Heights, posing no immediate threat. Therefore, the Israelis directed their first ground attacks against the Egyptian forces in the Sinai Peninsula. The two sides enjoyed roughly equal numbers of front-line troops, and the Egyptians actually possessed greater firepower, but without air support their tanks became metal coffins. Israeli armor spearheads penetrated deeply into the Sinai on several fronts, and General Ariel Sharon's division performed a technically complicated assault on the major Egyptian fortress complex. As historian Howard Sachar has noted: "The operation was to become known as a classic of tactics, and in ensuing years would be studied in military academies throughout the world."

Field Marshal Abdel Hakim Amer, the Egyptian commander in chief and a close personal friend of President Nasser, had been caught in the air on a routine reconnaissance during the preemptive strike. Back on the ground, he apparently fell apart as the scope of the Israeli attack became clear. On the morning of the second day, June 6, he ordered all Egyptian ground units to withdraw from the Sinai, back across the Suez Canal. The Israelis, however, raced the retreating Egyptians to the strategic Mitla and Gidi Passes that control the entrance and exit from the Sinai. A handful of Israeli tanks pushed eighty miles in twenty-four hours, along the same congested roads and tracks the Egyptians were using, to reach the Mitla Pass in the evening of June 7. With timely assistance from the air force, they choked off the Egyptian retreat at this bottleneck. However, the Gidi Pass remained open and many Egyptian soldiers retreated safely, leaving behind much of their equipment. In fact, only about a hundred of the estimated thousand Egyptian tanks in Sinai made it back across the Suez Canal.

The Israelis had not originally intended an advance all the way to the canal. In fact, Defense Minister Moshe Dayan repeatedly warned his commanders not to go near it, fearing that an approach to the international waterway would trigger unwelcome warnings from the superpowers. However, in the midst of the Egyptian collapse and withdrawal, individual commanders found the canal line irresistible, and Dayan eventually stopped trying to restrain them. By June 8, when the Egyptians accepted a cease-fire, Israeli forces controlled nearly the whole east bank of the Suez Canal.

Jordan would have been well advised to stay out of this war, but King Hussein had promised President Nasser that his forces would participate, and he kept his word. Neither side committed great numbers of troops on this front, but both Jordan and Israel sought an important political-symbolic goal, the unification of Jerusalem. The 1949 partition of Palestine had divided Jerusalem, a city holy to three world religions, into an Arab eastern sector and an Israeli-controlled western portion. The holy places — the al-Aqsa mosque, the Western Wall of Herod's Temple, and the Via Dolorosa — all lay in the Old City of East Jerusalem, under Arab control. At the beginning of the war, on the afternoon of June 5, Jordan's army captured a strategic ridge overlooking the city; but the Israelis took it back almost immediately, then began sealing off the city from outside attack. Small armored companies seized control of the hills surrounding Jerusalem, and the air force destroyed or disabled most of the Jordanian tanks approaching from the east. With the war going so well on the Sinai front and the Jordanians helpless to relieve Jerusalem, the Israeli cabinet on June 7 authorized the occupation of East Jerusalem, but without the benefit of air or artillery fire, so as not to damage the holy places. One of the few religious believers in the elite parachute brigade reached the Western Wall first, where he was soon joined in prayer by rabbis and politicians. In the meantime, the Israelis had also improvised a series of strikes into the Jordanian West Bank, and by June 7 the Arab defenders were in full flight across the Jordan River. King Hussein accepted a cease-fire on the evening of June 7, with Israel in firm control of Jerusalem and the entire West Bank.

Having knocked Egypt and Jordan out of the war, Israel could now direct attention to the Syrian front. The Golan Heights dominated the border between Syria and Israel and from this escarpment the Syrians had long rained artillery fire down on kibbutzes and villages below. In order to reduce the formidable defenses on the heights, the Israelis directed their entire air force against the Golan on the morning of June 9. With the defenders pinned down in their bunkers, five Israeli columns moved up the heights, probing for weak spots in a series of flexible attacks that could be exploited or broken off as circumstances dictated. The difference between Israeli and Arab tactics showed most clearly on the Syrian front. The Israeli commanders valued boldness, flexibility, and

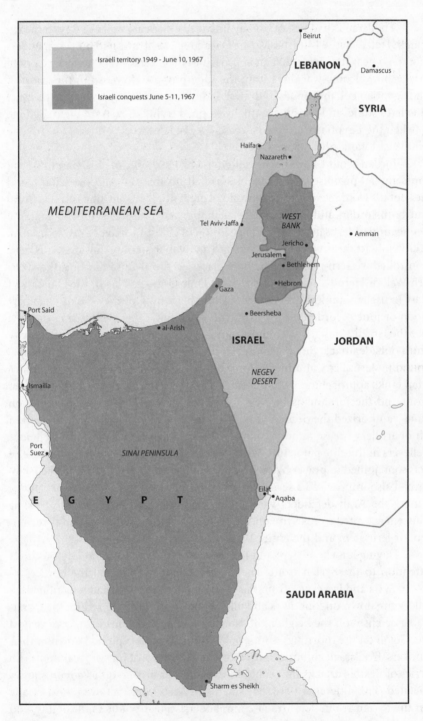

Greater Israel after the 1967 War

maneuverability above all, whereas the Syrians adhered to a more rigid, defensive doctrine. Individual Syrian units did not come to each other's aid for they had been ordered to defend a fixed zone, and the higher commanders were confused by the multiple attacks and did not know where to commit their reserves. By the end of June 10, the Israelis controlled the entire Golan Heights and Syria accepted a cease-fire.

The June 1967 war lasted just six days and resulted in a total victory for Israel over three neighboring Arab countries. The combined Arab losses totaled about 18,000 killed, whereas Israel suffered between 750 and 800 fatalities. Egypt, Jordan, and Syria lost their entire air forces and most of their tanks. Israel expanded its borders dramatically, occupying the vast expanse of the Sinai Desert up to the Suez Canal, the Golan Heights overlooking Syria, the West Bank of the Jordan Valley, and the entire city of Jerusalem. During the Egyptian campaign, Israel also captured the strongpoint commanding the Strait of Tiran and reopened that waterway to its shipping. In the course of its victory, Israel had unwittingly become an empire, acquiring political responsibility for about a million Palestinian Arab subjects in the occupied territories. The Six Day War pointed up Arab disunity and weakness and overcame any lingering feelings of inferiority in Israel, which now looked invincible.

The Israeli preemptive air strike and lightning ground attacks astounded the world. The war ended so quickly that the great powers did not get involved beyond requesting the United Nations to secure cease-fires on each of the fronts in turn. Using the hotline installed after the Cuban missile crisis, the Americans and the Russians coordinated their peacekeeping activity in the UN Security Council. Following up on his yellow light warning, President Johnson imposed an arms embargo on the Middle East and resisted Israeli requests for more weapons and ammunition. The Soviet Union did not support this embargo, but the war ended so quickly that re-supply of the Arabs proved impossible until after the fighting ceased.

Arabs everywhere felt deeply humiliated by the crushing defeat of June 1967. Nasser himself announced his resignation as president of Egypt on June 9, right after accepting the cease-fire in Sinai and while fighting still raged on the other fronts. The people of Cairo, however, rushed into the streets chanting Nasser's name and the Egyptian national assembly refused to accept his resignation. Journalist John Bulloch pointed out: "Without Nasser at that time, Egypt would have been lost. . . . Nasser was able to do things others would have found impossible: chief of these was his decision to establish just what had happened in the 1967 war." He discovered that the Egyptian military had been riddled with corruption and incompetence, and he forced his friend Field Marshal Amer to resign. When a cabal of officers plotted to reinstate the marshal, Nasser crushed their conspiracy and Amer committed suicide. One of Nasser's political associates, Anwar Sadat, remarked coldly: "It's the best decision Amer has taken as commander. . . . If I were him I would have done it on June 5."

The president of the Soviet Union, Nikolai Podgorny, visited Cairo two weeks after the war and affirmed his government's continued support for the Arabs. Though the Russians were skeptical of the Arabs' ability ever to win a war against Israel, they immediately replaced the military equipment that Egypt and Syria had lost, even providing newer and more deadly models of weapons. Nasser somewhat reluctantly met the other Arab heads of state at a summit conference in Khartoum, Sudan, at the end of August 1967. Crowds in the streets continued hailing him as a hero, and in the conference hall he won crucial financial support from the Arab oil states. Kuwait, Saudi Arabia, and Libya pledged to support the postwar reconstruction of Egypt and Jordan with an annual subsidy of 135 million pounds sterling. This marked the first significant political use of Arab oil wealth and a startling reconciliation between Nasser and the conservative monarchies. The Egyptian president had paved the way for this détente by withdrawing his troops from the smoldering civil war in Yemen.

The Khartoum conference ended with a ringing statement of three no's — no negotiations with Israel, no recognition of Israel, and no peace with Israel. Back in Egypt, Nasser then unleashed the War of Attrition, constantly shelling the Israeli positions on the east bank of the Suez Canal and mounting small-scale attacks into the Sinai. Israel, of course, retaliated with its superior airpower, launching deep penetration raids right into the heart of Egypt. Civilians suffered numerous casualties and Egypt's forces got much the worse of the fighting during the War of Attrition, yet the struggle wore down Israel as well. Over the next three years, from 1967 to 1970, Israel suffered more casualties in the Sinai than it had during the Six Day War. Many historians label the War of Attrition the fourth Arab-Israeli War.

Nasser, however, pursued a more flexible policy than the three no's and the War of Attrition might indicate. His government accepted United Nations Resolution 242 of November 1967 as a basis for discussion. Resolution 242 called for "withdrawal of Israeli armed forces from territories occupied in the recent conflict" and "acknowledgment of the sovereignty, territorial integrity, and political independence of every State in the area and their right to live in peace, within secure and recognized boundaries free from threats or acts of force." Though somewhat ambiguous, the resolution implied that the Arab-Israeli conflict could be settled if Israel would trade land for peace, withdrawing from its occupied territories in exchange for recognition by the Arabs and security guarantees from the great powers. Nasser might ultimately have accepted this deal, but first he wanted to rearm and unite the Arab nations so that he could deal from strength. The Soviet Union had provided Egypt with the latest models of SAM, ground-to-air missiles, but Nasser was unable to move them up to the Suez Canal while the War of Attrition raged across that waterway. Therefore, in August 1970 he accepted an American proposal for a cease-fire, and Israel followed suit. Nasser's aide, Abdel Magid Farid, has recently revealed what many suspected at the time: that Nasser accepted the cease-fire primarily so he could move the new anti-aircraft missiles into place along the Canal.

Israel, meanwhile, had built a complicated series of fortifications along and behind the Suez Canal, called the Bar-Lev line for Chief of Staff Chaim Bar-Lev. The Israeli military kept only small numbers of troops in the fortifications, relying on them to slow down invaders while they mobilized their airplanes and tanks for a counterattack. Finally enjoying some strategic depth, Israel could afford to give ground in an initial attack since the Sinai Desert was virtually unpopulated. Indeed the strategic situation had now reversed itself on the small Mideast planet. Nasser bluntly told the Soviets on one occasion: "You withdrew to the Volga River. For us, there is no Volga. There are only 100 kilometers behind these positions before the center of Cairo is reached." Israel's strategy made sense for a nation with military superiority but limited manpower; however, it unwittingly imparted a defensive turn of mind and reinforced Israeli complacency.

With the battle lines frozen at the Suez Canal and no prospect of ousting Israel in sight, a ferment of change bubbled through the Arab world. Yet another military coup in Syria brought air force general Hafez al-Assad to power. With Assad the revolving door at the top of Syria's government stopped turning, for the Syrian president remains in power at the end of the century. Assad is just as authoritarian and anti-Israel as any other Syrian leader, but considerably more intelligent and pragmatic, well aware of the need for Arab unity. Coups also toppled conservative governments in Sudan and Libya. The Sudanese leader Colonel Jaafar Numeiry became a staunch ally of Egypt's, but Libya's Muammar Gaddafi proved something of a loose cannon. Nasser indulged him, saying, "You remind me of myself when I was young," but did not trust him as an ally.

Palestinians realized after the Six Day War that the Arab states were unable, and perhaps unwilling, to do much for their cause, so they began relying more on their own resources. Yasser Arafat and a group of Fatah activists infiltrated the occupied West Bank right after the war ended, trying to raise a full-scale uprising. Israeli authorities, however, detained more than a thousand suspects and demolished the homes of guerrilla sympathizers. Arafat, therefore, called off the abortive guerrilla campaign at the end of 1967 and reverted to the usual hit-and-run commando raids. In March 1968, an Israeli reprisal on the Jordanian village of Karameh unexpectedly gave the Palestinian cause a new lease on life. A column of fifteen thousand Israeli soldiers marched against the

369

village but was ambushed by about three hundred Palestinian guerrillas, backed by the artillery of the Jordanian army. The Israelis withdrew after suffering relatively heavy losses. "Karameh" means "dignity" or "honor" in Arabic, and the Palestinians believed they had won back their dignity in this battle. Fatah's volunteer fighting strength soared from only about two thousand militants to more than fifteen thousand within three months of Karameh. A year later, in February 1969, Fatah took over the PLO by electing Yasser Arafat chairman of the organization. Nasser had already made Arafat a protegé, taking him along to Moscow in July 1968.

The growing prestige and activity of the Palestinian guerrillas posed a major challenge to Jordan's King Hussein, whose kingdom was divided between a native Bedouin population and a nearly equal number of Palestinian refugees. Arafat could not control all the splinter groups of guerrillas, many of whom wished to overthrow Hussein and take over his kingdom. After an unsuccessful assassination attempt, Hussein reluctantly decided to crush the Palestinian "state within a state." Had he not done so, his own military might have toppled him. In September 1970, the Jordanian army ruthlessly smashed the camps of armed Palestinians, setting off a brief civil war. Nasser hastily summoned an Arab summit conference and won a Jordanian cease-fire, but he died of a heart attack the day the conference ended, September 28, 1970.

To the outside world, the Arabs seemed divided, weak, and mindlessly violent. Splinter groups of Palestinian terrorists, calling themselves Black September in memory of their defeat in Jordan, mounted random attacks on airplanes and murdered Israeli athletes at the 1972 Olympic Games in Munich. Yet important changes had occurred in the Arab world. Though not yet ready to say so publicly, some Arabs would probably recognize Israel if its military withdrew from the occupied territories back to the pre-1967 borders. After the Six Day War Arafat's Fatah had redefined its ultimate goal from "the liberation of Palestine," which meant the extinction of Israel, to the establishment of a "secular, democratic state" in Palestine, open to Muslims, Christians, and Jews alike. Later, in 1974, the Fatah-dominated PLO simply called for the establishment of "a Palestinian national authority in any Palestinian areas liberated from Israeli control." These changes meant that the leading Palestinian organization had adopted a realistic, nationalist goal, the erection of their own national state side by side with the Jewish national state. Israel and the rest of the world largely ignored this change, but the Palestinians were putting forth a negotiable goal, rather than an impossible dream.

At the same time that the Palestinians were becoming more realistic, the Arab states were coming together. Nasser had begun to heal the rift between conservative and radical states, winning the financial support of the oil monarchies and literally dying to make peace between King Hussein and the Palestinian guerrillas. His successor, Anwar Sadat, completed the work of forging an alliance of all Arabs against Israel. Sadat was one of the original Free Officers who overthrew the Egyptian monarchy in 1952. Born in a peasant village but raised in the city of Cairo, his social background was strikingly similar to Nasser's. Though he had held a series of high offices in the Egyptian regime, few observers took Sadat seriously. Indeed, his fawning loyalty to Nasser earned him the nickname "Colonel Yes-Yes." Nasser had named Sadat vice president in 1969, seemingly on a whim, as he went off to an Arab summit conference where he feared he might be assassinated; yet it was unclear if he really meant to anoint him as successor. In any case, Nasser died before he could sort out the succession question and Sadat ascended to the presidency, hemmed in by other Nasser loyalists intent on running the government behind the scenes.

In May 1971, President Sadat staged a bloodless preemptive coup against his opponents in the government, dismissing his vice president, Ali Sabry, and other officials inherited from Nasser. He now felt free to pursue his own policies. Most importantly, he was determined to end the situation of "no war, no peace" between the Arabs and the Israelis. He dramatically announced that 1971 was the "Year of Decision" in which Egypt would either make peace with Israel or go to war against her. However, neither the Israelis nor the Americans took him seriously, feeling no sense of urgency to end the status quo. The Soviets, for their part, also underestimated Sadat and did not believe he was capable of challenging Israel. So 1971 passed with no decision, and Sadat looked like a fool. In July 1972 he unexpectedly expelled all the Soviet advisors who had swarmed over Egypt in previous years, a move wildly popular in Cairo. This action further misled the Israelis and Americans who believed that Egypt was incapable of military action on its own.

In May 1973, Anwar Sadat traveled secretly to Riyadh for a key meeting with King Feisal of Saudi Arabia. Feisal, whose kingdom was based on religion and oil, felt the loss of the holy places in Jerusalem very keenly and was willing to use his country's oil resources as a weapon to regain the lost territory. He pledged financial support to Egypt and a cutback in oil sales to Israel's allies as his country's contribution to a future war. By this time, Sadat had united all the Arab states, except Libya and Iraq, whose leaders he did not trust, behind a decision to attack Israel. The Arabs hoped that by ending the military stalemate in the Middle East they would force the Israelis to negotiate seriously and finally withdraw from the territories occupied in 1967.

Presidents Sadat of Egypt and Assad of Syria coordinated their military plans very closely, finally choosing October 6, 1973, as the day of attack. Since October 6 was Yom Kippur, the holiest day in the Jewish calendar, the two presidents hoped to catch the Israelis off guard. Yet they must also have been aware that their own troops would not be at peak condition, since October 6 fell within Ramadan, the Muslim month of fasting. In the final analysis, the usual military considerations of weather and phases of the moon proved decisive in choosing this date. Sadat and Assad kept their plans completely secret and disguised their war preparations with a series of deceptions. Twice during 1973 Egyptian troops massed near the Suez Canal and Israel mobilized its reserves, but nothing happened. When Egyptian forces advanced to the canal again in October, the Israeli military thought it was just another ruse. Also, Palestinian terrorists hijacked a trainload of Russian Jewish immigrants in Austria during September 1973. When Israel threatened reprisals, Syria and Egypt moved more troops toward the border. The Israelis misinterpreted these movements as defensive measures dictated by the heightened tensions. Even the one serious disagreement between Sadat and Assad worked in their favor. The Egyptian military originally planned the attack for sunset, when Israeli defenders would be blinded looking to the west, but the Syrians, who would be attacking from the east, wanted to jump off at dawn. They finally compromised and scheduled the H-hour for two in the afternoon. Israeli intelligence picked up reports of the original sunset time, so they were not prepared when the attack came at 2:00 P.M. on October 6.

Syrian tanks advanced in force across the Golan Heights on October 6, but desperate Israeli defenders, relying on hit-and-run tank attacks and superior air power, managed to stop them before they advanced into Israel proper. Three days later, Israel mounted a counterattack that threw the Syrians back off the Golan. The Egyptians, meanwhile, surprised the defenders of the Sinai Peninsula with a daring crossing of the Suez Canal which the Israelis did not believe them capable of. First, commandos plugged up the spigots that were supposed to spew flaming napalm over the waters of the canal, then about eight thousand elite troops crossed in small boats and scrambled up ladders over the sand ramparts on the east bank. Some of these soldiers attacked the undermanned fortresses of the Bar-Lev line with flame-throwers, but most bypassed the forts, waiting for the Israeli tanks to come forward. They surprised the tank commanders by firing brand new, Soviet-made hand-held missile launchers, swiftly destroying the Israeli spearhead and leaving the east bank open to a full-scale invasion. Within twenty-four hours Egyptian engineers, working under the cover of advanced Soviet anti-aircraft missiles, had thrown portable bridges across the canal, allowing tanks and heavy artillery to cross. They then blasted holes in the sand ramparts with high-pressure water hoses. Within three days, the Egyptians had moved two full armies across the canal and consolidated control of a ten-mile-wide strip on the east bank. Initial Israeli counterattacks failed.

Military observers have often remarked that Egypt should have advanced all the way to the Mitla and Gidi Passes in those initial days of the war. However, the Egyptian generals still held a healthy respect for Israeli air power and felt reluctant to advance beyond the range of their anti-aircraft batteries. Unlike Israel at the beginning of the Six Day War, they had not destroyed the enemy's air force upon initiating hostilities. Furthermore, Sadat's war aims remained political, rather than purely military, so he did not believe he had to advance his troops very far or fast to make his point. By the time Egypt's troops moved toward the passes, on October 14, a week after the war started, the Israelis had fully mobilized their armored battalions. The largest tank battle since World War II ended in an Egyptian defeat. Now the Israelis boldly counterattacked. Finding a lightly guarded seam on the boundary between the two Egyptian armies, General Ariel Sharon recklessly pushed his troops across the Suez Canal at the Great Bitter Lake. The Egyptians, overconfident after their initial successes, did not immediately realize the seriousness of the crossing, thinking it only a commando raid. By the time they reacted, the Israelis had reinforced their beachhead so they could fight off all attempts to throw them back. By October 20, the Israelis were rapidly taking control of the west bank of the canal, cutting off the Egyptian Third Army in the southern Sinai on the east bank.

President Assad of Syria had wanted a cease-fire after only a few days of battle, but Anwar Sadat resisted all pleas to stop fighting until October 21, when the precariousness of his troops' positions finally became evident. The next day, the UN Security Council passed a resolution calling for a cease-fire within twelve hours. Both sides accepted the resolution verbally but violated it in practice. A second cease-fire resolution finally took hold at 5:00 P.M. on October 24. Israel had suffered three times as many battle fatalities in 1973 as it had in 1967 (about 2,500); Arab losses were fewer (about 10,000 dead compared to 18,000). Yet in purely military terms, Israel had turned initial setbacks into a victory. Israeli troops held more Syrian territory on the Golan Heights at the end of the war than they had at the beginning, and they secured an enormous foothold on the west bank of the Suez Canal, marooning an entire Egyptian army and threatening Cairo. Still, the initial Arab victories, especially the surprise crossing of the Suez Canal by Egyptian forces, won back a great deal of pride and respect that had been lost in the Six Day War. World opinion turned about so completely that early in the war, with Israeli spokesmen still predicting an easy victory, some journalists proclaimed that the Israelis had learned to lie like the Arabs but the Arabs had learned to fight like the Israelis.

The Arabs had also learned to stick together. Egypt and Syria bore the brunt of the fighting, but ten other Arab states sent token military contingents to the two fronts. More importantly, King Feisal of Saudi Arabia kept his pledge to unleash the oil weapon. On October 16, just as the war was turning around in Israel's favor, six member states of the Organization of Petroleum Exporting Countries (OPEC) met in Kuwait to coordinate strategy. OPEC had been founded in September 1960 by the major oil-exporting nations in an attempt to win a greater share of oil profits from the international corporations that controlled the trade. They had not enjoyed much success during their first decade, due mainly to a worldwide oil glut that depressed prices. By the time of the October 1973 war, however, demand in the industrial nations had soaked up excess supply and begun putting upward pressure on prices, setting the stage for the oil shocks of the 1970s.

On October 16 the OPEC meeting in Kuwait raised the posted price of oil by 70 percent, to over five dollars per barrel. The oil minister from Iran then withdrew and the Arab members of OPEC took a purely political action, cutting their oil production by 5 percent and vowing to continue cutting it 5 percent per month until the Arab-Israeli conflict was settled to their liking. Saudi Arabia and a few other countries increased the initial shock by cutting production by 10 percent immediately, rather than 5 percent. Finally, the Arab oil states decreed a total embargo of oil to the United States and any other country that backed Israel. Together, the embargo, the cutbacks, and price increases set off a consumer panic in the United States, Japan, and Western Europe at the end of 1973. The initial military successes of the Arabs might not have been sufficient to force serious negotiations and possible concessions from Israel and her superpower supporter, the United States, but in conjunction with the oil weapon they served as a wake-up call, which is what Anwar Sadat intended.

The two superpowers had been cautiously edging towards détente in the early 1970s, and both found the Mideast status quo of "no war, no peace" after the June 1967 war suited their interests. The Soviets kept the Arab states well supplied with weapons but had no faith in their fighting ability, so they did not encourage them to go to war. A peace settlement, on the other hand, would reduce the need for Soviet support and thus reduce Soviet influence in the Arab world. The United States government, for its part, supplied advanced weapons to the Israelis and felt satisfied that the strategic depth provided by the occupied territories was more important than a peace treaty. They cautioned Israel, however, not to launch a preemptive attack a second time if they wanted to keep American support. Richard Nixon and Henry Kissinger, therefore, let Middle East policy drift after the 1970 cease-fire in the War of Attrition, consistently underestimated Anwar Sadat, and were completely surprised by the Yom Kippur attack on Israel. The leaders of the Soviet Union knew about the Arab attack in advance, but they were just as surprised as the Israelis and the Americans at the initial Arab successes.

At first, the Russians called for a quick cease-fire, while the Arabs were winning, but the Americans stalled until Israel could counterattack. Then, when the Arabs started losing but showed their ability to brandish the oil weapon, both the United States and the Soviet Union pushed for a cease-fire.

Henry Kissinger flew to Moscow at the suggestion of Russian ambassador Anatoly Dobrynin on the weekend of October 20-21 and worked out the terms of the UN resolution with Leonid Brezhnev and the other Soviet leaders. Resolution 338, passed by the Security Council, called for an end to the fighting and an immediate start of direct negotiations aimed at a "just and durable peace settlement" along the lines of the previous Resolution 242, whereby Israel would trade the occupied territories for recognition and peace.

Shortly after Kissinger returned to Washington, with the Mideast armies still resisting the cease-fire, one of the most curious incidents of the Cold War took place, showing how events on a small neighboring planet could have dangerous repercussions for the larger world. Anwar Sadat wanted both Russians and Americans to send troops or observers to police the cease-fire, and the Russians were ready to oblige. The United States, on the other hand, declined direct involvement and asked the UN to send peacekeepers from neutral states. On the evening of October 24, General Secretary Brezhnev sent a sharp note to the American government strongly urging joint superpower action to ensure an end to the fighting. In order to emphasize the urgency of the matter, Brezhnev included the following sentence in his note: "I will say it straight that if you find it impossible to act jointly with us in this matter, we should be faced with the necessity urgently to consider taking appropriate steps unilaterally."

There is no evidence the Russians were threatening war. Yet Henry Kissinger, who was virtually running the U.S. government while President Nixon dealt with the political consequences of the Watergate break-in, convinced the National Security Council to place American forces worldwide on a heightened state of alert, known as Defense Condition III (Defcon III). Nuclear-armed missiles and bombers were standing by for a possible retaliation against any Soviet moves in the Mideast, and the world stood closer to nuclear war than at any time since the Cuban missile crisis. Kissinger may have known there was no threat but was simply acting tough for domestic political consumption and to show the world that Watergate had not weakened U.S. resolve. It seems likely that if President Nixon were in full control of his own government he would probably not have approved the alert. Fortunately, Brezhnev chose to ignore the American nuclear alert and not inflame the situation further. However unwise the wording of his communiqué threatening unilateral action, he had good reason for concern. Though Kissinger had signed an understanding in Moscow that both the United States and the Soviet Union would actively participate in Mideast peace negotiations, he consistently cut the Russians out of the proceedings over the next several years.

The two superpowers jointly convened a general peace conference on December 21, 1973, but at American urging it adjourned after only one day of empty, symbolic speeches and never reconvened. In the first part of 1974 Secretary of State Henry Kissinger engaged in one-man "shuttle diplomacy," conveying proposals back and forth between Tel Aviv and Cairo, and later between Tel Aviv and Damascus. As a result, Israel and Egypt signed a disengagement agreement on January 18, 1974, whereby the two forces withdrew several miles from each other's positions in the Sinai. At Anwar Sadat's urging, the Arab states terminated the oil embargo and production cutbacks on March 18, 1974. Meanwhile, Kissinger flew to Moscow once more and stonewalled the Russians when they tried to convince him to reconvene the Geneva conference and hammer out a comprehensive settlement for the Mideast. Instead, he continued his shuttle diplomacy and finally secured a disengagement agreement between Syria and Israel on May 31, 1974. Richard Nixon took advantage of Kissinger's successful diplomacy to indulge in a final round of foreign visits during the month of June 1974. He was greeted like a hero in Cairo. Just two months later, on August 9, 1974, the threat of impeachment for Watergate-related offenses forced Nixon to resign. Kissinger remained secretary of state under Nixon's successor, Gerald Ford, and he secured one further agreement between Egypt and Israel whereby the Israelis pulled their troops back even farther, beyond the Mitla and Gidi Passes. The October 1973 war and its diplomatic aftermath had restored a rough balance of forces in the Mideast, with UN peacekeepers separating the Arabs and the Israelis, but no overall peace settlement was in sight.

Anwar Sadat made one further, heroic effort to end the Arab-Israeli conflict by flying to Jerusalem in November 1977 and personally pleading for an overall settlement before the Israeli legislature. Nothing immediately came of his initiative, but in September 1978 President Ford's successor, Jimmy Carter, invited Sadat and Israeli prime minister Menachem Begin to meet with him at his private retreat, Camp David, Maryland. Carter practiced a short-distance version of shuttle diplomacy, passing messages back and forth between Begin and Sadat, who rarely met together during the nearly two weeks they were sequestered. At the end of the bargaining, the Americans announced that both sides had agreed to the Camp David accords. After further details were refined, Begin and Sadat signed a peace treaty at the White House on March 26, 1979. Over the next three years, the Israelis withdrew all their troops from the Sinai Peninsula and Egypt recovered sovereignty over the territory it had lost in the 1967 war. However, the Egyptian-Israeli treaty fell far short of a comprehensive settlement of the Arab-Israeli conflict, for neither Jordan nor Syria participated in the negotiations and neither recovered their occupied territories from Israel. Sadat tried hard to gain concessions for the Palestinians in the Camp David accords, but could only win some vague language about possibly increased autonomy on the West Bank and in the Gaza Strip. In the end, Anwar Sadat settled for a separate peace with Israel; and even this cost him his life. Extremist members of the Muslim Brotherhood in Egypt assassinated him on October 6, 1981.

Two full-scale Mideast wars, plus the intervening War of Attrition, provide vivid examples of "new complexities but old responses" in the twentieth century. Israel's daring preemptive strike in June 1967 and its brilliant military tactics in both wars won it more territory but no greater security. Historian Frank Aker concluded that "one of the world's most militarily competent nations ironically is proving to be one of the world's most politically incompetent." Egypt and Syria's military comeback in the October 1973 war gained some revenge and an increase in Arab pride and self-respect, but would have resulted in a second defeat had it not been for superpower intervention that forced a cease-fire. Both superpowers were caught flat-footed by the initiatives of Israel in 1967 and the Arabs in 1973. Brezhnev's and Kissinger's heavy-handed diplomacy and President Nixon's distraction by his own personal political problems in 1973 led the world into a nuclear alert that could have had disastrous consequences.

The Arabs did attempt some original political initiatives, most obviously the Arab oil embargo and Sadat's heroic bid for a comprehensive peace. OPEC would brandish the oil weapon repeatedly in the 1970s, eventually bumping the price of oil up to a high of thirty-two dollars per barrel by 1980, ten times higher than its price a decade earlier. Eventually, however, new sources of supply and the inability of OPEC to enforce its own policies on its member states blunted the impact of the oil shocks. By the end of the century, oil prices had reverted to very moderate levels. Thanks to the courage of President Sadat, Egypt won a separate peace for itself, permitting it to divert some of its military spending to peaceful projects. Both Sadat of Egypt and the mainstream Palestinian leadership had abandoned the unrealistic position of not admitting Israel's existence. Yet neither the superpowers nor Israel responded creatively by recognizing the right of the Palestinian people to their own nation-state. As a result, the core issue at the heart of the Arab-Israeli conflict, the status of the Palestinians, remained unresolved.

Thanks to Kissinger's maneuverings and their own clumsiness, the Soviets became largely irrelevant in the Mideast after the Yom Kippur War. Kissinger, for his part, never understood nor sympathized with the cause of Palestinian nationalism, and he was irritated by the symbolic gains the Palestine Liberation Organization made after October 1973. An Arab summit at Rabat, Morocco, in October 1974, unanimously endorsed the PLO as the sole legitimate representative of the Palestinian people. Two weeks later, on November 13, 1974, Yasser Arafat appeared before the United Nations and his organization was granted permanent observer status at the world body. In Israel, however, a conservative political coalition led by Menachem Begin came to power in 1977, and thereafter the Israelis steadfastly refused to consider trading land for peace. Over a decade was lost in old responses to the new complexity of growing Palestinian nationalism and increasing Arab realism. Not until after Begin's coalition had left office, the superpower Cold War had ended, and the Palestinians had mounted an uprising in the Israeli-occupied territories, was further progress possible toward peace on a small neighboring planet.

PART SIX

THE WALLS COME TUMBLING DOWN

The twentieth century had a (relatively) happy ending! In November 1989 the Berlin Wall fell; and shortly thereafter, Communist rule in the Soviet Union and the Eastern European satellite states was terminated. Other symbolic and political walls also tumbled, most notably the apartheid system of racial segregation in South Africa. These revolutionary developments were not the product of incremental reforms; rather they came like an earthquake, in a series of "tectonic shifts," to use the terminology of historian John Lewis Gaddis. Even more unexpectedly, the end-of-the-century changes were nonviolent, for the most part. In Poland, the Soviet Union, South Africa, and the Philippines, moral and spiritual force vanquished military and political power, vindicating the strategies of Mohandas Gandhi and Martin Luther King. To be sure, not all change came peacefully at the end of the twentieth century. The breakup of Communist Yugoslavia led to a bloody civil war, and the various states of Central Africa have been ravaged by genocidal massacres. Yet overall, the most bloody century in human history ended with a remarkable triumph of morality over violence.

Of the "terrible isms" that reigned at the beginning of the century, only nationalism remained potent at the end. Anarchism had long ceased to inspire social or political movements, though it still remained as an undercurrent of protest against organized bigness. Both imperialism and socialism were decisively discredited during the second half of the twentieth century. When the European colonial empires and the Communist imperium crumbled, new or previously submerged national states took their place. At the end of the century, over 185 countries were recognized as members of the United Nations, and more will likely come into existence as large, unwieldy political entities continue to fragment.

Yet despite the centrifugal force of nationalism, large parts of the world also seem to be moving closer together. The end of the Cold War terminated one artificial division between peoples, and the successor states to the Soviet Union are striving to function as "normal" societies, that is, societies similar to those in Western Europe, North America, or East Asia. American popular culture has penetrated the most remote areas of the world, with African and Asian youths proudly wearing T-shirts from U.S. sports teams. Within some regions of the world, economic common markets are bringing formerly hostile peoples together. Europe, which dominated the world politically, economically, and militarily at the beginning of the century, then plunged humanity into two devastating world wars, has again taken the lead at the end of the century, peacefully this time. Unlike the cataclysmic end of the Soviet empire or the apartheid system, the formation of the European Union has been a slow, gradual, sometimes almost imperceptible process. Yet a single European economy has been forged. Elsewhere, free trade areas and measured steps toward political cooperation are also emerging. Federalism is providing an important counterbalance to nationalism. On the verge of the new century, therefore, the world is simultaneously coming apart yet coming together.

CHAPTER TWENTY

The Revolution of Memory and Morality

C ommunism failed in the Soviet Union and Eastern Europe. Journalist David Remnick, in his award-winning book *Lenin's Tomb,* provided a striking metaphor for the death-throes of Soviet Communism:

> In the years after Stalin's death, the state was an old tyrant slouched in the corner with cataracts and gallstones, his muscles gone slack. He wore plastic shoes and a shiny suit that stank of sweat. He hogged all the food and fouled his pants. Mornings, his tongue was coated with the ash-taste of age. He mumbled and didn't care. His thoughts drifted like storm clouds and came clear only a few times a year to recite the old legends of Great October and the Great Patriotic War. . . . The state was nearly senile but dangerous enough. . . . Now and then he had fits and the world trembled.

The United States did not win the Cold War; rather the Soviet Union lost it, for Communist power collapsed economically, environmentally, politically, and above all, morally.

Economic failure was an underlying cause of the Soviet demise. The gross national product of the Soviet Union had increased robustly in the decades after World War II, growing at an average annual rate of 6 percent in the 1950s and 5 percent in the 1960s. When Leonid Brezhnev took power from Nikita Khrushchev in the mid-1960s, he stepped up military spending and tried to buy off whole segments of society. The state granted limousines and summer homes to the top bureaucrats, and the prices of basic household necessities were kept artificially low for ordinary citizens. A stroke of good luck, the Arab oil embargo which raised the price for Soviet exports of crude oil, allowed the Brezhnev deal to continue in the 1970s; but luck ran out when bad harvests and reduced demand for oil slowed economic growth nearly to a halt in 1978. Yet even in comparatively good times, the Soviet economy suffered from distortions and strains. Brezhnev's government reached military parity with the United States, with an overall economy about half the size of America's. Somewhere between 15 to 25 percent of economic production was plowed into the defense sector, leaving too little to satisfy the needs of the Russian people.

Historian Stephen Kotkin lived in Magnitogorsk, Stalin's premier industrial city tucked away in the Ural Mountains, just before the collapse of the Soviet Union and found that people spent at least two hours a day waiting in lines for meager supplies of food and other necessities. Though nearly everyone had a TV and a radio, only 22,000 of the city's 438,000 inhabitants owned private cars, few businesses enjoyed access to computers, and even the public library did not operate a photocopier. Toxic emissions from the steel mills devastated a strip of land 120 miles long and 40 miles wide, where nothing could grow, and at least one-third of the city's people suffered from chronic respiratory diseases. Kotkin summarized the dreary life of Magnitogorsk: "Extended alcoholism, recurrent shortages of consumer goods, a severe housing crisis extending well into the future, a ubiquitous black market, a crumbling or nonexistent urban infrastructure, almost unfathomable pollution, and a health catastrophe impossible to exaggerate — such was the predicament of this once-showcased Soviet steel town."

Yet Soviet socialism could have limped along in this manner for decades longer had it not also failed on moral grounds. Most people grumblingly accepted the shortages because their basic needs were met by cradle-to-grave socialism. There were no homeless people, and no one suffered unemployment in Magnitogorsk or anywhere else in the Soviet Union. The lack of BMWs and VCRs did not doom socialism, for many Russians and Eastern Europeans thought they were better off without them. The constant assault on human dignity and identity took a much larger toll. Russians and Eastern Europeans lived double lives. Unable to tell if their neighbors or even members of their own family were informing on them to the authorities, they kept their deepest thoughts to themselves. Czech dissident Václav Havel once remarked: "The worst thing is that we live in a contaminated moral environment. We fell morally ill because we became used to saying something different from what we thought." History was also falsified. When Americans quip that someone or something "is history," they imply that it is irrelevant; but actually just the opposite is true. Czech novelist Milan Kundera has stated that "the struggle of man against power is the struggle of memory against forgetting." For example,

Stephen Kotkin found that the official history of Magnitogorsk told a heroic tale of young idealistic Communists building the steel town in the 1930s. This uplifting story, however, omitted the thirty thousand displaced peasants who had worked as forced laborers on the city's construction as well as the brutal purges that had decimated the local leadership. Shortly before Kotkin left Russia, Magnitogorsk's mayor begged him to translate sections of his work so that the mayor could "put an end once and for all to the damned silences."

When drastic change finally came to the Soviet Union and Eastern Europe in the late 1980s, people recovered historical truth and personal integrity, confronting Communist dominance with a revolution of memory and morality. Two men were the primary catalysts for this revolutionary change, Pope John Paul II and Mikhail Gorbachev, though Gorbachev did not intend to terminate the Communist system and even the pope could not have foreseen the extent of change his words and actions would inspire.

The election of Karol Józef Wojtyła, archbishop of Kraków, as Pope John Paul II on October 16, 1978, sparked a series of events in Poland that served as a dress rehearsal for the overthrow of communism. Born in 1920 in the foothills of the Carpathian Mountains, Wojtyła originally trained as an actor and considered pursuing a career in the theater. During the Nazi occupation of his country, he was compelled to labor in a quarry, but he also participated in highly political underground theater performances and began secretly to study for the priesthood. Ordained in 1946, he followed in the footsteps of his mentor, Cardinal Adam Sapieha, and was named archbishop of Kraków in 1963.

Both the Catholic Church and the working class of Poland had resisted total domination by the Communist government, carving out areas of independence unique in Eastern Europe. The church conducted vigorous programs of religious education, most farmers remained outside the system of collective farms, and workers went on strike whenever the government threatened to raise consumer prices. After a series of violently suppressed strikes in December 1970 brought Edward Gierek to power in Poland, the party first secretary paid off workers through a policy of massive borrowing in Western Europe and the United States. The Polish economy surged ahead at a rate of 10 percent per year between 1971 and 1975. Then the debt service bills started coming due. Gierek tried to raise consumer prices in 1976, but the workers went on strike, only to be suppressed again. This time, however, a group of intellectuals, inspired by the human rights provisions of the Helsinki Accords signed by the United States and the Soviet Union in 1975, founded a Workers' Defense Committee. At the same time, the Catholic hierarchy of Poland, renewed by fresh thinking from the Second Vatican Council, also spoke out against the regime's repression. Thus a potentially fruitful alliance of church, intellectuals, and workers was taking shape when Wojtyła's selection as the first non-Italian pope in centuries propelled a surge of national pride through Polish society.

When the church and the nation had celebrated the one-thousandth anniversary of Poland's conversion to Christianity in 1966, the government had refused Pope Paul VI a visa to preside at the religious ceremonies. Shortly after the election of John Paul II, however, the Polish pope declared his desire to visit Poland in 1979 for the nine-hundredth anniversary of St. Stanisław's martyrdom. St. Stanisław was not only the patron of Poland and Wojtyła's predecessor in the archdiocese of Kraków, but also a powerful symbol of resistance to tyrants, for he had been martyred by the king of Poland. The government dared not prevent this pope's pilgrimage, though it stalled, dragged out the negotiations, and changed the date of his arrival. John Paul II spent nine triumphant days in his homeland, from June 2 to 10, 1979, celebrating mass before crowds of over a million people on several occasions. The Communist government kept a low profile and let church volunteers keep order, which proved surprisingly easy as Poles abstained from vodka and displayed astonishing good humor and patience.

Austrian Cardinal Franz König called Pope John Paul's Polish pilgrimage a "psychological earthquake." The state had systematically downplayed the role of the Catholic Church in Polish history, yet the popular outpouring in June 1979 showed how Catholic society remained. The peaceful organization of the crowds demonstrated that Poles could function as a civil society outside of state control. The pope's boldly repeated message, "Be not afraid," and the crowd's experience of community and solidarity proved a refreshing antidote to the fear, lies, and double lives Poles usually experienced. The pope's visit stimulated historical memory and provided a model of non-violent civil protest in Poland.

The following summer, Gierek's government raised the price of meat nearly 100 percent, and a wave of strikes followed. One such protest, an occupation or sit-down strike in the Lenin Shipyard of Gdańsk on the Baltic coast, sparked a mass movement. The Gdańsk shipyard workers walked out on August 14, 1980, after the management fired a popular co-worker, Anna Walentynowicz, for preparing candles in memory of the workers killed in December 1970. They demanded a raise in wages, the reinstatement of "Pani Anna," and the building of a monument to the martyred workers. Management nearly bought them off with a wage hike, but another dismissed worker, Lech Wałęsa, climbed over the shipyard fence and started haranguing his fellows. By the evening of August 17 the strike had spread to at least 750,000 workers at other factories and had expanded its list of demands to twenty-one. The first two demands defined the fundamental goals of the expanded strikes: recognition of independent trade unions and a guarantee of the right to strike. At the end of August the government capitulated, and on September 6 Gierek was replaced as Communist first secretary. Drawing on the heady experience of community at both the pope's pilgrimage and the shipyard strike, workers and intellectuals founded a federation of unions called *Solidarność,* or Solidarity, on September 17 in Gdańsk. Solidarity was more than just a trade union; it was what journalist Timothy Garton Ash has characterized as a "civil crusade for national regeneration."

The Gdańsk shipyard strike had economic causes and goals, but the workers' dogged insistence on building a monument to the earlier worker martyrs showed the significance of memory and human dignity as well. A thirst for truthful information marked Solidarity as much as a desire for better wages. Timothy Garton Ash remarked that "there were queues in front of newspaper kiosks as long as those before the butchers.'" The strike, moreover, was saturated with religious symbolism. Lech Wałęsa's parish priest at St. Brigid's Church, Fr. Henryk Jankowski, celebrated daily mass inside the Lenin Shipyard; and the striking workers decorated the yard's main gate with pictures of the pope and Our Lady of Częstochowa and festooned it with flowers, symbolizing the workers' commitment to non-violence. The official logo that *Solidarność* adopted displayed the letters of the group's name leaning against one another. No letter, or person, can stand alone, but needs support from a neighbor. Three months after the Lenin Shipyard strike ended, the workers unveiled their long-awaited monument — three tall crosses, symbolizing faith and sacrifice; three anchors, standing for hope and work; and an eternal flame of life and rebirth.

Solidarity lasted for nearly a year and a half, eventually becoming a powerful organization enrolling about nine and a half million of Poland's twelve and a half million workers. Though its national commission under Lech Wałęsa's chairmanship was often wracked by factionalism and quarrels, it demonstrated on several occasions that it could shut down nearly all of Poland with "warning general strikes." Solidarity did not attack the Communists' right to rule the country or their dependent alliance with the Soviet Union, but they insisted on forming an independent civil society that could play a role in political life. Far from seeking only bread-and-butter gains, like American trade unions, Solidarity was willing to support an austerity program in Poland, provided the government gave it a partnership role in economic planning.

The Russians were sufficiently alarmed by the implications of such independence that they massed troops on Poland's borders in December 1980 and summoned General Wojciech Jaruzelski, the Polish prime minister, to Moscow in March 1981. Jaruzelski harbored a healthy fear of the Russians. He had been deported to Siberia with his family during the Second World War, and the distinctive dark glasses he wore constantly were not a fashion statement but the result of Siberian snow blindness. The cautious general would have preferred to co-opt Solidarity rather than suppress it, but Wałęsa, the workers and intellectuals, and the Polish church, publicly backed by Pope John Paul II in Rome, refused to be co-opted.

So in the middle of the night on December 12-13, 1981, Poland invaded itself. General Jaruzelski declared martial law and instructed the Polish army to cut off all telephone communications with the outside world and seal off the major cities. Nearly all the Solidarity leaders were arrested between 2 and 3 A.M. December 13. Though Solidarity workers resisted through sit-down strikes across the country, the dreaded ZOMO riot police stormed the factories one by one. Jaruzelski defended his actions as a necessary evil to prevent a Soviet invasion, which probably was imminent had he not acted. Solidarity went underground and the Poles consoled themselves by telling ZOMO jokes:

> Two Zomos were patrolling the streets of Warsaw five minutes before curfew, when a young man raced by on a bicycle. One of the Zomos raised his rifle and shot the man. His partner exclaimed: "Why did you shoot him? There's still five minutes until curfew." The first Zomo replied, "I knew where he lived. He'd never make it in time."

Jaruzelski won the battle, but he released Wałęsa and the other political prisoners a year later, and the pope visited Poland twice more during the 1980s.

An unnamed worker in Poznań, according to Timothy Garton Ash, labeled the Solidarity movement a "revolution of the soul." The disruption of strikes, Soviet economic pressure, and the refusal of non-communist states to lend Poland more money actually led to a lowering of the standard of living, indeed a sharpening economic crisis in Poland, during the year and a half of Solidarity's independence. Polish workers would have to answer Ronald Reagan's famous question, "Are you better off now than before?" with a resounding "no." Yet they felt better and freer. Even after the imposition of martial law, Poles did not return completely to their previous double lives. A non-violent assertion of civil society had helped them recover their memory and dignity, and furnished them a model for the overturn of communism, next time.

The next time came sooner than anyone expected. Shortly after the suppression of the Prague Spring in 1968, Eastern European historian Ferenc Fejtő wrote: "One may hope — certainly the people of Eastern Europe hope — that the next Dubček will appear in the nerve center of the system: Moscow." In March 1985 the Russian Dubček showed up, when Mikhail Gorbachev was chosen as general secretary of the Communist Party in the Soviet Union.[1] Born in 1931 in the Stavropol region of southern Russia, Gorbachev was relatively young

---

1. Leonid Brezhnev served as general secretary from October 1964 until his death in November 1982. He was succeeded by former KGB chief Yuri Andropov, who died just fifteen months later on February 9, 1984. The ill and elderly Konstantin Chernenko succeeded him, but died after only thirteen months, on March 10, 1985.

as Soviet leaders go. He belonged to a generation known as the *shestidesyatniki,* "men of the sixties," who had come to political maturity during the brief Khrushchev "thaw" and liked the dynamism and openness of that era. During the long period of stagnation under Brezhnev, Gorbachev and his contemporaries became, in the words of David Remnick, "half-brave, half-cynical careerists," living the double life of most Soviet citizens at the highest levels of government. Like Dubček in Czechoslovakia, Gorbachev did not want to overthrow the Communist system but revitalize it and give it a human face.

Gorbachev faced massive economic and moral problems. The centrally planned command economy of the Soviet Union had worked wonders during Stalin's lifetime because it addressed massive but relatively straightforward tasks, such as building hydroelectric dams and steel mills, or winning the war against Germany. Furthermore, Stalin's terror provided powerful incentives for Soviet citizens to work hard and produce results. If they did not, they not only lost their jobs, they lost their lives. With the easing of terror under Khrushchev and the buying off of the populace under Brezhnev, the Soviet system possessed neither carrots nor sticks. The top party bureaucrats enjoyed a lavish lifestyle, no matter what they did, while ordinary citizens suffered shortages but had their basic needs fulfilled. If anyone worked harder or produced more, he or she was no better off for there was nothing much to buy with increased wages. Without economic incentives, people adopted a cynical motto: "We pretend to work and they pretend to pay us." The malaise was moral or spiritual as much as economic.

Gorbachev hoped to energize both Communist cadres and ordinary citizens to work harder and catch up with the United States in sophisticated technological fields, such as computers, where Russia had fallen far behind. He started fairly cautiously and traditionally, first consolidating his power by wholesale firings of top bureaucrats. During his first year in office he dismissed about 40 percent of the top party officers, and he even eased the long-standing foreign minister Andrei Gromyko into the purely ceremonial post of president. Then he adopted an essentially moralistic approach to the economic mess by urging an "acceleration" of hard work and a crackdown on laziness. He also mounted an anti-alcohol campaign, for excessive drunkenness was reportedly reducing Soviet productivity by as much as 10 percent. The acceleration drive, from March 1985 until the middle of 1986 proved a dismal failure, and the anti-alcohol campaign became as unpopular as Prohibition had been in the United States.

In 1986, Gorbachev's second year in power, the general secretary upped the reform ante with twin policies of *perestroika* (restructuring) and *glasnost* (openness). *Perestroika* entailed greater responsibility and new incentives for factory managers to produce goods more efficiently, as well as a tentative introduction of private enterprise in services. It also cut down excessive bureaucratic layers in the planning process. *Glasnost* introduced greater freedom of speech and the press and encouraged the founding of "informal organizations" outside the Communist Party. In an attempt to earn some moral legitimacy for his reforms, Gorbachev also reached out to religious leaders of the Orthodox Church, permitting the reopening of five hundred to seven hundred churches during the year of 1988 alone. In effect, Gorbachev and his fellow reformers were trying to create a "civil society" from the top down, rather than from the ground up as Solidarity had done in Poland. As historian Mark Galeotti has written, "Gorbachev saw *glasnost'* as a way to create a nation of whistle-blowers who would work with him to keep the *apparatchiki* [party bureaucrats] in line."

This second phase of reform did not work out the way Gorbachev hoped. *Perestroika* appealed to the intellectual proletariat, well-educated professionals who knew that the United States and Western Europe enjoyed a technological lead over the Soviet Union, but it held little allure for ordinary workers. Factory operatives understood that efficiency reforms might mean the shuttering of their plants and the downsizing of work forces, just like in the United States. Furthermore the only effect that private enterprise seemed to have on the service economy was a sharp rise in prices. In a perverse way, therefore, the working class held just as big a stake in the existing system as the party bureaucrats did.

Glasnost, however, proved widely popular. Intellectuals, of course, reveled in the new freedom to publish and to organize a civil society outside the party and to recover their historical memory. One of the most popular of the new informal organizations, "Memorial," was organized in August 1987 to mount a petition drive for the exposure of Stalin's crimes and the erection of a monument to his victims. Even ordinary workers enjoyed the freedom to grouse openly. Stephen Kotkin found in Magnitogorsk that despite widespread dissatisfaction with the standard of living, what really agitated people was the corruption at high levels in the party. Gorbachev hoped to harness this sentiment for his own purposes, but it soon proved uncontrollable. Once people started criticizing the system openly, they realized that it was rotten to the core. A bitter joke combined both the material and the moral critique of the regime: "Why is there no soap or laundry powder in the Soviet Union? Because the party is trying to wash itself clean."

In order to recapture the initiative, Gorbachev extended *perestroika* to the realm of politics. At a party conference in the summer of 1988 he announced free elections for a Congress of People's Deputies which would, in turn, elect from among its ranks a new Supreme Soviet as a legislature for the Soviet Union. The election process was complicated and unwieldy. One-third of the 2,250 seats in the Congress were not subject to popular election but were reserved for delegates from major social organizations, most of them party-controlled. Another third were elected from "national-territorial" districts drawn in such a way that compact ethnic minorities would be assured of representation. The rest of the Congress deputies were elected from standard districts, apportioned according to population as in parliamentary democracies. Despite the unfamiliarity and clumsiness of the process, Soviet citizens responded enthusiastically, with an 89 percent turnout at the first round of balloting in March 1989. When the Congress assembled on May 25, 1989, nearly 87 percent of the delegates were members of the Communist Party; but the minority of non-Communists proved vocal, and even some of the Communists kept open minds. Television carried the Congress debates live, and for two weeks Russia's factories and collective farms virtually shut down as everyone stayed home to watch the "democrats," as the minority began calling themselves, upstage Chairman Gorbachev.

Andrei Sakharov, Russia's most distinguished nuclear physicist and a long-time political dissident, provided moral leadership to many Congress deputies who considered him a "secular saint." After his release from the Gulag in 1986, Sakharov had chaired numerous informal organizations, including Memorial, and had won election to the Congress. He advocated democracy because he believed it was in tune with the complex, scientific society of the late twentieth century and was more responsive to human needs. He died of a heart attack at the end of 1989, but not before handing Gorbachev a massive petition asking for the end of the Communist Party's monopoly on political power.

If Sakharov was the conscience of the democratic movement in Russia, Boris Yeltsin was the political technician. Born the same year as Gorbachev, Yeltsin shared the party leader's frustration with the system, but he had a more pragmatic temperament and a common touch. During his ten years as party secretary in the Ural Mountains district of Sverdlovsk, he regularly traveled about on public transportation to take the pulse of the citizenry. In Moscow during the early days of *perestroika*, he angered Gorbachev by openly criticizing the slow pace of reform. In the 1989 Congress elections, Boris Yeltsin won 90 percent of the vote in the election district that included most of Moscow. Shortly after the Congress closed in July, Yeltsin convened an interregional group of deputies that in effect formed the nucleus of an opposition political party. That same month, coal miners in Siberia and across the country mounted massive strikes to protest the meager economic payoff of *perestroika*. With his earthy manner and his lifelong commitment to social justice, Yeltsin established immediate rapport with the striking workers. Gorbachev felt the moral, political, and economic leadership of the Soviet Union slipping out of his control. As historian John Dunlop has concluded, "to use a West Coast image, he became a surfboarder of events."

Though absorbed with internal reforms, Gorbachev had also tried to liquidate Cold War baggage in foreign policy. He ended the Vietnam-type nightmare in Afghanistan by withdrawing all Soviet troops in February 1989. Desperate to reduce defense spending, he engaged in vigorous arms-control negotiations with President Ronald Reagan and then his successor, George Bush. In June 1989, just after the Congress of People's Deputies had adjourned, Gorbachev startled the chairman of the American Joint Chiefs of Staff, Admiral William Crowe, by referring to his relationship with the United States as a "partnership." At the end of the year, Bush and Gorbachev met for their first formal summit conference aboard a naval vessel near the island of Malta. The weather proved so stormy that journalists dubbed the meeting the "seasick summit," but the two leaders found that they actually liked each other. At the end of the summit, Gorbachev's spokesman, Gennadi Gerasimov, declared: "We buried the Cold War at the bottom of the Mediterranean Sea."

As these dramatic events unfolded in the Soviet Union and between the superpowers, the aborted revolution in Poland resumed, soon spreading to the rest of Eastern Europe. In the years since the lifting of martial law in Poland, the regime of General Jaruzelski had limped along, without an economic plan or any moral legitimacy. In the meantime, Solidarity flourished as an underground network of intellectuals and trade unionists, with certain key religious sites, such as Lech Wałęsa's parish church of St. Brigid's, enjoying what historian George Weigel has called "moral extraterritoriality." Within these shrines, activists pretended to be free and the government pretended not to notice. When Gorbachev opened the floodgates of *glasnost* in Russia, the Polish authorities began to negotiate with Solidarity again. Talks between Jaruzelski and the newly legalized Solidarity dragged on from February 6 to April 5 in 1989, resulting in an agreement to hold partially free elections that summer. Solidarity never regained the nine million members it had possessed in 1981 and it no longer functioned like a trade union. It had become, instead, an organized movement for democratization and an embryonic political party.

Jaruzelski, like Gorbachev, hoped to co-opt political reformers by conceding an element of democracy but retaining control in his own hands. The parliamentary elections of June 1989 permitted only one-third of the delegates for the lower house of parliament to be elected freely, whereas the rest would still be appointed by the party. All one hundred seats in the upper house, however, became elective. Solidarity won across the board, winning all but one senate seat and nearly all the elective house positions. Only 62 percent of eligible Poles voted, however, a much lower turnout than in the Soviet Union's Congress elections. The long, frustrating career of Solidarity may have made Poles more cynical, or perhaps their society was already "normal," for the 62 percent turnout approximates the figures for American elections. Solidarity had not believed they could take power in 1989, and they held only 161 out of 460 seats in the rigged lower house, but the election showed that they enjoyed far greater credibility and legitimacy than the Communists. Eventually they struck a deal with Jaruzelski, electing him president, but then organizing a coalition government under Prime Minister Tadeusz Mazowiecki, one of the leading intellectuals in the Solidarity camp. Mazowiecki took power on September 12, 1989, the first non-Communist premier in Eastern Europe in forty years. The country moved rapidly toward a free market economy and fully free elections in the following years.

Hungary also ended one-party government by drawing on the memory and traditions of an earlier, failed attempt to resist Soviet domination. On the thirtieth anniversary of the execution of Imre Nagy and his companions, June 16, 1988, the Committee for Historical Justice conducted a memorial service for the victims of the failed Hungarian uprising in the 1950s. A year later, they finally obtained permission to rebury the bodies with dignity, and a crowd of 200,000 turned out at Budapest's Heroes' Square on June 16, 1989. The ceremony was nationalist, not religious, but it demonstrated a civic independence and moral consciousness similar to the pilgrimage of the Polish pope a decade earlier. The Communist leader who had suppressed the Hungarian rising, János Kádár, died three weeks after the Nagy reburial, and the party then began a gradual process of democratization. Tortuous negotiations from June to September resulted in a deal for fully free elections, unlike the partially rigged Polish plebiscite. Hungarian democrats won the elections held in March of 1990.

The gradual loosening of Communist rule in Hungary held explosive consequences for East Germany. About the time of the Nagy reburial, the Hungarian authorities had begun dismantling the barbed wire that separated their country from neighboring Austria and allowing their citizens the right to travel. Germans saw this breach in the former Iron Curtain and tried to dash through it by crossing Hungary. At first the Hungarian government honored its treaty obligations with a fellow member of the Soviet bloc and interned the fleeing East Germans at camps in Budapest, but in September 1989 they released the flood of refugees to Austria. More than fifty thousand Germans took advantage of this escape valve by the end of October 1989.

As the Iron Curtain parted, East Germans organized peaceful protests against Communist rule. Protestant church activists had begun Monday evening "prayers for peace" in the square outside Leipzig's Church of St. Nicholas during the summer, but their numbers swelled throughout the autumn until they reached at least 300,000. Mikhail Gorbachev visited East Germany in early October, saw the crowds, and counseled the hardline German party secretary, Erich Honecker, to pursue a path of reform before it was too late. The German party got the message and replaced Honecker with the former security chief, Egon Krenz, on October 18. Then Gorbachev made official a policy that had become increasingly obvious to Eastern Europeans: the Russians would no longer intervene militarily to prevent the erosion of Communist rule in the satellite states. During a state visit to Helsinki on October 25, Gorbachev publicly renounced the Brezhnev Doctrine and held out his host country, Finland, as a model of peaceful neutrality and coexistence. Gorbachev's spokesman Gerasimov joked to reporters that the new policy could be called the "Sinatra Doctrine," for the Eastern Europeans were now free to do it "their way." Egon Krenz's government responded to the peaceful demonstrations of his people and the none-too-subtle hints from Gorbachev by dismantling the hated Berlin Wall that had divided Germany since 1961. On November 9, 1989, young people hacked and clawed the wall into rubble and about two million East Germans walked across for a stroll in West Berlin. One joyous reveler told a reporter he had counted twenty-eight years and ninety-one days since the wall went up.

The last Communist ruler of East Germany resigned on December 6, and free elections were held in March of 1990. The Christian Democratic chancellor of West Germany, Helmut Kohl, pushed vigorously for the reunification of the two Germanys. Though the Russians resisted at first, Gorbachev finally reached an agreement with Kohl in July 1990. Kohl allayed Russian fears of a revived, militarized Germany by pledging to hold the reunited country's armed forces below 400,000, and he offered a carrot of three billion dollars in credits to cover the cost of withdrawing Soviet troops from East Germany. A few months later, on October 3, 1990, Germany reunited.

A week after the fall of the Berlin Wall, on November 17, 1989, a Czech youth organization in Prague staged a demonstration in memory of a student murdered by the Nazis fifty years before. The government panicked and unleashed the special police, who beat the demonstrators with heavy truncheons. This "November massacre" touched off the so-called Velvet Revolution in Czechoslovakia. Intellectuals supported the students, with the theater people playing a major role by offering their auditoriums as sanctuaries and meeting places. Playwright Václav Havel organized an umbrella group called Civic Forum, which led three weeks of demonstrations and negotiations with the government.

On November 24, Alexander Dubček, the leader of the failed Prague Spring reforms of 1968, appeared with Havel on a balcony overlooking Wenceslas Square. An underground Catholic priest joined them and read a message of support from the ninety-year-old cardinal of Prague, František Tomášek. A Communist reformer, an intellectual dissident, and the Catholic hierarchy had united in moral leadership of the democracy movement. On December 10, Gustáv Husák, who had repressed the Prague Spring, resigned as president of Czechoslovakia and a coalition government was sworn in. The parliament elected Alexander Dubček as their speaker and Václav Havel as president of the republic. Havel delivered a dramatic inaugural address on New Year's Day calling the citizens of Czechoslovakia to forgiveness and reconciliation.

Bulgaria fell in line with the peacefully falling dominoes by sacking its long-time party boss, Todor Zhivkov, reorganizing the party on a democratic basis, and holding free elections in June 1990. Only in Romania did the Communist authorities resist violently. The family dictatorship of Nicolae Ceauşescu unleashed its security forces against the democratic reformers, but the army and the party bureaucrats deserted Ceauşescu, who was eventually captured and executed on December 25, 1989. Eastern Europe had undergone a thorough revolution by the end of 1989, a revolution that was non-violent everywhere except in Romania.

The collapse of Communist rule in Eastern Europe demonstrated that the Russians had been right all along to fear any loosening of the system, for freedom and democracy proved contagious. Poland's example of a mobilized, independent civil society and Gorbachev's revocation of the Brezhnev Doctrine set in motion a series of events that toppled the Communist satellite governments like dominoes. Even more than in Russia, the revolution of 1989 in Eastern Europe was a movement of memory and morality. Seventy years of official atheism had dulled religious consciousness in Russia, where the reform impetus came from idealistic Communists, such as Gorbachev, and secular moralists like Sakharov. In Poland and Czechoslovakia, however, Catholic leaders proved to be crucial allies of the students, intellectuals, and workers, whereas Protestant believers spearheaded the demonstrations in East Germany. The recovery of historical memory was a necessary, though painful, process in the Soviet Union, where the horrors of Stalinism and Soviet imperialism had been long suppressed. Yet in countries such as Poland, Hungary, and Czechoslovakia, many of the recovered memories were glorious reminders of national resistance in the past. The Czechs delightedly pointed out that '89 was '68 upside down!

Gorbachev realized that the Soviet Union could no longer afford its imperial dominance in Afghanistan and Eastern Europe, but he was determined to retain the "inner empire," the constituent republics of the Soviet Union that had non-Russian populations. The survival of the Union of Soviet Socialist Republics, as well as a sharp power struggle with Boris Yeltsin and with hardline Communist conservatives, preoccupied Gorbachev during his last two years in power.

The Baltic states of Lithuania, Latvia, and Estonia, which Stalin had forcibly incorporated into the Soviet Union at the time of his nonaggression pact with Hitler in 1939, were the first Soviet republics to claim independence. During the years of *glasnost* in the late 1980s, Soviet authorities had finally confessed Stalin's secret dealings with Hitler and had released the documentary evidence. Outraged at this confirmation of their worst suspicions, the Lithuanians, on August 22, 1989, declared the Soviet annexation of their country illegal. On March 11, 1990, Lithuania declared its independence, and the Latvian parliament followed suit in May; but Gorbachev denounced both actions as "illegal and invalid." In the Soviet republics that had a European orientation but spoke non-Slavic languages — the three Baltic states, plus Moldavia, Georgia, and Armenia — local elections in the spring of 1990 brought independence-minded leaders to power. Leaders of the Slavic republics of Ukraine and Bielorussia and the Muslim republics in central Asia were still biding their time to see whether Gorbachev and the central power in Moscow would survive.

Boris Yeltsin viewed the rise of nationalism in the various republics as a golden opportunity. At the beginning of 1990 he abandoned the politics of the Soviet central government and cast his lot with the huge Russian republic, which encompassed about two-thirds of the Soviet Union's populace and sprawled from European Russia to Siberia. In March 1990, Yeltsin's old district of Sverdlovsk gave him a landslide victory as a deputy to the Russian (not the Soviet) parliament, and on May 29, 1990, that parliament selected him as its speaker. In mid-summer he decisively cut his ties with the past by formally resigning from the Communist Party. Gorbachev had not been idle while Yeltsin built up his power base. Still in control of the Soviet (not the Russian) Congress, the Communist general secretary convinced legislators to create a new, stronger office of president, modeled on the French presidency of Charles de Gaulle, and appoint him to that post. The Congress named Gorbachev president of the Soviet Union in March 1990. The formerly monolithic Russian/Soviet state now had two leaders vying for influence as the force of nationalism contended with the waning powers of socialism and imperialism.

Alarmed by the centrifugal spin of the republics, Communist conservatives attempted to suppress the independence movements and depose Boris Yeltsin. As early as 1989 the KGB chairman Vladimir Kryuchkov had written a memo declaring that "the chief task of the KGB at the present time is not to permit the creation of a political opposition . . . [and] to discredit the leaders of the democratic movement. . . ." KGB operatives conspired to kill Yeltsin several times, but all their plots failed. Gorbachev's 1990 deal with Helmut Kohl for the reunification of Germany and its eventual entry into NATO outraged the conservatives, who felt humiliated. A hotheaded Communist colonel in the special forces, Viktor Alksnis, told an American journalist: "The West now thinks it can talk down to us. They used to think of the Soviet Union as Upper Volta with missiles. Now they just think of us as Upper Volta." Toward the end of 1990, Gorbachev made a tactical shift to the right, trying to co-opt the conservatives. He sacked most of his cabinet, replacing reformers with hardliners. The Soviet foreign minister, Eduard Shevardnadze, a committed reformer who had forged a strong relationship with American president George Bush and his secretary of state James Baker, resigned in protest against Gorbachev's conservative tilt.

The government of the Soviet Union then moved forcibly against the Baltic secessionists, replacing the elected parliaments of the republics with "committees of national salvation." On January 13, 1991, Colonel Alksnis's forces stormed the parliament building and the television broadcasting headquarters in Vilnius, capital of Lithuania. Fourteen people died and 580 were wounded on this "Bloody Sunday." A week later a similar force attacked the Latvian parliament. Gorbachev had probably given at least tacit consent to these assaults, but resistance in the Baltic republics was so widespread and international protest so vocal that he backed down. Unlike previous Soviet leaders, Gorbachev always avoided large-scale bloodshed and repression, but his attempt to make a surgical strike against Baltic independence and his subsequent retreat made him look weak and confused. He feigned innocence, declaring: "The report about the tragedy came as a surprise to all. I learned about it only later, when they woke me up." This was a lose/lose response. Either Gorbachev was lying or he had lost control. The original Bloody Sunday in 1905 had seriously damaged the prestige of Nicholas II, the last tsar of Russia, and the Vilnius Bloody Sunday similarly wounded the last Communist "tsar."

As Gorbachev's power waned, Yeltsin's increased. During the Baltic crisis, the Russian leader flew to Estonia, which had not yet been attacked by Soviet forces, and signed a mutual support pact with the three rebellious republics. Gorbachev desperately attempted to hold the union together by restructuring it into a somewhat looser federation. He conducted a referendum in March 1991 in which Soviet citizens approved his new union treaty, but Yeltsin won something for himself by inserting a second referendum question authorizing direct presidential elections in the Russian republic. In June 1991, Yeltsin was triumphantly elected as Russian (not Soviet) president. He now enjoyed something Gorbachev manifestly lacked, a popular mandate, for the Soviet president had still not won a popular election to any office.

By this time, the three Baltic republics, plus Armenia and Moldavia (now called Moldova), considered themselves independent, but had not yet made good their claims. The remaining republics continued to negotiate details of the revised union treaty with Gorbachev during the summer of 1991. Finally reaching an agreement that would drastically curtail the power of the central government, Gorbachev scheduled a treaty signing for August 20 in Moscow, then went on vacation at Foros in the Crimea. KGB chief Kryuchkov and the other hardliners Gorbachev had invited into his cabinet the previous winter decided to act, before it was too late to save the authority of the central government.

The coup d'état that the Communist rearguard mounted in August 1991 is surrounded by almost as much mystery and controversy as the Kennedy assassination in the United States. On August 18, 1991, a delegation of conspirators confronted Mikhail Gorbachev at his summer home in the Crimea. Gorbachev says he refused to sanction their plot and they therefore cut off his communications and kept him under house arrest. Many Russians believe that Gorbachev was actually a silent partner in the coup, waiting in the wings to resume control no matter which side won the struggle. In any case, the general secretary remained isolated at Foros during the coup and the "State Committee for the State of Emergency" in Moscow acted in his name, claiming that he was ill.

At 6:00 A.M. on August 19, the Moscow conspirators declared a state of emergency. Boris Yeltsin, staying with many members of the Russian republic's government at a guest house about twenty miles from Moscow, heard the news a few minutes later and made a dash for the city center. The same elite troops that had stormed the Vilnius parliament on Bloody Sunday had surrounded his house, but they failed to capture him, apparently due to dissension among the commanders. Arriving at the Russian parliament building in Moscow, the so-called Russian White House, Yeltsin defied the coup plotters and appealed to the Russian people for support. About fifty thousand demonstrators turned out to ring the White House, mostly young people but also some Russian Orthodox clergy and a number of democratic luminaries, such as Yelena Bonner, the widow of Andrei Sakharov. Veterans of the Afghanistan war, who had returned home disillusioned, instilled discipline into the youthful volunteers and organized the construction of twelve barricade lines around the White House. Eduard Shevardnadze, Gorbachev's former foreign minister, addressed the demonstrators in person. Shevardnadze's appearance vindicated the strategy of principled protest he had pursued the previous December. Rather than go quietly as Gorbachev veered to the right, he had spoken out, and therefore he could exercise moral leadership during the coup.

The coup plotters failed to assault Yeltsin's stronghold on the night of August 19 because they could not be certain of the loyalty of their troops. When they had finally positioned loyal units on the night of August 20, a torrential rainstorm prevented helicopters from launching an all-out attack. Preliminary probes against the barricades resulted in the death of three defenders, who were immediately lauded as martyrs for Russian democracy. With the failure of the attack and the loyalty of the soldiers increasingly in doubt, the conspirators decided to remove all military forces from Moscow on August 21. This effectively ended the coup. Two groups of politicians, one representing the conspirators and another delegated by Boris Yeltsin's government of the Russian republic, boarded planes and raced to Foros for meetings with Gorbachev. The general secretary refused to parley with the coup plotters, but accompanied the victorious Russian delegation back to Moscow.

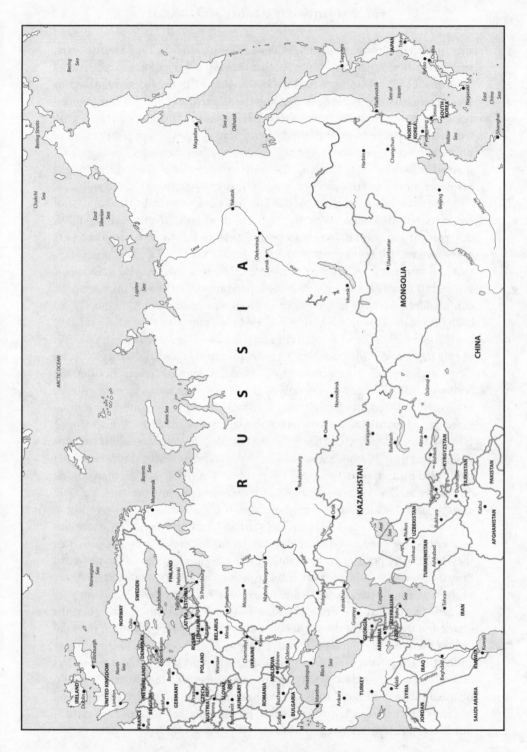

The New States of the Former Soviet Union

Though Mikhail Gorbachev officially resumed direction of the Soviet Union, the August coup and Boris Yeltsin's dramatic resistance against it had rendered him irrelevant. Gorbachev immediately resigned as general secretary and disbanded the Communist Party. He continued to talk and bargain with American leaders as president of the Soviet state and searched desperately for a new treaty formula to preserve some semblance of federal union. However, at the beginning of December, the presidents of the two Slavic republics, Ukraine and Bielorussia (which renamed itself Belarus), declared independence, and Boris Yeltsin recognized their actions. The other republics followed suit, preserving only a symbolic shell of federation in a "Commonwealth of Independent States." Gorbachev, whose country had disappeared from under him, resigned as Soviet president on December 25, 1991; and the Soviet Union formally ceased to exist on January 1, 1992.

In retrospect, a number of dates might be put forward to mark the end of the Cold War that dominated world politics for over forty years. Most Americans probably consider the fall of the Berlin Wall on November 9, 1989, as the most appropriate terminal date. Others might hold out for the reunification of Germany on October 3, 1990, as the completion of a process that the wall's collapse only symbolized. Yet another possibility would be the Malta summit on December 2-3, 1989, when Gorbachev and Bush declared that their countries were no longer rivals, but partners for peace. Finally, a strong case could be made for the failed coup of August 1991, which triggered the demise of the Russian Communist Party and the Soviet Union. Each of these dates possesses a certain poetic resonance. The Berlin Wall so dominated popular consciousness of the Cold War, on both sides of the divide, that its demolition and the resurrection of one Germany might well be considered the most important turning points. If the Bush-Gorbachev summit is considered the final act, then the Cold War could be said to run from "Yalta to Malta." Yet, since Communist power in Russia began with a coup, in October 1917, it somehow seems fitting that it also ended with a coup, an unsuccessful one this time, in August 1991. In any case, the Cold War came to a close sometime between 1989 and 1991, and few would disagree with President George Bush's statement on Christmas night, 1991: "That confrontation is over." Or, as he might have said, "It's history!"

The nations of the former Soviet empire are now "normal" states, which means that they possess democratically elected governments but are wracked by enormous economic and political problems. Boris Yeltsin proved that he was a ruthless and determined leader, thoroughly in the Russian tsarist tradition, by ordering tanks to fire on the parliamentary opposition in October 1993, and then winning reelection to a second term as president in 1996. Neither Russia nor the former satellite states has reverted to one-party dictatorship, though in several countries the former Communist Party has returned to office democratically, under a new name. Free-market economic reform has proceeded rapidly in Poland, Hungary, and the Czech Republic, and less successfully in Russia and other countries.

Yet historical and moral issues still remain salient. As archives are opened to historians, Russians and Eastern Europeans pen attacks on their Stalinist past that surpass in vitriol the works of American right-wingers during the Cold War. All of the survivors of communism are wrestling with ghosts as they confront the guilt of collaborators and informers. Czechoslovakia, Germany, and Bulgaria all passed laws of *lustrace,* or cleansing, which ban anyone whose name appears in secret police files from public office or government employment. The Communist police cast such a wide net and kept such meticulous records that great numbers of ordinary people, and even famous dissidents, appear tainted. Such supposedly guilty parties are not jailed, but they suffer public humiliation and great difficulty in obtaining employment. The Polish government indicted General Jaruzelski for declaring martial law, and the Germans prosecuted Erich Honecker for ordering border guards to shoot at escapees over the Berlin Wall, but neither government obtained a conviction. In Germany, however, a number of border guards were jailed for following orders. Tina Rosenberg, whose book *The Haunted Land* examines the moral dilemmas of East Europeans after the fall of communism, suggests that a government inquiry, or truth commission, might be a better way to exorcise ghosts from the past rather than a draconian *lustrace* law or selective prosecutions. Since the cataclysm that toppled communism was a revolution of memory and morality, a search for historical truth and a generous policy of reconciliation would seem most appropriate.

400

CHAPTER TWENTY-ONE

Generations of Struggle

The white-ruled government of South Africa constructed the closest approximation to a totalitarian state outside the Communist bloc. White supremacists separated the races and suppressed the black majority far more rigorously than in the American South or in other European settler colonies, enforcing the system of *apartheid* (apartness) with the powers of a ruthless police state. Resistance and struggle against white supremacy began as soon as the racist trend became clear, but it took nearly a century until apartheid was overthrown.

The black liberation movement in South Africa can be compared to an entertainer who achieves sudden fame and recognition on stage or screen. Indeed the first black president of South Africa, Nelson Mandela, became an international superstar, pursued by the news media and hailed by world leaders. However, a movie star usually becomes an overnight success only after years of labor in obscure entertainment venues. So too, Mandela and the African National Congress overcame apartheid suddenly and unexpectedly, but only after decades of fruitless and frustrating struggle. Mandela himself spent twenty-seven years in prison before emerging to international acclaim. Indeed, the South African freedom movement went on for such a long time that it mirrored many of the major trends of the twentieth century. South Africa's generations of struggle grew out of the country's unusual local conditions but also recapitulated the history of the world in the twentieth century.

At the beginning of the century, a "tribe" of whites who called themselves Boers or Afrikaners was defeated by the British in the Anglo-Boer War of 1899-1902 (see chapter 1, volume 1). Descendants of Dutch, Germans, and French Huguenots who had begun settling the southern tip of the African continent in

401

1652, the Afrikaners did not consider themselves colonists, but white, native Africans, locked in struggle against both the English imperialists and rival black African tribes. Though defeated in battle, the Afrikaners swiftly outmaneuvered the English; and in 1910, the four provinces of the Cape, Natal, Orange Free State, and Transvaal federated into the Union of South Africa, a self-governing dominion within the British Commonwealth. At the time of the Union whites numbered just 1.25 million of South Africa's nearly 6 million inhabitants (under 20 percent of the total). Nearly two-thirds of the population, about 4 million individuals, were black Africans, who spoke one of at least a dozen different languages, such as Zulu, Xhosa, or Sotho. A half million South Africans were considered "coloreds," that is, the product of mixed marriages or sexual liaisons between whites and blacks, whereas a small minority of about 150,000 Indians from Asia lived mainly in the province of Natal.

South Africa's system of white supremacy had its origins in fear and greed. Whites of both Afrikaner and English descent feared that they would be overrun politically, culturally, economically, and biologically by the black African majority. Above all, they had an almost pathological fear of racial mixing, miscegenation. Shortly after defeating the Boers, the English government appointed a native affairs commission which in 1905 recommended a fundamental sorting out of the country into black and white areas, with a mechanism for labor exchange between the two. Despite their desire to keep the races apart, Afrikaner farmers relied on the casual labor of black Africans; and after gold and diamonds were discovered in the late nineteenth century, the mining industry, largely owned by English entrepreneurs, required great numbers of workers. Therefore, about the time of South African Union, the Afrikaner and English whites joined together to create a system of exploited black labor that lasted through most of the twentieth century.

White farmers and mine owners pressured the new Union government to evict black African peasant farmers, many of whom had become moderately prosperous and were successfully competing with white agriculture, and to bar them from owning land in most of South Africa. The Native Land Act of 1913 restricted African land ownership to the "native reserves," fragments of territory left untouched by white conquest in the nineteenth century, much like Indian reservations in North America. These native reserves amounted to only 13 percent of the country's land for two-thirds of its people. Not all Africans were expected to reside on the reserves. Indeed the whites wanted black laborers on their own farms and in the mines. However, they decreed that blacks living off the reserves would be considered temporary migrants, whose labor would be carefully controlled by the "pass laws." Any African caught without a labor pass would be sent back to the appropriate native reserve. Historian Leo Marquard accurately captured the essence of the labor control system: "The Reserves are

[were], in fact, vast rural slums whose chief export is [was] their man-power. . . ." The dual economy that resulted from the Native Land Act was not the legacy of "traditional" or "backward" African practices, but a consciously conceived and ruthlessly imposed policy of white supremacy.

The displaced black landowners protested the discriminatory policies even before the Native Land Act was officially promulgated. A group of middle-class, educated, and largely Christian Africans formed the South African Native National Congress on January 8, 1912, at a conference in the city of Bloem-fontein. (It was later renamed the African National Congress, ANC.) Modeled explicitly on the Indian National Congress, which had been founded in 1885, the ANC was a gathering of the African elite including prosperous farmers, tra-ditional native chiefs, and the intellectual proletariat of teachers and other pro-fessionals. Like their counterparts in India before Mohandas Gandhi turned the Congress into a mass movement (see chapter 3), they politely and respectfully petitioned the South African government to restore and protect their basic rights. When that failed, they appealed over the heads of the Union government to the British in Westminster. None of their petitions elicited any concessions or changes in the emerging system of labor exploitation and white supremacy. The ANC continued to meet annually, but it remained ineffective during the interwar years.

After World War I, white immigrants from Europe and white migrants from rural areas swelled the populations of South African cities and developed a white working class in the growing industries of the country. At the same time, blacks also abandoned the native reserves, with or without passes, and tried to find work in the cities. This rural-to-urban migration threatened to de-plete the pool of casual labor on which white farmers depended. Therefore, in the 1920s a coalition of white rural landowners and white urban workers pres-sured the government to pass "color bar" legislation reserving skilled industrial jobs for whites. The pass laws were tightened up, and blacks were limited to un-skilled urban or rural labor. In the words of economic historians Anton D. Lowenberg and William H. Kaempfer, "modern industrial-age apartheid amounted to racial socialism," or, perhaps, affirmative action for white Afrikaners. The word *apartheid* was not actually coined until 1943, by an Afri-kaner journalist, but the concept and the system were already well developed between the two world wars. The few white liberals who dissented from this policy were primarily English or Jewish European immigrants; but most white South Africans, whether Afrikaners, English, or other Europeans, agreed with the emerging consensus on "native affairs."

The Afrikaners who dominated the South African government during the first half of the twentieth century were divided into two parties. The moderate South African Party was led by Jan Christian Smuts, a former Boer general who

became an Anglophile and an internationally recognized statesman, the confi-
dant of world leaders such as Winston Churchill and Franklin Roosevelt. The
opposing Nationalist Party, founded by Barry Hertzog in 1913, advocated a narrower, inward-looking Afrikaner nationalism. The Nationalists opposed South
African participation in the world wars on the side of the English, but Smuts
and his fellow Anglophiles led the country into war on both occasions. Both
parties agreed on the policy of racial segregation and labor control, but the Nationalists defended it more stridently and openly. During World War II, industrial demand sparked a mass influx of black laborers into the cities, and a governmental commission appointed by Smuts in 1948 found more than half of
black Africans actually were residing in white areas. The commissioners concluded that it was physically impossible to shove them all back into the native
reserves. Smuts then called a general election to renew his mandate. Terrified by
the commission's implications of drastic change in racial policy, Afrikaner voters defeated Smuts and brought the Nationalist Party to power in 1948. Led by
D. F. Malan, a former minister in the Dutch Reformed Church, the triumphant
Afrikaner Nationalists, who believed that white supremacy represented divine
will, tightened up and intensified the existing system of labor control and race
relations. Nationalist apartheid was not a new policy but rather a series of old
practices, customs, and laws carried to their logical, and chilling, conclusions.

The Nationalist Party, supported by an increasingly prosperous whites-
only electorate, ruled South Africa from 1948 until 1994. During its first two decades in power it closed all the loopholes in existing segregation practices and
codified in law what had previously been customary behavior. For example, the
1949 Prohibition of Mixed Marriages Act speaks for itself, and the 1953 Reservation of Separate Amenities Act forbade racial mixing in public accommoda-
tions, much like the Jim Crow system of segregation in the American South. In
addition, the government extended to colored and Indian populations most of
the restrictions that had previously applied only to black Africans. The Group
Areas Act of 1950 divided the major cities into racially exclusive zones for each
of the four major population groups. Africans had long been confined to
shantytowns on the outskirts of cities, but in the 1950s a number of these were
destroyed and their populations uprooted to make room for exclusive white
suburbs. Furthermore, coloreds and Indians were forced to move out of mixed
neighborhoods and consolidate their residences in ghettoes of their own. Under the Group Areas Act, only about 2,000 white families were compelled to
move but 35,000 Indians and 75,000 coloreds were relocated. The coloreds were
also deprived of the right to vote in the Cape Province in 1956, just as Africans
had been in 1936. No Africans or coloreds had ever possessed the political franchise in the other provinces.

The government of Henrik Verwoerd, who was elected prime minister in

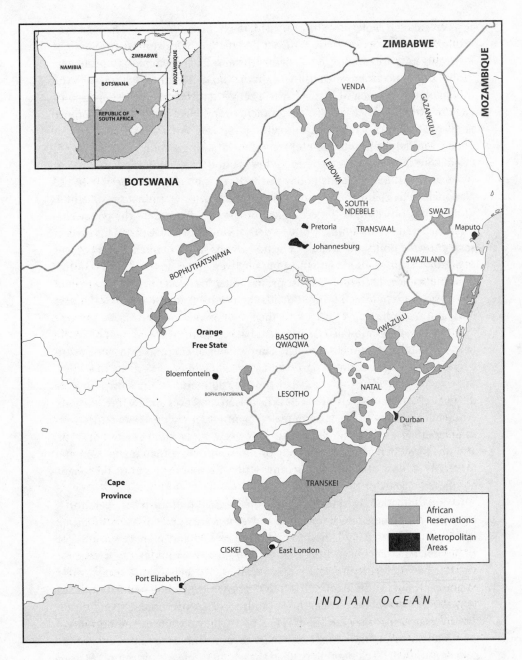

South Africa and Its Native "Homelands"

1958, erected the centerpiece of apartheid, the homelands policy. The 1959 Promotion of Bantu Self-Government Act designated the existing native reserves as ten separate tribal homelands, or Bantustans. Each member of a particular "tribe" or ethnic group, such as the Zulu or Xhosa, no matter where he or she lived, became a citizen of his or her respective homeland and was deprived of citizenship in South Africa. The government promised to grant these ten homelands political independence eventually, and indeed three were declared independent in the 1970s and one more in 1981. Not a single country of the world, besides South Africa, ever recognized these Bantustans as independent nations. Nevertheless, the homelands policy was a clever subterfuge that permitted the Nationalists to claim they were promoting the self-determination of ethnic groups and contributing to decolonization. Some advocates of the policy sincerely believed this, but most white leaders, including Verwoerd and his successors, knew the policy was a sham. The homelands still contained just 13 percent of South African territory, and most of them were not even territorially contiguous but scattered across the landscape in numerous small pockets. The majority of Africans continued to live outside the reserves under control of the pass laws, and many had never even seen their supposed homeland.

Finally, the Nationalist government backed up the whole system of apartheid with police state measures. The Suppression of Communism Act of 1950 banned the local communist party; and succeeding internal security measures, drawing on Cold War hysteria, labeled nearly all manifestations of protest or dissent as "communist-inspired." Besides prison sentences and torture, the government also employed the technique of "banning" individuals. A banned person was either exiled to a remote district or kept under house arrest, or both, and was forbidden to speak in public or meet with more than one person at a time. The subject of a banning became a non-person, in the most thoroughgoing Soviet sense of the term.

In summation, the system of apartheid rested on four pillars: territorial segregation into separate homelands and group areas; exploitation of cheap, unskilled black labor and the reservation of skilled and managerial jobs for whites; total disfranchisement of non-whites; and numerous laws providing for separate but decidedly unequal public facilities. The evil essence of apartheid can be captured in a series of ratios: 5 to 1, non-white to white population; 87 to 13, white to non-white ownership of land; 10 to 1, government spending on white versus non-white education; 13 to 1, non-white to white infant mortality.

Shortly before the white Nationalist government came to power, a younger generation of black nationalists had shaken up the nearly moribund African National Congress, turning it into an instrument of challenge and defiance against apartheid. Inspired by the "Africanist" philosophy of a former schoolteacher, Anton Lembede, young men such as Oliver Tambo, Walter Sisulu, and

Nelson Mandela founded the ANC Youth League on Easter Sunday, April 1944. As young people usually do, the Youth Leaguers rejected the strategy employed by their elders — polite, deferential petitions to the authorities. Yet they had not found a strategy of their own and they were deeply divided ideologically. The Africanists who followed Lembede's philosophy most closely asserted a "black power" vision of Africa for the Africans, arguing that black Africans must rely on their own resources and not depend on alliances with white liberals. A more pragmatic, nationalist wing of the Youth League was willing to accept assistance and alliances anywhere they could find them and hoped to build a non-racial South Africa. The individuals in both wings, however, were intense and idealistic, aspiring members of the intellectual proletariat, like their counterparts in European colonies such as the Gold Coast or Kenya. Oliver Tambo has reminisced about the Youth League: "We were never really young. There were no dances, hardly a cinema, but meetings, discussions, every night, every weekend."

The early death of Anton Lembede in 1947 and the harsh imposition of apartheid after 1948 tipped the balance in the ANC Youth League toward the pragmatic strategy of making alliances with other groups, regardless of race. Furthermore, the non-violent campaigns of Mohandas Gandhi, leading to Indian independence in 1948, gave the ANC a model of successful protest. At the African National Congress session of December 1949, the Youth Leaguers took over the organization, electing Walter Sisulu the secretary-general, placing most of their key members on the national executive committee, and adopting a non-violent "Program of Action" as official policy. On the day that the government passed the Suppression of Communism Act, June 26, 1950, the ANC prematurely mounted a nationwide non-violent protest, but it was poorly organized and only brought out large crowds in some areas of Natal, where the Indian population already had considerable experience with such actions. Exactly two years later, however, on June 26, 1952, the ANC kicked off the "Defiance Against Unjust Laws Campaign" that turned their organization into a mass movement, just as Gandhi's salt march in India had galvanized the Indian National Congress.

Relying on public, symbolic actions and the force of moral example, the leaders of the ANC presented themselves for arrest after openly breaking the unjust laws of apartheid. In the five months from July to November 1952, eight thousand people were arrested, charged under the Suppression of Communism Act, and jailed for weeks at a time. The Defiance Campaign did not effect any changes in the government's policy of racial segregation, but it boosted the ANC's membership from about 7,000 to over 100,000. The campaign also led to the formation of a multiracial Congress Alliance, linking the ANC with like-minded groups such as the Colored Organization, the Indian Congress, and the

407

largely white Congress of Democrats. In June of 1955, the organizations in this alliance sent delegates to a mass meeting on a football field in Kliptown, near Johannesburg, where they adopted the "Freedom Charter." In reflecting on the Defiance Campaign and the Freedom Charter, Nelson Mandela's biographer, Martin Meredith, has concluded: "The singular achievement of the ANC and its white allies in the 1950s was that they established a multiracial tradition in politics strong enough to withstand all attempts by the government to obliterate it."

Most of the Freedom Charter was written in vague, inspirational language, setting out democratic goals taken for granted in more fortunate countries, such as the right to vote and equality before the law. However, the charter also included a call for public ownership of the mines and other monopoly industries in South Africa and for redistribution of land. These latter clauses prompted the government to brand the Freedom Charter a communist manifesto and to arrest 156 activists for treason and conspiracy the following year. Charges were dropped against some of those arrested, but ninety-five individuals, including Nelson Mandela, endured over four years of court appearances in the infamous treason trial. Though the accused were eventually acquitted, this long-running legal harassment sapped the strength of the ANC.

In fact, the government charge of an ANC alliance with the Communists was true. The African National Congress and the South African Communist Party (SACP) had quite separate origins and early histories, but they came together after the party's banning in 1950. The Communists adopted a policy of "entryism," that is, infiltration into legal organizations, so that they could survive after the government suppressed their own party. The white Congress of Democrats, which formed part of the Congress Alliance during the Defiance Campaign, was a pure Communist front, and many individual black Communists also belonged to the ANC. With the Cold War heating up during the 1950s, the government made the most of these close alliances to whip up a red scare that made McCarthyism in the United States look tame. Yet the black nationalists of the ANC did not need white Communists to tell them they were oppressed, for that was patently obvious. Nelson Mandela stated openly at one of his courtroom appearances that he was influenced by Marxist thought but also admired the democratic customs of Britain and America. "I have been influenced in my thinking by both West and East," he avowed. Black activists did find the SACP appealing for its multiracial composition and the unfeigned friendship that white Communists extended to blacks. Put simply, the Communists were the only white South Africans willing to socialize with blacks and treat them as equals. Furthermore, the official Communist line set down by Moscow for the SACP emphasized the liberation struggle of blacks as a necessary first step before working for a socialist revolution, so the two organizations agreed on their immediate goals. As a result, a symbiotic relationship developed between the ANC and the SACP. The two organizations remained technically separate, but they increasingly overlapped in their membership.

Neither the Communists nor the ANC, however, made any headway against apartheid during the 1950s. Their campaigns of non-violent protest failed, and the leaders eventually wound up banned, arrested, or exiled. The black liberation movement also remained divided between multiracialists and black power Africanists. A leading Africanist, Robert Sobukwe, broke away from the ANC in 1959 to found the Pan African Congress (PAC), which mounted a major protest against the pass laws. One anti-pass demonstration, at the town of Sharpeville on March 21, 1960, drew a larger than expected crowd. Growing increasingly nervous, the police fired on the demonstrators and continued firing as the crowd broke and ran. Sixty-seven Africans were killed, most of them shot in the back, and 186 were wounded. The ANC quickly mounted a one-day national strike in support of the victims, and the Sharpeville massacre drew international condemnation of South Africa's racial practices for the first time.

Frustrated at the failure of their Gandhian tactics and finding themselves challenged by the militant PAC, the ANC leaders decided to mount a campaign of violent sabotage against the regime. After his acquittal in the treason trial on March 29, 1961, Nelson Mandela went underground and began organizing Umkhonto we Sizwe (the Spear of the Nation) as a military wing of the ANC. The Communist Party, with more than a decade of clandestine experience, helped him obtain weapons from the Soviet Union and other Communist bloc states. The sabotage campaign, aimed at symbolic targets such as government buildings and power stations and carefully limited to prevent civilian casualties, kicked off in December 1961, but it soon fizzled. In June 1962, the Nationalist government passed a draconian Sabotage Act, allowing the police to arrest and hold suspects without charges or trials. The passage of this act marked the final transformation of South Africa into a police state. Though Oliver Tambo slipped across the border into British Bechuanaland (now Botswana) to keep the ANC alive in exile, Sisulu, Mandela, and six other top leaders were arrested; and in 1964 they were sentenced to life imprisonment on Robben Island, South Africa's version of Alcatraz, off the coast near Cape Town.

The twists and turns in the policy of the African National Congress were primarily dictated by local circumstances, but they also vibrated to international rhythms. The success of Gandhi's *satyagraha* in India in the 1940s suggested the early strategy of the ANC Defiance Campaign, and the relatively peaceful decolonization of Ghana and other African colonies in the 1950s imparted a heady optimism to the movement that proved unrealistic. Then in the 1960s, as the guerrilla tactics of Fidel Castro and Che Guevara in Cuba seemed more effective than non-violence, the ANC turned to revolutionary violence. The early non-violent campaigns in South Africa also ran parallel to the civil rights movement in the United States, though the American example seems unlikely to have affected South Africans very much. The Defiance Campaign preceded the Montgomery bus boycott in Alabama (1955-56) that launched Martin Luther King's movement in the American South.

The outstanding difference between the American and South African movements, however, is that one was successful and the other was not. Non-violent protest in South Africa lacked charismatic, spiritual leadership like that of Gandhi in India or Dr. King in the United States. Oliver Tambo and Nelson Mandela were both believing Christians, but they adopted non-violence simply as a pragmatic tactic, much like Nkrumah in Ghana, rather than a lifelong commitment. The president of the ANC from 1952 until his death in 1967 was the Zulu chief Albert Luthuli, a man of great moral authority and a recipient of the Nobel Peace Prize in 1961; but he was banned and kept under house arrest during most of these years so his voice did not resonate as loudly as it might otherwise. Luthuli heard of the ANC's decision to pursue a sabotage campaign second-hand, for the government did not permit him to attend meetings. He eventually consented to this decision, but only on condition that Umkhonto we Sizwe remain separate from the main ANC organization.

The failure of non-violence in South Africa in the 1950s and 1960s, however, owed more to circumstances than to any lack of leadership. Critics of Gandhian protest often assert that non-violence only works against "civilized, humane" government authorities like the British or the Americans. Nelson Mandela even asserted this argument when he founded Umkhonto we Sizwe, remarking that non-violence requires both sides to play by the same rules. This allegation, however, does not stand up to inspection. Neither the British in India nor the white supremacists in Mississippi and Alabama were civilized or humane; they harassed, arrested, tortured, and murdered protesters. The Amritsar massacre of 1919 (see chapter 3), which helped launch Gandhi's movement, far surpassed the Sharpeville massacre in ferocity. British soldiers and American police followed no rules but their own.

The major reason for the failure of non-violent protest in South Africa was the lack of an effective audience with both the power and the willingness to force change. Non-violence works best when its protests reach an audience far enough away not to be threatened, yet connected enough to be inspired and moved by the moral force of the protest. Gandhi could appeal to the consciences of the English, who lived far from the scene but possessed the power to change policies in India. In the United States, confrontations between civil rights marchers and brutal Southern sheriffs shocked white Northerners who were not directly affected by the Jim Crow system and could afford to be gener-

ous. In the South African case, however, no audience possessed sufficient leverage to force change. Theoretically, Great Britain retained some responsibility
for a Commonwealth nation, but after the Union of South Africa in 1910 they
consistently declined involvement. When, after the Sharpeville massacre, public
opinion in England became outraged, the South African government simply
withdrew from the Commonwealth and became a republic in 1961. World opinion elsewhere did not mobilize against South Africa in an effective fashion until
several decades later.

Furthermore, soul force proves most effective when the government authority is unexpectedly vulnerable or already inclined toward change. Gandhi
and English public opinion did not force the British government to leave India;
the British were exhausted by world wars and less dependent economically on
Indian trade than they had previously been, so they were ready to quit. Likewise, white farmers had mechanized cotton agriculture in the American South,
so the American economy no longer needed a pool of cheap rural labor. The
South African government and its white constituency, however, resolutely resisted any concessions to the black majority. White Afrikaners considered
themselves a beleaguered band of pioneers, circling their wagons into a *laager*,
or defensive formation, against the tide of African "savagery." With no mother
country to return to, they intended to resist until the bitter end.

The conclusion seems inescapable that non-violent protest against an
oppressive government will likely succeed only when an outside audience is
positioned to force change and when the government loses its nerve or self-
confidence. If this seems to place stringent limits on the strategy of non-
violence, it is worth pointing out that similar conditions limit violent resistance as well. The guerrilla forces of Castro and Guevara succeeded in Cuba
because Batista's dictatorship collapsed. Cuban communism endured after its
victory mainly because of massive outside support from the Soviet Union.
Castro's imitators, and Guevara himself in South America, could not repro-
duce the Cuban model of violent revolution, just as the ANC did not match
Gandhi's non-violent success. Indeed, when the ANC itself turned to violence
in the 1960s, the new strategy failed as abysmally as the old. Both non-violent
and violent change require the appropriate historical circumstances, which
had not yet arrived in South Africa.

The African National Congress literally wandered in the wilderness for
over twenty-five years after Mandela and his associates were sentenced to
Robben Island in 1964. Oliver Tambo and other exiles set up headquarters first
in Julius Nyerere's Tanzania, then later in the newly independent state of Zam-
bia, a bit closer to South Africa. In exile the ANC changed from a non-violent
mass movement to a small, clandestine clique dedicated to guerrilla warfare
and the violent overthrow of the government. It also became more heavily de-

411

pendent on the Soviet bloc for weapons and economic support. Though the exiled South African leaders managed to create a presence at the United Nations, securing official observer status in 1974, they felt frustrated at the lack of interest in their cause at the UN and in the United States throughout the 1960s and 1970s. ANC reliance on communist states, therefore, developed out of pragmatic necessity as much as ideological affinity. Historian Scott Thomas has concluded: "The ANC preferred communist assistance to that provided by international organisations. The communist sources provided funds at short notice, when they were really needed, and without a lot of bureaucratic meddling."

Developments within South Africa during the 1970s rescued the ANC from irrelevance or oblivion. A new generation of activists, drawn mainly from the student population, organized a black consciousness movement that was heavily influenced by black power advocates in the United States. Mimicking the mannerisms, lingo, and even the "Afro" hairstyles of the American Black Panthers, black consciousness leaders such as Steven Biko broke away from the liberal, integrated university students' union and founded an all-black South African Students' Organization (SASO). When the government began requiring the use of Afrikaans as well as English and African languages in the schools and universities, SASO spearheaded a school boycott in Soweto, the black shantytown southwest of Johannesburg. Beginning on June 16, 1976, the student revolt virtually shut down black schools. The police engaged in running battles with student militants, and before the revolt died down at the end of 1976 at least six hundred Africans were killed, most of them children, and four thousand more were injured. Six thousand leaders were arrested, many were tortured, and some died in prison, including Steven Biko.

The Soweto revolt was sparked by youths with no memory of the ANC's Defiance Campaign. One of their number, Murphy Morobe, later admitted: "We thought we were the first people to fight the government." Yet the ANC made the most of the new situation, recruiting thousands of students forced into exile by the suppression of the Soweto disturbances. After training the recruits at camps in Angola, the ANC infiltrated them back into South Africa to perform spectacular deeds of "armed propaganda," such as the torching of a coal liquification plant on June 1, 1980. The South African government, however, retaliated massively against the so-called front-line states that harbored ANC guerrilla bases and swiftly neutralized this latest wave of sabotage.

Perhaps the most effective ANC recruitment in the wake of the Soweto revolt took place on Robben Island, where Nelson Mandela inspired the younger generation of militants. Already forty-six years old when he disappeared into South Africa's gulag, Mandela had been born on July 18, 1918, and given the Xhosa name Rolihlala, which can be roughly translated as "troublemaker." His

Christian mother, however, sent him to a Methodist mission school where he was baptized with the English name Nelson. His father belonged to a minor branch of the Thembu royal family, and Nelson Rolihlala was trained to be a counselor of the Thembu paramount chief. He fled to Johannesburg, however, to escape an arranged marriage and fell in with Walter Sisulu, six years his senior, who became his mentor in ANC politics. Just one of many leaders during the Defiance Campaign, Mandela first gained notoriety when he dodged police for months as underground leader of Umkhonto we Sizwe and then delivered a ringing defense speech at his 1964 trial. Yet it was in prison that he showed his rare leadership qualities. Withdrawing deeply within himself, he developed a cool reserve and immense self-control that, added to his already royal bearing, imparted great authority. Viewing Robben Island as a microcosm of apartheid society, where whites held all the power, he led a slow, steady campaign of stubborn resistance and timely negotiation that gradually eased the harsh conditions of prison life. He and his associates also won the right to study in their cells, so when the Soweto prisoners arrived in 1976 their elders turned Robben Island into a virtual university of ANC principles and strategy. Then, beginning in 1980, the exiled ANC leaders mounted an international "Free Mandela" campaign that eventually transformed the imprisoned leader into an icon of rebellion.

While the ANC continued its covert work in prison and exile, both legal and illegal protests escalated within South Africa. Numerous groups of business, labor, and church leaders, both white and non-white, formed an umbrella coalition called the United Democratic Front (UDF) in 1983. Intentionally keeping its distance from the banned ANC so that it could operate above ground, the UDF followed the policies of non-racialism and non-violent protest that the African National Congress had pioneered. One of the UDF religious leaders, Desmond Tutu, the Anglican archbishop of Cape Town, received the Nobel Peace Prize in 1984, as Albert Luthuli had a generation earlier.

That same year, the black masses in the shantytowns erupted in revolt again, this time hoping to overthrow the entire apartheid system. The newest township rebels, many of whom belonged to a "lost generation" that had been out of school since the Soweto revolt of 1976, organized rent strikes, forced their neighbors to boycott white stores, and viciously hunted down government informers. Many Africans believed to be collaborating with the white government were tortured and killed with flaming "necklaces," rubber tires thrown around victims' necks, filled with gasoline, then ignited. The ANC had not prompted the township revolt but nevertheless welcomed it as the "people's war" they had been proclaiming since the 1960s. One of the younger ANC exiles, Thabo Mbeki, coined a slogan that summed up the goal of the new war, "We shall make South Africa ungovernable." It seemed for a time that they might succeed,

413

as the militants in the shantytowns terrorized and neutralized the police net-work of informers. In 1986, however, President Pieter W. Botha, who had culti-vated close ties with the army and its network of government supporters dubbed "securocrats," declared a nationwide state of emergency. Soldiers re-placed policemen in the black townships, detaining thousands of people with-out trial. With the liberal use of torture and terror, the military suppressed the township revolt by the end of 1986. The United Democratic Front mounted protest marches against the state of emergency, but in February 1988 Botha banned the UDF. This generation of struggles, both violent and non-violent, seemed as unsuccessful as the previous ones had been.

Yet by the 1980s important changes had taken place, both within South Africa and outside it. Just as in the Soviet Union, "tectonic shifts" tilted the landscape dramatically towards a political revolution. The township revolts and the Free Mandela campaign finally energized public opinion in the United States and other non-communist nations. Spurred by both moral outrage and economic fears, businesses began withdrawing from South Africa, and govern-ments slapped economic sanctions on the country. The Reverend Leon Sullivan in the United States fashioned a code of conduct, usually referred to as the Sullivan Principles, for American corporations doing business in South Africa. This and similar codes adopted in England and the European Community tried to make foreign-owned businesses agents for social change in South Africa. Then in 1985, the violence in the townships scared American and European banks into withdrawing their short-term loans to the white Nationalist govern-ment, and the following year the U.S. Congress passed the Comprehensive Anti-Apartheid Act, imposing numerous trade and investment sanctions. Finally, in 1987, Reverend Sullivan declared his principles a failure and called on American businesses to disinvest, to get rid of their financial stakes in South Af-rica altogether. Under political and shareholder pressure, most large corpora-tions complied. White South Africa became an international pariah.

Sanctions by themselves did not bring down the Afrikaner Nationalist government, but they exacerbated problems inherent in the South African economy. Racial socialism, or affirmative action for Afrikaners, had succeeded almost too well, and by 1980 over two-thirds of the whites were employed as technical, professional, managerial, or skilled crafts personnel. Since the black majority was deprived of technical and higher education, the South African economy developed a skilled labor shortage. Furthermore, the pathetically low wages paid to blacks prevented them from developing much purchasing power, so South Africa's economy suffered from overproduction and under-consumption, much like the United States and the industrialized world during the Great Depression of the 1930s. Realizing that apartheid was proving to be bad for business, many white industrialists bankrolled the United Democratic

Front's legal demonstrations calling for an easing of the segregationist regime. Sanctions, therefore, struck against a vulnerable economy, which depended on exports to sop up excess production and to pay the interest on foreign debts.

Another external occurrence, the end of the Cold War, finally precipitated dramatic changes in South Africa. When F. W. de Klerk replaced P. W. Botha as state president in August 1989, he realized that Mikhail Gorbachev's revolution in Russia had presented him with an unprecedented opportunity. In the late 1980s the Soviet Union and the United States had begun to coordinate their Third World policies, liquidating a civil war in Angola between American-backed and Communist guerrillas. The Angolan settlement deprived the ANC of their base camps in that country and promised to dry up further financial and military aid from the Soviet Union. The African nationalists felt pressed to terminate their armed struggle now that they could not depend on Soviet support. At the same time, the easing of guerrilla pressure on South Africa made stringent security measures less necessary for the government. Since the Soviet menace had disappeared with the end of the Cold War, de Klerk could reach out to the ANC without fear of a new red scare among his white constituency. Economic historians Lowenberg and Kaempfer sum up the changed reality: "The expected net utility to South Africa's rulers of maintaining apartheid was falling at the same time as the net gain to the ANC of negotiating in good faith was rising."

In fact, de Klerk's predecessor had already extended tentative feelers to the imprisoned Nelson Mandela in response to the international Free Mandela campaign. As early as 1982, Mandela's jailers had transferred him from Robben Island to Pollsmoor prison on the mainland near Cape Town, and beginning in 1985 government ministers conferred with their famous prisoner, sometimes even taking him for long drives in the country. Curious bystanders never recognized him since he had been imprisoned for so long. During these secret talks, the government remained as much Mandela's prisoner as he was theirs, since they wanted to release him but could not figure out how to do so without losing face. In December 1988 the prison authorities transferred him again, to a minimum-security facility in the Paarl wine district; and on July 5, 1989, he was transported to President Botha's office for a face-to-face meeting. Yet nothing happened until de Klerk forced Botha out of office in August 1989. Pieter W. Botha resembled Yuri Andropov in Russia; he was aware of the need for change but unwilling to take the risks.

Frederik Willem de Klerk was born on March 18, 1936, to a politically active family of Afrikaners. His father had been appointed a cabinet minister in three different Nationalist governments and an uncle had briefly served as prime minister. Frederik was first elected to parliament in 1972 and held a variety of cabinet posts over the next two decades. Curiously, however, he was

415

largely unknown when he became president, and a Johannesburg newspaper compared him to American president George Bush as a "man who left no footprints." In fact, he was considered a member of the conservative wing of the party and no one expected him to push radical reforms once he was elected. De Klerk, however, like Mikhail Gorbachev in Russia, believed that reform was necessary or his long-entrenched system of government would collapse. He did not intend to hand over power to the black majority, but hoped to forge a power-sharing arrangement which would retain considerable influence, if not an outright veto, for the white minority. Again like Gorbachev, he failed; for he unwittingly set in motion a chain of events that resulted in black majority rule.

Once installed as South African president, de Klerk permitted the banned UDF to mount protest marches once more, and he released all the political prisoners from the 1964 trial except Nelson Mandela. Then on February 2, 1990, the president astounded the nation and the world with an inaugural speech, in which he announced the legalization of the ANC and the South African Communist Party and promised an end to apartheid and negotiations for power-sharing with the black majority. On February 11, 1990, the seventy-one-year-old Nelson Mandela walked out of Victor Verster prison farm a free man for the first time in twenty-seven years. He was flown to Cape Town for a raucous rally that evening and then a triumphant international press conference the following day. For the next four years, the freed black prisoner and the white Afrikaner president were, in the words of *Washington Post* journalist David Ottaway, "chained together." "Like two escaping convicts . . . they needed one another to make good their run to freedom." They jointly shared the Nobel Peace Prize in 1993, the third Nobel awarded to South Africans during their generations of struggle.

The road to a new South Africa turned out to be longer and more violent than either man expected in 1990. Serious constitutional talks did not even begin until the end of 1991, for both Mandela and de Klerk faced serious divisions within their own constituencies. The first open conference of the African National Congress in a generation, held in July 1991, elected Mandela as president to replace the seriously ill Oliver Tambo and confirmed his policy of negotiations with de Klerk. Yet it also purged about half of Mandela's aging contemporaries from the national executive council, replacing them with younger militants. Cyril Ramaphosa, a thirty-eight-year-old trade unionist, became secretary-general of the ANC, took over the day-to-day work of the organization, and kept open secret channels of negotiation with the white government. For his part, de Klerk held a national, all-white referendum in March 1992 that gave him a thumping mandate for constitutional negotiations. Still the talks dragged on, with many adjournments, through 1992 and 1993.

Continuous violence marred the process of constitutional change. Many

ANC militants resented the slow process of negotiations, preferring to press the "people's war" to a triumphant overthrow of the government. Over Mandela's objections, a program of mass action was mounted in 1992 that quickly turned ugly. A more important source of violence was the Inkatha Freedom Party organized by Zulu leader Mangosuthu Buthelezi. Chief Buthelezi, whom journalist David Ottaway called "the most unpleasant politician on the African continent," was the prime minister of the largest Bantustan homeland, Kwa Zulu in the province of Natal. As the leader of seven million Zulus, he had a vested interest in preserving apartheid in some form, forging his own alliance with de Klerk, and preventing the ANC from taking power. Throughout the early 1990s, Zulu warriors carrying traditional spears and other weapons ruthlessly attacked ANC supporters throughout Natal and in the townships surrounding Johannesburg, accounting for six to ten deaths per day on the average. Mandela charged that the South African police were conniving with Inkatha to torpedo the constitutional negotiations, and he eventually became disillusioned with de Klerk, who seemed unwilling or unable to stem the violence. A commission of inquiry chaired by Justice Richard Goldstone at the end of 1992 found considerable evidence that government security forces did aid and abet Inkatha in its attacks on the ANC. President de Klerk was probably not responsible for these police actions, but he was unable to control the "securocrats" who had become entrenched in the government under his predecessor, P. W. Botha.

Finally, a summit conference between de Klerk and Mandela, on September 26, 1992, got the constitutional negotiations back on track, but by this time de Klerk had lost control of the process. The ongoing violence, the revelations of the Goldstone Commission, and Mandela's insistence on majority rule prompted de Klerk to abandon his power-sharing fantasy. When a young ANC militant, Chris Hani, was assassinated by a fanatical white in April 1993, Mandela, not de Klerk, calmed the populace and prevented an explosion of revenge and hatred. The white community realized, perhaps for the first time, that Nelson Mandela provided their best security against chaos as apartheid fell apart. Legitimacy and authority were already shifting to Mandela from de Klerk just as they passed from Gorbachev to Yeltsin after the abortive coup in Moscow.

The negotiators completed a provisional constitution on November 18, 1993, providing for elections the following April to a four-hundred-member House of Assembly and a ninety-member Senate, consisting of ten members each from nine newly constituted provinces. In a concession to whites, a number of cabinet positions and one of two deputy presidents were reserved for minority parties during the five-year tenure of the first government. After that, however, beginning with the second election in 1999, elections would be conducted on the basis of one-person one-vote, with no minority guarantees or power-sharing mechanisms. On four days in late April 1994, black and white voters waited patiently for up to six or seven hours in lines that stretched the length of whole villages. The African National Congress won 62 percent of the vote and elected 252 delegates to the Assembly. They also controlled the provincial governments and the national Senate seats of seven provinces, while Inkatha won in Kwa Zulu and the white Nationalists managed a victory in the Western Cape Province around Cape Town. Nelson Mandela took office as president of South Africa on May 10, 1994, with an ANC assistant, Thabo Mbeki, and the Afrikaner F. W. de Klerk as his deputy presidents. Even before the five-year term of office expired, however, de Klerk found himself redundant and irrelevant, so he resigned in 1996 as the new constitution was being drafted in final form. President Mandela signed the new constitution on December 10, 1996, at the town of Sharpeville, where white police had massacred blacks almost forty years before.

The white supremacist regime fell from power in South Africa because it was economically dysfunctional and increasingly out of step with world public opinion. The generations of struggle by the African National Congress did not force white Afrikaners to relinquish control, but they did establish black Africans on the moral high ground where they were assured of eventual success. Nelson Mandela candidly remarked to a white general:

> If you want to go to war, I must be honest and admit that we cannot stand up to you on the battlefield. . . . But you must remember two things. You cannot win because of our numbers: you cannot kill us all. And you cannot win because of the international community.

Fortunately, white South Africa produced a Gorbachev-figure, F. W. de Klerk, who recognized these realities and negotiated himself out of a job.

The South African freedom movement mirrored many trends and events of the twentieth century, but in one respect it was quite out of step with the rest of the world. For one of the few times in the century's history, communists played a creative and morally inspiring role. Indeed, the final anti-apartheid coalition united Christian believers, such as Archbishop Desmond Tutu and the secretary of the South African Council of Churches, Frank Chikane, with non-believers and atheists. Joe Slovo, the white general secretary of the South African Communist Party, once commented that "there are only two sorts of people in life that you can trust — good Christians and good Communists." The martyred Chris Hani was raised a Roman Catholic and once considered becoming a priest, but he eventually fell away from religion. A few months before his assassination, he told an interviewer, "I . . . admired the selflessness of the priests who worked among us. They lived alone, frugal and puritan in their life style. . . . My political involvement was a natural outworking of my religious convictions. . . ." Nelson Mandela provided the ecumenical leadership needed to head up such a coalition. Never a communist himself and originally opposed to the alliance with the SACP, he came to admire the Communists' ideals and dedication and to value their company. Raised a Methodist, he admitted in an interview about his beliefs that "I am not particularly religious or spiritual. . . . The question concerning the existence of God is something I reflect on in solitude." During his prison years, he attended church services conducted by all the different denominations, and once liberated he valued religious individuals and groups primarily for their contributions to social and political justice.

As president, Mandela made reconciliation between whites and blacks, former oppressors and their victims, his personal crusade. He brought together the spouses of black activists and apartheid leaders for "reconciliation lunches" and publicly embraced the prosecutor who had tried to impose the death penalty in his 1964 trial. Instead of exacting revenge in "Nuremberg Trials" for members of the previous regime, he appointed Archbishop Tutu to head a Truth and Reconciliation Commission, which issued its final report in 1998. The commission afforded apartheid leaders an opportunity to confess their crimes and then apply for amnesty. Controversially, it also condemned incidents of violence committed by the African National Congress. Even Mandela thought this went too far, but after failing to block the report's release, he accepted the commission report publicly. Archbishop Tutu concluded: "We have looked the beast in the eye. We will have come to terms with our horrendous past, and it will no longer keep us hostage."

In 1999, Nelson Mandela declined to run for another term as president. Thabo Mbeki ran as the ANC candidate and was elected with a large majority. Mandela's retirement was an almost unique example of a revolutionary leader voluntarity relinquishing power. In the final analysis, the twentieth century's longest struggle for self-determination, though marred by violence, provided a model for the principled exercise of power.

CHAPTER TWENTY-TWO

Non-Violent and Violent Change around the World

Toward the end of the century, dictators were on the run as an unprecedented wave of non-violent change swept around the world. Indeed, one remarkable example, the "People Power" revolution in the Philippines, preceded the collapse of Soviet Communism and of apartheid in South Africa by several years.

A colony of the United States from 1898 to 1946, the Philippine Islands had inherited both American political institutions and a heavy economic dependence on the former mother country. With its entire period of political independence engulfed by the Cold War, the country had become a pawn in the superpower rivalry. The United States retained five military bases on the Philippines, including Clark Air Field near Manila and the gigantic Subic Bay naval base, headquarters of the U.S. Seventh Fleet and home to sophisticated Polaris submarines armed with nuclear-tipped missiles. The U.S. government influenced Philippine elections to ensure that staunchly anti-communist presidents were chosen. One such president, Ferdinand Marcos, elected with American backing in 1965, declared martial law in 1972, suspending the constitution and extending his personal dictatorship indefinitely. The American president at the time, Richard Nixon, did not publicly endorse Marcos's coup, but the U.S. government continued to funnel military and economic aid to his regime. Ronald Reagan, who had embarked on a fact-finding mission to the Philippines in 1969 and became U.S. president in 1981, considered himself a personal friend of Ferdinand Marcos and his flamboyant wife, Imelda.

The Marcos administration systematically stripped the Philippines of its assets. The dictator's personal wealth was estimated at about 10 billion dollars, and his cronies were believed to have extorted at least as much from the government. Imelda Marcos amused Americans and shocked Filipinos with her extravagant shopping sprees in New York. The former beauty queen eventually accumulated over three thousand pairs of shoes and a thousand formal gowns. Such conspicuous consumption caused widespread anger in a nation constrained by a largely one-crop (sugar) economy and wracked by endemic poverty. A communist guerrilla movement flourished in the countryside throughout the islands, and a separatist rebellion of Muslims also flared up on the large southern island of Mindanao. Marcos's military became a haven for cronies, promoted beyond their qualifications and kept on after their normal retirement ages, and an instrument of oppression. The military perpetrated at least two thousand murders during the Marcos dictatorship.

Reformers in the Philippines had long pinned their hopes on a charismatic politician named Benigno "Ninoy" Aquino. A member of the same landowning elite as Marcos, Aquino had begun his political career as a lawyer and a senator in the 1950s. Journalists pointed out that the two men, Marcos and Aquino, were strikingly similar in many ways — gregarious, ambitious, ruthless — but their wives made them different. Imelda Romualdez Marcos was a poor girl who got lucky, and consequently she played on the insecurity and ambition of her husband. Corazon Cojuangco Aquino, born to wealth and security, was driven primarily by her Catholic religion and a sense of duty, bringing out the best in her spouse. Marcos jailed Senator Aquino in 1972 after he declared martial law, keeping him behind bars for seven and a half years. The outgoing Aquino nearly went crazy as long stretches of solitary confinement cut him off from human contact, but he apparently underwent a religious experience that helped him retain his sanity. Pressure from the human rights campaign of President Jimmy Carter convinced Marcos to release Aquino for medical treatment in the United States in 1980. The opposition politician then decided to return to the Philippines and take his chances in 1983.

Aquino suspected the worst but calculated that if he were jailed or kept under house arrest, he would become a symbol of opposition to Marcos, and if he were killed he would become a martyr. He calculated correctly. The moment his airplane touched down at Manila airport on August 21, 1983, military officers boarded it, took Aquino off, and shot him in the head before he reached the tarmac. They then unloaded their machine guns into a drifter they had brought with them and proclaimed him the assassin, and a communist as well. In an overwhelmingly Catholic nation (roughly 85 percent), Aquino's Christlike sacrifice had the same impact as the abortive Easter Rising in Ireland, seventy years previously (see chapter 13, volume 1). It provides another striking example of the "triumph of failure." Theologian Walter Wink has concluded:

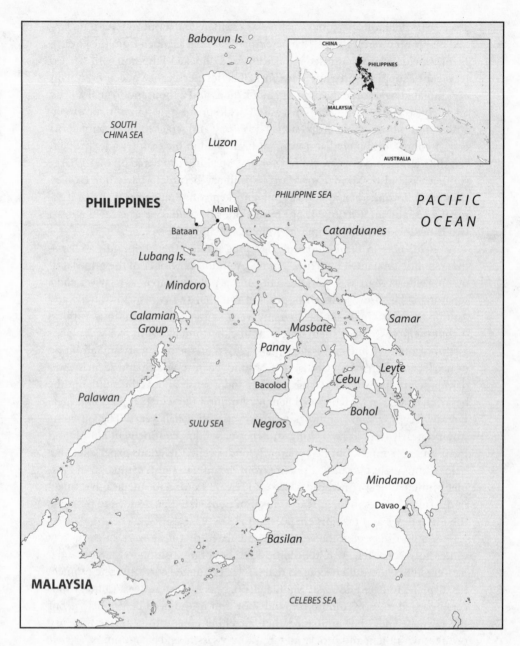

The Philippines

His death changed nothing. Marcos was more powerful than ever, having disposed of his only rival. Yet his death changed everything. Two and a half years later, Marcos was nonviolently removed from power. . . . Jesus's death was like that, only he took on more than a single ruler.

The Aquino assassination outraged the hierarchy of the Catholic Church in the Philippines, particularly Cardinal Jaime Sin of Manila. Cardinal Sin had long faced an agonizing "effectiveness dilemma," like Pope Pius XII during World War II or American officials who privately opposed the Vietnam War. He often criticized the corruption and abuses of the Marcos regime, but in order to retain his own personal and institutional freedom, and thus remain "effective," he spoke in measured tones without naming names. Yet Aquino's murder emboldened him, and he eventually convinced the martyr's widow that she would make the most effective opposition candidate if Marcos should call an early election. When the dictator did gamble on a snap election, called in late 1985 for February 7, 1986, Cardinal Sin brokered a compromise between Corey Aquino and a seasoned opposition politician, Salvador Laurel. Aquino ran for president with Laurel as her vice-presidential running mate. Marcos committed massive electoral fraud and claimed a victory, but Aquino's supporters, backed by international observers, counted the votes independently and proclaimed her in the lead. Neither side ever completed the vote count and both contenders claimed to be president.

Corey Aquino, drawing on her religious beliefs and supported by the hierarchy of the Catholic Church, proclaimed a non-violent campaign of protests, boycotts, and demonstrations against Marcos's fraudulent presidency. Then, on Saturday, February 22, a military rebellion against Marcos transformed the situation. Generals Juan Ponce Enrile and Fidel Ramos had joined an existing conspiracy of lower-level officers who felt humiliated by the dictator's political appointments in the army and frustrated that their own advancement was blocked. Enrile had been a staunch supporter of Marcos, one of the architects of martial law, and Ramos was a cautious and non-political soldier; but both men joined the rebels when they began to fear for their lives in the Marcos regime. When the dictator discovered their plans, they put the rebellion into effect prematurely on February 22, withdrawing defensively to two military installations, Camp Aguinaldo and Camp Crame, in the Manila area. Had Marcos acted decisively, or had the Philippine people not supported the rebels, the military coup would have been suppressed. But the president hesitated on February 22, and Cardinal Sin appealed to Manila's citizens to surround the besieged camps with a human barricade.

The decisive confrontation occurred on the morning of Sunday, February 23. A convoy of tanks and armed commandos was proceeding along the broad boulevard that Manilans call Edsa *(Epifanio de los Santos Avenida)* when they were stopped by a line of nuns kneeling and praying the rosary. Other citizens surged forward, handing flowers to the soldiers and begging them not to fire on their brothers and sisters. If the protesters had been armed, the tanks would have swept them aside and crushed the rebellion at the military camps. However, the soldiers hesitated at the sight of praying demonstrators, and finally their commander ordered a retreat. From that time on, more and more detachments of soldiers defected to the rebels. Finally, when the United States government made it clear to Marcos that it would not support a violent suppression of the revolt, the Philippine president resigned; and on the night of Tuesday, February 25, 1986, American military helicopters took Ferdinand and Imelda Marcos into exile in Hawaii. Corey Aquino had already been sworn in as president earlier that day.

Though the new president proved unable to meet the sky-high expectations of her supporters for all the reforms the country needed, she did survive numerous attempts by the exiled dictator, and even by some of her military supporters, to overthrow her. She served out her term of office and passed the presidency on peacefully to a successor. Her administration also negotiated an end to the American military presence in the Philippines.

During the remarkable days of February 1986, People Power protected the rebellious Philippine military and convinced the United States to abandon its longtime client-dictator. The Philippine people looked to inspired and principled leaders, and they drew on their own religious beliefs and an outraged sense of nationalism. The Marcos dictatorship had profoundly humiliated the citizens of the Philippines. Benigno Aquino himself, before returning to his country, publicly questioned "whether the Filipino is worth suffering, or even dying for. Is he not a coward who would readily yield to any colonizer, be he foreign or homegrown?" Aquino finally decided "I have come to the conclusion that he is worth dying for," and the Filipinos themselves stood up and proved him right. The morning that Marcos left the country, the *Manila Times* editorialized: "We have redeemed ourselves before the world. . . . No one will ever refer to our race as being made up of so many millions of cowards." Peaceful protest can draw on nationalist emotions as much as warfare can.

Yet more than religion or the quasi-religious feeling of nationalism is required for a successful movement of non-violent change. The Philippine People Power revolution falls into a tradition begun with Sinn Fein in Ireland and Mohandas Gandhi's *swaraj* campaigns in India. The civil rights marches of Martin Luther King in the United States, the Solidarity movement in Poland, and the African National Congress's anti-apartheid struggle also fit the pattern. In all or most of these cases, the oppressive authorities were already weakened by internal doubts, economic troubles, and an unfavorable trend in international opinion. Mass non-violent protest proved successful at overthrowing dictators and oppressive governments when crucial elites, such as the military and the church in the Philippines, or business leaders in South Africa, defected from the regime. Michael Randle, an activist who has written a definitive account of non-violent resistance, sums up the essentials of such protests:

> The short answer is that a government is only as powerful as its ability to command the loyalty and obedience of key state institutions — the army, the police, the civil service — and, beyond that, to secure the cooperation or at least the compliance of the majority of the population. . . . Governments need people more than people need governments.

Another important factor suggested by the historical record is a hint or threat of violence accompanying the non-violent protests. None of the regions that experienced peaceful change in the twentieth century — Ireland, India, the American South, Poland and Eastern Europe, South Africa, or the Philippines — remained wholly free of violence. Indeed, a "good cop/bad cop" effect often seemed at work. The non-violent Sinn Fein of the 1920s made a worthy negotiating partner for the British, in part because of the threat of the IRA if negotiations failed. The peaceful protests inspired by Corey Aquino and Cardinal Sin went hand in hand with a military uprising.

The historical reality that non-violent protest seems most effective when backed by a threat of violence poses a moral challenge to non-violent leaders. Indeed, Gandhi often suspended his campaigns when violence broke out. Albert Luthuli, the Nobel Prize-winning leader of the African National Congress in South Africa, agonized over Nelson Mandela's adoption of violent sabotage as a strategy in the early 1960s. He finally rationalized a compromise with his conscience by not denouncing the violent actions but insisting that they be carried out by a separate organization. Perhaps it would have been better had he not compromised. Violence is so prevalent in the world, especially in crisis situations, that it will always remain a threat. It may sound cynical, but if moral leaders hold their supporters faithful to the path of non-violence, they can always be sure that "bad cops" will still lurk in the background making them appear moderate. The historical record suggests that non-violent protest shadowed by a threat of violence is more powerful than either peaceful protest or violent rebellion alone. Corey Aquino's People Power would probably not have overthrown Ferdinand Marcos if the military had not rebelled, but the dictator would have crushed the military rebels if the unarmed people had not protected them.

In the late twentieth century this dynamic of peaceful protest backed by a threat of violence swept away other dictators besides Marcos. On the very day in 1986 that the Filipinos conducted their dramatic election, the long-time dictator of Haiti, President-for-Life Jean-Claude Duvalier, was forced into exile. In the 1990s, formerly one-party regimes in South Korea and Taiwan implemented democratic reforms and allowed opposition parties to contend freely. In 1997 a formerly imprisoned Korean opposition leader, Kim Dae Jung, won a free election and was inaugurated as president. Then in May 1998 widespread student protests in Indonesia forced General Suharto, the country's dictatorial president for thirty-two years, to step down. Suharto's regime resembled that of Marcos in the Philippines in many respects, though it was even longer-lived. The *Washington Post* accurately described his government as one marked by "rampant corruption, monopolies, nepotism, and crony capitalism." Yet largely peaceful and principled protest finally toppled him.

Nevertheless, not all the oppressive regimes fell by century's end. In the euphoria generated by the end of the Cold War and the collapse of the Soviet Union, commentators sometimes heralded the end of communism. Yet the largest nation on earth remains a communist dictatorship. When Chinese pro-democracy protesters, inspired in part by the wave of non-violent change sweeping Asia and the world, mounted massive demonstrations in 1989, the Chinese Communist government brutally suppressed them.

Students and intellectuals had traditionally provided the moral leadership for Chinese society, but Mao's disastrous Cultural Revolution of the 1960s and 1970s (see chapter 4) humiliated the intellectuals, deposing them from positions of influence and forcing them to work at manual labor in the countryside. Mao's successor, Deng Xiaoping (Teng Hsiao-p'ing),[1] attempted to modernize and liberalize the Chinese economy while still maintaining a one-party dictatorship. He realized that he needed the expertise of intellectuals for economic growth, but he did not encourage them to resume their moral and political roles. As a result, tension built up between the intellectual proletariat and the Communist Party.

Deng's halfway reforms resulted in greater prosperity among enterprising peasants and city entrepreneurs, but they also led to great economic disparities and a raging inflation. Communist Party leaders and many officers of the People's Liberation Army took advantage of their privileged positions to engage in smuggling and profiteering. Furthermore, a greater openness to foreign invest-

---

1. In this chapter, I am reversing my previous conventions for dealing with Chinese names. Previously, I employed the old style of transliterating Chinese into English, since most historical sources used these older forms. However, in dealing with recent events, the new style *(pinyin)* of transliteration is firmly established; therefore, in this chapter, I use the new style English forms (e.g., Deng Xiaoping) and give the old style (Teng Hsiao-p'ing) in parentheses, wherever possible. In many cases, however, only the new style names are readily available.

ment under Deng's government inevitably led to a penetration of China by foreign ideas of democracy and liberty. Finally, the party leadership seemed split between reformers, such as Hu Yaobang and Zhao Zhiyang, and more traditional authoritarians, with Deng holding a deciding vote between the factions. China, therefore, seemed to be experiencing economic difficulties and a weakening of leadership sufficient for fundamental, non-violent change. Influenced by the example of Corey Aquino in the Philippines and Mikhail Gorbachev in Russia, China's intellectuals published appeals for greater intellectual and political freedom and an end to corruption.

The balance of power within the government, however, had already begun to tip back toward a cautious conservatism. Hu Yaobang was dismissed from his post as party secretary in 1987, leaving only Zhao Zhiyang as a possible Gorbachev-figure. In the meantime, Deng Xiaoping was slowly withdrawing from public view but retaining absolute power behind the scenes. After 1987 the "Paramount Leader," as he was called, held no governmental or party position, and was not even a member of the Politburo; however, he remained chairman of the Central Military Commission, which meant he controlled the ultimate arbiter in an authoritarian society, military force. Unlike Soviet Russia at the same time, therefore, the Chinese Communist state had not rotted from within. A small coterie of eighty-year-olds, who had embarked with Mao on the Long March of the 1930s, still controlled everything.

In the spring of 1989, the students and intellectuals of China's capital, Beijing (Peking), mounted an escalating series of demonstrations aimed at fundamental reforms. The demonstrations would have started on May 4, the seventieth anniversary of a seminal event in modern Chinese history, the anti-Japanese protests of May 4, 1919, which led to both a cultural renaissance and the founding of the Chinese Communist Party (see chapter 20 of volume 1). However, the death of Hu Yaobang on April 15 presented the dissidents with an opportunity they could not pass up. On April 18, 1989, university students staged a sit-in at Tiananmen Square, the great central space of Beijing facing the old Imperial Palace and the Communists' Great Hall of the People. The demonstrators voiced seven demands, including a rehabilitation of Hu Yaobang's reputation, such self-interested policies as an increase in the education budget, and moral and political reforms, especially an end to official corruption and greater freedom of speech and the press. Though they called on individual Communist leaders to step down, few of the protesters advocated an overthrow of the entire system.

The demonstrations swelled in number to about 200,000 by the time of Hu's funeral on April 22. Then in the weeks that followed, journalists, teachers, and other professionals, as well as many ordinary citizens of the capital, began joining the students at the daily demonstrations in Tiananmen Square. As

427

many as a million people mingled in the square on some days. The government stalled for time, since it had scheduled two major international events in the capital, a meeting of the Asian Development Bank on May 4 and a summit meeting with Mikhail Gorbachev on May 15. Over a thousand foreign correspondents in China for these events reported the remarkable demonstrations in Tiananmen Square to an amazed world. Deng Xiaoping, however, made it clear to the Chinese leadership as early as April 25 that the demonstrations must be suppressed, violently if necessary. So after Gorbachev left China in mid-May, the party eased Zhao Zhiyang, who had made conciliatory statements about the student demonstrations, out of his positions of authority and decided to terminate the demonstrations.

At first, the military found the citizens of Beijing blocking their way whenever they attempted to move troops towards the city center. Beijing had stayed at peace for over three hundred years, even while the rest of China had been torn by civil war and revolution. The sight of the People's Army violating their "home village" outraged inhabitants of the capital. Unlike in the Philippines, however, the Chinese Communist leadership finally ordered the military to roll over the non-violent protests. In the early morning hours of June 4, 1989, tanks and troop carriers headed for Tiananmen Square, blowing up barricades and engaging in running battles along the way. They surrounded the square and ordered the students to disperse. In the melees that followed, at least a thousand people died. The government then began a hunt for student leaders, arresting and executing any that fell into their hands. People Power failed in China as decisively as it succeeded in the Philippines.

The tragic events of Tiananmen Square present sobering lessons to advocates of non-violent political change. Though China's government was divided in the 1980s, a hardline faction won the internal power struggle and no significant sector of the elite defected from the authoritarian government. Above all, the army remained loyal to Deng Xiaoping and did not hesitate to suppress non-violent protests, in direct contrast to the Philippine situation. Any government that retains the loyalty of the power elites in its society can defy international public opinion and forcibly repress non-violent demonstrations (or violent rebellion, for that matter). China's leaders have not been the only ones to do so in recent years. A ruthless military regime in Burma crushed non-violent demonstrations in 1988, then overturned the results of an election the following year. They kept the leader of the non-violent resistance, Aung San Suu Kyi, under house arrest for the rest of the century, even after she was awarded the Nobel Peace Prize.

The conclusion seems simplistic but unavoidable: a government cannot be overthrown, either by violence or non-violence, until it is ready to collapse. Movements for fundamental change, therefore, must be long-term commitments. Solidarity did not succeed in Poland on its first try in 1980; it only toppled the Communist regime a decade later when Gorbachev withdrew his support from the Polish leadership. Benigno Aquino did not overthrow Ferdinand Marcos; his widow and Marcos's own military did, a few years after his assassination. Mounting a non-violent challenge to oppressive governments requires as much courage, determination, and perseverance as winning a war.

Despite the continued existence of oppressive regimes, the scope of political change in the latter years of the twentieth century still was remarkable. Dictators or oppressive systems of government were dispatched in the Soviet Union, Eastern Europe, South Africa, the Philippines, Indonesia, Chile, and the Congo. A widespread revulsion against violence, which traces back to the two world wars; a worldwide hunger for democratic freedoms and consumer prosperity; and the apparent failure of communism created favorable conditions for these striking changes. The walls indeed came tumbling down.

Though most political change in the late twentieth century occurred with a minimum of violence, people sometimes got crushed as the walls tumbled down. The two major sources of violence remaining at the end of the century were oppressive governments that resisted the forces of change and the sharp rivalries of competing ethnic or religious groups in unstable societies. The violence that did occur during the fall of the Soviet Union, for example, was either perpetrated by the government or the result of ethnic quarrels. Gorbachev sent in troops against the Baltic states of Latvia and Lithuania in early 1991, before deciding to back off. Hardline Communists took over the Soviet government briefly in August 1991 and unsuccessfully attempted to halt the forces of change. Later, as the Soviet Union fragmented, several instances of ethnic rivalry, most notably between Armenia and Azerbaijan, marred the largely peaceful separation of the various republics. Likewise, the liberation of South Africa was scarred by ethnic violence between the Zulu-based Inkatha movement and the African National Congress. In the South African case, the two major causes of violence blended together, for the apartheid state encouraged the black-on-black killing as a way of dividing the opposition. The most horrendous cases of violent change in the last decade of the twentieth century, however, took place in Yugoslavia and Rwanda. The break-up of Yugoslavia proved far more violent and chaotic than the fragmentation of the Soviet Union, and the ethnic violence in Rwanda assumed genocidal proportions.

Yugoslavia was an unstable amalgam of numerous ethnic groups first created after World War I and then re-created by the independent Communist regime of Marshal Joseph Broz Tito (see chapter 2). The three major ethnic groups — the Serbs, Croats, and Slovenes — were all South Slavs (or *Yugo* Slavs), who spoke similar languages but had different religious and cultural backgrounds. Numerous minority nationalities also lived in parts of Yugoslavia, such as the Albanians of Kosovo and the Muslims of Bosnia (descendants of South Slavs who had converted to Islam during the Ottoman Turkish occupation of their land). Tito and the Communist Party had worked hard to transcend ethnic divisiveness by stressing Yugoslav identity and communist internationalism, but at the same time they had organized the government along federal lines. Tito's Yugoslavia consisted of six constituent republics — Serbia, Croatia, Slovenia, Montenegro (a formerly independent principality whose inhabitants were ethnically Serbian), Macedonia (a territory with a late-developing, but separate ethnic identity), and Bosnia-Hercegovina (divided between Serbs, Croats, and Muslims) — and two autonomous provinces within Serbia — Kosovo and Vojvodina (both with mixed populations). This balancing act held the country together until Tito's death in 1980, but the dictator's successors accentuated the natural divisions of the country for their political advantage, playing on nationalist emotions in the constituent parts of Yugoslavia.

The two most vociferous nationalist leaders were Slobodan Milošević of Serbia and Franjo Tudjman of Croatia. Milošević was born in 1941 and worked his way up through the League of Communists of Yugoslavia (as the Communist Party was officially titled by Tito), taking over the party leadership of Serbia in 1986. He then manipulated growing unrest in the province of Kosovo to bolster his political support. Kosovo was sacred ground to Serbs, the site of their climactic battles with the Turks in the fourteenth century (see chapter 6 of volume 1), but over the centuries most Serbs had migrated out of the territory and it had become nearly 90 percent Albanian. After Tito's death the Albanians of Kosovo began agitating for greater freedom from Serb control or even independence, but Milošević whipped up Serbian emotions and removed Kosovo's existing autonomous powers. On June 28, 1989, the six-hundredth anniversary of the Serbian-Turkish battle of Kosovo Polje, Milošević harangued a crowd of a million Serbs who had made a pilgrimage to the hallowed ground. Sheer repression kept the lid on Kosovo for nearly a decade, but fierce fighting finally broke out there in 1998. In the meantime, however, Milošević's nationalist demagoguery made his position unassailable in Serbia. Franjo Tudjman was a decade older than Milošević and had fought with Tito's Partisans during World War II against the Nazis and many of his fellow-Croatians who formed a semi-fascist regime under Nazi domination. He became a historian after the war and gradually fashioned a revisionist account of the struggle, minimizing the atrocities committed by Croats. He was jailed by Tito in 1970 but after his release two years later he continued his historical revisionism and anti-Serbian agitation. By the time the Cold War came to an end in 1989, Yugoslavia was heading for a breakup. Milošević had already ridden the wave of nationalism to power in Serbia, and Tudjman was poised to do likewise in Croatia.

The initial impetus for Yugoslavia's dismemberment, however, came from Slovenia, a tiny republic of about two million Catholics, tucked away in the foothills of the Alps. Unlike the Serbs and Croats, Slovenians had never known national independence, but they had developed their own national consciousness in the nineteenth and twentieth centuries and considered themselves culturally more European than their Balkan neighbors. Bolstered by healthy trading relationships with Italy and Austria, Slovenia produced 18 percent of Yugoslavia's gross national product and contributed 25 percent of the federal budget, though it only had 8 percent of the federation's population. As the communist economy deteriorated in the 1980s, Slovenes resented the subsidies they provided to less productive regions. Milan Kučan, a communist-turned-nationalist like Milošević and Tudjman, proposed a looser federal system for Yugoslavia in 1989 and steered a resolution through his republic's legislature asserting a right of secession from the federation. Adding insult to injury, Kučan and the Slovenian nationalists also supported the Albanian protests against Serbian rule in Kosovo. In January 1990, when Kučan was unable to secure approval for a looser federal system from the Yugoslav Communist Party Congress in Belgrade, he walked out of the meeting followed by the Croatians. This effectively ended the unity of Yugoslav communism and precipitated the breakup of the federation.

Slovenia held free elections in April 1990. The voters chose Kučan as president but sharply defeated his Communist compatriots in the legislative voting, electing a moderate coalition of democratic politicians. Croatia then held elections in May, throwing out the Communists and bringing Franjo Tudjman and his Christian Democratic Union into power in a landslide. Neither Slovenia nor Croatia opted immediately for independence, and negotiations for a new form of federal system dragged on through the early part of 1991. When the talks finally deadlocked, the governments of Slovenia and Croatia coordinated a joint announcement of independence on June 25, 1991. The European countries closest to the scene — Italy, Austria, and Germany — seemed content to let Yugoslavia disintegrate into its component parts, but the great powers of the world were more disturbed by this development. American secretary of state James Baker visited Belgrade on June 21, 1991, just before the Slovenian and Croatian independence declarations, and tried to talk them out of it. This American intervention may have inadvertently signaled the Serbian-dominated Yugoslav military to try and abort secession.

The Yugoslav army invaded Slovenia the day after its declaration of independence. To the surprise of most observers, however, the Slovenians resisted skillfully with a combination of guerrilla warfare and massive civilian noncooperation. Since Slovenia did not share a common border with Serbia and had few Serbs or members of other minority ethnic groups within its territory, the invaders withdrew after ten days of warfare and only minimal casualties.

Slovenia made good its independence about as non-violently as the rest of Eastern Europe, but unfortunately the Yugoslav army felt humiliated and determined to recapture its prestige in battle.

After the relatively easy separation of Slovenia from Yugoslavia, the federation dissolved into three savage wars that raged until 1995 and witnessed the worst atrocities in Europe since World War II. The first war pitted Serbs against Croats and raged throughout the second half of 1991. Newly independent Croatia had a large Serbian minority clustered in thirteen communes. The Serbian-dominated Yugoslav military, therefore, attacked Croatia, aiming to link up the republic of Serbia with these communes and create a Greater Serbia. After ferocious fighting that resulted in 10,000 deaths, 30,000 injuries, and 750,000 refugees, a UN cease-fire stopped the fighting in November 1991. Croatia remained independent but lost about one-third of its territory to the Serbs, who began a systematic policy of "ethnic cleansing," eliminating non-Serbs from the area. Then Bosnia exploded.

Bosnia-Hercegovina was the most ethnically heterogeneous of all the Yugoslav republics. The 1991 census counted a population of 4,364,574, consisting of 43.7 percent Muslims, 31.4 percent Serbs, and 17.3 percent Croats. (A brave minority of 5.5 percent identified themselves simply as "Yugoslavs.") Poised between the warring Serbs and Croats, a shaky coalition of three ethnic parties in Bosnia tried to stay out of the fray but found it could not. Milošević and Tudjman, foreseeing the imminent breakup of Bosnia, had already met in secret in September 1991 and agreed to divide the territory between them when the time was right. The Bosnian government finally declared independence on April 6, 1992, and fighting broke out almost immediately when the Serbs attacked, trying to unite various ethnic pockets of their countrymen into the growing region of Greater Serbia.[2] During the first year of fighting, nearly all the hostilities were between Serbs and the government of Bosnia, now backed only by Muslims and Croatians. The Croats' adherence to a unified Bosnian state remained shaky, however, and in spring 1993 the former allies, Croats and Muslims, began fighting each other.

The major world powers — France, Germany, Great Britain, the United States, and Russia — who had looked on rather passively and uncertainly as the three wars of Yugoslav succession raged, finally formed what was called the Contact Group in March 1994 and brokered a new alliance between Muslims and Croats. This tipped the balance in the wars against the Serbs, who were now placed on the defensive. With tacit great power support, the Croats mounted two offensives, in May and August 1995, that cleared their own country of Serbian

2. Macedonia also declared its independence in 1992, so a rump version of Yugoslavia, consisting only of Serbia and Montenegro was proclaimed on April 27, 1992.

troops and reduced the number of Serbian civilians from 600,000 to 150,000. Then renewed offensives in Bosnia, backed by NATO air strikes, forced the Serbs to negotiate. All the warring parties in Bosnia agreed to an American-brokered peace plan at Dayton, Ohio, in November 1995, and 60,000 NATO troops, including 20,000 Americans, kept an uneasy peace thereafter. Bosnia remained technically one state, but it was in effect partitioned into two nearly autonomous entities, a Muslim-Croat federation and a Serbian republic. This peace plan for Bosnia effectively followed the Milošević-Tudjman partition agreement of 1991 and was probably available any time after that meeting. However, the Bosnian Muslims and the great power governments tried futilely to keep Bosnia united until three and a half years of savage war convinced them otherwise. Between 145,000 and 250,000 people perished in Bosnia between 1992 and 1995, and more than a million more had been forced into exile. Mass rape, concentration camps, and civilian massacres, usually initiated by the Serbs but amply repaid by the other two ethnic participants, marked the struggle.

The horrors of the struggle in Bosnia shocked the world. American and European journalists wrote passionate accounts of the slaughter, implying that the Balkans were inhabited by savages impelled by age-old tribal hatreds. To counteract this impression, most historians and some journalists developed a standard script arguing that the people of Bosnia and all of Yugoslavia normally lived in peace but that evil politicians, particularly Serbia's Slobodan Milošević, had deceived and incited them to violence. A synthesis between these rival interpretations seems the best explanation for the Yugoslav tragedy. People of the Balkans had lived together in peaceful coexistence most of the time, for the various ruling regimes — Ottoman, Austrian, Communist — kept them apart as much as possible and severely repressed any ethnic dissidence. However, deep-seated ethnic hostilities did exist and they tended to erupt at times of crisis for the ruling authorities. For example, Serbs and Croats rioted and attacked each other in Sarajevo after the assassination of the Austrian archduke in 1914, and later the Nazi invasion of World War II triggered horrendous massacres of Serbs by the Croatian Ustasha. It is not surprising, therefore, that more violence would break out as the Communist regime disintegrated. Nationalist politicians, however, did fan the flames of ethnic resentment. In particular, Serbian president Milošević used his tight control of the media in Belgrade to whip up fears of renewed Croatian terrorism, harking back to the horrors of the Ustasha. The Muslims of Bosnia tended to get caught in the middle of these fierce, politically accentuated quarrels between Serbs and Croats. One Bosnian Muslim politician remarked astutely: "Bosnia is the kind of country in which your neighbor may be your friend, but also a savage enemy. . . . The thread of peace is a thin one and there are problems that have to be handled carefully, and never played around

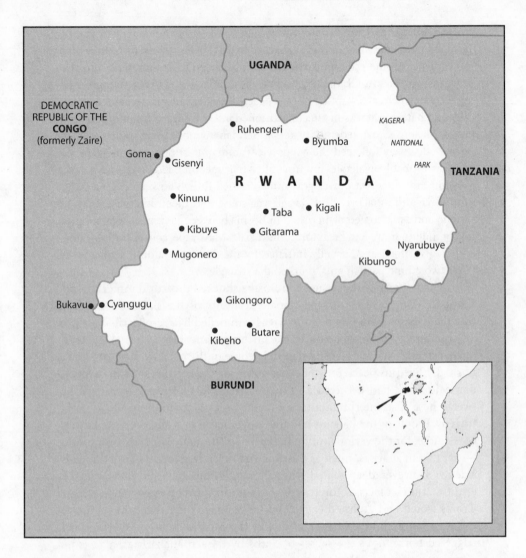

Rwanda

with." Unfortunately, political leaders could not resist the temptation to "play around" with them.

The genocidal massacres in the central-African state of Rwanda in 1994 eclipsed the horrors of Yugoslavia in their ferocity, yet drew much less international attention. A picturesque "land of a thousand hills," Rwanda is a country about the size of Vermont, but with a population equivalent to that of New York City — about seven to eight million people. Along with neighboring Burundi, Rwanda was colonized by Germany in the 1890s then entrusted to Belgium as a League of Nations trust territory after World War I (the two territories were known at that time as Ruanda-Urundi). The population of both countries encompassed two ethnic groups, the majority Hutu and the minority Tutsi. Both groups spoke the same language, Kinyarwanda, and shared similar cultural and religious practices. They were Christianized by European missionaries in roughly the same proportions, about 62 percent Catholic and 18 percent Protestant. Yet the two groups remained distinct, primarily because of their differing economic pursuits. Traditionally, the Tutsi were cattle herders and the Hutu agriculturists. Like farmers and cowboys the world over, the two groups often quarreled, and since African culture valued cattle raising more than farming, the Tutsi belonged to an elite class or caste that generally ruled the two kingdoms.

Finding this feudal arrangement in place when they arrived, Europeans misunderstood and exaggerated it. Anthropologists hypothesized that the tall, light-skinned "obviously superior" Tutsi must be "honorary white men," possibly a lost tribe from Ethiopia with Caucasian blood. Therefore, the Belgian government overtly favored the Tutsi in education and employment and imposed a racial identity card system, similar to South Africa's. Whereas Hutu and Tutsi often intermarried and the caste system remained rather porous before colonization, it now became rigid and all encompassing. When the Belgians hastily granted independence in the early 1960s, the Tutsi of Burundi maintained their leadership and dominance of the state, but Rwanda experienced a violent revolution in which the Hutu overthrew and massacred the Tutsi. Though the Belgians had contributed greatly to the problem of Tutsi dominance, they rapidly changed sides and supported the principle of majority, Hutu rule. With Belgian connivance, the Hutu deposed the Tutsi king and declared Rwanda a republic in 1961. It became an independent state on July 1, 1962.

A series of military dictators turned the former caste system on its head, favoring the Hutu, who comprised about 85 percent of the population. At times of depression or unrest, the government instigated massacres of Tutsi to distract the populace from their problems. A Hutu general, Juvenal Habyarimana, seized power in 1973 and stopped the massacres, devoting his government's attention to economic development. Habyarimana remained in power over twenty years, building roads, schools, and health clinics, and winning favor with the international aid community. Still the country remained poor, densely populated, and rigidly divided into two castes, with the authoritarian government favoring Hutus in education and employment. Then in the late 1980s the price of coffee, the country's main export, plummeted, and widespread drought increased the economic misery. Across the border in Uganda, a group of Rwandan refugees from the earlier massacres organized the Rwandese Patriotic Front (RPF) to overthrow Habyarimana. Though the RPF was composed mainly of Tutsis, it also included some Hutus, and it did not aim at reinstating the Tutsi monarchy. Rather the rebels hoped to introduce a democratic regime that would end the discriminatory dominance of one group over another.

RPF troops crossed the border on October 1, 1990, sparking a civil war. Pressured by European donor nations, Habyarimana introduced some political reforms and negotiated with the rebels, but Hutu extremists in the military short-circuited any concessions made to the RPF or the Tutsi minority. Rwanda's Hutu Power advocates broadcast vicious propaganda on both private and government-owned radio stations, branding all Tutsi in the country as a treasonous fifth column for the RPF, bent on slaughtering Hutus if they ever returned to power. Occasional massacres of Hutus in neighboring Burundi gave these claims some credibility, and Hutu refugees from Burundi fanned the flames higher. The military organized citizen militias to harass and terrorize the Tutsi of Rwanda and began plotting the systematic destruction of the Tutsi community. When President Habyarimana signed a peace agreement with the RPF at Arusha, Tanzania, in August 1993, calling for a coalition government marked by power-sharing between Hutus and Tutsis, the extremists decided to act in order to preserve exclusive power.

On April 6, 1994, two guided missiles downed a French jet carrying both Rwanda's president Habyarimana and the president of Burundi home from a peace conference in Tanzania. Responsibility for the assassinations has never been conclusively determined, but it is widely suspected that the Hutu extremists, possibly aided by foreign mercenaries, did the deed. In any case, the Hutu Power advocates in the Rwandan government and military took advantage of the president's death the same way Hitler capitalized on the burning of the Reichstag. They used it as an excuse to unleash the Hutu militias in a genocidal fury against Tutsi civilians. Hacking their victims to death with machetes, the Hutus murdered about 800,000 people in a period of three and a half months. They actually began the slaughter by picking out individual Hutus in the government and military who might oppose their conspiracy; but about 97 percent of the victims were Tutsis, including women and children who had taken refuge in churches, orphanages, and hospitals. About half the Tutsis resident in Rwanda died.

The international community remained passive during the months of genocide. Since Rwanda's government enjoyed a good reputation prior to 1994, many countries supported it against the RPF, with France in particular supplying arms and military advisors. When rumors of massacres first surfaced, many believed they were simply the inevitable fallout from a civil war. The United Nations had already organized a small peacekeeping force to police the Arusha agreements between the two warring parties; but after the assassination of President Habyarimana, the Hutu extremists murdered ten Belgian peacekeepers in cold blood, prompting the Belgian government to pull out from the UN force. Neither the United States nor any other major power wished to become involved, so the UN Security Council actually reduced the peacekeeping force to a token size and stood on the sidelines. The killing only ended when RPF troops overpowered the Rwandan military, winning the civil war in mid-July 1994.

The defeated government leaders and their murderous militias urged all Hutus to flee the invaders, and at least two million Rwandans poured across the border into neighboring Zaire (Congo), where they lived for two and a half years in squalid refugee camps. The new Rwandan government pursued a moderate policy, with relatively few revenge slayings of Hutus. However, it did provide military muscle for Laurent Kabila's rebellion in Zaire that finally overthrew the long-ruling dictator, Joseph Mobutu, from power. U.S. and European governments, who had propped up Mobutu throughout the Cold War, were amazed. As journalist Philip Gourevitch remarked: "The thought of Rwanda invading Zaire was a bit like Liechtenstein taking on Germany or France. Mobutu sponsored invasions of his neighbors, not the other way around." Nevertheless, with Rwandan aid the wave of political change sweeping the world toppled Mobutu in May 1997. The Congo dictator had supported the genocidal Hutu Power advocates in Rwanda and helped the defeated Hutu militias control and terrorize the refugee camps in his own country. So in the process of overthrowing Mobutu, a force of Rwandans and Congo rebels smashed the Hutu militias once again and finally sent the Rwandan refugees streaming back home in November 1996. Armed with a special genocide law, the Rwandan government aimed to arrest and punish the main organizers of the genocide but offered relatively lenient sentences to lower-level perpetrators who confessed their crimes. Rwanda faces an enormous task of reconciliation in the new century.

The massacres in both Rwanda and the former Yugoslavia fit the United Nations definition of genocide, that is, "intent to destroy, in whole or in part, a national, ethnical, racial or religious group." They also conform to the conditions for genocide advanced by Robert Melson, which I have used throughout this study: revolution in time of war, or war in time of revolution. The killings in Rwanda, however, were far more extensive and constitute a more clear-cut case of genocide. The murders of Serbs by Croatians and of Croatians by Serbs were intended, for the most part, to chase the other ethnic group away into the neighboring nation-state, not to exterminate it. Many Muslims of Bosnia got caught in the crossfire. In contrast, the Rwandan massacres were conceived as a "final solution," the total elimination of the Tutsi minority. A Seventh Day Adventist pastor who participated in the carnage told one of his parishioners point blank: "Your problem has already found a solution. You must die."

Leadership, or the lack thereof, matters. Both Rwanda and the former Yugoslavia illustrate the murderous results of latent ethnic tensions manipulated by unscrupulous political leaders fearful of losing power. Corey Aquino and Cardinal Sin in the Philippines managed to direct the anti-dictatorial outrage of the populace in a non-violent direction. Serbian president Milošević and Croatian president Tudjman in the former Yugoslavia and the Hutu Power extremists in the Rwandan government chose to enflame nationalist passions in a brutal fashion. Philip Gourevitch wisely notes that "there was nothing inevitable about the horror [in Rwanda]. . . . It required a dogged uphill effort for Habyarimana's extremist entourage to prevent Rwanda from slipping toward moderation." Significantly, even though the president of Burundi, a Hutu, died in the same plane crash that killed Rwanda's Habyarimana, the political leadership of Burundi kept calm and prevented any massive outbreak of violence.

International responsibility also matters. The United States belatedly, but decisively, abandoned its former client, Ferdinand Marcos, in the Philippines and provided crucial support for Boris Yeltsin when he faced down the military rebels in Moscow. However, both Americans and Europeans dithered as Yugoslavia fragmented in a series of violent wars and did nothing to help the United Nations in Rwanda. Political scientist Lenard Cohen explains the failure of international action: "The violent disintegration of Yugoslavia occurred just as the Cold War was drawing to an end but before mechanisms for conflict management had been established to deal with a crisis of such proportions." Another political scientist, Arthur Klinghoffer, makes a similar point about Rwanda: "The UN and major world powers were spread too thinly at the time, dealing simultaneously with crises in Bosnia, Somalia and Haiti." African-American congressman Alcee Hastings concluded less charitably that the world would have reacted in one day had the same thing happened in England or France. "It is numbing to see this take place and for us not to do one damned thing." The American government did eventually assume a leadership role in the Yugoslav imbroglio, brokering the Dayton Peace Agreement for Bosnia in 1995. President Bill Clinton actually apologized for the American neglect of the Rwandan genocide on his trip to Africa in March 1998. Perhaps in compensation for its earlier inaction, the United Nations set up International War Crimes Tribunals for both Bosnia and Rwanda. This marked the first attempt by the international organization to prosecute individuals under its 1948 Genocide Convention.

Then in 1999 the United States led a NATO air offensive against Serbian troops committing atrocities in Kosovo. At first the massive bombardment produced the result it was designed to prevent. The majority of Albanians in Kosovo fled the province due to Serbian atrocities and NATO bombs. After massive damage was inflicted on the infrastructure of Serbia, however, the Serbian president, Slobodan Milošević, capitulated, and the Albanian population returned under NATO protection.

In summation, as the twentieth century came to an end, a wave of political change was sweeping the world, and the United Nations and the world's major powers had a hard time keeping up. Many of the changes were remarkably non-violent, but genocide, the distinctive brand of the twentieth century, marked two of them. Clearly one task for the international community in the new century is to organize a mechanism for timely intervention before genocide or crimes against humanity take place, rather than dealing tardily with their aftermath. The United Nations has played an important role in peace*keeping* operations over the past half century, but it desperately needs to develop more effective mechanisms of peace*making* to prevent future crimes against humanity such as took place in Rwanda and Yugoslavia.

CHAPTER TWENTY-THREE

Coming Apart, Coming Together

During the second half of the twentieth century, the countries of the world seemed to be coming apart. First the world split into two rival blocs, led by the United States and the Soviet Union, the only powers left standing after World War II. Then, as the former colonies of Asia and Africa freed themselves from European empires, a Third World of proudly nationalist but very poor countries emerged as well. Despite the efforts of Yugoslavia's Tito and Indonesia's Sukarno to organize a nonaligned nations movement, these Third World countries did not form a cohesive bloc but often wound up fighting each other over boundaries and scarce resources. The Cold War rivalry between the superpowers aggravated and exaggerated these conflicts.

When the Cold War ended, several multinational states that had been held together by communist dictatorship fragmented. The Soviet Union was replaced by fifteen separate countries, and Yugoslavia violently exploded into six different states. The citizens of Czechoslovakia voted to split in two, forming the Czech Republic and Slovakia. On the other side of the Cold War boundary, no nation had divided by the end of the century, but a tendency toward decentralization also set in. The United Kingdom moved tentatively toward lesser unity when the Labour government of Tony Blair voted to "devolve" significant government powers to Scotland, Northern Ireland, and Wales, reversing a three-hundred-year-old policy of centralizing government authority in London. The federal states of Canada and Belgium were continually threatened with secession by their minority ethnic components. More violently, the former Belgian Congo (Zaire), now named the Democratic Republic of Congo, teetered on the edge of fragmentation after the overthrow of its long-time dictator Joseph Mobutu. The world indeed seemed to be coming apart.

Many politicians, journalists, and scholars lamented that the Cold War had been replaced by a chaos of competing nationalisms making the world more unstable and dangerous than it had been during the superpower rivalry. When I mentioned to friends and colleagues that I saw a happy ending to the twentieth century, many responded with disagreement. Nostalgia for the certainties of the Cold War had set in. Yet without minimizing the horrors of Yugoslavia or Rwanda, which were largely caused by irresponsible politicians enflaming nationalist passions, I believe that a very positive trend has developed which partially counters the centrifugal force of nations flying apart. Though countries may fragment, they cannot physically separate from each other, and in the twenty-first century the world is too tightly bound together by trade and communications for them to remain wholly isolated. As the world is coming apart, it is simultaneously coming back together.

Many observers lamented that some of the new nations which emerged from the wreckage of communism, such as Estonia, Latvia, Lithuania, or Slovenia, were too small to be viable. In defense, the Slovenian government frequently claims that its country of just under two million inhabitants is actually larger than sixty members of the United Nations. My inspection of a recent world atlas revealed that this is not literally true, but is close enough. By my count, about forty-nine independent countries are smaller than Slovenia. Furthermore, Slovenia has proven more peaceful and economically successful than the other states of the former Yugoslavia. In the Baltic region, Estonia, Lithuania, and Latvia are markedly more democratic and prosperous than their former overlord, Russia. Size does not matter all that much. Close trading relations and cultural affinity with Western European neighbors have made some of these small successor states viable. And few if any of them wish to remain isolated. Nearly all of the former Communist satellite nations are clamoring for entry into the NATO security alliance or the European Union, or both. As nations fly apart, their leaders realize that they must also come together. Federalism and regionalism are two "isms" that may temper the excesses of nationalism in the twenty-first century.

The European Union represents the outstanding example of nations coming together after flying apart. Europeans ruled the world at the beginning of the twentieth century, impelled by buoyant economies, political acumen, and a soaring sense of cultural superiority. Yet rivalries for dominance on the home continent tore the world apart in two horrendous conflagrations during the first half of the century, and it took most of the century's second half to mend the damage. By century's end, however, a Europe that was no longer dominant politically or militarily had fashioned a new way for nations to come together that just might prove a model for the world. Ironically, in its weakness and defeat, Europe may have made a useful contribution to world politics.

441

The European economic community,[1] or Common Market, first took effect on January 1, 1958, with six original founding members — France, West Germany, Italy, Belgium, Netherlands, and Luxembourg. The Common Market had grown out of the earlier European Coal and Steel Community organized by Jean Monnet in the early 1950s. (See chapter 2 for background on Monnet and the Common Market.) The driving impulse for economic union was a desire to overcome the disastrous rivalry between France and Germany that had torn Europe apart twice in the first half of the century. Following Monnet's lead, the French foreign minister Robert Schuman and the German chancellor Konrad Adenauer decided to make France and Germany partners rather than rivals. This required vision and courage, but it was also a pragmatic decision taken in each country's national interest. As British diplomat and historian David Harrison has pointed out: "The European Community can be seen as a pact whereby those who take part expect to obtain benefits which are greater than those given up. . . . Those who take part do so on the basis of a rational expectation of gaining more than they lose." The fundamental economic trade-off which made the European Community work was a protected and guaranteed market for the large, but inefficient, French agricultural sector and a much expanded market for German industries. The smaller countries of Europe wished to join the Big Two so that they would not be left out of their large markets.

The European Community was a roaring success in its early years. Trade between the six member states surged ahead at an annual rate of 28.4 percent between 1958 and 1967, whereas trade with the rest of the world increased only 10 percent each year. The Treaty of Rome that had organized the EC called for the construction of a customs union, with no tariffs on trade between member states and a common external tariff against the rest of the world, by January 1, 1970, at the latest. In fact, the customs union was completed eighteen months early, on July 1, 1968. In the meantime, the guaranteed high prices for agricultural products had made the EC self-sufficient in most basic foodstuffs, and booming trade and industry had raised the standard of living. The EC completed the reconstruction of Western Europe that had begun with the Marshall Plan.

Progress toward "ever closer union," as called for in the Treaty of Rome, nevertheless stalled for nearly a generation after 1970, and even in the 1960s political problems had made the EC's path rocky. President Charles de Gaulle of France recognized the economic benefits in EC membership, but he resisted all attempts to move from an economic union to a political union. In 1965 France

---

1. The official name for the European Common Market was the European Community (EC), but this was changed in 1993 to the European Union (EU). I will use EC for events before 1993 and EU for those afterward.

boycotted the central governing body of the EC for over half a year in protest over budgetary matters. The French only returned when the other members informally agreed to take all important decisions by unanimous consent, rather than a weighted majority vote, as called for in the Treaty of Rome. De Gaulle also vetoed the British application for entry into the EC on two occasions, in 1963 and 1967.

The French president's resignation in 1969 finally cleared the way for expansion of the European Community, and Great Britain, Denmark, and Ireland joined on January 1, 1973. Greece was admitted to membership in 1981, followed by Spain and Portugal in 1986. However, the EC continued to stagnate. The oil shocks and other economic problems of the 1970s pushed European national governments into narrowly self-interested reactions and little progress was made toward closer cooperation in political and diplomatic relations. Furthermore, Great Britain proved to be a stubbornly independent member. After a change of government in London, the British insisted on renegotiating the terms of their accession to the EC in 1975. Then after Margaret Thatcher became prime minister in 1979, she noisily insisted that Britain was paying too much in subsidies to other member states and the terms should be renegotiated once again. This BBQ, or "Bloody British Question," was only settled in 1984 with the provision of a substantial rebate of British fees to the EC. In the meantime, a state of "Europessimism" or "Eurosclerosis" had set in throughout the community. The original plans of economic union had envisioned complete freedom of movement for goods, persons, services, and capital, but through the 1970s and 1980s only goods could move without hindrance throughout the community. Immigration and customs posts still dotted the borders between countries, and each nation retained its own currency and a host of regulations that prevented common investment policies.

French initiative and German cooperation finally moved the EC toward a complete economic union with the passage of the Single European Act in 1986, which committed the member states to dismantle the remaining economic barriers by the end of 1992. The fall of the Berlin Wall and the reunification of Germany gave an unexpected push to this effort. Reunited Germany would be a colossus, accounting for more than a quarter of the EC's population and economic output. Chancellor Helmut Kohl realized that other states would fear German dominance and therefore determined to bind Germany firmly into a united Europe. He adopted the slogan "not for a German Europe, but for a European Germany." The resulting Maastricht Treaty, negotiated by the heads of EC member state governments in December 1992, put the finishing touches on this deeper economic unity and renamed the European Community the European Union. After a scare, in which the voters of Denmark first refused to ratify the Maastricht Treaty, it finally took effect in November 1993 after approval in a second Danish referendum. Two years later the EU grew to a total of fifteen members, with the accession of Austria, Sweden, and Finland. The Common Market then stretched from the Arctic to the Mediterranean and from the Alps to the Atlantic. (See map in chapter 2.)

The "new Europe" that emerged from the Single European Act and the Maastricht Treaty adopted "three pillars" of unity — a much enhanced economic community, plus cooperation in foreign policy and consultation on matters of justice and internal police affairs. The most important measure provided for complete monetary union, the forging of a common currency for use by member states. The first phase of monetary union kicked in as planned on January 1, 1999, with the creation of the "euro" as an accounting mechanism, widely used by banks and investors in eleven of the fifteen EU countries (Britain, Denmark, Greece, and Sweden chose to opt out, at least for the time being). The replacement of national currencies by the euro was scheduled to take place three years later in 2002. Yet already at the end of the century, citizens of the European Union could move freely from state to state without pausing at borders to show passports and could trade goods, sell their services, or invest freely in any of the member states. If they used credit cards or travelers' checks they could purchase goods in euros, rather than francs or marks. Generally speaking, any economic activity that was legal in one member state was legal in all.

The European Union is not a supranational state, though it has some of the powers and trappings of one and its most enthusiastic supporters would like it to become one. Rather it is a union of still-sovereign national states that agreed, in their own self-interest, to delegate some of their powers in the economic realm. The EU has a complicated structure that evolved through innumerable political compromises. A European Commission in Brussels functions as an executive for the Union, with its own civil service or bureaucracy; but the real power is reserved for the Council of Ministers, in which the ministers of each member state meet regularly and make regulations for the whole community. The European Parliament, which has been directly elected since 1979, is the weakest of the quasi-governmental bodies; and despite its name, it is not really a legislature but primarily an advisory council. One of the most important, though least well known, structures of the Union is the European Court of Justice, which has built up an impressive body of case law dealing with economic questions. In its relatively narrow field of competence, the European Court of Justice can apply laws directly to individuals of the various member states, and European laws take precedence over national laws. If, for example, a monopoly practice sanctioned by law in one member state conflicts with a Union-wide regulation, a citizen can sue and invoke the Union-wide case law. This gives the economic common market teeth, and is probably the most significant supranational power of the European Union.

In most other ways, however, the EU functions like an intergovernmental alliance of sovereign states. Though it has an independent source of financial support in customs duties and a share of the individual countries' value added taxes, the EU's budget and expenditures are tiny compared to those of the individual states. Its expenditures represent only about 1 percent of gross domestic product, compared to around 20 percent of GDP spent by the United States or other national states. About 97 percent of government spending in Europe is appropriated by individual national governments, not by the EU. Furthermore, the second and third pillars of the Maastricht Treaty, increased coordination of foreign policy and consultation over domestic justice affairs, are purely voluntary and conducted on a state-to-state basis. They represent little more than statements of good intentions. The EU has no military, since a common European Defense Force failed to secure ratification in the 1950s. When they wish to use force, European states cooperate with the United States and Canada in the NATO alliance, and sometimes with Russia too, as in the Contact Group for Bosnia.

The structure of the European Union, therefore, contains a mix of both supranational and intergovernmental elements. Its very illogicality adds to its strength. Rather than an oppressive super-government imposed by force or chicanery, the European Union represents a pragmatic series of bargains entered into democratically through a political process of constant compromise. In his original proposal for the Coal and Steel Community Jean Monnet stated his hope for a future European federation, but he added that "I do not attempt to imagine its political framework. . . . What we are preparing, through the action of the Community, has probably no precedent." Monnet was right. Fifty years ago, no one could have imagined the shape the European Union would eventually assume, and nobody today believes its structure is ideal. Yet Monnet imagined that a federation of Europe could come into existence, and pragmatic politicians made it happen over the span of half a century. The result is a peaceful, if often quarrelsome, union of countries that matches the United States in economic production and surpasses it in population.

The European Union's example of trade liberalization has been influential and infectious, though its exact mix of centralism and decentralization has not been reproduced anywhere else. In 1992, the United States, Canada, and Mexico signed a North American Free Trade Agreement (NAFTA), which went into effect on January 1, 1994. NAFTA, however, is not really comparable to the European Union, as it only provides for free trade in goods and capital, not a complete customs union. In a customs union, the partners eliminate tariffs between themselves, erect a common external tariff against the rest of the world, and coordinate or merge their currency exchange relations. In a free trade agreement such as NAFTA, however, each partner can pursue its own tariff and currency policies with third countries that are not partners to the agreement. A free trade arrangement, therefore, is much looser than a customs union. NAFTA established no quasi-governmental central institutions comparable to the European Commission or the European Court of Justice. Moreover, NAFTA is much less a partnership of equals than the EU. The United States is much larger than its two partners combined, in both population and economic production, and Mexico remains far less developed economically than either Canada or the United States.

NAFTA proved very controversial in all three countries. Independent presidential candidate Ross Perot proclaimed in 1992 that NAFTA would produce a "giant sucking sound" of jobs heading south to the low-wage economy of Mexico. American environmentalists predicted that the Mexican border would become a toxic dumping ground for inefficient, low-wage industries. Mexicans, for their part, feared that American corporations would buy up their assets and repatriate all the profits to the United States. Canadians harbored similar economic concerns, but they also feared that American popular culture would overwhelm Canada's fragile cultural identity. All the parties, therefore, imbedded protections and reservations in the NAFTA treaty. Mexico retained the government's monopoly over oil production, for oil had become a symbol of national independence after it was nationalized in the 1930s. Canada obtained a cultural exemption, allowing it to insulate Canadian magazines, newspapers, and broadcast outlets against American competition. The United States negotiated side agreements with Mexico aimed at raising wages and environmental standards in Mexican industries.

None of the three countries has been completely satisfied with NAFTA. By century's end neither the high hopes of some nor the dire predictions of others had been fulfilled. Trade between the United States and its two partners nearly doubled between 1993 and 1998, and Mexico replaced Japan as the second most important American trading partner (Canada had long been America's largest trading partner). Yet it was not clear how much economic benefit either side obtained from this increased trade. American manufacturing jobs were definitely lost to Mexico, but higher-skilled technical and managerial jobs were also created. The Mexican border has become the home of very low-wage and environmentally harmful industries, despite the side agreements in NAFTA. Canadians feel more beleaguered than ever, a mouse sleeping next to an economic and cultural elephant, in the words of one of their former prime ministers. Several successive end-of-the-year assessments by economists and journalists have concluded that "the impact of the NAFTA has been thought to be minimal." The substantial inequality between the trading partners in NAFTA may render it ineffectual.

A closer analogue to the European Union than NAFTA is the South

American common market, named MERCOSUR (an abbreviation of the Spanish words *Mercado Comun del Sur,* which is usually translated as "Common Market of the Southern Cone"). Brazil, Argentina, Paraguay, and Uruguay signed an economic treaty in 1991 that established most features of a customs union, including a common external tariff, on January 1, 1995. A complete economic union was scheduled to be phased in over the next ten years. Chile, emerging from its disastrous years of dictatorship, joined MERCOSUR as an associate member in 1996. The five member countries comprise a potentially large market of about 200 million people, nearly half of Latin America's population and more than half its industrial production. The general level of economic production in the MERCOSUR countries is roughly equivalent to Mexico's but far below that of Canada and the United States. It seems unlikely, therefore, that MERCOSUR and NAFTA will merge into a Western Hemisphere common market, as politicians in both North and South America have sometimes proclaimed. The union of the Southern Cone, however, will likely expand to other Latin American nations and develop deeper institutions of integration, such as those that have been constructed over the past half century in Europe. The EU has taken MERCOSUR under its wing, so to speak, training its administrators and forging close trading relationships with it. As unlikely as it may seem, a common market between Europe and Latin America may come sooner than a union between North and South America.

Elsewhere in the world, economic integration and incipient federal relations between states have proceeded at varying speeds. The so-called Commonwealth of Independent States that replaced the Soviet Union in 1992 has so far proven to be worth little more than the paper it was written on. Yet Russia has begun to forge strong ties with its closely related Slavic neighbors of Belarus and Ukraine. At the same time, the Turkic speaking states of central Asia, such as Kazakhstan and Uzbekistan, are building economic and cultural relations between themselves and with Turkey as well. The free-enterprise states of the Pacific Rim in Asia have formed a loose consultative relationship with Canada and the United States, called the Asian Pacific Economic Cooperation Forum (APEC).

At first sight, the formation of regional trading blocs such as the EU, NAFTA, and MERCOSUR may seem uncomfortably reminiscent of the 1930s, when nations of the world raised trade barriers and tried to build exclusive regional empires, such as Japan's Greater East Asia Co-Prosperity Sphere. However, the political context was completely different at century's end. First, the new regional economic spheres have been constructed democratically, by negotiation and agreement, rather than by force. Second, the regional trading unions were embedded in a wider system of trade relations that some economists call "Open Regionalism." Since the Second World War, most of the non-communist nations of the world have been committed to freer trade and have negotiated a series of common tariff reductions in the General Agreements on Tariff and Trade (GATT). The general level of tariff protection worldwide fell from about 40 percent of the value of goods traded to less than 5 percent by century's end. Free trade has become the gospel of the post-Cold War world.

Yet free trade and regional economic unions should not be considered panaceas. When all the nations of a region are small and economically underdeveloped, pooling their misery does little good. The nations of the Caribbean, for example, have been negotiating economic and political union since the 1960s, but still have little to show for it. Furthermore, economic unions between unequal partners, such as the NAFTA agreement, do not seem very promising. Finally, there is no guarantee that economic union will inevitably lead to political merger. Europe's leaders have recognized the continuing strength of nationalism and have not forced the pace of political integration.

The European Union remains a delicate mix of centralism and decentralization that may yet prove unworkable. Its success so far lies in the balance between centrifugal and centripetal forces. Nations of Europe are simultaneously coming apart and coming together. The EU does not represent a model that can be applied by rote worldwide, but rather one example of peaceful negotiations between formerly hostile states. It is not a finished product to be exported but a process to be loosely imitated. Jean Monnet believed that this process was based on three essential principles: rules of conduct between nations rather than force; equality of treatment rather than domination; and common objectives pursued in the common interest rather than a quest for individual, selfish advantage. Europe did not have any unique advantages in pursuing the course of peaceful economic integration. In fact, it was operating against all odds. France and Germany were deadly enemies who had torn Europe and the world apart on more than one occasion. Furthermore, for such a small continent, Europe has been fragmented into many small nation-states, with no common language. The business of the EU has to be translated into eleven different languages. Other regional blocs, such as Latin America, will actually start with more advantages than Europe did.

Historians cannot foretell the future any more than other individuals can, but they can assess present trends in light of recent history. At the end of the twentieth century, the world is simultaneously coming apart yet beginning to come together. World leaders need not look back nostalgically to the rigid certainties of the Cold War but should look optimistically to a future of simultaneously centralized and de-centralized political relations. Regionalism and federalism are *not inevitable* solutions to world political problems, but they are *available* and partially proven processes for peaceful relations between nations. Rather than striving to abolish nationalism, world leaders might do well to tame it and harness it in regional federations and common markets. Nationalism expressed imperialistically and violently made the twentieth century a bloody hundred years. Perhaps there is hope that the future century will be marked by nationalism expressed cooperatively and peacefully.

Suggestions for Further Reading

Note: Books considered "must reading" are marked with an asterisk (*), those which are unusually accessible for a popular audience are marked with a plus sign (+). A few happy hybrids bear both marks!

Chapter 1. The Grand Alliance Flies Apart

A series of readable, thought-provoking books by John Lewis Gaddis makes a very good starting point for exploring the history of the Cold War. Gaddis's *The United States and the Origins of the Cold War, 1941-1947* (New York: Columbia University Press, 1972), was one of the first studies to transcend the rather sterile debate between those who blamed the Russians for starting the Cold War and the so-called revisionists who blamed the Americans. His collection of essays, *The Long Peace: Inquiries into the History of the Cold War* (New York: Oxford University Press, 1987), is filled with wisdom, even though I disagree with the theme of his title essay, that the forty-year-long American-Soviet rivalry should be considered a "long peace" rather than a "cold war." A more recent collection of essays, *The United States and the End of the Cold War: Implications, Reconsiderations, Provocations* (New York: Oxford University Press, 1992), contains some interesting second thoughts suggested by the end of the Cold War. It's a satisfying experience to read the work of a top scholar, such as Gaddis, who has lived through the entire length of the period he is writing about and can reflect on both its beginning and its end.

*Walter LaFeber, *America, Russia, and the Cold War: 1945-1992* (New York: McGraw-Hill, Inc., 1993), is a widely used textbook that has been frequently re-

450

vised and updated, most recently since the end of the Cold War. A more read-able survey by an English journalist, +Martin Walker, *The Cold War: A History* (New York: Henry Holt and Company, 1993), is particularly useful for its En-glish point of view and its emphasis on the economic aspects of superpower ri-valry. Ritchie Ovendale, *The English-Speaking Alliance: Britain, the United States, the Dominions and the Cold War, 1945-1951* (London: George Allen & Unwin, 1985), also provides an English point of view, but just on the formative years of the rivalry. Pierre de Senarclens, *From Yalta to the Iron Curtain: The Great Powers and the Origins of the Cold War,* trans. Amanda Pingree (Oxford: Berg Publishers Limited, 1995), analyzes the first few years of the Cold War from a French point of view.

George Frost Kennan, "America's global planner" during the formative years of the containment policy, has been a prolific author in his own right. He wrote *American Diplomacy: 1900-1950* (Chicago: University of Chicago Press, 1951) during a leave of absence from the State Department in 1950-51 and deliv-ered its contents as the Charles R. Walgreen Lectures. The book includes a re-print of the original 1947 X-Article from *Foreign Affairs.* Kennan has also writ-ten two volumes of highly readable *Memoirs, 1925-1950* (Boston: Little, Brown, 1967), and *1950-1963* (Boston: Little, Brown, 1972). President Harry S. Truman also published two volumes of memoirs: *1945: Year of Decision* (New York: Time Inc., 1955), and *1946-1952: Years of Trial and Hope* (New York: Time Inc., 1956). *Wilson D. Miscamble, *George F. Kennan and the Making of American Foreign Policy, 1947-1950* (Princeton: Princeton University Press, 1992), is a very compre-hensive and balanced study of Kennan's role as a policymaker.

+Charles L. Mee, *The Marshall Plan: The Launching of the Pax Americana* (New York: Simon and Schuster, 1984), is a readable, provocative narrative of the origins of the Marshall Plan. Michael J. Hogan, *The Marshall Plan: America, Britain, and the Reconstruction of Western Europe, 1947-1952* (Cambridge, En-gland: Cambridge University Press, 1987), is far more comprehensive, but quite ponderous and tedious. It will be of interest only to specialists.

+Henry Ashby Turner, Jr., *Germany from Partition to Reunification* (New Haven: Yale University Press, 1992), is a brief textbook, whose opening chapter makes a good introduction to the postwar issues surrounding defeated Ger-many. John H. Backer, *The Decision to Divide Germany: American Foreign Policy in Transition* (Durham, N.C.: Duke University Press, 1978), is an important study, but rather technical in its economics and assuming a fairly good back-ground in general history. *+Ann and John Tusa, *The Berlin Airlift* (New York: Atheneum, 1988), is a readable and comprehensive narrative account of an im-portant and dramatic incident.

During all the Cold War years, historians were handicapped by being able to research only half of the story, the Anglo-American side, since Soviet archives were inaccessible. *William Taubman, *Stalin's American Policy: From Entente to Detente to Cold War* (New York: W. W. Norton & Company, 1982), was a courageous and lively attempt to fill this gap through an imaginative reconstruction of Stalin's mindset. Since the opening of Russian archives at the end of the Cold War, however, two young Russian historians, Vladislav Zubok and Constantine Pleshakov, have published a riveting account of the Kremlin policymakers' motives and policies, *+*Inside the Kremlin's Cold War: From Stalin to Khrushchev* (Cambridge, Mass.: Harvard University Press, 1996). The melancholy story of Stalin's imposition of Soviet rule on Poland was written, largely from Polish sources, by Krystyna Kersten, *The Establishment of Communist Rule in Poland, 1943-1948*, trans. John Micgiel and Michael H. Bernhard (Berkeley: University of California Press, 1991).

Finally, the important case study of Finland has been examined in great detail by Tuomo Polvinen, *Between East and West: Finland in International Politics, 1944-1947*, trans. D. G. Kirby and Peter Herring (Minneapolis: University of Minnesota Press, 1986), and more briefly and accessibly in *+Roy Allison, *Finland's Relations with the Soviet Union, 1944-84* (New York: St. Martin's Press, 1985).

Chapter 2. Cracks in the Iron Curtain

*+Jasper Ridley, *Tito* (London: Constable, 1994), is a model biography, readable and fair minded, which supersedes the previous biographies of the Yugoslav leader, most of which were written by his followers or sympathizers. Milovan Djilas, *Tito: The Story from Inside*, trans. Vasilije Kojic and Richard Hayes (New York: Harcourt Brace Jovanovich, 1980), is still worth reading, however, as much for its insights into the character of the author, who became a conscience-stricken dissident in Yugoslavia, as for its puritanical comments about Tito and his lifestyle. I hesitate to recommend Richard West, *Tito and the Rise and Fall of Yugoslavia* (London: Sinclair-Stevenson, 1994), since the author is clearly obsessed with Catholic guilt for the Ustasha genocide and because the book rambles badly in its final hundred pages. Yet the author, a British journalist, clearly knows Yugoslavia and his book does contain many insights and nuggets of wisdom.

Duncan Wilson, *Tito's Yugoslavia* (Cambridge, England: Cambridge University Press, 1979), is a good historical overview of the nation's history, but it was written before the country fell apart in the early 1990s. *Aleksa Djilas, *The Contested Country: Yugoslav Unity and Communist Revolution, 1919-1953* (Cambridge, Mass.: Harvard University Press, 1991), is a superb study of Yugoslavia's ethnic divisions up to the time of the Tito-Stalin split. The author is the son of

Milovan Djilas, Tito's top lieutenant and most important dissident, and the book was written at the time of the tragic break-up of his country. *Stefan Pavlowitch, *Tito: Yugoslavia's Great Dictator, A Reassessment* (Columbus: Ohio State University Press, 1992), admirably and briefly summarizes the state of historical knowledge about Tito after the fall of the Communist empire in Eastern Europe.

Wayne S. Vucinich, ed., *At the Brink of War and Peace: The Tito-Stalin Split in a Historical Perspective* (New York: Columbia University Press, 1982), contains the proceedings of a historical conference held to mark the thirtieth anniversary of the Tito-Stalin split. It is loaded with information, but its interpretations are dated since history has moved on swiftly since 1982. The last article in the volume is the very interesting memoir of Hungarian general Bela Kiraly, who discusses Stalin's plan for an invasion of Yugoslavia. Beatrice Heuser, *Western "Containment" Policies in the Cold War: The Yugoslav Case, 1948-1953* (London: Routledge, 1989), is a solid, but dull, study of British, French, and American reactions to the Tito-Stalin split. The book is clearly marked by its origins as a doctoral dissertation. Wilson D. Miscamble, *George F. Kennan and the Making of American Foreign Policy,* and Vladislav Zubok and Constantine Pleshakov, *Inside the Kremlin's Cold War* (both cited in chapter 1), contain some useful material on the American and Russian responses (respectively) to Tito's break with Stalin.

Two biographies make a good introduction to the nationalist General Charles de Gaulle. +Charles Williams, *The Last Great Frenchman* (New York: John Wiley & Sons, 1993), is a lengthy but readable narrative; whereas *Andrew Shennan, *De Gaulle* (London: Longman, 1993), is brief, highly interpretive, and insightful.

*Derek Urwin, *The Community of Europe: A History of European Integration since 1945* (London: Longman, 1991), is a useful overview of the European unification movement, though unfortunately it was written before the latest moves toward a single Europe in the 1990s. *François Duchêne, *Jean Monnet: The First Statesman of Interdependence* (New York: W. W. Norton & Company, 1994), provides an excellent narrative biography as well as an insightful analysis of Monnet's political techniques. Douglas Brinkley and Clifford Hackett, eds., *Jean Monnet: The Path to European Unity* (New York: St. Martin's Press, 1991), brings together articles written by friends of Monnet as well as by scholars. The reference to George Ball in my chapter text comes from the introduction that Ball wrote for this volume. *John Gillingham, *Coal, Steel, and the Rebirth of Europe, 1945-1955: The Germans and French from Ruhr Conflict to Economic Community* (Cambridge, England: Cambridge University Press, 1991), is a long, dense, and definitive study of the origins of the ECSC. He outlines his analysis more succinctly in a chapter of the Brinkley and Hackett collection cited above.

Chapter 3. Soul Force versus the British Raj

A possible starting point for the history of this region is Hugh Tinker, *South Asia: A Short History* (Honolulu: University of Hawaii Press, 1990). The book is brief and readable, but it is so crammed with information about five countries (India, Pakistan, Bangladesh, Ceylon, and Burma) that it might be better to read this book later, after acquiring some familiarity with the region. That is the way I read it. Either way, the book is useful in providing the big picture.

*Judith M. Brown, *Modern India: The Origins of an Asian Democracy* (Oxford, England: Oxford University Press, 1994), is a wide-ranging overview of India's recent history; and the same author's *Gandhi: Prisoner of Hope* (New Haven, Conn.: Yale University Press, 1989) is an outstanding full-scale biography of the Indian leader. +Calvin Kytle, *Gandhi, Soldier of Nonviolence: An Introduction* (Cabin John, Md.: Seven Locks Press, 1982) is a briefer biography by an American who was involved in the civil rights movement; and Joan V. Bondurant, *Conquest of Violence: The Gandhian Philosophy of Conflict* (Princeton, N.J.: Princeton University Press, 1958), provides an insightful analysis of Gandhi's ideas and techniques.

Since Judith Brown's history of India consciously downplays the political story which was central to my chapter, I consulted two works of political history by the Australian historian Jim Masselos: *Indian Nationalism: An History* (New Delhi: Sterling Publishers, 1985); and a collection of essays by various historians that Masselos edited to commemorate the one-hundredth anniversary of the Indian National Congress, *Struggling and Ruling: The Indian National Congress 1885-1985* (New Delhi: Sterling Publishers, 1987). Sankar Ghose, *Jawaharlal Nehru: A Biography* (New Delhi: Allied Publishers, 1993), is a readable and balanced biography of Gandhi's major disciple, who became the first prime minister of independent India; and B. R. Nanda, P. C. Joshi, and Raj Krishna, *Gandhi and Nehru* (Delhi: Oxford University Press, 1979), is a brief collection of lectures comparing the two Indian leaders. Ayesha Jalal, *The Sole Spokesman: Jinnah, the Muslim League, and the Demand for Pakistan* (Cambridge, England: Cambridge University Press, 1985), is not an easy book to read, but it provides an important corrective to the overly negative views of Jinnah, the founder of Pakistan, usually found in Indian works. H. V. Hodson, *The Great Divide: Britain — India — Pakistan* (London: Hutchinson, 1969), furnishes a lengthy, detailed account of the final days of the British Raj, primarily from the British point of view.

Salman Rushdie, an Indian Muslim by birth but an English agnostic by choice, has stirred much controversy with his fictional writings on Islam. *The Moor's Last Sigh* (New York: Pantheon Books, 1995) is an entertaining, kaleidoscopic story of one Indian extended family. The quotations from Rushdie in my chapter are drawn from this book. *+R. K. Narayan, *Waiting for the Mahatma* (Chicago: University of Chicago Press, 1981), is a brief, haunting novel which wraps the career of Mohandas Gandhi around a love story involving two ordinary Indian youths. Most Americans, however, will still acquire their knowledge of India's freedom struggle from Richard Attenborough's 1982 motion picture, *Gandhi*. Though many important incidents are omitted and time is telescoped, this film stays truer to historical reality than most screen biographies and presents a remarkably full exploration of Gandhi's religious and political ideas.

Chapter 4. The World Turned Upside Down

Two firsthand accounts of the Chinese Revolution by American participant-observers give a feel for both the idealism and the violence of the revolutionaries: *+Jack Belden, *China Shakes the World* (New York: Harper & Brothers, 1949), and *+William Hinton, *Fanshen: A Documentary of Revolution in a Chinese Village* (New York: Monthly Review Press, 1966). *Lucien Bianco, *Origins of the Chinese Revolution, 1915-1949*, trans. Muriel Bell (Stanford, Calif.: Stanford University Press, 1971), and *Maurice Meisner, *Mao's China and After: A History of the People's Republic* (New York: The Free Press, 1986), are both classic historical accounts that have held up well despite their basically sympathetic attitude toward the Chinese Communists. *John King Fairbank's last book, *China: A New History* (Cambridge, Mass.: Harvard University Press, 1992), has an advantage over both Bianco and Meisner since much new evidence has appeared in recent years.

I garnered a great deal of essential information from three specialized works by professional historians, but unfortunately none of the three makes for interesting reading. All three fall into the category of books that I read so that you don't have to: Tetsuya Kataoka, *Resistance and Revolution in China: The Communists and the Second United Front* (Berkeley: University of California Press, 1974); Suzanne Pepper, *Civil War in China: The Political Struggle, 1945-1949* (Berkeley: University of California Press, 1978); and Kathleen Hartford and Steven M. Goldstein, eds., *Single Sparks: China's Rural Revolutions* (Armonk, N.Y.: M. E. Sharpe, Inc., 1989).

*+Ross Terrill's *Mao: A Biography* (New York: Harper & Row, 1980) is extremely readable and informative, but it is beginning to appear dated as new information surfaces about Mao's atrocities. Stuart R. Schram wrote an even earlier biography of Mao, which I did not read, but I did consult his brief update of his work, *Mao Zedong: A Preliminary Reassessment* (New York: St. Martin's Press, 1983). As of the writing of this book, Schram still believed that "Mao's

455

merits outweighed his faults," but in my opinion his own evidence disproves this.

The early works of academic China-watchers were largely favorable (as I have indicated) to Mao Tse-tung and the Chinese Revolution, but in the years following the suppression of anti-democracy demonstrations in 1989, a flood of negative accounts have appeared. *Zhang Xianliang's novel, *Getting Used to Dying,* trans. Martha Avery (New York: Harper Collins, 1991), is the best of these critical works that I consulted. A haunting, largely autobiographical story, it conveys the terror felt by the intellectuals in Mao's China. +John Byron and Robert Pack, *Claws of the Dragon: Kang Sheng — The Evil Genius Behind Mao — and His Legacy of Terror in People's China* (New York: Simon & Schuster, 1992), is a very readable, though somewhat exaggerated, exposé of a Mao henchman. Zheng Yi, *Scarlet Memorial* (Boulder, Colo.: Westview Press, 1996), relates the shocking story of cannibalism in Kwangsi Province. I did not have the stomach to read it but contented myself with the foreword by Ross Terrill. I also did not read much of +Dr. Li Zhisui, *The Private Life of Chairman Mao: The Memoirs of Mao's Personal Physician,* trans. Tai Hung-chao (New York: Random House, 1994), because I don't care much more about the private life of Mao than I do about the private life of John or Ted Kennedy. The book does appear, however, to be an easy, if overly long, read.

Chapter 5. Unity in Diversity

There are not an overwhelming number of books about Indonesia in English, but most are of high quality. Unfortunately, I didn't find any of them interesting enough to recommend for a popular audience. The biography of Sukarno, by John David Legge, comes closest.

*M. C. Ricklefs, *A History of Modern Indonesia: c. 1300 to the Present* (Bloomington: Indiana University Press, 1981), and *Bernhard Dahm, *History of Indonesia in the Twentieth Century,* trans. P. S. Falla (London: Pall Mall Press, 1971), are very comprehensive introductions to the history of this country, though they make slow reading. *J. [John] D. [David] Legge, *Sukarno: A Political Biography* (Sydney, Australia: Allen & Unwin, 1984), is a sympathetic but not uncritical life story.

Benedict R. O'G. Anderson, *Java in a Time of Revolution: Occupation and Resistance, 1944-1946* (Ithaca, N.Y.: Cornell University Press, 1972), is a long, detailed, but fascinating portrait of the radical youth of Java during the revolution. Anderson has also written a highly influential study of modern nationalism, *Imagined Communities: Reflections on the Origin and Spread of Nationalism* (London: Verson, 1983), which draws on his knowledge of Indonesia. Anthony

Reid, *The Indonesian National Revolution, 1945-1950* (Hawthorn, Victoria: Longman Australia, 1974), admirably summarizes the events of the revolution in a brief volume, and Audrey Kahin, ed., *Regional Dynamics of the Indonesian Revolution: Unity from Diversity* (Honolulu: University of Hawaii Press, 1985), presents brief articles by individual scholars exploring the complexities of the revolution in various regions of the country.

The Modern Indonesia Project of Cornell University published a translation series of crucial Indonesian documents and scholarly studies. I consulted Sukarno's key address, "Nationalism, Islam and Marxism," translated by Karel H. Warouw and Peter D. Weldon, no. 17, published in 1969. Herbert Feith and Lance Castles, eds., provide another way to sample primary sources in *Indonesian Political Thinking, 1945-1965* (Ithaca, N.Y.: Cornell University Press, 1970). Most of Sukarno's major addresses from this period are included. Eka Darmaputera, *Pancasila and the Search for Identity and Modernity in Indonesian Society: A Cultural and Ethical Analysis* (Leiden, Netherlands: E. J. Brill, 1988), is a doctoral dissertation in religious studies and reads that way, but it explores some fascinating and provocative ideas about Indonesian society and culture. Mochtar Lubis, *A Road with No End,* trans. Anthony H. Johns (Chicago: Henry Regnery, 1970), is a brief, fascinating novel about fear and courage during the time of the Indonesian revolution. Peter Weir's 1982 film *The Year of Living Dangerously* is not a historical documentary, though the details of Sukarno's "guided democracy" era are presented fairly and accurately. The film presents a routine love/adventure story against the backdrop of the 1965 army takeover that brought down Sukarno. It is worth viewing for the portrayal of a Eurasian character by Linda Hunt, which deservedly won her an Oscar for best supporting actress.

I developed my definition of nationalism more fully in chapter 2 of volume 1. It is based primarily on Ernst Renan's classic lecture, *"Qu'est-ce qu'une nation?,"* which can be found in an abridged English version in Hans Kohn, *Nationalism: Its Meaning and History* (Princeton, N.J.: Van Nostrand, 1955).

Chapter 6. Tigers and Elephants

*+Walter Laqueur, *Guerrilla: A Historical and Critical Study* (Boston: Little, Brown and Company, 1976), is a masterly survey of the theory and practice of guerrilla warfare throughout history. Franklin Mark Osanka, ed., *Modern Guerrilla Warfare: Fighting Communist Guerrilla Movements, 1941-1961* (New York: The Free Press, 1962), on the other hand, is a dated collection of Cold War essays. It still retains some usefulness, however, as a primary source; and both the introduction by Samuel Huntington and two irreverent articles by Paul M. A.

Linebarger, about Indochina and Malaya, are quite striking. *Sir Robert Thompson, *Defeating Communist Insurgency: The Lessons of Malaya and Vietnam* (New York: Frederick A. Praeger, 1966), is a classic analysis, marred but not destroyed by its very British "I told you so" tone.

*K. G. Tregonning, *A History of Modern Malaya* (London: Eastern Universities Press, 1964), and *Barbara Watson Andaya and Leonard Y. Andaya, *A History of Malaysia* (New York: St. Martin's Press, 1982), are equally good overviews of Malayan history, though both books are fairly ponderous to read. William R. Roff, *The Origins of Malay Nationalism* (New Haven, Conn.: Yale University Press, 1967); Albert Lau, *The Malayan Union Controversy, 1942-1948* (Singapore: Oxford University Press, 1991); and James P. Ongkili, *Nation-building in Malaysia, 1946-1974* (Singapore: Oxford University Press, 1985), are detailed, specialized monographs on their subjects. +Harry Miller, *Prince and Premier: A Biography of Tunku Abdul Rahman Putra Al-Haj, First Prime Minister of the Federation of Malaya* (London: George G. Harrap & Co., Ltd., 1959), provides a brief, journalistic, but quite perceptive biography of the Tunku.

*Anthony Short, *The Communist Insurrection in Malaya, 1948-1960* (London: Frederick Muller Ltd., 1975), provides the most comprehensive study of the Malayan Emergency, but it is very long and frustratingly dull. A novel by Han Suyin, *And the Rain My Drink* (London: Jonathan Cape, 1956), paints a much darker picture of the Emergency's impact on the Chinese community than either Short or Thompson (above).

American academia has made the Vietnam War into a massive growth industry. Most of the numerous general histories of the American war in Vietnam provide some background on the earlier French struggle. Two of the best are: *Marilyn B. Young, *The Vietnam Wars, 1945-1990* (New York: Harper Collins, 1991), and George C. Herring, *America's Longest War: The United States and Vietnam, 1950-1975* (New York: John Wiley and Sons, 1979).

Joseph Buttinger wrote a two-volume history of the nation of Vietnam, entitled *Vietnam — The Smaller Dragon* (1958) and *Vietnam: A Dragon Embattled* (1967). I consulted his one-volume, condensed version of this work, *Vietnam: A Political History* (New York: Frederick A. Praeger, 1968). *William J. Duiker, *The Rise of Nationalism in Vietnam, 1900-1941* (Ithaca, N.Y.: Cornell University Press, 1976), is an admirably brief and balanced study. *Ellen J. Hammer, *The Struggle for Indochina, 1940-1955* (Stanford, Calif.: Stanford University Press, 1966), is the standard overview of the First Indochinese War, remarkably sympathetic to the peoples of Indochina.

There is a big biography of Ho Chi Minh by Jean Lacouture (New York: Random House, 1968), but I was unable to obtain a copy at either bookstore or library. The book is out of print and the copy in my university library was stolen. All of the works on Vietnam cited in this section give considerable biographical information on Ho, especially Duiker's book. The American journalist David Halberstam has provided a very brief, readable sketch of the Vietnamese leader, simply entitled +*Ho* (New York: Random House, 1971).

*+Bernard Fall, *Street Without Joy: Insurgency in Indochina, 1946-63* (Harrisburg: The Stackpole Company, 1963), is a classic account by a French participant observer, and +Jules Roy, *The Battle of Dienbienphu*, trans. Robert Baldick (New York: Harper & Row, 1965), is a comprehensive and impassioned account of that tragic battle. Finally, Regis Wargnier's 1993 film *Indochine* is the kind of sprawling epic drama that American filmmakers rarely make anymore. It vividly depicts the human impact of French colonialism and Vietnamese revolution.

Chapter 7. Drawing a Line

The news media call Korea the "forgotten war," but it has not been neglected by historians. The general books cited in chapter 1, Walter LaFeber, *America, Russia, and the Cold War;* Martin Walker, *The Cold War: A History;* and John Lewis Gaddis, *The Long Peace: Inquiries into the History of the Cold War,* all contain interesting and important material about the Korean War. In fact, chapter 3 of Walker's book, "The Cold War Goes Global — and Comes Home," is as fine a brief history of the Korean War as can be found.

Unfortunately, until very recently historians could only research one side of the war in detail, the American side, since Soviet and Chinese archives were closed. Nonetheless, much fine work was done before the end of the Cold War made Communist documentation available. *John Merrill, *Korea: The Peninsular Origins of the War* (Newark, Del.: University of Delaware Press, 1989), though not very readable, provides an excellent analysis of the causes of the war. Burton I. Kaufman, *The Korean War: Challenges in Crisis, Credibility and Command* (Philadephia: Temple University Press, 1986), adequately summarizes the diplomatic record from the American point of view. *+Max Hastings, *The Korean War* (New York: Simon and Schuster, 1987), gives the best overview of the whole war, with emphasis on the military history.

Three books that have appeared since the end of the Cold War do much to fill in the blanks about the Korean War. Vladislav Zubok and Constantine Pleshakov, *Inside the Kremlin's Cold War: From Stalin to Krushchev* (cited in chapter 1), tells the Soviet side of the story. *Sergei N. Goncharov, John W. Lewis, and Xue Litai, *Uncertain Partners: Stalin, Mao, and the Korean War* (Stanford, Calif.: Stanford University Press, 1993), draws on Soviet and Chinese sources to give the best account of the Communists' decisions to date. If you don't want to read their fairly heavy academic prose, you can cheat and get the gist of their findings in the review article written by John Lewis Gaddis, "Who Really Started the Korean War?", *Atlantic Monthly* (May 1994). *William Stueck, *The Korean War: An International History* (Princeton, N.J.: Princeton University Press, 1995), is an overview of the whole war that draws together the latest research from all sides. It is encyclopedic in scope and difficult to read, but a good all-around summation. For the general reader, however, I would recommend Hastings's book for the military history and the Goncharov, Lewis, Xue volume for the latest archival finds.

Finally, a number of books that I consulted proved useful, but would likely be of lesser use to the general reader. Bruce Cumings, a leading scholar on the Korean War who has written a number of weighty tomes that I did not consult, recently attempted a popular history of Korea, entitled *Korea's Place in the Sun: A Modern History* (New York: W. W. Norton & Company, 1997). The book is too chatty and rambling to be entirely successful but does contain a passionate defense of the Korean people. Ramon H. Myers and Mark R. Peattie, eds., *The Japanese Colonial Empire, 1895-1945* (Princeton, N.J.: Princeton University Press, 1984), publishes the proceedings of a scholarly conference and provides important background on Japan's colonial rule in Korea and Taiwan. Finally, two books by Michael Schaller contain nuggets of information that I found helpful: *The American Occupation of Japan: The Origins of the Cold War in Asia* (New York: Oxford University Press, 1985), and *Douglas MacArthur: The Far Eastern General* (New York: Oxford University Press, 1989). Both are heavy to read and poorly edited.

Chapter 8. Family, Religion, and Nation in the Arab Heartland

Albert Hourani, *A History of the Arab Peoples* (Cambridge, Mass.: The Belknap Press of Harvard University Press, 1991), and +Peter Mansfield, *The Arabs* (London: Penguin Books, 1992), provide extensive background. Mansfield's book is far more appropriate for the general reader. A. A. Duri, *The Historical Formation of the Arab Nation: A Study in Identity and Consciousness,* trans. Lawrence I. Conrad (London: Croom Helm, 1987), and *C. Ernest Dawn, *From Ottomanism to Arabism: Essays on the Origins of Arab Nationalism* (Urbana: University of Illinois Press, 1973), analyze the various dimensions of Arab nationalism. Dawn's book also contains an excellent essay on Sherif Hussein and the Arab Revolt. Ami Ayalon, *Language and Change in the Arab Middle East: The Evolution of Modern Political Discourse* (New York: Oxford University Press, 1987), dissects the changing meanings of various Arabic words. Though I didn't use much material directly from this book, I found it fascinating, and I wish there were a similar book for each of the languages and cultures I have researched for this world history.

At least one good historical study has been written in English for each of the major countries of the Arab heartland. *Mary C. Wilson, *King Abdullah, Britain, and the Making of Jordan* (Cambridge, England: Cambridge University Press, 1987), is a solid, readable historical monograph. *Philip S. Khoury, *Syria and the French Mandate: The Politics of Arab Nationalism, 1920-1945* (Princeton, N.J.: Princeton University Press, 1987), is longer and more detailed than the general reader will appreciate, but is highly interpretive and full of insights. *+Patrick Seale, *The Struggle for Syria: A Study of Post-War Arab Politics, 1945-1958* (New Haven, Conn.: Yale University Press, 1987), deals mainly with a later period than I discuss in this chapter, but is very readable and perceptive. +Helena Cobban, *The Making of Modern Lebanon* (London: Hutchinson, 1985), provides a brief introduction for the general reader. *Phebe Marr, *The Modern History of Iraq* (Boulder, Colo.: Westview Press, 1985), is longer, more detailed, and less readable. The oil crisis of the 1970s occasioned the writing of two very long, popular histories of Saudi Arabia: *David Holden, Richard Johns, *The House of Saud: The Rise and Rule of the Most Powerful Dynasty in the Arab World* (New York: Holt, Rinehart and Winston, 1981), and *Robert Lacey, *The Kingdom* (New York: Harcourt Brace Jovanovich, 1981). The book by Holden and Johns is a little more serious and Lacey's more breezy and chatty, but both are informative and enjoyable. *David McDowell, *A Modern History of the Kurds* (London: I. B. Tauris, 1996), is a detailed, impassioned chronicle of the long-suffering Kurdish minorities of Turkey, Iran, and Iraq.

Three books that survey the broad sweep of events in the Middle East during the years considered in this chapter are: *+Elizabeth Monroe, *Britain's Moment in the Middle East, 1914-1956* (Baltimore: Johns Hopkins Press, 1963); Yehoshua Porath, *In Search of Arab Unity, 1930-1945* (London: Frank Cass, 1986); and Ritchie Ovendale, *Britain, the United States, and the Transfer of Power in the Middle East, 1945-1962* (London: Leicester University Press, 1996). The latter two are more ponderous and academic than Monroe's older, but still delightful, overview. Finally, the story of the oil industry in the twentieth century is admirably narrated in *+Daniel Yergin, *The Prize: The Epic Quest for Oil, Money, & Power* (New York: Simon & Schuster, 1991).

Chapter 9. A Settler Colony with a Difference

Two large overviews that survey the founding of the state of Israel are +Howard M. Sachar, *A History of Israel from the Rise of Zionism to Our Time* (New York: Alfred A. Knopf, 1996), and *Christopher Sykes, *Cross Roads to Israel* (London: Collins, 1965). Both are openly sympathetic to Zionism, but Sykes's book is more balanced and insightful, full of interesting asides and moral musings. It is the single best book on Zionism that I encountered.

461

Yehoshua Porath, *The Emergence of the Palestinian-Arab National Movement, 1918-1929* (London: Frank Cass, 1974), and *The Palestinian Arab National Movement: From Riots to Rebellion, 1929-1939* (London: Frank Cass, 1977); and Kenneth W. Stein, *The Land Question in Palestine, 1917-1939* (Chapel Hill: University of North Carolina Press, 1984), are useful, detailed, but rather dull academic studies.

*Bernard Wasserstein, *The British in Palestine: The Mandatory Government and the Arab-Jewish Conflict, 1917-1929* (London: Basil Blackwell, 1991), and *Wm. Roger Louis and Robert W. Stookey, eds., *The End of the Palestine Mandate* (Austin: University of Texas Press, 1986), analyze British policy in Palestine as fairly as possible. The Louis and Stookey volume also contains essays on American and Russian policy towards the emerging state of Israel.

*Ann Moseley Lesch, *Arab Politics in Palestine, 1917-1939* (Ithaca, N.Y.: Cornell University Press, 1979), is a fascinating study of the Arab side of the Palestine question, set in a larger context of imperialism and the dynamics of settler colonies. Philip Mattar, *The Mufti of Jerusalem: Al-Hajj Amin al-Husayni and the Palestinian National Movement* (New York: Columbia University Press, 1988), is a brief, sympathetic biography of an unsympathetic historical character. Readers who find the mufti portrayed as a virtual Nazi in the standard Zionist sources should read this book as an antidote.

+Michael Bar-Zohar, *The Armed Prophet: A Biography of Ben-Gurion*, trans. Len Ortzen (London: Arthur Barker, 1967), is a popular, readable biography by an unabashed admirer of the Israeli leader. Ronald W. Zweig, ed., *David Ben-Gurion: Politics and Leadership in Israel* (London: Frank Cass, 1991), presents a collection of less readable, but more sober, historical essays on Ben-Gurion.

Finally, *Simha Flapan, *The Birth of Israel: Myths and Realities* (New York: Pantheon Books, 1987), and *Benny Morris, *The Birth of the Palestine Refugee Problem, 1947-1949* (New York: Cambridge University Press, 1987), are fascinating, revisionist accounts of the birth of Israel by Israeli scholars. Both explode many myths of the usual celebratory Zionist accounts and focus on the creation of the refugee problem in the 1947-48 war.

Chapter 10. The Life-Line of Imperialism

Nearly any book of history covering the mid-century contains some mention of the Suez crisis, including the general histories of the Cold War listed in chapter 1. Two excellent short accounts of the crisis can be found in Daniel Yergin, *The Prize* (cited in chapter 8), and *Henry S. Wilson, *African Decolonization* (London: Edward Arnold, 1994).

Three surveys cover the broad sweep of modern Egyptian history admirably: *+Arthur Goldschmidt Jr., *Modern Egypt: The Formation of a Nation-State* (Boulder, Colo.: Westview Press, 1988); Selma Botman, *Egypt from Independence to Revolution, 1919-1952* (Syracuse, N.Y.: Syracuse University Press, 1991); and *Derek Hopwood, *Egypt: Politics and Society 1945-1984* (Boston: Unwin Hyman, 1985). Peter Mansfield wrote a short, laudatory biography of Gamal Abdul Nasser just before the Egyptian president's death, +*Nasser* (London: Methuen Educational Ltd., 1969); and *P. J. Vatikiotis, *Nasser and His Generation* (New York: St. Martin's Press, 1978), presents a more critical analysis.

To my surprise, no one has written a full-scale study of the Bandung Conference. Perhaps it seems too ephemeral an event, filled with speeches and photo opportunities, or possibly the necessity of analyzing twenty-nine different countries' policies may have daunted historians. In any case, two brief works written shortly after the conference provide useful information: George McTurnan Kahin, *The Asian-African Conference: Bandung, Indonesia, April 1955* (Ithaca, N.Y.: Cornell University Press, 1956), contains a brief synopsis of the conference along with some documents, including Sukarno's keynote speech and the final communiqué; whereas Richard Wright, *The Color Curtain: A Report on the Bandung Conference* (Cleveland: The World Publishing Company, 1956), presents a highly personal reaction by a noted African-American novelist.

Everything you ever wanted to know about the Suez crisis but were afraid to ask can be found in just two books: *Keith Kyle, *Suez* (New York: St. Martin's Press, 1991), a definitive narrative history; and *Wm. Roger Louis and Roger Owen, eds., *Suez 1956: The Crisis and Its Consequences* (Oxford, England: Clarendon Press, 1989), a collection of articles by a variety of scholars and participants in the event. Of course, each book runs over five hundred pages, but who's counting?

Chapter 11. Terror and Torture

Peter Mansfield, *The Arabs* (cited in chapter 8), and H. S. Wilson, *African Decolonization* (cited in chapter 10), present useful introductions to the French presence in North Africa. Wilson's book contains a particularly good section on the "lost opportunity" of the Blum-Violette bill. *John Ruedy, *Modern Algeria: The Origins and Development of a Nation* (Bloomington: Indiana University Press, 1992), provides a good overview of the nation's history; and *+Alistair Horne, *A Savage War of Peace: Algeria, 1954-1962* (New York: Viking Press, 1977), is an outstanding, nearly definitive narrative history of the Algerian war of independence. William B. Quandt, *Revolution and Political Leadership: Algeria, 1954-*

1968 (Cambridge, Mass.: M.I.T. Press, 1969), analyzes the various generations of leaders who participated in Algeria's liberation struggle.

Walter Laqueur, *The Age of Terrorism* (Boston: Little, Brown and Company, 1987), is an updated and expanded version of a 1977 book and a companion piece to his volume on guerrilla warfare (cited in chapter 6). *Martha Crenshaw Hutchinson, *Revolutionary Terrorism: The FLN in Algeria, 1954-1962* (Stanford, Calif.: Hoover Institution Press, 1978), focuses specifically on the FLN as a case study. Frantz Fanon, *The Wretched of the Earth,* trans. Constance Farrington (New York: Grove Press, 1966), is still worth reading for its many insights, but is not convincing in its main argument. Rita Maran, *Torture: The Role of Ideology in the French-Algerian War* (New York: Praeger, 1989), is a maddeningly academic tome. I am tempted to say that it was torture to read it. It does contain much useful information.

General Charles de Gaulle figures prominently in all the general treatments of the Algerian war. I consulted a recent biography by Charles Williams and an interpretive study by Andrew Shennan (both cited in chapter 2).

Jean Lartéguy's two-volume novel about the French paratroopers is enjoyable: *+*The Centurions,* trans. Xan Fielding (New York: E. P. Dutton & Co., 1962), and +*The Praetorians,* trans. Xan Fielding (New York: E. P. Dutton & Co., 1963). *The Centurions* is more interesting, a big, brash, swashbuckling story of men at war. *The Praetorians* reads more like a piece of journalism than a fully realized novel. Both volumes, however, provide sharp insights into the minds of the French soldiers who fought in Vietnam, at Suez, and in Algeria. *+Albert Camus, *The First Man,* trans. David Hapgood (New York: Alfred A. Knopf, 1995), brilliantly captures the life of a "native" French Algerian. Camus's proposal for a civil truce and other writings about Algeria are contained in his collection of essays, *Resistance, Rebellion, and Death,* trans. Justin O'Brien (New York: Alfred A. Knopf, 1960). Gillo Pontecorvo's film *The Battle of Algiers* (1967) is a highly effective piece of propaganda, in a documentary style.

Chapter 12. Tribes, Nations, and States

Many overall histories of Africa have been published in the last thirty or forty years. I consulted two of these for general background on the continent: Roland Oliver and J. D. Fage, *A Short History of Africa* (London: Penguin, 1995), and *+Basil Davidson, *Africa in History: Themes and Outlines* (New York: Macmillan, 1991). Patrick Manning's superb study, *Slavery and African Life: Occidental, Oriental, and African Slave Trades* (Cambridge, England: Cambridge University Press, 1990), is essential for understanding the legacy of slavery. Bill Freund, *The Making of Contemporary Africa: The Development of African Soci-*

ety since 1800 (Bloomington: Indiana University Press, 1984), is useful as an introduction to the most recent period of African history.

Books that survey the broad sweep of decolonization (the British spell it decolonisation) are usually written from the point of view of the colonial power and are stupefying in their encyclopedic breadth; nonetheless, it is useful to read some of them for the "big picture." I consulted R. F. Holland, *European Decolonization, 1918-1981: An Introductory Survey* (New York: St. Martin's Press, 1985); John Darwin, *Britain and Decolonisation: The Retreat from Empire in the Post-War World* (New York: St. Martin's Press, 1988); Raymond F. Betts, *France and Decolonisation, 1900-1960* (New York: St. Martin's Press, 1991); *John D. Hargreaves, *Decolonization in Africa* (London: Longman, 1988); and *H. S. Wilson, *African Decolonization* (cited in chapter 10). Prosser Gifford and Wm. Roger Louis, eds., *The Transfer of Power in Africa: Decolonization, 1940-1960* (New Haven, Conn.: Yale University Press, 1982), provides a collection of scholarly essays.

Elizabeth Isichei, a Nigerian Ibo scholar, has written a fine overview of the region of West Africa, *History of West Africa since 1800* (New York: Africana Publishing Company, 1977). John D. Hargreaves, *The End of Colonial Rule in West Africa: Essays in Contemporary History* (London: Macmillan, 1979), is a series of personal reflections rather than a complete history of decolonization in the region.

*+Basil Davidson, *Black Star: A View of the Life and Times of Kwame Nkrumah* (New York: Praeger, 1973), is a sympathetic but not wholly uncritical biography of the Ghanaian *Osagyefo*. Kofi Buenor Hadjor, *Nkrumah and Ghana: The Dilemma of Post-Colonial Power* (London: Kegan Paul International, 1988), is quite adulatory but still full of insights. Jon Woronoff, *West African Wager: Houphouet versus Nkrumah* (Metuchen, N.J.: Scarecrow Press, 1972), is a fascinating comparative study of Ghana and the Ivory Coast. I wish something like it had been done more recently. I found the book more critical of Nkrumah than the two previous biographies.

James S. Coleman, *Nigeria: Background to Nationalism* (Berkeley: University of California Press, 1963), is another old but useful study, delivering exactly what its title and subtitle promise. *John Hatch, *Nigeria: A History* (London: Secker & Wartburg, 1971), is a model national overview. *+John de St. Jorre, *The Brothers' War: Biafra and Nigeria* (Boston: Houghton Mifflin, 1972), is a fascinating narrative account of the Nigerian civil war by a journalist who witnessed it firsthand.

My discussion of "tribalism" and nationalism in Africa relies heavily on *+Basil Davidson, *The Black Man's Burden: Africa and the Curse of the Nation-State* (New York: Times Books, 1992); and my perception of Ibo society was shaped by Chinua Achebe's classic novel, *+ *Things Fall Apart* (New York:

Ballantine, 1959), probably the best known of all African novels, a staple of high school and college reading lists. Achebe's sequel, *No Longer at Ease* (New York: Ballantine, 1960), provides a vivid dramatization of the rampant corruption in Nigeria that led to the coups and civil war of the 1960s; and Buchi Emecheta, *The Joys of Motherhood* (New York: George Braziller, 1979), shows the female side of the society that Achebe portrays in his novels.

Chapter 13. Land and Freedom

Bethwell A. Ogot is the dean of East African historians. He and his colleagues in Nairobi have produced many collaborative volumes that explore the social and economic as well as the political history of the region. I consulted *B. A. Ogot and J. A. Kieran, eds., *Zamani: A Survey of East African History* (Nairobi: East African Publishing House, 1968), for a basic introduction to the region; and *William R. Ochieng, ed., *A Modern History of Kenya, 1895-1980, in Honour of B. A. Ogot* (London: Evans Brothers, 1989), for an overview of that country's history. *B. A. Ogot and W. R. Ochieng, *Decolonization & Independence in Kenya, 1940-93* (London: James Currey, 1995), brings the story of Kenya's development nearly up to date.

Apparently a biography of Jomo Kenyatta exists — Jeremy Murray-Brown, *Kenyatta* (London: George Allen & Unwin, 1972) — but I was unable to track it down. I found the basic facts of Kenyatta's life in a biography intended for young people, Dennis Wepman, *Jomo Kenyatta* (New York: Chelsea House Publishers, 1985). Kenyatta is so central to Kenya's independence movement, however, that he is extensively discussed in all the general books about Kenya. His anthropological treatise, *Facing Mount Kenya* (London: Secker and Warburg, 1938), is still fascinating and well worth reading. Kenyatta's younger lieutenant and sometime rival, Tom Mboya, has been the subject of a very good biography, David Goldsworthy, *Tom Mboya: The Man Kenya Wanted to Forget* (London: Heinemann, 1982). I read and enjoyed this book, but unfortunately did not have sufficient space to work Mboya into my narrative.

Two recent books narrate the broad sweep of the Mau Mau movement: *+Robert Edgerton, *Mau Mau: An African Crucible* (New York: The Free Press, 1989), an admirable journalistic account; and *Wunyabari O. Maloba, *Mau Mau and Kenya: An Analysis of a Peasant Revolt* (Bloomington: Indiana University Press, 1993), a more academic study. Both books take the movement seriously as a revolutionary struggle, something which older studies do not. If you wish to sample the style of academic historians today, read the article by John Lonsdale, "Mau Maus of the Mind: Making Mau Mau and Remaking Kenya," *Journal of African History*, 31 (1990): 393-421, which contains precious little information on Mau Mau but a lot about the language, or "discourse" as it is fashionably termed, used in talking about Mau Mau.

*John Iliffe, *A Modern History of Tanganyika* (Cambridge, England: Cambridge University Press, 1979), is a long, comprehensive study of colonial Tanganyika, emphasizing the environment and the economy more than politics. Iliffe's book is a real tour de force, and my only complaint is that it ends just when the story is getting interesting, at independence. William Redman Duggan and John R. Civile, *Tanzania and Nyerere: A Study of Ujamaa and Nationhood* (Maryknoll, N.Y.: Orbis Books, 1976), is a far less sophisticated study than Iliffe's; and the second section, an analysis of Nyerere's Christian socialism by Civile, proves disappointing, as the author merely matches quotes from Nyerere with quotes from the modern popes. The first section by Duggan, however, contains much information that is especially useful since no full biography of Nyerere exists. Nyerere's ideas are best sampled directly in his short, readable collection, *Ujamaa — Essays on Socialism* (London: Oxford University Press, 1968). *Ahmed Mohiddin, *African Socialism in Two Countries* (London: Croom Helm, 1981), compares the economic experiences of Kenya and Tanzania during their first fifteen years of independence. The book is academic and ponderous but very insightful. As with Jon Woronoff's study comparing Ghana and the Ivory Coast (cited in chapter 12), I only wish someone had done such a study more recently.

Isak Dinesen, *Out of Africa* (New York: Random House, 1938), and the 1985 movie based on it, directed by Sydney Pollack and starring Meryl Streep and Robert Redford, are interesting for their lush descriptions of the African landscape and for their insights into the stunted mind of settler colonialism. In this case, the Hollywood movie improves on the book by focusing mainly on the love story and mercifully downplaying Dinesen's attitudes toward Africans. Grace Ogot, the wife of historian B. A. Ogot, has written an interesting novel, *The Promised Land* (Nairobi: East African Publishing House, 1966), which illustrates the frontier nature of East Africa by portraying the immigration of an African family from western Kenya to western Tanganyika shortly after World War II. The book resembles the many immigration novels written about Europeans settling in the New World, except that the sea journey in this case stretches only across Lake Victoria rather than the Atlantic.

Chapter 14. Chaos and Cold War

*+Thomas Pakenham's brilliant narrative history, *The Scramble for Africa: White Man's Conquest of the Dark Continent from 1876 to 1912* (New York: Avon Books, 1991), weaves the incredible story of Belgian King Leopold II through

the book as a recurring nightmare for Africans. *Roger Anstey, *King Leopold's Legacy: The Congo Under Belgian Rule, 1908-1960* (London: Oxford University Press, 1966), offers a thorough, slightly dull history of the Congo after Leopold relinquished control to the Belgian government. *Crawford Young, *Politics in the Congo: Decolonization and Independence* (Princeton, N.J.: Princeton University Press, 1965), is an old, but still unrivaled, analysis of the Congo's politics and society at the time of independence.

Amazingly, there is no book-length narrative history of the Congo crisis in English, as historians have not been much drawn to this event. However, *+Stanley Meisler, *United Nations: The First Fifty Years* (New York: Atlantic Monthly Press, 1995), contains an excellent chapter entitled "The Battles of Katanga and the Crash of Hammarskjöld," which summarizes the crisis admirably. Sandra W. Meditz and Tim Merrill, *Zaire: A Country Study* (Washington: The Library of Congress, 1994), provides a handbook on the country's history and society in a volume commissioned by the U.S. Army. Its statistical information and thumbnail history of the independence crisis are very useful.

In addition, I have read more memoirs of participants than I usually do. *Thomas Kanza, *The Rise and Fall of Patrice Lumumba: Conflict in the Congo* (Boston: G. K. Hall, 1972), is not a full biography but more of a memoir by a devoted friend. It is not complete or objective, but I have relied heavily on it for vivid, firsthand impressions of Lumumba. *Brian Urquhart, *Hammarskjöld* (New York: Harper & Row, 1972), is a more traditional biography, but also a work produced by a devoted friend of the subject. Urquhart's later autobiography, *A Life in Peace and War* (New York: Harper & Row, 1987), is slightly more readable than his first study and contains a few additional tidbits about the Congo crisis. Indar Jit Rikhye, *Military Adviser to the Secretary-General: UN Peacekeeping and the Congo Crisis* (London: Hurst, 1993), is a stolid and earnest tome, with a few valuable insights. Conor Cruise O'Brien, *To Katanga and Back: A UN Case History* (London: Hutchinson, 1962), stands on a different level from the other memoirs. In many respects it resembles Winston Churchill's massive histories of both world wars. Like Churchill's studies, O'Brien's book is primarily intended as self-justification, but he is such a keen observer and good writer that the book often sparkles with insights when the author is writing about someone other than himself.

*+Sean Kelly, *America's Tyrant: The CIA and Mobutu of Zaire* (Washington: American University Press, 1993), would probably be the most interesting book on the Congo for a contemporary audience. It not only summarizes the events of the Congo crisis but also brings the story of Mobutu's American-backed tyranny almost up to date. It was published just a few years before Mobutu's overthrow and death. Finally, *Madeleine G. Kalb, *The Congo Cables: The Cold War in Africa — From Eisenhower to Kennedy* (New York: Macmillan,

1982), admirably analyzes the Cold War context of the Congo affair, from both the American and the Russian points of view.

Chapter 15. Khrushchev, Kennedy, and Castro at the Brink

The general histories of the Cold War cited in chapter 1 are all useful for this continuation of the story, especially John Lewis Gaddis, *The Long Peace;* Walter LaFeber, *America, Russia and the Cold War;* and Vladislav Zubok and Constantine Pleshakov, *Inside the Kremlin's Cold War.*

After his forced retirement, Nikita Khrushchev tape-recorded a long series of memoirs that his son Sergei smuggled out to the United States for publication. They were published in three pieces over a long period of time as *Khrushchev Remembers, Khrushchev: The Last Testament,* and *Khrushchev Remembers: The Glasnost Tapes.* I read only the last volume, the shortest and most recent (Boston: Little, Brown, 1990), but all three works have been thoroughly mined by the secondary sources I consulted. *William J. Tompson, *Khrushchev: A Political Life* (New York: St. Martin's Press, 1995), is a brief and well-balanced biography. James G. Richter, *Khrushchev's Double Bind: International Pressures and Domestic Coalition Politics* (Baltimore: Johns Hopkins University Press, 1994), on the other hand, is boringly academic, though it does advance some important arguments and interpretations. *Martin McCauley, *The Khrushchev Era, 1953-1964* (London: Longman, 1995), is a very good survey, but the general reader does not need to consult both Tompson and McCauley. Take your choice. I found myself relying very heavily on Jack M. Schick, *The Berlin Crisis, 1958-1962* (Philadelphia: University of Pennsylvania Press, 1971), even though the book is old and not very interesting. Historians have not written much recently about this particular Berlin crisis.

Castro's revolution is voluminously detailed in Hugh Thomas, *The Cuban Revolution* (New York: Harper & Row, 1977), which, despite its great length, forms only half of a larger work, *Cuba: The Pursuit of Freedom.* General readers will probably prefer the equally long but more recent and more journalistic biography by *+Tad Szulc, *Fidel: A Critical Portrait* (New York: William Morrow and Company, 1986). Despite the subtitle, the work is not very critical of Castro. +Paco Ignacio Taibo II, *Guevara, Also Known as Che,* trans. Martin Michael Roberts (New York: St. Martin's Press, 1997) is a fascinating account of Guevara's life which probably tells us more about the Argentine revolutionary than we really need to know.

The "court histories" of the Kennedy presidency, Arthur M. Schlesinger, Jr., *A Thousand Days: John F. Kennedy in the White House* (Boston: Houghton Mifflin, 1965), and Theodore C. Sorensen, *Kennedy* (New York: Harper & Row,

1965), are fun to read. Both authors write extremely well; Schlesinger is a noted historian in his own right and Sorensen was Kennedy's speechwriter and the ghostwriter of his published books and articles. However, the reader should approach these books more as historical novels than objective history. I was particularly amused by the fact that Schlesinger's thousand-page book devotes, in effect, one page to each day of Kennedy's presidency. If I could indulge this luxury in writing my two-volume history of the twentieth century, the two books would total 36,525 pages!

I will readily admit that I have not attempted to keep up with the enormous deluge of Kennedy literature over the years, and I am not the slightest bit interested in the conspiracy theories surrounding JFK's death. However, a volume in the prestigious History of the American Presidency series, *James N. Giglio, *The Presidency of John F. Kennedy* (Lawrence: University Press of Kansas, 1991), provides a well-balanced account of what most historians believe about Kennedy. *Thomas G. Paterson, ed., *Kennedy's Quest for Victory: American Foreign Policy, 1961-1963* (New York: Oxford University Press, 1989), provides a much more critical look at the foreign policy of the Kennedy administration, including the Berlin and Cuban crises, by various authors.

It's important to rely primarily on recent works concerning the Cuban missile crisis, since much new data has been revealed from both Soviet and American sources in the past decade or so. Among the older works, however, Robert Kennedy, *Thirteen Days: A Memoir of the Cuban Missile Crisis* (New York: W. W. Norton, 1969), remains fascinating since Bobby Kennedy was the president's alter ego on the ExComm. This is as close to a memoir by the president himself as we will ever get. A more recent memoir by two generals, one Russian and one American, is also informative: Anatoli I. Gribkov and William Y. Smith, *Operation Anadyr: U.S. and Soviet Generals Recount the Cuban Missile Crisis* (Berlin: Edition q, 1994). *+Mark J. White, *The Cuban Missile Crisis* (London: Macmillan, 1996), is a model study of this dramatic affair — graceful, balanced, and thoroughly grounded in the latest research. I don't believe it found a wide audience, but it should have!

Chapter 16. The War of Illusions

The sources on Vietnam cited in chapter 6 provide useful background for this chapter, especially Marilyn Young's excellent overall history of the conflict, *The Vietnam Wars, 1945-1990*.

I cannot claim objectivity in the writing of this chapter, since I was part of the generation of American males directly affected by the Vietnam War. I did not serve in the military during the war, or at any other time. The war itself helped me crystallize my own religious beliefs as a pacifist and therefore I filed for conscientious objector status. One of my proudest possessions is a letter written by a close friend, who had just returned from military service in Vietnam, attesting to the sincerity of my pacifist beliefs. The Selective Service Administration, however, never processed my application as a CO, since in the meantime I flunked the draft physical. In any case, most, but not all, of the sources I consulted reflect in a general way my anti-war views. This is unremarkable, for the mainstream academic sources, such as Marilyn Young's book, are nearly all anti-war in tone and interpretation.

Three sources written while the conflict still raged remain enormously useful: +David Halberstam, *The Best and the Brightest* (New York: Random House, 1972); +Frances Fitzgerald, *Fire in the Lake: The Vietnamese and the Americans in Vietnam* (Boston: Little, Brown, 1972); and the internal history of the war compiled at Robert McNamara's direction in the Department of Defense and leaked to the *New York Times* by Daniel Ellsberg, *The Pentagon Papers* (New York: New York Times, 1971).

Two essential historical studies view the key military and political decisions from opposite sides of the war: *George McT. Kahin, *Intervention: How America Became Involved in Vietnam* (New York: Alfred A. Knopf, 1986), and *William J. Duiker, *The Communist Road to Power in Vietnam* (Boulder, Colo.: Westview Press, 1981). Loren Baritz, *Backfire: A History of How American Culture Led Us into Vietnam and Made Us Fight the Way We Did* (New York: William Morrow and Company, 1985), is impassioned but disappointing, as it does not really live up to its impressive subtitle. It is best read as a gauge of the mainstream academic obsession with the Vietnam War rather than as a useful interpretation in its own right.

There is an enormous memoir literature that I have only sampled. Robert McNamara's *In Retrospect: The Tragedy and Lessons of Vietnam* (New York: Random House, 1995) is an agonized admission by the former defense secretary that he was wrong about the Vietnam War. This is useful for the record, but it would have been more productive if he had admitted his mistake twenty-five years earlier when it might have affected policy. Clark Clifford's recollections about the war are more meaty and satisfying. I did not read his entire book of memoirs, *Counsel to the President* (New York: Random House, 1991), but consulted the three excerpts dealing with Vietnam published in *The New Yorker,* May 6, 13, and 20, 1991. Doris Kearns, *Lyndon Johnson and the American Dream* (New York: Harper & Row, 1976), is virtually a memoir, for the ex-president unburdened himself to the author, a former White House intern, as she sat at the foot of his bed. The book is far more revealing than Johnson's official presidential memoirs.

Novels about the war are at least as numerous as memoirs. I decided to

471

read Chicago author Larry Heinemann's *Close Quarters* (New York: Farrar, Straus and Giroux, 1977), rather than the more celebrated Philip Caputo's *Rumor of War*. The Heinemann novel is unpleasant and episodic, presumably reflecting the episodic and unpleasant nature of the war. Caputo's novel was made into the riveting movie *Platoon* by director Oliver Stone. As a fictional window on the Vietnam War I still prefer Graham Greene, *The Quiet American* (London: William Heinemann and the Bodley Head, 1955), written with great insight and foresight at the very beginning of American involvement in the war.

*+William Shawcross, *Sideshow: Kissinger, Nixon and the Destruction of Cambodia* (New York: Simon and Schuster, 1979), is an almost perfect piece of investigative journalism, which provides essential background on Cambodia and indicts both President Nixon and Henry Kissinger for the roles they played in the Cambodian tragedy. Wilfred P. Deac, *Road to the Killing Fields: The Cambodian War of 1970-1975* (College Station: Texas A & M University Press, 1997), provides a less critical view of American policy in Cambodia than Shawcross, but interestingly most of the facts chronicled in the two books are the same, only the spins are different. *Karl D. Jackson, ed., *Cambodia 1975-1978: Rendezvous with Death* (Princeton, N.J.: Princeton University Press, 1989), is a very impressive collection of essays about Pol Pot's regime and the Cambodian genocide. My final thoughts about Cambodia are drawn from *Robert Melson, *Revolution and Genocide: On the Origins of the Armenian Genocide and the Holocaust* (Chicago: University of Chicago Press, 1992).

Chapter 17. The Shark and the Sardines

Eduardo Galeano, an Uruguayan journalist, has written a remarkable trilogy on Latin America, entitled *Memory of Fire*. I read his twentieth-century volume, *+*Century of the Wind*, trans. Cedric Belfrage (New York: Pantheon Books, 1988), as my introduction to Latin America. Galeano pens brief one- or two-paragraph vignettes of individuals, events, and countries, year by year through the century. His point of view is impassioned and radical, but he writes beautifully and captures much of the tragic essence of Latin American history. *Thomas Skidmore, Peter H. Smith, *Modern Latin America* (New York: Oxford University Press, 1989), is a very good, academic overview of recent history, with case studies of several countries, including Chile, Cuba, and Guatemala. Lester D. Langley presents a sweeping overview of the relations between the United States and Latin America in *America and the Americas: The United States in the Western Hemisphere* (Athens: University of Georgia Press, 1989); and *Walter LaFeber provides a stinging critique of U.S. policy in one part of Latin America in *Inevitable Revolutions: The United States in Central America* (New

York: W. W. Norton & Company, 1983). I took my chapter title from Juan José Arevalo, *The Shark and the Sardines,* trans. June Cobb and Raul Osegueda (New York: Lyle Stuart, n.d.).

Political scientist Cole Blasier provides an excellent framework for understanding the Cold War confrontation in Latin America in two books: *The Hovering Giant: U.S. Responses to Revolutionary Change in Latin America, 1910-1985* (Pittsburgh: University of Pittsburgh Press, 1985), and *The Giant's Rival: The USSR and Latin America* (Pittsburgh: University of Pittsburgh Press, 1983). Both scholars and participants took a look back at the Alliance for Progress on the twenty-fifth anniversary of its proclamation. Ronald L. Scheman has edited the proceedings of this conference, *The Alliance for Progress: A Retrospective* (New York: Praeger, 1988).

Two good books examine the Dominican intervention of 1965, which I only had space to mention briefly in the text of my chapter: Abraham F. Lowenthal, *The Dominican Intervention* (Cambridge, Mass.: Harvard University Press, 1972), and Piero Gleijeses, *The Dominican Crisis: The 1965 Constitutional Revolt and American Intervention* (Baltimore: Johns Hopkins University Press, 1978). Likewise, two excellent books detail the history of the Guatemalan revolution and its overthrow. Richard H. Immerman, *The CIA in Guatemala: The Foreign Policy of Intervention* (Austin: University of Texas Press, 1982), is useful for its examination of American policy. His book has generally been superseded, however, by *Piero Gleijeses, *Shattered Hope: The Guatemalan Revolution and the United States, 1944-1954* (Princeton, N.J.: Princeton University Press, 1991). Gleijeses writes with both passion and perception. He is critical of American policy, but he was honest enough to discover and demonstrate that Arbenz was indeed a communist (which Immerman and other liberal Americans have generally denied). I have not compiled a top ten list of books in this bibliography, but if I did this book would be on it.

Henry Butterfield Ryan has written a concise study of Che Guevara's final campaign in Bolivia, *The Fall of Che Guevara: A Story of Soldiers, Spies, and Diplomats* (New York: Oxford University Press, 1998). Ryan astutely comments that the Guevara literature belies the usual dictum that "history is written by the victors." Except for Ryan's own book, Guevara's story has been chronicled by his admirers. A good example is *+Paco Ignacio Taibo, *Guevara, Also Known as Che* (cited in chapter 15).

Paul Sigmund, *The United States and Democracy in Chile* (Baltimore: Johns Hopkins University Press, 1993), provides a good overview of recent Chilean history and relations between Chile and the United States. Investigative journalist Seymour M. Hersh pens a biting critique of Henry Kissinger's role in the overthrow of Allende in two chapters of his biography, *The Price of Power: Kissinger in the Nixon White House* (New York: Summit Books, 1983). Remarkably, the best study of Allende's presidency available in English was written by the American ambassador to Chile, *Nathaniel Davis, *The Last Two Years of Salvador Allende* (Ithaca, N.Y.: Cornell University Press, 1985). I almost missed this book, because I assumed it would be an apologia for the Nixon administration. Davis does defend American policy and I disagree with his point of view, but the body of his book is a balanced and very readable history of the Allende regime. Fernando Alegria was authorized by Allende to write his biography, but after the Chilean president's death, his friend chose to write his story in slightly fictionalized form, *Allende: A Novel*, trans. Frank Janney (Stanford, Calif.: Stanford University Press, 1993). Finally, +Pamela Constable and Arturo Valenzuela, *A Nation of Enemies: Chile Under Pinochet* (New York: W. W. Norton & Company, 1991), admirably examines the military regime which overthrew and succeeded Allende.

Chapter 18. The Bear and Her Cubs

*Karen Dawisha, *Eastern Europe, Gorbachev and Reform: The Great Challenge* (Cambridge, England: Cambridge University Press, 1988), though written specifically in response to Gorbachev's *perestroika* campaign in the Soviet Union, actually provides a wise and insightful introduction to the problems of the Soviet empire. *Ben Fowkes, *The Rise and Fall of Communism in Eastern Europe* (New York: St. Martin's Press, 1993); and Geoffrey Swain and Nigel Swain, *Eastern Europe since 1945* (New York: St. Martin's Press, 1993), both survey the history of the major portion of that empire, the Eastern European satellites. The Swain volume is more interpretive, with a heavy emphasis on ideology and economics, whereas Fowkes's book is more accessible for the general reader. Charles T. Baroch, *The Soviet Doctrine of Sovereignty (The So-Called Brezhnev Doctrine)* (Chicago: American Bar Association, 1970); and John Norton Moore and Robert F. Turner, *International Law and the Brezhnev Doctrine* (Lanham, Md.: University Press of America, 1987), are both disappointing Cold War tracts, but the latter volume contains the full text of the Brezhnev Doctrine.

Miklós Molnár, *From Bela Kun to Janos Kadar: Seventy Years of Hungarian Communism*, trans. Arnold J. Pomerans (New York: Berg, 1990), surveys the broad sweep of Hungarian Communist history, but this former insider's account is occasionally confusing and unclear. *Charles Gati, *Hungary and the Soviet Bloc* (Durham, N.C.: Duke University Press, 1986), delivers far more than its title indicates. Gati's book is not only a good study of the Soviet intervention in Hungary, but also a penetrating analysis of Soviet policy toward the satellites in general. *Bill Lomax, *Hungary 1956* (New York: St. Martin's Press, 1976), provides an excellent narrative account of the Hungarian revolution and Soviet intervention. It includes the best introduction to an academic treatise I have ever read, with the author alleging that "the inspiration for this book was first provided by a considerable quantity of red wine in a continental express train, after which I awoke to find myself speeding towards Budapest." *Khrushchev Remembers* (Boston: Little, Brown, 1970), presents an interesting but very defensive account of the Soviet decision to intervene. An academic conference in Finland, whose proceedings were published partly in English and partly in German by Paula Hihnala & Olli Vehvilainen, eds., *Hungary 1956* (Tampere, Finland: University of Tampere, 1995) presents the fruit of research into newly opened Soviet archives. This work affords a fuller view of the decision-making process but does not greatly change the overall picture.

*Kieran Williams, *The Prague Spring and Its Aftermath: Czechoslovak Politics, 1968-1970* (Cambridge, England: Cambridge University Press, 1997), is the most recent study of the Czech intervention and largely supersedes previous accounts. Still, *+William Shawcross, *Dubček* (New York: Touchstone, 1990), is well worth reading, particularly the revised and updated 1990 edition, which includes material from interviews with Dubček after the fall of the Soviet Union. Karen Dawisha, *The Kremlin and the Prague Spring* (Berkeley: University of California Press, 1984), provides a lengthy account of the Soviet decision-making process that most readers will find too detailed. However, the book does list the fifty-one major Soviet decisions regarding Czechoslovakia in 1968 in tabular fashion, and it presents a common-sense theory of decision making. The non-violent resistance of the Czechs has been insufficiently studied. All of the works cited above mention it, but seem not to know what to make of it. Only specialists in the subject of non-violence recognize its significance. See *Philip Windsor, Adam Roberts, *Czechoslovakia 1968* (New York: Columbia University Press, 1969); the introduction to Adam Roberts, *Civilian Resistance as a National Defense* (Baltimore: Penguin, 1969); and *Gene Sharp, *Civilian-Based Defense: A Post-Military Weapons System* (Princeton, N.J.: Princeton University Press, 1990).

The decidedly violent Afghan resistance to Soviet invasion has been extensively studied, though, of course, all books on the subject are dated since none of them can know how the continuing civil war in Afghanistan will turn out. *Anthony Hyman, *Afghanistan under Soviet Domination, 1964-91* (London: Macmillan, 1992), provides the best overview, though it is a little repetitious and disorganized. *+Edward Girardet, *Afghanistan: The Soviet War* (New York: St. Martin's Press, 1985), is a vivid narrative account, though unfortunately it is more dated than other accounts published later. Milan Hauner, *The Soviet War in Afghanistan: Patterns of Russian Imperialism* (Lanham, Md.: University Press of America, 1991), is an unusually readable political science treatise that sets the Afghanistan invasion in a long historical context.

Chapter 19. War on a Small Planet

Three general histories cited earlier provide good background reading for this chapter: Peter Mansfield, *The Arabs* (cited in chapter 8); Howard Sachar, *A History of Israel* (cited in chapter 9); and Daniel Yergin, *The Prize* (cited in chapter 8). Malcolm H. Kerr, *The Arab Cold War: Gamal 'Abd al-Nasir and His Rivals, 1958-1970* (London: Oxford University Press, 1971), and Miriam R. Lowi, *Water and Power: The Politics of a Scarce Resource in the Jordan River Basin* (Cambridge, England: Cambridge University Press, 1993), flesh out the details of Arab politics before the June 1967 war.

The Six Day War itself has been meticulously studied both by military and diplomatic specialists and by historians writing for a general audience. Michael Brecher with Benjamin Geist, *Decisions in Crisis: Israel, 1967 and 1973* (Berkeley: University of California Press, 1980), puts the Israeli decision-making process in both wars under a microscope. Karen Dawisha's study of the Prague Spring cited in the previous chapter was consciously modeled on Brecher's book. Both contain too much detail but are valuable sources. +Eric Hammel, *Six Days in June: How Israel Won the 1967 Arab-Israeli War* (New York: Charles Scribner's Sons, 1992), contains more purely military information than I cared for and is basically pro-Israeli, yet the book is still fundamentally fair-minded and quite readable. Ian Lustick, ed., *From War to War: Israel vs. the Arabs, 1948-1967* (New York: Garland Publishing, 1994), reprints numerous articles by different authors. I found *Charles Yost's "The Arab-Israeli War: How It Began," originally published in *Foreign Affairs* 46 (1968): 304-20, the best brief overview of the causes of the Six Day War.

Abdel Magid Farid, *Nasser: The Final Years* (Reading, England: Ithaca Press, 1994), is an insider's account of Egyptian policymaking during the War of Attrition. The book consists largely of meeting records copied down by the author, who served as Nasser's chief secretary. +John Bulloch, *The Making of a War: The Middle East* (London: Longman, 1974), is a journalist's pro-Arab, pro-Sadat account of the events leading to the Arab comeback in the October 1973 war. *Frank Aker, *October 1973: The Arab-Israeli War* (Hamden, Conn.: Archon Books, 1985), provides an unusually concise account of the war itself.

*+Victor Israelyan, *Inside the Kremlin During the Yom Kippur War* (University Park: Pennsylvania State University Press, 1995), offers a fascinating glimpse at Soviet policymaking by a member of the Politburo's four-man task force that assisted Brezhnev during the war crisis of 1973. *William Quandt, *Peace Process: American Diplomacy and the Arab-Israeli Conflict since 1967* (Washington: Brookings, 1993), is an updated version of the author's standard study of Kissingerian diplomacy, *Decade of Decisions*. Quandt is both a professional political scientist and a former staff member of the National Security

476

Council. His book provides a comprehensive and balanced overview of American diplomacy in the Middle East. Ian Lustick, ed., *From Wars Toward Peace in the Arab-Israeli Conflict, 1969-1993* (New York: Garland Publishing, 1994), is a further selection of articles supplementing the volume cited above. Finally, *Helena Cobban, *The Palestine Liberation Organization: People, Power and Politics* (Cambridge, England: Cambridge University Press, 1984), is a rather ponderous but balanced appraisal of the PLO.

Chapter 20. The Revolution of Memory and Morality

Two popular books by journalists make a good starting point. *+David Remnick, *Lenin's Tomb: The Last Days of the Soviet Empire* (New York: Random House, 1993), is the best overview of the fall of communism that I have seen; and *+Tina Rosenberg, *The Haunted Land: Facing Europe's Ghosts after Communism* (New York: Random House, 1995), examines the moral dilemmas that communism left behind as its legacy. Historian Robert V. Daniels, who spent his life studying communism, has written a very thoughtful essay, *The End of the Communist Revolution* (London: Routledge, 1993), which sets the events of 1989 in a long historical perspective. *George Weigel, *The Final Revolution: The Resistance Church and the Collapse of Communism* (New York: Oxford University Press, 1992), makes a strong case for the moral dimensions of the anti-communist revolutions.

*+Timothy Garton Ash, *The Polish Revolution: Solidarity* (New York: Charles Scribner's Sons, 1983), presents a lively narrative and insightful commentary on Solidarity's brief moment of glory and its suppression. The second section of Tina Rosenberg's book (cited above) provides a concise overview of the Polish events, including a penetrating portrait of General Jaruzelski. Two journalistic biographies survey the life and times of the Polish pope: +Tad Szulc, *Pope John Paul II: The Biography* (New York: Scribner, 1995), and +Carl Bernstein and Marco Politi, *His Holiness: John Paul II and the Hidden History of Our Time* (New York: Doubleday, 1996). Jan Kubik, *The Power of Symbols Against the Symbols of Power: The Rise of Solidarity and the Fall of State Socialism in Poland* (University Park: Pennsylvania State University Press, 1994), buries a fascinating subject in academic prose but contains some interesting visual material.

*Mark Galeotti, *Gorbachev and His Revolution* (New York: St. Martin's Press, 1997), is an admirably brief, concise, and clear overview of Gorbachev's life and times; but *John B. Dunlop, *The Rise of Russia and the Fall of the Soviet Empire* (Princeton, N.J.: Princeton University Press, 1993), digs deeper. Stephen Kotkin, *Steeltown, USSR: Soviet Society in the Gorbachev Era* (Berkeley: University of California Press, 1991), presents a fascinating case study of life at the grassroots (though the grass was blasted by pollution) during the time of *perestroika*.

The two general histories cited in chapter 18, Ben Fowkes, *The Rise and Fall of Communism in Eastern Europe*, and Geoffrey and Nigel Swain, *Eastern Europe since 1945*, both contain good, brief accounts of the end of Soviet domination in Eastern Europe. *+Timothy Garton Ash, *We the People: The Revolution of '89 Witnessed in Warsaw, Budapest, Berlin, & Prague* (Cambridge, England: Granta Books, 1990), is a fascinating eyewitness account of East Europe's liberation. The book is better known in the United States under its American title, *The Magic Lantern*.

Michael Beschloss and Strobe Talbott, *At the Highest Levels: The Inside Story of the End of the Cold War* (Boston: Little, Brown and Company, 1993), presents a lengthy narrative history of the Cold War's end from the perspective of American politics and foreign policy, an aspect of the story I have slighted in my chapter. John Lewis Gaddis, *The United States and the End of the Cold War: Implications, Reconsiderations, Provocations* (New York: Oxford University Press, 1992), collects some insightful essays, including one originally written in 1987 that includes the author's later notes commenting on his failure to foresee the end of the Cold War.

Chapter 21. Generations of Struggle

I have been reading and teaching about South Africa for a long time, so some of the background texts I relied on are a bit out of date. Nonetheless, although they didn't predict the happy ending of the struggle, many of the older works still are useful for their portraits of the entrenched apartheid system. See in particular Leo Marquard, *The People and Policies of South Africa* (London: Oxford University Press, 1969); T. R. H. Davenport, *South Africa: A Modern History* (London: Macmillan, 1977); and Leonard Thompson and Andrew Prior, *South African Politics* (New Haven, Conn.: Yale University Press, 1982). In fact, any book by Leonard Thompson would be worth reading for wise background history on South Africa. Two books that appeared in the early 1980s develop fascinating comparisons between the systems of white supremacy in South Africa and in the American South: John W. Cell, *The Highest Stage of White Supremacy: The Origins of Segregation in South Africa and the American South* (Cambridge, England: Cambridge University Press, 1982), and *+George M. Frederickson, *White Supremacy: A Comparative Study of American and South African History* (New York: Oxford University Press, 1981). Cell's book is insightful, but fairly narrow and academic; whereas Frederickson's sweeping survey of the two nations' racial history must surely appear on just about anyone's top ten list of historical works.

Among the numerous studies of the African National Congress and the black liberation movement, the best I encountered was *Stephen Ellis and Tsepo Sechaba, *Comrades Against Apartheid: The ANC and the South African Communist Party in Exile* (London: James Currey, 1992), the product of a collaboration between a freedom fighter and a journalist. Ellis and Sechaba brilliantly analyze the symbiotic relationship between the ANC and the SACP without either romanticism or red-baiting. Dale T. McKinley, *The ANC and the Liberation Struggle: A Critical Political Biography* (London: Pluto Press, 1997), is heavily Marxist in its interpretation, criticizing the ANC for selling out its socialist principles. Unlike much ideologically inspired writing, however, McKinley's book is clear, interesting, and useful. Scott Thomas, *The Diplomacy of Liberation: The Foreign Relations of the African National Congress Since 1960* (London: I. B. Tauris Publishers, 1996), is a pedestrian account of an important and fascinating subject. Julie Frederikse, *The Unbreakable Thread: Non-Racialism in South Africa* (Bloomington: Indiana University Press, 1990), is a collection of interviews and documents from ANC history, including, for example, the text of the Freedom Charter; whereas Charles Villa-Vicencio, *The Spirit of Freedom: South African Leaders on Religion and Politics* (Berkeley: University of California Press, 1996), presents interviews with twenty-one anti-apartheid leaders, probing their religious and spiritual attitudes.

*+Martin Meredith, *Nelson Mandela: A Biography* (New York: St. Martin's Press, 1997), provides more than the story of one man's life. In classic life-and-times fashion, Meredith pens a complete history of the South African liberation struggle. Two accounts by journalists detail the final years of the struggle, when Nelson Mandela was released from prison and forged his uneasy relationship with F. W. de Klerk: *+Allister Sparks, *Tomorrow Is Another Country: The Inside Story of South Africa's Road to Change* (New York: Hill and Wang, 1995), and *+David Ottaway, *Chained Together: Mandela, de Klerk, and the Struggle to Remake South Africa* (New York: Times Books, 1993). Finally, *Anton D. Lowenberg and William H. Kaempfer, *The Origins and Demise of South African Apartheid: A Public Choice Analysis* (Ann Arbor: University of Michigan Press, 1998), is a highly technical treatise on economic history, but I found its analysis of the causes of apartheid's decline and of the role of sanctions in the process extremely valuable.

Chapter 22. Non-Violent and Violent Change around the World

*Michael Randle, *Civil Resistance* (London: Fontana Press, 1994), is a marvelous survey of the many instances in which non-violent techniques have been used effectively; and Walter Wink, *Engaging the Powers: Discernment and Resistance in a World of Domination* (Minneapolis: Fortress Press, 1992), probes deeply into the theology of non-violence. Both +Lewis Simons, *Worth Dying For* (New York: William Morrow and Company Inc., 1987), and *John Lyons and Karl Wilson, *Marcos and Beyond: The Philippines Revolution* (Sydney, Australia: Kangaroo Press, 1987), provide readable, insightful accounts of the Philippines People Power revolution.

The final chapter of John K. Fairbank, *China: A New History* (cited in chapter 4), contains a brief account of the Tiananmen Square incident. Much fuller accounts are *Nan Lin, *The Struggle for Tiananmen: Anatomy of the 1989 Mass Movement* (Westport, Conn.: Praeger, 1992), and Chu-Yuan Cheng, *Behind the Tiananmen Massacre: Social, Political, and Economic Ferment in China* (Boulder, Colo.: Westview Press, 1990).

Fortunately, there is a good guide through the minefield of the literature on Yugoslavia's breakup: Gales Stokes et al., "Instant History: Understanding the Wars of Yugoslav Succession," *Slavic Review* 55 (spring 1996): 136-60. As Stokes and her colleagues indicate, there is an enormous journalistic literature of impassioned hand-wringing. +Misha Glenny, *The Fall of Yugoslavia: The Third Balkan War* (London: Penguin, 1992), is one of the best journalistic accounts, and several updated versions have been issued since its first release. *Carole Rogel, *The Breakup of Yugoslavia and the War in Bosnia* (Westport, Conn.: Greenwood Press, 1998), provides an admirable, brief survey in a textbook format, complete with selected documents, brief biographies of the main characters, and a very good review of the literature. Lenard J. Cohen, *Broken Bonds: Yugsoslavia's Disintegration and Balkan Politics in Transition* (Boulder, Colo.: Westview Press, 1995), is an overly long, rather dull academic study. Its very dullness, however, is refreshing and useful as a contrast to the over-heated nature of most writing on the subject.

*+Philip Gourevitch, *We Wish to Inform You that Tomorrow We Will Be Killed with Our Families: Stories From Rwanda* (New York: Farrar, Straus and Giroux, 1998), is a positively riveting account of the Rwandan genocide by a *New Yorker* reporter. It is easily one of the best, most humane, and most important books on any subject in this entire bibliography. Arthur Jay Klinghoffer, *The International Dimension of Genocide in Rwanda* (New York: New York University Press, 1998), by contrast, is quite dull and academic, but it does provide a useful exploration of the international ramifications of the genocide. *The United Nations and Rwanda, 1993-1996* (New York: United Nations, 1996), is an official compilation that does not indicate how slowly and ponderously the UN reacted to the Rwanda genocide. The volume, however, does contain useful, brief background chapters and a full chronology of UN decisions during the crisis.

Chapter 23. Coming Apart, Coming Together

François Duchêne's biography of Jean Monnet (cited in chapter 2) is worth reading more than once. A spate of books analyzing the European Union came out right after the passage of the Maastricht Treaty in 1992; undoubtedly updated versions and new studies will appear in the wake of the euro currency's introduction. Desmond Dinan, *Ever Closer Union? An Introduction to the European Community* (Boulder, Colo.: Lynne Rienner Publishers, 1994), remains a solid, if overly long and dull, study, including both a history of the European Union and a profile of its operations. General readers will far prefer +Dick Leonard, *"The Economist" Guide to the European Union* (London: Hamish Hamilton, 1994), which also includes both history of the Union and a profile of its workings, but in briefer and more sprightly fashion. *D. M. Harrison, *The Organisation of Europe: Developing a Continental Market Order* (London: Routledge, 1995), is not easy reading, but it contains a very insightful analysis of the European Union's strengths and weaknesses.

I happened to be in Europe when the euro was first introduced, so I collected all the newspaper clippings I could find. Most of my information about NAFTA is also derived from newspaper articles appearing during the time of its formation in the 1990s. In addition, a series of academic articles collected by Theodore Georgakopoulos, Christos C. Paraskevopoulos, and John Smithin, eds., *Economic Integration between Unequal Partners* (Aldershot, England: Edward Elgar Publishing Limited, 1994); and a second collection by Peter Coffey, ed., *Latin America — Mercosur* (Boston: Kluwer Academic Publishers, 1998), provided vital information about a number of common markets and free trading areas. I would not recommend either of these books to the general reader.

Index